Rethinking Trade and Commercial Policy Theories

To all from whom I had the privilege to learn and draw inspirations

Rethinking Trade and Commercial Policy Theories

Development Perspectives

P. Sai-wing Ho

Associate Professor of Economics, University of Denver, USA

Edward Elgar

Cheltenham, UK • Northampton, MA, USA

Published by
Edward Elgar Publishing Limited
The Lypiatts
15 Lansdown Road
Cheltenham
Glos GL50 2JA
UK

Edward Elgar Publishing, Inc.
William Pratt House
9 Dewey Court
Northampton
Massachusetts 01060
USA

A catalogue record for this book
is available from the British Library

Library of Congress Control Number: 2009940979

ISBN 978 1 84064 942 0

Printed and bound by MPG Books Group, UK

Contents

Abbreviations

AER	*American Economic Review*
CTT	Commodity terms of trade
CVD	Countervailing duties
ECLA	Economic Commission for Latin America
EOI	Export-oriented industrialisation
EP	Export promotion
FDI	Foreign direct investment
FTT	Factoral terms of trade
GATT	General Agreement on Tariffs and Trade
GSP	Generalized System of Preferences
H–O–S model	Heckscher–Ohlin–Samuelson model
HPAEs	High-performing Asian economies
ILPES	Latin American Institute for Social and Economic Planning
IMF	International Monetary Fund
IPR	Intellectual property rights
IS	Import substitution
ISI	Import-substituting industrialisation
ITT	Income terms of trade
MNCs	Multinational corporations
MTNs	Multilateral trade negotiations
NICs	Newly industrialising countries
PST	Prebisch–Singer thesis
QRs	Quantitative restrictions
SDT	Special and differential treatment
SCM	Agreement on Subsidies and Countervailing Measures
SEUM	Society for Establishing Useful Manufactures
TNCs	Transnational corporations
TRCB	Trade-related capacity building
TRIMs	Agreement on Trade Related Investment Measures
TRIPs	Agreement on Trade Related Aspects of Intellectual Property Rights
UN	United Nations
UNCTAD	United Nations Conference on Trade and Development
WIPO	World Intellectual Property Organization
WTO	World Trade Organization

Preface

In hindsight the rethinking of trade and commercial policy theories from development perspectives that is discussed in the following pages first took germination in Chapter II of the dissertation that I wrote at Stanford University (Ho 1989) and that chapter is titled, 'International technological differences and uneven accumulation in a classical production model'. Before it was published several years later (Ho 1997), I devoted time to read more of the works of the classical economists, adding those of Torrens. These efforts resulted in Ho (1996a, 1996b).

The period between the latter part of the 1980s and the mid-1990s roughly coincided with the Uruguay Round of multilateral trade negotiations (MTNs) which resulted in the establishment of the World Trade Organization in 1995. The North–South divide that emerged from that round and the controversy surrounding some of the agreements reached appear to me to be quite readily comprehensible within the uneven development framework that I had partly constructed by then. Nevertheless, beginning from the mid-1990s I devoted time to educate myself about the history of the General Agreement on Tariffs and Trade, especially focusing on the issue of Special and Differential Treatment (see, for instance, Ho 1998b).

It should not be surprising that how one appraises the outcome of different rounds of MTNs depends on one's theoretical perspective. Nevertheless, it served as a reminder that there was more that I needed to do to further construct the framework of uneven development. Thus, although back in 1994 I had drafted a research paper (which has not been published) that reappraised the theory of domestic divergences and considered its limitations on shedding light on the process of development, there is a more thorough story yet to be told. If the mainstream of the economics profession has been unable, or has refused, to recognise that there is an alternative framework to stitch together the works of the classicists, might there be a similar inability or refusal when it comes to the works of the so-called 'protectionists'?

Beginning from the late 1990s, but before the protests in Seattle in 1999, I thus turned my attention to the original works of these so-called 'protectionists' or supporters of import substitution. When Edward Elgar Publishing kindly offered me the opportunity in 2001 to submit a proposal to write a book, I connected all of these different pieces together into a plan. That is essentially what the reader will find in the ensuing pages.

The chief reason why it has taken so many years before the book could be completed is because in spring 2001 I became the Department Chair and, save for the 2004–2005 academic year, had remained in that capacity until June 2010. The administrative work involved and the orchestrating effort that was necessary to strengthen what might otherwise become a 'soft' department (in the sense which Myrdal referred to certain nation states) had at times proved to be excessively demanding and draining. That had inevitably slowed down the completion of the project. Thanks to the University of Denver Administration, I was granted a sabbatical for two academic quarters between autumn 2004 and winter 2005. I was also allowed to take two halves of a mini-sabbatical, while remaining as the Chairperson, in each of the winter quarters of 2007 and 2010 respectively. Those periods of time off were helpful, though the project would necessitate much more. I want to thank Edward Elgar Publishing for kindly showing its understanding of the situation that I have been in and for allowing me the time that it takes to prepare the manuscript.

Given the current trend and emphasis in the mainstream of the economics profession, writing a book of this nature has understandably been quite a lonesome experience. Hence, it is particularly important for me to give thanks to those who have offered their kind encouragement and support. First and foremost I want to thank my teacher at Stanford University, Donald Harris, who supervised my dissertation research. It was through the courses that I took with him and through his supervision of my research that I came to read more about alternative approaches to economic analysis, and learned to appreciate their strengths and weaknesses. He, together with Amit Bhaduri and Medhi Shafaeddin, kindly read the whole or parts of the manuscript for this book and offered many helpful suggestions for revision. Needless to say, all remaining errors are my sole responsibility.

I also want to thank Ha-Joon Chang for allowing me, given my citizenship, to attend the 2002 Cambridge Advanced Programme on Rethinking Development Economics as an observer. That turned out to be a most important occasion for me to compare my way of thinking with that of many of the scholars and researchers whom he had invited to lecture. Over the years I have also been fortunate to get on the programmes of various conferences to present early drafts of my work and I want to thank the conference organisers involved. Back in 2001 it was at one such conference that, through Andrea Maneschi, I was introduced to Mr Edward Elgar. I want to thank Andrea for that introduction and for, prior to that occasion, pointing me to the works of John Rae. For students in my senior-/graduate-level course on trade theories and policies, I want to thank them for allowing me to test my alternative developmentalist interpretation in front of them.

Given the voluminous amount of reference materials to consult, not all of which were easily obtainable, I have sought the help of many at the University of Denver Penrose Library, especially those who have worked at the Inter-Library Loan Department. I want to thank them for the patient assistance that they have kindly lent me. I want to thank Christopher Brown, Reference Technology Integration Librarian, for putting his nifty searching skills to use on many occasions to help me hunt down documents that are difficult to locate. Mary Sue Brown, Software Training Specialist, University of Denver Technology Services, provided ample help when I prepared the camera ready copy that conforms to the guidelines provided by Edward Elgar Publishing.

I would like to acknowledge the kind permissions to reproduce passages from the following books or articles:

- Adam Smith, *An Inquiry into the Nature and Causes of the Wealth of Nations*, Liberty*Classics* reprint of the Oxford University Press edition, published in 1976 and reprinted with minor corrections in 1979, Indianapolis: Liberty*Classics*, reproduced by permission of Oxford University Press.
- David Ricardo, *On the Principles of Political Economy and Taxation*, vol. I of *The Works and Correspondence of David Ricardo*, edited by Piero Sraffa and Maurice H. Dobb (Indianapolis: Liberty Fund, 2004), originally published by Cambridge University Press in 1951, reprinted by permission of Liberty Fund via license from the Royal Economic Society.
- John Stuart Mill, *Principles of Political Economy with Some of Their Applications to Social Philosophy*, vols. II and III of *The Collected Works of John Stuart Mill*, edited by John B. Robson, published 1965, Toronto: University of Toronto Press, reprinted with permission of the publisher.
- Alexander Hamilton, *The Papers of Alexander Hamilton*, vol. X, edited by Harold C. Syrett and Jacob E. Cooke, published 1966, New York: Columbia University Press, reproduced with permission of the publisher.
- Raúl Prebisch, *Towards a New Trade Policy for Development*, © United Nations, published 1964, reproduced with permission.
- Gunnar Myrdal, *An International Economy*, published 1956, New York: Harper & Brothers, reproduced with permission of HarperCollins *Publishers*.
- Gunnar Myrdal, *Economic Theory and Under-Developed Regions*, originally published by Gerald Duckworth in 1957, later published Methuen & Co. Ltd. in 1963, reproduced with permission of Gerald Duckworth & Co. Ltd.
- Gunnar Myrdal, *Asian Drama: An Inquiry into the Poverty of Nations*, vols. I–III, published 1968, New York: Pantheon, reproduced with permission of the Board of Culture, City of Stockholm, Sweden.

- Hans W. Singer, *The Strategy of International Development*, published 1975, London: Macmillan, reproduced with permission of Palgrave Macmillan.
- P. Sai-wing Ho, 'Rethinking classical trade analysis within a framework of capitalist development', *Cambridge Journal of Economics*, **20**, 4 (July 1996), 413–32, used by permission of Oxford University Press.
- P. Sai-wing Ho, 'Reappraising Torrens's contributions to the analysis of trade, growth, and colonisation', *Contributions to Political Economy*, **15** (1996), 1–31, used by permission of Oxford University Press.
- P. Sai-wing Ho, 'Distortions in the trade policy for development debate: a re-examination of Friedrich List', *Cambridge Journal of Economics*, **29**, 5 (2005 September), 729–45, used by permission of Oxford University Press.
- P. Sai-wing Ho, 'An institutionalist's policy advice to address international inequalities: the contributions of Gunnar Myrdal', from *Journal of Economic Issues*, **43**, 2 (June 2009), 337–44. Copyright © 2009 by the Association for Evolutionary Economics, used by permission of M.E. Sharpe, Inc.

Every effort has been made to trace all the copyright holders but if any has been inadvertently overlooked, the publisher will be pleased to make the necessary amendments at the first opportunity.

Last but not least I want to thank my wife, Martha, for all her support of my indulgence in this undertaking. She understands that I dedicated myself to it because of my passion to learn and to discover. With much sacrifice on her part she had kindly provided me the space to carry it out and bring it to fruition.

1. Introduction

1.1 THIS BOOK'S CONCEPTION

To most readers it is probably too obvious to point out that a substantial portion of the rationale behind the push toward globalisation – in its trade or trade-related aspects – is based, directly or indirectly, upon the mainstream or orthodox trade and commercial policy theories that have long exercised dominance within the economics profession.[1] Nevertheless, as trite as that observation may sound, it usefully reminds one that any serious voice of caution against those aspects of the globalisation process must necessarily take on those theories.

For the sake of discussion they can be grouped into two intimately connected sets that essentially constitute two sides of the same coin. One set has to do with the illustration that free trade is, under assumptions that are widely regarded by the economics mainstream as standard and innocuous, the 'best' or 'most efficient' trade policy.[2] In the rest of this book these are referred to as the static classical trade theories.[3] The flip side, the other set, relates to the claim that deviations from free trade would, under the same list of assumptions made in the first set of theories, not be efficient as a trade policy. Even if there are 'market failures', deviations from free trade would in most cases fare no better than 'second-best'. In the rest of this book this set is referred to as the theory of commercial policy, or more technically known as the theory of domestic divergences or distortions.[4] In both cases, though with obvious differences in details, lineage has been traced by mainstream historians of economic thought all the way back to the great classical economists, namely Adam Smith, David Ricardo, and John Stuart Mill.[5] It is this most impressive lineage that partly lends dominance to the theories and it gives pause to anyone who dares to question them.[6]

Previous attempts to challenge the development implications of these theories have taken place on two fronts, namely theoretical and empirical.[7] What is conspicuously missing in these attempts, unfortunately, are efforts that quite comprehensively research into alternative versions of history of economic thought on the subject of development and trade. To be sure, alternative interpretations of the works of some of the authors re-examined in the rest of this book have occasionally been advanced.[8] However, without a more systematic effort to stitch together the insight of these authors, one passes up the possibility of uniting the strong and thoughtful voices to counter the mainstream theorists on the theoretical front of the debate. And without respectable theoretical justifications, any challenge on the empirical front may come across as not firmly grounded.

Hence, while there have been scores of books published in recent years that cast doubt on the implications for development with the push toward globalisation, what seems to be missing is a comprehensive and exhaustive effort to critically re-examine the mainstream theories upon which the push is significantly based.[9] That is not to suggest that the scepticism toward the developmental effects of globalisation, or toward the speed at which it has been pushed, which has been expressed in these publications is not well-founded.[10] But had the critical re-examination been undertaken, the case for caution could perhaps be more forcefully made and could perhaps better withstand the dismissal by the supporters of globalisation.

Indeed, among those in the economics mainstream who have appeared to be willing to engage the sceptics, one readily notes simple reiterations of such theories in their rebuttals and then the debate is brought back to square one. Deardorff (2003) expresses this in a most telling way and is worth quoting at full length:

> [W]e [economists] … tend to believe in the power of competition among … firms to render their greed harmless and in fact to turn it into an engine for making people better off. We have this model, you see, in which competition among firms leads in a perfect world to economic efficiency. And while the world is obviously imperfect in many ways, we still tend to believe that this force for good usually plays the dominant role.
> … We have built our academic careers on the foundation of this model, and it has served us well… When confronted with those who disagree with us, we almost always can find elements of their arguments that are contrary to fact – or if not to fact, then to theory – and we marshal our own arguments in the comfortable context of our theory without really hearing what others are saying. (p. 642)

To him (and many others in the economics mainstream), 'complaints about globalisation … seem to emerge from a different world' than one with which he is familiar (ibid., p. 640).[11]

This book is an attempt to fill the void. It purports to take a serious step toward re-examining the history of economic thought on the subject of development and trade, and advances an alternative developmentalist version of that history. It is an understatement to characterise the literature in this area as huge and enormous, and it is hence impossible for a book of this length to be adequately comprehensive in that regard. But to the extent that a preponderant portion of that literature has, directly or indirectly, grown from the mainstream version of the history of thought pertaining to that area, the advancement of an alternative developmentalist version of that history could, if it proves to be compelling, give reason to rethink that whole literature. It is with that strategy in mind that this book focuses on some of the key figures in this literature.

Given that mainstream theories are placed into the two aforementioned sets, this book is accordingly divided into two parts. Part I challenges the perception created by the subscribers to the static classical trade models that these were largely all that the classical economists had written about as they made their case for free trade.[12] It argues that the lineage to classical economics built by the mainstream actually rests upon an extremely narrow reference to the original works by the classicists. By meticulously re-examining these original works – those by Smith, Ricardo, Mill, and adding those by Robert Torrens – it is argued that a model of growth, trade, and foreign investment can be shown to run through many parts of their works. Most importantly, this model engenders uneven development among the participating countries in an expanding trade and investment network. During the times of the classical economists England exploited various advantages that she enjoyed as the first to industrialise, and widened and consolidated her lead, especially in a technological sense, over the others in that network. Putting this polarising tendency slightly differently, while England reaped most of the benefits, many other countries and regions were mired in the trap of underdevelopment and technological backwardness. So, after all, maybe there are good reasons to be sceptical about the benefits of free trade from the perspective of certain countries, and this scepticism is derived from having meticulously perused the original works of the same classical economists who are claimed to be the first to have systematically illustrated the mutual benefits of free trade! But it bears emphasising that the issue is not just about trade policy. To the extent that concomitant with uneven development are widening technological gaps across countries, and associated with foreign investment by the advanced countries in the less-developed ones are controversies relating to the distribution of gains from (including the extent of technology transfer through) such investment, this alternative developmentalist approach to linking up the classicists, unlike the mainstream one, much more readily highlights certain issues that were at first somewhat latent, but have erupted in the more recent rounds of multilateral trade negotiations (MTNs) (on which more later).

A corollary from the above is that the classical economists were either oblivious or apathetic to the possibly polarising developmental effects of trade and investment. Unfortunately, it is mostly the parts of their works that pertain to the non-polarising, equilibrating or equalising effects of trade and investment that have been extended and refined into modern mainstream trade and commercial policy theories.[13] The framework for analysing the economic development of the relatively backward countries that is based upon such theories is consequently also oblivious to the polarising effects of trade and investment.[14] Technological gaps across countries are treated as given and unchanging in the static classical trade models.[15] Capital is either assumed to be internationally immobile[16] or the possible negative impact of its mobility downplayed.[17] While widening technological gaps and the adverse impact of hosting unregulated FDI have thus received far less attention than they deserve, a huge amount of time and effort has been invested in analysing the effects of commercial policy within the equilibrium framework, giving rise to the theory of domestic divergences.[18]

While these blind spots have been inherited and retained by the modern mainstream, over the course of more than two centuries since the publication of Smith's *Wealth of Nations* countless sceptics of free trade and unbridled *laissez-faire* have expressed concerns with the process of uneven development between the rich and the poor countries.[19] The more thoughtful and sophisticated among these sceptics studied the mechanisms that have aggravated such development. Then they explored ways to shape certain market and social forces, resulting in proposals of different state-aided efforts to spur development and technological-capability cultivation so that the uneven development process could be arrested and the gaps between the two groups of countries could be narrowed, even if not completely closed. In the rest of this book they are often referred to as the *developmentalists*.

How, then, has the economics mainstream maintained the dominance of its trade and commercial policy theories despite the onslaught by these developmentalists? It has selectively distilled elements from their works, represented these as treatable within its equilibrium framework, and illustrated that they typically did not draw the first-best policy conclusions. The distillation has enabled the mainstream to categorically label them as 'protectionists' or supporters of 'import-substitution' (IS); the prominent usual suspects include Alexander Hamilton, Friedrich List, Mihaïl Manoïlesco, Raúl Prebisch, Gunnar Myrdal, Hans Singer, and others. By attaching such labels, attention is focused on the trade protection policies that they allegedly support and is diverted from their broader development programmes – which often comprise, among other elements, domestic policies, technological-capability cultivation policies and (for Prebisch, Myrdal, and Singer) policies that regulate foreign direct investment (FDI) – of which trade policies only constitute a part. The distilled elements are then treated under the aforementioned second set of mainstream theories, namely the theory of domestic divergences. Specifically, the various 'cases for protection' have been subjected to diagnosis using mainstream analytical tools that are geared toward detecting circumstances under which otherwise efficient equilibrium outcomes from resource allocation are not obtained under free market conditions. Such circumstances are collectively known in the mainstream as 'market failures'. Invoking the 'principle of targetting', the next step in the treatment of their cases is to portray these 'protectionists' as knowing nothing better than using trade protection to target the correction of market failures.[20] For according to the theory of domestic divergences, there are, for most market failures, typically some non-trade policy instruments that could more precisely target the sources of those failures. Put differently, market failures are typically not best corrected by trade protection. The case for free trade that is supported by mainstream trade and commercial policy theories thus appears to remain intact.

Part II of this book challenges the perception, created by these critics of protectionism and IS, that what they have focused on accurately depicts the thoughts of the developmentalists. It argues that their depiction actually rests upon an extremely narrow reference to the original works by these authors. Through meticulous re-examinations of these original works, it illustrates how that depiction has seriously distorted and misrepresented their ideas, and has thus obfuscated the questions posed by them. There have thus been processes of distortions and misrepresentations that resemble each other that Parts I and II of the present work seek to correct. In both cases the distortions and misrepresentations result when the economics mainstream narrowly focuses on just certain passages in the otherwise voluminous amount of works of the classical economists as well as the prominent developmentalists.

Unlike Part I where the smaller number of economists re-examined and the relatively shorter time that their lives collectively spanned allow for an easier summary, Part II poses more of a challenge. Nevertheless, the following should highlight the major findings. Most fundamentally, the developmentalists were all concerned with the uneven development process from the vantage point of those countries that were lagging behind. That is, they drew attention to the problem of lack of development in precisely those countries or parts of the world that the classical economists re-examined in Part I did not pay adequate attention to. To them (excepting Manoïlesco, on which see Chapter 9 below), the problem of underdevelopment was never conceived as treatable within the mainstream equilibrium framework. That is, development was not conceptualised as simply a matter of attaining static efficiency through an instantaneous resource reallocation from an initial inefficient situation that obtains due to a market failure.[21]

While there are hints in their works that they might have stumbled upon barriers and obstacles to development some of which appear to be akin to the mainstream notion of market failures, these barriers and obstacles are not situated in equilibrium frameworks.[22] Importantly, they were not studied in the compartmentalised ways that are typical of treatments of market failures under the theory of domestic divergences. Instead, their interconnections are always at least implicitly recognised, thereby giving rise, in some cases, to notions of circular and cumulative causation, especially in the works of Myrdal and Singer, and to some extent also in those of List and Prebisch. But precisely because the obstacles to development are intimately intertwined, the process of overcoming them has to be multifaceted, and in some sense, sequenced. This process will by no means be realised through an instantaneous reallocation of resources.

Indeed, these developmentalists have generally thought through arguments for state-aided development that are much more sophisticated than the mainstream treatment has made them out to be. Part of this sophistication is reflected by the fact that, contrary to mainstream portrayal that presents them as knowing no better than relying on trade protection to correct 'market failures', they have invariably considered deploying other instruments, including subsidies. In fact, two of them – Hamilton and List – can be regarded to have anticipated insights that later came to be known as the 'principle of targetting'.[23] Besides, all of them had expressed a healthy dose of caution against some possible side-effects from state support of developmental efforts (for example, the inefficiencies that might be bred). While all of them advocated the promotion of industries, all (excepting Manoïlesco) were also careful, in one way or another, to point out that agricultural growth should not be neglected. And while all intended the industries that would be promoted should serve the domestic market, most of them also emphasised the importance of interweaving IS with export promotion (EP). More fundamentally, these developmentalists did not merely confine themselves to 'protectionist' policies as traditionally defined by the economics mainstream. Instead, some of them (Prebisch, Myrdal, and Singer) also gave thoughts to how to better reap developmental benefits from hosting FDI. Last but not least, they all concerned themselves with closing or narrowing the technological gaps between the rich and the poor countries, through trade policies as well as other technological-capability cultivation policies. This cultivation has never been an instantaneous event in any country. Some aspects of it and the subsequent technological upgrading are processes that necessitate purposeful state support and encouragement. They require time to take root, and so do the social and institutional changes that accompany them.

The mainstream critic may counter that the developmentalists have not refined their analyses to the point where they could obtain clean and precise policy conclusions. To be sure, many of their arguments remain to be refined and developed into more elaborate analyses.[24] The mainstream of the economics profession has, however, not taken a constructive step in this direction. Instead, it has constructed a straw-man – the 'protectionist' –

whenever it finds room to attach that label. It has then developed an elaborate analytical machine – the theory of domestic divergences – to annihilate this straw-man. But having originated from frameworks that are quite blind to polarising developmental forces, one wonders if this theory might also be handicapped when applied to analyse the development-promoting effects of various policies.[25] Indeed, have the mainstream theorists gained elegance and precision in their results only at the expense of relevance to the full complexity of underdevelopment? By only focusing on development barriers and obstacles that are akin to the mainstream notion of market failures, and then by treating the latter in compartmentalised manners while disregarding their inter-related nature (and their interconnections with other barriers and obstacles), has the mainstream derived policy conclusions that, while elegant and precise, are oversimplified and have quite limited applicability? If the developmentalists considered these barriers and obstacles at both the local and global levels more broadly than the mainstream notion of market failures, and also gave recognition that they are intertwined in a complex web, then would it be highly misleading for the mainstream to judge the merit of their policy programmes by narrowly focusing on just the trade protection aspect and also to misrepresent the trade policies as simply intending to correct such simplified notions of market failures?

These critical questions align with one of the points made by Stiglitz and Charlton in their recent book, *Fair Trade for All: How Trade Can Promote Development*. One example they give is if the diagnosis that employs the theory of domestic divergences reveals that the very source of a market failure is traceable to imperfect capital markets, then according to that theory 'the [preferred] solution was to create perfect capital markets'. But unfortunately, this conclusion 'made the critical error of treating the distortion almost as if it was an accidental mistake, which government could easily correct'. One should bear in mind, they thus caution, that 'in many cases the market failure might be endemic or not readily able to be countered by government action' (2005, p. 31).[26]

The fact that Part II of this book seeks to clarify the ideas of the developmentalists might be misconstrued as nothing but support for 'protectionism', where the latter is defined in the mainstream sense of the term. If this book has even some success in accomplishing what it seeks to accomplish, the reader should be in a better-informed position to decide that the traditional debate on free trade versus protection has a misplaced focus as far as engendering development is concerned. This traditional debate is able to sustain itself in that form thanks to the peculiar nature of mainstream trade and commercial policy theories. For in these theoretical frameworks, where among other suppositions the production process has been compressed into well-behaved production functions which represent some given level of technological capability, the central focus is on exchange and allocation under competitive conditions and the efficiency results that arise therefrom. Restricted exchange will, under the given assumptions, result in misallocation and inefficiencies. Therein the 'debate' on free trade versus protection would appear to be the only way that it can be waged.

But when that production process is not thus compressed, when resources have to be mobilised not just economically but socially, when technological learning has to take place and technological capability has to be cultivated and continually upgraded, when market institutions have yet to be more fully established and some markets remain to be created, it becomes more obvious that while some trade and exchange are essential to certain phases of the complex process of development, engendering development takes much more than just trade and exchange. Development as a multifaceted process could be aided via multiple supports, involving both non-trade as well as trade instruments. Certain commercial policy instruments, if employed with appropriate checks and balances, could play a role in helping this process along. However, commercial policy by itself, even if appropriately deployed, will be far from adequate.[27] Clearly, this whole set of considerations cannot simply be tagged under the banner of a free trade versus protection debate. In that connection, the subtitle of the present book that indicates that theories of trade and commercial policy are rethought from 'development perspectives' is not trivial.

Indeed, it is not an accident that, apart from the caution against liberalising trade too rapidly, most less-developed countries have also been cautious toward the rapid extension of the agenda at the recent rounds of MTNs held under the auspices of the General Agreement on Tariffs and Trade (GATT) and the World Trade Organisation (WTO). Those in the mainstream who had become too confined and accustomed to the traditional free trade versus protection debate were at first caught off guard by this extension.[28] But not surprisingly, well before the controversy surrounding the negotiations on the Agreement on Trade Related Investment Measures (TRIMs) and the Agreement on Trade Related Aspects of Intellectual Property Rights (TRIPs) erupted during and after the Uruguay Round of MTN (1986–1994),[29] many of the aforementioned developmentalists had already considered circumstances under which technological gaps, and the distribution of gains from FDI, between the rich and the poor countries could be widened in the one case and be unevenly obtained in the other. They went on to propose ways to close those gaps and measures to render the distribution less uneven. But thanks to the selective treatment of their ideas so as to fuel the free trade versus protection debate, these contributions have been swept aside and ignored! The rethinking exercise conducted in this book is intended to contribute to the debate on the wisdom of such an agenda from the perspective of the less-developed countries. It is in that regard that it could shed some useful light on certain aspects of the current debate on the merits of globalisation.

While such policy considerations are indeed discussed in especially the last chapter, the primary task in the chapters before then is to establish an alternative developmentalist version of history of thought on the subject of development and trade. Let it be reiterated that this book is only taking one step, albeit a serious one, toward re-examining that history. A sense of some possible limitations of this first step can be gained by clarifying what significant elements, which authors, or what important works have been left out.

Firstly, it would have been of interest to compare and contrast the growth, trade, and investment process discussed in Chapters 4 and 5 in Part I with the literature on imperialism.[30] Secondly, it could be illuminating to compare and contrast the ideas re-examined in Part II with the literature on mercantilism. But limited by the scope of the present work, these would have to await future research. While Smith, Ricardo, Mill and, to a lesser extent, Torrens, are indeed the most appropriate economists whose works should be the focus of Part I, there are some names that could, with fairly easy justification, be added to Part II were it not for space limitation. These include, but are not restricted to, John Rae, Henry Carey, Frank Graham, Paul Rosenstein-Rodan, W. Arthur Lewis, Ragnar Nurkse, and Albert Hirschman.[31] The first two do receive some coverage in Chapter 6 below, but the remaining four receive no, or only scarce, mention.[32] Lastly, because of the language barriers faced by the present author, to the extent that there are non-English works published by five of the six developmentalists in Part II that have not been translated into English, they have not been included among the materials consulted.[33]

With these omissions noted, the rest of the book is organised as follows.

1.2 ORGANISATION OF DISCUSSION BY CHAPTERS

Part I begins with a short chapter, Chapter 2, that reviews the interpretation in the mainstream history of economic thought that gives currency to the static classical trade models. That chapter also serves as a reference point for comparison and contrast when the alternative developmentalist interpretation is advanced in Chapters 3 to 5.

Chapter 3 focuses on Smith's and Ricardo's analytical frameworks for studying capitalist development, and the former's 'productivity theory' (Myint 1958) is stitched up with the latter's argument against the Corn Laws.

That produces a compelling two-pronged case for pursuing free trade by the England of their times. In particular, by specialising in manufactures and exporting them, she could harness the benefits from division of labour that are richly associated with those products. At the same time, by importing food and raw produce, she could circumvent the problem of rising wages and cost of production that are inevitable due to the 'natural impediments' to the procurement of those commodities.

With the benefit of hindsight, Smith's observation on how the improvement of the productive powers of labour in agriculture does not always keep pace with their improvement in manufactures (section 3.3 in Chapter 3) turns out to be a most consequential one. If one accepts it, and if one considers a two-country model of pure trade with no foreign investment and the two goods – agricultural and manufactured – have identical income elasticity of demand, then the country that specialises in manufactures, thanks to its more rapid productivity improvements, would experience a declining commodity terms of trade (CTT) over time.[34]

Torrens and Mill were both cognizant of the aforementioned observation made by Smith. Apparently neither made distinctions between agricultural and manufactured goods in terms of their income elasticity of demand.[35] Hence, both anticipated that England's future relied on more than just trade. Specifically, while subscribing to Smith's 'productivity theory' and Ricardo's argument against the Corn Laws, both concluded that the pattern of trade that they (Smith and Ricardo) proposed would engender a situation of uneven development, with England leading the rest of the world. In that context and given the trade pattern, she would increasingly run into problems of finding markets for her manufactures as well as finding supplying countries that would augment their production of food and raw produce at a fast enough pace to satisfy her voracious demand. Torrens's route to this discovery is outlined in Chapter 4. His policy response was to advocate 'commercial reciprocity' and he also re-dedicated himself to the colonisation movement. Mill's extension of Smith and Ricardo is represented in Chapter 5. Unlike Torrens, he was much more focused on England's need to augment supplies of food and raw produce. To this end he recommended the 'perpetual overflow of capital' from England to either help raise the production in other countries or to establish new colonies with the same purpose in mind. Their response to the incipient declining CTT for England was to increase the flow of English capital to others, as the coloniser or the foreign investor. In the process one moves beyond the two-country confine of the typical trade model and trade is also no longer the only activity that is involved.

While England's growth and development was thus amply nourished in this expanding trade and investment (colonial) network, there were plenty of other countries and territories in that network that were lagging behind, and were envious, if not resentful, of her. It was in that context of uneven development, a context that has been bequeathed down to the present (though England has been joined by other countries in the group of economically advanced countries or industrial 'centres'), that the developmentalists sought to find ways for the 'less-developed' countries or regions to catch up, be it with England when it was still the nineteenth century or with the developed countries in today's world. Their ideas are re-examined in Part II.

Chapter 6 partly serves the same function for Part II as Chapter 2 does for Part I. Thus, while Ricardo's England–Portugal model is the anchor in the story told in Chapter 2, Mill's oft-quoted qualified-endorsement passage for infant-industry protection is in many ways the focal point in Chapter 6. But while in Part I it is not until Chapters 3 to 5 that an alternative interpretation is advanced, in Part II some seeds for alternatives are sown in Chapter 6. The chapter thus reviews the interpretation in the mainstream history of economic thought that gives currency to the theory of domestic divergences and it takes the discussion back to the classical period. It draws attention to the faith on the part of the classical economists in the spontaneity and automaticity of structural changes under free trade conditions in the primary-producing countries that traded with England. This explains their objection to a reliance on regulation and protection to promote manufactures. Mill was to break ranks and offered a qualified endorsement of infant-industry protection. However, his lack of direct familiarity with Hamilton's and List's works, and his narrow reference to Rae (and Carey), are all noted so as to set the stage for the discussions in Chapters 7 to 12. Despite his lack of familiarity and appreciation of these people's ideas, his own fame has lent tremendous authority to his representation of them. It is in consideration of this that two features of his endorsement passage deserve attention in particular. One is that it only refers to import duties as the instrument for promoting 'infant industries', thus giving the impression that, according to the most powerful minds among the 'protectionists', that was the best policy instrument of which they could conceive. The other feature is that without specifying the wider economic and technological environment within which one or some such infant industries are situated (and if more than one industry, any possible inter-industry dynamics), the passage is of extremely limited use in shedding light on the process of development. The first feature is still a major part of what drives today's debate on trade policies. The second feature, sadly speaking, has been bequeathed down to modern times so that within the economics mainstream an overwhelming amount of attention is afforded to static efficient resource allocation, and along the way development as a process has been portrayed in the most trivialised manner.

Chapter 7 re-examines Hamilton's approach to promoting American development. Smith's observation on the greater scope for division of labour in manufactures did not escape his attention. He thus deplored an America that was predominantly agricultural and anticipated some of the drawbacks of relying excessively on primary exports that more than one-and-a-half centuries later Prebisch, Myrdal, and Singer were to stress (on which see Chapters 10 to 12 below). He shrewdly noted that structural changes involving the establishment of manufactures would not occur spontaneously in the course of free trade. State aid to enhance her technological capability and to support her nascent manufactures would be needed. Contrary to the portrayal by the economics mainstream,[36] he showed a keen awareness of the advantages of deploying bounties. Nevertheless, his realisation of their own drawbacks and his understanding of the public-finance constraint on deploying them put him in a more pragmatic position. He thus saw the importance and necessity of also relying on tariffs as well as several other instruments, including, significantly, those that would encourage technology acquisition through inventions, discoveries and technology piracy.

Chapter 8 considers List's programme of development promotion. Smith's observation on more opportunities for division of labour in manufactures also did not escape his attention. His warning of the danger of remaining predominantly agricultural again touched upon some issues that a little over a century later occupied the attention of Prebisch, Myrdal, and Singer. Not surprisingly, his case for diversifying into manufactures resembles that of Hamilton, but he moved beyond the latter by incorporating 'productive powers' (the 'power of producing wealth') and 'reciprocal effects' into the discussion. Similar to Hamilton, he was sceptical toward free trade as a measure to promote structural changes. Like Hamilton, he was not single-mindedly pushing for tariffs as the means of encouragement. Instead, he proposed many forms of state aid to cultivate and invigorate productive powers through the encouragement of manufactures. Last but not least, there is one portion of his policy programme that relates to EP, including an element that anticipates the 'import substitution as export promotion' idea of Krugman (1984).

Manoïlesco, the focus of Chapter 9, attempted to make a case for state support for expanding the superior (that is, industrial) sectors by employing a slightly augmented textbook Ricardian model. The latter has the property of confining the user's attention to static allocative issues and his adoption of it has thus an unfortunate consequence. It has led mainstream interpreters to conclude that it has to be a market failure of some sort that prevented more workers from being allocated from the agricultural to the superior sectors. It thus reinforces the illusion that the needed structural changes for development is only one market-failure correction away. However, upon closer examination his augmentation of the textbook Ricardian framework is flawed in the first place, and his conclusion, contrary to his wish, would turn out to be no different than what has been drawn from the unaugmented model. While his discussions of it thus amounted to much ado about nothing, the mainstream has seized the one-market failure idea, added elegance to the scaffolding that surrounds it, and perpetuated the illusion that development – in the form of static efficient resource allocation – is merely one market-failure correction away. Despite all this, the mainstream's criticism that instead of protection Manoïlesco should have simply proposed using a subsidy is somewhat misplaced, because he did indicate an awareness of possibly relying on 'subventions' (and a few other measures) to encourage the expansion of the superior sectors. Nevertheless, from the perspective of this book's thesis, he is the weakest link among the group of six in Part II.

Smith's observation on the greater scope for division of labour in manufactures also caught Prebisch's and Singer's attention. However, contrary to the prediction that emerges out of the two-country and two-good (identical income elasticity) pure-trade framework that was alluded to in the early part of the present section, both drew attention to the problem of declining CTT for the less-developed countries. Many have since christened the thesis of declining CTT for those countries as the Prebisch–Singer Thesis (PST).[37] Both noted that historically the advanced industrial countries had invested in (or sometimes colonised) underdeveloped territories and regions in order to augment the production of primary products, *à la* Torrens's and Mill's prescription (although it is doubtful if Prebisch and Singer were aware of this aspect of their works). Both recognised the generally higher income elasticity of demand for manufactured than agricultural products. Finally, both also teased out a possible implication of Smith's observation on division of labour, namely that such division in manufactures could, and did actually, advance to a stage where a new industry emerges to produce synthetic substitutes for their natural counterparts.[38] More generally, new techniques and production processes could be, and have indeed been, introduced that economise on the use of raw materials. All said, both found even more reasons than Hamilton and List for the less-developed countries to diversify their economies, upgrade their technologies, and undo the hindrances to development that earlier FDI which largely focused on primary production had brought about.

Prebisch, the focus of Chapter 10, thus also advocated industrialisation. However, coming right after the chapter on Manoïlesco, one can sense that his works reveal a much deeper appreciation of the obstacles to development and their interconnectedness. While the mainstream has become fixated on the PST, he was actually more broadly concerned with the uneven (technological) development between the centre and the periphery. He thus advocated improving peripheral productivity in both agriculture and industries, and infusing 'dynamism' into the development process. The interconnected obstacles that he paid more attention to were the 'chronic savings gap', 'persistent disequilibrium in balance of payments', lack of industrialisation, and inadequate 'technological densities' in the periphery. Seen in that light, the reduction of his case for protection to one akin to an optimal-tariff case for a primary exporting country with monopoly power has done him great injustice. There are signs, even if limited, that he was aware of the importance of comparing the sensibility of different policy instruments in certain situations. Thanks to his focus on the interconnected obstacles, he was not single-mindedly advocating IS. Early on he advocated the promotion of manufactured exports.

Chapter 11, one focused on Myrdal, is placed before the ensuing one on Singer given the influence that the former had on the latter. Like Prebisch, Myrdal advocated both IS and EP, and he showed in several instances an ability to sensibly compare different policy instruments. However, he was not naïvely expecting industrialisation by itself would ensure that 'international inequalities' between the advanced and underdeveloped countries would be reduced, let alone eliminated. Thanks to his holistic approach to research that embodies the principle of circular and cumulative causation, he emphasised much more explicitly than Prebisch the inter-linkages of various obstacles to development. Thus, policies to promote industrialisation and trade policies are only part of a broader plan that aims at moving the entire social system upward. He was not under the illusion that the implementation would be simple and success would come easily. In fact, he was alert to the problem of corruption, or more generally the problem with 'soft states'. However, unlike many mainstream economists who subsequently attended to the problem of 'rent-seeking' and decided that practically one should simply throw in the towel and not try to interfere with anything, Myrdal would only support sensible policy 'retrenchment' but would otherwise continue to support state actions in the underdeveloped countries that harness the spread effects while curtailing the backwash effects of economic expansions in the industrial centres.

As Chapter 12 illustrates, despite being associated with Prebisch regarding the PST, the more interesting parallel between Prebisch and Singer is found in their broader frameworks of development analysis. While the former concerned himself with centre–periphery uneven technological development, the latter focused on 'international dualism' especially with respect to the capacity to use science and technology. Though less explicitly than how Prebisch had expressed his concern with the persistent external disequilibrium in many countries in the periphery, Singer also put more stress on the income terms of trade (ITT) than the CTT faced by many less-developed countries. On the other hand, Prebisch's rather subtle emphasis on indigenous 'technological densities' contrasts with the stark importance that Singer placed on an indigenous 'capacity to create wealth' (and on this, one wonders if he might have been influenced by List's notion of the 'power of producing wealth'). Both, perhaps slightly more so in the case of Singer, expressed caution toward the role that FDI could play in technology transfer and the tackling of international dualism. Both supported IS while being alert to its shortcomings, and both recognised the importance of interweaving EP with IS. Finally, in depicting international dualism as a consequence of how 'divergent' forces had tended to dominate over 'convergent' forces, and in quite frequently invoking the principle of cumulative and mutual causation in connecting various factors that contributed to that dualism, it is clear that Singer was strongly influenced by Myrdal.

Chapter 13 sums up the discussion. Embedded in mainstream trade and commercial policy theories is a conceptualisation of development as attaining efficient static resource allocation under freely operating market forces, with allowance for market failures that impede such efficient allocation but where those failures are mainly treated in compartmentalised manners. The developmentalist version of history of thought advanced in the present work leads to an alternative conceptualisation. Instead of an equilibrium framework, one is confronted with all kinds of backwash/polarising and spread effects that obtain under the free functioning of market forces. Operating in accordance with the principle of circular and cumulative causation, the process of development is uneven across countries and between regions within countries. After summing up such differences in the two conceptualisations, the chapter teases out some implications for interpreting the outcomes of MTNs, especially regarding whether special and differential treatment (SDT) should be offered to the less-developed countries. In the pre-Uruguay Round period SDT chiefly concerned the right of the state in the less-developed countries to enjoy relative autonomy in employing policies of all sorts to promote their development. For that period a distinction can be drawn between GATT-defined SDT and implicit SDT. The former element essentially relates to the flexibility on the part of the less-developed countries in employing trade instruments and how they expect 'non-reciprocity' in trade negotiations. Informed by its own version of history of economic thought, this former element is what the mainstream has focused on and is what it regards as harmful to development. The latter element relates to the policy space to deploy non-trade instruments (especially subsidies), cultivate technological capabilities, and regulate FDI, all of which were largely implicitly available prior to the Uruguay Round of MTNs. Could the countries that have enjoyed success in development since World War II be so regarded because they have sensibly exploited both

GATT-defined and the implicit SDT? If so, is it a grave mistake for the mainstream to narrowly focus on GATT-defined SDT? The Uruguay Round of MTNs rolled back GATT-defined SDT, made explicit the heretofore implicit forms of SDT, and put substantial restrictions on them. Is the outcome of that round then strongly anti-development? In the post-Uruguay era, SDT has come to mean assisting the less-developed countries to build capacity for integration into the world trading system. What could be the implication of that definition of SDT for development? What have been the ongoing battles to switch some significant elements of SDT back to the right of states to development promotion? There are questions here that are beyond the scope of this book to address thoroughly. The hope is that the message from the alternative developmentalist version of history of thought proposed here and the conceptualisation of development contained therein offers the reader a meaningful alternative to think about these questions.

The challenge set forth in the present work is formidable given how deeply ingrained in the minds of mainstream economists their version of history of thought is. If the alternative version advanced here is worth its label, the readers' familiarity with it cannot be assumed. Instead, proposing it necessitates a lot of textual support from the original works of those that are being re-examined. Hence, the reader should be prepared to come across a large amount of direct quotations. These can be tedious at times, but they are indispensable for a work of this nature.

NOTES

1. Writing around the dawn of the current globalisation debate, Bhagwati – who was subsequently to become the Economic Policy Advisor to the Director General of the General Agreement on Tariffs and Trade, Special Adviser to the United Nations on Globalisation, and External Adviser to the Director General of the World Trade Organisation – succinctly put it thus: 'the theory of trade and welfare provides the underpinnings for the general principles that underlie GATT' (1987b, pp. 551–2).
2. Such illustrations and the assumptions which they rest upon can readily be found in the chapters on trade models in various standard textbooks on International Economics.
3. Mainstream trade theories have certainly found expressions in more than just the static classical trade models, for instance, in the Heckscher–Ohlin–Samuelson (H–O–S) model. But as Haberler aptly observed, 'A very large part of classical, neo-classical and modern theory of international trade is based on the doctrine of Comparative Cost or Comparative Advantage as originally presented in Chapter VII of David Ricardo's *Principles of Political Economy*', and 'the family resemblance of the modern version or versions with their Ricardian prototype is unmistakable, just as a modern Cadillac or Rolls Royce belongs to the same family as the Model T Ford' (1964, pp. 130–31). '[D]espite the author's protestations', Haberler further remarked in another discussion, 'B. Ohlin's important contribution does not fall outside the main current of classical thought' (1954, p. 544). For the present discussion it is important to recognise that, in assuming factor endowments to be given and technology to be identical across countries, the H–O–S model is of limited relevance for understanding the process of development. To be sure, it has been employed to explore the effects of trade protection. However, those effects pertain to the static results

in resource allocation, especially as they relate to income distribution, rather than to impinging upon the process of development. For these considerations the H–O–S model will only receive occasional mentioning in the rest of this book.

4. For two excellent references on this, see Corden (1997) and Bhagwati, Panagariya and Srinivasan (1998), as well as the reference lists therein.
5. For three recent exercises of this nature, see Irwin (1996), Maneschi (1998), and Gomes (2003). Of these, the first tows the mainstream line the most religiously. The second actually expresses some thoughtful doubts regarding the mainstream version of the history of thought on this subject. The last is essentially a combination of Gomes (1987, 1990) with some updates and extensions, and is quite in harmony with mainstream interpretations of the history of thought.
6. As Krugman (1992a, p. 424) states it in a most telling manner, 'An understanding of the principle of comparative advantage, and an appreciation of the virtues of Free Trade, are key dividers between trained economists and the Gentiles; even brash young theorists are hesitant to risk excommunication by challenging these tenets directly'.
7. These are too numerous to mention. See section 2.1 below for further reference to the theoretical challenges. The latter part of section 13.3 lists some significant empirical challenges.
8. The two companion volumes, Sundaram (2005) and Sundaram and Reinert (2005), usefully re-examine the works of some pioneers and the origins of development economics respectively, but the focus of each is not so much about rethinking trade and commercial policy theories. See also Sundaram and Fine (2006).
9. Again, these are too numerous to mention. With the onset of the globalisation debate, there has definitely been a massive proliferation of books published with the word 'globalisation' in the title. According to Scholte (2008, p. 1472), the entries for 'globalisation' in the USA Library of Congress skyrocketed from 34 in 1994 to 5,245 in 2005!
10. The present author realises that not all efforts that caution against globalisation are equally thoughtfully undertaken. It is, however, not within the scope of this book to make comparisons among them.
11. See also Bhagwati (2002a, Lecture 1; 2004, Ch. 5) and Irwin (2002a, Ch. 2).
12. The present author is well aware that the more careful mainstream researchers have noted other insights that can be found in the works of the classicists. Nevertheless, these are generally recognised in isolation without a systematic effort to stitch them together and then to explore their implications for uneven development. See Ch. 2 below.
13. One direction of extension was to add an additional factor of production and jettison the labour theory of value. The H–O–S model that ultimately emerges supports, under certain assumptions, the factor-price equalisation theorem, which is an internationally equalising effect *par excellence*!
14. Mainstream trade theories are built upon the operation of equilibrating forces which, under free and competitive market conditions without market failures, allegedly bring about equilibrium results that have some desirable normative properties. Unfortunately, the implication of its reliance on equilibrating processes has not been adequately fathomed. While some economic adjustments under free market conditions do tend to bring convergence, if not equality, of certain economic outcomes, it is a gross mistake to ignore disequilibrating forces that tend to polarise such outcomes. This is where the prominent developmentalists re-examined in Part II of the present book enter into the discussion.
15. In fact, the subscribers to these models precisely pride themselves in being able to illustrate that even the country that possesses absolute disadvantages in producing all goods – that is, the technological laggard – can still gain from trade so long as it possesses comparative advantage in producing something. See the discussion in Ch. 2 below. It also bears repeating that in the H–O–S model, technology is assumed to be identical across countries.
16. See section 3.8 in Ch. 3 below.
17. This is reflected by the very limited coverage of topics like foreign direct investment and the activities of transnational or multinational corporations in standard textbooks on International Economics. Besides, in that very limited coverage the significance of those activities tends to be belittled. Thus, as Krugman and Obstfeld (1991, pp. 168–9) contend,

'[M]uch of what multinationals do could be done without multinationals, although perhaps not as easily. ... [T]he shift of labor-intensive production from industrial countries to labor-abundant nations, and capital flows from capital-abundant countries to capital scarce countries ... reflect the "location" aspect of our theory of multinationals, which is really no different from ordinary [that is, H–O–S] trade theory. If multinationals were not there, the same things would still happen, though perhaps not to the same extent. This observation leads international economists to attribute less significance to multinational enterprise than most lay observers'.

18. Examples of strong insistence that evaluation of cases for protection should be conducted within the equilibrium framework can be found in Baldwin (1969, p. 238) and Srinivasan (1985, pp. 38–9).
19. There were, of course, also the mercantilists. Limited by space, their ideas will not be considered in this book.
20. For an oft-cited reference, see Baldwin (1969). See also the introductory sections in Chs. 7, 8, and 9 below for additional references.
21. Labelling the analysis of the 'welfare and structural aspects of the theory of international trade' as 'pure reallocation analysis', Linder (1961, pp. 12, 11) laments that such analysis 'has not provided proper guidance in explaining reality' and notes that '[t]he more essential task of studying ... the impact of trade on the processes of growth and stagnation receives scant attention'. 'Lack of reallocative ability', he believes, 'might exclude any reallocation gains from trade' (ibid., p. 12). He proceeds to construct two alternative models that are based on differential treatment of the 'adjustment process' subsequent to the opening-up of trade for two groups of countries. The distinction between them is based upon the 'ability or lack of ability ... to reallocate resources' (p. 14). However, it should be noted that for the model of the 'growth countries', he draws on the 'traditional reallocation analysis' such that 'reallocation takes place instantaneously' (ibid.) The other model is designed for what he calls 'u-countries', those that are 'supposedly bearing some similarity to the underdeveloped countries of the present-day world' and where the 'absence of growth capacity implies a lack of reallocative capacity' (p. 13). See n. 2 in Ch. 10 below for further description of this latter model, including how Linder considers it to be capturing some aspects of the Prebisch–Singer–Myrdal thesis.
22. While certain economic terminologies are found commonly employed across distinct analytical frameworks, the fact that they are rooted in such different frameworks usually implies that they play different conceptual roles and assume different analytical meanings. Thus, in mainstream equilibrium analysis a market failure arises in a situation where free operation of market forces does not result in a Pareto efficient equilibrium outcome. If, as this book contends, the developmentalists, excepting Manoïlesco, were seeking to study underdevelopment outside the equilibrium framework, then 'market failures' that result in inefficiencies in a Paretian sense have no role to play in their analyses. Lall and Latsch (1999) offer a thought-provoking challenge to the usefulness of the mainstream notion of 'market failure' in development studies that pertains to the consideration here and is worth quoting at full length: 'There is ... a wider question of whether the "market failure" terminology is appropriate for analysing issues that go well beyond achieving a static optimum. Government interventions can go beyond correcting for existing market deficiencies to changing the parameters within which markets function, by creating new factor endowments, institutions and market structures. It is difficult to describe the latter set of interventions as remedying "market failures" in the neoclassical sense, that is with reference to a competitive equilibrium. In principle, markets can clear *within* a given set of endowments and parameters, even if these occur at low levels of income and growth. The conventional market failure approach has little to say on changing those endowments and raising the economy beyond "low level equilibrium". Yet changing endowments and developing new market structures is what development policy is all about. Most governments seek to dynamise their economic growth, create new sources of comparative advantage, deepen the industrial structures and expand their base of technological capabilities. In addition they often aim to develop specific industries and enter into new groups of activities that are believed to be more conducive to growth, competitiveness and

technological progress than others' (ibid., p. 46, n. 33, italics original). On the subject of technology policy R. Nelson (2009) similarly argues that efforts to build 'effective innovation systems' is far from the same as correcting 'market failures' in static frameworks. C. Wolf (1979) proposes to employ the notion of 'market inadequacies' instead of 'market failures'. But what counts as inadequate will still depend on the analytical framework employed. As additional examples of how the analytical framework matters, consider how notions like 'external economies' and 'increasing returns' have been variously defined, and assumed different shapes and forms in different models.

23. It should be stressed that the 'principle of targetting' is not an insight that is unique to mainstream economics. Thus, to claim that some of the developmentalists have anticipated this principle in no way suggests that their works have in some ways validated mainstream economic analysis. Rather, the 'principle of targetting' *per se* is a commonsensical idea that can find application in other frameworks and fields. Consider, for instance, advising patients on medical treatment. It certainly makes sense for a physician to prescribe a treatment that targets as closely as possible the source of the patient's problem and which causes no or minimal undesirable side-effects (while ignoring in this brief consideration the differences in monetary cost in alternative treatments). Interestingly, even in this context one can easily relate to something akin to the Theory of Second Best (on which more in section 6.5 in Ch. 6 below). Thus, if the only problem experienced by a patient were obesity, then the first-best advice could simply be exercise. But if in addition to obesity the patient had a serious heart problem, then perhaps exercising would no longer be the first-best treatment. It should then be obvious why mainstream treatments of market failures often involve comparmentalisation. That is practised because otherwise second-best complications would render it quite impossible to obtain clean and precise policy rankings.
24. The same applies to the dynamic classical analyses. Thus, while the developmentalist interpretation of the works of the classical economists advanced in Part I focuses attention on uneven development, one should not easily feel contented that the mechanisms engendering that outcome have been fully and adequately spelled out by them. Future research should consider what other mechanisms might have been at work, and thus what remains to be refined and extended in that framework.
25. The excitement about 'increasing returns', and the effort that sprang from it to construct the 'new trade theory' and to design 'strategic trade polices' soon became subdued by the old guards in the mainstream. The tool to achieve this was none other than the theory of domestic divergences. See, for instance, Bhagwati (1989, section VI). With specific reference to those models that claim to incorporate increasing returns with monopolistic competition, Ocampo and Taylor (1998, pp. 1524–5) critically point out that '[t]he main response to decreasing costs on the part of mainstream "new" trade theory has been to muffle the impact of scale economies by "convexifying" assumptions, e.g. the Dixit–Stiglitz (1977) model of monopolistic competition in which firms' profitability gains from returns to scale are strictly limited by consumers' desires for product diversity. Protection to force big cost reductions from long product runs cannot pay off. It makes little sense to introduce one more yuppie automobile marque if its intended consumers' preferences for diversity are going to limit sales to an uneconomical 100,000 units per year'.
26. Stiglitz's own emphasis is chiefly on 'information imperfections' as added complications to the standard problems of market failures. The developmentalists re-examined in Part II of the present work did not conceptualise the problem of underdevelopment with this emphasis.
27. This should serve as a reminder that all so-called 'protectionists' are not alike. Some are far more sophisticated than others. It is a grave mistake to lump them together, although doing so has provided some tactical advantages to the economics mainstream.
28. Thus, Bhagwati (2002b) can be regarded as playing 'Monday morning quarterback' with regard to the Agreement on Trade Related Aspects of Intellectual Property Rights, specifically concerning patents. For playing a similar position with respect to the Uruguay Round Agreements more generally, see Finger (2001), and Finger and Nogués (2002).
29. Further negotiations in both areas have occasionally been pushed in the Doha Round of MTNs that is ongoing while this book was written.

30. One contemporary of Torrens and Mill whose works should also be re-examined is Edward Gibbon Wakefield.
31. Some might also wonder if Alfred Marshall should be a noticeable part of the discussion in Ch. 6. He was familiar with some of List's works and showed some admiration of his ideas. He was quite curious about the American protectionists and had an opportunity to meet Carey during his visit to America. Few can deny that his conceptualisation of external economies, though in some respects obscure, has provided strong inspiration to certain prominent development economists. Nevertheless, a thorough and balanced treatment is well beyond the scope of the present work.
32. There is also a fairly sizeable literature produced chiefly in the 1950s and 1960s that cast doubt on the automaticity of structural changes in the primary exporting countries in the course of trade. See, for instance, Baldwin (1956), Rollins (1956), Levin (1960), Watkins (1963), Seers (1964), Caves (1965), and Hirschman (1977).
33. One further omission that is in a sense too big to mention is the evolving international monetary and financial framework within which various countries have been seeking to develop and trade. There is certainly a history-of-thought project concerning that area that is extremely worthy of pursuit. See Gomes (1993) for a serious attempt to do so.
34. The assumption of identical income elasticity of demand is unnecessarily strong and can certainly be relaxed. However, how much variation in magnitude can be accommodated depends on, *inter alia*, consumption patterns, input-use patterns (if applicable), and relative growth rates of the two countries.
35. Some have suggested that the differences in income elasticity of demand between agricultural and manufactured products did not become consequential until the gaps in living standards between the developed and less-developed regions had widened to what was witnessed in the twentieth century. Rosenstein-Rodan (1943, p. 209) thus notes that, 'International trade in the nineteenth century functioned more or less smoothly because all countries had a high income elasticity of demand for imports. On the higher standard of living in the rich countries of the twentieth century the income elasticity of demand for imports may be lower'.
36. Irwin (1996) as an exception is duly noted in Ch. 7 below.
37. See Toye and Toye (2003) for a discussion of the origins and interpretation of the PST.
38. Hufbauer (1966, pp. 38–46) provides a short history of the emergence of the synthetic materials industry and its structural features among the major industrial countries up to the 1960s.

PART I

Re-interpreting Classical Trade Theories in a Simple Framework of Capitalist Development

2. The Mainstream Interpretation of Classical Trade Theories

2.1 INTRODUCTION[1]

Until the construction of the so-called 'new trade theory' beginning from the late 1970s,[2] different models of trade were (and often still are) typically distinguished from each other according to what inter-country difference is assumed to be initially given in providing an explanation of why international trade takes place. Seldomly, if ever, have these models been differentiated according to the kind of international development process which they can accommodate into their analyses. In almost all cases, there is no development process whatsoever while the focus is largely on static resource reallocation through trade. A development process, should one be incorporated, inevitably entails modifications and alterations of some of the initial inter-country differences in the course of development and trade, and yet these are precisely what most trade models have little or nothing to describe about. The argument in these models is simply, but strictly, one way from inter-country differences to trade. Mutually beneficial results from re-allocation of resources called for by trade are guaranteed when certain assumptions are made.[3]

Thus, consider the classical trade theories. Technological differences among countries figure prominently in explaining why trade takes place. In the standard framework employed to illustrate the mainstream version of the theories (in which framework it is assumed that labour is the only factor-input and it operates with constant returns to scale), such differences are represented by given differences in the direct labour coefficients. While the trade which arises is shown to be mutually beneficial to the trading countries, the 'gains' are merely consumption (static welfare) gains and they have absolutely no modifying effects on the given technological differences. Obviously, if the latter remain constant over time, the outcomes which are theorised to depend upon them (that is, the pattern, volume, and benefits of trade) would likewise be unchanging. For instance, if trade conferred a certain amount of gains on the trading countries when it was first opened up, then barring the introduction of any exogenous changes in the initially given data, the same amount of gains will be accorded to them, and the proportion in which these gains are shared among them will remain fixed, forever after.

Yet, as Williams incisively remarked long ago, '[i]t is one question whether these conclusions follow logically from these premises. It is a more important question whether these are the premises best calculated to illuminate the subject-matter' (1929, pp. 195–6). If the subject matter is the process of development, then it is unmistakable that concomitant with the process of trade and investment expansion, technological and other differences (for example, relative growth rates) among certain countries have been widened, while those among other countries have been narrowed.

Thus, consider the time back when England was the most advanced capitalist country. The world was then in a unique 'uneven' state which could be characterised, in a drastically simplified way, by the technological superiority of England over the rest of the world.[4] The former was then in the process of phasing out various protectionist measures bequeathed from the mercantilist era, and she was preaching the virtues of free trade to the rest of the world. She dominated in manufactured exports while she imported mostly food and primary products. Her enhanced scale of capital accumulation increasingly drew various countries and regions into a network of new or expanded trade and investment.[5] However, the process of an expanding trade and investment network is alien to the static classical (and for that matter, other mainstream) trade models, where the consideration typically involves a two-country situation where a hypothetically no-trade situation is juxtaposed with one that is with-trade. As a result, the implications of this expansion, which has been far from happening at a uniform pace over the course of history and had even occasionally been reversed, have not been adequately fathomed.

Concomitant with this expansion process of the trade and investment network, the technological lead of England over some countries or regions was extended, while it was gradually reduced in other cases. Pollard (1981), together with Hobsbawm (1968, Ch. 9), and Landes (1969, Chs. 3 and 4) portrayed the catching up by the United States and some European countries in especially the latter decades of the nineteenth century. Kaldor concluded that 'Britain's example in industrialisation was followed, *with the assistance of protective tariffs*, by Germany, France, the US and finally Japan (plus a number of smaller European countries)' (1980, p. 88, italics added). Chang (2002, Ch. 2) takes that a step further, includes the East Asian 'newly industrialising countries' (NICs), and contends that '[a]lmost every successful country used infant industry protection *and* other activist ITT [industrial, trade and technology][6] policies when they were "catching-up" economies' (ibid., p. 59, italics added). As these took place, 'while the trade between the different regions of the globe was greatly intensified the differences in wealth and living standards became considerably larger and not smaller' (Kaldor 1980, p. 89). Again, it is not obvious that the static classical trade models would readily allow one to account for these developments.[7]

This part of the book, after a quick review of the static classical trade models, advances an alternative interpretation that places the classical theories within the simple framework of capitalist development that the classical economists worked with in their analyses of the growth and progress of nations. Section 2.2 of this chapter describes how the mainstream interpretation of the classical models came to be consolidated, where attention is particularly drawn to the fact that in that interpretation, the classical trade theories are related to portray the emergence and extension of the two-party exchange analysis which is so fundamental to mainstream economics. Section 2.3 briefly considers the chief implications of the mainstream interpretation. Chapters 3, 4, and 5 in the rest of Part I present the alternative interpretation.

2.2 THE MAINSTREAM APPROACH TO LINKING UP CLASSICAL TRADE THEORIES

The mainstream approach to linking up the classical trade theories employs Ricardo's England–Portugal model (Ricardo [1821] 2004, p. 135) as its anchor. Differences in the pre-trade relative prices are indications that both countries can (assuming that neither of them is too 'large' in relation to the other) specialise and trade to augment their consumption sets, and thereby attain higher welfare levels. In terms of its conclusion, it thus harmonises neatly with that of the neoclassical two-party production-and-exchange analysis, which is itself an extension of the two-party exchange analysis that is so fundamental to mainstream economics.

The thorny problem is that the difference between the pre-trade relative prices in the two countries, which reflects relative differences in their technological capabilities, is founded upon the simple labour theory of value. As Knight remarked, 'historically the whole doctrine of comparative cost was a prop for a labor cost theory of value' (1924, p. 599, n. 5). Writing in the 1930s Viner observed that there was then 'almost universal and vigorous rejection of the labor-cost theory' and he lamented that the 'historical association with that theory is proving for the comparative-cost doctrine a hindrance rather than an aid to its general acceptance' ([1937] 1975, p. 491). To remove that hindrance he offered that,

> The association ... is a historical accident, a result merely of the fact that Ricardo, in his pioneer exposition of it, expressed real costs in terms of quantities of labor. ... [I]t is therefore important to emphasize that the doctrine of comparative costs has for most of its exponents derived its cogency from their acceptance of a real-cost theory of value which was not simply a labor-cost theory of value, even when expressed in its terms. (Ibid., pp. 490–91)[8]

Writing at almost exactly the same time, Haberler expressed even more succinctly that that value theory should not be a cause for too much concern.[9] Thus,

> [i]n spite of the defectiveness of this theory, we shall adopt it as our provisional point of departure. It will greatly facilitate the analysis, and, fortunately, we shall be able to show that the deductions obtained with its aid do not depend for their validity upon its assumptions. We shall end by discarding the theory, with all its assumptions, without having to discard the results obtained from it: these will remain, just as a building remains after the scaffolding, having served its purpose, is removed. (1937, p. 126)

Unlike Viner's resort to a 'real-cost theory of value', Haberler followed the Austrian school in measuring costs, with accommodation for many different factors of production, by the alternatives forgone in deriving 'substitution-ratios' between commodities (ibid., p. 177, including n. 5). When all modifications have been introduced, one can safely claim that it is because of the conclusion that one can draw from it that the survival of Ricardo's England–Portugal model in the mainstream trade literature has been ensured!

With recognition thus accorded to this model of Ricardo, economists after him are judged by whether they have improved on the 'special case' to bring it closer to a full-blown neoclassical general equilibrium model. That is the principal reason why Mill has received so much credit for resolving the problem of determining international values. Indeed, Ch. XVIII of Bk. III of his *Principles*, titled 'Of International Values', has been eulogised as the 'great chapter' by Edgeworth (1894a, p. 38).[10] And according to Samuelson (1982, p. 36), 'Mill's chapters on international values provide the first complete model of general equilibrium – one essentially isomorphic with Jevons' chapters a generation later on competitive exchange and with Walras's equilibrium'.[11]

Also, with this recognition of his England–Portugal model, economists before Ricardo are judged, when international trade is concerned, by how close they came to stumbling upon the principle of comparative advantage. That is the reason why Smith has been snubbed, for instance, by Bloomfield (1975, p. 455), who also cites Bastable, Robbins, and Viner to show how they had slighted Smith's contributions to the 'pure theory of international trade'. In the meantime Torrens, Ricardo's contemporary, has been accorded a certain amount of recognition because he is regarded by some to have antedated Ricardo in the discovery of the comparative advantage principle. Gomes (1987, p. 141), for example, notes that Seligman, J. Hollander, Viner, Schumpeter, and Robbins had all acknowledged Torrens's priority.[12] According to Schumpeter (1954, p. 608), he might be the first to suggest (in print) 'reciprocal demand' as the mechanism which would solve the international value problem. Also, as Viner had clarified, Torrens was among the first to discuss the possibility that a tariff might turn the terms of trade in favour of the country imposing it ([1937] 1975, pp. 298–9, 322).

The mainstream interpretation of an area in the history of economic thought – namely international trade theory – is thus established for the classical period. Specifically, Smith recognised the benefits of specialisation and trade based on the principle of 'absolute advantage'. His insight, however, was surpassed by that of Ricardo, who illustrated that it is possible to have mutually beneficial trade based on the principle of 'comparative advantage'. This was in turn improved upon by Mill, who grappled with the problem which went 'unnoticed' by Ricardo – the determination of international values.[13] As this interpretation gains currency, other contributions made by these classical economists to trade (and development) analysis, as well as modern attempts to revive or extend them, have tended to be neglected or even banished. Occasionally, some of these other contributions or insights may be listed as add-ons after the static principle of comparative advantage has been established or asserted.[14] However, the reader is typically not alerted to the fact that the model that is employed to illustrate that principle will have to be drastically reformulated, if not abandoned, had those other contributions (for example, increasing returns) been recognised right from the start when a model is constructed. This is comparable to what Myrdal characterised as 'throw[ing] the yeast into the oven after the bread has been baked', on which see section 11.2 below.

2.3 IMPLICATIONS FOR THE REST OF THE BOOK

In a mutually reinforcing manner this mainstream version of history of economic thought has directed attention to the static classical trade models and their modern-day descendants in the form of mainstream trade models. Collectively, these are models that focus on improving static efficiency (welfare) levels through the opening of trade between countries. As indicated in Chapter 1, they thus shape and freeze debates involving trade policies into ones that pit free trade against protection. They can only be claimed to address development issues if one conceives of development as nothing other than a static allocation process, where all the intricate circular and cumulative results that can arise from allocation are suppressed by the use of given 'well-behaved' functions that pertain to production and to the derivation of utility. Indeed, the mainstream approach to studying 'development' proceeds from 'the crowning achievement of neoclassical economics, namely the two fundamental theorems of welfare economics'. These theorems 'set the stage for an analysis of the role of the state' and '[t]he more thoughtful among the advocates of the free market or of the need for intervention in markets explicitly, or more often implicitly, base their case on these theorems' (Srinivasan 1985, pp. 38, 39). Geared with 'standard' assumptions, the models can illustrate that trade is mutually beneficial. In a static way, by hypothetically considering different possible terms of trade, one can demonstrate different possible distribution of gains between two countries. This is what Mill did, among other things, in Essay I of his *Some Unsettled Questions of Political Economy* (Mill [1874] 1974). Otherwise, uneven development as a process totally eludes these models.

Not surprisingly, these static classical trade models are not without their share of critics, from both within, though mostly from without, the economics mainstream. Along the line mentioned in the introductory section, most of these attacks have centred around its static nature (including its assumption of constant costs)[15] and its lack of attention to the impact of trade on England's trading partners.[16] It has also been criticised for its assumption of factor immobility across countries and its inability to address distributional issues.[17] While these criticisms have for years triggered numerous responses, either to improve or to abandon the theory, few of them (that is, the criticisms) seem to have considered that in the first place Ricardo's England–Portugal model, the anchor in the mainstream interpretation, can be argued to be quite seriously taken out of context.[18]

The three chapters in the rest of this part of the book constitute an alternative framework to relate the classicists that would render their analyses accommodative to the process of uneven development. But it is one thing to be able to accommodate such a process, it is an entirely different matter whether the classicists themselves fully utilised that capacity to investigate the problem of underdevelopment among the trading partners of, or (in the case of Torrens and Mill) recipients of investment from, England. Those three chapters will show that they did not. There are instances in their works where one could detect their apathy to or oblivion of the problem. In other instances, those which will be discussed in the early part of the lead chapter in Part II of the present book, they showed a rather naïve conception of how structural changes would occur spontaneously in the less-developed countries or regions under free trade conditions.

NOTES

1. Sections 2.1 and 2.2 are largely a revised version of sections 1 and 2 in Ho (1996a).
2. For references on this theory, see Krugman (1987, 1992a).
3. For these assumptions, consult the chapters on trade models in any standard textbook on International Economics.
4. See Hobsbawm (1968, Chs. 2 and 3), Landes (1969, Ch. 2), and Pollard (1981, Ch. 1) for discussions of the Industrial Revolution in Britain, and see Hobsbawm (ibid., Ch. 6) for a discussion of the 'second phase' of that process.
5. For a very concise description of British commercial policy and its changes in the mid to late nineteenth century, see McCloskey (1980, pp. 305–9). For an examination of such a policy, but including those practised by other European nations between the early nineteenth to early twentieth centuries, see Bairoch (1989; 1993, Ch. 2). On the expansion of Britain's trade and investment (or colonial) network during this period, see the discussion in Gallagher and Robinson (1953), and see also Fieldhouse (1966, Chs. 11 and 12), Hobsbawm (op. cit., Ch. 7), Pollard (op. cit., Ch. 4), Bagchi (1982, pp. 74–98), and Findlay and O'Rourke (2007, Chs. 6 and 7).
6. The ITT abbreviation is here employed by Chang (2002) to stand for industrial, trade and technology policies. However, for the present book ITT is the abbreviation for income terms of trade.
7. Of course, one can appeal to the so-called 'infant-industry argument' for protection in an attempt to explain some of these. However, see the critical discussion of the development of this argument in Ch. 6 below. In that connection, notice that Chang (op. cit.) does not only mention infant industry protection.
8. See Viner (op. cit., pp. 438, 492) for further elaboration of the real-cost theory of value.
9. For Haberler's own criticisms of the labour theory of value, see Haberler (1937, pp. 126–7, 132, 175, 178).
10. However, Edgeworth indicated that he was not impressed by the three sections that Mill added to that chapter beginning with the third edition of the *Principles* in 1852 (Edgeworth 1894b, p. 609). For a brief discussion of that evaluation and others' reaction to those three sections, see Maneschi (2001, pp. 609–10), who goes on to contend that Mill should share the distinction of formulating the law of international values with Whewell. See also Creedy (1992) for an earlier argument along similar lines.
11. Haberler described the transition to general equilibrium analysis and its ramifications more fully in the following way: '[I]n the classical and modern literature the simplifying assumptions have been gradually replaced by more realistic ones... The labour theory of value underlying Ricardo's model has been dropped and the modern theory of general equilibrium substituted. ... While in the old classical theory the doctrine of comparative cost occupied a special place outside and apart from the general body of the classical theory – because of the inapplicability of the labour theory of value to international trade in view of the absence of mobility of labour as between countries – today the theory of international trade and the doctrine of comparative cost have been completely assimilated into the general body of economic theory' (1964, pp. 130–31). Also recall n. 3 in Ch. 1 above.
12. See, specifically, Seligman (1903, pp. 344–5), Viner ([1937] 1975, pp. 441–4), Schumpeter (1954, p. 607), and Robbins (1958, pp. 21–4). See also Chipman (1965, pp. 480–82). It is not clear that J. Hollander (1911), despite being mentioned by Gomes (1987), has acknowledged Torrens's priority. Thus, Seligman's award of priority to Torrens was ensued by a brief exchange between himself (1911) and J. Hollander (ibid.). For a case for James Mill's role in the early development of the doctrine, see Thweatt (1976). Gomes (1987, p. 144) regards it to be a case of multiple discovery.
13. As will be shown in Ch. 9 below, Manoïlesco also saw the contributions by Smith, Ricardo, and Mill to be linked in the manner that is laid out here. Seeing Ricardo's England–Portugal model as the anchor, he constructed his attack on the classicists by first attempting to reformulate that model of Ricardo.
14. See, for instance, Irwin (2002a, Ch. 2).

15. Haberler (1961, p. 4) remarks that 'the classical theory of "comparative cost," and the more modern version which succeeded and elaborated it, are static general equilibrium theories. ... There exist only rudiments of truly dynamic analysis in the field of non-monetary trade theory'. For an early and forceful critique on the static nature of the theory, see Williams (1929). As for the assumption of constant costs, the most recent criticism is launched by the 'new trade theorists'. But recall n. 25 in Ch. 1.
16. Smith's free-trade message was not well received in America and many parts of Europe in the late eighteenth century. Into the nineteenth century, even with the addition of the contributions by Ricardo and Mill, there were still many pockets of scepticism and resistance. Today, sceptics are easily heard in especially the less-developed countries.
17. Among other economists, the alleged inability to address distributional issues was the focus of attack by two Swedish economists, Heckscher and Ohlin. When the former broke fresh ground with his 1919 paper on a trade model based on the Marginalist theoretical structure, it was titled: 'The effect of foreign trade on the distribution of income'. And when that paper was selected to be included in the American Economic Association's *Readings in the Theory of International Trade*, he claimed in the prefatory note that his attempt was 'one of the first to combine foreign trade with distribution of income or, perhaps better, with the prices of the agents of production' ([1919] 1949, p. 272).
18. See Maneschi (1992) for a cogent argument along this line to clarify Ricardo's trade theory.

3. Smith and Ricardo: Trade and Uneven Development

3.1 INTRODUCTION

One corollary that follows from the discussion in section 2.1 is that, for a model to be capable of analysing the changing impact of trade on various countries' progress, it must accommodate development into its analysis. To do so, what matters is perhaps not so much which specific inter-country difference is assumed to begin with. Rather, it is the structure of the underlying theoretical framework within which an inter-country difference is rooted that is relevant.

It is with this in mind that this and the following two chapters attempt to reinterpret the classical economists' trade (and in the case of Torrens and Mill, trade and investment) theories within a simple framework of capitalist development. At the risk of oversimplifying their differences, one can suggest that the classical economists were all interested in studying the capitalist growth and development process, especially that in England.[1] They did put different emphases on the factors which pertain to that process so that when they extended their analyses to the international context, they made different contributions to a better understanding of growth, development, and trade. Nevertheless, because of their common interest in examining that process, and because of the strong influence which Smith and Ricardo had exerted on Torrens and Mill, their analyses can neatly be stitched together within a framework of their simple conception of capitalist development. The resulting theory comprises what Myint (1958) has labelled as Smith's 'productivity theory', Ricardo's argument against the Corn Laws, Torrens's advocation of commercial reciprocity and colonisation, and Mill's reasoning that a fast growing capitalist country would have to undertake foreign investment in other countries or to colonise 'uninhabited regions'.

Smith's productivity theory has been revived by Myint (1958, 1977), S. Hollander (1973), and Bloomfield (1975), and something akin to it has received a lot of attention in the literature on the 'new trade theory' that proliferated since the late 1970s. In the 1990s Elmslie and James (1993) and Elmslie (1994) re-examined it slightly more broadly as 'positive feedback mechanisms' to constitute, among other things, an account of uneven development between rich and poor countries. Meanwhile, Ricardo's argument against the Corn Laws has been extended in different directions in the works of Steedman and Metcalfe (1973), Findlay (1974, 1984), Steedman (1979), Walsh (1979), Maneschi (1983), Burgstaller (1986, 1987), and Evans (1989). However, until the present author proposed it in Ho (1996a), there had not been any attempt to link the insight of Smith and Ricardo, as well as to tie their contributions to the discussions by Torrens and Mill, in the manner that is presented here in this part of the book.[2]

This alternative approach to relating classical trade theories could constitute a more fruitful one to follow through the logic of the uneven technological start that was enjoyed by England. Even though it is again 'technological differences' among various countries which have driven them to trade,[3] thanks to the simple framework of capitalist development within which those differences are now rooted, it is no longer a one-way argument. Thus, because of the incorporation of Smith's productivity theory and Ricardo's argument against the Corn Laws, there are mechanisms in the theory that could be suggestive of how England had further enhanced her technological capabilities and augmented her growth rate by expanding trade. These will be further examined in the rest of this chapter. Then because of the inclusion of Torrens's and Mill's support for 'sending capital abroad', there are mechanisms in the theory that could be suggestive of why England had enlarged her international investment network and these are considered in Chapters 4 and 5 below.

The rest of this chapter is organised as follows. Section 3.2 outlines the classical economists' simple conception of capitalist development. Sections 3.3 and 3.4 briefly represent Smith's 'productivity theory' and Ricardo's argument against the Corn Laws, respectively. These are integrated in section 3.5. Section 3.6 considers where the principle of comparative advantage might fit into this framework. Smith's and Ricardo's oblivion of the implications of uneven development, with England further and further surpassing its trading partners, is discussed in section 3.7. While, unlike what Torrens and Mill would do later, they did not advocate sending English capital overseas, they were keenly aware of the possibility of international capital mobility. This awareness is illustrated in section 3.8.

3.2 THE CLASSICAL ECONOMISTS' SIMPLE CONCEPTION OF CAPITALIST DEVELOPMENT[4]

To the classical economists, the progress of capitalist countries closely depends on the process of accumulation of capital. Their analyses invariably involve class distinctions in societies and the income distribution based thereupon. Thus, capitalists are commonly regarded as constituting the 'progressive' class. Profits accrue to them and it is they who save and invest more so than others. However, their ability to do so clearly depends on, *inter alia*, the pattern of income distribution. Any factor that precipitates a fall in the rate of profits would in turn result in a slower rate of accumulation.

Leaving aside the problem of realisation,[5] the rate of profits would be governed by the productivity of the techniques of production (which pertain to the 'integrated wage-goods sector') and the real wage. Hence, two main focuses of analysis among the classical economists were how the techniques of production on the one hand, and wage costs on the other, would change in the course of capital accumulation, which focuses can, as the next two sections will show, be respectively traced to the analyses of Smith and Ricardo. Thus, Smith drew attention to how the techniques of production would change in the process of capital accumulation and the widening of the extent of the market, while Ricardo was concerned about increases in wage (and raw produce) costs during the same process. Not surprisingly, when they extended their respective analyses to the international context, they conceive of the benefits of trade rather differently.

3.3 SMITH'S 'PRODUCTIVITY THEORY'

As Eltis (1975, p. 449) observes, 'an account of *The Wealth of Nations* could hardly be produced which failed to attribute overwhelming importance to [capital] accumulation and what causes it'.

According to Smith, increases in the wealth of nations originate from improvements in the productivity of labour, a process that is limited by the 'extent of the market'. This extent of the market is in turn intimately connected with the scale of capital accumulation. It is in the process of capital accumulation and expansion of the extent of the domestic market that the techniques of production in the economy could become more productive. With a given real wage, the more productive the techniques of production (which apply to the integrated wage-goods sector), the higher the rate of profits (and accumulation) will be.[6]

It is a simple step to extend this argument to an international setting. In Smith's own words in the *Wealth of Nations*,

> By means of it [foreign trade], the narrowness of the home market does not hinder the division of labour in any particular branch of art or manufacture from being carried to the highest perfection. By opening a more extensive market ..., it encourages them [the trading countries] to improve its [their labour's] productive

> powers, and to augment its annual produce to the utmost, and thereby to increase the real revenue and wealth of the society. ([1776] 1979, pp. 446–7)

This extended argument has subsequently been labelled by Myint (1958) as Smith's 'productivity theory'. Smith regarded the discovery of a passage to the East Indies via the Cape of Good Hope as possibly, and the discovery of America as definitely, instances when new and inexhaustible markets were opened up that created ample opportunities for new divisions of labour and improvements of art ([1776] 1979, pp. 448–9).

Is that theory equally applicable to agricultural and manufacturing activities? Here Smith made an observation the significance of which was already noted in section 1.2 above. It was later repeated by Torrens and Mill, and it did not escape the attention of Hamilton, List, Prebisch, and Singer. Specifically, he observes early on in the *Wealth of Nations* that the nature of agriculture 'does not admit of so many subdivisions of labour, nor of so complete a separation of one business from another, as manufactures'. Hence, 'the improvement of the productive powers of labour in this art, does not always keep pace with their improvement in manufactures' (ibid., p. 16). Later in the same work, after pointing out that '[t]he improvement in the productive powers of useful labour depend[s], first, upon the improvement in the ability of the workman; and, secondly, upon that of the machinery with which he works', he goes on to add that, '[b]ut the labour of artificers and manufacturers, as it is capable of being more subdivided, and the labour of each workman reduced to a greater simplicity of operation, than that of farmers and country labourers, so it is likewise capable of both these sorts of improvement in a much higher degree' (ibid., p. 676). The message was that if England were to produce and export manufactures, she could reap larger benefits in the form of labour productivity improvements than if she were to specialise in agricultural activities. Notice that he made no distinction in the income elasticity of demand between the two types of products. That distinction would become central in the works of Prebisch, and to a lesser extent in those of Singer, as discussed in Chapters 10 and 12 below.

3.4 RICARDO'S ARGUMENT AGAINST THE CORN LAWS

Smith's observation that manufacturing activities have more room for improvements in productivity than agriculture was made at a time when '[i]n all the great countries of Europe ..., much good land still remains uncultivated, and the greater part of what is cultivated is far from being improved to the degree of which it is capable' (ibid., p. 374). However, the situation had become quite different by Ricardo's time. As Nurkse (1962, p. 283) dramatises it, 'In England at the time of Ricardo the margin of cultivation was creeping up the hillsides into poorer and poorer land'. The concern of Ricardo was thus: given that the dominant wage-good item was corn, and given that in the course of growth in England the more infertile land had to be cultivated, there would be an increase in the cost of producing corn. Given a social subsistence level for the workers, this would then translate into higher wage costs, entailing a fall in the rate of profits, and hence, a slower rate of accumulation.

The implication of this for an open economy is obvious. Hence, as Ricardo states it in his *Principles of Political Economy and Taxation* (hereafter abbreviated as *Principles*),

> It has been my endeavour to shew throughout this work, that the rate of profits can never be increased but by a fall in wages, and that there can be no permanent fall of wages but in consequence of a fall of the necessaries on which wages are expended. If, therefore, by the extension of foreign trade, or by improvements in machinery, the food and necessaries of the labourer can be brought to market at a reduced price, profits will rise. If, instead of growing our own corn, or manufacturing the clothing and other necessaries of the labourer, we discover a new market from which we can supply ourselves with these commodities at a cheaper price, wages will fall and profits rise. ([1821] 2004, p. 132)

The same conclusions were drawn earlier by him in his *Essay on Profits*[7] ([1815] 1951a, pp. 22–3, 26).

3.5 STITCHING TOGETHER THE TWO ARGUMENTS

It seems that if this insight of Ricardo is combined with that contained in Smith's productivity theory, then free trade can be rendered an even more appealing policy from England's viewpoint. Thus, while free importation of corn into England would circumvent the problem of diminishing returns and check increases in wage costs, the productive powers of the English labourers would rapidly improve if the extent of the market for her exports – manufactures – could be widened!

It is true that Ricardo did not devote any chapter in his *Principles* to principally, let alone exclusively, consider Smith's discussion of the division of labour and how that relates to the widening of the extent of the market. This is despite the observation made by Sraffa (1951a, p. xxiii) that for some parts 'the order of the chapters [in the *Principles*] coincides closely with the order in which the topics are treated in the *Wealth of Nations*'. But while there is no reference to Smith's pin-manufacture example, there is a passage on the manufacture of stockings in the first chapter of the *Principles* that reflects a substantial understanding and appreciation of division of labour in the economy of a fairly advanced kind of his time. To quote this description at length,

> [I]n estimating the exchangeable value of stockings, ... we shall find that their value, comparatively with other things, depends on the total quantity of labour necessary to manufacture them, and bring them to market. First, there is the labour necessary to cultivate the land on which the raw cotton is grown; secondly, the labour of conveying the cotton to the country where the stockings are to be manufactured, which includes a portion of the labour bestowed in building the ship in which it is conveyed, and which is charged in the freight of the goods; thirdly, the labour of the spinner and weaver; fourthly, a portion of the labour of the engineer, smith, and carpenter, who erected the buildings and machinery, by the help of which they are made; fifthly, the labour of the retail dealer, and of many others, whom it is unnecessary further to particularize. ([1821] 2004, pp. 24–5)

Ricardo did not go on to consider how this division of labour would become more elaborate should there be a widening of the extent of the market for stockings. What he did was to hypothetically consider improvements in the different parts of this production process and how the value of stockings would be lowered (ibid.). It was not until four chapters later, and by then stated generally and not with reference to stockings, that he observed that,

> The natural price of all commodities, excepting raw produce and labour, has a tendency to fall, in the progress of wealth and population; for though, on one hand, they are enhanced in real value, from the rise in the natural price of the raw material of which they are made, this is *more than counterbalanced* by the improvements in machinery, by the better division and distribution of labour, and by the increasing skill, both in science and art, of the producers. (Ibid., pp. 93–4, italics added)

Indeed, Ricardo was quite sensitive to the technological changes and productivity improvements occurring in England during his time, observing at one point in the rough draft of *Absolute Value and Exchangeable Value* that, 'In our own times great improvements have been made in the mode of manufacturing cloth, linen and cotton goods, iron, steel, copper, stockings – great improvements have been made in husbandry all which tend to lower the value of these goods and of the produce of the soil' ([1823] 1951a, p. 374). In fact, one frequently comes across references in his works to instances, both hypothetical and actual, of improvements in arts and machinery and the associated improvements in productivity. These span across mining, agriculture, and manufacturing activities (references to these three respective areas of which can be found, for instance, in Ricardo [1821]

2004, pp. 18–19; 15, 79–80; 16, 145). He even admitted that the onset of the stationary state had been 'happily checked at repeated intervals by the improvements in machinery, connected with the production of necessaries, as well as by discoveries in the science of agriculture' ([1821] 2004, p. 120). In this connection, one should take note that improvements in machinery in producing food and necessaries have, to Ricardo, the same significance as extension of foreign trade to acquire cheaper imports of such items, as is evident in the quotation provided in section 3.4 above.[8]

These all suggest that Ricardo was not oblivious to Smith's productivity theory. Earlier on, at one point in the *Essay on Profits*, he thus claimed that 'nations are benefited by the extension of commerce, by the division of labour in manufactures, and by the discovery of machinery, – they all augment the amount of commodities, and contribute very much to the ease and happiness of mankind' ([1815] 1951a, pp. 25–6). Somehow this element has been overshadowed in Ricardo's discussions by his own contributions to trade theories, namely, his argument for the repeal of the Corn Laws,[9] and let it not be forgotten, his illustration of comparative advantage as a basis for trade.[10] Had he given it more emphasis, and had he built a connection with his recommendation to freely import corn to bypass the insurmountable 'natural impediments' in agriculture, his argument for free trade could even be more forceful from the perspective of England. As the discussion in Chapters 4 and 5 below shows, this was left for Torrens and Mill to achieve. In doing so, both concluded that new obstacles to sustaining England's growth rate could arise.[11]

3.6 A PLACE FOR COMPARATIVE ADVANTAGE

Where, then, does that leave Ricardo's static model of trade that embodies the principle of comparative advantage? To put it in a better perspective, one should pay attention to the way that his discussion of the gold specie flow mechanism was set up in the same chapter that contains that model, although it appeared later. There he considered a country that was experiencing improvements in manufacture, drawing to itself more gold, raising its general price level (including the price of corn), and thereby putting itself in a position that was more in need of importing corn from other countries. This consideration can then be tied together with what he argued in a footnote that was inserted right after the England–Portugal model was introduced. In his words in that footnote,

> It will appear then, that a country possessing very considerable advantages in machinery and skill, and which may therefore be enabled to manufacture

> commodities with much less labour than her neighbours, may, in return for such commodities, import a portion of the corn required for its consumption, *even if its land were more fertile, and corn could be grown with less labour than in the country from which it was imported.* (Ibid., p. 136n, italics added)

Which country could that be? He specifically put down in one instance in the pages where he discussed the specie flow mechanism, 'If England were the manufacturing country' (ibid., p. 146). What is more, earlier in this same chapter in the *Principles*, Ricardo reasoned that,

> Under a system of perfectly free commerce, each country naturally devotes its capital and labour to such employments as are most beneficial to each. ... By stimulating industry, by rewarding ingenuity, and by using most efficaciously the peculiar powers bestowed by nature, it distributes labour most effectively and most economically ... It is this principle which determines that wine shall be made in France and Portugal, that corn shall be grown in America and Poland, and that hardware and other goods shall be manufactured in England. (Ibid., pp. 133–4)

In fact, as early as 1815, in a letter dated 13 January to Malthus where he responded to his (Malthus's) supposition of 'a great foreign demand for our raw produce', he countered that '[s]uch a demand cannot exist in the present situation of the world. Raw produce is always imported into the relatively rich country, and never exported from it, but on occasions of dearth or famine' (Ricardo 1951c, p. 171).

Some might argue, as hinted at by Viner ([1937] 1975, p. 530), that the several instances when Ricardo mentioned increases in the 'mass' or 'quantity of commodities' and 'sum of enjoyments' ([1815] 1951a, pp. 25–6; [1821] 2004, pp. 128, 132–4, 319) are indications that his England–Portugal model indeed plays a role that its mainstream interpreters have made it out to be, namely that trade according to the pattern of comparative advantage between two countries will expand the consumption sets in both and their welfare levels. Ricardo's message, however, appears to be as follows. In his *Essay on Profits* he points out that there are two ways in which a country may be benefited by trade:

> one by the increase of the general rate of profits, which, according to my opinion, can never take place but in consequence of cheap food, which is beneficial only to those who derive a revenue from the employment of their capital, either as farmers, manufacturers, merchants, or capitalists, lending their money at interest – the other by the abundance of commodities, and by a fall in their exchangeable value, in which the whole community participate. In the first case, the revenue of the country is augmented – in the second the same revenue becomes efficient in procuring a greater amount of the necessaries and luxuries of life. ([1815] 1951a, p. 25)

But would the whole community in fact share the second kind of benefit when one keeps in mind Ricardo's class-based analysis and the behavioural assumptions for each class that he made? The distinction between luxury imports and imports of food and necessaries is important to remember here. The landlords would like to keep the Corn Laws in place and would benefit from having cheaper luxuries imported. If cheaper corn were to be allowed to be imported, then they would suffer a drop in corn rent, although, if cheaper luxuries could still be imported, their sufferings could be ameliorated to some extent. The labourers might, given any level of money wage, temporarily enjoy cheaper imported food and necessaries. However, when the Malthusian mechanism kicks in, as Ricardo often considered to be the case, then the good time is not going to last. By definition, luxury imports would not be purchased by them. Finally, for the capitalists, they might 'indulge themselves in the purchase of an additional quantity' (*Notes on Malthus*, quoted in Viner [1937] 1975, p. 530). Otherwise, they would have 'an increased means of making savings from their expenditure' (ibid.). Thus, of those two benefits that Ricardo identified, the former augments the rate of accumulation, while the latter 'affords ... incentives to saving, and to the accumulation of capital' ([1821] 2004, p. 133, see also pp. 131–2), and it is no exaggeration to claim that he attached a tremendous amount of significance to the impact of trade on the ability of a country to accumulate capital.

3.7 ENGLAND'S TRADING PARTNERS

Did Smith and Ricardo explore the dynamic implications of the trade pattern proposed in section 3.5 above for England's trading partners?

Smith was oblivious to the implications of his productivity theory for England's trading partners but one can perhaps make the excuse that he did not come out quite explicitly as Ricardo did in advocating the trade pattern described in section 3.5.[12] Nevertheless, in enumerating several reasons at one point in Bk. IV in the *Wealth of Nations* as to why he regarded the 'agricultural systems'[13] to be defective, he considered the advantage that a manufacturing country could possess over those that produced and exported raw produce. That passage is worth quoting at full length:

> A small quantity of manufactured produce purchases a great quantity of rude produce. A trading and manufacturing country, therefore, naturally purchases with a small part of its manufactured produce a great part of the rude produce of other countries; while, on the contrary, a country without trade and manufactures is generally obliged to purchase, at the expence of a great part of its rude produce, a very small part of the manufactured produce of other countries. The one exports

> what can subsist and accommodate but a very few, and imports the subsistence and accommodation of a great number. The other exports the accommodation and subsistence of a great number, and imports that of a very few only. The inhabitants of the one must always enjoy a much greater quantity of subsistence than what their own lands, in the actual state of their cultivation, could afford. The inhabitants of the other must always enjoy a much smaller quantity. ([1776] 1979, pp. 677–8)[14]

Eltis concluded from this that, to Smith, 'a country which successfully develops its industry can attain far more favourable terms of trade between agricultural produce and manufactures than one that is still without a substantial industrial sector' (1988, p. 283).

As Part II of this book shows, this kind of consideration did not escape the attention of Hamilton, List, Manoïlesco, and Prebisch. Singer himself (and working with collaborators in another instance) was to hark back to Smith's observation that there was more room for division of labour in manufactures, and thus opportunities to reap benefits from 'increasing returns, improvement in skills, technological innovations, etc.' (Sapsford, Sarkar and Singer 1992, p. 316; Singer 1991a, p. 339). Without referring to the above quotation from the *Wealth of Nations*, he and his collaborators inferred that 'in the dynamic sense he [Smith] advised industrialization [in developing countries] so as to reap the advantages of technological progress'. In that sense, he thought that he, together with Prebisch and Myrdal who also advocated those countries to industrialise, 'were taking up a line of reasoning derived from Adam Smith' (Sapsford, Sarkar and Singer 1992, p. 316).[15]

In spite of the above passage, Smith thought that 'landed nations', those that consisted in a great measure of proprietors and cultivators, ought to 'allow the most perfect freedom' to the trade of the mercantile nations. For, as Chapter 6 below will further illustrate, he believed that as the surplus produce of their land increased in the course of trade, part of the growing capital 'would naturally turn itself to the employment of artificers and manufacturers at home'. Though they started out 'with much less art and skill', their advantage in serving the home market lay in not having to incur as large a transportation cost as their counterparts who exported from the mercantile states. And 'as their art and skill improved' they would compete strongly with the foreign artificers' and manufacturers' products in the home market and would even drive them out of it. In fact, in further consequence of 'the gradual improvements of art and skill', they would extend their sale beyond the home market and rival with the exports of the mercantile nations (Smith [1776] 1979, pp. 670–71). Notice, however, that a substantial portion of this outcome hinges on a strong protection of the home market that was offered by its supposedly long distance from the mercantile states. This transportation-cost afforded protection has since largely disappeared so that the 'new trade theorists' have to resort to 'strategic trade policies' of some sort (for instance, Krugman 1984) so as to accomplish something akin to what Smith had thought attainable through a 'perfect freedom of trade'. As will be illustrated in Chapter 8 below, it was List who anticipated one such strategic policy and proposed a way for some late industrialising countries to catch up with England.

More fundamentally, the discussions in Part II will remind the reader that it should not be taken for granted that the improvements in 'productive powers' and 'art and skill' envisaged by Smith will happen spontaneously with the extension of the market (be it through free trade as in his 'productivity theory' or through temporary but deliberate creation with the use of strategic trade policies). In his time England was the leading industrial country. Relative to other countries, she had much further cultivated what List called 'the power to produce wealth' (Ch. 8 below) and what Singer would later label as 'the capacity to create wealth' (Ch. 12 below). As such, she was in a unique position to enjoy 'virtuous circles' *à la* Young (1928, p. 539), where the extension of markets allowed her to benefit from further division of labour, and the additional division of labour in turn enabled further extension of her markets. Unfortunately, as the discussion in Part II will explain, the less-developed countries could, instead of virtuous circles of progress, be mired in 'vicious circles' of underdevelopment.

As for Ricardo, regarding his analytical framework, the implication of the trade pattern for the corn-exporting country is very obvious. So did he really turn a blind eye to it? Maneschi (1992, p. 433, n. 2) thinks so when he writes, 'Being primarily concerned with England, Ricardo ignored the possibly adverse dynamic effects of trade on corn-exporting countries'.

As it turns out Ricardo did consider the situation of the corn-exporting countries in his *Principles*, although he tiptoed around the key dynamic implications. For instance, in Chapter XXII he considered the implications of a bounty on the exportation of corn. The hypothetical situation was such that England was the corn-exporting country, while France was the importing country. For reasons that the reader can only speculate, Ricardo assumed that England's farmers could produce corn at constant costs in the discussion spanning the first ten pages or so of that chapter, despite the fact that in the close to 300 pages up to that point, he incessantly drew the reader's attention to the increasing-costs nature of corn production. Thus, within the context that he was reasoning, and after inferring that a bounty on England's corn exports would extend the demand for British corn, he stated that,

> This extension of demand for British corn could not fail to raise its price for a time in the home market ... But the causes which would thus operate on the market price of corn in England would produce no effect whatever on its natural price, or

> its real cost of production. To grow corn would neither require more labour nor more capital. ([1821] 2004, p. 301)

Why would neither more labour nor more capital be required?

> In this account of the effects of a bounty, nothing has been supposed to occur to raise the natural price of corn …; for it has not been supposed, that any additional labour would be required on the land to insure a given production, and this alone can raise its natural price. … So, in the supply of corn, although we should export 2, 3, or 800,000 quarters annually, it would ultimately be produced at its natural price, which never varies, unless a different quantity of labour becomes necessary to production. (Ibid., pp. 303–4)

It was not until a little more than halfway through the chapter that Ricardo finally relaxed the assumption. Nevertheless, he then surprisingly referred only to the implications for rent but not for the rate of profits. Thus, he conceded that,

> But the natural price of corn is not so fixed as the natural price of commodities; because, with any great additional demand for corn, land of a worse quality must be taken into cultivation, on which more labour will be required to produce a given quantity, and the natural price of corn will be raised. By a continued bounty, therefore, on the exportation of corn, there would be created a tendency to a permanent rise in the price of corn, and this … never fails to raise rent. (Ibid., p. 312)

Curiously, in the same 1815 letter to Malthus that was alluded to in section 3.6 above, when he briefly went along with Malthus's supposition of a 'great foreign demand' for England's raw produce, he concluded that 'there can be no question that more capital would be employed on the land, and I think profits would fall' (1951c, p. 171).

Nevertheless, as the discussion in that section indicates, Ricardo did not feel that under a free trade situation England would be a corn-exporting country. In fact, in his *Essay on Profits* he anticipated at one point that 'if it [the English legislature] were to allow a permanently free trade, and did not with every variation of price, alternately restrict and encourage importation, we should undoubtedly be a regularly importing country' ([1815] 1951a, p. 27).

He further regarded France as being one of the exporting countries (ibid., p. 30). This pattern of corn trade was briefly discussed in Chapter XXVIII of the *Principles*. When Ricardo then considered that England might demand a hypothetically large quantity of corn from France, he admitted 'it is probable that, owing to the necessity under which France would be, of having recourse to land of a worse quality, to furnish this large supply, the natural price would rise in France' ([1821] 2004, p. 374). But again, he failed to conclude, as he could easily have done, on the impact of this for France's general rate of profits and hence rate of accumulation.[16] Interestingly, in the 1815 letter to Malthus that has twice been referred to above he stated, 'I have no doubt that if the free importation of corn is allowed into this country, inasmuch as it will direct foreign capital to foreign land, it will tend to lower foreign profits' (1951c, p. 171). He drew a similar conclusion at one point in *Notes on Malthus* when he followed along with Malthus's supposition of a 'prosperous commercial city, greatly excelling in some manufactures' and was purchasing corn from abroad. He posed the question of whether the foreign countries could supply additional quantity without taking new land into cultivation should England's demand double. 'If they can', he concluded, 'I can see no reason for the rise in the price of their corn, if they cannot it will rise and the result will be a fall of profits in both countries' (Ricardo [1928] 1951b, p. 289).[17]

Smith's and Ricardo's oblivion of the dynamic impact of trade on England's trading partners is neatly summed up by de Cecco:

> Adam Smith had considered increasing returns to scale; he had not, however, recognised the revolutionary implications of this feature of manufacturing production. Nor had he, or David Ricardo for that matter, drawn the conclusion that an imperialistic division of labour would obtain for the world as a whole, and a chasm would open between developed and under-developed countries. (1974, p. 10)[18]

This oblivion, as Chapters 4 and 5 below show, would be shared by Torrens and Mill.

3.8 INTERNATIONAL CAPITAL MOBILITY

As the discussion inches closer to Chapters 4 and 5, where it will be shown that Torrens and Mill both considered 'foreign investment' in addition to trade, it is only appropriate to re-examine what Smith and Ricardo had said, even if minimally, about such capital flow.

Here one is reminded that mobility of factors of production across countries is assumed away in the static classical trade models. That model is typically set up with only one factor of production, labour. Nevertheless, in generalising its conclusions and referring to capital as an additional factor of production, the following passage from Ricardo's *Principles* is often quoted to justify the assumption of international factor immobility:

> Experience ... shews, that the fancied or real insecurity of capital, when not under the immediate control of its owner, together with the natural disinclination which

> every man has to quit the country of his birth and connexions, and intrust himself with all his habits fixed, to a strange government and new laws, check the emigration of capital. ([1821] 2004, p. 136)

But as Williams observed, even before the nineteenth century international trade 'strikingly displays a movement of the factors of production underlying, requisite to and proceeding out of the anticipation of profits to be made by international extension of markets and raw material resources'. Among writers (Smith included) and statesmen, he added, there was general recognition 'that the same profits motivation which moved goods could move also the labour and capital requisite to produce them effectively' (1929, p. 206). So what did Smith have to say? And what else, other than the passage quoted above, did Ricardo say on this subject?

At one point in the *Wealth of Nations* Smith had this to offer on the mobility of merchants, and thus on the mobility of their capital:

> A merchant, it has been said very properly, is not necessarily the citizen of any particular country. It is in a great measure indifferent to him from what place he carries on his trade; and a very trifling disgust will make him remove his capital, and together with it all the industry which it supports, from one country to another. ([1776] 1979, p. 426)

While that remark was made in Bk. III, later, in Bk. V, when considering the wisdom of a direct taxation on the interest of money, he generalised from merchants to the 'proprietor of stock'. Thus,

> [t]he proprietor of stock is properly a citizen of the world, and is not necessarily attached to any particular country. He would be apt to abandon the country in which he was exposed to a vexatious inquisition, in order to be assessed to a burdensome tax, and would remove his stock to some other country where he could, either carry on his business, or enjoy his fortune more at his ease. (Ibid., pp. 848–9)

In parallel with his prediction regarding the merchant, Smith feared that such removal of the proprietor's stock 'would put an end to all the industry which it had maintained in the country which he left' (ibid.).[19]

While the passage from Ricardo's *Principles* quoted at the beginning of this section indicates that the considerations contained therein would 'check the emigration of capital', it does not go so far as to claim that such emigration would consequently be stopped completely. Indeed, at another point in the same work, while also hypothetically considering as Smith did the burden from taxes, albeit in the context of servicing a national debt, he considered the 'temptation' to remove oneself and one's capital to another country so as to avoid such burdens. '[A]ssuredly there are limits to the price, which in the form of perpetual taxation', he thus reasoned, 'individuals will submit to pay for the privilege merely of living in their native country' ([1821] 2004, p. 249). Indeed, the temptation to emigrate with one's capital could become 'at last irresistible, and overcomes the natural reluctance which every man feels to quit the place of his birth, and the scene of his early associations' (ibid., pp. 247–8).[20]

But it is what Ricardo states at one point in his *Essay on Profits* that relates capital exports to his argument against the Corn Laws and thus places him even closer to the discussions in the next two chapters of the present book. 'It cannot be doubted', he thus contends, 'that low profits, which are the inevitable effects of a really high price of corn, tend to draw capital abroad'. More exactly, 'after profits have very much fallen, accumulation will be checked, and capital will be exported to be employed in those countries where food is cheap and profits high' ([1815] 1951a, p. 16n). For those who did not wish to see capital exported for this reason, 'this consideration ought therefore to be a powerful reason to prevent us from restricting importation [of corn]' (ibid.).[21] But the 'low profits' here were the hypothetical results of the maintenance of the Corn Laws. Free importation of corn could avert that, except that Ricardo did not take into consideration that even that solution could have its own limitation when England would lead over her trading partners in an uneven growth and development situation. That is, he did not really anticipate what Torrens and Mill were to concern themselves with. He did argue, also in his *Essay on Profits*, that '[i]f in the progress of countries in wealth and population, new portions of fertile land could be added to such countries, with every increase of capital, profits would never fall, nor rents rise' (ibid., p. 18).[22] Nevertheless, this isolated thought of land addition through colonisation or sending capital abroad was not further developed and was rather left for Torrens and Mill to work on. It is to these that the discussion would now turn.

NOTES

1. It should be pointed out that Smith has expressed other views on development in his *Wealth of Nations*. Thus, in Bk. III, Ch. I he describes the 'natural course' for the greater part of 'the capital of every growing society' as, 'first, directed to agriculture, afterwards to manufactures, and last of all to foreign commerce' (Smith [1776] 1979, p. 380). As Blecker (1997, pp. 531–2) remarks, this is tantamount to saying that 'each country develops autonomously along a natural path that is largely if not entirely independent of its external trade relations'. Clearly, it is at odds with how the world trade and investment network expanded during the time when England surged from the rest and became the workshop of the world. To be fair to Smith, he does add that this 'natural order' of things 'has, in all the modern states of Europe [during his time], been, in many respects, entirely inverted', manifesting in the process an 'unnatural and retrograde order' (Smith, ibid.). Specifically, '[t]he foreign commerce of some of their cities has introduced all their finer manufactures,

or such as were fit for distant sale; and manufactures and foreign commerce together, have given birth to the principal improvements of agriculture' (ibid.).

2. After discussing the influence of exports and imports on growth, where Smith's productivity theory and Ricardo's corn model are mentioned, Bloomfield (1981, pp. 111, 118) does briefly refer to Mill's awareness of the insufficiency of merely repealing the Corn Laws and hence the need to export British capital. He also briefly refers to Torrens's argument for colonisation (ibid., pp. 116–17). However, the purpose of his paper is to conduct a general survey of British thought on the influence of foreign trade and investment on growth. The aforementioned dynamic notions, together with other contributions made by the same as well as other classical authors, are summarised as 'widely scattered throughout the nineteenth-century British economic literature' and 'were never developed systematically' (ibid., p. 120). For an earlier attempt to formalise the discussion (without Smith's productivity theory), see Ho (1989, Ch. II), which was subsequently extended and published as Ho (1997). The model in these earlier publications was inspired by Harris (1978), Pasinetti (1977), and Garegnani (1984).
3. Some might argue that when Ricardo's reasoning against the Corn Laws is included in the theory, then the different 'endowments' of the primary factor 'land' constitute another inter-country difference. For attempts which link Ricardo with Ohlin or the 'factor proportions theory of comparative advantage', see Findlay (1974) and Evans (1989).
4. This section and sections 3.3 and 3.4 below are partly based on section 3 in Ho (1996a).
5. The 'excuse' for this is that in general, the classical economists seemed to subscribe to Say's Law. However, see the discussion in Chs. 4 and 5 for later signs of modification in Torrens's and Mill's positions.
6. Smith did not have as complete a theory of distribution as Ricardo. He had made claims that the competition of capital would drive down the rate of profits, claims with which both Ricardo and Mill disagreed. On his influence on the early thoughts of Torrens, see section 4.2 in Ch. 4 below.
7. The full title is: *An Essay on the Influence of a Low Price of Corn on the Profits of Stock.*
8. Chs. 10 and 12 below respectively indicate that Prebisch and Singer had drawn attention to technological improvements that economised on the use of certain raw materials, often through the discoveries of synthetic substitutes.
9. Indeed, Tucker (1960, p. 121) concludes that 'the question of the Corn Laws may have been indirectly responsible for the summary treatment of the effects of technical improvements in his [Ricardo's] later work [after the *Essay on Profits*]'.
10. For a discussion of the possible harmony, as opposed to rivalry, between Smith's productivity theory and the Ricardian comparative cost doctrine, see Parrinello (1988).
11. Given that both Torrens and Mill had extended Smith's and Ricardo's analyses in similar directions, there can arise a question of priority. A full-scale investigation into that is beyond the scope of the present work; it is simply drawing attention to the fact that they both sensed the need for an extension.
12. With respect to America, however, Smith ([1776] 1979, p. 367) has this piece of advice to offer at one point in the *Wealth of Nations*: 'Were the Americans, either by combination or by any other sort of violence, to stop the importation of European manufactures, and, by thus giving a monopoly to such of their own countrymen as could manufacture the like goods, divert any considerable part of their capital into this employment, they would retard instead of accelerating the further increase in the value of their annual produce, and would obstruct instead of promoting the progress of their country towards real wealth and greatness. This would be still more the case, were they to attempt, in the same manner, to monopolize to themselves their whole exportation trade'. It should also be recalled that in his consideration of the significance of the commerce between the town and the country in a civilised society, which Smith likens to trade between neighbouring states, the exchange consists of manufactured goods for rude produce (ibid., pp. 376–8, 677, 686).
13. This is the system that 'represents the produce of land as the sole source of the revenue and wealth of every country' (op. cit., p. 663).
14. The second half of n. 12 above reminds the reader of Smith's consideration of the 'gains' from the commerce between the town and the country. Yet he has this to observe on this

trade at one point in the *Wealth of Nations*: 'That the industry which is carried on in towns is, every-where in Europe, more advantageous than that which is carried on in the country ... In every country of Europe we find, at least, a hundred people who have acquired great fortunes from small beginnings by trade and manufactures, the industry which properly belongs to towns, for one who has done so by that which properly belongs to the country, the raising of rude produce by the improvement and cultivation of land. Industry, therefore, must be better rewarded, the wages of labour and the profits of stock must evidently be greater in the one situation than in the other' (op. cit., p. 142). See Hamilton ([1791b] 1966, p. 289, n. 190), where the editors of that version of his *Report on Manufactures*, Syrett and Cooke, point out in referring to Smith's passage that is quoted here that 'H[amilton], in this instance, agreed with Smith'. See also section 7.2 in Ch. 7 below. Manoïlesco suggested in a similar manner that '*it is the nature of international exchange which is the determining factor of the wealth of nations*' (1931, p. xiii, italics original). 'The country becomes rich', he observed, 'if it exports goods of high productivity [industrial products] and imports goods of small productivity [agricultural products]' (ibid., p. 168). See section 9.2 in Ch. 9 below.

15. Singer might have gone too far when he claimed that the policy conclusion from his (and Prebisch's) works that developing countries should industrialise rather than chiefly rely on primary production 'would be fully approved by ... Ricardo, Malthus, John Stuart Mill et al.' in addition to Smith (1991a, pp. 339–40).
16. There was some sort of a Freudian moment in the chapter 'On Colonial Trade' in his *Principles*, when Ricardo considered whether a mother country might sometimes be benefited by the restraints to which she would subject her colonial possessions. 'Who can doubt, for example', he thus questioned, 'that, if England were the colony of France, the latter country would be benefited by a heavy bounty paid by England on the exportation of corn, cloth, or any other commodities?' ([1821] 2004, p. 339).
17. Malthus's original supposition was such that the commercial city was purchasing *all* its corn from abroad. Ricardo changed that to less than all (op. cit., pp. 287–8).
18. De Cecco added that 'Smith on colonies is complementary to Smith on free trade' (op. cit.). By that he was probably referring to Smith's belief that the effects of the colony trade 'are always and necessarily beneficial', although he (Smith) took pains to distinguish between those effects from others that were due to 'the monopoly of that trade' (Smith [1776] 1979, p. 607).
19. According to Williams (1929, p. 207, n. 2), J. S. Nicholson cited Smith's recognition of the international mobility of capital as one of his significant 'lost ideas'.
20. As Maneschi (1992, pp. 432–3) notes, Ricardo also implied that capital would likely move away from a nation that discourages the adoption of machinery to another that does not. See Ricardo ([1821] 2004, pp. 396–7).
21. Tucker (1960, p. 169) sums it up this way: 'But the reduction of the incentive to save was not the most pressing evil that had been produced by the Corn Laws; their more immediate effect was to induce capitalists to invest a portion of their savings in other countries'.
22. If these 'new portions of fertile land' were added through the creation of enclaves via foreign investment, then this is another moment when Ricardo failed to consider the impact of England's action on, in this case, her investment partners. More than 130 years after this passage appeared in the *Essay on Profits*, Singer lamented that, 'Where the purpose and effect of the investments was to open up new sources of food for the people and for the machines of industrialized countries, we have strictly domestic investment in the relevant economic sense, although for reasons of physical geography, climate, etc., it had to be made overseas' (1950, p. 475). See section 12.4 in Ch. 12 below for further discussion on this point.

4. Torrens: Trade, Uneven Development, Commercial Reciprocity, and Colonisation

4.1 INTRODUCTION[1]

As noted in section 2.2 above, when the mainstream interpretation of the history of classical trade theories gains currency, the contributions to developing mainstream trade analysis by other 'minor figures' can readily be assessed. To repeat, in the case of Torrens he has been partially rehabilitated in the mainstream economists' esteem because he is regarded by some to have antedated Ricardo in the formulation of the doctrine of comparative advantage. He might be the first to think of 'reciprocal demand' as constituting the solution to the international value problem and was among the first to consider the possibility that a tariff might turn the terms of trade in favour of the country imposing it.

However, these rehabilitation exercises have only aimed at singling out those contributions of his which are related to mainstream trade theories. Not surprisingly, Torrens's analyses have typically been removed from the original context of discussion, and this has inevitably obfuscated some of his messages. Even Robbins (1958), who has by far offered the most comprehensive assessment of Torrens's works,[2] does not seem to constitute an exception. Specifically, while he ardently directs attention to Torrens's discussion of the *static* gains from trade (ibid., Ch. II, parts 4 and 6), he does not seriously heed the role played by his (Torrens's) distribution theory in shaping his trade analysis.[3] In a footnote attached to the end of the first paragraph of Ch. III (ibid.), a chapter in which Torrens's contributions to 'Central Classical Theory: Distribution and Value' are being examined, and one in which the Corn Laws debate is referred to, Robbins thus allows that,

> This chapter, although dealing with problems central to the main Classical theories of value and distribution and therefore inevitably occupying this place in the development of the story, may be found to have rather less interest than its fellows for the reader who is not a specialist in the history of thought. It may be omitted without prejudice to what follows. (Ibid., p. 36)

Although he is quick to add that the omission 'is not recommended', his inability to grasp the significance of the role of Torrens's distribution theory has prevented him from pinpointing the framework of capitalist development within which Torrens developed his growth–trade analysis, and with which a common thread to piece it together with his other contributions (which pertain to commercial reciprocity and colonisation) could be provided. Not surprisingly, Torrens's discussion of the *dynamic* benefits from trade is being downplayed, and he could not clearly discern from Torrens's argument the relationship between these benefits from trade for England and the resulting urgency felt by her to further open up markets which were protected by 'hostile tariffs', as well as to expand trade by undertaking colonial investment abroad.

What follows is a reappraisal of Torrens's contributions to the analysis of growth, trade, and colonisation. To give full recognition to his concern for England's economic progress (and hence his interest in her dynamic gains from trade), these contributions are presented, and are thus linked together, within a framework of his simple conception of capitalist development.

In line with classical economists like Smith and Ricardo, Torrens regarded the rapidity of that development process to be closely related to the speed of capital accumulation, the latter of which is in turn dependent upon the rate of profits. Smith had emphasised the importance of improvements in production techniques and in the productivity of labour in the course of expansion of the market. Ricardo had raised concerns about increasing wage costs (due to insurmountable natural impediments) in the course of accumulation. Torrens, by focusing on two 'powerful' determinants of the rate of profits – namely the 'degree of skill with which labour is applied' and the 'natural productiveness of land' – was able to combine the Smithian and the Ricardian insight to make a forceful two-pronged case for free trade from England's viewpoint.

However, thanks to the unleashing of productive forces in manufactures and the bypassing of the growth obstacle in agriculture, an 'uneven accumulation' type of situation (with England in the lead) would be engendered. Torrens concluded that trade *per se* would not be a sufficient guarantee for England's prosperity. Her trading partners would not be supplying food and raw produce at the rate that she demanded, nor would they be purchasing manufactured products at the rate that she supplied. To him, the problems attendant upon this unevenness would be aggravated if the trading partners were to employ hostile tariffs and to locally work up the materials. It was in the debate on the relief of this distress that he later emerged as a champion of commercial reciprocity and also re-dedicated his support to the colonisation movement.

Apart from showing how Torrens stitched together the Smithian and Ricardian insight into the dynamic benefits of trade, and then provided a sequel to the attendant 'uneven growth' outcome, the reinterpretation advanced in this chapter could in several other ways serve to distinguish the nature and significance of some of Torrens's contributions from other commentaries on him that have hitherto been written. Thus, in his discussion of trade between 'old countries' he observed that trade would not always be mutually beneficial: depending on which one of them exports food and raw produce, it would actually suffer from trade! To the extent that these countries trade with each other manufactures that are 'not applicable to reproduction', he opined that the gains from trade have been 'exaggerated'. Regarding the international value problem, unlike Mill, it was not out of curiosity of how the static gains from trade would be divided that Torrens studied it. Rather, his involvement sprang from an interest in understanding how, due to the 'uneven accumulation' alluded to above (and other factors), the dynamic gains from trade for England would diminish over time. In this connection, the 'relative degrees of demand' to which he referred in the process of grappling with the problem was principally integrated with the uneven rates of accumulation in different countries, and not with the different 'inclinations of consumers'. Related to the subject of unevenness, it was with an aim of providing relief to the distress arising therefrom, and not because he thought England could exploit any monopoly power to extract further static gains from trade, that Torrens started to advocate the principle of commercial reciprocity beginning from the late 1820s and early 1830s.

The rest of this chapter is organised as follows. Section 4.2 examines what Torrens regarded to be the principal determinants of the rate of profits, and what he observed to be the 'antagonistic' tendencies between two of them in particular. On the basis of that observation, he constructed a powerful two-pronged case for free trade from England's viewpoint. Section 4.3 describes his subscription to Smith's 'productivity theory'. Section 4.4 then shows that Torrens essentially adopted Ricardo's argument against the Corn Laws. It was after he combined the Smithian and the Ricardian insight into the benefits from trade that Torrens started to sense that trade by itself could not sufficiently guarantee lasting prosperity for England. That prompted him to study the determining circumstances of, and the causes of changes in, the terms of international exchange. His conclusions are presented in section 4.5. Based on them, and as section 4.6 illustrates, Torrens argued that in order to relieve England's distress, she would have to enforce the principle of commercial reciprocity, as well as to practise extended colonisation. Section 4.7 provides a summary and concluding remarks.

4.2 DETERMINANTS OF THE RATE OF PROFITS

Smith's and Ricardo's Influences[4]

In the early part of his career as an economist, Torrens's understanding of the forces which determine the rate of profits was quite clearly shaped by Smith.[5] For instance, in his first publication as an economist, *The Economists Refuted*, he states in Smithian fashion that, 'Every increase of capital increases the competition amongst the capitalists, and consequently, diminishes the profits of stock' ([1808] 1993, p. 16).[6] This conception is carried over to his reasoning against the Corn Laws in the first edition of the *External Corn Trade*. There he argues that free importation of corn would reduce wages and heighten the productive powers of industry. '[T]hese heightened powers [would then] accelerate the accumulation of stock; and ... this accumulation lowers the rate of profit. A free external trade in corn, then, would effect a reduction in rents, wages, and profits: – that is, would reduce all the component parts of natural price, and enable us to sell every article at a cheaper rate' (1815, p. 298).[7]

Five years later, however, in the second edition of the *External Corn Trade*, Torrens is found to be acknowledging his indebtedness to Ricardo's 'original and profound inquiry into the laws by which the rate of profit is determined' (1820, p. xix, quoted in de Vivo 1985a, pp. 89–90), and there is a suggestion of an awareness of the need for 'the correction of certain erroneous doctrines respecting the rate of profit, to which the authority of Adam Smith has given currency' (ibid., pp. xvi–xvii, quoted in Robbins 1958, p. 52).[8]

In fact, in an article contributed to the *Edinburgh Review* two months before the publication of the second edition of the *External Corn Trade*,[9] Torrens has already spelled out three circumstances that would influence the rate of profits, which circumstances, according to Langer, 'are basically those given by Ricardo in his *Essay on Profits*' (1982, p. 398).[10] These are: 'the quality of the Soil under cultivation',[11] 'the degree of Skill and economy with which labour is employed', and 'the real amount of Wages, or the quantity of the products of labour advanced to the labourer while performing his work'[12] ([1819] 1993, pp. 85–6, see also p. 87).

These circumstances are repeated in the second edition of the *External Corn Trade* (1820, p. 405, quoted in de Vivo 1985b, p. 200). By the fourth edition of the same title, his restatement reads that,

> The circumstances which determine the rate of profit are, the natural productiveness of the land ... which is resorted to for obtaining the necessaries of life; the degree of skill with which labour is applied, whether in raising raw produce, or in preparing wrought goods; and the real rate of wages, or the quantity

> of the products of labour which the capitalist expends in supporting his labourers. (1827, pp. 94–5, see also pp. 110, 117)

Note that despite Langer's claim that, in the forms stated in Torrens ([1819] 1993) these three circumstances are essentially those discussed by Ricardo in his *Essay on Profits*, Torrens had from the very beginning incorporated 'manufactures' or 'wrought goods' into many of his illustrations.[13] In the case of Ricardo, as Sraffa (1951a, p. xxxii) points out, it was not until he wrote the *Principles*, and after frequent attacks by Malthus, that he (Ricardo) started to include manufactures in wages. Even after that, 'the degree of skill with which labour is applied in preparing wrought goods' does not seem to have received a lot of coverage.[14] As will be illustrated in section 4.3 below, it is this incorporation by Torrens that has allowed him to give a prominent role to Smith's 'productivity theory' in his trade analysis.[15]

Interaction among the Determinants

Torrens was fully aware that the three causes which regulate the rate of profits 'may act, either in conjunction with, or in opposition to, each other' ([1829] 1972, p. 110). Subsequent to stressing that the 'natural productiveness of the land' and the 'degree of skill with which labour is applied' are the two causes which would exert a much more 'powerful and permanent influence' on the rate of profits ([1819] 1993, p. 87; [1829] 1972, pp. 117–18),[16] he went on to point out the 'antagonistic' tendencies between these two causes. As it was his shrewdness in perceiving these tendencies which underlay his powerful two-pronged case for free trade, his description is worth quoting at full length:

> [I]n the progress of society, the two main causes which determine the rate of return upon productive capital, are as antagonist muscles, modifying and balancing the action of each other. As increasing population compels us, on the one hand, to resort to inferior soils, and thus raises the natural price of raw produce, so it leads, on the other, to more accurate divisions of employment, and to that extension of machinery which is at once their cause and their effect, and thus lowers the natural price of all wrought goods. ... But ... increased facility in producing wrought necessaries, has the same effect in raising the rate of profit, which diminished facility in producing food and material has in lowering it.[17]

This passage is immediately ensued by the following rather optimistic prediction:

> And hence it will frequently happen, that a greater degree of economy and skill in the application of labour may completely counteract the effects of resorting to inferior soils; and that the return upon productive capital may rise, on the whole, though the difficulty of obtaining food and material should increase. ([1819] 1993,

pp. 87–8; repeated with slight rewording in [1829] 1972, pp. 119–20, see also p. 110)[18]

The optimism, it should be noted, is immediately curtailed in the next sentence, which expresses that, 'Such a process, however, could not continue long' ([1819] 1993, p. 88; omitted in [1829] 1972).

Declining Rate of Profits, the Stationary State, and the Corn Laws

Thus, in the progress of society, 'with respect to agricultural industry ... upon every increased quantity of labour and capital applied to the soil, we obtain a less proportional return' ([1821] 1965, p. 111). Concomitantly, the cultivation of inferior soils and the improving powers of manufacturing industry would result in 'a constant tendency to raise the value of raw produce in relation to wrought goods' ([1829] 1972, p. 79). In fact, according to Torrens, of all the countries in the world, England was then exhibiting the most striking practical example of the natural tendency of raw produce to rise in value as compared with wrought goods (ibid., p. 81). Now, to him, '[i]t is a principle capable of the most rigid and perfect demonstration, that increasing the productive cost and exchangeable value of food, and the materials of wrought necessaries, depresses the rate of profit' (ibid., p. 125, see also pp. 110–11, and [1834] 1969, p. 100). So this rate 'will constantly diminish, until that stationary state is attained, in which no additional capital can be employed, and all tendency to increased population must be checked by famine' ([1819] 1993, p. 88; repeated in [1829] 1972, p. 120, see also pp. 323 and 381–4).

Based on the discussion so far, it is easy to imagine where Torrens stood in the Corn Laws debate. Thus, he warned that the gradual approach of the 'stationary and melancholy state' could be 'prodigiously accelerated ... and forced prematurely upon us by *unwise Commercial Regulations*' ([1819] 1993, p. 89, italics original). He concluded that, 'if we persist in excluding the raw products of other countries, and consequently force our capitalists to employ their stock in a comparatively disadvantageous production, it requires very little sagacity to foresee that we must continue to languish and decline' ([1819] 1993, p. 90). To continue the 'barbarous' and 'disgraceful' system of the Corn Laws, he accordingly declared, would be tantamount 'to apply[ing] the axe to the roots of England's prosperity' ([1829] 1972, p. 332).[19]

On to a Two-Pronged Case for Free Trade for England

It was obvious to Torrens that the growth obstacle posed by the 'natural productiveness of the land' could easily be bypassed through allowing freer importation of food and raw produce. In addition, the circumvention of that obstacle would mean that the greater degree of economy and skill in the application of labour in manufacturing would no longer be counteracted by the effects of resorting to inferior soils. Thus, should England specialise in the export of manufactures in return for food and raw produce, her rate of profits would no longer be depressed and might very well be raised. It was on the basis of this conviction that Torrens constructed a two-pronged case for free trade for England.

4.3 SUBSCRIPTION TO SMITH'S 'PRODUCTIVITY THEORY'

Torrens subscribed to the 'productivity theory' that was outlined in section 3.3 in the previous chapter. Indeed, as Robbins observed at one point, 'It is very clear that Torrens was a willing inheritor of the general theory of division of labour and the market' (1958, p. 237). However, elsewhere he also stated that, 'On this plane of generality Torrens' arguments were simply a series of variations on a thesis that was already established' (ibid., p. 19).

Based on the discussion in the previous section, this trivialisation of Torrens's adherence to the theory could be very misleading. For he was fully aware of the theory's relationship to one of the two powerful determining circumstances of the rate of profits, and hence, the rate of accumulation. When his discussion of, and reference to, the theory is interpreted, as Robbins did, outside of his framework of analysis, it is not surprising that the fuller and more dynamic consequences of his adoption of the theory could not be discerned.[20]

Now returning to Torrens's subscription to the theory, he asserts in *The Economist Refuted* that 'the division of labour augments in a very considerable degree the productiveness of human industry' ([1808] 1993, p. 8; see also [1821] 1965, p. 155). The famous example given by Smith of the pin-maker ([1776] 1979, pp. 14–15) is briefly mentioned in the *Production of Wealth* ([1821] 1965, p. 156). He also adhered to Smith's discussion of the circumstances which would bring about such productivity augmentation, namely 'the increase of dexterity in every particular workman'; 'the saving of the time which is commonly lost in passing from one species of work to another'; and 'the invention of ... machines which facilitate and abridge labour' (Smith [1776] 1979, pp. 17–21; Torrens [1808] 1993, pp. 8–9, and [1821] 1965, pp. 90, 155–6, and 206).

As for the relationship between the degree of the division of labour and the extent of the market, Torrens is very explicit, in his [1819] 1993 article in the *Edinburgh Review*, in acknowledging the insight of Smith. He thus concurs that,

> The great cause which increases the powers of manufacturing industry is the division of labour; and the division of labour, as Adam Smith long ago demonstrated, is limited by the extent of the market. ... It is precisely because [of these relationships] ... that roads are constructed, bridges erected, canals opened, and every possible means resorted to, in order to facilitate the intercourse between one district and another. (Ibid., pp. 94–5)

He elaborates on this theme in the *Production of Wealth*, explaining that, 'Where the market is very small, no person can have any encouragement to devote himself entirely to one employment, for want of the power to exchange all that surplus part of his own labour which is over and above his own consumption, for such parts of the produce of other men's labour as he may have occasion for' ([1821] 1965, pp. 160–61).[21] It was partly because of this awareness of the significance of the extent of the market that he constantly distinguished thinly- from densely-peopled regions or countries in his discussions.

Like Smith, Torrens clearly extended the principle to the international context. '[E]very ... branch of mercantile industry', he indicates in the *Production of Wealth*, 'gives occasion to divisions of employment, and thus heightens the productive powers of labour and capital' ([1821] 1965, p. 228). Next, in the *External Corn Trade*, he asserts that,

> The first principle of political economy informs us, that the divisions of employment, whether established between the individuals of the same country, or between the individuals of different countries, are the sources from which every considerable improvement in the productive powers of industry is derived. Now, the people who deprive themselves of foreign trade, deprive themselves of the benefits of the foreign divisions of employment. ([1829] 1972, pp. 380–81)

To this principle Torrens continued to hold, reiterating in *The Budget* that, 'International divisions of employment are as efficacious in multiplying the productive powers of labour, as divisions of employment between the inhabitants of the same estate' ([1844] 1970, p. 48).

But between agriculture and manufactures, in which sector would the 'productivity theory' operate with more vigour? Torrens's answer, that '[c]ombination of labour, and division of employment, increase the productive powers of non-agricultural industry in a much greater proportion than they increase the productive powers of agricultural industry' ([1835] 1962, p. 38, see also pp. 37, 39), undoubtedly resonates with Smith's observation alluded to in section 3.3 above. Hence, for an 'old and advanced' country like England, which, 'in consequence of denser population, and larger accumulations of capital, employment is more subdivided, and machinery better applied' than most other countries, she would stand to benefit significantly from further labour productivity improvements if other countries would subscribe to the idea of free trade and allow her to expand her exports of manufactured products.

4.4 FREER CORN TRADE: BENEFITS FOR ENGLAND, POSSIBLE LOSSES FOR THE EXPORTER

However, for an old country, 'the necessity of resorting to inferior soils, and of applying additional portions of capital to the best, renders it daily more difficult to raise an increased supply of agricultural produce' ([1821] 1965, p. 253). This difficulty was aggravated by restrictions on the importation of corn. In this connection, Torrens basically followed the analysis and policy conclusion of Ricardo with respect to the effects of the Corn Laws.[22] He thus concurred that, 'If we restrict importation, or grant bounties, or in any way turn capital from its most beneficial occupation, we check the progress of wealth, and the further accumulation of capital'. Such 'forced and artificial encouragement' afforded to agriculture would consequently be 'much too dearly purchased' ([1829] 1972, p. 53). On the other hand, if free trade in corn and raw produce were allowed, both static and dynamic benefits would be reaped for the corn-importer (that is, England).

For the Corn-Importer

The discussion of the static benefit here will be brief and is not aimed at shedding new light on the question of priority. The reader who is interested in that can refer to Gomes (1987, pp. 141–4) and Maneschi (1998, pp. 52–7). Nor will the familiar England–Poland example, initially introduced in the first edition of the *External Corn Trade* (1815, pp. 263–5) and then consolidated in the fourth edition of the same title (1827, pp. 401–3, see also pp. 49, 364), be repeated here. Nevertheless, for those who are interested in an exceptionally clear statement, more on the circumstances giving rise to trade based on comparative advantage and less on the benefits arising therefrom, there is the following example of trade between England and France from the *Letters on Commercial Policy* which is worth quoting at full length:

> If, in England, any given quantities of corn, of cotton, and of linen, were produced by 100 days' labour; and if, in France, the same quantities of these articles were produced by 200 days' labour; then, in the two countries, the *absolute cost of production* would be *different*, while the *relative cost of production* would be equal. But if, in France, commodities in general required for their production double the quantity of labour requisite for their production in England, while some particular commodity, say corn, produced in England by 100 days' labour, could be produced in France by 150 days' labour, then, though the *absolute cost* of production would be *greater* in France than in England, yet the *relative cost* of production it would be *less* in France than in England. Under such circumstances, the value of corn in relation to other commodities, would be lower in France than in England; and, consequently, corn could be imported with a profit from France into England, though the *absolute cost* of producing it was 50 per cent. higher in France than in England. ([1833] 1958, p. 17n, italics original)

As will be explained more carefully in the next subsection, Torrens did not believe the trade between England and France could be that beneficial to both in practice. In fact, it could even be harmful to France! The discussion of the dynamic benefits of the corn trade will set the stage for that consideration.

Thus, if corn could be freely imported, 'there would be no increase in the cost of obtaining corn, and hence no diminution in the productive powers of industry, and in the rate of profit ..., and capital would continue to accumulate as rapidly as before' ([1829] 1972, p. 386).[23] In this manner, 'in an old and well-peopled country, the free importation of foreign agricultural produce ... keeps the rate of profit high, and flings into viewless distance the ultimate limits of national prosperity and wealth' (ibid., p. 323; see also [1821] 1965, pp. 257–9).[24]

Tying the argument with Smith's 'productivity theory', Torrens continued to say that '[a]s capital [thus] accumulated [with no diminution in the rate of profit], and as commerce extended, more accurate divisions of employment would multiply and cheapen all wrought goods' ([1829] 1972, p. 386).

Would England be able to export the larger quantity of wrought goods that could thus be produced? Torrens's answer at this stage (*circa* the late 1820s) still appeared to be in the affirmative. Thus, 'every addition made to the quantity of agricultural produce imported, would, while it gave employment to a greater number of workmen, create, in the foreign market, an additional demand for the equivalents which purchased it. – The limits of commercial prosperity cannot be assigned' (ibid., p. 388). The curtailment of this optimism will be illustrated in section 4.5 below.

For the Corn-Exporter: New versus Old Countries

What about the benefits of trade for the corn-exporter? Here one should take note of Torrens's distinction between new (thinly-peopled) and old (densely-peopled) countries as the trading partners of England. In order to establish a benchmark for comparison, he first portrayed a situation of trade between an old country and that of a new one. 'Of all kinds of commerce', he maintained, 'that is the most eminently beneficial, which is carried on between old and new countries, and which consists of the interchange of manufactured goods, and agricultural produce' ([1833] 1958, p. 63). The circumstances surrounding an old country like England and the benefits which it could derive by exporting manufactures in exchange for raw produce have already been considered in the last subsection. As for the new countries, '*where it is not necessary to cultivate inferior lands*, or to cultivate the better soils in an expensive manner, the productive powers of agricultural industry are extraordinarily high; while, from the population being thin and scattered, and from capitals being little accumulated, the application of machinery, and the division of mechanical employment are imperfect; and consequently, the productive powers of manufacturing industry are extraordinarily low' ([1821] 1965, p. 253, italics added). Now, the difficulty of working up raw produce in these countries could be 'completely obviated by those international divisions of employment which foreign trade establishes' (ibid., p. 254; see also [1808] 1993, pp. 89–90; [1829] 1972, pp. 120–21; [1833] 1958, pp. 63–4; and [1844] 1970, pp. 268–9, and 408).

As far as the static aspect of the gain for the corn-exporting new country is concerned, the reasoning on which it is based is exactly the same as that applied to the corn-importer (see [1829] 1972, pp. 42–3). As for the dynamic gain, Torrens echoed Smith (section 6.2 below) and suggested that,

> perfect liberty to export the produce of the soil, accelerates the period of manufacturing prosperity in an agricultural country. In such a country, when capital[, which can be most rapidly accumulated under unrestricted commerce,] begins to exceed what, at the existing price of produce, can be beneficially vested in the soil, it will seek other employment, and invest itself in the working up of the raw material. (Ibid., p. 44)[25]

Having portrayed the circumstance under which the 'most beneficial commerce' could occur, one can imagine that it was but one small step for Torrens to conclude that 'the least beneficial is that which is carried on between two densely peopled countries, neither of which is in a condition to export raw produce' ([1844] 1970, p. 270). Thus, in considering free trade between England and France, where both were regarded by him to be old countries, he suggested that, 'The opinions entertained, respecting the advantages of a free trade with France, are in the highest degree exaggerated' ([1833] 1958, pp. 50–51).

Two scenarios were considered. The first one involved the exchange of manufactures for raw produce and it is in this situation that free trade would not be mutually beneficial; it would instead be harmful to the corn-exporter. Thus, supposing England to be the exporter of manufactures, Torrens concluded that it was beyond all doubt that this species of commerce would be highly beneficial to her. But for France, 'it would be so highly injurious, so perfectly ruinous ... that those who conceive its introduction practicable, must either have lost their own senses, or must proceed upon the supposition, that the people of France have lost their's' ([1833] 1958, pp. 53–4). According to Torrens, there are those who hold that 'the principles of free trade are liable to no limitations and exceptions', and they would insist that if England could manufacture more cheaply than France, it would be in the interest of France to receive her wrought goods from England, and to transfer to her soil the labour and capital previously employed in her manufacturing towns. However, these 'extreme advocates of free trade' seem to have forgotten that,

> in transferring the industry of a country from manufactures to agriculture, there must be disposable *land* ... France has no extensive tracts of fertile and unappropriated soil, over which cultivation could be advantageously extended. In the existing state of agricultural skill, inferior lands could not be reclaimed, nor heightened tillage bestowed upon the better soils, without a reduction of the profit upon the capital employed in these operations. ... [W]hile England became the workshop of France, France would be converted into a corn-field for England.
>
> When a country has arrived so near the limits of her territorial resources that, in the actual state of her agricultural knowledge, the last quality of land resorted to yields the lowest rate of increase for the sake of which capital will be applied; then, in such a country, a system of free trade, permitting the importation of manufactured goods in exchange for food and raw materials, must occasion the most calamitous diminution of wealth and population. ([1833] 1958, pp. 54–5)[26]

It is no wonder why right from the beginning, Torrens categorically ruled out the possibility that England be the exporter of raw produce,[27] implying at one point that a corn-exporting England would be 'bankrupt and depopulated, sunk from her place in Europe, and, perhaps, deprived of her existence as an independent nation' (1815, p. 256).

What if, as in the second scenario, the two countries trade with each other manufactures that are 'not applicable to reproduction'? In Torrens's opinion, this species of trade 'cannot enlarge the field of employment' ([1844] 1970, p. 274).[28] Hence, if England supplied France with cottons while France supplied England with silks, then even though silks would be rendered cheaper in England, and cottons cheaper in France,

> [t]here will be no increase of employment, of profit, or of wages; and the whole of the benefit will consist in the gratification which the consumer may derive from the use of those luxuries, which the fall in the price of silks enables him to procure. … [T]his is the *sole* advantage which England could derive from a free trade with France. ([1833] 1958, p. 53, italics added, see also p. 51; and [1844] 1970, pp. 270–71 and 276)[29]

That is why he regarded the benefit of this kind of trade to be 'exaggerated'.

4.5 TERMS OF INTERNATIONAL EXCHANGE: DETERMINANTS, CHANGES, AND THE IMPACT ON ENGLAND'S GROWTH

In section 4.3, Torrens's rationale for free trade *à la* Smith's 'productivity theory' was laid out, and that involved England specialising in manufactures to take advantage of their larger scope for productivity improvements. In section 4.4, his other rationale for unrestricted trade, *à la* Ricardo's argument against the Corn Laws, was presented, and that entailed England to be importing food and raw produce to circumvent the increasing cost problem in their procurement domestically. If England's trade could be expanded in these manners, then based on the discussion in section 4.2 the forces unleashed in the one and the obstacle bypassed in the other would tend to raise the rate of profits in England, and hence to augment her rate of accumulation. Torrens, to his credit, followed through the logic of combining the Smithian and Ricardian insight, and foresaw that perhaps trade *per se* could not be a sufficient guarantee of lasting prosperity for England. It was to this end that he devoted a significant amount of effort in studying what had caused changes in, and thus what were the determining circumstances of, the terms of international exchange.

In this connection it cannot be overemphasised that his motive for investigation was sharply distinct from that of Mill (on which see section 5.7 below). Thus, the latter picked up from where Ricardo left off in his England–Portugal model to show how different terms of trade would result from the various 'inclinations and circumstances of the consumers' in the two trading countries, and to illustrate what these different terms of trade would imply in terms of the static gain from trade for each ([1874] 1974, Essay I). In contrast, Torrens, who had consistently maintained an interest in the prospect of growth for England, and hence in the conditions affecting the pattern of income distribution in that country, firmly believed that,

> an accurate knowledge of the circumstances which determine the relative value of the products of foreign and of domestic labour is indispensably necessary, in order

> to enable us to ascertain the laws which govern the amount of wages, the rate of profit, and the incidence of import duties. ([1844] 1970, p. v)

It is not to be disputed that in the hands of Mill, the problem of determining international values was most ably worked out in a manner which pioneered its modern mainstream formulation and solution.[30] Nevertheless, as far as credit for attempting to grapple with the problem in a manner that is more focused on issues which logically follow from the dynamic classical trade analyses, it should be awarded to Torrens.

The Determining Circumstances of the Terms of International Exchange

Torrens also took notice of what he had dubbed the 'Ricardo doctrine of international exchange', namely that, 'The same rule which regulates the relative value of commodities in one country, does not regulate the relative value of the commodities exchanged between two or more countries' (Ricardo [1821] 2004, p. 133; see Torrens [1844] 1970, p. v for his explicit reference to it). This 'rule' stipulates that commodities produced in the same country exchange with each other in proportion to the 'cost' of their production.[31] However, since 'labour and capital cannot be so easily transferred from one country to another, and therefore competition cannot operate', it could not be applied to the exchange of commodities produced in different countries ([1833] 1958, pp. 16–17; see also [1835] 1962, pp. 159–61, and [1844] 1970, p. 333 of Postscript to Letter IX).

What then are the determinants of the terms of international exchange? As early as the fourth edition of the *External Corn Trade*, Torrens spells out that, apart from the relatively minor considerations of 'carriage and merchant's profit' (which subsequently did not receive much further treatment), the circumstances include 'the difference between the comparative cost of producing commodities in one country, and the comparative cost of producing them in others'[32] and 'the relative degrees in which different countries demand the commodities of each other' (1827, pp. 401, 407; see also [1833] 1958, p. 17). Notice that these were stated roughly two years before Mill drafted the essays that were to be published in his *Essays on Some Unsettled Questions of Political Economy*, the first of which addresses international values and some related subjects.[33]

Changes in the Circumstances

With the determinants thus spelled out, it was natural for Torrens, in his diagnosis of England's distress in those years (1830s to 1840s), to identify the causes to be:

> the participation by other manufacturing countries in those advantages which, while exclusively possessed by England, rendered the produce of British more valuable than the produce of foreign labour; – an increase in the capital and labour employed in preparing goods for foreign markets more rapid than the contemporaneous increase in the capital employed in foreign countries in supplying us with the elements of reproduction; – and the disadvantageous terms upon which the imposition of heavy import duties compels the British manufacturer to dispose of his fabrics in foreign markets. ([1844] 1970, p. 284)

In short, the distress had been the result of 'foreign competition', the 'powers of production outgrowing the field of employment', and 'hostile tariffs' ([1844] 1970, pp. 250–52). In relation to the determinants of the terms of trade spelled out in the previous subsection, the first cause of distress would directly result in changes in the 'comparative difference in productive cost', while the latter two would directly lead to alterations in the 'relative degrees of demand' in England and her trading partners for different commodities. Thus, unlike Mill who related reciprocal demand to the 'inclinations of the consumers' in the trading countries, Torrens integrated the relative degrees of demand to a set of forces which was determined by the comparative rates of accumulation in, as well as the dissimilar duty rates imposed by, those countries.

Regarding the first cause of distress, Torrens had elsewhere expressed that it was 'the employment of superior machinery, greater energy and skill in the application of manual labour, and the possession of more accessible coal mines' which accounted for the comparative efficacy of England's industries (ibid., p. 235, see also p. 234). Although she still enjoyed the 'natural advantage' of having accessible coal fields, the same could not be said for the 'artificial advantages'. For,

> [i]n the actual state of knowledge and of international communication, the adoption of the latest improvements in scientific power cannot be confined to any particular country. A rigid enforcement of laws against the exportation of machinery might possibly retard, but could not ultimately prevent the inevitable result. ... As regards energy and skill in the application of manual labour, it would be presumptuous to assume that the English operative will continue ever superior to the robust and persevering German. (Ibid., pp. 235–6)

To put it simply, England could not for long maintain the artificial advantages over the 'rival nations'.

While the treatment of this first cause of distress was rather brief, Torrens devoted much more attention to the other two causes. A careful appreciation of his analysis of these is a prerequisite to a fuller understanding of his policy proposals for their removal.

Powers of Production Outgrowing the Field of Employment

Unlike the first cause of distress, the second cause directly follows from the discussion in sections 4.2 to 4.4 above. As was mentioned there, Torrens followed through the logic of combining the Smithian and Ricardian insight, and predicted that trade by itself could not guarantee lasting prosperity for England. Why? The unleashing of productive forces when England specialised in manufactures, and the bypassing of the growth obstacle when she could more freely import food and raw produce, would tend to augment her rate of accumulation. Her lead in this respect over most, if not all, of her trading partners would be further extended. Hence, Torrens observes in the *Colonization of South Australia* that,

> it is ... a fact established by experience, and universally admitted, that in countries in different states of improvement capital may increase in different ratios. ([1835] 1962, pp. 241–2; repeated in [1844] 1970, p. 92, and again, with minor changes, in ibid., p. 240)

Then in *The Budget*, referring specifically to England, he points out that,

> The enormous sums advanced in foreign loans, invested in foreign securities, and hazarded in the execution of internal improvements in foreign lands, supply a practical demonstration that the ratio at which capital increases is higher in this, than in foreign countries. ([1844] 1970, p. 242)[34]

To modern development economists, these observations would smack of what is today termed 'uneven accumulation'.

What would be the consequences of this 'unevenness'? Keeping in mind that England was the exporter of manufactured products and that it imported mostly food and raw produce from its trading partners, this was a situation in which 'the capital employed in preparing [wrought] goods for the foreign market increases faster than the capital employed in foreign countries in raising raw materials, and in exchanging them for finished goods' ([1835] 1962, p. 262, see also p. 243; and [1844] 1970, pp. 93, 241). It is no wonder why '[t]he quantity of capital, employed in producing manufactured goods, for the foreign market, bears a greater proportion than before, to the quantity of capital employed in foreign countries, in raising the articles which replace the elementary cost of preparing the manufactured goods' ([1835] 1962, p. 245; repeated verbatim in [1844] 1970, p. 95).

Would England's trading partners be able to absorb the manufactured products at the rate that she was supplying? Would they be capable of supplying food and raw produce at the rate that she was demanding? With a sense of helplessness, Torrens answered that,

> The inventions of Watt, of Arkwright, and of Crompton, increased, in almost a miraculous degree, the productive power of manufacturing industry in England. But these inventions did not, and could not, increase, in a corresponding degree, the productive powers of the foreign agricultural industry which raises the materials and the equivalents of British manufactured goods. The consequence was, a divergement from that due proportion between the industry which works up raw materials, and the industry which raises them, upon which the permanent well-being of a manufacturing population necessarily depends. ([1835] 1962, pp. 268–9; repeated verbatim in [1844] 1970, pp. 101–2)[35]

Consequently '[t]he supply of British fabrics was increased beyond the demand, and the demand for raw materials was increased beyond the supply' ([1835] 1962, p. 269; repeated verbatim in [1844] 1970, p. 102).[36]

Torrens specifically exemplified the seriousness of the situation by referring to the history of cotton manufacture in England, in the course of which he observed that '[t]here was a rapid increase in the foreign demand; but there was an increase still more rapid in the supply' ([1835] 1962, pp. 238–9; repeated verbatim in [1844] 1970, pp. 89–90). In order to dramatise the problem, he employed an illustration in which there was an increase in England's production of cotton goods but the demand for such goods in America remained stationary. In predicting the necessary consequences, Torrens clearly demonstrated that he was concerned with the distributional implications of the uneven growth process. Thus, he anticipated that,

> the value of English cottons will fall in the markets of America, and that the value of American produce, cotton wool, and other materials, will rise in the markets of England. This fall in the value of manufactured goods [of cotton], in relation to the raw produce expended on their production, is the same thing as a fall in the rate of manufacturing profit [in the cotton industry]. ([1835] 1962, pp. 234–5; repeated with minor changes in [1844] 1970, p. 87)

Miserably, 'causes similar to those which produce these effects in the cotton trade, may, at the same time, be producing similar effects in the silk trade, in the linen trade, in the woollen trade, and in all the other branches of industry in which goods are made for foreign markets' ([1835] 1962, p. 242; repeated verbatim in [1844] 1970, p. 93, and then, with slight changes, in ibid., p. 240). He thus reiterated that, more generally, '[i]n a country depending upon foreign commerce, if manufacturing capital and labour increase faster than the foreign demand for finished goods expands, the employment of such increased capital and labour, must, of necessity, occasion a fall in the price of [wrought] goods [in relation to the elementary cost of their production], and a reduction in profits, and in wages' ([1835] 1962, p. 236; repeated with emphasis throughout in [1844] 1970, pp. 88–9).[37]

Employing terms which were to prompt writers like Robbins (1958, Ch. VI, part 6) and Ghosh (1967, pp. 165–78) to conclude that he might have anticipated the 'stagnation theory', Torrens declared that,

> the single fact, that the manufactures of a country exchange, in the foreign market, for a less quantity than before, of the articles expended in preparing manufactured goods, is in itself a demonstration, that there is, in relation to the demand of the foreign market, a redundancy, a general glut of capital, over-trading, or home competition. ([1835] 1962, p. 245; repeated verbatim in [1844] 1970, p. 95)

Prices, profits, and wages would all be lowered during this period of 'embarrassment and revulsion' ([1835] 1962, pp. 261–2).[38]

Hostile Tariffs Aggravating the Problem

To Torrens, the problems created by the third cause of England's distress – the proliferation in the use of hostile tariffs by her trade rivals – follow directly from the difficulties associated with the 'uneven growth' discussed in the previous subsection. Thus, 'the disproportionate increase of the capital and labour employed in foreign trade compels us to force our fabrics into markets where they are met by hostile tariffs' ([1844] 1970, p. 252). English manufacturers were put in a situation in which they had to dispose of their goods at disadvantageous terms. But that was not all.

> [T]he lines of circumvallation drawn around us by hostile tariffs, show us, in a way which cannot be mistaken, that it has become the established policy of foreign countries to employ their *relatively slow increase of capital* in manufacturing for themselves, and not in raising additional supplies of raw produce to be exported in exchange for British fabrics. By the operation of a two-fold cause, the supply of British goods is kept in excess of the foreign demand. ([1844] 1970, p. 242, italics added)

The force that was turning the terms of international exchange against England would thus be intensified.

4.6 POLICY RESPONSE: COMMERCIAL RECIPROCITY AND EXTENDED COLONISATION

In what ways then could the fall in profits be averted? Following from his diagnosis, it is not surprising that Torrens first considered the further extension of markets in foreign countries.[39] However, he quickly realised that such extensions would depend on two circumstances, over which England could not control. Thus,

> We cannot cause the capital, employed by foreign countries in producing raw materials, to increase in the same proportion in which the manufacturing capital employed in preparing goods for the foreign market may increase.

Even if that could be accomplished,

> we could not cause the increasing supplies of raw produce to be offered as the equivalents for our increased supply of wrought articles; for we could not prevent foreign countries from imitating the example we have set them, and from imposing high protecting duties on the importation of manufactured goods, and thus forcing their increasing supplies of food and materials to be worked up at home. ([1835] 1962, p. 247; repeated verbatim and with some emphases in [1844] 1970, p. 96, see also p. 98)

Sensing England's helplessness under these circumstances, Torrens started to advocate the principle of commercial reciprocity and he also re-dedicated his support for the colonisation movement.

Commercial Reciprocity

Torrens's analysis of commercial policy has over time attracted some attention because it seems to be a precursor to the celebrated argument for the 'optimal tariff' (Viner [1937] 1975, pp. 298–9, 322; Robbins 1958, p. 182; Bhagwati 1994, p. 566). For instance, at one point in *The Budget* he argues that,

> [I]mport duties, imposed upon one side, and not upon the other, diminish, by their amount, the demand for the products of the country against which they are levied, without diminishing, in that country, the demand for the productions of the country by which they are imposed; and that this alteration in the reciprocal relations of demand and supply, alters the terms of the international exchange in favour of the country imposing the adverse duty, and to the disadvantage of the country upon whose productions the adverse duty is levied. ([1844] 1970, p. 343 of Postscript to Letter IX)

This certainly sounds as if he was supporting the levying of import duties to turn the terms of trade in England's favour (see also ibid., pp. 344–5 of Postscript to Letter IX).[40]

However, as Robbins had partially clarified, 'Torrens was not concerned with any proposal that, starting from a free trade position, we should endeavour by widespread resort to import duties to turn the terms of trade in our favour'.[41] 'The discussion of the effects of tariffs on the terms of trade was not an exercise in abstract analysis', he continued to point out, 'it was [rather] all part and parcel of the explanation and apologia of a particular form of commercial policy'. That policy, according to Robbins, was the policy of reciprocity (1958, pp. 225–6).

Upon closer examination, Torrens was in fact trying to illustrate how, from an initial situation in which both England and her trading partners were employing tariffs, the former would be sunk into deeper distress if she would unilaterally lower her duties. Obviously, if attention is merely called to the 'optimal tariff' implication from his analysis, his motive for getting into the policy controversy in the first place – which was defensive rather than offensive – would be misconstrued, and the reader would be misled as to what course of commercial policy action he was actually recommending.

Why then did Torrens get into the debate about commercial reciprocity? It is Robbins's interpretation that, 'He was interested ... in the way in which we endeavoured to get to a free trade position, the benefits of which he never ceased to emphasize ... The inventor of the phrase "territorial division of labour" never went back on his original contention that the wider the areas of such co-operation, the better for *all* concerned' (ibid., pp. 226–7, italics added). While this certainly harmonises with his (Robbins's) emphasis of the static gains from trade for all in his interpretation of Torrens's contributions to trade analysis, it does not accord well with the reinterpretation advanced so far in this chapter.

Were the implementation of the principle of commercial reciprocity to create a wider market to which England could export her manufactures, and from which she could import food and raw produce, Torrens would readily agree that she would be better off. However, given this pattern of specialisation and trade, and based on the discussion in the second subsection in section 4.4, he would not say the same for the other 'old' countries. As for the 'new' countries, given that they were lagging behind England in terms of growth (see the third subsection in section 4.5) and they were not able to satisfy her voracious demand for raw produce, the condition for structural change to take place in these countries (namely, 'when capital begins to exceed what, at the existing price of produce, can be beneficially vested in the soil' ([1829] 1972, p. 44, quoted in section 4.4 above)) would simply not be realised. Thus, while he indeed pressed for the opening of foreign markets, abandoning his earlier unilateral free-trade position[42] and subscribing to the principle of commercial reciprocity, it can perhaps be claimed that in doing so, he was only certain of (if not solely interested in) the dynamic benefits for England.

Moreover, it was only when his attention was drawn to the problems that were associated with England's relatively rapid growth that Torrens started to urgently feel the need to respond to hostile tariffs. Thus, in the light of the discussion in last two subsections in section 4.5, it follows *a fortiori* that,

> Were we to open our ports to the produce of foreign countries, while these countries retain their hostile tariffs, the British demand for foreign produce would be increased in a greater proportion than the foreign demand for British goods; and ... the value of the produce of British labour would be still further depressed in relation to the produce of foreign labour. ([1844] 1970, p. 254)[43]

This lowering of import duties upon the productions of those countries which retained their hostile tariffs would, 'instead of affording relief, ... aggravate the general distress, by occasioning ... a deeper decline in prices, in profits, [and] in wages' (ibid., p. 29). Moreover, 'an unconditional remission of import duties upon our part, could have no ... effect [of presenting to foreign countries an inducement to mitigate their tariffs]. It would have a directly contrary effect. It would be a bounty upon the continuance of hostile tariffs' (ibid., p. 345 of Postscript to Letter IX, see also p. 354 of that Postscript, and pp. 62, 405–6).

What exactly would be involved in the enforcement of the principle of commercial reciprocity? Torrens proposed that England should 'lower the import duties upon the goods produced in countries receiving British goods upon terms equally favourable', 'impose high or prohibitory duties upon goods, the produce of countries imposing high or prohibitory duties upon British goods',[44] and 'admit, duty free, all raw materials employed in the processes of reproduction' ([1844] 1970, pp. 47–8; see [1833] 1958, p. 6, for an earlier statement of these).[45]

Although the enforcement of these elements of the principle would aid in averting the distressing situation in England, from the beginning when they were conceived Torrens did not seem to believe that carrying them out alone would be sufficient to solve her problems. He was thus resigned to the conclusion that,

> To create an extension of the foreign market proportionate to the increasing powers of production in this country, is beyond our power. It is not to foreign countries that we must look, in order to prevent our accumulating capital from becoming redundant, and occasioning a decline in profits and in wages. ([1835] 1962, p. 247; repeated, with emphasis throughout, in [1844] 1970, pp. 96–7, see also p. 242)

This brings the discussion to his renewed support for the colonisation movement.

Re-dedication to the Colonisation Movement[46]

Not giving much hope to what the practice of commercial reciprocity could accomplish, Torrens came to believe that 'the only possible means by which we can avert a fall of profits and of wages, is, to find for the superabundant capital and labour other fields of profitable employment. The great practical problem is, to find where these other fields exist' ([1833] 1958, pp. 248–9; see also [1844] 1970, p. 98).

In the manner that Torrens conceived of it, such 'fields' were to be created through colonisation:

> [I]t is only with the foreign dependencies of the British Crown that England can purchase increased quantities of raw produce with increased quantities of finished goods. *Extended colonisation is the only practicable means by which we can create expanding fields of employment for the redundant capital and labour which must otherwise melt away and perish through bankruptcy and destitution.* ([1844] 1970, p. 98, italics original)

How would the fall of profits and wages be averted?

> [A]bstracting the redundancy [of capital and labour] for the purpose of planting new nations ... restores that equal proportion between the supply of goods and the demand for them, upon which commercial prosperity depends, and [thus] averts that fall of profits, and of wages, which inflicts embarrassment and privation upon the producing classes. ([1835] 1962, p. 261)[47]

Harking back to the Smithian and Ricardian themes discussed earlier in sections 4.3 and 4.4, Torrens projected that,

> This discovery [of the true principles of colonisation] gives us the same unlimited power, with respect to the production of raw materials, which the inventions of Watt, and Arkwright, and Crompton, gave us with respect to the production of wrought goods. ([1835] 1962, p. 269; see also [1844] 1970, p. 102)

An expanding field of beneficial employment capable of receiving 'indefinite additions' of capital and labour would hence be opened. 'England might become a vast industrial metropolis, and the colonies agricultural provinces of unlimited extent' ([1844] 1970, p. 177).

Typical of his style of exposition, Torrens illustrated his argument with an example, and this time it was in the woollen trade. Initially, the greater increase in capital and labour employed in manufacturing woollens in England for the foreign market than the capital and labour hired in foreign countries in raising the equivalents for woollen goods had resulted in distress for the woollen industry along the line of the discussion in section 4.5, namely, a fall in prices, profits, and wages. Then he considered withdrawing the 'redundant' capital and labourers from England and planting them in an Australian colony, 'where they would become demanders, and not suppliers, of the finished fabric, and suppliers, not demanders, of the raw materials'. As a result of this effort,

> the increase in the supply of the raw material, and in the demand for the finished article, would occasion a rise of profits and an advance of wages in the woollen trade, and these would cause in that trade an increase of capital and of hands. But the increasing numbers would not now perish by the increase of bankruptcy, and of mortality, because they could now be beneficially employed in manufacturing woollens for Australia, where the planting of the capital and labour, formerly redundant in England, had created the materials and equivalents which constitute effectual demand.

This woollen trade example, as Torrens also claimed, was equally applicable to all the other staple manufactures of the United Kingdom, including linens, silks, cottons, and so on ([1835] 1962, pp. 263–6; [1844] 1970, pp. 99–101).

In addition to the above benefits, expanded trade through the creation of colonies could neutralise the effect of hostile tariffs because 'the English manufacturer would no longer find it necessary to export his goods to foreign countries, except at prices sufficiently high to cover the amount of the import duties which foreign countries might impose' ([1844] 1970, p. 294).[48] More importantly,

> By extending our colonial system, and opening new and expanding markets in our trans-marine dependencies, coupled with the rigid enforcement of the principle of reciprocity, we may arm ourselves with accumulating force to break down hostile tariffs, and to establish free trade throughout the world. ([1844] 1970, p. 66)

England's influence in negotiating commercial treaties with foreign states would be preponderant.[49]

4.7 SUMMING UP

The reappraisal of Torrens's works in this chapter has proceeded from the contention that, thanks to the eagerness on the part of mainstream economists to close the chapter on the history of thought in classical trade theories, the thrust and the richness of the classical approach to distribution, growth, and trade have been subverted.

Torrens, like Smith and Ricardo, was interested in the process of capitalist development, especially of that in England. He understood the key to be capital accumulation, and hence the factors affecting the rate of profits. Of these factors, he emphasised the 'degree of skill with which labour is applied' and the 'natural productiveness of land', related them to each other by noting the opposing effects they could have on the rate of profits, and built upon them a two-pronged case for free trade from the viewpoint of England. His distribution (and growth) theory thus provided a framework within which he stitched together Smith's productivity theory and Ricardo's argument against the Corn Laws. Needless to say, this feat of his has escaped the attention of those who are more than ready to toss out his distribution theory.

But Torrens did not stop there. For while England's growth rate could be augmented through the further unleashing of productive forces in manufactures and the bypassing of the natural impediments in the primary producing sector, her trading partners would be trailing behind in terms of their rates of accumulation. Upon perceiving this development and the attendant distress for England, he started to argue for commercial reciprocity and he renewed his support for the colonisation movement, all for the sake of more aggressively opening markets for English products as well as tapping new or expanded sources of supply to satisfy her needs for raw products. In doing so, he provided a most interesting sequel to Smith's and Ricardo's analyses of the process of capitalist development in an international context. Unfortunately, this accomplishment has also not been appreciated.

These contributions by Torrens are not the only pieces of evidence to suggest that the mainstream assessment has not done him justice. One should also recall that he did not believe free trade to be always mutually beneficial. Despite his reference to the 'relative degrees of demand' in determining the values of international exchange, he principally integrated it not to the 'inclinations of consumers' in the trading countries, but to the comparative rates of accumulation in those countries. Finally, his discussion of the monopoly power of trade should not be misconstrued as a desire on his part to see England exploit her market power; he was rather concerned with the intensification of her distress if she were to lower her duties, while her trading partners were to retain theirs.

Lest there are those who would dismiss this reappraisal of Torrens by reminding that he was after all just a minor figure, it should be pointed out that Mill, quite apart from all that he has been acclaimed for by mainstream trade theorists, had actually attempted to relate Smith and Ricardo in a manner very similar to that by Torrens. Furthermore, he had also provided a sequel to that unified analysis which is also very comparable to that of Torrens. These are the subjects of discussion in the following chapter.

NOTES

1. Except for some minor revisions, including those necessitated by placing it as a part of the present book, this chapter is essentially a reproduction of Ho (1996b).
2. Two of his works, *An Essay on External Corn Trade* and *An Essay on the Production of Wealth*, will hereafter be referred to, respectively, as *External Corn Trade* and *Production of Wealth*. The reader should take note that, as Robbins (1958, p. 273) has pointed out, the fourth (1827) edition of *External Corn Trade* was reproduced unaltered in the first 450 pages of the fifth (1829) edition of the same title. The reader should also pay attention to the

fact that the Postscript to Letter IX in *The Budget* is given page numbers which are duplicated in the first portion of Letter X contained in the same publication. To avoid confusion, the Postscript is explicitly mentioned whenever reference is made to it. Finally, Torrens had a high propensity to repeat his own passages. For those that were reproduced, whether verbatim or with minor changes, their source(s) and page references will be indicated.

3. Let it be stressed that Torrens's view on distribution had changed over time. This is not surprising given that his works were put together and published over an exceptionally long period. Section 4.2 below briefly describes this change from a Smithian to a Ricardian position. For an earlier description of the development of Torrens's position on distribution, which includes an excellent discussion of the changes in his view on value from a Smithian to a Ricardian, and then to an anti-Ricardian, position, see de Vivo (1986). Notes 10 and 15 below refer to the weaknesses and limitations in his treatment of distribution. It should be added, however, that after the 1820s Torrens's attention was predominantly switched to monetary issues, commercial policies, and the practice of colonisation.
4. Torrens's deep respect for the two is reflected in this observation which is registered in his introduction to the *Production of Wealth*: 'Mr. Ricardo has done more for the science of Political Economy than any other writer, with the single exception perhaps of Dr. Adam Smith' ([1821] 1965, p. iv).
5. According to Meenai (1956, p. 49, n. 5), Professor George Pryme, who was the first Professor of Political Economy at Cambridge University, recalls in his autobiographic recollections that, 'He [Torrens] told me the origin of his introduction to the science, that being appointed to the command of some lonely place, he took with him the *Wealth of Nations*, and a few other books on political economy and there mastered the subject' (1870, p. 286). Groenewegen (1993, p. xii), in his introduction to *The Economist Refuted and Other Early Economic Writings by Torrens*, describes the source more fully as the *Autobiographical Recollections of George Pryme edited by his daughter* (*Mrs. Alicia Boyne*), Cambridge. For additional biographical information on Torrens, see, apart from Meenai (ibid.), Robbins (1958), and Fetter (1962, 1990).
6. Smith's original claim was: 'The increase of stock, which raises wages, tends to lower profit. When the stocks of many rich merchants are turned into the same trade, their mutual competition naturally tends to lower its profit; and when there is a like increase of stock in all the different trades carried on in the same society, the same competition must produce the same effect in them all' ([1776] 1979, p. 105, see also pp. 352–3).
7. Taking the earliest advertisement, which stated 'this day is published' and gave the price of the book, as an indication of the date of publication, Sraffa (1951b, pp. 4–5) suggests that the first edition of the *External Corn Trade* was probably published on the same day as Ricardo's *Essay on Profits*.
8. For the likely role that Ricardo and his *Essay on Profits* had played in this switch of Torrens, see de Vivo (op. cit., pp. 91–2).
9. The article is titled: 'Mr. Owen's plans for relieving the national distress'. For the timing of its publication in relation to the second edition of the *External Corn Trade*, and for the references pertaining to the controversy surrounding its authorship, see de Vivo (1985b). The present author takes the position that the article was indeed written by Torrens.
10. Langer (op. cit., p. 397) further claims that Torrens's article 'details a "corn model" theory of profits in much more explicit terms than does Ricardo's *Essay on Profits*'. In one of Torrens's examples, Langer (ibid., pp. 398–9) even detects the presence of 'the germ of Sraffa's "Standard Commodity"', concluding that 'it may not … be inappropriate to designate both Ricardo and Torrens as anticipators of Sraffa's construction'. However, as de Vivo (1986) has meticulously argued, Torrens was able to determine the rate of profits in his numerical examples only when he assumed conditions of production that involved a physical homogeneity between capital and product either at the economy level or in the agricultural sector.
11. According to Seligman (1903, p. 341), Torrens discovered the law of rent 'independently of Malthus and Ricardo'. To Gomes (1987, p. 173), it was 'discovered jointly by Malthus, West, Torrens, and Ricardo'. See Torrens (1827, pp. 130–37) for a lengthy, but not his

earliest, discussion on the subject. The errors which he pointed out in Ricardo's treatment of the subject of rent (ibid., pp. 137–50) were later retracted in *The Budget* ([1844] 1970, pp. xvi–xxii). See also Robbins (1958, pp. 41–7).

12. According to Torrens, the level of real wages is determined by 'climate and custom' and the 'habits of living', and it is not fixed or immutable ([1829] 1972, pp. 84, 460–61; [1834] 1969, pp. 11–13). As Sraffa had pointed out, upon Torrens's complaint, Ricardo inserted a note beginning from the second edition of his *Principles*, acknowledging that, 'The whole of this subject is most ably illustrated by Colonel Torrens'. See Ricardo ([1821] 2004, p. 97). Notice that Torrens defined real wages as the *quantity* of necessaries and comforts which the labourer receives ([1829] 1972, pp. 83–4, 454; [1834] 1969, p. 5). He found it confusing for Ricardo to discuss the level of wages in terms of 'proportions in which the produce of industry is distributed', instead of 'quantities' of commodities. See Torrens ([1829] 1972, p. 455; [1834] 1969, p. 6; [1835] 1962, pp. 24–33; and [1844] 1970, pp. xxiii–xxvii). Nevertheless, he seemed to be more disputing Ricardo's usage of terms and less squabbling with the latter's conclusion with regard to the relationship between wages and profits.
13. It should be stressed that Torrens included only those wrought goods that would enter directly or indirectly into the necessaries for labourers. He thus stated in very clear terms that, 'An increase in the value of superfluities has no real effect in absorbing profit' (1827, p. 170, see also p. 171). However, manufactures were not incorporated into all illustrations. See, for instance, those numerical examples of his which are cited by Langer (1982) and de Vivo (1985a) in substantiating their claims that Torrens had subscribed to Ricardo's corn-ratio theory of profits. Torrens had also asserted at one point that, 'Of all the articles which enter into the labourer's subsistence, food is the most considerable and the most important' ([1829] 1972, p. 84).
14. For some situations where he did show some considerations, see section 3.5 above.
15. However, this also opens up the possibility of making errors in determining the relative price of the agricultural and manufactured elements in the wage-basket, which errors Torrens indeed committed. See de Vivo (1985a, p. 91; 1986).
16. The reason why the real wage rate was left out appeared to be a faith on the part of Torrens in the rapidity in the operation of the Malthusian mechanism, in which case the third determining circumstance of the rate of profits could be regarded as very stable and unchanging. See Torrens ([1829] 1972, pp. 117–18).
17. This type of relationship between the agricultural and manufacturing sectors has actually been referred to by Torrens in a lot of other instances. See, for instance, Torrens ([1821] 1865, pp. 133, 138, and 206–7; [1829] 1972, pp. 134, 163; and [1834] 1969, p. 38).
18. For a formal illustration of how increasing returns in particularly the capital goods sectors can contribute to sustaining long period growth in an economy, even though land is fixed and there exists no technical progress in the agricultural sector, see Canning (1988).
19. The benefits which would accrue to the landed interest should the duties be continued earned this harsh reaction from Torrens: 'To increase the rent-roll of proprietors, by compelling all other members of the community to pay more for their corn than they otherwise need to do, would be as gross a violation of natural justice as it is possible for the mind to conceive. ... It would be nothing better than legalised robbery, taking the money out of the pockets of the poor and of the industrious, in order to lavish it on the idle and the rich' ([1829] 1972, pp. 375–6).
20. What Robbins did was to direct attention to Torrens's discussion of the benefit of a 'territorial division of labour' (1958, pp. 20–21). See Torrens ([1808] 1993, p. 9; 1821 [1965], pp. 156–7) for the original discussions. His motive is transparent: he wanted to illustrate that this was a step which subsequently 'led [Torrens] to conclusions which ... were to underlie one of the most famous propositions of the Classical system [namely the theory of comparative advantage]' (ibid., p. 21). While in doing so he might be portraying certain phases of Torrens's thought process, in calling undue attention to that he had distorted the thrust of Torrens's trade analysis.
21. For this elaboration, however, he was no longer explicit in his acknowledgement and has appeared to plagiarise Smith (see Smith [1776] 1979, p. 31). The passage concerned is

immediately followed by a description by Torrens of how impractical it would be to carry out division of labour in 'thinly-peopled districts' (op. cit., p. 161). It also appears here that Torrens was plagiarising Smith (ibid., pp. 31–2). Nevertheless, when Torrens described as a contrast the situation in 'populous districts' (op. cit., pp. 162–4), his discussion appears to be original.

22. Recalling the discussion in section 4.2, Torrens was for a short while opposing the Corn Laws on terms that were more Smithian than Ricardian. See the discussion in Torrens (1815, pp. 297–9). However, in a few years' time from the publication of the first edition of the *External Corn Trade*, he started to adopt the Ricardian argument.
23. This principle of free trade in corn, Torrens added, 'is more or less applicable to every species of agricultural produce, as well as to every description of raw material, whether derived from the soil, from forests, from mines, or from fisheries. It is applicable in a peculiar manner to sugar, as a general article of food; and to timber, and iron, as important ingredients of capital' ([1829] 1972, p. 436).
24. Torrens also painstakingly tried to convince the 'interests of agriculture' that the repeal of the Corn Laws would *ultimately* not be injurious to them ([1829] 1972, pp. 49–54, 156–73, 374–9, and 386–7; see also [1844] 1970, pp. 82–3).
25. Notice that there was a faith on the part of Torrens that a structural change in the economy of the corn-exporting new countries would take place rather spontaneously under free trade conditions. It will be contended later in sections 4.5 and 4.6 below that the 'uneven growth' which he observed between England and these countries actually implied the reason for that structural change to take place would not even materialise.
26. Compare with Kaldor's reconsideration of Ricardo's England–Portugal model, in which diminishing, instead of constant, returns to scale in viniculture in Portugal is recognised, and there is a 'land-constraint' in that country. In that situation, the latter 'could well end up by being a much poorer country than before [trade with England was opened up] – there would be less employment and less output' (1980, p. 87). See also Ballance, Ansari and Singer (1982, p. 14).
27. For instance, he simply insists in the *Letters on Commercial Policy* that, 'Were a free trade established between England and France, England would not send food and raw materials to France, in exchange for manufactured goods; the commerce between the two countries would consist either in the interchange of those manufactured goods in which they respectively excel, or else in the barter of the food and raw materials raised in France for the fabrics prepared in England' ([1833] 1958, p. 51).
28. Torrens regarded this claim to be 'practically proved' by England's trade with the United States and with China, from which cotton wool and tea were respectively imported. (Tea, though not a manufactured product, was chosen because it was not applicable to reproduction.) In his typical magniloquent style, he reasoned thus: 'Stop our imports from the United States, and our manufacturing millions perish; suspend our imports from China, and not a hand will be thrown out of work' (op. cit., p. 275).
29. While in his time silk was regarded as a luxurious item, Torrens must also have assumed, albeit implicitly, that cotton did not enter directly or indirectly into the French worker's wage-basket. Notice also how this conclusion was reached not from France's, but from England's, viewpoint. Some would accuse Torrens of failing to foresee the possibility, and the associated advantage, of what is known today as 'intra-industry trade'. This would seem to be quite unfair to him at a time when 'inter-industry' trade was clearly the relatively more important species of international commerce. Besides, neither were Smith, Ricardo, and Mill able to foresee it.
30. But recall n. 10 in Ch. 2 above.
31. Even though Torrens had by the late 1810s developed his so-called 'capital theory of value', he seemed to be ready to fall back on the labour theory of value, at least for making his point when he called attention to the problem of determining international values. See, for instance, Torrens ([1833] 1958, p. 17).
32. 'The power of any one country in commanding the productions of other countries', he thus maintained, 'must be in proportion to the facilities which it possesses for producing commodities extensively demanded in other countries' ([1835] 1962, pp. 148–9). It should

be added that 'skill and facilities in producing commodities' is a factor that was always brought up by Torrens in connection with a consideration of gold flows. See Torrens ([1829] 1972, pp. 410, 423; [1833] 1958, pp. 12, 18; [1835] 1962, p. 174; and [1844] 1970, pp. 26–7).

33. It was probably Torrens's reference to 'the proportion which exists between the demand for foreign commodities in the home market, and the demand for domestic commodities in foreign markets' (1827, p. 401) that prompted Schumpeter (1954, p. 608) to remark that he (Torrens) could be the first to employ 'reciprocal demand' in an effort to solve for the terms of trade. (The term 'reciprocal relations of demand and supply' did not appear until the publication of *The Budget* ([1844] 1970, p. 334 of Postscript to Letter IX).) Indeed, in the numerical illustration of a trade between England and Poland, Torrens made an attempt to show how, depending on the different 'extent of demand' in both countries, the terms of trade could either be pushed toward the domestic (autarkic) exchange ratio in England or be tilted toward that in Poland (1827, pp. 401–7). Unfortunately, partly because of the inclusion of 'carriage and merchant's profit', it is not as crisp an illustration as that of Mill's. See also the discussion in Torrens ([1835] 1962, p. 233, which is repeated verbatim in [1844] 1970, p. 86, and then repeated again with minor modifications in ibid., p. 238). As was cautioned earlier in this section, Torrens's interest in the problem should not be confused with that of Mill.
34. Referring again to England in the *Tracts on Finance and Trade*, Torrens contends that 'in a country possessing superior powers of production, there is a more rapid accumulation of capital ... than in less favoured countries; and this fact [is] practically verified ... by the vast amounts of British capital annually seeking more advantageous investments in foreign securities and foreign speculations' (1852, No. II, p. 22).
35. This concept of a 'due proportion between industries' appears to originate from Torrens's own discussion of the notion of 'effectual demand'. Thus, he observes in the *Production of Wealth* that in the 'improved and complex state' of society, in which the practice of divisions of employment had augmented the effective powers of human labour, 'the machine of society becomes infinitely artificial and complex, and a derangement in any of its nicer parts, not unfrequently impedes the working of the whole'. Consequently, in this state of society, 'the object is not merely to produce, but to produce in such proportions that the peculiar articles furnished by each class may be readily and profitably exchanged for the peculiar articles prepared by the others' ([1821] 1965, pp. 340–41).
36. This should be contrasted with the optimistic mood about England's trade prospect which appeared to have prevailed with him until the late 1820s. See the discussion at the end of first subsection in section 4.4 above.
37. See also Torrens ([1835] 1962, p. 269; [1844] 1970, p. 102). On occasion, Torrens had mentioned that wages would also fall when the rate of profits declined. This is because he believed that '[a]s profits fall, the capitalist is driven to press more and more heavily upon the operatives whom he employs. ... He therefore goes to the operative, and says, I cannot employ you on the same terms as before; you must consent to take less wages, or to work a greater number of hours' ([1833] 1958, p. 72; repeated verbatim in [1834] 1969, pp. 123–4). This pressure would especially be exerted on those labourers working for the 'inferior' capitalists who had not introduced productivity-improving methods ([1835] 1962, pp. 236–7; [1844] 1970, p. 89).
38. To the extent that Torrens had portrayed how, in an uneven economic expansion situation, the faster-growing country could experience a declining terms of trade against the slower-growing country, he might also be regarded as anticipating what Bhagwati (1958) has dubbed the situation of immiserising growth. However, the immiserising-growth literature has tended to focus on spelling out, within the standard framework of the neoclassical trade model (and not the classical framework of capitalist development employed by Torrens), the *conditions*, but not the *causes*, under which that kind of growth would occur. It has also tended to be confined to ascertaining the effect of growth on the real income for a country, rather than on the distribution of income between profits and wages. Understandably, the policy conclusions drawn from the literature are very different from those of Torrens (see section 4.6 below).

39. He concluded early on that the remedy was not to be found in transferring capital from one branch of manufacture to another, because the 'contemporaneous over-trading' affected all the departments of industry supplying goods to the foreign market ([1835] 1962, p. 243; [1844] 1970, p. 94).
40. As early as the *Production of Wealth*, Torrens shrewdly observes that 'a country which possesses commodities peculiar to herself, and generally desired, may render other countries tributory to her by imposing duties on the exportation of those things in the production of which she has a natural monopoly, either partial or complete' ([1821] 1965, p. 282, see also p. 281). This is enough evidence to refute the claim by Gomes, that 'although he [Torrens] was the first in print with the terms-of-trade argument, the idea was not original with him; for John Stuart Mill had formulated the argument on the economics of reciprocity since 1829, but only published it in 1844' (1987, p. 198).
41. Viner (1953, p. 39) similarly notes that Torrens was aware 'from the start that the unilateral substitution by a country of free trade for protection would move the terms of trade against that country'.
42. Roughly six years before he started to show signs of supporting commercial reciprocity (see n. 44 below), Torrens has thus asserts in the *Production of Wealth* that, 'It never could become necessary for the protection of domestic industry, that we should retaliate upon any foreign country the restrictive system which it may ignorantly enforce against us' ([1821] 1965, p. 275).
43. To more fully convince the reader about the change in the terms of trade when 'a duty [is] levied on one side, and not on the other', Torrens had employed several illustrations. See, for instance, Torrens ([1833] 1958, pp. 8–10; [1844] 1970, pp. 29, 51, 62, and pp. 335–7 of Postscript to Letter IX, which includes the well-known 'Cuba case').
44. An even earlier sign of this position can be detected in the fourth edition of the *External Corn Trade*, where Torrens suggests that, 'The subtraction of the precious metals ... and the consequent fall in general prices, might be prevented by retaliating the prohibitory system, and diminished by imposing duties on the importation of foreign commodities coming from countries refusing to act on the principle of reciprocity' (1827, p. 424).
45. This last element was initially insisted upon because, food and raw materials being the 'ultimate elements' and 'component parts of productive capital', duties upon them would 'increase the cost of production, and thereby diminish or destroy that superior facility in producing the articles demanded in foreign markets' ([1833] 1958, p. 24). However, there were signs later on that Torrens was inclined to extend the reciprocity principle even to the import of food and raw produce. See Torrens ([1844] 1970, pp. 409–13, 427).
46. In his early writings Torrens has showed some support for the colonisation movement as a measure to relieve the population pressure. See his argument in *A Paper of the Means of Reducing the Poors [sic] Rates and of Affording Effectual and Permanent Relief to the Labouring Classes*, which is discussed in Robbins (1958, Ch. VI, section 3) and Ghosh (1967, pp. 168–70). In fact, Ghosh even argued that Torrens might be said to have 'very crudely and imperfectly' anticipated in that 1817 pamphlet the idea of self-supporting emigration by means of the sale of unappropriated colonial lands (ibid., pp. 175, 170). His concern with the population problem again surfaced when, a few years later in the *Production of Wealth*, he refers to the need of a system of colonisation 'to relieve the mother country from superfluous numbers' ([1821] 1965, p. 232). However, it appears that he gradually turned to support the movement more as a means of creating new fields of employment for capital. Ghosh (ibid., pp. 172–3) has pointed out that Torrens's attention to 'surplus capital' could be noticed in as early as his 1827 speech to the House of Commons. Nevertheless, having observed that '[t]he capitalist can emigrate – the labourer cannot' ([1835] 1962, p. 18), labourers continued to remain in the picture, as when he got very involved in advocating a 'well-regulated system of colonization'. With regard to the latter, the influence on him by Wakefield beginning in the 1830s is unmistakable. See, for instance, the discussion in Robbins (1958, Ch. VI, parts 4 and 5) and Ghosh (1967, pp. 176–8). Since that has more to do with the 'practice', but not the 'rationale', for colonisation, it will not be further discussed here.

47. In an effort similar to the one employed when he persuaded them not to oppose the repeal of the Corn Laws, Torrens also spelled out the benefits of extended colonisation for the landed proprietors. See, for instance, Torrens ([1835] 1962, pp. 271–81; [1844] 1970, pp. 177–85, 296).
48. Torrens was assuming that free trade could be established between England and her colonies, as well as among the colonies. This was clearly suggested when he claimed that, 'The prosperity of the country cannot be arrested by the hostile tariffs of foreign rivals, if England will establish throughout her wide-spread empire a British commercial league – a colonial Zollverein' ([1844] 1970, p. 102). For more indications of his support of free trade within the 'British commercial league' at round this point of his career, see Torrens (ibid., pp. 64–5, 176, 304, 392; 1852, No. II). To contrast with his earlier discussion of the different effects of various commercial arrangements between mother countries and their colonies, see Torrens ([1808] 1993, pp. 26–8; [1821] 1965, pp. 233–46).
49. Torrens also briefly discussed the benefit of an extended colonial trade in 'neutralizing foreign competition', which competition, to recall the discussion in the subsection that is titled 'Changes in the Circumstances' in section 4.5, was a cause of England's distress. See Torrens ([1844] 1970, pp. 290–93).

5. Mill: Trade, Uneven Development, and Perpetual Overflow of Capital from England

5.1 INTRODUCTION[1]

While Torrens is commonly treated as a 'minor figure' in the mainstream interpretation of the history of international trade theories, John Stuart Mill, as noted in section 2.2 above, is highly esteemed because of the contributions that he made in moving Ricardo's England–Portugal model in the direction of a simple general equilibrium system. Along the way he also introduced a rudimentary demand–supply analysis in the determination of both international and domestic values.[2] These are more than sufficient to ensure an important place for him in that mainstream interpretation. But Mill brought more. He is regarded as having pioneered the analysis of the optimal-tariff case for trade protection, although credit here is sometimes shared with Torrens. Last, but not least, he cogently expressed the infant-industry case for trade protection, a subject which will be further examined in section 6.4 in the following chapter.[3]

These recognitions, however, have only focused on those contributions of his which are related to mainstream trade theories. Can one argue with equal force, as was done in the case of Torrens in Chapter 4 above, that the other contributions of Mill have been ignored because the original context of his discussion has been swept aside? There are some difficulties here because that original context of discussion, while basically Ricardian, has many 'new' elements added to it. These, to borrow an expression from Bharadwaj (1978), were to pave the way for Marshall and others to 'subvert classical analysis'.[4] It is then not surprising that over time the Ricardian framework in which many of Mill's trade analyses were (or could be) situated has been ignored by most mainstream economists. Some, like Schumpeter (1954, pp. 529–30), even grunt about the unnecessary 'filial respect' that Mill had shown toward Ricardo. S. Hollander (1982) argues that there is an 'essential continuity of nineteenth century doctrine'. That is, 'the economics of Ricardo and J. S. Mill ... comprises in its essentials an exchange system consistent with the neo-classical elaborations' (S. Hollander 1985, p. 931).[5] Given that the anchor that brings together Chapters 3 and 4 above is the Ricardian framework as outlined in section 3.2, Mill's filial respect of it should be recognised and properly documented so that his contributions to trade analysis could be re-appraised.

What follows is such a reappraisal of Mill's contributions to the analysis of growth, trade, and foreign investment. To give due recognition to his concern for England's economic progress (and hence his interest in her dynamic gains from trade), these contributions are presented, and are thus linked together, within the Ricardian framework of capitalist development that he employed in many parts of his works.

Like Smith and Ricardo (and, following the discussion in Chapter 4 above, Torrens), Mill regarded the rapidity of that development process to be closely related to the speed of capital accumulation, the latter of which is in turn dependent upon the rate of profits. Thus, in an unsigned contribution to the *Westminster Review* in April, 1825, that is titled 'The Corn Laws' (reprinted in Mill's *Collected Works*, vol. IV, pp. 46–70), he declared that '[i]t is the rate of profits which constitutes the inducement to accumulation, and, whatever be the advantage of a rapid accumulation, the advantage of high profits is the same. But it is on the accumulation of capital that the advancement of the national wealth is wholly dependant' (ibid., p. 50).

Two changing determinants of the rate of profits that Mill emphasised – 'an increased difficulty of producing ... some article which the labourer habitually consumes' and 'the successive introduction of improvements in agriculture, *and* in the production of those manufactured articles which the labourers consume' ([1874] 1974, pp. 105–6, italics added) – enabled him to stitch together the Smithian and Ricardian insights into the dynamic benefits of trade. His case for free trade is multi-pronged, but it is unmistakable that two of the more powerful prongs (from England's viewpoint) have been derived from Smith and Ricardo.

Like Torrens, Mill detected an 'uneven growth' outcome and provided a sequel to it. It was seen in the previous chapter that Torrens devoted attention to both how England's trading partners would not be supplying food and raw produce at the rate which she demanded as well as how they would not be purchasing manufactured products at the rate which she supplied. Mill, on the other hand, appeared to be exclusively preoccupied with the former problem in concluding that trade *per se* would not be a sufficient guarantee for England's lasting prosperity. This prompted him to advocate the 'perpetual overflow of capital [from England] into colonies or foreign countries' ([1871] 1965, p. 746). Based on his diagnosis of England's distress Torrens also advocated commercial reciprocity. Mill supported it too, although a little bit less actively.

The rest of this chapter is organised as follows. Section 5.2 examines what Mill regarded as the principal determinants of the rate of profits and what he observed to be the 'antagonist' tendencies between two of them in particular. On the basis of that observation he constructed a powerful two-pronged case for free trade from England's viewpoint. Section 5.3 describes his adoption of Smith's 'productivity theory'. Section 5.4 then illustrates Mill's subscription to Ricardo's argument against the Corn Laws. Section 5.5 shows his consideration of the impact of trade on some of the corn-exporters and reveals his concern regarding their limited ability to step up their exports to meet England's rapidly expanding demand. As section 5.6 demonstrates, this concern prompted him to recommend the 'perpetual overflow of capital' from England to foreign countries and colonies. Section 5.7 compares his support of commercial reciprocity with that of Torrens. The discussion is summed up in section 5.8.

5.2 DETERMINANTS OF THE RATE OF PROFITS

Ricardo's Influences

Unlike Torrens, who in the early years of his career as an economist was for a short while influenced by Smith's view on the rate of profits, Mill recognised that the doctrine that 'competition of capital lowers profits by lowering prices' was 'unsound in principle' ([1871] 1965, p. 734). He doubted if Smith had really held that doctrine, 'for his language on the subject is wavering and unsteady, denoting the absence of a definite and well-digested opinion'. He further noted that it was when Smith ([1776] 1979, p. 109) spoke of the rate of profit in new colonies that he seemed 'on the very verge of grasping the complete theory of the subject'. He even conjectured that if Smith had 'meditated longer on the subject, and systematized his view of it by harmonizing with each other the various glimpses which he caught of it from different points', he would have perceived that 'the true cause of the fall of profits usually consequent upon increase of capital' was because soil inferior in quality and not as conveniently situated had to be cultivated ([1871] 1965, pp. 734–5). In other words, for 'the complete theory of the subject', one should turn to Ricardo.[6]

It is in one of the essays in his *Essays on Some Unsettled Questions of Political Economy* (hereafter abbreviated as *Some Unsettled Questions*), titled 'On Profits and Interest', that Mill makes an early attempt to state in his own words Ricardo's theory of profits.[7] Concerned with the confusion surrounding the latter's use of the term 'wage', he switches to 'the cost of production of wages' and declares that the rate of profits depends on this cost ([1874] 1974, pp. 97, 104–5).[8] He then goes on to spell out that,

> The cost of production of the wages of one labourer for a year, is the result of two concurrent elements or factors, – viz., 1st, the quantity of commodities which the state of the labour market affords to him; 2ndly, the cost of production of each of those commodities. It follows, that the rate of profits can never rise but in conjunction with one or other of two changes, – 1st, a diminished remuneration of the labourer; or, 2ndly, an improvement in production, or an extension of commerce, by which any of the articles habitually consumed by the labourer may be obtained at smaller cost. ...[9]
>
> So, on the other hand, the rate of profit cannot fall, unless concurrently with one of two events: 1st, an improvement in the labourer's condition; or, 2ndly, an increased difficulty of producing or importing some article which the labourer habitually consumes. (Ibid., p. 105)

The first 'factor' can be compared with what Torrens referred to as the 'real rate of wages' (see section 4.2 above). As for the second factor, it will be illustrated in the following subsection that it corresponds with the other two determinants listed by Torrens.

By the time that he wrote the *Principles* Mill started employing the term 'the cost of labour'[10] and in the chapter on 'Profits' (Bk. II, Ch. XV) he describes it thus:

> The cost of labour ... is ... a function of three variables: the efficiency of labour; the wages of labour (meaning thereby the real reward of the labourer); and the greater or less cost at which the articles composing that real reward can be produced or procured. ... These, therefore, are also the circumstances which determine the rate of profit; and it cannot be in any way affected except through one or other of them. ([1871] 1965, p. 414)

It is not clear why Mill separates the first and the third variables in this passage when he has stated elsewhere that 'the increasing power which mankind are constantly acquiring over nature, increases more and more the efficiency of human exertion, or in other words, diminishes cost of production' (ibid., p. 710).[11] Indeed, in the final chapter of Book III of his *Principles* he writes,

> There are two modes in which the Cost of Labour, which is correctly represented (money being supposed invariable) by the money wages of the labourer, may be increased. The labourer may obtain greater comforts; wages in kind – real wages – may rise. Or the progress of population may force down cultivation to inferior soils, and more costly processes; thus raising the cost of production, the value, and the price, of the chief articles of the labourer's consumption. On either of these suppositions, the rate of profit will fall. (Ibid., p. 698)

This is essentially repeating the description from the essay 'On Profits and Interest' quoted above.[12]

'Antagonist' Tendencies between the Determinants

Assuming the 'standard of comfort' of the labouring class to be given[13] and assuming money to be an 'invariable standard', 'money wages depend on the money price, and therefore on the cost of production, of the various articles which the labourers habitually consume'. In this part of his discussion, Mill might have used a little exaggeration when he describes that '[o]f these articles, food and other agricultural produce are so much the principal, as to leave little influence to anything else' ([1871] 1965, pp. 696–7). In a Ricardian fashion he then goes on to argue,

> The cost of production of food and agricultural produce ... depends on the productiveness of the least fertile land, or of the least productively employed portion of capital, which the necessities of society have as yet put in requisition for agricultural purposes. The cost of production of the food grown in these least advantageous circumstances, determines ... the exchange value and money price of the whole. (Ibid., p. 697)

Momentarily regarding 'food and agricultural produce' as principally making up the entire wage-good basket, Mill draws the reader's attention to how 'the force which urges cultivation in this downward course, is the increase of people; while the counter-force which checks the descent, is the improvement of agriculture science and practice, enabling the same soil to yield to the same labour more ample returns' (ibid.). Not much further in the *Principles*, he labels the 'increase of population' on the one hand and 'improvement in agricultural skill' as two 'antagonist agencies' (ibid., p. 713).

But his consideration of these 'antagonist' forces was to broaden in other situations to include manufactures in the wage-good basket or manufactured means of production that enter, directly or indirectly, into both agricultural and manufactured wage-good items. Thus, continuing right at the end of the second paragraph in the quotation on the 'cost of production of labour' (see the previous subsection) Mill adds that,

> The progress of population and cultivation has a tendency to lower profits through the latter of these two channels [an increased difficulty of producing some article which the labourer habitually consumes], owing to the well known law of the application of capital to land, that a double capital does not *ceteris paribus* yield a double produce. There is, therefore, a tendency in the rate of profits to fall with the progress of society. But there is also an antagonist tendency of profits to rise, by the successive introduction of improvements in agriculture, *and* in the

> production of those manufactured articles which the labourers consume. ([1874] 1974, pp. 105–6, italics added)

'Supposing', he continues, 'that the actual comforts of the labourer remain the same, profits will fall or rise, according as population, or improvements in the production of food *and* other necessaries, advance fastest' (ibid., p. 106, italics added). Thus, it is conceivable that '[t]he increased cheapness of clothing and lodging might make up to them [the poorest class] for the augmented cost of their food' ([1871] 1965, p. 183).[14]

Then in some parts of the *Principles* Mill gets into the situation of manufactured means of production. 'There is another agency', he thus proclaims at one point, 'in habitual antagonism to the law of diminishing return from land ... It is no other than the progress of civilization' (ibid., p. 179). He employed this 'general and somewhat vague expression' because the considerations included under it 'are so various'. He then proceeded to spell out these considerations, noting that 'the most obvious is the progress of agricultural knowledge, skill, and invention' (ibid., pp. 179–80).

Mill distinguishes between two kinds of improved processes in agriculture.[15] One 'enable[s] the land to yield a greater absolute produce, without an equivalent increase of labour' (for example, the disuse of fallows by crop rotation or the introduction of new crops). The second kind of improvement diminishes the 'labour and expense' but 'without increasing the capacity of the land to produce' and includes the 'improved construction of tools' and the 'introduction of new instruments'. It is here that Mill reminds the reader that,

> many purely mechanical improvements, which have, apparently at least, no peculiar connexion with agriculture, nevertheless enable a given amount of food to be obtained with a smaller expenditure of labour. A great improvement in the process of smelting iron, would tend to cheapen agricultural implements, diminish the cost of railroads, of wagons and carts, ships, and perhaps buildings, and many other things to which iron is not at present applied, because it is too costly; and would thence diminish the cost of production of food. (Ibid., p. 181)[16]

He admits that not all 'manufacturing improvements' can 'be made instrumental to facilitate, in any of its stages, the actual production of food, and therefore [some such improvements] do not help to counteract or retard the diminution of the proportional return to labour from the soil' (ibid., p. 185). However, to the extent that manufacturing improvements indirectly cheapen the production of manufactured wage-goods, then they have an effect 'which is practically equivalent'. 'What they do not prevent', Mill proposes, 'they yet, in some degree, compensate for' (ibid., pp. 181–2).[17] Thus,

> [t]he steam-engine, and every other invention which affords a manageable power, are applicable to all things, and of course to those consumed by the labourer. Even the power-loom and the spinning-jenny, though applied to the most delicate fabrics, are available no less for the coarse cottons and woollens worn by the labouring class. All improvements in locomotion cheapen the transport of necessaries as well as of luxuries. Seldom is a new branch of trade opened, without, either directly or in some indirect way, causing some of the articles which the mass of the people consume to be either produced or imported at smaller cost. It may safely be affirmed, therefore, that improvements in production generally tend to cheapen the commodities on which the wages of the labouring class are expended. (Ibid., p. 724)

Referring again to the 'clothing and lodging' that was earlier referred to as non-food wage-good items, he thus predicts that 'almost all improvements in machinery cheapen the labourer's clothing or lodging, or the tools with which these are made' (ibid., p. 751).

It is with recognition of the 'antagonist principle' in the broader sense that Mill's discussion of the determinants of the rate of profits is rendered comparable with Torrens's consideration of the 'natural productiveness of land' and the 'degree of skill with which labour is applied [in both agriculture and in producing wrought goods]' (see section 4.2 above).

Declining Rate of Profits and the Stationary State

Mill was impressed by the increasing power which mankind was constantly acquiring over nature during his time. This 'increases more and more the efficiency of human exertion, or ..., diminishes cost of production' ([1871] 1965, p. 710). However, 'diametrically opposite' to this is a tendency 'in the case of the most important classes of commodities, food and materials ... The cost of production of these commodities tends to increase' (ibid., 712). This is where the 'general law of agricultural industry' (alternatively referred by Mill as the 'general law of diminishing return from land' or the 'law of production from the land') kicks in, when, 'for the purpose of raising an increase of produce recourse is had to inferior land'. With some exaggeration he referred to this as 'the most important proposition in political economy' (ibid., pp. 174, 177). Specifically,

> [w]hen ... population increases ..., the demand for most of the productions of the earth, and particularly for food, increases in a corresponding proportion. And then comes into effect that fundamental law of production from the soil...; the law, that increased labour, in any given state of agricultural skill, is attended with a less than proportional increase of produce. The cost of production of the fruits of the earth increases, *cæteris paribus*, with every increase of the demand. (Ibid., p. 712)

That is, the conflict in agriculture and mining between the two tendencies – 'the one towards an increase of productive power, the other towards a diminution of it' – could, unlike in manufactures, be dominated by the latter with 'every addition of population' (ibid., p. 713).[18]

At times Mill exhibited ambivalence regarding which of these tendencies would win. 'I do not assert', he thus maintained at one point, 'that the cost of production, and consequently the price, of agricultural produce, always and necessarily rises as population increases. It tends to do so; but the tendency may be, and sometimes is, even during long periods, held in check' (ibid., p. 179). Indeed, a strong impulse towards agricultural improvement had 'shown itself in Great Britain during the last twenty or thirty years [leading up to the middle part of the nineteenth century]' (ibid., p. 713; see also p. 190). Elsewhere, however, he also noted that, 'Agricultural skill and knowledge are of slow growth, and still slower diffusion. Inventions and discoveries, too, occur only occasionally, while the increase of population and capital are continuous agencies'. In fact, agricultural improvement 'seldom lowers rent, ... it seldom cheapens food, but only prevents it from growing dearer; and seldom, if ever, throws land out of cultivation, but only enables worse and worse land to be taken in for the supply of an increasing demand. ... [It] may ... be considered to be not so much a counterforce conflicting with increase of population, as a partial relaxation of the bonds which confine that increase' (ibid., pp. 729–30).

Mill then wrote a controversial passage in which he referred to a country where 'the means have long existed of making a great annual addition to capital' but which does not have 'a large reserve of fertile land still unused'.[19] It is one of the characteristics of such a country, he lamented, that 'the rate of profit is habitually within, as it were, a hand's breadth of the minimum, and the country therefore on the very verge of the stationary state' (ibid., 738). Although he clarified he did not mean by that that this state would 'be soon actually reached' in any of the great countries of Europe. 'My meaning is', he explained, 'that it would require but a short time to reduce profits to the minimum' and '[t]he expansion of capital would soon reach its ultimate boundary', if 'the boundary itself did not continually open and leave more space' and if 'capital continued to increase at its present rate, and no circumstances having a tendency to raise the rate of profit occurred in the meantime' (ibid., pp. 738–9).

Two such circumstances follow directly from his consideration of the determinants of the rate of profits alluded to above and they form two powerful prongs in a multi-pronged case for free trade made by Mill.

5.3 SUBSCRIPTION TO SMITH'S 'PRODUCTIVITY THEORY'

Early on in his *Principles* Mill devotes a chapter, 'Of Co-operation, or the Combination of Labour' (Bk. I, Ch. VIII), to reiterate many of the points that Smith made in the first few chapters of his *Wealth of Nations*, chapters which relate to the subject of the division of labour.[20]

Smith's pin-making example is transcribed (and so are Say's example of the manufacture of playing cards and Babbage's watchmaking example) ([1871] 1965, pp. 122–4). Mill offers his own portrayal of a situation of division of labour in the manufacture of a coat (ibid., pp. 117–18) and, at an earlier point in the *Principles*, a situation of bread-making (ibid., p. 31). He reproduces the three causes advanced by Smith why a division of labour would raise productivity (ibid., pp. 124–9). He also agrees with Smith that the division of labour is limited by the extent of the market (ibid., pp. 130–31), saying at one point that 'the division of labour, and its skilful and economical distribution, depend on the extent of the market, and on the possibility of production in large masses' (ibid., p. 182).

Like Smith and Torrens, Mill extends the principle to the international context. He regards the dynamic benefit that follows from this extension to be an 'indirect effect' of foreign trade but 'which must be counted as benefits of a high order'. Specifically,

> [there is] the tendency of every extension of the market to improve the processes of production. A country which produces for a larger market than its own, can introduce a more extended division of labour, can make greater use of machinery, and is more likely to make inventions and improvements in the processes of production. Whatever causes a greater quantity of anything to be produced in the same place, tends to the general increase of the productive powers of the world. ([1871] 1965, p. 593)[21]

But between agriculture and manufactures, in which sector would the 'productivity theory' operate more powerfully? Mill notices that the division of labour is in many cases also limited by the nature of the employment. 'Agriculture', he thus claims, 'is not susceptible of so great a division of occupations as many branches of manufactures, because its different operations cannot possibly be simultaneous' (ibid., p. 130). On the other hand '[m]anufactures are vastly more susceptible than agriculture, of mechanical improvements, and contrivances for saving labour' (ibid., p. 182). This perfectly resonates with Smith's observation alluded to in section 3.3 above and predisposed Mill to advocate England to export manufactures. Specifically, by extending the market for manufactures through exports and reaping the benefits of manufacturing improvements arising therefrom, wage-good items that are manufactures could be cheapened. Alternatively, manufactured means of production that enter directly or indirectly into the production of all wage goods – agricultural and manufactured items alike – could be produced more cheaply. All this would push off the onset of the stationary state because '[t]here is ... no possible improvement in the arts of production which does not in one or another mode exercise an antagonist influence to the law of diminishing return to agricultural labour' (ibid., p. 183). For this effect Mill dubs 'improvements in production' as a 'counteracting circumstance' or 'resisting agency' against the 'downward tendency of profits' (ibid., pp. 741, 742–3).

5.4 SUBSCRIPTION TO RICARDO'S ARGUMENT AGAINST THE CORN LAWS

England as the Corn-Importer

Mill started writing on different subjects of political economy well before the Corn Laws were repealed in 1846. Not surprisingly, based on the discussion in section 5.2 above, one of these subjects was making a case for the repeal. Thus, in the 1825 *Westminster Review* article mentioned in section 5.1 he argues,

> There is no fact in political economy better established than the tendency of every tax on the necessaries of life, to produce a rise of wages. ... While however, the labourer continues to receive the same quantity of necessaries as before, corn (the most important of those commodities) has risen in value. He must, therefore, receive a greater *value*, in order to command the same quantity: his money wages must rise. The manufacturers and other capitalists are thus compelled to give a greater value to their labourers, without having a greater value for themselves. They are, therefore, obliged to forego a portion of their profits. And thus we see that a high price of corn, which is a cause of high rent, is a cause of low profits. It is as prejudicial to the capitalist as it is beneficial to the landlord. (*Collected Works*, vol. IV, pp. 49–50)

Given the central role played by capital accumulation in promoting the national wealth of England, and given that 'the rate of profits ... constitutes the inducement to accumulation', a policy 'which consists in lowering profits for the purpose of raising rents, must be, at best, of very doubtful expediency' (ibid., p. 50–51).

Mill continued to emphasise the importance of a sustained free importation of food and necessaries to England's well-being even after the repeal of the Corn Laws in 1846. He thus contends in the *Principles* that,

> If necessaries are cheapened, whether they are so by improvements at home or importation from abroad, is exactly the same thing to wages and profits. Unless the labourer obtains, and by an improvement of his habitual standard, keeps, the whole benefit, the cost of labour is lowered, and the rate of profit raised. As long as food can continue to be imported for an increasing population without any diminution of cheapness, so long the declension of profits through the increase of population and capital is arrested, and accumulation may go on without making the rate of profit draw nearer to the minimum. ([1871] 1965, pp. 743–4)

It is on this ground that the repeal of the Corn Laws could be regarded to have opened England to 'a long era of rapid increase of capital with an undiminished rate of profit' (ibid.). For this, the free importation of cheaper food and necessaries is labelled by Mill as another 'counteracting circumstance' or 'resisting agency' to the downward tendency of profits (ibid.).

Furthermore, based on his understanding of the need of manufactured inputs in the production of food and materials (see section 5.2 above), Mill added to Ricardo's argument against the Corn Laws by clarifying that, 'When foreign trade makes room for more capital at the same profit, it is by enabling the necessaries of life, or the habitual articles of the labourer's consumption, to be obtained at smaller cost', and it may accomplish this in two manners: 'by the importation either of those commodities themselves, or of the means and appliances for producing them' (ibid., p. 744).[22]

Putting Mill's Discussion of Comparative Advantage in Perspective

Although in the celebrated Essay I in *Some Unsettled Questions* Mill employs an England–Germany model to restate and extend Ricardo's England–Portugal model where England exports cloth in exchange for Germany's linen, and despite the reproduction of this model in the *Principles*, it is safe to say that he had in mind as the reality that England would export manufactures (like cloth, iron, cottons) while 'other commercial countries' would export things like corn, timber, sugar, wool, hides, tallow, hemp, flax, raw cotton, wine, and tobacco ([1871] 1965, pp. 595, 620–21). In fact, in addition to making and reiterating the case against the Corn Laws above, he illustrates the case in static manners and the illustrations, though very brief and not as rigorous as the England–Germany model, lend further support to the trade pattern suggested above.

Thus, in the same *Westminster Review* article referred to twice already in the present chapter Mill argues that if the Corn Laws were retained,

> a portion of the labour and capital of the country is diverted out of a more into a less advantageous employment: a quantity of labour is employed in growing corn, which would otherwise have produced, not only cloth, or hardware, sufficient to

> purchase the same quantity of corn in the foreign market, but much more. That corn which could be obtained abroad, in exchange for the produce of the labour of 100 men, is compelled to be produced at home, by that of 120, 130, or 140. (*Collected Works*, vol. IV, p. 52)

As if he was simply turning to the flip-side of the same illustration, he compares cheaper import of food to an agricultural invention in one instance in the *Principles* and explains that '[t]he return was before [trade was opened up], so much food for so much labour employed in the growth of food: the return is now, a greater quantity of food, for the same labour employed in producing cottons or hardware or some other commodity, to be given in exchange for food' ([1871] 1965, pp. 190–91).

Was the dynamic impact of such trade on the corn-exporting countries ever considered?

5.5 THE CORN-EXPORTING COUNTRIES: TRADE'S IMPACT ON THEM AND THEIR LIMITED CAPACITY TO INCREASE EXPORTS

Mill's discussion of the impact of trade on the corn-exporting countries can neither be regarded as extensive nor penetrating. Whatever discussion there was reveals more his concern of their limited capacity to supply corn to England than how they might reap dynamic benefits from such trade.

These corn-exporting countries were divided into two groups. One was the old countries, like the Russia, Poland, Hungary, and Spain of his time. Mill believed that they would not be able to rapidly augment their food exports and the reasons he gave are as follow:

> In those regions the effective desire of accumulation[23] is weak, the arts of production most imperfect, capital scanty, and its increase, especially from domestic sources, slow. When an increased demand arose for food to be exported to other countries, it would only be very gradually that food could be produced to meet it. The capital needed could not be obtained by transfer from other employments, for such do not exist. ... If a greater outlay of capital is relied on as the source from which the produce is to be increased, the means must either be obtained by the slow process of saving ... or must be brought in from foreign countries. ([1871] 1965, p. 192)[24]

Could the increase in demand for food exports be met through 'great improvements in their agriculture'? His view was again pessimistic, saying that any such improvement 'is likely to be a very slow process, from the rudeness and ignorance of the agricultural classes' in those countries (ibid., p. 745). He noted in passing that these countries were in a position to export food (however limited a capacity they might have) 'only because their industry is in a very backward state' (ibid., p. 192). What he did not consider was their dynamic paths of development and their employment situations should free trade be opened up with England, where the latter's superior manufactured products would surely wipe out their 'backward' industries.

The other group is the new countries of his time like Canada, the United States, and Australia. Unlike the old countries, here 'the effective desire of accumulation is strong'. Hence, given that they 'are already in possession of most of the improvements yet made' in agriculture, 'capital increases fast ... [except that] population also increases with extraordinary rapidity' (ibid., pp. 191–2, 745). This observation led Mill to voice in one instance the concern for corn-exporting countries that logically follows from the Ricardian reasoning. Thus,

> [t]heir agriculture has to provide for their own expanding numbers, as well as for those of the importing countries. They must, therefore, from the nature of the case, be rapidly driven, if not to less fertile, at least what is equivalent, to remoter and less accessible lands, and to modes of cultivation like those of old countries, less productive in proportion to the labour and expense. (Ibid., p. 192)

Disappointingly, he did not follow through to conclude on the impact on the rate of profits and accumulation in these corn-exporting countries. One also wonders why he chose to recognise this problem in connection with his discussion of the new countries, granted that, if any country were to feel the problem, the old and typically smaller countries would feel it much sooner than the new ones. In another instance, specifically with reference to the USA, Mill noted that a portion of America's annual savings which could have been deployed in augmenting food production and exports to England 'has heretofore been applied to increasing the manufacturing establishments' and that 'free trade in corn may possibly divert from that purpose to growing food for our market' (ibid., p. 745).[25]

5.6 PERPETUAL OVERFLOW OF ENGLAND'S CAPITAL INTO FOREIGN COUNTRIES AND COLONIES

Thanks to the 'counteracting circumstances' presented in sections 5.3 and 5.4, the downward tendency of England's rate of profits could temporarily be resisted. But thanks to them and also thanks partly to England's strong 'effective desire to accumulate',[26] there arose a situation of uneven growth where its capital 'increases faster than that of its neighbours' (ibid., p. 745).

Mill was to argue that trade by itself would not be an adequate guarantee of England's prosperity.

Augmenting Supply of Food and Materials to England

Although he regarded the ability to import cheaper food as 'equivalent to an agricultural invention' that cuts its cost of production domestically,[27] Mill also realised that while '[t]he one improvement, like the other, throws back the decline of the productive power of labour by a certain distance: but in the one case as in the other, it immediately resumes its course; the tide which has receded, instantly begins to re-advance' ([1871] 1965, p. 191). With an exaggeration that might not be as great as it first appears, Mill pointed out that England 'no longer depends on the fertility of her own soil to keep up her rate of profits, but on the soil of the whole world' (ibid., p. 745). Yet, as described in section 5.5, the prospect of rapid agricultural improvements and application of additional capital to agriculture in the food-exporting countries appeared to be too bleak for them to supply every year England's demand that was 'considerably beyond that of the year preceding'. 'It remains to consider', he worried, 'how far this resource can be counted upon, for making head during a very long period against the tendency of profits to decline as capital increases' (ibid.). He drew the conclusion that there had to be a 'perpetual overflow of capital into colonies or foreign countries'. In his words, 'if our population and capital continue to increase with their present rapidity, the only mode in which food can continue to be supplied cheaply to the one, is by sending the other abroad to produce it' (ibid., pp. 746, 745).[28]

Mill believed that this 'resisting agency' had for many years been one of the principal causes by which the decline of profits in England had been arrested.[29] It served a 'twofold operation': it carried off a part of the increase of capital from which the reduction of profits proceeded, and it was chiefly employed either in founding colonies (which would become exporters of agricultural products), or in extending and perhaps improving the agriculture of older communities. He concluded that,

> It is to the emigration of English capital, that we have chiefly to look for keeping up a supply of cheap food and cheap materials of clothing, proportional to the increase of our population; thus enabling an increasing capital to find employment in the country, without reduction of profit, in producing manufactured articles with which to pay for this supply of raw produce. Thus, the exportation of capital is an agent of great efficacy in extending the field of employment for that which remains: and it may be said truly that, up to a certain point, the more capital we send away, the more we shall possess and be able to retain at home. (Ibid., p. 746)

Near the very end in the *Principles* Mill reiterates that, 'There needs be no hesitation in affirming that Colonization, in the present state of the world, is the best affair of business, in which the capital of an old and wealthy country can engage' (ibid., p. 963).[30]

Clearly Mill was no longer confined to a two-country framework, nor was trade the only economic activity that was taking place. Instead, this is one which has many countries or regions, with England extending its trade and investment network to incorporate more and more of them over time. This would also seem to provide an answer to the puzzle that was alluded to at the end of section 5.5 above, that is, why Mill did not consider the rising price of corn in England's trading partners. But why would that price rise when she kept adding suppliers of corn to the trade and investment network? Here is what Mill considered at one point,

> It might seem, indeed, that when a country draws its supply of food from so wide a surface as the whole habitable globe, so little impression can be produced on that great expanse by any increase of mouths in one small corner of it, that the inhabitants of the country may double and treble their numbers, without feeling the effect in any increased tension of the springs of production, or any enhancement of the price of food throughout the world. (Ibid., p. 191)[31]

Indeed, as Haberler observed, in the first half of the nineteenth century England obtained her grain from the German states. Then it reached out to Russia, the United States, and then Canada and Argentina (1937, p. 287).

Creating Export Markets for England's Manufactures?

Thus far, the rationale offered by Mill for colonisation can be said to overlap with one of Torrens's reasons for supporting the same undertaking, namely that the pursuit of free trade *per se* would not guarantee that England's trading partners could supply food and raw produce at the rate which she demanded. However, the other reason voiced by Torrens – that those trading partners would not be purchasing manufactured products at the rate which England supplied – was left unmentioned by Mill. This is despite the fact that in the first indented quotation in the previous subsection he clearly indicated that the emigration of English capital would supposedly enable an increasing capital in England to find employment 'in producing manufactured articles with which to pay for this supply of raw produce'.

Also, in that same passage quoted above the term 'field of employment' is a clear reminder of the influence that Wakefield had exerted on Mill. The latter was very explicit in acknowledging this influence. Nevertheless, these acknowledgements have largely to do with the former's discovery of the art or a rational means of colonisation rather than his discussion of the rationales for pursuing it ([1871] 1965, pp. 120–21, 376, and 963–5). While indeed

Wakefield's use of the term field of 'employment' or 'production' was at times not sharply delineated (Tucker 1960, p. 182, n. 4) and while indeed he devoted more of his attention in clarifying his proposal for 'systematic colonization' than spelling out the rationales for colonisation, he did emphasise that the colonies to be planted or extended be 'nations of Englishmen born, and their descendants; using the English language; preserving English skill and English tastes; and, therefore, both *able and willing to purchase English goods* with cheap corn' (Wakefield [1834] 1967, p. 248, italics added).

Furthermore, for reasons that will become transparent in the following section, Mill had to be quite familiar with Torrens's arguments for extended colonisation, at least as presented in one of the letters in *The Budget*. Contained in those arguments are what, as first mentioned in section 4.5 in the previous chapter, Robbins (1958, Ch. VI, part 6) has referred to as early hints of a 'stagnation theory'. Could Mill, in not focusing on this rationale for colonisation, be attempting to smooth out the disagreement arising from the debate on the possibility of general gluts?[32] It is worth noting that after summarising Wakefield's explanation of the fall of profits at one point in the *Principles*, Mill interjects that the 'error' which seems 'imputable to Mr. Wakefield is that of supposing his doctrines to be in contradiction to the principles of the best school of preceding political economists, instead of being, as they really are, corollaries from those principles' ([1871] 1965, pp. 735–6). Such treatment and the ignoring of Torrens's discussions on the same subject have, according to D. Winch (1965, p. 139), prompted Robbins (1958, pp. 247–8) to conclude that Mill had completely overlooked the stagnationist position implicit in the arguments of Wakefield and Torrens.

5.7 INTERNATIONAL VALUES AND COMMERCIAL RECIPROCITY

In Chapter 4 the circumstances prompting Torrens to advocate commercial reciprocity were outlined. One of the letters that he penned between the end of 1842 and January 1843 to support this was addressed to the then Prime Minister, Sir Robert Peel, and was titled, 'On the condition of England; and on the means of removing the causes of distress' (which letter was subsequently published together with other letters in *The Budget* in 1844). In it Torrens argued that England's distress at that time was the result of three causes, namely the 'powers of production outgrowing the field of employment', 'hostile tariffs', and 'foreign competition' (see section 4.5 above). Upon seeing this letter (in the form of a pamphlet) Mill wrote some comments that appeared in late January 1843 in the *Spectator* under the title

'Torrens's letter to Sir Robert Peel' (*Collected Works*, vol. XXIV, pp. 836–41). How did he react to Torrens's account?

Powers of Production Outgrowing the Field of Employment

With respect to the first of these factors Mill appeared to be totally oblivious to Torrens's consideration of capital increasing at different rates in countries in different stages of improvement and the consequent 'contemporaneous overtrading throughout all the departments of manufacturing and commercial industry' (Torrens [1844] 1970, pp. 239, 240). Recall that when Torrens turned his attention to solutions that could counter those factors that had precipitated the distress, he considered colonisation and the means to do so in a way that closely resembled Wakefield's proposal of systematic colonisation. Mill seized the opportunity to shift the focus to such means. While Wakefield's name was never mentioned by Torrens in his letter, Mill did not miss the opportunity, noting that 'almost from the first promulgation of Mr. Wakefield's views, Colonel Torrens has been their earnest and intelligent apostle' ([1843] 1986, p. 840). He praised Torrens for his unwavering support of these views, adding that,

> Nowhere will the reader find more completely demonstrated than here, the reviving effect which would be produced upon the industrial state of a country in which both labour and capital are every year more and more redundant, by the transfer of large masses of both to her outlying possessions, there to raise raw produce *for exchange against the manufactures of the parent nation.* (Ibid., italics added)

This was as close as Mill reached in the *Spectator* article in acknowledging Torrens's other rationale for colonisation, namely the one arising from his concern that an England growing more rapidly than its trading partners would be exporting manufactures at a pace much faster than they would be prepared to demand.

On 22 April, 1843 Torrens sent to Sir Robert Peel a postscript to the aforementioned letter. In it he applied the 'reciprocal relations of demand and supply' to demonstrate that 'a reduction of the duties upon foreign productions, unaccompanied by a corresponding mitigation of the duties imposed by foreign countries upon British goods, would cause a further decline of prices, of profits, and of wages' (Torrens [1844] 1970, p. 331 of Postscript to Letter IX). Mill got a chance to peruse this when *The Budget* was published. Upon noticing that 'opinions identical in principle' with those promulgated by Torrens were contained in the postscript, and driven by the controversies surrounding commercial reciprocity that *The Budget* had excited, he decided to publish several essays that he wrote in 1829 and 1830 in the book *Some Unsettled Questions* ([1874] 1974, Preface). As is widely known, in Essay I therein, titled 'Of the laws of interchange between nations', Mill employed the 'principle of demand and supply' in an attempt to solve for international values.[33]

It was emphasised in section 4.5 above that Torrens's motive of investigating into the determining circumstances of the terms of international exchange should be distinguished from that of Mill. Thus, to the former, 'an accurate knowledge of the circumstances which determine the relative value of the products of foreign and of domestic labour is indispensably necessary, in order to enable us to ascertain the laws which govern [for England] the amount of wages, the rate of profit, and the incidence of import duties' ([1844] 1970, p. v). On the other hand, to Mill, '[i]f we know what this level [of international value] would be, we should know in what proportion the two *countries* would share the advantage of the trade' ([1874] 1974, p. 7, italics added).[34] Torrens's investigation, the conclusions drawn, and the policy recommendations he based thereupon were presented in sections 4.5 and 4.6 above. What did Mill obtain?

Having illustrated through his England–Germany model in Essay I in *Some Unsettled Questions* the result that the international value of two commodities would adjust in accordance with the 'inclinations and circumstances of the consumers' in both countries until an equality between quantities imported and quantities exported is reached (ibid., p. 12), one of the extensions that Mill made was to consider a situation where one of the two experienced an 'increase of wealth and population' and reached the conclusion that 'the division of the advantage becomes more and more favourable to a country, in proportion as the demand for its commodities increases in foreign countries', which in this case means the no-growth (or relatively slower growing) England (ibid., p. 33). Although in this context Mill hypothetically considered Germany to be the country that enjoyed the expansion in wealth and population, at the end of this essay it became clear that he had in mind another context, where England exported manufactures in return for food and materials from her colonies and other countries (ibid., pp. 45–6). The aforementioned conclusion was reiterated in the *Principles*, although the uneven growth context had then become muted. Hence, 'the countries which carry on their foreign trade on the most advantageous terms, are those whose commodities are most in demand by foreign countries, and which have themselves the least demand for foreign commodities'. From this one could infer 'that the richest countries, *cæteris paribus*, gain the least by a given amount of foreign commerce: since, having a greater demand for commodities generally, they are likely to have a greater demand for foreign commodities, and thus modify the terms of interchange to their own disadvantage' ([1871] 1965, p. 615, see also p. 602). How then could one reconcile this with another remark that Mill made in Essay I, that '[o]n the whole, England probably, of all the countries of Europe, draws to herself the largest share of the gains of international commerce: because her exportable articles are in universal demand, and are of such a kind that the demand increases rapidly as the price falls' ([1874] 1974, p. 45)? The answer may hinge on a distinction between whether he was basing his conclusion on two-country models or others of a higher dimension. Thus, one other extension that Mill made in that essay was to add a third country that would compete with Germany in exporting the same product (linen) to England (ibid., pp. 34–5). This extension was reproduced and refined in the *Principles*, where Mill drew the happy conclusion that,

> the opening of the third country makes a great difference in favour of England. There is now a double market for English exports, while the demand of England for linen is only what it was before. This necessarily obtains for England more advantageous terms of interchange. The two countries, requiring much more of her produce than was required by either alone, must, in order to obtain it, force an increased demand for their exports, by offering them at a lower value. ([1871] 1965, p. 603)

But is this not, after generalising to many countries and colonies, and substituting food and materials for 'linen', what the perpetual overflow of English capital overseas was supposed by Mill to accomplish?[35]

Hostile Tariffs

There are signs that the young Mill at one point leaned toward a support of England practicing free trade with the hope that that would induce other countries to do the same. Thus, in the article 'The Corn Laws' referred to earlier in this chapter he strikes the following analogy: 'every man would find it his interest, even if there were no laws, to refrain from picking his neighbour's pocket, lest by so doing he should provoke his neighbour to perform a similar *manœuvre* upon his' ([1825] 1967, p. 67). On that note he laments that, 'But for the parliamentary slang of protecting agriculture, America might never have conceived the ridiculous idea of protecting manufactures' (ibid.).

However, by the time he commented on Torrens's letter to Sir Rober Peel, Mill regarded 'hostile tariffs' as 'the real source of alarm', noting that '[i]f foreign nations generally adopt this policy and persevere in it, ... the train of consequences described and characterized by Colonel Torrens will then be inevitable' ([1843] 1986, p. 839).

Just a year later, in Essay I of *Some Unsettled Questions*, he extended his England–Germany model to determine if any country, 'by its own legislative policy, can engross to itself a larger share of the benefits of foreign commerce, than would fall to it in the natural or spontaneous course of trade' ([1874] 1974, p. 21). As pointed out in section 4.6 in the previous chapter this approach to the consideration is of an *offensive* nature whereas Torrens's approach is *defensive* from England's viewpoint. Seen in that light, Mill's caution on the use of export taxes or import duties to this end – nullification through foreign retaliation ([1874] 1974, p. 29; [1871] 1965, pp. 855–6, 916) and the relative ease to find substitutes when exports are restricted (18 August, 1867 letter to David Ames Wells, reprinted in *Collected Works*, vol. XVI, p. 1309) – thus appears to be missing the point from Torrens's perspective. His remark in the Preface to *Some Unsettled Questions* that those 'opinions identical in principle' with those of Torrens would probably differ 'to the extent of their practical application' also appears to show a misunderstanding of what he (Torrens) was seeking to advocate. Nevertheless, as Semmel (1970, p. 187) argues, it is clear that Mill's analyses in Essay I are 'capable of being extended ... into an argument in favour of reciprocity'. Indeed, at one point in that essay he voices support for such and declares that,

> A country cannot be expected to renounce the power of taxing foreigners, unless foreigners will in return practise towards itself the same forbearance. The only mode in which a country can save itself from being a loser by the duties imposed by other countries on its commodities, is to impose corresponding duties on theirs. ([1874] 1974, p. 29)

His only caution was that these duties should not be so high as to become 'protective'. Indeed, when this passage was reproduced almost verbatim in the *Principles*, Mill qualifies the duties as 'revenue duties' both times that the word appears in the passage ([1871] 1965, p. 856; see also [1874] 1974, p. vi).

Foreign Competition

The last factor leading to England's distress that was enumerated by Torrens, foreign competition, relates to his fear that its technological lead over other countries was rapidly disappearing. To this Mill suggested that 'the author, as is not unusual with him, seems to us to overstate the importance and urgency of a portion of his doctrines in their application to the immediate circumstances of the country' ([1843] 1986, p. 837). He granted to Torrens that there was indeed industrial progress in some other countries and the productiveness of their labourers had become less inferior than that of England's, '[b]ut there is still a large margin, on which it will take them many years, if not generations, seriously to encroach' (ibid., p. 838). With regard to 'mechanical inventions' Mill conceded that,

> It is true, inventions spread rapidly from country to country, but not so the power of bringing them into profitable use. In that respect, the advantage of having large masses of capital already accumulated is immense. There are as many inventions made on the other side of the Channel as on this; but it is to England that the inventors bring their inventions when they desire to make money by them. (Ibid., p. 839)[36]

He thus felt assured that if free trade were universally practiced, England would be 'tolerably secure of remaining for generations to come, the workshop of the world'. 'Not how to retain her natural superiority', he went on to warn, 'but how to make herself independent of the attempts of foreign governments to counteract it artificially by restrictive tariffs, is the problem for English politicians' (ibid.).

A year later, and here again referring to Essay I in *Some Unsettled Questions*, Mill briefly considered the wisdom of permitting the export of machinery from England. He recognised that allowing such exportation 'would alter to our disadvantage the division of the benefit of trade' unless England possessed as great an advantage in the production of the machinery itself as it had in the production of other articles by means of machinery. Nevertheless, he felt that restrictions on such export 'are not ... justifiable, either on the score of international morality or of sound policy' ([1874] 1974, p. 31). He, however, ventured that,

> The exportation of machinery may ... be a proper subject for adjustment with other nations, on the principle of reciprocity. Until, by the common consent of nations, all restrictions upon trade are done away, a nation cannot be required to abolish those from which she derives a real advantage, without stipulating for an equivalent. (Ibid., p. 32)

This is essentially consistent with his stance as expressed in the *Spectator* article.

5.8 SUMMING UP

This chapter has shown that, aside from having extended Ricardo's England–Portugal model and developing it into a simple general equilibrium analysis, Mill made some other significant contributions to trade and investment theories that the mainstream has tended to gloss over or even totally ignore. Despite signs of subverting certain aspects of classical analysis, he was nevertheless employing in many places Ricardo's theory of profits and thus the latter's simple framework for understanding the capitalist development of England. Like Torrens, he subscribed to both Smith's productivity theory and Ricardo's argument against the Corn Laws, and saw in that combination a powerful two-pronged case for free trade from England's perspective. Similar to Torrens, he clearly realised that trade *per se* would not ensure lasting prosperity for England, although in recommending a 'perpetual overflow of capital into colonies or foreign countries', he appeared to be mostly preoccupied with enhancing the supplies of food and raw produce for England. Finally, he also shared Torrens's concern with hostile foreign tariffs, though his formulation and solution of the international value problem – and for that matter the modern mainstream formulation and solution of it – is premised on quite a different set of considerations from that of his (Torrens's).

It is partly with reference to Mill's other contributions revived here that Williams found 'so strikingly in contrast with his (Mill's) general theory of international trade' (1929, p. 208). In fact, the alternative developmentalist interpretation of Smith's, Ricardo's, Torrens's, and Mill's contributions to trade and investment analyses that is constituted by stitching together their theories as presented in the last two chapters and the present one cannot be more strikingly in contrast with the mainstream interpretation. Britain was weaving together a trade and investment network that was rapidly expanding. But along the way pockets of underdevelopment had been carved out in many parts of the world.

Not surprisingly, it was initially largely left to those outside of Britain to question the benefit of a membership of this network that was subservient to that country. Some, Hamilton and List foremost among them (see Chapters 7 and 8 below), preached policy actions that were distinct from the free trade position prescribed by the classicists. Thanks partly to their recommendations for state action, development was indeed spurred on that resulted in the emergence of a group of second-tier industrial countries. Thence, the leadership in the trade and investment network started to consist of more than just one country. Nevertheless, the gap between that leading group of advanced, and the trailing group of less-developed, countries continued to widen in many cases.

Significantly, although he did not specifically allude to England, Prebisch noted at one point that as the Industrial Revolution got into full swing, '[l]arge numbers began to emigrate from the older regions of primary production in Europe ... to the newer areas which had become either complements or substitutes in the production of primary goods'.[37] He then added that,

> Productivity in the new lands was higher *per capita* than in the older regions, and progress in transport enabled goods from the former to reach the European markets easily and cheaply. It is possible that this increase in production, probably greater than that of demand at the centre, greatly influenced the deterioration of the terms of trade which occurred after the seventies of the last [nineteenth] century and continued until the First World War. (1951a, p. 51)[38]

Separately, Singer observed that 'the specialization of underdeveloped countries on export of food and raw materials to industrialized countries … [is] largely … a result of investment by the latter' (1950, p. 477). What one sees as the 'import of capital into underdeveloped countries' served, and still serves in many cases, the purpose of 'making them into providers of food and raw materials for the industrialized countries'. In passing, he mentioned as examples '[t]he tea plantations of Ceylon, the oil wells of Iran, the copper mines of Chile, and the cocoa industry of the Gold Coast' (ibid., p. 476).[39] These are events that fully corroborate with the scenarios considered by Torrens and Mill when they extended the Smith–Ricardo growth and trade analysis.

For both Prebisch and Singer, such investments by England and other industrial countries, together with considerations relating to the disparate income elasticity of demand between manufactured and primary products (which did not appear to be considered by the classicists), all enter into the mix as they sought to account for the deteriorating CTT for the primary exporting countries. As Chapters 10 and 12 show below, these are just parts of Prebisch's broader desire to infuse 'dynamism' into the economies of the peripheral countries and Singer's grander wish to tackle international dualism between the advanced and less-developed countries.

The stage is thus almost completely set to re-examine the ideas of these so-called 'protectionists', except that the manner in which the mainstream history of economic thought related to the theory of commercial policy has to be laid out. That is the subject of Chapter 6.

NOTES

1. A small portion of what is contained in this chapter was first outlined in Ho (1996a, subsection 3.5), although that spans no more than two pages. The present discussion is conducted in much greater detail.
2. Mill ([1871] 1965, Bk. III, Chs. II and III) divides commodities into three classes and in the case of domestic values he regarded the analysis to be applicable only to two of those three classes. For a consideration of how this division is attributable to the chapter 'On the Causes of Value' in Bailey (1825), see de Vivo (1981). For a critical discussion of this variance on the part of Mill with Ricardo, see Bharadwaj (1978, pp. 256–7).
3. Not restricting himself to trade analyses, Stigler (1955, pp. 297–9) lists several other of Mill's major contributions.

4. Dobb (1973, p. 122) concludes that 'in major respects his [Mill's] own work was much nearer to Marshall than it was to Ricardo'.
5. See the evaluation by de Marchi (1988) of this thesis and the response to it by S. Hollander (2000, Ch. 11). Jensen (2001, p. 506) contends that Mill had a 'Keynesesque vision of an ideal society' that 'cannot be judged a Ricardian prognostication'. This vision 'is a value-laden script for the casting of desirable characters, institutions and processes that fit a collectivist social economy'. And it was developed '[i]n spite of his occasional Ricardian lapses'.
6. Referring to the same passage by Smith that Mill referred to, Myint (1977, p. 236) concludes that the former had 'foreshadowed the later classical doctrine of a secular decline in the rate of profit brought about by the diminishing returns from land'.
7. For passages that indicate how he had followed Ricardo in 'getting rid of rent' in his discussion of distribution, see Mill ([1871] 1965, pp. 428–9, 490–91).
8. 'A rise of wages, with Mr. Ricardo, meant an increase in the cost of production of wages; an increase in the number of hours' labour which goes to produce the wages of a day's labour; an increase in the *proportion* of the fruits of labour which the labourer receives for his own share; an increase in the ratio between the wages of his labour and the produce of it' (Mill [1874] 1974, pp. 96–7). However, Mill also recognised that the outlay of the capitalist consisted not just wages, for 'profits ... also enter into the outlay itself' (ibid., pp. 98–9). Here, as Bharadwaj (1983, pp. 73–4) points out, Mill ran into some confusion with the problem of value. See also Dobb (1973, pp. 126–31).
9. It is clear that Mill was excluding luxuries from the discussion here. Indeed, he appended this to the passage just quoted: 'If the improvement be in any article which is not consumed by the labourer, it merely lowers the price of that article, and thereby benefits capitalists and all other people so far as they are consumers of that particular article, and ... increase ... not the rate of profit' (op. cit.).
10. *Principles* is the abbreviation for the full title, *Principles of Political Economy with Some of Their Applications to Social Philosophy*. In it Mill proposes that, 'Instead of saying that profits depend on wages, let us say (what Ricardo really meant) that they depend on the *cost of labour*' ([1871] 1965, p. 413, italics original).
11. This is a point that was also raised by Cairnes, who in late 1864 offered suggestions for revision to Mill as the latter prepared for the sixth edition of the *Principles* (*Collected Works*, vol. III, pp. 1048–50).
12. Elsewhere in the *Principles* Mill thus decides that, 'The cause of profit is, that labour produces more than is required for its support. ... To vary the form of the theorem: the reason why capital yields a profit, is because food, clothing, materials, and tools, last longer than the time which was required to produce them; so that if a capitalist supplies a party of labourers with these things, on condition of receiving all they produce, they will, in addition to reproducing their own necessaries and instruments, have a portion of their time remaining, to work for the capitalist. We thus see that profit arises, not from the incident of exchange, but from the productive power of labour' ([1871] 1965, p. 411). However, he also adopts Senior's 'well-chosen expression', namely that profits are a 'remuneration for abstinence', and he adds 'compensation for risk' and 'wages of superintendence' as further components into which profits resolve themselves (ibid., pp. 400–402).
13. For two representative discussions of how the labourer's 'habitual standard' of living was shaped, including references to the Malthusian mechanism, see Mill ([1871] 1965, pp. 159, 727–8).
14. When Mill made the distinction that, 'Improvements which only affect things consumed exclusively by the richer classes, do not operate ... in diminishing the cost of labour' (op. cit., p. 743), it is again clear that he separated luxuries from his discussion.
15. Compare the discussion here with a very similar one in Ricardo's *Principles* ([1821] 2004, p. 80). Mill briefly returns to this distinction in a later part of his own *Principles* ([1871] 1965, pp. 724–5).
16. Mill adds that, 'The same effect would follow from an improvement in those processes of what may be termed manufacture, to which the material of food is subjected after it is separated from the ground. The first application of wind or water power to grind corn,

tended to cheapen bread as much as a very important discovery in agriculture would have done; and any great improvement in the construction of corn-mills, would have, in proportion, a similar influence' (op. cit.).

17. Having discussed both agricultural and manufacturing improvements as elements of 'progress of civilization', Mill (op. cit., pp. 183–4) then brings in 'improvements in government', 'moral and social advancement', and 'improvements in education' as other elements of progress.
18. Although manufactures rely on materials produced from agriculture or mining, the small portion constituted by the crude material means that any increase in cost in that portion 'is much over-balanced by the diminution continually taking place in all the other elements; to which diminution it is impossible at present to assign any limit' (op. cit., p. 713). Mill also notes earlier in the *Principles* that in manufactures, 'the causes tending to increase the productiveness of industry, preponderate greatly over the one cause which tends to diminish it' (ibid., p. 182).
19. For two differently-focused reactions to this passage see Schumpeter (1954, p. 571) and D. Winch (1970, pp. 40–41).
20. Mill briefly followed Wakefield's suggestion that the division of labour is only a part of the whole subject. He thus drew a distinction in the manner of Wakefield between simple versus complex co-operations and associated Smith's discussion with the latter. However, he failed to argue convincingly why simple co-operation is worthy of a separate consideration.
21. There is a footnote right at the end of this passage where it appears in the *Principles*, referring the reader back to Bk. I, Ch. IX, § 1, that is, pp. 131–5, where, among other subjects, Mill considers situations of decreasing costs and how large establishments could undersell smaller ones.
22. See Steedman and Metcalfe (1973) for a formal illustration.
23. Spengler (1960, p. 133, n. 74) notes that Mill's account of the factors that determine the 'effective desire of accumulation' largely draws upon Rae's discussion, for a brief consideration of which see Spengler (1959, pp. 398–9).
24. Mill regretted that English investment would be 'attended with so many difficulties, as are equivalent to great positive disadvantages. It is opposed by differences of language, differences of manners, and a thousand obstacles arising from the institutions and social relations of the country…: so that, if it were not the almost only mode of introducing foreign arts and ideas, and giving an effectual spur to the backward civilization of those countries, little reliance could be placed on it for increasing the exports, and supplying other countries with a progressive and indefinite increase of food' (op. cit., pp. 192–3). The first part of this quotation resonates with Ricardo ([1821] 2004, p. 136), on which see section 3.8 above. The quotation is taken from the earlier part of Mill's *Principles*. As will be illustrated in section 5.6 below, he was to drop his reservations later in that work.
25. Across the other side of the Atlantic Ocean and before Mill wrote this, Hamilton had complained about the 'artificial impediments' against American export of agricultural products to Europe. As far as he is concerned, it is not clear that even if these impediments were removed, then he would stop championing for industrial development in America. See Ch. 7 below.
26. Mill observed that 'there are other countries, and England is at the head of them, in which neither the spirit of industry nor the effective desire of accumulation need any encouragement; where the people will toil hard for a small remuneration, and save much for a small profit; where … the spirit of accumulation in the more prosperous part of the community requires abatement rather than increase' ([1871] 1965, p. 187).
27. 'The abolition of corn laws, or of any other restrictions which prevent commodities from being produced where the cost of their production is lowest, amounts to a vast improvement in production' ([1871] 1965, p. 183).
28. Elsewhere, referring to the old countries Mill wrote that, 'If England is to obtain a rapidly increasing supply of corn from Russia or Poland, English capital must go there to produce it' (op. cit., p. 192).

29. This is the third out of four 'resisting agencies' that Mill discusses in the chapter, 'Of the Tendency of Profits to a Minimum', in his *Principles* (Bk. IV, Ch. IV). The last such agency, which is actually the first that was enumerated in that chapter, relates to 'the waste of capital in periods of over-trading and rash speculation, and in the commercial revulsions by which such times are always followed'. But while it 'is one considerable cause which arrests profits in their descent to the minimum', Mill also insists that 'this is not ... the principal cause' (ibid., pp. 741–2).
30. Near the end of section 3.8 above this passage from Ricardo's *Essay on Profits* was quoted: 'If in the progress of countries in wealth and population, new portions of fertile land could be added to such countries, with every increase of capital, profits would never fall, nor rents rise' ([1815] 1951a, p. 18). Mill, in regarding colonisation as involving emigration of 'increasing numbers' who pressed hard against the productive capacity of land, imagined at one point in his *Principles* that '[i]f Australia or the interior of Canada were as near to Great Britain as Wisconsin and Iowa to New York; if the superfluous people could remove to it without crossing the sea, and were of as adventurous and restless a character, and as little addicted to staying at home, as their kinsfolk of New England, those unpeopled continents would render the same service to the United Kingdom which the old states of America derive from the new' ([1871] 1965, p. 194). But as Mill observes later in the *Principles* with the West Indies as an example, the trade that arose between England and such colonies should actually be deemed 'home' rather than 'external' trade (ibid., p. 693).
31. See also the discussion in 'The Corn Laws' (*Collected Works*, vol. IV, p. 57).
32. Mill's consideration of 'commercial crisis' and/or 'commercial difficulties' are mostly to be found in Bk. III, Chs. XII, XIV, and XXII–XXIV of his *Principles*.
33. After Mill's *Some Unsettled Questions* was published Torrens had a chance to study at least Essay I therein. The latter had his *Tracts on Finance and Trade* published in 1852, in which he continued to advocate commercial reciprocity (though in a different international environment than in the early 1840s). In No. II of that publication he credited Mill for his 'masterly essays' and praised that '[t]he influence of relative demand upon the proportions in which the productions of one country will exchange for the productions of another, cannot be better illustrated' (Torrens 1852, p. 31). As illustration, he went on to quote a passage from Mill ([1874] 1974, pp. 43–4).
34. It is not clear whether the praises given by Torrens regarding Mill's illustration (see the previous note) suggests that Torrens himself did not see the distinction or that he might have some reason to just sing those praises despite the distinction.
35. Mill's reference to 'greater demand' should not be confused with the higher income elasticity of demand that Prebisch and Singer were to emphasise later when, as opposed to Mill's conclusion, they suggested that it was the richer countries that gained more from trade partly because their products generally enjoyed higher income elasticity of demand. See Chs. 10 and 12 below.
36. In this instance Mill appeared to be considering something akin to the discussion of 'technological capabilities'. See, for example, Lall (1992, 1993).
37. Prebisch understood that some of the countries that opened up to commerce at that time, including many in Latin America, had 'old settled populations' that potentially provided ample labour supply to engage in primary production (1951a, p. 52).
38. Without mentioning this discussion by Prebisch, Haberler observed that, 'When the United Kingdom's terms of trade improved in the last quarter of the nineteenth century as a consequence of the opening up of new sources of supply of agricultural products from the United States, Canada, and Argentina – that did not mean that this was an unfavourable change for the producers in those then under-developed areas, although they would have been still better off if the British market could have absorbed the additional supplies at unchanged prices' (1963, p. 286). Prebisch himself did not refer back to the scenario that was represented in the illustration just four pages earlier in the same work where there was productivity improvement in primary production.
39. Myrdal made quite a bit of reference to the colonial experience of many underdeveloped countries. See especially Myrdal (1956, [1957] 1963).

PART II

Re-examining 'Trade Protection' Arguments from Perspectives of Development

6. The Mainstream Conception of Spontaneous Structural Changes and Its Formulation of the Theory of Commercial Policy

6.1 INTRODUCTION

It should be clear from the discussions in Chapters 3 to 5 that Smith, Ricardo, Torrens, and Mill had devoted most of their attention to England's economic well-being, though the intensity of that devotion varies, with Torrens showing in his works the strongest nationalistic sentiments. This preoccupation with England implies, as was also argued in those chapters, a neglect of the development of its trading partners. As Myrdal remarked, 'When ... they [the classical economists] recommended free trade as a general policy, it was not on the ground that free trade would be to the good of the world but because it would be in the interest of their own country' ([1957] 1963, p. 146).[1]

This leading chapter in Part II of this book purports to show that the neglect is coupled with a simple-minded belief or faith in how structural changes in the food and raw produce (or primary) exporting countries would spontaneously take place under free trade conditions. This is contained in section 6.2, which also illustrates how that faith has been happily inherited by the mainstream economists. The four classical economists re-examined in the earlier chapters all opposed trade protection as an effort to promote structural changes and these oppositions are represented in section 6.3.

Among them, Mill was the one who accepted the so-called infant-industry argument for such protection. Section 6.4 explores the possible roots of his endorsement of this case and closely scrutinises it (the endorsement). The economics mainstream has portrayed Hamilton and List as the two 'protectionists' who played pivotal roles in popularising that argument for protection. Did Mill actually acquaint himself with their works? What influence might Rae's writings on development promotion have exerted on him?

The last part of section 6.4 also calls attention to two features of Mill's endorsement in the *Principles* that has far-reaching consequences for the debate on this subject. Firstly, he solely focuses on protective import duties in his endorsement. Secondly, he appears to have in mind an overly simplified development process that could either be spearheaded by one single industry the relationship to the rest of the economy of which was left unspecified, or by two or more industries the dynamic relationship between or among which was left unexplored. Together these features have shaped the course of the development of the mainstream theory of commercial policy. Section 6.5 outlines the formation of the mainstream version of the history of thought on this theory and the construction of the theory of domestic divergences or distortions beginning from the 1950s. It will be argued that that theory has a tendency to trivialise the development process.

Section 6.6 points out that there are passages and thoughts, even if quite isolated, in the works of the classical economists that expressed doubts on the spontaneity of structural changes in England's trading partners. These are some of the themes that would be amplified in different manners by the authors whose works are re-examined in Chapters 7 to 12.

6.2 SPONTANEOUS STRUCTURAL CHANGES: FAITH HELD BY THE CLASSICAL ECONOMISTS

Faith on the Part of the Classical Economists

While all four classical economists re-examined here were clearly aware that nations during their times had not advanced by the same degree, they did not concern themselves with determining how trading with England could possibly aggravate the uneven development. Rather, in the case of Smith, Torrens and Mill, a faith was expressed that suggested that manufacturing industries would quite spontaneously spread from England to other countries.

Thus, in explaining at one point in his *Wealth of Nations* the outlines of the 'ingenious' agricultural system, Smith portrays what a policy of 'perfect freedom of trade' practiced between landed nations on the one hand, which had essentially agricultural economies, and mercantile states on the other, would do to the former. 'This perfect freedom of trade', he predicts, 'would be the most effectual expedient for supplying them, in due time, with all the artificers, manufacturers and merchants, whom they wanted at home' ([1776] 1979, p. 670). The reason for the optimism is,

> The continual increase of the surplus produce of their land, would, in due time, create a greater capital than what could be employed with the ordinary rate of

> profit in the improvement and cultivation of land; and the surplus part of it would *naturally* turn itself to the employment of artificers and manufacturers at home. (Ibid., italics added)

Likewise, Torrens suggests in his *External Corn Trade* that a corn-exporting country should not prematurely divert capital to create 'manufactories' at home 'until a further accession of capital, sufficient for their establishment, has been previously accumulated', for then new lines of industries could be set up 'without breaking up the old' ([1829] 1972, pp. 43–4). Given that in that work he regarded capital to be most rapidly accumulated in the corn-exporting country when commerce was unrestricted, he thus predicts that,

> [P]erfect liberty to export the produce of the soil, accelerates the period of manufacturing prosperity in an agricultural country. In such a country, when capital begins to exceed what, at the existing price of produce, can be beneficially vested in the soil, it will seek other employment, and invest itself in the working up of the raw material. (Ibid.)

Yet, given the uneven growth that he was to later emphasise, where England's demand for food and materials would expand ever so rapidly, the farmers in the corn-exporting country may continue to find it beneficial to vest their capital in the soil. In other words, the condition for spontaneous structural change may simply not materialise in the way that he (and for that matter, Smith) believed it would.[2]

Before turning to Mill, Smith's faith in, and optimism about, spontaneous structural changes are worth a closer look. As first mentioned in section 3.7 above, this optimism on the part of Smith was largely based on the protection of domestic industries afforded by the high transportation costs incurred in bringing in competing imports (Smith [1776] 1979, pp. 670–71). It has to be this protection which allowed 'the gradual refinement of those household and coarser manufactures which must at all times be carried on even in the poorest and rudest countries' and are 'generally employed upon the materials which the country produces', so that manufactures 'fit for distant sale' appear to 'grow up naturally, and as it were of their own accord' (ibid., pp. 407–8).[3]

Smith, however, recognised that manufactures could be introduced into a country in a different way. Thus, '[s]ometimes they have been introduced ... by the violent operation ... of the stocks of particular merchants and undertakers, who established them in imitation of some foreign manufactures of the same kind' and their operation employed 'foreign materials' (ibid. p. 407).[4] Implicitly, such 'imitation' must be a process that can be effected very readily, if not instantaneously. Indeed, on two different occasions in the *Wealth of Nations* where Smith essentially refers to technology diffusion, the ease with which such could be effected in a situation of 'extensive commerce' is suggested. In one such occasion, where he imagines how the 'superiority of force' might become equalised between the East and West Indies on the one hand, and Europe on the other, he expresses that 'nothing seems more likely to establish this equality of force than that mutual communication of knowledge and of all sorts of improvements which an extensive commerce from all countries to all countries naturally, or rather necessarily, carries along with it' (ibid., p. 627).[5] Then, at another point while commenting on China's development, he predicts that,

> A more extensive foreign trade ... could scarce fail to increase very much the manufactures of China, and to improve very much the productive powers of its manufacturing industry. By a more extensive navigation, the Chinese would naturally learn the art of using and constructing themselves all the different machines made use of in other countries, as well as the other improvements of art and industry which are practiced in all the different parts of the world. (Ibid., p. 681)

Shielded by a protectionist barrier offered by transportation costs and blessed with the ease of technology diffusion, it is no wonder why Smith had faith in spontaneous structural changes in the 'poor and rude countries'.

In the Preliminary Remarks in his *Principles* Mill takes special note of the 'remarkable differences in the state of different portions of the human race, with regard to the production and distribution of wealth'. These existed not just between the hunting, nomadic, and feudal communities on the one hand and the industrial communities on the other, but also among countries within the latter group ([1871] 1965, pp. 19–20). This interest of Mill, as Schumpeter (1954, p. 543) remarks, 'is not in itself surprising in a work that aimed at doing again what A. Smith had done [in the *Wealth of Nations*]'. He proceeds to explore in some parts of this work the causes of these differences (see especially ibid., Bk. I, Chs. VII, VIII, and XI). Then in describing another 'indirect effect' of trade that involves 'benefits of a high order' (see section 5.3 above for the first such effect and benefit), he considers what trade conducted with an industrial community would do to one that is 'in an early stage of industrial advancement' and with a people 'in a quiescent, indolent, uncultivated state' and who 'may fail to put forth the whole of their productive energies for want of any sufficient object of desire'. He writes,

> The opening of a foreign trade, by making them acquainted with new objects, or tempting them by the easier acquisition of things which they had not previously thought attainable, sometimes works a sort of industrial revolution in a country whose resources were previously undeveloped for want of energy and ambition in the people: inducing those who were satisfied with scanty comforts and little work, to work harder for the gratification of their new tastes, and even to save, and

> accumulate capital, for the still more complete satisfaction of those tastes at a future time. ([1871] 1965, pp. 593–4)

Mill regards this to be applicable to India. He observes that it was above all, 'the deficiency of [its] town population which limits the productiveness of the industry'. That population did not grow up 'because the few wants and unaspiring spirit of the cultivators (joined until lately with great insecurity of property, from military and fiscal rapacity) prevent them from attempting to become consumers of town produce' (ibid., p. 121). He decides that,

> the best chance of an early development of the productive resources of India, consists in the rapid growth of its export of agricultural produce ... to the markets of Europe. ... [T]he market thus opened for surplus food will, if accompanied by good government,[6] raise up by degrees more extended wants and desires, directed either towards European commodities, or towards things which will require for their production in India a larger manufacturing population. (Ibid., pp. 121–2)

He also advocates the importation of foreign capital, believing that it

> renders the increase of production no longer exclusively dependent on the thrift or providence of the inhabitants themselves, while it places before them a stimulating example, and by instilling new ideas and breaking the chains of habit, if not by improving the actual condition of the population, tends to create in them new wants, increased ambition, and greater thought for the future. (Ibid., pp. 186–7)

This, of course, ties in with what he intended to be the result from the perpetual overflow of capital from England into foreign countries (and in this case, an old one). To sum it up for Mill, the key to igniting spontaneous structural changes was to excite through foreign trade and investment 'new wants' and 'ambition and energy'.[7]

Faith Shared by the Modern Mainstream Economists

The faith on the part of the classical economists in spontaneous structural changes in the exporters of food and materials has been readily shared by mainstream economists, in essence if not in details. This partly manifests itself in a frequently invoked response to two related but non-identical claims. One is more likely attributed to Hamilton, List, and Manoïlesco (see Chapters 7 to 9 below) and concerns the disadvantages of being 'merely agricultural states'. The other claim, attributed in its original form to Prebisch and Singer (see Chapters 10 and 12 below; some have argued that Myrdal also subscribed to it, on which see Chapter 11), is the PST.

For instance, in his lectures delivered at the National University of Brazil in 1950 and in a part where he responded to the PST, Viner predicted that,

> In a predominantly agricultural country rapid growth of population unaccompanied by proportionate growth in demand for its agricultural products will under free-market conditions bring *spontaneously* into action forces tending to industrialize the country, by making agricultural production relatively less remunerative. (1953, p. 113, italics added)[8]

More recently, answering a question that he himself rhetorically posed – 'why *encourage* industrialization?' – Rodrik noted that,

> There is a presumption that growing economies would industrialize over time even when policy is broadly neutral between industry and other sectors. ... [W]e are likely to observe a certain amount of import substitution in industry, quite independent from any role played by policy. ... [T]he issue is ... whether government intervention is desirable to alter the speed and character of the industrialization *likely to result naturally*. (1992, p. 310, italics added)

Addressing the PST, he thus contended that,

> A deterioration in primary commodity prices will *naturally* reorient an economy's resources toward industry (and services). Industrialization will be the *automatic* consequence of the shift in relative prices. That governments must speed up the process through industrial policies is by no means a logical corollary. (Ibid., italics added)[9]

Echoing Rodrik, Krueger reminded that 'without further assumptions, that argument [of deteriorating terms of trade] would not, even if factually correct, constitute a case for *protection*: market forces should provide for reallocation toward import-competing production over time' (1984, p. 526, n. 10, italics added). What 'further assumptions' could these be? They are nothing but those relating to 'specific market failures and externalities which, in the absence of corrective policies, may leave the industrial sector in command of a socially suboptimal share of the economy's resources' (Rodrik, ibid.).

Are there classical roots in the mainstream analyses of market failures and externalities that lend (or refuse, as the case might be) support for trade protection?

6.3 CLASSICAL ECONOMISTS' GENERAL REJECTION OF PROTECTION

The classical economists' rejection of trade protection, which, of course, is the natural flipside of their support of free trade, is widely known and can thus be afforded a brief representation here.[10]

A significant reason behind this rejection rests on static efficiency considerations, under the implicit assumption of full employment of resources and given technology. Thus, in the oft-cited Bk. IV, Ch. II of the *Wealth of Nations*, Smith declared that,

> No regulation of commerce can increase the quantity of industry in any society beyond what its capital can maintain. It can only divert a part of it into a direction into which it might not otherwise have gone; and it is by no means certain that this artificial direction is likely to be more advantageous to the society than that into which it would have gone of its own accord. ([1776] 1979, p. 453)

This was religiously echoed by Ricardo, Torrens, and Mill. The sole effect of high duties on importation or of bounties on exportation, Ricardo thus claimed, 'is to divert a portion of capital to an employment, which it would not naturally seek. It causes a pernicious distribution of the general funds of the society – it bribes a manufacturer to commence or continue in a comparatively less profitable employment' ([1821] 2004, p. 314). Similarly, Torrens lamented that when protection was pursued to set up manufactures, 'a number of hands will be employed in fabricating goods, inferior in quantity, or quality, to those which the same number of hands formerly enabled the people to procure by exchange from foreign countries' ([1829] 1972, p. 44). Finally, Mill pointed out that,

> To prohibit ... this importation [of foreign commodities], or impose duties which prevent it, is to render the labour and capital of the country less efficient in production than they would otherwise be; and compel a waste, of the difference between the labour and capital necessary for the home production of the commodity, and that which is required for producing the things with which it can be purchased from abroad. ([1871] 1965, p. 914)

Again, this is reasoning against protection based on the static efficiency consideration for supporting free trade.

But with respect to the contemporary trade pattern where England was the exporter of manufactures while her trading partners were largely exporting food and raw materials, one could ask if the advantages enjoyed by the former in manufacturing were permanent, or if they were capable of being 'acquired' or 'learned' by other countries. Should these trading partners adopt measures to hasten such acquisitions and learning? Quoting again from Bk. IV, Ch. II of the *Wealth of Nations*, Smith opines that '[t]he *natural* advantages which one country has over another in producing particular commodities are sometimes so great, that it is acknowledged by all the world to be in vain to struggle with them' ([1776] 1979, p. 458, italics added).[11] Here he illustrates the absurdity of a hypothetical attempt to grow grapes in

Scotland in an artificial environment created by 'glasses, hotbeds and hotwalls', and then generalises the conclusion by asserting that,

> Whether the advantages which one country has over another, be natural or acquired, is in this respect of no consequence.[12] As long as the one country has those advantages, and the other wants them, it will always be more advantageous for the latter, rather to buy of the former than to make. (Ibid.)

Although he does concede, '[b]y means of … regulations, … a particular manufacture may sometimes be acquired *sooner than it could have been otherwise*, and after a certain time may be made at home as cheap or cheaper than in the foreign country' (italics added), he cautions that

> it will by no means follow that the sum total, either of its industry, or of its revenue, can ever be augmented by any such regulation … [T]he immediate effect of every such regulation is to diminish its revenue, and what diminishes its revenue is certainly not very likely to augment its capital faster than it would have augmented of its own accord, had both capital and industry been left to find out their natural employments. (Ibid.)

In other words, manufactures would sooner or later spontaneously emerge and it was not clear to him that their emergence should be artificially hastened.

Early on in the *Principles*, based on the conviction that 'industry is limited by capital', Mill makes an argument that resembles the one made by Smith that was reproduced in the first quotation in this section. Specifically,

> Had legislators been aware that industry is limited by capital, they would have seen that, the aggregate capital of the country not having been increased, any portion of it which they by their laws had caused to be embarked in the newly-acquired branch of industry must have been withdrawn or withheld from some other; in which it gave, or would have given, employment to probably about the same quantity of labour which it employs in its new occupation. ([1871] 1965, p. 64)

It is not until near the end of the *Principles* that Mill breaks ranks by offering conditional support for infant-industry protection.

6.4 MILL'S ENDORSEMENT OF INFANT-INDUSTRY PROTECTION

As Viner ([1937] 1975, pp. 71–2) has meticulously documented, there were several early versions of the infant-industry argument for temporary public encouragement prior to Hamilton's *Report on Manufactures*. Judging from the acknowledgements that he gave in various publications, Mill apparently had not come across them, at least not directly. He had also apparently not read Hamilton's works.[13] Who else, as far as 'protectionists' are concerned who are regarded to be arguing for infant-industry protection, might he have been exposed to?

Distorted Ideas of List's *National System of Political Economy* Acquired via John Austin[14]

Although Sir William Ashley notes in the Bibliographical Appendix to his edition of the *Principles* that 'Mill makes no reference ... to the writings of Friedrich List' (Ashley [1909] 1987, p. 1003), as far as the latter's *National System of Political Economy* (hereafter *National System*) is concerned Mill mentioned in a March 1842 letter that that was a book 'the nature of which I well remember though I have forgotten the author' (*Collected Works*, vol. XIII, p. 506). That was written in a letter to Sarah Austin, whose husband, John, was then preparing a review of List's book. The review, 42 pages long, was published in the April–July issue of the *Edinburgh Review* of that same year (Austin 1842). It is clear that Mill studied it quite swiftly so that by early July 1842 he could write to the reviewer and complimented him thus:

> I have read the article on List & find it as good as even I expected. ... List seems to have as much confusion in his head as the advocates of prohibitions generally have, but the state of public feeling to which such a book recommends itself is a very serious consideration. (*Collected Works*, vol. XIII, p. 528)

But was Austin an objective reviewer and interpreter who portrayed List's ideas in undistorted ways?

List is the subject of Chapter 8 below and the features of his perspective on development will be presented there. Suffice it for just a few of these features to be mentioned here to suggest that the objectivity of Austin's review is highly suspect. While many have regarded List's critique of Smith to be sometimes unfair, the same can perhaps be said when one considers if Austin's review did justice to List. He thus labelled the *National System* a 'desultory volume' that was 'unworthy of notice' and 'unworthy of grave criticism' if not because of its 'incendiary' danger. Austin himself felt provoked by its 'pernicious tendency' and its 'malevolent spirit' so that he was urged to dispute its claims despite the fact that writing a critical review of it was 'painful and disgusting drudgery' (Austin 1842, pp. 521–3, 555). But prejudice and jealousy aside, what was the gist of his critique?

Austin firmly subscribed to that classical analysis from which is derived the static benefits of specialisation and trade. Based upon this he repeatedly pointed out the static inefficiency of the 'protective system' allegedly advocated by List. For instance, he explained at one point that,

> unless the nation has aptitudes for manufacturing, (or can produce manufactures more cheaply than she can buy them,) the protective system, instead of stimulating her industry, tends to discourage it. The capital and labour which she *unnaturally* turns to manufacturing, would be more productive if they were otherwise applied; and consequently their products would exchange for a quantity of manufactures larger than the quantity which they actually produced. (Ibid., pp. 530–31, italics added)

His firm subscription in turn rested on an unyielding belief that various nations of the trading world all have different natural aptitudes in producing different things. These are 'powers, bodily and mental, with which ... members are *naturally* endowed' and it so happened that England possessed 'unrivalled' and 'matchless' natural capacities for manufacturing and commercial industry (ibid., pp. 537, 542, 552, italics added).[15] Any country which adopted the protective system in an attempt to catch up with England would only be creating 'unnatural' or 'forced' manufactures, and would 'abridge the general productiveness of her labour and capital' by giving them a direction 'which they would not take spontaneously' (ibid., pp. 527, 532–4, 538).

Clearly, Austin did not address List's deep conviction that 'productive powers' for manufactures, at least for the temperate zone countries, could be acquired. He dismissed List's richly suggestive 'reciprocal effects' that would be ignited by the encouragement of manufactures (ibid., pp. 538–9). Rather, when he noticed that List's faith in acquiring such powers did not extend to the 'torrid zone' countries, he seized the opportunity (and rightly so!) to attack his inconsistency. However, instead of conceding the point that manufacturing productive powers could potentially be acquired by all, he pointed to List's unevenly attached faith as affirmation that 'the respective vocations of various nations are determined by their several aptitudes'. 'Now', he added, 'though he [List] applies it partially, this reasoning will hold universally. It is not more applicable to the nations of the torrid, than to the civilized nations of the temperate zones' (ibid., p. 531).

Given his predisposition, it is not surprising that Austin did not see any need to be patient with any test of a vocation to manufacture. He misrepresented List at one point by saying that '[h]e ... admits in effect ... that *every* branch of industry *which has not arisen spontaneously*, is presumptively an evil to the country which has forced it into existence' (1842, p. 528, italics in the original).[16] Elsewhere, he lamented that List's tests of vocation 'are too indeterminate to admit of application in practice. ... [T]he necessary vagueness of his tests proves the absurdity of his system' (ibid., pp. 535–6). However, he also made an unexpected confession that '[w]hether a country be fitted for manufacturing, is a question of infinite extent and invincible difficulty' (ibid.).

Finally, throughout the review Austin exclusively referred to 'prohibitory or restrictive tariffs' and 'import duties' as if they were the only instruments that List had proposed to employ to engender development. It will be argued in Chapter 8 that this did tremendous injustice to List.

Attention Drawn to Rae's *New Principles* by Nassau Senior[17]

Hence, Mill cannot be claimed to be influenced by Hamilton and List, not in the sense that he had actually read their works. Instead, in his *Principles* he credited Rae for contributions to several economic subjects, one of these instances being found in the former's endorsement of the infant-industry argument for trade protection. Specifically, he notes in the oft-quoted passage containing the endorsement (see the next subsection) that 'it is a just remark of Mr. Rae, that nothing has a greater tendency to promote improvements in any branch of production, than its trial under a new set of conditions' ([1871] 1965, pp. 918–19).[18]

Dimand (1998, p. 179) points out that the words 'of Mr. Rae' first appeared as an attribution in the fifth (1862) edition of Mill's *Principles*. Now it was Senior who drew Mill's attention to Rae's *New Principles* that was published in 1834 (James 1965, pp. 167–8), although it is not clear when he (Senior) did that exactly. James (ibid.) suggests that Senior himself appeared to have learned of Rae's book before 1847. Prior to the publication of the first (1848) edition of his *Principles*, an instance when Mill appeared to be considering breaking ranks with Smith and Ricardo on the subject of protection can be found in an 1845 letter to Carey (*Collected Works*, vol. XIII, pp. 658–60). He was replying to Carey's letter that acknowledged his receipt of a copy of the 1844 edition of *Some Unsettled Questions* and he took the opportunity to thank him (Carey) for sending him (Mill) his (Carey's) *Principles of Political Economy*. In the latter work Carey reviewed the thoughts of several classical writers and was generally critical of them. Nevertheless, at the time when he had this work published (1837–1840) he was not yet a protectionist.[19] Indeed, in a few instances he strongly supported the gradual, as opposed to sudden, removal of tariffs in England and the United States, including the Corn Laws. It was against this background that Mill wrote in the 1845 letter to Carey that,

> It is fortunate that political economists do not differ so radically in their conclusions, as the diversity of their premises might lead any one to expect, & that your doctrines point as directly as those of any follower of Adam Smith or Ricardo, to the gradual abandonment of the restrictive, or as it is improperly

> called, the protective policy – to which I am not the less rootedly hostile because I differ from you in thinking that in certain exceptional cases, the conditional maintenance of some part of the system may be justified or even required by self-protection. (Ibid., p. 659)

Whether this came after he read Rae's *New Principles* cannot be presently determined.

So what is Rae essentially arguing for in his *New Principles*? Distinguishing himself from Smith, he argues that 'the augmented wealth of the society cannot be said altogether to flow from the gradual increase of its capital by accumulation, the consequent division of labor, and the improvements thence resulting' ([1834] 1964, p. 68). To Smith, the invention and application of machinery 'seems to have been originally owing to the division of labour' ([1776] 1979, p. 20). For Rae, in contrast, the 'extended division of labor implies the existence of many arts, and of much intelligence'. If such arts and intelligence indeed exist, 'the inventive faculties will be generally active'. But the inventive activity, 'though a concomitant of the division of labor, is to be held as an effect, not of that division, but other causes themselves producing the division' ([1834] 1964, p. 357).[20] He thus believes that 'the gradual increase which the accumulation of capital produces on the productive powers of any society, is not alone sufficient to call forth all the resources which that society possesses' (ibid., p. 68). Instead, for countries that aspire to advance more rapidly, 'it is often necessary to seek in other countries for the means, which give these resources full efficiency' and the society could be 'dependent on the importation of new arts from other countries, for the means of being advantageously directed' (ibid., pp. 68, 45).

Implicit in this contention was Rae's deep conviction, again in contrast with Smith (see section 6.3 above), that while '*natural* advantages cannot be procured by an expenditure of revenue or capital, ... *acquired* advantages may often be got by means of a very small expenditure. ... [T]hey differ in this, that the latter can be transferred from one country to another, the former cannot' (ibid., pp. 71–2, italics added).[21] At a later point in his *New Principles* he asks rhetorically, 'Who can positively say what fifty years hence will be the productions of any country?' (p. 258).

Historically, Rae goes on to observe, manufacturing arts had only been successfully transferred from one country to another with the occurrence of 'some favorable conjuncture of events'. Firstly, artificers and artisans had expatriated themselves when persecuted or when adversely affected by wars and natural disasters (p. 49). Secondly, interruptions of commerce because of wars had gradually excited, in the countries to which the supplies had been cut off, imitations of foreign products (pp. 49–50). However, he downplays these, regarding them to be then 'continually diminishing in ... the vigour of their operations, and becoming more and more beyond the reach of our calculations' (p. 51).[22] Recognising that it would practically be impossible for any individual to attempt such transfers – given the tedious and expensive nature of the undertakings, and the concerns relating to adequately appropriating the benefits arising therefrom while preventing free-riding (pp. 51–2, 55–6) – Rae proposes that the 'legislators' should provide encouragements and support to accomplish such tasks for the good of the society. Note here that he is further distinguishing his position from that of Smith. Thus, recall the quotations in sections 6.2 (first subsection) and 6.3 above illustrating Smith's belief in the spontaneity in the emergence of manufactures in agricultural countries and hence there was no reason to artificially hasten their arrival. Rae, on the other hand, laments that 'a case of the circumstances of a country being so peculiarly favorable to the practice of a foreign art, that, in the very first essays it makes in it, it can successfully compete with another, where that art has been long established, is assuredly very rare' (p. 54). Again, state support would be needed.

How should the legislators set up a support system? They should, according to Rae, encourage manufactures 'by means of a system of premiums, bounties, and duties' (ibid., p. 74). Specifically, '[t]he legislator effects his purposes by premiums for successful individual imitations of the foreign article; by general bounties on the home manufacture; or by duties on that imported from abroad' (ibid., p. 368). Upon closer inspection, one can discern a two-step sequence in offering state support. First, the viability of the transfer of the foreign art should be determined. If that is feasible, then the second consideration is how to encourage and support its local practice and further growth. In his words,

> premiums ... are useful as testing the practicability of the transfer. That having been done, it having been made sufficiently apparent that nothing prevents the branch of industry in question being established, but the difficulties attending new undertakings, the want of skilled labor, and a sufficiently accurate knowledge of the properties of the materials to be employed in the formation of the new instruments, it is then proper to proceed to direct and general encouragements by bounties or duties. (Ibid.)[23]

Notice that he was not single-mindedly relying on protective duties in this recommendation.[24]

In funding the premiums, bounties, and the like, the whole society might thus effect the introduction of manufacture 'through the expenditure for a few years of a portion of its revenue, much less than what an equal number of years succeeding them will return to it in the diminished cost of the article' (ibid., p. 70). There is a faint hint here that state support would only be temporary, but it is otherwise left unspecified in the *New Principles* roughly how long the bounties or duties would be maintained.[25] He also appears to be employing some sort of cost–benefit calculus and he does so again on a few other occasions. Thus, in one instance when he engages himself with a likely challenge by the supporters of Smith's doctrines, he retorts that,

> If it be said by any supporter of these doctrines ... that the loss which the society sustains, by the destruction of the capital of the original introducer of the manufacture, must be allowed to be made up by the gain which it receives from the profits made by those who afterwards engage in it; I reply, that I perfectly agree with him in his conclusions. ... [T]he small present expenditure of the funds of the society which the project may occasion, may be more than repaid, by the large future revenue that it will bring in. ... I hold, that it would be more just and judicious that the necessary first cost of the scheme should be borne by the whole community. (Ibid., p. 53, see also pp. 16, 60, 68–70, 75)

The 'gain' in this quote takes the form of a 'larger future revenue'. Elsewhere, he indicates that he would regard the measures adopted by the legislators as 'completely successful ... when the commodity, the product of the art in question, comes to be made at the same cost in the country to which its manufacture is transferred, as in that from which it comes, or at less cost than there' (ibid., p. 364).

Lest the reader hastily compares this with what later came to be known as the 'Mill–Bastable test', it should be noted Rae immediately appends a point that there are three kinds advantages which the community could derive from such success (ibid., pp. 364–6). Firstly, transportation expenses would be economised (see also ibid., pp. 45–6, 57, 74). Secondly, any inconvenience associated with interruption of commerce by wars and other causes would be minimised. Last, but not least, the successful transfer of the manufacturing art would generate all kinds of indirect effects that would stimulate further inventions and improvements. Hence,

> [e]very useful art is so connected with many, or with all others, that whatever renders its products more easily attainable, facilitates the operations of a whole circle of arts, and introduces change – the great agent in producing improvements – under the most favorable form. ... Arts, too ..., when brought together pass into one another, and thus also improvements in old arts are produced, or new arts generated. Even their very existence in any society gives a powerful stimulus to the ingenuity of its members. (Ibid., p. 365)[26]

Rae apparently attaches quite a bit of importance to this last advantage, observing in another instance that,

> the variety of effects that may be generated, from the action, and reaction, on each other, of the numerous powers at its disposal, becomes illimitable. As in numbers,

> every addition multiplies amazingly the possible antecedent combinations, until at length the amount becomes too great to be ascertained. (Ibid., p. 115, see also pp. 23, 112, 259, 262, 303)

Thus, although he might appear to be employing a cost–benefit calculus in explaining his policy proposal, he was quite aware of the immense potential, a complex one indeed, on the benefit side. Put slightly differently, although he might advocate policy measures that were mainly targeted at a certain manufacture, it is clear that his attention was not confined solely to what would subsequently happen to that manufacture. He even sounded Listian in a couple of instances (see Chapter 8 below) by attempting to condense these complex beneficial effects as increases in the 'productive powers' of the community (ibid., pp. 69–70).

There are some signs Rae had wished that his recommendation would not be invoked carelessly, as when he emphasised that 'while the legislator is called on to act, he is also called on to act cautiously, and to regulate his proceedings by an attentive consideration of the progress of events' (ibid., p. 367). But there are also signs he thought that legislators should quite actively follow his advice and not be deterred by some unavoidable errors in the process. He thus explained,

> Like individual schemes their projects seem sometimes to have succeeded, and sometimes to have failed. But though, when he acts, it is incident to man's imperfect nature occasionally to err, to sit down therefore in resolute inactivity would be the worst error he could commit. (Ibid., p. 69)

Elsewhere, referring to the introduction of modern science and art into Egypt by its then ruler, Rae optimistically predicted that '[e]rrors, no doubt, may have been, and may be committed, but the good assuredly overbalances the evil' (ibid., p. 379).[27]

Mill's Qualified Endorsement of Infant-Industry Protection

Just several years after the release of Austin's review of List referred to above, the first (1848) edition of Mill's *Principles* was published. Therein, but late in the book, he provides an endorsement, albeit a qualified one, of protecting an infant industry. Although the passage in which Mill states this is most oft-quoted, it is reproduced here as it appears in that edition so that attention can be focused on a few features for further discussions. He thus asserts that,

> The only case in which, on mere principles of political economy, *protecting duties* can be defensible, is when they are imposed *temporarily* (especially in a young and rising nation) in hopes of naturalizing *a* foreign industry, in itself perfectly

> suitable to the circumstances of the country. The superiority of one country over another in *a* branch of production, often arises only from having begun it sooner. There may be no inherent advantage on one part, or disadvantage on the other, but only a present superiority of *acquired* skill and experience. A country which has this skill and experience *yet to acquire*, may in other respects be better adapted to the production than those which were earlier in the field: and besides, it is a just remark,[28] that nothing has a greater tendency to promote improvements in any branch of production, than its trial under a new set of conditions. But it cannot be expected that individuals should, at their own risk, or rather to their certain loss, introduce a new manufacture, and bear the burden of carrying it on, until the producers have been *educated up* to the level of those with whom the processes are traditional. (1848, Vol. II, pp. 487–8, italics added)

Thus far in the passage it is important to note that despite his compliments to Austin for his review, Mill takes the opposite position, as he was probably influenced by Rae, that skill and experience in industry could be acquired and producers could be 'educated up'. Also, he seems to concur with Rae on why individuals acting independently of each other could not be expected to effect the transfer of a manufacture. To continue with the endorsement,

> A *protecting duty, continued for a reasonable time*, will[29] sometimes be the least inconvenient mode in which the nation can tax itself for the support of such an experiment. But[30] the protection should be confined to cases in which there is good ground of assurance that *the industry* which it fosters will after a time be able to dispense with it; nor should the domestic producers ever be allowed to expect that it will be continued to them, beyond the time strictly necessary for a fair trial of what they are capable of accomplishing. (Ibid., p. 488, italics added)[31]

Having dissented from Austin on the subject of natural versus acquired advantages, Mill was to qualify his endorsement by proposing that the trial be only temporary and in the process put emphasis on something that Rae did not pay much attention to in his *New Principles*. What instrument was to be adopted to render that trial possible? He only mentioned the protecting duty in this passage, despite Rae's reference to employing a system of measures involving also premiums and bounties.[32] By omitting premiums, Rae's two-step sequence in promoting manufactures is also reduced to just one step, as if the skill and experience involved in certain production processes can entirely be cultivated domestically.[33]

One final feature in this endorsement that is at least as consequential as others is its reference to encouraging just *one* industry. It is not clear how the promotion of merely one industry in an economy can hasten economic development. A lot depends on how that single industry is considered to be situated in a broader economic and technological environment that characterises the stage of economic development, and how its progress might spill over to, and ignite further progress in, the rest of the economy. But these are unfortunately left unconsidered by Mill, at least in this part of his *Principles*.[34] One can perhaps argue that the focus on a stand-alone industry is consistent with the formulation of Ricardo's England–Portugal model (and Mill's own England–Germany model). Some might point out that the mentioning of 'protecting duties' in the first sentence in the endorsement passage indicates that he was allowing for the promotion of two or more industries more or less simultaneously. Even so, it is still unclear how those industries relate to the rest of the economy, and how they relate to each other and perhaps feed on each other's progress. Rae's 'variety of effects' that generate 'actions, and reactions, on each other', and which arise from further inventions and improvements is no where to be found. Viewed as such, the passage contains an extremely narrow focus if one aims at engendering development by adopting a more holistic approach. The main directions in which mainstream economists have extended their analyses from this narrow focus will be indicated in the next section.[35]

6.5 DEVELOPMENT OF THE MAINSTREAM THEORY OF COMMERCIAL POLICY

The endorsement of a case for protection by a most notable English economist of that time had, not surprisingly, attracted a huge amount of attention. There were many, especially in the United States and Australia, who were anxious to take advantage of it. In fact, quite a few even misused it, much to the chagrin of Mill. In several letters in the mid to late 1860s he described his despair upon learning that behind the shield of his endorsement some 'vulgarest and most exploded fallacies' and 'false and pernicious doctrines' in support of protection had been revived. Also, while he emphasised that the protecting duty should be a temporary one, that message had become buried and duties were imposed by some Australian protectionists with the intention that these be permanent.[36]

Subsidy versus Tariff: Is the Tariff the Best Instrument that the 'Protectionists' could come up with?

In some of the same correspondence Mill confessed that the opinion that he stated in the *Principles* had been 'greatly shaken'. He indicated that he was leaning toward advocating the replacement of the protecting duty by a subsidy, 'which is far less likely to be continued after the conditions which alone justified it have ceased to exist'.[37] To the mainstream theorists on commercial policy, Mill had thus redeemed himself and was rescued from the 'protectionists'. For according to the mainstream analyses that have subsequently been developed, the best way to correct the market failures and externalities that Rodrik alluded to at the end of section 6.2 above is typically not through trade protection but rather through some sort of non-trade interventions, including many types of subsidies.[38]

The mainstream version of the history of economic thought on this subject – theory of commercial policy – has thus taken shape. Just as the story of the evolution of mainstream analysis supporting free trade is anchored by Ricardo's England–Portugal model (Chapter 2 above), the story of the evolution of analysis offering qualified state support for industry promotion is anchored by Mill's endorsement passage and the indication in some of his correspondence of an awareness of the superiority of a subsidy over a tariff for such promotion.

One would expect that, geared with this version of history of thought the mainstream theorists would then determine if various 'protectionists', writing both before and after Mill, had made arguments that are similar to or different from Mill's. In addition, one would also expect that they would ascertain if the 'protectionists' were solely thinking of promoting industries through the imposition of protective duties.

But thanks to Mill's reputation and hence the ready popularisation of his endorsement passage, learning the case as cogently stated by him has been regarded as a substitute for carefully perusing other authors' argumentations for promoting development. Knowing the case as presented by him has come to be regarded as knowing the strongest case that 'protectionists' anywhere could present. As Kemp (1960, p. 65) puts it when referring to Mill's account of the infant-industry dogma, 'it is brief and has hardly been improved upon'.

Recall that one important feature in Mill's endorsement passage is that he only refers to a protecting duty as *the* instrument to promote an infant industry. When almost exclusive attention has been focused on this passage, mainstream theorists on commercial policy have arguably been lulled into believing that the duty was the best instrument that the usual suspects who allegedly advocated protectionism had to offer. An impression has become deeply ingrained among those theorists that the 'protectionists' know nothing better than advocating the use of protective duties to promote industrial development.[39] The re-examination of Hamilton, List, and Myrdal in Chapters 7, 8, and 11 (and, to a lesser extent, Manoïlesco in Chapter 9) below will reveal otherwise. (Recall also that the examination of Rae in section 6.4 above shows that he did not confine himself to the use of protective duties.)

Diagnosing Arguments for Protection as Situations of Market Failures: The Theory of Domestic Divergences or Distortions

Armed with the mainstream version of history of thought, the mainstream theorists have certainly proceeded to trace how Mill's qualified endorsement, including his suggestion of the superiority of subsidies over protective duties, has been refined and extended.

Specifically, aided by some strong assumptions the alleged superiority of certain subsidies (or some other forms of 'non-trade' intervention) over protective duties was confirmed by some mainstream theorists shortly after World War II as they developed and refined what later became the theory of domestic divergences or distortions. This theory facilitates the ranking of different policy instruments that could be employed in correcting various market failures. Obviously, this presupposes that the different arguments for protection allegedly made by various 'protectionists' can neatly be reduced to the distinct standard cases of market failures. Such ranking is obtained based on how closely each instrument targets, in accordance with the 'principle of targetting', the very source of each situation of market failure while minimising by-product distortions. The strong assumptions are made precisely to guarantee that while a protective duty's by-product distortions are starkly highlighted, those associated with non-trade interventions are essentially swept under the rug.

By far, Corden, in his *Trade Policy and Economic Welfare*, is the most candid about these assumptions and admits that 'in spite of the surfeit of articles in the economic journals on the "theory of domestic distortions," no one other than Meade ... has found it necessary to remove or review these assumptions' (1997, p. 33).[40] He proceeds to offer a very careful scrutiny of such assumptions, devoting a whole chapter in the book to examining four assumptions upon which he regards the conclusion of the theory to be dependent. These assumptions maintain that: subsidies can be financed by 'non-distorting' taxes;[41] taxation involves no collection costs;[42] there are no costs of disbursement of subsidies; and the income distribution effects of various policies can be neglected.[43] He reaches the rather lenient verdict that 'the central argument is unshaken' by removing the first and the last of these assumptions; discarding the second assumption 'slightly dents it', while abandoning the third assumption 'does affect it' (ibid.).[44] Keesing (1974, p. 209), after rethinking the second and the third assumptions, echoes by concluding that,

> A somewhat more complete theory ... would take into account the social costs of collecting taxes by various means and the social costs of intervention to influence incentives through subsidies and similar measures. As a matter of logic, what start

as first-best and second-best solutions under the original assumptions may well reverse their rank order when new cost equations are added.

Regrettably, in the unqualified form that it is usually being stated and applied, the theory is founded upon 'an unrealistic model of public finance'.[45]

Associated with these strong assumptions is a rather implicit element or assumption that should also be made more explicit. Collectively, these assumptions amount to saying that there are no 'constraints' that would render unavailable a 'first-best' policy instrument in correcting an isolated market failure. Corden (1965, p. 47) broadly classifies them into 'economic-environment constraints' (including market failures additional to the one under consideration) and 'government-policy constraints'. Should there be more than one market failure, then '[t]he optimal correction required for one particular divergence may well depend on whether another divergence has been corrected' (Corden 1997, p. 18). Put alternatively, 'if several failures occur simultaneously it can be misleading to analyse them one-by-one' (Stern 1989, p. 617). Should a government-policy constraint exist, then what was ranked the 'first-best' policy instrument to correct a divergence in the hypothetically no-constraint situation is no longer necessarily superior to what was previously ranked as 'second-best'.[46]

Thus, for the theory of domestic divergences to yield unambiguous ranking of policy instruments, it relies on the aforementioned strong assumptions and it hinges on the assumption that each case for protection originates from one and only one market failure. Different types of market failures are identified and treated through a process of compartmentalisation. That is, each type of market failure is compartmentalised from the rest,[47] so that a clean ranking of policy instruments in each situation becomes possible.[48]

It is here that a second feature in Mill's endorsement passage might be regarded, even if remotely, to have played a contributory role, namely that it refers to only one industry. By thus referring to only one narrow portion of a developing economy, namely one infant industry, it can be argued to have the unintended effect of facilitating the compartmentalisation by the theory in its treatment of market failures as obstacles to development. It certainly has the obvious effect of trivialising the complex process of development. By separating the types of market failure by which an industry is exactly being hindered from emerging, those who apply the theory to refine and extend Mill's endorsement of infant-industry support might, at first sight, appear to be situating the consideration of the development process in some slightly broader contexts. But upon closer examination, the trivialisation of the development process is maintained. This is because, by compartmentalising market failures and by claiming the theory of domestic divergences as a significant portion of the literature on trade and development, it is as if engendering development is just one remaining market-failure correction away. If only it were that simple! (Recall the recognition and criticism by Stiglitz and Charlton (2005) of this kind of trivialisation in Chapter 1 above.)[49]

But if one were prepared to ignore these problems in the theory, then it appears that it can handle many cases for protection other than Mill's formulation of the infant-industry argument. A quick perusal of the literature indicates that most of the attention has been centred on capital market failures, labour market failures (of which Manoïlesco's case is represented as one), and imperfect information.[50] Some consideration has been given to external economies, except that, to ensure manageability, such economies have been rather narrowly characterised as production externalities.[51] It is through this exercise, backed by the aforementioned strong assumptions, that the conclusion is reached that under almost all circumstances the protective duty does not emerge as a first-best policy instrument.[52] The most notable exception is regarded as having classical roots (on which see Chapters 4 and 5 above) and is where a tariff turns out to be the 'first-best' instrument. This is the so-called optimal-tariff applied in a situation where a country possesses monopoly power in trade.[53] Some in the mainstream suggests that it could be what Prebisch and Singer were implicitly advocating the primary exporting countries to do, a claim which will be scrutinised in Chapters 10 and 12 below.

6.6 SELF-DOUBT AMONG CLASSICAL ECONOMISTS ON SPONTANEOUS STRUCTURAL CHANGES?

With the passage of time and improvements in transportation, the transportation-cost afforded protection that Smith could count on has become less and less effective. And the technology diffusion that he occasionally portrays in the *Wealth of Nations* to 'naturally' occur between countries (see section 6.2 above) does not, after all, take place that naturally. Regarding two channels for such diffusion, namely the 'exportation of the instruments of trade', and the exercising and teaching of certain trades abroad by English artificers, Smith acknowledged that their effectiveness had been restricted or their operation had been prohibited by regulations ([1776] 1979, pp. 659–60).[54] Torrens and Mill were also aware of these regulations, especially as Bloomfield (1978, p. 631) points out, it was between the 1820s and 1840s that there emerged a lively debate in England on the pros and cons of removing those restrictions.[55]

Regulations aside, Smith indicates in one instance in 'An Early Draft of Part of *The Wealth of Nations*', that 'a nation is not always in a condition to imitate and copy the inventions and improvements of its more wealthy neighbours; the application of these frequently requiring a stock with which it is not furnished'.[56] Interestingly, as first quoted in section 5.7 above, Mill also recognised with regard to 'mechanical inventions' that '[i]t is true, inventions spread rapidly from country to country, but not so the power of bringing them into profitable use. In that respect, the advantage of having large masses of capital already accumulated is immense'. He went on to add that, 'There are as many inventions made on the other side of the Channel as on this; but it is to England that the inventors bring their inventions when they desire to make money by them' ([1843] 1986, p. 839).[57]

To be sure, these seeds of doubt from within the works of the classical economists are, unlike the voluminous amount of textual evidence presented in Chapters 3 to 5, insufficient to constitute an alternative interpretation of their thoughts on commercial policy and technology acquisition. They nevertheless serve as some significant points of departure or attack by the authors that are re-examined in the following chapters as they put forth their thoughts on engendering development. In general, it is not the belief of these authors that technological-capability cultivation, structural changes, and economic development in the less-developed countries that traded and received investment from the economically advanced countries would spontaneously and naturally take place under free trade (market) conditions.

NOTES

1. Williams (1929, p. 206) labels Smith 'a nationalist of nationalists'. Robbins (1998, p. 241) admits that 'Smith's attack on the mercantile system of wealth is based on the view that the mercantile system of wealth was inimical to the British nation', while he also allows, when commenting on List's critique of the author of the *Wealth of Nations*, that Smith 'doubtless was cosmopolitan in sympathy'. Robbins is in fact cited by Myrdal (1956, p. 339, n. 2) in illustrating the nationalistic concern among the classical trade theorists. See also Irwin (1996, p. 76, n. 4), who quotes a passage from Smith's *Theory of Moral Sentiments* to illustrate the latter's nationalistic feelings. Contrast with Viner's position that, 'The English classical school in general took a cosmopolitan approach, not because they were not patriotic Englishmen, but because as they saw things they were advocating as desirable policy for England what was also in the interest of the world at large, so that as a rule there was no need for deliberate choice between a national approach and a conflicting cosmopolitan approach. I think that they were substantially correct in this regard in their own time' (1953, p. 5).
2. Torrens did not consider the scenario when growth had occurred to the point where differences in income elasticity of demand between manufactures and primary products would kick into play.
3. 'In this manner have grown up naturally, and as it were of their own accord, the manufactures of Leeds, Halifax, Sheffield, Birmingham, and Wolverhampton. Such manufactures are the offspring of agriculture' (op. cit., p. 409).

4. As examples, Smith referred to the ancient manufactures of silks, velvets, and brocades that flourished in Lucca during the thirteenth century (op. cit.).
5. Myint (1977, p. 247) cites this as proof that Smith 'believed that the "educative effect" of an open economy would be greater [than that which obtains through "infant industry" protection]'.
6. By 'better government', Mill was proposing a more complete security of property, moderate taxes (and freedom from arbitrary exaction under the name of taxes), and a more permanent and more advantageous tenure of land. He also considered it important to improve the 'public intelligence': 'the decay of usages or superstitions which interfere with the effective employment of industry; and the growth of mental activity, making the people alive to new objects of desire' (op. cit., p. 186).
7. Meier (2005, p. 34) observes that '[a]lthough Mill was officially associated for 35 years with the India Office, his writings about Indian affairs were confined to routine administrative details, and he showed no general concern with problems of development in non-European countries'. Based on the passages from his *Principles* quoted in the present discussion he did show some concern, although it was drowned by some rather simpleminded beliefs. Spengler (1960, p. 117) points out that while '[l]arge portions of the Principles are devoted to economic development', Mill 'did not make extensive reference to non-European countries, other than India'.
8. See Viner (op. cit., pp. 44, 46) for lamenting that some, like Manoïlesco and Prebisch, were demonstrating a 'dogmatic identification of agriculture with poverty'.
9. This was Rodrik's position as of the early 1990s. For an example of a later and very different stance, see Rodrik (2001), and that would continue to evolve afterwards, even if in subtler ways.
10. Allowances were granted by Smith ([1776] 1979, pp. 463, 465) for protection under national defence considerations and for equalising the tax treatment of domestic and foreign products. As discussed in Chs. 4 and 5 above, Torrens and Mill supported commercial reciprocity, and, in a sense, so did Smith (ibid., pp. 467–8).
11. But contrast this suggestion made early on in the *Wealth of Nations* with: 'The difference of natural talents in different men is, in reality, much less than we are aware of; and the very different genius which appears to distinguish men of different professions, when grown up to maturity, is not upon many occasions so much the cause, as the effect of the division of labour' (op. cit., p. 28).
12. It is of immense consequence, as Rae and List would later counter. For Rae's attack on this point, see section 6.4 below. For List's criticism, see section 8.4 in Ch. 8.
13. The several times that Hamilton's name is mentioned in volumes XV, XVI, and XIX of Mill's *Collected Works* have nothing to do with his *Report on Manufactures* or his 'protectionist' ideas.
14. Austin first became an acquaintance of the Mills in the early 1820s. Subsequently the junior Mill at a young age received instructions from him on some subjects. The more mature junior Mill still showed a lot of respect to this former instructor. See Mill's *Autobiography*.
15. While alluding to 'natural' aptitudes numerous times in his review, Austin only referred once each to 'acquired aptitudes' and to the 'acquisition of factitious means' (op. cit., pp. 529, 532). He appeared to have done so unintentionally, for he never dwelled on them.
16. How much time List was prepared to offer to such tests will be mentioned in the last subsection in section 8.5 below.
17. The full title of the *New Principles* is *Statement of Some New Principles on the Subject of Political Economy, Exposing the Fallacies of the System of Free Trade, and of Some Other Doctrines Maintained in the "Wealth of Nations"*.
18. At one point in his *New Principles* Rae mentions Hamilton and quotes a couple of passages from the latter's *Report on Manufactures* ([1834] 1964, pp. 365–6). Nevertheless, even if Mill did not skip those pages, they could in no way provide a decent representation of his (Hamilton's) thoughts on development promotion.
19. Among the American 'protectionists', the one that Mill paid the most attention to other than Rae was Carey. While in the late 1830s Carey was not a protectionist, the mid-1840s was roughly when he became converted (Dorfman [1946] 1966, pp. 790, 794–5). The

protectionist sentiment is unmistakable when he published the *Principles of Social Science* in three volumes between 1858 and 1859. For Carey's expressions of such sentiments in publications prior to the *Principles of Social Science*, see Kaplan (1931, pp. 48–54) and Kaiser ([1934] 1939, pp. 128–32).

20. This is a difference between Smith and Rae that is also briefly considered by Spengler (1959, p. 395). Smith conjectured that '[m]en are much more likely to discover easier and readier methods of attaining any object, when the whole attention of their minds is directed towards that single object, than when it is dissipated among a great variety of things' (op. cit.). Rae quoted from another part of the *Wealth of Nations* to contradict Smith: 'The man whose whole life is spent in performing a few simple operations, of which the effects too are, perhaps, always the same, or very nearly the same, has no occasion to exert his understanding, or to exercise his invention in finding out expedients for removing difficulties which never occur. He ... generally becomes as stupid and ignorant as it is possible for a human creature to become' (Smith [1776] 1979, p. 782, quoted in Rae op. cit., p. 356).
21. S. Hollander (1998) seeks to illustrate 'how close – despite appearances – Smith and Rae were *in practice*' (p. 199, italics original). The reader is invited to contrast that claim with the discussion in the rest of the present section.
22. The second of these two events, in the form of Napoleon's 'Continental blockade', was what, according to List, enabled 'German manufactures of all and every kind for the first time to make an important advance' ([1841] 1991, p. 85). It was also partly how, as Prebisch was to observe, Latin America was thrust into IS about a century later.
23. This suggests that Rae had in mind a plan to promote development that was more sophisticated than protecting an infant industry. As further evidence, one should note that early on in the *New Principles* he lists promoting the progress of science and art, encouraging the discovery of new arts or improvements in the arts already practiced in the country, and encouraging the discovery of how to adapt arts that were already practiced in other countries to domestic circumstances as areas that if the 'legislator' could so direct his power, it would 'at least seem not improbable, that ... [it] might be beneficial' ([1834] 1964, pp. 15–6).
24. In his *Sketches of the Origin and Progress of Manufactures and of the Policy Which Has Regulated Their Legislative Encouragement in Great Britain and in Other Countries* (hereafter *Sketches of Legislative Encouragement*) Rae had a very elaborate programme to advocate. See Rae ([1825] 1965, pp. 200–206).
25. The temporary nature is suggested in Rae's *Sketches of Legislative Encouragement*. See, for instance, Rae ([1825] 1965, pp. 200, 202).
26. Rae acknowledges that this last part was considered by Hamilton in his *Report on Manufactures*. See Hamilton ([1791b] 1966, p. 256).
27. Contrast with the interpretation advanced by S. Hollander (1998, pp. 212–15).
28. The words 'of Mr. Rae' were inserted here beginning from the fifth (1862) edition.
29. The word 'will' was replaced by 'might' by the seventh (1871) edition.
30. The words 'it is essential that' were inserted here by the seventh (1871) edition.
31. In the sixth edition of Mill's *Principles* one finds three new paragraphs inserted right after the one in which the endorsement of infant-industry protection was given. These comment on the protectionist ideas spelled out by Carey in his *Principles of Social Science* (see n. 19 above). As revealed in a December 1864 letter to Cairnes (*Collected Works*, vol. XV, p. 968), Mill read that work while preparing the sixth (1865) edition of his own *Principles*. He confessed to Cairnes that he felt compelled to do so because Carey's attack on Ricardo and on free trade was starting to generate noticeable influence, especially among the French political economists, and was 'helping to muddle their ideas'. He further indicated that he was only going to critique certain parts of Carey's 'speculations', specifically 'the best parts, as it was not worth while to notice any of his errors but those which had some affinity with truths' (ibid.). He begins the first of these new paragraphs by referring to Carey as '[t]he only writer, of any reputation as a political economist, who now adheres to the Protectionist doctrine'. He then represents Carey's defence of the doctrine, 'in an economic point of view, [as resting] principally on two reasons' ([1871] 1965, p. 919). The first of

these is 'the great saving in cost of carriage, consequent on producing commodities at or very near to the place where they are to be consumed', while the second concerns how countries that export agricultural produce 'send away their soil: the distant consumers not giving back to the land of the country, as home consumers would do, the fertilizing elements which they abstract from it' (ibid., pp. 919–20). By thus teasing out two reasons from an otherwise complex amalgam of arguments in Carey's *Principles*, Mill is able to reject them within the framework of static classical trade analysis. Hence, a country like America 'would not persist in exporting raw produce and importing manufactures, any longer than the labour she saved by doing so exceeded what the carriage cost her, so when it became necessary for her to replace in the soil the elements of fertility which she had sent away, if the saving in cost of production were more than equivalent to the cost of carriage and of manure together, manure would be imported; and if not, the export of corn would cease' (ibid., p. 920). Having thus satisfied himself with these answers, he declares 'Mr. Carey's economic arguments for Protectionism to be totally invalid' (ibid., p. 921). But immediately after declaring victory, Mill concedes that '[t]he economic ... is far from being the strongest point of his [Carey's] case. American Protectionists often reason extremely ill; but it is an injustice to them to suppose that their Protectionist creed rests upon nothing superior to an economic blunder'. Labelling Carey as the head of these protectionists, he refers back to Carey's complex amalgam of arguments and describes them (the protectionists) as 'deem[ing] it a necessary condition of human improvement that towns should abound; that men should combine their labour, by means of interchange – with near neighbours, with people of pursuits, capacities, and mental cultivation different from their own, sufficiently close at hand for mutual sharpening of wits and enlarging of ideas – rather than with people on the opposite side of the globe. They believe that a nation all engaged in the same, or nearly the same, pursuit – a nation all agricultural – cannot attain a high state of civilization and culture' (ibid., p. 921). Mill portrays these as considerations 'for the higher interests of humanity' rather than 'purely economic reasons' for a protectionist stance (ibid.). But in doing so could he be accused of mislabelling Carey's references to economic linkage and spill-over effects of all kinds, however convoluted and discursive they may be? There are indeed, for lack of a better term, non-economic considerations embedded in Carey's ideas. However, there is also more economic reasoning than Mill has teased out. Some commentators have labelled Carey's as a 'home market argument' for protection. See, for instance, Kaplan (1931, p. 83), Kaiser ([1934] 1939, p. 130), and Dorfman ([1946] 1966, p. 791). Whether his infant-industry argument could be rendered to accommodate Carey's considerations was, unfortunately, a question that Mill never sought to answer. He was anxious to see someone thoroughly ridicule Carey's arguments, although he did not want to undertake the monumental task himself. Thus, in the December 1864 letter that he sent to Cairnes he intimated that 'it really would be a useful exercise for any clearheaded and painstaking student of political economy to shew up the book [Carey's *Principles of Social Science*]' (*Collected Works*, vol. XV, p. 968). More than five years went by and no one obliged. In an April 1870 letter to Cairnes, he brought up the book by Carey again and dubbed it 'the very worst book on political economy that I ever toiled through', repeating that 'the only thing I wish to do with it is to find somebody who will take the trouble to write a detailed exposure of it, for the American public, on whom I believe it has really some influence'. This time Mill dangled a small incentive, offering that '[i]f you know of any person competent and willing to perform this irksome but useful service, it would be a great satisfaction to me to make him a present of my copy' (*Collected Works*, vol. XVII, pp. 1713–14).

32. Beginning in the sixth edition, in the latter part of the paragraph that immediately follows the endorsement statement, there is an abbreviated version of the endorsement where Mill again refers to using a 'protecting duty' (op. cit., pp. 919–20).
33. But see n. 55 and n. 57 below.
34. One may say that this is a little puzzling or even disappointing especially because, as the discussion in Ch. 5 above shows, Mill was quite aware of certain inter-industry considerations when he spelled out his theory of profits.

35. One important exception to these departures that maintain a relatively narrow focus is Marshall, specifically those parts of his works that are on the subject of external economies. In that connection, it is worth noting that in some sense he was quite impressed by certain insights of List. See Ch. 8 below.
36. See, for instance, the letters to Frederick Milnes Edge, George Kenyon Holden, Archibald Michie, and Edward William Stafford in Mill (*Collected Works*, vol. XVI, pp. 1150, 1420, 1515–16, and 1520–21).
37. See the letters to Michie and Stafford that are mentioned in the previous note. Prior to those letters, Mill had indicated in an 1865 letter to Henry Soden that the 'temporary aid' to support an infant industry could be 'either of a subsidy from the Government or of a protecting duty' (*Collected Works*, vol. XVI, p. 1044).
38. Corden (1997, pp. 34, 42) dubs it a '"subsidy-biased" approach'.
39. For one of the best representations of this type of thinking, see Baldwin (1969).
40. The reference to Meade is with respect to Meade (1955). It should be noted that the second edition of Corden (op. cit.) was published in 1997. The observation stated here in the main text was originally made in that book's first (1974) edition.
41. Thanks to *ad hoc* or fictional assumptions made by the subscribers to the theory, the distortion costs of non-trade taxes have been rendered totally non-existent. Thus, as Corden (1984, p. 97) points out, 'A striking feature of the standard theory of domestic distortions is the assumption that lump-sum taxes are available and will be used to finance subsidies, or alternatively, that the elasticity of supply of effort is zero, so that it is possible to raise non-lump-sum taxes without creating a distortion relative to leisure'. See Johnson (1965, p. 8) for essentially making these assumptions. One can also find zealous assertion, like the one made by Bhagwati and Ramaswami (1963, p. 50), that, 'The contention that the payment of subsidies would involve the collection of taxes which in practice cannot be levied in a non-distortionary fashion is fallacious. A tax-cum-subsidy scheme could always be devised that would both eliminate the estimated divergence and collect taxes sufficient to pay the subsidies'. Yet, even Meade (1955, p. 186) admits that assumptions like those above are 'hopelessly unrealistic'. As Bhagwati would later confess, 'let it be admitted, revenue cannot in practice be raised by lump-sum taxes' (1968, p. 8, n. 7). But see n. 43 below.
42. With regard to such collection costs in the less-developed countries, Johnson (1965, pp. 7–8) dismisses the concern this way: 'This consideration [that poor countries have considerably greater difficulty in levying taxes to finance subsidies than they have in levying tariffs on imports] is of practical rather than theoretical consequence, and to constitute a case for tariffs requires supplementation by empirical measurement of both the relative administrative costs and the economic effects of the alternative methods of promoting favored industries'. With the onus of proof thus unilaterally assigned to those favouring the use of trade taxes, most subscribers to the theory could afford to ignore the collection costs of taxes and to neglect the administrative aspects of fiscal systems in general (Corden op. cit., p. 49).
43. In the chapter that leads to the cluster of chapters mentioned in n. 47 below, one titled 'Distortions: departures from free-trade optimality', the authors thus declare: 'We will use Samuelsonian social-indifference curves, so we will not consider income-distributional questions directly. Nor will we consider questions of second-best analysis which arise from not being able to utilize lump-sum transfers (questions that arise because otherwise the collection of revenue to pay for subsidies itself can create a distortionary loss). Nor will we consider the direct costs of raising revenues and disbursing them' (Bhagwati, Panagariya and Srinivasan 1998, p. 286).
44. There is at least one other quite consequential assumption that Corden was aware of that could be added to the four that he discussed. Thus, as he noted, the revenue role of trade taxes is typically ignored by the subscribers to the theory of domestic divergences (1984, p. 97). In his *Trade Policy and Economic Welfare* he acknowledges in one instance that the revenue raised from 'taxes' (with no distinction made by him in that context between different kinds) might be used 'to finance public goods, to finance subsidies to correct domestic divergences, to finance social services, or to finance capital accumulation' (1997, p. 46). Yet, in setting out the basic framework of the theory, he also states that '[v]arious

effects connected with the use of customs revenue will be ignored' (ibid., p. 10). On his part, Meade (1955, p. 158) admits that in analysing the economic effects of an import duty it is essential to take into account the effects of the use by the taxing authority of the revenue collected by means of the duty, and that the neglect of this side of the question is 'a frequent source of muddle and error'. He immediately adds, however, that for the discussion in his *Trade and Welfare*, 'we shall be primarily interested in the use of import duties as protective devices, that is to say, as instruments designed to reduce the demand for certain foreign products in favour of certain home-produced products. In order to isolate, as far as possible, these aspects of import duties we shall neglect the ... possible uses of the revenue from import duties [to add to the taxing government's budget surplus, or to use the revenue to increase its own consumption of goods and services]' (ibid., p. 161). He consequently restricts the use of the revenue to reducing other forms of taxation and, in particular, a general income tax (ibid.).

45. Bliss (1989, p. 1216) admits that the theory hinges on 'optimistic assumptions concerning the fiscal instruments available' to various governments. See also Anand and Joshi (1979) for aptly reminding that the need for revenue to fund subsidies can be subject to underestimation.
46. This is the Theory of Second Best in mainstream economics. The classic discussion is, of course, Lipsey and Lancaster (1956–57). For a concise explanation, see Corden (1965, pp. 46–9).
47. For an excellent example of such compartmentalisation, done largely on a chapter-by-chapter basis, see Bhagwati, Panagariya and Srinivasan (1998, Chs. 21–30).
48. The compartmentalisation is largely inserted so as to avoid complications that arise from second-best considerations. Thus, if more than one market failure exists, then the otherwise clean and precise policy ranking obtained when such failures are considered one separately from the other may no longer obtain. Recall the medical treatment analogy considered in n. 23 of Ch. 1 above.
49. Myint (1963, p. 175) critically observes that 'in tearing the protectionist argument from its original context and applying it to minor deviations from the static optimum on the basis of a very narrow concept of "infant industry", the orthodox economists have, not surprisingly, reduced it to the status of a theoretical curiosity; and that it is only when the protectionist argument is reconsidered in its proper setting of the present-day under-developed countries that it can be restored to its full stature having important applications to the broader structural and dynamic problems of the economic development of these countries'. Díaz-Alejandro (1975, p. 97) similarly laments that 'different assumptions regarding the availability, effectiveness, and real costs of different policy instruments can yield a disconcerting variety of heterodox conclusions ... [A]ny bright graduate student, by choosing his assumptions regarding distortions and policy instruments carefully, can produce a consistent model yielding just about any policy recommendation he favored at the start'. 'Algebra and consistent models', he cautions, 'can prove nothing about the real world, but perhaps the major contribution of these models, and of those sure to follow them, is to force a discussion of the realism of assumptions that are crucial to theoretical demonstrations'.
50. See, for instance, Corden (1997, pp. 139–50).
51. See, for instance, Bhagwati, Panagariya and Srinivasan (1998, Ch. 22).
52. As Myint (1987, p. 114) succintly sums it up, the theory 'cuts the ground under all the arguments for tariff protection which purport to correct the misallocation of resources'.
53. See Corden (1997, Ch. 6).
54. Commenting on such regulations, Smith lamented that the 'liberty of the subject' was sacrificed to the 'futile interests of our merchants and manufacturers' (op. cit.). Ricardo did not seem to have expressed an opinion on the issue, although Bloomfield (1978, pp. 634–5) points out that according to Sraffa, shortly before his death Ricardo had promised his friend Joseph Hume that he would assist him in his proposed motion before the House of Commons, which motion was against the regulations restricting the export of machinery, the emigration of artisans, and the combination of workers.

55. Torrens was initially supportive of continuing those restrictions. This is the conclusion reached by Bloomfield (op. cit., p. 632) after examining an early (1826) statement by Torrens, in which he argued that the principle of free trade ought to be limited by the rule that each country should reserve to itself the sole benefit of those exclusive advantages that it happened to enjoy. But Torrens later conceded that, 'A rigid enforcement of laws against the exportation of machinery might possibly retard, but could not ultimately prevent the inevitable result. If the exportation of our machines could be prevented, the makers of our machines would be induced to emigrate; and in the long run, we should lose the advantage of manufacturing superior machines for the foreign market, without being able to secure their exclusive application' ([1844] 1970, p. 236). Hence, his position appeared to have softened over time. Mill did not find the restrictions on the exportation of machinery to be justifiable, 'either on the score of international morality or of sound policy'. But he also suggested that it might be 'a proper subject for adjustment with other nations, on the principle of reciprocity' ([1874] 1974, pp. 31–2).
56. This is quoted in Elmslie (1994, pp. 263–4).
57. This was written prior to the following passage in his *Principles*: 'But the economical advantages of commerce are surpassed in importance by those of its effects which are intellectual and moral. It is hardly possible to overrate the value, in the present low state of human improvement, of placing human beings in contact with persons dissimilar to themselves, and with modes of thought and action unlike those with which they are familiar. Commerce is now what war once was, the principal source of this contact. Commercial adventurers from more advanced countries have generally been the first civilizers of barbarians. And commerce is the purpose of the far greater part of the communication which takes place between civilized nations. Such communication has always been, and is peculiarly in the present age, one of the primary sources of progress' (Mill [1871] 1965, p. 594).

7. Hamilton: Promoting Development of America through a Multitude of Policy Instruments

7.1 INTRODUCTION

With the history of the formulation of the mainstream theory of commercial policy portrayed in the previous chapter, the time has arrived for a meticulous re-examination of the works of the so-called 'protectionists'. Were they, as the history of that mainstream theory has represented, simple-minded protectionists who supported solely the use of protective duties to promote infant industries? If not, what exactly did they advocate?

This chapter re-examines the developmental ideas of Hamilton.[1] As is well known, his lineage in the evolution of the infant-industry argument for protection in accordance with the mainstream version of the history has been claimed. Thus, Bastable noted that Hamilton's answer to those who maintained that manufactures would arise 'under the normal action of individual interest' was by 'anticipating the "infant industry" argument familiar to readers of J. S. Mill's *Political Economy*' (1912, pp. 120–21). Separately, Haberler concluded that, 'The infant-industry argument for tariffs was clearly formulated as early as 1790 by Alexander Hamilton in his Report on Manufactures' (1937, p. 278). To this Robbins added that 'he made out a very powerful case [for protection of industry], a case which was accepted by John Stuart Mill' (1998, p. 240). Similarly, but perhaps attracting greater attention, Baldwin (1969) affirms that lineage in his oft-cited article in the literature of trade and development, 'The case against infant-industry tariff protection'. In his words,

> The essential point stressed by infant-industry proponents since Hamilton (1791) and List (1856) first wrote on the subject is that production costs for newly established industries within a country are likely to be initially higher than for well-established foreign producers of the same line, who have greater experience and higher skill levels. However, over a period of time new producers become 'educated [up] to the level of those with whom the processes are traditional' … and their cost curves decline. (Ibid., p. 296)

The portion of the last sentence in quotation marks is, of course, from Mill's oft-quoted endorsement of the infant-industry argument as dissected in the last chapter.[2]

With the lineage thus claimed, the next step in completing the mainstream story is to label Hamilton as a proponent of solely *tariff* protection. As Haberler put it, Hamilton was asserting the possibility 'that a *tariff* may help an industry to survive the weaknesses of infancy' (1937, p. 281, italics added). The attribution made by Baldwin (1969) is perhaps more consequential, again because of how widely referenced that article has been. Thus, '[t]he infant industry argument states that during the temporary period when domestic costs in an industry are above the product's import price, a *tariff* is a socially desirable method of financing the investment in human resources needed to compete with foreign producers' (ibid., p. 297, italics added).

In what ways are these claims doing justice to Hamilton and in what ways has he been distorted and misrepresented? The rest of this chapter is organised as follows. Section 7.2 discusses the disadvantages he regarded to be experienced by a country that was predominantly agricultural while it also brings out what he considered to be the advantages of diversifying into manufactures. Section 7.3 examines the key reasons why he was sceptical of the benefits of free trade for America. Some policy instruments that he considered for engendering diversification into manufactures, of which protective duties were not even his preferred choice, are enumerated in section 7.4. The final section, 7.5, sums up the discussion in this chapter.

7.2 REMAINING PREDOMINANTLY AGRICULTURAL VERSUS DIVERSIFYING INTO MANUFACTURES

When it comes to agricultural products Hamilton understood the specific nature of the demand for them and was aware of the various 'artificial impediments' imposed by foreign nations on the exportation of such from America during his time. His consideration of the nature of demand and the implications for balance of trade to some extent anticipates what would one-and-a-half centuries later be amplified by Prebisch and Singer (see Chapters 10 and 12 below).

Thus, '[i]ndependently ... of the artificial impediments ..., there are natural causes tending to render the external demand for the surplus of agricultural nations a precarious reliance'. This is because annual fluctuations in foreign harvests would be translated into wild fluctuations in their demand for American supplies. Given this 'great inequalities resulting from difference of seasons', the 'uniformity of demand on one side, and unsteadiness of it, on the other, must necessarily have a tendency to cause the general course of the exchange of commodities between the parties, to turn to the disadvantage of the merely agricultural States' (Hamilton [1791b] 1966, pp. 258, 288). Another consideration concerns the risk of putting all eggs in one basket for a predominantly agricultural country. Thus, 'stagnations of demand for certain commodities' had been experienced that 'interfere[d] more or less with the sale of all'. In that event,

> [t]he Nation which can bring to Market, but few articles is likely to be more quickly and sensibly affected by such stagnations, than one, which is always possessed of a great variety of commodities. The former frequently finds too great a proportion of its stock of materials, for sale or exchange, lying on hand – or is obliged to make injurious sacrifices to supply its wants of foreign articles, which are Numerous and urgent, in proportion to the smallness of the number of its own. (Ibid., pp. 288–9)[3]

Hamilton believed that this kind of 'difference of situations' could have 'immensely different effects upon the wealth and prosperity of Nations' (ibid.).[4] Interestingly and significantly, it is in this part of his *Report* that he also claims that 'there is always a higher probability of a favorable balance of Trade, in regard to countries in which manufactures founded on the basis of a thriving Agriculture[,] flourish, than in regard to those, which are confined wholly or almost wholly to Agriculture' (ibid., p. 289).[5] This rhymes with Prebisch's concern with the 'persistent tendency towards external imbalance' on the part of many primary exporting countries.

The want of a secure and stable demand for domestic agricultural products, and the desire to reduce risks associated with over-reliance on such, translate into one of the several reasons why Hamilton ardently supported the encouragement of manufactures in the United States (ibid., pp. 257–60). Not only would this support, he emphasised, not weaken the agricultural sector, it would be conducive to a flourishing state of it. This is because, 'by their tendency to procure a more certain demand for the surplus produce of the soil, they [manufactories] would, at the same time, cause the lands which were in cultivation to be better improved and more productive'. It is for this consideration that the establishment of manufactures 'is calculated not only to increase the general stock of useful and productive labour; but even to improve the state of Agriculture in particular' (ibid., pp. 259, 261).[6]

More generally, Hamilton believed that the founding and locating of manufactures in America would much more powerfully invigorate various linkage effects between the manufacturing and primary producing (including the agricultural and fishery) sectors. Thus, 'it is known that the oils, bones and skins of marine animals, are of extensive use in various manufactures.

Hence the prospect of an additional demand for the produce of the Fisheries' (ibid., p. 292).[7] In such a manner he further identified a lengthy list of other primary products – timber, flax, hemp, cotton, wool, raw silk, indigo, iron, lead, furs, hides, skins, and coals – the production of which could likewise be stimulated and supported (ibid., p. 294).[8]

A depiction of the rich linkages between various branches of primary production on the one hand and the multifarious branches of manufactures on the other presents an opportunity for one to consider the economies of division of labour. Indeed, Hamilton observed that 'the mere separation of the occupation of the cultivator, from that of the Artificer, has the effect of augmenting the productive powers of labour, and with them, the total mass of the produce or revenue of a Country' (ibid., p. 251). This observation was made as he enumerated several 'principal circumstances' to explain why 'manufacturing establishments not only occasion a possitive augmentation of the Produce and Revenue of the Society, but … they contribute essentially to rendering them greater than they could possibly be, without such establishments' (ibid., p. 249)[9] and the first circumstance that he listed was division of labour.[10]

As Bourne (1894, pp. 338–40) points out, and as is obvious to those who are familiar with Bk. I, Ch. I of the *Wealth of Nations*, Hamilton's consideration of this is simply a repetition of Smith.[11] In particular, he repeated the three reasons put forward by the latter why a great increase of the quantity of work could be performed through such division, namely the 'greater skill and dexterity naturally resulting from a constant and undivided application to a single object', the 'economy of time', and an 'extension of the use of machinery' ([1791b] 1966, pp. 249–51).

Of these, he treated the last as a separate circumstance exerting a significant influence on the total mass of industrious effort in a society. To Smith, '[t]he nature of agriculture … does not admit of so many subdivisions of labour, nor of so complete a separation of one business from another, as manufactures … [and so] the improvement of the productive powers of labour in this art, does not always keep pace with their improvement in manufactures' ([1776] 1979, p. 16). To Hamilton, who paraphrased Smith (ibid., p. 676), '"the labour of Artificers being capable of greater subdivision and simplicity of operation, than that of Cultivators, it is susceptible, in a proportionably greater degree, of improvement in its productive powers, … from an accession of Skill, or from the application of ingenious machinery"' ([1791b] 1966, p. 239). Hence, '[i]t shall be taken for granted … that manufacturing pursuits are susceptible in a greater degree of the application of machinery, than those of Agriculture'. That also means if instead of establishing manufactures domestically a country were to import from others, it would 'transfer to foreign nations … the advantages accruing from the employment of Machinery, in the modes in which it is capable of being employed, with most utility and to the greatest extent' (ibid., pp. 251–2).

Having borrowed that much from Smith, Hamilton was, however, to stop short of expanding the possible scope of the economies by not mentioning that the division of labour is limited by the extent of the market.[12] Nevertheless, there were two other circumstances out of the seven that he listed that could perhaps be generously interpreted as vague hints of some sort of external economies arising from economic diversification and differentiation. One is his belief that the results of human exertion may be 'immensely increased by diversifying its objects'. With the creation of all kinds of industries in an economy, 'each individual can find his proper element, and can call into activity the whole vigour of his nature. And the community is benefitted by the services of its respective members, in the manner, in which each can serve it with most effect' (ibid., p. 255).[13] The other concerns how diversifying into manufactures would afford 'a more ample and various field for enterprise'. He then stated the benefits as follow:

> To cherish and stimulate the activity of the human mind, by multiplying the objects of enterprise, is not among the least considerable of the expedients, by which the wealth of a nation may be promoted. ... Every new scene, which is opened to the busy nature of man to rouse and exert itself, is the addition of a new energy to the general stock of effort.
>
> The spirit of enterprise ... must necessarily be contracted or expanded in proportion to the simplicity or variety of the occupations and productions, which are to be found in a Society. It must be less in a nation of mere cultivators, than in a nation of cultivators and merchants; less in a nation of cultivators and merchants, than in a nation of cultivators, artificers and merchants. (Ibid., p. 256)[14]

Significantly, these passages are quoted in full by Rae ([1834] 1964, pp. 365–6) when he articulates the insightful point that '[a]rts, ... when brought together pass into one another, and thus also improvements in old arts are produced, or new arts generated. Even their very existence in any society gives a powerful stimulus to the ingenuity of its members' (ibid., p. 365). This, and related observations, were noted in section 6.4 above and they serve as powerful reminders that the benefit accruing to infant-industry promotion is, for Hamilton (and for Rae), far more than a reduction in the cost of producing the product concerned. Indeed, at one point he indicated that whatever 'temporary expence' has to be incurred in promoting manufactures would be 'more than compensated, by an increase of industry and Wealth, by an augmentation of resources and independence; & by the circumstance of eventual cheapness' ([1791b] 1966, p. 302).

Some may belittle all these discussions of the 'principal circumstances' why encouraging domestic manufactures would exert a significant influence on the total mass of industrious effort in a society by charging that they are too vague and general, and has not moved much beyond Smith's consideration of the benefits of an extended division of labour. Nevertheless, it should be remembered that Hamilton's *Report* was published only 15 years after the appearance of the *Wealth of Nations*. Well into the nineteenth century not even someone like Mill was able to take the consideration contained in the first few chapters in that classic much further. With respect to these circumstances, Hamilton concluded that '[e]ach ... has a considerable influence upon the total mass of industrious effort in a community. *Together, they add to it a degree of energy and effect, which are not easily conceived*' (ibid., p. 249, italics added). Writing at the time and in the context that he did, there is no need for any apology for the lack of definiteness in this observation.

7.3 SCEPTICISM TOWARD FREE TRADE

For obvious reasons, of the four classical economists re-examined in detail in Part I of this book, Hamilton could only refer to the works of one of them. That was Smith, and not surprisingly, it was his *Wealth of Nations* that Hamilton had studied. It is thus safe to assume that when he alluded to the 'respectable patrons of opinions, unfriendly to the encouragement of manufactures' ([1791b] 1966, p. 231), one such patron was Smith.[15]

Although Hamilton made no reference to the beneficial specialisation and trade among the 'taylor', 'shoemaker', and 'farmer' portrayed by Smith ([1776] 1979, p. 456), he showed a grasp of the static argument of the benefits of trade by claiming that,

> In such a state of things [where perfect liberty to industry and commerce were the prevailing system of nations], each country would have the full benefit of its peculiar advantages to compensate for its deficiencies or disadvantages. If one nation were in condition to supply manufactured articles on better terms than another, that other might find an abundant indemnification in a superior capacity to furnish the produce of the soil. And a free exchange, mutually beneficial, of the commodities which each was able to supply, on the best terms, might be carried on between them, supporting in full vigour the industry of each. ([1791b] 1966, p. 262)[16]

He even granted that *if* such a state of things were in existence, 'the arguments which dissuade a country in the predicament of the United States, from the zealous pursuit of manufactures would doubtless have great force' (ibid.). Such great force, alas, was not powerful enough to change his position.[17] Besides, he was to point out that a system of perfect liberty of industry and commerce simply did not exist during his time. These are explained, respectively, in the remainder of this section.

Structural Changes not Spontaneous

Chapter 6 above alludes to the fact that Smith's argument for free trade dovetails with his rejection of attempts to artificially bring about or support manufactures in otherwise agricultural nations and he was clearly one of the 'patrons' who had an opinion that was unfriendly to the encouragement of manufactures.[18] Hamilton's representation of this opinion in his *Report* thus reads, '"it can hardly ever be wise in a government, to attempt to give a direction to the industry of its citizens"', for it entails a '"misdirection of labour"'. On the other hand, '"under the quicksighted guidance of private interest, ... if left to itself, [the industry of its citizens would] infallibly find its own way to the most profitable employment ... To leave industry to itself ... is ... the soundest as well as the simplest policy"' ([1791b] 1966, p. 232). Then more than 30 pages later, he returns to this theme and makes reference, even if an implicit one, to Smith's faith in the spontaneity of structural changes (see section 6.2 above). Thus, 'Industry, if left to itself, will naturally find its way to the most useful and profitable employment: whence it is inferred, that manufactures, without the aid of government will grow up as soon and as fast, as the natural state of things and the interest of the community may require' (ibid., p. 266). However, as Hamilton would contend, '[a]gainst the solidity of this hypothesis, in the full latitude of the terms, very cogent reasons may be offered' to suggest why structural changes – in the form of new branches of manufacture – would simply not take place spontaneously (ibid.).

Firstly, any 'spontaneous transition to new pursuits, in a community long habituated to different ones', may be attended with great difficulty because

> [e]xperience teaches, that men are often so much governed by what they are accustomed to see and practice, that the simplest and most obvious improvements, in the most ordinary occupations, are adopted with hesitation, reluctance and by slow gradations. ... When former occupations ceased to yield a profit adequate to the subsistence of their followers, or when there was an absolute deficiency of employment in them, owing to the superabundance of hands, changes would ensue; but these changes would be likely to be more tardy than might consist with the interest either of individuals or of the Society. In many cases they would not happen, while a bare support could be ensured by an adherence to ancient courses; though a resort to a more profitable employment might be practicable. (Ibid., pp. 266–7)

The incitement by, and patronage of, the government may consequently be needed to hasten the desirable changes.

Secondly, and as a 'more serious impediment', there is the 'apprehension of failing in new attempts'. Here Hamilton argued it was important that 'the confidence of cautious sagacious capitalists[,] both citizens and foreigners, should be excited'. Specifically, a strong signal should be sent to those considering the undertaking of 'new' and 'precarious' projects that there is 'the prospect of such a degree of countenance and support from government, as may be capable of overcoming the obstacles, inseparable from first experiments' (ibid., p. 267).

Thirdly, an even 'more formidable obstacle' existed in the form of the 'superiority antecedently enjoyed by nations, who have preoccupied and perfected a branch of industry' over a country which had just introduced that same branch. 'To maintain [in such a situation] … a competition upon equal terms, both as to quality and price, is in most cases impracticable [because] [t]he disparity in the one, or in the other, or in both, must necessarily be so considerable as to forbid a successful rivalship'. Again, Hamilton insisted that 'the extraordinary aid and protection of government' would be indispensable (ibid., p. 268).

Note was taken in Chapter 6 that there is no sign that Mill had read Hamilton's *Report*. Nevertheless, the first two of these three aforementioned reasons can arguably be related to the part of Mill's endorsement statement where he proclaims 'it cannot be expected that individuals should, at their own risk, or rather to their certain loss, introduce a new manufacture' ([1871] 1965, p. 919). As for the third reason, although it is not clear in this context that the superiority enjoyed by one would over time be eroded when the other acquired the pertinent skills and experience (in which case the 'aid and protection' would no longer be necessary), elsewhere Hamilton did imply that that was what he believed would happen. Thus, '[w]hen a domestic manufacture has attained to perfection, and has engaged in the prosecution of it a competent number of Persons, it invariably becomes cheaper'. Hence, '[i]n a national view, a temporary enhancement of price must always be well compensated by a permanent reduction of it' ([1791b] 1966, p. 286). Later in the *Report* he also argued that 'it is the Interest of the society … to submit to a *temporary* expence' incurred in the aid and protection, resulting, among other benefits, in 'eventual cheapness' (ibid., p. 302, italics added). Taking these together with the third reason, it seems to resonate with the observation in Mill's endorsement that '[t]he superiority of one country over another in a branch of production, often … only [represents] a present superiority of acquired skill and experience' ([1871] 1965, p. 918). Indeed, if one focuses only on these three reasons, it seems not unreasonable to claim that, despite not appearing to have read Hamilton, Mill's infant-industry-protection endorsement passage could have been partly inspired by the former's *Report*.[19] But Hamilton had more to offer.

Free Trade was not Practised by Other Countries

In addition to the three reasons mentioned already, Hamilton named a fourth one to explain why it would be difficult for structural changes to occur spontaneously. Deeming this 'the greatest obstacle of all', he lamented the fact that 'bounties[,] premiums[,] and other aids' were granted by the nations that had already established the branch of industry but which the United States was just freshly introducing. As a result, 'the undertakers of a new manufacture have to contend not only with the natural disadvantages of a new undertaking, but with the gratuities and remunerations which other governments bestow'. It is evident, Hamilton concluded, that the interference and aid by the American government was essential ([1791b] 1966, p. 268). As he elaborated,

> The existence or assurance of aid from the government of the country, in which the business is to be introduced, may be essential to fortify adventurers against the dread of such combinations [by those engaged in a particular branch of business in one country, to frustrate the first efforts to introduce it into another], to defeat their effects, if formed and to prevent their being formed, by demonstrating that they must in the end prove fruitless. (Ibid., p. 269)

This last part even smacks of a 'strategic trade policy' consideration.

This fourth reason also serves as a reminder that the system of 'perfect liberty to industry and commerce' is 'far from characterising the general policy of Nations' (ibid., p. 262). As illustrated at the beginning of this section, he had granted that the existence of universal free trade might weaken, though by no means refute, the arguments for encouraging manufactures. But when it actually did not exist, he felt emboldened to make his case.

And not only were foreign governments supporting and encouraging their manufactures, they were also discouraging the importation of American agricultural products through the 'artificial impediments' mentioned in passing at the beginning of section 7.2 above. The net result was that 'the United States ... can indeed, without difficulty obtain from abroad the manufactured supplies, of which they are in want; but they experience numerous and very injurious impediments to the emission and vent of their own commodities'. The danger, as Hamilton perceived it, was that '[a] constant and encreasing necessity, on their part, for the commodities of Europe, and only a partial and occasional demand for their own, in return, could not but expose them to a state of impoverishment' (ibid., p. 263).[20] This hardened his belief that the USA should not remain a predominantly agricultural nation and should diversify into manufactures. But if that diversification were not to take place spontaneously, what policy actions should be taken to engender it?

7.4 A MIXTURE OF BOUNTIES, TARIFFS AND OTHER INSTRUMENTS IN THE POLICY PROPOSAL

While sections 7.2 and 7.3 illustrate that Hamilton's case for promoting manufactures rests on rationales that are broader than that portrayed in the standard textbook (Mill's) version of the infant-industry argument, this section shows that his policy-instrument proposal is much more sophisticated than the common misrepresentation in the trade literature, namely that he was solely relying on protective duties.

In the latter half of his *Report*, Hamilton devotes a substantial amount of space to a consideration of the relative merits and demerits of a total of 11 different policy instruments or actions (ibid., pp. 296–311). These are what he characterises as the 'principal' ones 'which have been employed with success in other Countries'. Space limitation does not allow reproducing all of them here. The following subsection reports on his comparison that is of greater interest to the present discussion, and that is between 'protecting duties' and 'bounties' (subsidies). The subsection after that focuses attention on his desire to acquire the advanced technologies of his time that would allow the USA to narrow its technological gap with England as well as to partly solve the problem of 'scarcity of hands'. This he sought to accomplish through various means to encourage 'new inventions and discoveries' and the 'introduction into the Untied States of such'.[21]

Bounties versus Tariffs[22]

Although he reminded the reader that bounties had not yet been offered by the American government, Hamilton proclaimed that '[t]his has been found one of the most efficacious means of encouraging manufactures, and it is in some views, the best' (ibid., p. 298). He said so for four reasons. First, '[i]t is a species of encouragement more positive and direct than any other, and for that very reason, has a more immediate tendency to stimulate and uphold new enterprises', increasing the chances of making profits for otherwise risky 'first attempts' (ibid., p. 299). On this count 'protecting duties' as a species of encouragement 'evidently amount to a virtual bounty on the domestic fabrics since[,] by enhancing the charges on foreign Articles, they enable the National Manufacturers to undersell all their foreign Competitors' (ibid., p. 296). However, and that brings up the second reason for favouring a bounty, '[i]t [a bounty] avoids the inconvenience of a temporary augmentation of price ... or it produces it to a less degree; either by making no addition to the charges on the rival foreign article, as in the Case of protecting duties, or by making a smaller addition'.[23] Here Hamilton showed that he was not skirting the issue of having to raise funds for the bounty. The final result on prices would depend on which 'objects' were taxed and on the nature of those objects (ibid., p. 299).[24] Third, '[b]ounties have not[,] like high protecting duties, a tendency to produce scarcity' (ibid.). Lastly, and this is just a part of what he had put down as the fourth reason,[25] while an import duty levied on a certain article could 'aid the domestic production of it, ... [i]t can have no influence upon the advantageous sale of the article produced, in foreign markets; no tendency, therefore[,] to promote its exportation' (ibid., p. 300). By implication, a bounty, if properly deployed, could promote exports.

The possible disadvantages of, and limitations in, using bounties did not escape Hamilton's attention. 'It is a familiar objection to them', he pointed out, 'that they are difficult to be managed and liable to frauds', although he quickly added that 'neither that difficulty nor this danger seems sufficiently great to countervail the advantages of which they are productive, when rightly applied'.[26] He recommended that it would be 'necessary to guard, with extraordinary circumspection, the manner of dispensing them' ([1791b] 1966, p. 336). Hamilton then indicated that he had thought of the 'requisite precautions', but limited by the scope of the *Report*, would not go into the details. Nevertheless, he proposed that

> any bounty, which may be applied to the manufacture of an article, cannot with safety extend beyond those manufactories, at which the making of the article is a regular trade.
> It would be impossible to annex adequate precautions to a benefit of that nature, if extended to every private family, in which the manufacture was incidentally carried on, and its being a merely incidental occupation which engages a portion of time that would otherwise be lost, it can be advantageously carried on, without so special an aid. (Ibid., p. 337)

This relates to a consideration against bounty that Corden identified as the disbursement costs of subsidies (1997, pp. 37–9).

In considering protecting duties Hamilton noted their 'recommendation of being a resource of revenue' ([1791b] 1966, pp. 296–7). This consideration further led him to distinguish between 'protecting duties' and 'prohibitions ... or duties equivalent to prohibitions'. While noting the latter could be 'an efficacious mean[s] of encouraging national manufactures', he cautioned that they would 'only fit to be employed when a manufacture, has made such a progress and is in so many hands as to insure a due competition, and an adequate supply on reasonable terms' (ibid., p. 297). The former, while of relatively moderate nominal levels, could nevertheless afford some useful protection. In a passage that Coxe penned in his draft of the *Report*, he observes that 'the duties already imposed by the legislature, tho principally for the purposes of Revenue, afford very considerable and certain advantages to the American manufacturer'. '[I]t may be very doubtful', he adds, 'whether general addition to these duties be necessary further to encourage the manufactures of the United States', though he suggests that 'it is humbly conceived a few articles may be very properly aided by a moderate encrease' ([1790] 1979, p. 637). Although this passage was not incorporated into the final version of the *Report*, Hamilton brought up the consideration of the 'expense of transportation', including 'insurance and other incidental charges'. These constitute 'a sum of extra charge on the foreign fabric, which cannot be estimated, at less than from 15 to 30 per Cent. on the cost of it at the manufactory' ([1791b] 1966, p. 273).[27] All noted, moderate duties could be quite potent in his time in affording encouragements to manufactures.[28]

But perhaps more dominating in Hamilton's consideration was the fact that prohibitive duties could not generate revenues.[29] In that connection '[t]he possibility of a diminution of the revenue may also present itself as an objection to the arrangements, which have been submitted [for employing bounties]' (ibid., p. 337). Indeed, one should not ignore the dire need of funding the public debt at that time. Hence, '[i]n Hamilton's opinion … the industrial policy should be carried out in concert with the policy of public credit' (Tajima 1985, p. 146)[30] and the *Report* 'cannot be divorced from Hamilton's view of public credit and banking' (Syrett and Cooke 1966, p. 3).

While one thus detects a 'practical compromise' (Irwin 1996, p. 122) in the *Report*, one can also sense a certain amount of optimism on Hamilton's part that his industrial policies would not worsen the debt situation. For if, as he believed, the bounties succeeded in promoting an increase of national industry and wealth, then the 'capacity … to contribute to the public Treasury' would also be augmented. 'The measures …, taken aggregately', he thus optimistically predicted, 'will, for a long time to come rather augment than decrease the public revenue' ([1791b] 1966, p. 337).

In fact, if one specifically focuses on the aspect of Hamilton's programme that relates to protecting duties, one notices that it involves the 'abolition in some instances, and a reduction in others' on the one hand, and the imposition of 'additional duties' on the other.[31] The appropriation of revenues from the latter would, according to him, not only be sufficient 'to replace all defalcations, which may proceed from any such abolition or diminution …, but will yield a considerable surplus' (ibid.). He proposed that a part of this surplus be set aside for 'paying the bounties',[32] while the use of the other part will be considered in the following subsection.

Aside from the above public finance considerations, Hamilton on many occasions paired bounties and tariffs for one other reason. Earlier in this subsection when the four reasons that he gave for preferring bounties over tariffs were mentioned, only a part of the fourth reason was reproduced. The reasoning behind the remaining part actually surfaces several times throughout the *Report*. Specifically, he contended that '[b]ounties are sometimes not only the best, but the only proper expedient, for uniting the encouragement of a new object of agriculture, with that of a new object of manufacture' (ibid., p. 300). He had thus in mind situations where the production of a manufactured product and the principal raw material(s) that it used would both have to be promoted to rival with competing imports. Should protective duties be applied to both the manufactured and raw products? Hamilton recognised that '[i]t is the interest of the manufacturer to have the material abundant and cheap'. Hence,

> [i]f prior to the domestic production of the Material, in sufficient quantity, to supply the manufacturer on good terms; a duty be laid upon the importation of it from abroad, with a view to promote the raising of it at home, the Interests both of the Farmer and Manufacturer will be disserved. By either destroying the requisite supply, or raising the price of the article, beyond what can be afforded to be given for it, by the Conductor of an infant manufacture, it is abandoned or fails; and there being no domestic manufactories to create a demand for the raw material, which is raised by the farmer, it is in vain, that the Competition of the like foreign article may have been destroyed. (Ibid.)

What he proposed, instead, was to impose a protective duty on the imports that compete with the manufactured article, the revenue derived from which would pay for a bounty for either encouraging the domestic production of the raw material and/or the manufactured article itself (where the bounty to the manufacturer could be conditioned upon the use of domestically produced raw materials) (ibid.).[33]

In the last part of his *Report* where Hamilton considered how 16 objects could be promoted, he specifically pointed out that the duty on the foreign grown cotton was 'undoubtedly a very serious impediment to the progress of those manufactories [that use it]'. He argued that a repeal of the then levied duty on imported cotton is 'indispensable' and it would be better to substitute that by a bounty on the domestically grown cotton 'when wrought at a home manufactory' (ibid., pp. 328–9). Similar considerations were extended to flax and hemp (ibid., pp. 325–6, but recall n. 31 above). In general, he very much favoured encouraging the augmentation in the supplies of various raw materials through the use of bounties and/or premiums where the USA had the capacity to furnish them. That by itself, he seemed to believe, should provide a very powerful inducement for forward linkages to materialise.

Where they did not, then encouragements in the form of protective duties were usually proposed.

Hamilton preoccupied himself with relatively simple processing of raw materials into some sort of manufactured articles. That reflects the relatively primitive state of manufacturing activities of his time. Considerations that involve further phases in the processing are few and far between, one example being the printing and staining of cottons and linens in their white state. The latter 'partakes of the Nature of a raw material' and though a protective duty would be proper to promote their domestic manufacture, '[a] drawback of that duty is proper to encourage the printing and staining at home of those which are brought from abroad'.[34] And when cottons and linens in their white state have attained sufficient maturity in a country to furnish a full supply for the printing and staining industry, 'the utility of the drawback ceases' (ibid., pp. 306, 307).

Technology Acquisitions: Inventions, Discoveries, and Piracy

While assistance and protection can thus be afforded to manufacturers through bounties and protecting duties, the activities thence encouraged would, in Hamilton's opinion, still be handicapped by America's relative technological backwardness and their expansion be hindered by the problem of 'scarcity of hands', especially the skilled ones. His strong desire to acquire the superior technologies of his time as well as to partly alleviate the labour-shortage problem can be inferred from some of the other nine policy instruments that he had enumerated in the *Report* for the promotion of manufactures.[35]

Thus, in discussing the 'encouragement of new inventions and discoveries, at home, and of the introduction into the United States of such as may have been made in other countries; particularly those, which relate to machinery', Hamilton regarded it to be 'among the most useful and unexceptionable of the aids, which can be given to manufactures' (ibid., p. 308). The usual means involved 'pecuniary rewards' and perhaps 'exclusive privileges'. Regarding the latter he noted that some provisions had already been made by law for 'authors and inventors'. However, that was not adequate. He added that 'it is desireable in regard to improvements and secrets of extraordinary value, to be able to extend the same benefit to Introducers, as well as Authors and Inventors; a policy which has been practiced with advantage in other countries' (ibid.).[36]

In the previous subsection it was indicated that a part of the surplus in tariff revenue that Hamilton optimistically predicted to arise would, according to his plan, be set aside for funding bounties. The other part of it would 'constitute a fund for the operations of a Board, to be established, for promoting Arts, Agriculture, Manufactures and Commerce' (ibid., p. 338). This board would be managed by commissioners, who would be empowered to

> apply the fund confided to them – to defray the expenses of the emigration of Artists, and Manufacturers in particular branches of extraordinary importance – to induce the prosecution and introduction of useful discoveries, inventions and improvements, by proportionate rewards, judiciously held out and applied – to encourage by premiums both honorable and lucrative[,] the exertions of individuals, And of classes, in relation to the several objects, they are charged with promoting – and to afford such other aids to those objects, as may be generally designated by law. (Ibid., p. 338)

In some respects these goals resemble those that he enumerated when he considered what the dispensation of premiums might accomplish. Thus, premiums, which 'are of Nature allied to bounties', could 'serve to reward some particular excellence or superiority, some extraordinary exertion or skill, and are dispensed only in a small number of cases'. Designed to be 'both honorary and lucrative, they address themselves to different passions; touching the chords as well of emulation as of Interest'. Indeed, they could be 'a very economical mean[s] of exciting the enterprise of a Whole Community' (ibid., p. 304).[37] At the end of the *Report* Hamilton specifically singles out the Pennsylvania Society for the Promotion of Manufactures and useful Arts, a society which dispensed premiums to such ends, as doing something 'truly invaluable'. Nevertheless, in view of the relatively limited private wealth in the United States at that time, he decided that 'voluntary contributions of patriotic individuals' to fund such societies must be limited and 'the public purse must supply the deficiency of private resource' (ibid., p. 340).

In gathering information as he prepared his *Report* Hamilton consulted manufacturers who had established factories (Hamilton [1928] 1968). Some of the more successful among them attributed their success to their ability to pirate British technology, primarily by enticing skilled British artisans to emigrate.[38] For those who sought to 'introduce' useful 'discoveries, inventions and improvements' made in other countries, Hamilton himself, or his department, had in some cases lent assistance or provided support. For instance, he enticed Thomas Marshall, a British master craftsman who supposedly had superintended some of Arkwright's mills, to emigrate, and later recruited him to supervise the SEUM (Parks [1963] 1977, p. 133; Shankman 2003, p. 334). He supported William Pearce's application for a patent in textile operation, even though he was aware that the latter was merely introducing to America techniques that were already under protection in England (Ben-Atar 1995, p. 404). The living expenses of George

Parkinson, an English weaver whom Coxe had contracted[39] to construct a mill that was based on his claim of knowledge of Arkwright's machine, were defrayed by Hamilton's Treasury Department. He later worked for the SEUM and was indeed granted a patent by the USA Patent Office for 'introducing' a version of Arkwright's flax-spinning machine that was only marginally improved over the original (ibid., p. 389). These were just some of the many instances in which that Department during Hamilton's years 'organized and supported raids on Britain's industry preeminence' (Cooke 1975, p. 381; Ben-Atar 1995, pp. 390–91). Thus, in practice, the encouragement of emigration of 'manufacturers' and 'artists' in 'branches of extraordinary importance' with the hope that they would 'introduce' useful 'discoveries, inventions and improvements' made in other countries had sometimes amounted to what Ben-Atar (1995) has dubbed 'technology piracy'.

While undermining other nations' effort to prohibit the export of implements and machines, Hamilton noted that there were 'already objects for a similar regulation in the United States; and others may be expected to occur, from time to time'.[40] While understanding that the adoption of such regulation could be dictated by the 'principle of reciprocity', he also realised that it could 'tend to increase the advantages of those by whom they [the improvements made at home] may have been introduced; and operate as an encouragement to exertion' ([1791b] 1966, pp. 308–9).

7.5 CONCLUDING REMARKS

Hamilton's penetrating discussion (by the standard of his time) of the advantages and disadvantages of using bounties to promote manufactures should correct, once and for all, the distortion and misrepresentation that he knew nothing better than the deployment of protective duties. In offering that, he could be argued to have anticipated some of the elements of what is known today as the 'principle of targetting'.

Alarmingly, it has taken the mainstream trade theorists more than two hundred years to come to this realisation, and even then, not among more than a handful of them. Thus, Irwin admits in his *Against the Tide: An Intellectual History of Free Trade* that Hamilton's study of policy instruments 'is quite insightful for this period' (1996, p. 122).[41] But that is all the credit that was belatedly given.[42] Compare that with all the praises that have been lavished upon Mill, all for merely mentioning the word 'subsidy' in several pieces of personal correspondence. Given how widespread the distortion and misrepresentation of Hamilton's ideas continue to be, it is obvious that that realisation has not yet been widely disseminated.

Nor did Hamilton believe that bounties and duties would be adequate even if both were deployed. Equally, if not more, important would be state-supported purposeful technological acquisition, including technology piracy.

No claim is made here that he had figured out the 'optimal' instrument to deploy to engender American development. Given the complexity of the 'underdevelopment' situation, which might be likened to a situation of multiple and perhaps (in some instances) interlocking market failures, and missing markets and institutions, it is meaningless to talk of *an* optimal policy instrument. Rather, the pragmatist[43] in him understood that it had to be a combination of instruments and actions, and he spelled out a number of considerations in packaging them into a programme.

These discussions and considerations have clearly shown that Hamilton was a much more sophisticated proponent for encouraging development than the mainstream label of a 'protectionist' would convey. Although there are a few points in his arguments where one could detect resemblance with Mill's endorsement passage for infant-industry protection, his framework is broader and richer. This especially relates to his vision of promoting development on a broad (but selective) front rather than a single industry. Critics might point out that while considering multiple branches of industries, he failed to portray the intricate inter-industry connections among them that were to develop later. In his defence, manufactures throughout the world were during his time still at their relatively early stage of development. Besides, he did exercise some insightful imagination when he suggested that circumstances like a more ample and various field for enterprise, greater division of labour, more extensive use of machinery, and others would add a degree of energy and effect to the total mass of industrious effort in a community ([1791b] 1966, pp. 249–61). It was left for other so-called 'protectionists' to further consider these economies. List made an attempt and it is to his works that the discussion turns.

NOTES

1. The ensuing discussion is principally based on a re-examination of Hamilton's *Report on the Subject of Manufactures* (hereafter abbreviated as *Report*), which he submitted to the USA Congress in December, 1791, in his capacity as the first Secretary of Treasury of the country. That document went through four drafts before the final version was submitted. The first draft is largely based upon what Tench Coxe, Assistant Secretary for Hamilton's Treasury Department, had himself drafted in 1790. Common themes of significance between Coxe's draft and Hamilton's final version will be pointed out in some endnotes below. Syrett and Cooke (1966, p. 12) observe that the final version of Hamilton's *Report* 'differs markedly in both emphasis and substance from Coxe's draft and from Coxe's other writings on manufactures'. However, when Coxe's manuscript collection subsequently became available, Cooke restudied the subject and came to a different conclusion. Specifically, Coxe 'was the one individual who most decisively influenced Hamilton's

Report on Manufactures', having 'made few proposals that did not wind up, although usually in different stylistic garb and occasionally in expanded form' therein (Cooke 1975, pp. 369, 376–7, see also p. 372, n. 9). He 'provided the inspiration for the SEUM [Society for Establishing Useful Manufactures] and played an important part in arrangements for its organization, incorporation, location, and operations'. In short, his role in the *Report* and SEUM was 'instrumental' (ibid., p. 369). Notwithstanding, 'Hamilton's unique accomplishment ... was to present the case for manufactures not only in practical but in theoretical terms. The written record contains no hint that Coxe, although a close student of European political economists, contributed to Hamilton's exposition of economic theory' (ibid., p. 375). On that last note Syrett and Cooke (1966, pp. 7–8) point out that the *Report* 'contains considerable evidence of Hamilton's reliance on those European writers from whom he had drawn material in some of his earlier papers and reports'. Other than Smith, these include Jacques Necker, Sir James Steuart, Malachy Postlethwayt, Emeric de Vattel, Charles de Secondat, baron de Montesquieu, and David Hume. They (Syrett and Cooke) provide useful suggestions of parallels between the *Report* and some of the works of these European thinkers. Reference is made to their edition of the *Report* (Hamilton [1791b] 1966), although the notations that they employ to distinguish between Hamilton's and others' handwritings will be omitted in the passages quoted.

2. Others who subscribe to this include, for instance, Little, Scitovsky and Scott (1970, p. 118), Johnson (1972c, p. 308), and Corden (1997, p. 139).
3. Compare with these statements: 'It is a position in commerce of indisputable "truth" that the greatest resort will ever be to those marts wherein the supplies while equally valuable are most various. Each difference of kind holds out their proper inducements to those who need or desire it' (Coxe [1790] 1979, p. 633).
4. Recall in n. 14 in Ch. 3 above that Smith appears to be admitting this in one instance in his *Wealth of Nations*.
5. 'The importations of manufactured supplies', Coxe believed, 'incessantly drains the merely agricultural people of their wealth'. '[N]or is there any instance of a country', he put it differently, 'which does not manufacture that can retain its Specie' ([1790] 1979, p. 634).
6. Cole ([1928] 1968, p. 237) associates this with the 'home market' plea for protection, 'which in the hands of Henry C. Carey and others came to have exceptional influence in American thought'. In that connection, it should be added that Hamilton was not oblivious to the burden of transportation costs incurred through foreign trade ([1791b] 1966, pp. 291–2), a burden which Carey was very anxious to lessen by advocating the promotion of domestic manufactures ([1858–59] 1873, Vol. I, Chs. VIII and XVI). As indicated in n. 12 in Ch. 3 above, the 'gains' from trade between the town and the country received not a small amount of attention in Smith's *Wealth of Nations*. This is a fact that did not escape the attention of Carey. These benefits are also considered in Mill's *Principles* ([1871] 1965, pp. 120–21).
7. This point, in particular the reference to fisheries, was raised in Coxe ([1790] 1979, p. 633).
8. See the discussion in the latter part of the subsection that is titled 'Bounties versus Tariffs' in section 7.4 below for more about his consideration of such linkage effects.
9. Even though Syrett and Cooke (1966, p. 6, n. 10) claim that 'there is no reason to believe that H[amilton] had read the works of Quesnay, Turgot, or others of the "économistes"', the shrewd reader would have detected that Hamilton was attempting, partly by drawing upon Smith, what Cole ([1928] 1968, p. 235) has dubbed 'a thoroughgoing demolishment of the Physiocratic position'. By adding this critique to the *Report*, which was not in Coxe's draft, it constitutes a 'major difference' between the two documents (Tajima 1985, p. 145).
10. Hamilton spelled out a total of seven such circumstances ([1791b] 1966, pp. 249–61), five of which are discussed in the present section. The one that concerns the benefits of how encouraging domestic manufactures would engender a new and stable demand for domestic agricultural produce has already been mentioned earlier in the present section. The two that are left out are how encouraging manufactures would give occasion to the exertion of a greater quantity of industry and how it would promote emigration from foreign countries (ibid., pp. 252–4).

11. Parks ([1963] 1977, Ch. V) argues that Bourne (1894) does not carefully point out where Hamilton was sometimes, while paraphrasing Smith, actually disagreeing with him.
12. It should, however, be noted that one of the 11 courses of action that Hamilton considered for encouraging manufactures was 'facilitating ... the transportation of commodities' ([1791b] 1966, pp. 310–11). That, if implemented, would effect domestic market integration and thus the extension of the domestic market.
13. This benefit resembles one that Mill, in his *Principles*, credited Babbage for noticing. He (Mill) puts it as 'the more economical distribution of labour, by classing the work-people according to their capacity' or 'the advantage which consists in extracting the greatest possible amount of utility from skill' ([1871] 1965, pp. 128–9). Interestingly, he mentions this right after discussing the three reasons that Smith put forward to explain why a great increase of the quantity of work could be performed through a division of labour.
14. Elsewhere Hamilton also opined that there seemed to be 'a moral certainty, that the trade of a country which is both manufacturing and Agricultural will be more lucrative and prosperous, than that of a Country, which is, merely Agricultural' and that 'the field of enterprise must be enlarged to the Merchants of a Country, in proportion to the variety as well as the abundance of commodities which they find at home for exportation to foreign Markets' (op. cit., pp. 287, 288). Compare with Coxe ([1790] 1979, p. 635), who states that 'when the variety of human talent is duly remembred, and it is considered that minds of the strongest & most active powers for their proper objects, may fall below mediocrity, or labor without effect, if confined to incongenial pursuits, it will appear unwise so to arrange our political œconomy as to impel to agriculture the whole body of the people'.
15. According to Syrett and Cooke (1966, pp. 5, 6), two other 'patrons' could well be Lord Sheffield and Etienne Clavière.
16. Earlier in his *Report* Hamilton also represents the patrons' opinion as, '"we should procure, in exchange for its [US agricultural] productions, the commodities, with which foreigners are able to supply us in greater perfection, and upon better terms"' ([1791b] 1966, p. 235).
17. Parks ([1963] 1977, p. 137) suggests that this 'admission' of the theoretical validity of the free trade argument, when compared with what Hamilton argues for in *The Continentalist No. IV* regarding the necessity for the confederation to regulate trade (see n. 21 below), would appear to be one 'glaring inconsistency'. He suggests that Hamilton's position on free trade in this part of the *Report* 'was one of expediency'; the *Report* would stand 'a greater chance of acceptance and adoption if it coincided with the opinions of important national leaders'.
18. For the cases for which Smith would grant exceptions to protection, see Smith ([1776] 1979, pp. 463–72).
19. While it is not clear what exactly led Bastable (1912), Haberler (1937), Robbins (1998), and Baldwin (1969) to link Mill to Hamilton (see the passages quoted in the introductory section of the present chapter), in the case of Cole ([1928] 1968, pp. 237–8), it clearly has to do with the first two reasons listed in the discussion here.
20. This is not a reference to the disparities in income elasticity of demand that Prebisch was to emphasise (see Ch. 10 below), but it can be translated into differences in import coefficients, which he also alluded to.
21. In *The Continentalist No. IV*, the fourth in a series of six articles that appeared in 1781–82, which was roughly a year or so before he was appointed to Congress, Hamilton argues for the necessity to augment the powers of the confederation. The first such power that he enumerates is the power of regulating trade, 'comprehending a right of granting bounties and premiums by way of encouragement, of imposing duties of every kind, as well for revenue as regulation' ([1781] 1961, p. 670). He reiterates this necessity in the beginning sentence of *The Continentalist No. V* ([1782] 1962, pp. 75–6).
22. Hamilton indicates in his *Report* that the 'propriety' of 'protecting duties' as a 'species of encouragement' need 'not be dwelt upon' as it is 'a clear result from the numerous topics which have been suggested' ([1791b] 1966, p. 296).
23. While generally referring to 'measures, which serve to abridge the free competition of foreign Articles' rather than specifically to protecting duties, Hamilton optimistically granted 'though it were true, that the immediate and certain effect of regulations controlling

the competition of foreign with domestic fabrics was an increase of price, it is universally true, that the contrary is the ultimate effect with every successful manufacture. When a domestic manufacture has attained to perfection, and has engaged in the prosecution of it a competent number of Persons, it invariably becomes cheaper. ... The internal competition which takes place, soon does away every thing like Monopoly, and by degrees reduces the price of the Article to the minimum of a reasonable profit on the Capital employed' ([1791b] 1966, pp. 285, 286).

24. Contrast with the considerations in notes 41–43 in Ch. 6 above. The similarity and differences between a bounty and a duty noted by Hamilton up to this point can be roughly compared with Corden's decomposition of a tariff into a production subsidy for, and a consumption tax on, a product (1997, pp. 34–5). In *The Continentalist No. V* Hamilton briefly considered how the division of a duty between the 'merchant' and the 'consumer' 'turns upon the quantity of goods at market in proportion to the demand' ([1782] 1962, p. 80).
25. The remaining part will be discussed later in the present subsection.
26. Writing in the late 1990s, more than 200 years after Hamilton's *Report*, Krueger (1997, p. 5, n. 14) concedes in a rare moment that '[m]ore recent analyses would ... point to the greater potential for corruption inherent in production subsidies as yet another reason [besides the revenue constraint] why [tariff] protection might be preferable'.
27. American fabrics 'are free from the heavy expences of importation, which rival foreign goods sustain to the amount, of fifteen, and twenty five per Cent on their Value according to their bulk' (Coxe [1790] 1979, p. 638).
28. Not to be left out is the consideration of the effective rate of protection of manufactures. See the ensuing discussion of the remaining part of the fourth reason for preferring bounties over tariffs, where Hamilton showed that he would not support applying protective duties to both a manufactured good and the raw produce that enters into it as an input.
29. In *The Continentalist No. V* Hamilton makes this observation: 'Experience has shown that moderate duties are more productive than high ones. When they are low, a nation can trade abroad on better terms – its imports and exports will be larger – the duties will be regularly paid, and arising on a greater quantity of commodities, will yield more in the aggregate, than when they are so high as to operate either as a prohibition, or as an inducement to evade them by illicit practices' ([1782] 1962, pp. 78–9). In *The Continentalist No. VI* he repeats that 'moderate duties ..., without being injurious to commerce, are allowed to be the most agreeable species of taxes to the people' ([1782] 1962, pp. 99–100).
30. J. Nelson (1979) seeks to appraise Hamilton's effort to encourage manufactures 'from the angle of public debt' (Tajima op. cit., p. 135, n. 32) and arrives at a disapproving conclusion of it.
31. An examination of the 22 pages near the very end of the *Report*, which Hamilton devotes to a consideration of how 16 or so 'objects' could be promoted, reveals that in general the abolition and reduction of duties were largely proposed in relation to the procurement of raw materials (the domestic production of which would then be encouraged by bounties or premiums) whereas additional duties generally applied to manufactures that employed those raw materials. See also the discussion in the latter part of the present subsection. Irwin (2004) provides a meticulous documentation of the changes in USA tariffs in the immediate aftermath of the submission of the *Report* by Hamilton, observing that he 'worked to ensure that Congress enacted virtually every tariff recommendation in the report within five months of its delivery' (ibid., p. 801). He also notes that resistance in Congress to the use of public funds to subsidise a particular industry became evident in early 1792 (ibid., p. 806).
32. This is one area where Hamilton and Coxe appeared to differ, where the latter decided that 'under the present circumstances of this country the Secretary cannot discover sufficient inducements to these expensive encouragements to justify a strenuous recommendation of them to the consideration of the legislature' (Coxe [1790] 1979, p. 638). This difference is also noted by Cooke (1975, p. 377).
33. With rare exceptions, one of which was encouraging the growth of flax and hemp as well as the manufacture of items like sail-cloth, Hamilton did not recommend offering bounties to

the two stages of production. That could be because of the systemic budgetary implications of this approach.

34. Coxe briefly proposed a drawback on imported raw materials that were used in manufacturing articles for exports ([1790] 1979, pp. 639–40).
35. In the *Prospectus of the Society for Establishing Useful Manufactures* that was issued four months before the *Report* was submitted to Congress, Hamilton stresses that as soon as capital could be raised for the Society, 'means ought to be taken to procure from Europe skilful workmen and such machines and implements as cannot be had here in sufficient perfection', and that 'the employment of the labor-saving mills and machines is particularly contemplated' ([1791a] 1965, p. 147). As Cooke (1975, p. 386) notes, Coxe's 'Plan for a Manufacturing Society' was included in the *Prospectus*, 'although in amplified and occasionally modified form'. Some have emphasised that Hamilton and Coxe shared an interest in employing power-driven machines (Hamilton [1791b] 1966, pp. 251–2, n. 155).
36. Coxe conceived of a 'landed fund' that was for 'rewarding the first introducers or establishers of new and useful manufactories, arts[,] machines, & secrets not before possessed, known or carried on in the United States'. In addition, he thought that acts could be passed to allow the 'granting to the introducers such exclusive privileges for a term of years as would have been secured by patent had they been the inventors' ([1790] 1979, p. 639). Hamilton did not include the 'landed fund' idea in his *Report*. According to Ben-Atar (1995, p. 405), he 'feared that immigrant artisans would yield to the temptation of bucolic life and not remain in urban centers to develop their trades'.
37. Recall the discussion of Rae in section 6.4 above how he emphasised the importance of employing premiums to facilitate and hasten the transfer of foreign arts. He regarded that transfer as enabling the test of the 'practicality' of producing certain products, the passing of which would be followed by further encouragement in the form of bounties and/or duties. This two-stage approach cannot be discerned explicitly in Hamilton's *Report*.
38. One such immigrant was Samuel Slater, who became known as 'America's most famous industrial recruit' (Ben-Atar 1995, p. 395, including n. 33).
39. According to Ben-Atar, Coxe 'had come out publicly for state and federal support of industrial piracy as early as 1787' (op. cit., pp. 395–6).
40. In Coxe's draft he suggests that, 'The peculiar value to the U.S. of improved implements and machinery for manufacturing, and the inducements to export those we have already obtained or may hereafter procure, which the interest of our competitors obviously creates, seem to render a penalty for such exportations an eligible measure[, although i]t is ... proper to guard carefully against extending this further than is absolutely necessary' ([1790] 1979, p. 643).
41. Of the four reasons that Hamilton offered for favouring bounties over tariffs Irwin (op. cit.) has either subsumed the second reason under the third one, or he has, for whatever reason, simply left it out.
42. Others who are aware that Hamilton had considered providing bounties include Bastable (1912, p. 122) and Kaplan (1931, p. 20). Those who have pointed out his insight of how bounties might possess some advantages over protective duties include Lunt (1895, pp. 301–2), Cole [1928] 1968, p. 242), and Dorfman ([1946] 1966, p. 411).
43. This is a label that Parks ([1963] 1977) regards to be most appropriate.

8. List: Unleashing Productive Powers and Reciprocal Effects through a Multitude of Policy Instruments

8.1 INTRODUCTION[1]

Just as the lineage of the infant-industry argument for trade protection was claimed by the mainstream to have descended from Hamilton's *Report*, a similar assertion has been made with respect to List's works.[2]

Thus, as Bastable put it, 'It is hardly necessary to remark that List's doctrines are a development of those of Hamilton' (1912, p. 126). 'All that is really suggestive and powerful in protectionist theory', he added, 'can be traced back to Hamilton and List' (ibid.). Having attributed the 'infant-industry argument for tariffs' to Hamilton's *Report* (see section 7.1 above), Haberler went on to argue that the ideas contained therein 'were brought to Germany by Friedrich List.[3] In his celebrated *National System of Political Economy* he expounds and popularises them with wearisome verbosity and a vast display of historical "illustrations"' (1937, p. 278). Baldwin's similar affirmation of this in his oft-cited (1969) article has already been quoted in section 7.1 above and does not need to be repeated here.[4] Not surprisingly, List's name is sometimes paired with the postwar policy of development that is known as IS (Balassa 1989, pp. 68–9).

Just as in the case of Hamilton, the next step in composing this mainstream story of the lineage of the infant-industry argument is to label List as a proponent of solely *tariff* protection. Bastable thus observed that '[t]he system advocated by List contains the leading ideas that have influenced continental, American, and colonial statesman in adopting the tariff systems' (1912, p. 123). Haberler similarly stated that, 'List arrives at the conviction … [of] fostering manufacturing … through protective tariffs' (1937, p. 279).[5] For their part, Gide and Rist remarked that, 'The tariff, apparently, is the only method of raising the wind [that bears the seed from one region to another, i.e. to help spread industries from one country to another]' (1948, p. 283).[6] Baldwin's attribution of the tariff recommendation to both Hamilton and List has been illustrated in section 7.1 above and needs no repetition. Irwin, after crediting Hamilton for his 'quite insightful' study of policy instruments, went on to criticise that, 'Unlike ... Hamilton, List did not mention any preference for subsidies over tariffs as the way to promote industry' (1996, p. 127).

There are others, however, who have suggested that List had a more sophisticated argument to make on how to promote development than the narrow notion of infant-industry protection (Henderson 1983a, p. 6). For instance, Gomes argued that 'List was concerned with the development of productive powers and its role in propelling economic growth' and that '[p]rotection was not central to List's argument' (1987, pp. 269–70). Haddad contended that 'the conventional association of List with "the infant industry case" and protection is too narrow an interpretation and a superficial assessment of his contribution to economics'. His argument is, contrary to the mainstream view, 'more than an exception to free trade. ... [I]t forms the general case for industrial development and economic growth' (1987, p. 17). Maneschi echoed this by pointing out that '[h]is primary interest was the economics of development rather than international trade' and that although his justification for protection 'is at first reminiscent of the infant industry argument ..., [t]he end-product of List's vision, for which protection would act as a midwife, was the creation of a modern, urbanized society with the associated cultural and geopolitical characteristics' (1998, pp. 92, 94). Dissenting similarly from the mainstream interpretation, Dosi, Pavitt and Soete reasoned that List's view 'involves much more than an "infant industry argument", the idea being that the long-term position of each country depends jointly on its degrees of capital accumulation, its global, technical and learning capabilities, and a set of institutional factors (social consensus, factory discipline, political conditions)' (1990, p. 28). Alas, with the refinement and subsequent rise to dominance of the theory of domestic divergences since the 1960s and 1970s as discussed in section 6.5 above, the so-called 'protectionist' ideas of people like List are regarded as having been exposed as imprecise and the policy prescriptions drawn therefrom as far from 'first best'. Not surprisingly, the aforementioned developmentalist interpretations of List's works have in the meantime been ignored, and hence, not been further clarified.[7]

The rest of this chapter is organised as follows. Section 8.2 refers to List's distinction between different stages of development and presents his case for diversifying into manufactures in a fashion that is parallel to that of Hamilton. In considering his discussion of 'productive powers' and 'reciprocal effects', section 8.3 indicates where and how he took his case beyond that of Hamilton. Section 8.4 then shows why he was sceptical toward free trade under conditions that obtained during his time. His policy proposals for cultivating and invigorating productive powers through the encouragement of manufactures are presented, and their salient features will be examined, in section 8.5. Section 8.6 looks at the portion of his policy programme that relates to EP, including an element that anticipates the 'import substitution as export promotion' idea of Krugman (1984). Section 8.7 is for concluding remarks.

8.2 STAGES OF DEVELOPMENT: THE DRAWBACKS OF BEING A PURELY AGRICULTURAL NATION

It is well-known that List had portrayed the development of nations as progressing through stages, namely 'original barbarism, pastoral condition, agricultural condition, agricultural–manufacturing condition, and agricultural–manufacturing–commercial condition' ([1841] 1991, p. 177).[8] Nevertheless, the main focus of his works was placed on how the temperate zone countries, especially France, the German states, and the United States, could make a transition from the third to the fourth and fifth stages.

The Drawbacks of Being a Purely Agricultural Nation

But why make the transition? What is wrong with remaining in the agricultural condition? List's answer to these questions are very much in line with what Hamilton had argued, although the latter did not conceptualise the process of development in terms of stages.

Thus, '[a] merely agricultural state is dependent for its market as well as for its supply on foreign laws, on foreign goodwill or enmity' ([1827] 1996, p. 31). Reminiscent of Hamilton's reference to the 'artificial impediments' imposed by the European nations, List lamented that the nations exporting agricultural products 'are exposed to the danger of being totally ruined' in their trade with the manufacturing nations 'by wars, or new foreign tariff regulations whereby they suffer the double disadvantage of finding no buyers for their surplus agricultural products, and of failing to obtain supplies of the manufactured goods which they require' ([1841] 1991, p. 180).[9]

List also showed some awareness of the specific nature of the demand for raw produce, noting that the purely agricultural nations were 'dependent for their power of effecting sales on the chances of a more or less plentiful harvest in the agricultural–manufacturing nations ... [and] they have to compete in these sales with other purely agricultural nations, whereby their power of sale, in itself very uncertain, thus becomes still more uncertain' (ibid.).[10] At one point in the *Outlines*, while referring to the attempt of the 'southern states' in America to grow more cotton to make up for low prices in the European markets, he mentioned in passing a situation of a low price elasticity of demand for that raw product. Specifically, 'the prices fell in consequence in the same proportion in which the quantity had increased, and the planters received not a cent more for their increased quantity than in the preceding year' ([1827] 1996, p. 139).[11] He added that similar difficulties were encountered by the 'grain-growing states' (ibid.). Similar to Hamilton's suggestion of the lower probability for 'wholly, or almost wholly', agricultural countries to enjoy favourable balance of trade (see section 7.2 above), List noted that, 'Experience has proved repeatedly ... that in agricultural nations, whose manufacturing market is exposed to the free competition of a nation which has attained manufacturing supremacy, the value of the importation of manufactured goods exceeds frequently to an enormous extent the value of the agricultural products which are exported' ([1841] 1991, p. 271). A little over a hundred years later his concerns with the nature of the demand for raw produce exported by, and with the balance of trade of, these countries would be shared by Prebisch and Singer (see Chapters 10 and 12 below).

To prepare himself to bring out the advantages of a domestic presence of manufactures, List went on to condemn that,

> People who depend entirely upon farming and are scattered over a wide area, live in isolation and cannot meet one another. ... They are ignorant folk who have no appreciation of the arts and they do not enjoy any personal liberty. Such people cannot hope to make progress ...
>
> ... Nothing encourages them to improve their situation and so they carry on with the dull routine of labour from one generation to another ... Their physical and mental powers are never adequately used or properly developed. ([1837] 1983, p. 53)[12]

He lamented that under such circumstances, 'inefficiency, prejudices, bad habits, and vices survive for centuries' (ibid., p. 54). The isolation of the agriculturist rendered him dependent on the landed proprietor while 'caprice and slavery, superstition and ignorance, want of means of culture, of trade, and of transport, poverty and political weakness exist' ([1841] 1991, p. 141, see also p. 203).

List concluded with the incisive comparison that,

> A nation which exchanges agricultural products for foreign manufactured goods is an individual with *one* arm, which is supported by a foreign arm. This support may be useful to it, but not so useful as if it possessed two arms itself, and this because its activity is dependent on the caprice of the foreigner. ... [I]t can merely produce as much surplus as foreign nations do not care to produce for themselves, and which they are obliged to buy from another country. (Ibid., pp. 160–61, italics original)

In receiving support from the foreign arm, it 'cannot make sure of the use of it in all cases' (ibid., p. 180). Hence, '[*a*] *nation which only carries on agriculture, is an individual who in his material production lacks one arm*', whereas 'an agricultural–manufacturing nation is an individual who has *two* arms *of his own* always at his disposal' (ibid., pp. 160, 180, italics original).

The Importance of Manufactures

List's argument for diversifying into manufactures again shows some parallel with that of Hamilton. Recall the discussion in section 7.2 where the latter spelled out several 'principal circumstances' to suggest why encouraging domestic manufactures would exert a significant positive influence on the 'total mass of industrious effort' in a society. Although List did not justify his position in as systematic a fashion as Hamilton did, it is clear that he subscribed to at least four among these 'circumstances', namely, how when domestic manufactures had been established, there are tremendous benefits arising from the new and stable demand for domestic agricultural produce, division of labour, extension of the use of machinery, and a more ample and various field for enterprise.[13]

Thus, he points out in his *Natural System* that 'it is necessary that agriculture and industry should be physically close together and that their close co-operation should not be interrupted by natural causes or by any political action' so that 'the agriculture of a country can flourish, can expand, can gain security for the future, and can be protected against every relapse and every crisis' ([1837] 1983, p. 61).[14] Then he adds in his *National System* that 'the closer the manufacturer is to the agriculturist, the more will the former offer to the latter both an inducement to consume and means for consumption, the more also will the latter feel himself stimulated to greater production' ([1841] 1991, p. 306).

With regard to division of labour, he essentially subscribed to the theme that is common to Smith and Hamilton, namely that there is more scope for such division in manufactures.[15] In his words,

> A division of labour can be usefully developed in agriculture only insofar as it is brought about and stimulated by differences of soil and climate. On the other hand the various branches of industry can give unlimited scope for the division of labour. The productive powers of agriculture are scattered over a wide area. But the productive powers of industry are brought together and are centralised at one place. This process of concentration eventually creates an expansion of productive powers which grow in geometric rather than in arithmetic proportion. ([1873] 1983, pp. 68–9)[16]

Extending this to the application of machinery, List asserted that '[a] manufacturing nation has a hundred times more opportunities of applying the power of machinery than an agricultural nation' ([1841] 1991, p. 201).

Finally, while Hamilton believed that the 'spirit of enterprise' must necessarily expand 'in proportion to the ... variety of the occupations and productions, which are to be found in a society' ([1791b] 1966, p. 256), List had this to offer:

> [T]he separation and variety of the operations of business, and the confederation of the productive powers, press with irresistible force the various manufacturers towards one another. Friction produces sparks of the mind, as well as those of natural fire. Mental friction, however, only exists where people live together closely, where frequent contact in commercial, scientific, social, civil, and political matters exists, where there is large interchange both of goods and ideas. The more men live together in one and the same place, the more every one of these men depends in his business on the co-operation of all others, the more the business of every one of these individuals requires knowledge, circumspection, education. ([1841] 1991, p. 204)

He reasoned that it was in such manners that civilisation had emanated from towns.

The representation of List's ideas up to this point was deliberately made in a way to show how they resemble many of those of Hamilton. However, he was to add substance to them.

8.3 PRODUCTIVE POWERS AND RECIPROCAL EFFECTS

Just as Hamilton took time to counter Smith, one of the 'respectable patrons of opinions unfriendly to the encouragement of manufactures', List also devoted quite a few passages to criticising Smith. Furthering the discussion in the previous section, the criticism outlined here concerns the alleged lack of a 'theory of productive power' in the *Wealth of Nations*.

Theory of Exchange Value is No Theory of Productive Powers

Thus, while reading the 'Introduction and Plan' of Smith's classic, List noticed the author indicated that the causes of improvement in the 'productive powers of labour' would be part of the subject of Bk. I (Smith [1776] 1979, pp. 10–11). For that reason he did not deny that Smith might have 'recognise[d] the significance of productive power for the creation of material wealth' ([1837] 1983, p. 37). However, as List was to allege, 'Smith was too exclusively possessed by the cosmopolitical idea of the physiocrats, "universal freedom of trade," and by his own great discovery, "the division of labour," to follow up the idea of the importance to a nation of its *power of production*' ([1841] 1991, pp. 134–5). He illustrated 'solely by exchange, augmentation of material capital, and extension of markets' and allowed his mind to be 'dominated by the idea of "value," "exchangeable value," ... [and] thus fell into the mistake of explaining mental forces from material circumstances and conditions' (ibid., p. 137).

List then broadened his criticism to 'Smith's school', accusing it of teaching 'nothing else than the theory of values' and giving a misleading definition to the science of political economy. With regard to the latter, he cited Say as having defined it as 'that science which teaches how riches, or exchangeable values, are produced, distributed, and consumed' (ibid., p. 138).[17] But he hastened to emphasise that '[t]his is undoubtedly not the science which teaches how the *productive powers* are awakened and developed, and how they become repressed and destroyed' (ibid., italics original) and it does not show 'how the productive powers of an entire nation can be called into existence, increased, maintained, and preserved – for the special benefit of its civilisation, welfare, might, continuance, and independence' (ibid., p. 350, see also p. 259).[18] It 'lays far greater stress upon material objects than upon the creative power which makes possible the production of material goods' ([1837] 1983, p. 180).[19]

List thus concluded that Smith had given the *Wealth of Nations* a misleading title when the first half of it reads '*An Inquiry into the Nature and Causes*'. Without a theory of productive powers, would not the *causes* actually remain to be fully explored? This is where he proclaimed that,

> *The causes of wealth* are something totally different from *wealth itself.* A person may possess wealth, i.e. exchangeable value; if, however, he does not possess the power of producing objects of more value than he consumes, he will become poorer. A person may be poor; if he, however, possesses the power of producing a larger amount of valuable articles than he consumes, he becomes rich.
> *The power of producing wealth* is therefore infinitely more important than *wealth itself.* ([1841] 1991, p. 133, italics original)

With productive powers adequately cultivated, a nation's possession would thus not only be insured against possible losses (say, due to natural calamities), it is also assured of future increases of such possessions (ibid.).[20] As Chapter 12 below shows, this distinction that List drew would resurface 120 years later when Singer emphasised the importance of cultivating an indigenous 'capacity to create wealth' in the less-developed countries.

List regarded the subject matter of the first few chapters of Bk. I of the *Wealth of Nations*, namely the division of labour, to be a good point to commence on a consideration of the cultivation of productive powers. Smith himself, according to List, did not carry out the analysis. Just what did he think should be done to extend Smith's discussion?

Division of Labour, Union of Labour, and Balance of Productive Powers

Smith's school, as List declares at one point in his *National System*, 'has committed the error of applying it [the division of labour or operation] merely to the separate manufactory or farm; it has not perceived that the same law extends its action especially over the *whole manufacturing* and *agricultural power,* over *the whole economy of the nation*' ([1841] 1991, pp. 150–51, italics original, see also pp. 350–51). Several pages later he continues thus,

> The whole social state of a nation will be chiefly *determined by the principle of the variety and division of occupations and the co-operation of its productive powers.* What the pin is in the pin manufactory, that the national well-being is to the large society which we term 'the nation'. (Ibid., p. 159, italics original)[21]

He then made some broad distinctions between 'occupations' and 'productive powers in material production', claiming that, '*The most important division of occupations in the nation is that between the mental and material ones*' while '*[t]he most important division of occupations, and the most important co-operation of productive powers in material production, is that of agriculture and manufacture*' (ibid., pp. 159–60, italics original). Part of his reasoning behind the claim concerning agriculture and manufacture could be inferred from the discussion in section 8.2. However, the complete reasoning behind both claims involves what he referred to as 'mutual dependence' or 'reciprocal' effects among the occupations and productive powers, and these will be examined in the next subsection.

While those claims were made at what could be characterised as a rather aggregate level, it is unmistakable that List was no less interested in seeing division of labour practised among different branches of industry.[22] And this is where he pointed out that an emphasis on the 'union of labour' and 'balance of productive powers' is lacking in Smith.

Thus, List noticed Smith was aware that '"[t]he necessaries of life of the lowest members of society are a product of *joint* labour and of the co-operation of a number of individuals"' but lamented that he 'did not follow out this idea ... of *united labour*' (ibid., p. 150, italics original).[23] To List, what is important not to ignore is that there is

> not merely *a division of labour,* but *a division of different commercial operations between several individuals,* and at the same time *a confederation or union of various energies, intelligences, and powers on behalf of a common production.* The cause of the productiveness of these operations is not merely that *division,* but essentially this *union.* (Ibid., pp. 149–50, italics original)

Referring back to Smith's pin-manufactory, List thus remarked that as it could only prosper 'by the confederation of the productive force of the individuals, so does every kind of manufacture prosper only by the confederation of its productive forces with those of all other kinds of manufacture' (ibid. p. 151). To illustrate, he considered how the success of a 'machine manufactory' would depend on the supply of some necessary materials from the mining and metal works industries, and that there should be plenty of manufactories in various industries which would require and buy the machines that it assembled together (ibid.).[24] Generalising this observation, he thus argued that '[a]s in the pin manufactory, so also in the nation does the productiveness of every individual – of every separate branch of production – and finally of the whole nation depend on the exertions of all individuals standing in proper relation to one another', and he labelled this relation as 'the *balance* or the *harmony of the productive powers*' (ibid., p. 160, italics original).

As it is the nature of this 'union' of, and 'balance' between, different branches of manufactures that will resurface in section 8.5 below when List's policy proposals are examined, this prediction of his in the *Natural System* should be noted:

> The fullest development of manufacturing industry ... will take place only when various branches of industry are so intimately linked that one process can follow another as closely as possible. The principle of co-operation is as indispensable to steady regular industrial growth as the principle of the division of labour. ([1837] 1983, p. 28)[25]

Later in the same work he could thus say, without exaggeration, that 'the success of one branch of industry always depends upon the success of another branch of industry' (ibid., p. 72).[26]

Reciprocal Effects and Actions

The representation of List's case for the creation of a 'variety and division of occupations' and his emphasis on the 'co-operation of productive powers' has thus far left out one key ingredient that he had considered. He had indeed looked at the individual elements of this matrix. Yet, 'the aggregate of the productive powers of the nation is not synonymous with the aggregate of the productive powers of all individuals, each considered separately' ([1841] 1991, p. 170). This is where he brought in considerations which he dubbed 'reciprocal' or 'mutual dependence' effects.

Thus, within the manufacturing sector,

> all individual branches of industry have the closest reciprocal effect on one another; … the perfecting of one branch prepares and promotes the perfecting of all others; … no one of them can be neglected without the effects of that neglect being felt by all; … in short, the whole manufacturing power of a nation constitutes an inseparable whole. (Ibid., p. 387)[27]

In this manner, 'by the establishment and continuance of industry one branch of trade originates, draws after it, supports and causes to flourish many others' (ibid., p. 298).

At least as important are the multifarious reciprocal effects between manufactures and other parts of the economy and society. Thus, '[m]anufactures everywhere first brought into operation improved means of transport, improved river navigation, improved highways, steam navigation and railways'[28] and these constitute the 'fundamental elements of improved systems of agriculture' (ibid., p. 109).

> By these [improvements] … the surplus produce of the agricultural land [could be] converted into machinery for yielding income, … [and] the powers of labour of those who are employed by it brought into activity …
> Through the introduction of manufactures, a demand for a quantity of articles of food and raw materials is created, to the production of which certain districts can be far more profitably devoted than to the growth of corn … The demand which now springs up for milk, butter, and meat adds a higher value to the existing pasture land, and leads to the breaking up of fallows and the erection of works of irrigation. The demand for fruit and garden produce converts the former bare agricultural land into vegetable gardens and orchards. (Ibid., pp. 211–12)[29]

Improved transportation also made possible fuller utilisation of different kinds of natural resources, for 'all minerals, all metals, which heretofore were lying idle in the earth are now rendered useful and valuable' and '[a]rticles which could formerly only bear a freight of a few miles, such as salt, coals, stone, marble, slate, gypsum, lime, timber, bark, &c., … formerly quite valueless, can now assume a degree of importance in the statistical returns of the national produce' (ibid.).[30]

Furthermore, '[m]anufactures are at once the offspring, and at the same time the supporters and the nurses, of science and the arts'. Referring to yet another example of reciprocal effects, List thus pointed out that '[i]n the manufacturing State the industry of the masses is enlightened by science, and the sciences and arts are supported by the industry of the masses' (ibid., p. 200, see also [1837] 1983, p. 64). Concomitantly,

> [t]he necessity for education and instruction, through writings and lectures by a number of persons who have to bring into practice the results of scientific investigations, induces men of special talents to devote themselves to instruction and authorship. The competition of such talents, owing to the large demand for

> their efforts, creates both a division and co-operation of scientific activity, which has a most beneficial influence not merely on the further progress of science itself, but also on the further perfection of the arts and of industries. ([1841] 1991, p. 201)[31]

And arts and science are by no means the only areas of 'mental production' that are stimulated by manufactures. For instance, better transport facilities necessitated by manufactures 'are a powerful means of improving a people's level of culture' ([1837] 1983, p. 53). Similarly, 'a vigorous middle class … could only have been called into existence by the establishment of an internal manufacturing power' ([1841] 1991, p. 186).[32]

More generally, the 'mental and material occupations' (see the previous subsection) are 'mutually dependent' on each other.

> The more the mental producers succeed in promoting morality, religion, enlightenment, increase of knowledge, extension of liberty and of perfection of political institutions – security of persons and property within the State, and the independence and power of the nation externally – so much greater will be the production of material wealth. On the other hand, the more goods that the material producers produce, the more will *mental production be capable of being promoted.* (Ibid., p. 159, italics original)

Keeping in mind the key role played by the establishment of manufactures in enabling the materialisation of these effects, it is no wonder why List proclaims in the *Natural System* that '[i]ndustry is the mother and father of science, literature, the arts, enlightenment, freedom, useful institutions, and national power and independence' ([1837] 1983, p. 66). 'Manufactories and manufactures are', as he essentially reiterates in the *National System*, 'the mothers and children of municipal liberty, of intelligence, of the arts and sciences, of internal and external commerce, of navigation and improvements in transport, of civilisation and political power. They are the chief means of liberating agriculture from its chains' ([1841] 1991, pp. 141–2, see also p. 186).[33] It is now also clear why he writes in the latter work that a nation derives its productive power 'from the mental and physical powers of the individuals; from their social, municipal, and political conditions and institutions; from the natural resources placed at its disposal, or from the instruments it possesses as the material products of former mental and bodily exertions (material, agricultural, manufacturing, and commercial capital)' (ibid., p. 224).[34]

8.4 SCEPTICISM TOWARD FREE TRADE IN MANUFACTURES

Political or National versus Private and Cosmopolitical Economy

Continuing with his criticism that the 'school' has offered a misleading definition of political economy and that what is conspicuously missing is a theory of productive powers, List lamented that '*political economy* is not … that science which teaches only how values in exchange are produced by individuals, distributed among them, and consumed by them' ([1841] 1991, p. 356, italics original). Rather,

> a statesman will know and must know, over and above that, how the productive powers of a whole *nation* can be awakened, increased, and protected, and how on the other hand they are weakened, laid to sleep, or utterly destroyed; and how by means of those national productive powers the national resources can be utilised in the wisest and best manner so as to produce national existence, national independence, national prosperity, national strength, national culture, and a national future. (Ibid., italics original; see also [1827] 1996, p. 25)

But in following their definition the followers of 'Smith's school' had reached 'erroneous conclusions'. In particular, they have concluded that 'since goods can be bought only in exchange for other goods, the exchange of products by foreign trade is always desirable' ([1837] 1983, p. 181). To List, the object of political economy is, instead, to gain productive and political power by means of exchange with other nations, and when and where appropriate, 'to prevent the depression of productive and political power, *by restricting that exchange*' ([1827] 1996, p. 57, italics added). When questions of international trade are the subject of discussion, List proclaimed, 'the theory of value should be regarded as subordinate to the theory of productive powers' ([1837] 1983, p. 190).

This is also where List distinguished *political* or *national* economy from *individual* and *cosmopolitical* economy, insisting that 'the object of political economy … is not *to gain matter, in exchanging matter for matter*, as it is in individual and cosmopolitical economy' ([1827] 1996, p. 57, italics original). In response to Smith's oft-quoted teaching that '[i]t is the maxim of every prudent master of a family [be that a taylor, shoemaker, or farmer], never to attempt to make at home what it will cost him more to make than to buy' and that '[w]hat is prudence in the conduct of every private family, can scarce be folly in that of a great kingdom' ([1776] 1979, pp. 456–7), List retorted,

> that may be wisdom in national economy which would be folly in private economy, and *vice versâ*; … that a tailor is no nation and a nation no tailor, that

> one family is something very different from a community of millions of families, that one house is something very different from a large national territory. Nor does the individual ... by striving to further them [his own interests], if left to his own devices, always further the interests of the community. ([1841] 1991, pp. 165–6)

With respect to cosmopolitical economy, he observed that no 'universal union' or 'world republic' existed at his time. 'If the whole globe were united by a union like the 24 States of North America', he hypothesised, 'free trade would indeed be quite as natural and beneficial as it is now in the Union' ([1827] 1996, p. 21). However, instead of such a union there are *nations*.

It should be noted List was prepared to grant that specialisation and trade would indeed be mutually beneficial if only natural-resource-based products were involved.[35] This is because each region is suited to whatever its climate and soil would allow it to produce, and humans can do little to modify natural processes ([1837] 1983, p. 87). However, he took issue with Smith ([1776] 1979, p. 458, illustrated in section 6.3 above) when the latter generalised from his observation that it would not make economic sense to grow grapes in Scotland (under artificially sheltered conditions created by 'glasses, hotbeds, and hotwalls') to all kinds of situations involving 'regulations' to encourage activities, regardless of whether the activities concerned involve 'natural or acquired' advantages (List [1841] 1991, pp. 213–14, 227). '[O]ne must appreciate', List demanded, 'that agriculture is in quite a different position from industry' and 'the two forms of production are governed by quite different laws' ([1837] 1983, pp. 87, 88). Most countries, excepting those in the torrid zones (see section 8.6 below), 'are potentially capable of establishing and developing all kinds of industries' (ibid., p. 87) and 'have equal capability provided that they possess the necessary material, mental, social, and political qualifications' ([1841] 1991, p. 385). England 'never received at the hands of Nature a perpetual right to a monopoly of manufacture, but which merely gained an advance over others in point of time' and '[i]t is absurd to attribute specially to the English greater mechanical talent, or greater skill and perseverance in industry, than to the Germans or to the French' (ibid., pp. 127, 386). One can only imagine how he would have rebutted Austin in response to the latter's review of the *National Economy* (see section 6.4 above)!

But would free trade spontaneously bring about a diversification into manufactures in an otherwise agrarian nation? Would, as the 'cosmopolitan theorists' have assumed, 'adopting the policy of free trade and ... leaving individuals to pursue their own private interests ... automatically secure the development of those branches of manufacture' which are best suited to a nation's own particular situation (List [1837] 1983, p. 70)?

Structural Changes not Spontaneous (after a Point)

List allowed that free trade would raise an agrarian nation 'from a state of barbarism' ([1841] 1991, p. 115). Referring to the stages of development that he had identified, he thus advanced that,

> The industrial history of nations ... proves that the transition from the savage state to the pastoral one, from the pastoral to the agricultural, and from agriculture to the first beginnings in manufacture and navigation, is effected most speedily and advantageously by means of free commerce with further advanced towns and countries ...
>
> The less any nation's agriculture has been perfected, and the more its foreign trade is in want of opportunities of exchanging the excess of native agricultural products and raw materials for foreign manufactured goods, the deeper that the nation is still sunk in barbarism and fitted only for an absolute monarchical form of government and legislation, the more will free trade ... promote its prosperity and civilisation. (Ibid., pp. 177–8)

During this period 'a nation's industries begin to develop'. New products were brought into the country and awakened the desire to buy and even make them. To meet the growing demand for manufactured products, some 'native industries' emerged; some of these products 'may be made more cheaply at home than abroad because of the country's resources, the existence of a low level of wages, or other circumstances' ([1837] 1983, pp. 56, 98).[36]

But before long 'this relationship becomes a burden which hampers the development of its own manufacturers' and the latter 'realise that their progress is being restricted by the import of foreign goods' (ibid., p. 155, 56; see also List [1841] 1991, pp. 16, 178).[37] Speaking for the agrarian nations that had arrived at this stage, List predicted that '[u]nder such circumstances it is quite impossible that in ... [these] nations, "in the natural course of things" (as Adam Smith expresses himself),[38] merely in consequence of their progress in agriculture, *immense* manufactures and works should be established'[39] ([1841] 1991, p. 299, italics added). But what exactly are these circumstances?

To List, these circumstances are internal and external with respect to the country concerned. Collectively, they roughly correspond to the four 'cogent reasons' put forward by Hamilton to explain why structural changes in a predominantly agricultural country would not be spontaneous (see section 7.3 above).

To recapitulate, under free trade the agrarian nation might be awakened to utilise its local advantages – specific resources, low wages, proximity to domestic market, and so on – to commence on some manufacturing activities. Yet, to List, these could not become 'immense' manufactures if free trade were to continue. This emerging nation 'could never secure to itself an acquired perfection' in manufactures without protective measures ([1827] 1996, p. 97).

Within the country, '[e]very new business is connected with great losses by want of experience and skill for a considerable time'. Hence, '[t]he more knowledge, experience, and skill are wanted for a particular business, the less individuals will be willing to devote themselves to it, if they have not a full assurance of their being able to make a living by it for their whole lifetime' (ibid.; see also [1841] 1991, p. 294). Lest these appear to the subscribers to the theory of domestic divergences as nothing but references to labour and capital market failures, it should be emphasised that List, consistent with his broad-based discussion of productive powers, did not lose sight of how the obstacles to structural changes are interconnected.[40] Thus,

> *[t]he advancement of every kind of manufactories, depends upon the advancement of many other kinds*, upon the proper construction of houses and works, of instruments and machinery. All this makes the commencement of a new undertaking extremely difficult, whilst the undertakers have to contend with a want of labourers of skill and experience. ([1827] 1996, p. 97, italics added)

Besides, there might 'not [be] a sufficient knowledge of the ways and means to get the first materials profitably'. New businesses also had to win over domestic customers who might be prejudiced in favour of foreign products (ibid., pp. 97, 99).

Coming from outside the agrarian nations was the threat of competition posed by England's 'commercial and industrial supremacy'. Consistent with his discussion of productive powers in broad terms rather than in terms of a single branch of industry, List referred to the multiple ingredients of this supremacy, including the abundance of 'skilled and experienced workmen', the availability of 'the best technical men and foremen' and 'the most perfect and the cheapest machinery' in that country. Besides, it enjoyed 'the greatest benefit in buying and selling advantageously', 'the cheapest means of transport', more extended credit for the manufacturers 'at the lowest rates of interest', and 'greater commercial experience, better tools, buildings, arrangements, connections'. Last but not least, it is blessed with 'an enormous home market' and 'a colonial market equally enormous' ([1841] 1991, p. 300; see also [1827] 1996, p. 99).[41]

By implication, all other nations lagged behind on all these counts so that 'in competition with such a power it is simply foolish to rest our hopes on the operation of "the natural course of things" under free competition' (ibid.). Here List made another incisive comparison, noting that 'a child or a boy in wrestling with a strong man can scarcely be victorious or even offer steady resistance' ([1841] 1991, pp. 299–300). What is worse, in many instances that 'strong man' was alarmingly supported by his own protective duties and drawbacks ([1827] 1996, p. 101; see also [1841] 1991, pp. 168–9).

Arresting Uneven Development between England and Other Nations

Part I of this book has advanced a re-interpretation of classical growth and trade analyses that portrays an uneven development outcome with England in the lead. The implication of this process for the trailing group of countries did not attract much attention from the classical economists. It received some timely treatment in the hands of Hamilton and much further treatment in the hands of List. And the latter seldom failed to find strong words, sometimes to underscore the dire situation, and other times to incite fear and jealously.

Thus, List warned, 'There is … a real danger that the strongest nations will use the motto "Free Trade" as an excuse to adopt a policy which will certainly enable them to dominate the trade and industry of weaker countries and reduce them to a condition of slavery'. Such a trade arrangement 'permits foreign competitors to ruin native industry' ([1837] 1983, pp. 24–5). The result would be 'a universal subjection of the less advanced nations to the supremacy of the predominant manufacturing, commercial, and naval power' ([1841] 1991, p. 126); they would merely become the 'satellite dependency of a foreign power' ([1837] 1983, p. 96).

What could be done by the 'less advanced nations' to arrest such uneven development? Here List employed an analogy that offers the followers of 'Smith's school' the benefit of doubt that the 'natural course of things' would indeed result in the spread of industrial development, albeit extremely slowly, from England to the other temperate zone nations. Specifically, he granted, 'It is true that experience teaches that the wind bears the seed from one region to another, and that thus waste moorlands have been transformed into dense forests' ([1841] 1991, p. 110). Then he posed the rhetorical questions: Would it be wise 'for the forester to wait until the wind in the course of ages effects this transformation?' Or '[i]s it unwise on his part if by sowing and planting he seeks to attain the same object within a few decades?' (ibid.).

It was with reference to this analogy that Gide and Rist, in labelling List as an advocate solely of the tariff, remarked that, 'The tariff, apparently, is the only method of raising the wind' (1948, p. 283, quoted in section 8.1 above). But as it turned out, List had more up his sleeve.

8.5 SOME SALIENT FEATURES OF LIST'S POLICY AGENDA

A Broad Set of Policy Actions to Promote Industries[42] and to Cultivate Productive Powers (Technological Capabilities)

While List did attach quite a bit of importance to tariffs as an instrument to promote industries in the advanced agricultural societies in the temperate zone, he also proposed to deploy a variety of other instruments, including subsidies.

Thus, very early on in the cluster of chapters relating to tariffs and protection in his *Natural System* (Chs. 21–25),[43] List proclaims that,

> There are *many ways* in which industrialisation can be promoted. They include the establishment of technical schools; the granting of financial assistance to enable scientists to travel abroad; the holding of industrial exhibitions at which new inventions can be shown; the establishment of companies to promote industry and internal commerce by regulating rivers and by constructing highways, canals, railways and steamships; the granting of honours to those who advance scientific knowledge or establish new industries; the payment of generous *subsidies* for new industries, new processes, new plants, and new efficient factories; and the granting of state loans to industrial enterprises. But all these measures will have little effect unless they are supported by a tariff. ([1837] 1983, p. 106, italics added)

Then in his *National System*, he basically repeats this list and adds that some on the list were not given detailed treatment in that book because of their obvious effects. In his words,

> It is not part of our plan to treat of those means of promoting internal industry whose efficacy and applicability are nowhere called in[to] question. To these belong e.g. educational establishments (especially technical schools), industrial exhibitions, offers of prizes, transport improvements, patent laws &c.; in short, all those laws and institutions by means of which industry is furthered, and internal and external commerce facilitated and regulated. We have here merely to speak of the institution of customs duties as a means for the development of industry. ([1841] 1991, p. 308)

It thus seems fair to say that List was definitely aware of the multifarious ways of industry promotion. However, given what he perceived to be the key in winning the battle against the ideas of the 'school', one of the most deeply entrenched of which was the principle of free trade, he probably decided to devote most of his effort in examining the roles that customs duties could play in industrial promotion while leaving the other instruments with obvious effects untreated.

But does it mean that List attached more importance to the tariff instrument in some sense? The ending sentence of the first of the two passages just quoted seems to suggest that that was the case. However, it also unequivocally indicates that the institution of tariffs was not all that needed to be done; they were instituted to support the operation of these other instruments. Moreover, the support is not just one-way. Rather, tariff protection is in turn supported by at least some of these instruments. Thus, in considering how the fundamental conditions of manufacturing power might be judged to be lacking after tariff protection has been afforded at certain levels for some time, List reminded the reader that '[t]he causes of such incapacity can be removed more or less readily: to the class more readily removable belong want of internal means of transport, want of technical knowledge, of experienced workmen, and of the spirit of industrial enterprise' (ibid., p. 313).

Recall from the discussion in the second subsection of section 7.4 above that Hamilton was anxious to acquire superior foreign technology for America. According to List and as the discussion in section 8.3 above indicates, industry promotion awakes productive powers. In that connection Freeman (1995) observes that List 'advocated not only protection of infant industries but a broad range of policies', most of which 'were concerned with learning about new technology and applying it' (ibid., p. 5). He 'anticipated many contemporary ideas about "national systems of innovation" including the crucial importance of technological accumulation through a combination of technology imports with local activities and pro-active interventionist policies to foster strategic "infant" industries' (ibid., p. 19). Indeed, one can detect from his 'many ways' of promoting industries as well as some of his ideas illustrated in the last subsection in the present section (see below) that he can be regarded as proposing an approach that is 'similar to the theory of "capability-building" in the context of state-directed economic development' (Shafaeddin 2005b, p. 47).

Awareness of the Possible Need to Compare Some Policy Alternatives

While this complementary relationship among policy instruments was noted here and elsewhere, List was also alert to the fact that in some situations one would have to consider certain instruments as alternatives to each other.

One such situation relates to his discussion of export bounties, which he regarded as 'objectionable as permanent measures to render the exports and the competition of the native manufactories possible with the manufactories of further advanced nations in neutral markets', and they are 'still more objectionable as the means of getting possession of the inland markets for manufactured goods of nations which have themselves already made progress in manufactures' (ibid., p. 314). Nevertheless, there are cases where they could be justified as temporary means of encouragement, 'namely where the slumbering spirit of enterprise of a nation merely requires stimulus and assistance in the first period of its revival, in order to evoke in it a powerful and lasting production and an export trade to countries which themselves do not possess flourishing manufactures'. However, he went on to clarify that,

> even in these cases it ought to be considered whether the State would not *do better* by making advances free of interest and granting special privileges to individual men of enterprise, or whether it would not be *still more to the purpose* to promote the formation of companies to carry into effect such primary experimental adventures, to advance to such companies a portion of their requisite share capital out of the State treasury, and to allow to the private persons taking shares in them a preferential interest on their invested capital. (Ibid., p. 315, italics added)

As precedents, List pointed to the experimental undertakings in trade and navigation to distant countries to which private persons had not yet attempted; the establishment of lines of steamers to distant countries; and the founding of new colonies (ibid.).

In another situation there was a consideration of whether coal or pig iron should be produced domestically. Obviously, as List reasoned, one must determine if the necessary natural resources are available. If not, the country should simply import and 'there is no point in levying import duties' on those items ([1837] 1983, p. 116). If, on the other hand, the resources are available, then one could impose import duties to encourage the opening of coalmines and the establishment of ironworks. However,

> [t]he *best* policy would be for the state to foster these industries by improving internal communications – canals and railways – as much as possible. And if there is not enough private capital available for the development of the mining industry the state should itself invest in joint stock mining companies and it should forego any dividend on its shares so long as private investors are not receiving any interest on their capital. (Ibid., italics added)

In the event that duties are imposed, 'they should not be so high as to reduce consumption' because coal and pig iron are materials that are indispensable to the expansion of the economy (ibid.).

A third situation deals with whether the importation of machinery should be subject to duties in countries 'which have not yet made considerable advances in technical art and in the manufacture of machinery'. In such cases 'it would be foolish to impose high import duties'; such machinery should be imported 'free of duty' or there should only be 'a small duty' imposed. This is because,

> Machine manufactories are in a certain sense the manufacturers of manufactories, and every tax on the importation of foreign machinery is a restriction on the internal manufacturing power. ... [Hence], this particular branch of manufacture has very special claims for the direct support of the State in case it should not be able under moderate import duties to meet competition. The State should at least encourage and directly support its home manufactories of machinery. ([1841] 1991, p. 314)

One course of action is for the state 'to foster the establishment of joint stock companies to set up model engineering workshops for the construction of machinery' ([1837] 1983, p. 117).

It is interesting to note that in all of these three situations discussed above, it is clear List was aware that there could be better actions than a direct trade intervention.[44] While most commentators are aware that List was strongly opposed to protecting the agricultural sector,[45] the aforementioned third situation also serves as a reminder that List was not supportive of protecting the entire manufacturing sector in the initial phase of industry promotion.

Protection of Manufactures should not be 'in the Same Degree'

As early as his *Outlines* List proclaims that, 'It is bad policy to regulate everything and to promote everything, by employing social powers, where things may better regulate themselves and can be better promoted by private exertions; but it is no less bad policy to let those things alone which can only be promoted by interfering social power' ([1827] 1996, p. 85). When this principle became incorporated in his proposals to protect industries, it resulted in the declaration in his *Natural System* that, 'No country should try to promote the immediate expansion of all branches of manufacture. At first ... it should attempt to stimulate only those industries which have an assured home market and appear to have the best chance of success' ([1837] 1983, p. 115).[46] These industries would be those supported 'by a great internal consumption', and that produce 'the first necessaries of life' or 'articles of general consumption', examples of which include, in List's time, cotton, woollen and linen manufactures, hardware, iron, and earthenware ([1841] 1991, pp. 179, 311; [1827] 1996, p. 79).

One category of products that would initially be left unprotected is the 'finer' or more 'luxurious' products, the rationale being that,

> the total value of ... industrial products [of general consumption] is incomparably greater than the total value of the much more expensive fabrics of luxury. The former class of manufactures, therefore, brings into motion large masses of natural, mental, and personal productive powers, and gives – by the fact that it requires large capital – inducements for considerable saving of capital, and for bringing over to its aid foreign capital and powers of all kinds. The development

> of these branches of manufacture thus tends powerfully to promote the increase of population, the prosperity of home agriculture, and also especially the increase of the trade with foreign countries, inasmuch as less cultivated countries chiefly require manufactured goods of common use, and the countries of temperate climates are principally enabled by the production of these articles to carry on direct interchange with the countries of tropical climates. ([1841] 1991, p. 311)

Note that the last part of this quotation suggests that List was not advocating industry promotion purely for serving the domestic market. This is a feature of his policy agenda that will be discussed in section 8.6 below.

But some of these finer products would eventually be promoted also, for '[e]very improvement must be advanced by steps' and '[t]he tariff legislation must advance as the national industry advances if it is rightly to fulfil its purpose' ([1827] 1996, pp. 77, 79; [1841] 1991, p. 403).[47] Initially, before protection is conferred upon them,

> [t]hese articles of comfort and luxury, if imported cheaper than we can manufacture them, get in use among all labouring classes, and act as a stimulus in exciting the productive powers of the nation. Its consumption becomes by and by more important, and by and by time will arrive when these articles, with a moderate encouragement, will be manufactured too within our limits. ([1827] 1996, p. 79)

In his *National System* List thus approves of the policy of the German Customs Union of encouraging and protecting the printing of cloths and then weaving, while importing the medium and finer yarns relatively duty free. However, in view of the tremendous potential benefits that could accrue with the local establishment of the 'great and fruitful' spinning industry, he laments that that policy would not be 'the right one for all time' ([1841] 1991, p. 403). Specifically,

> the spinning factories, quite apart from their importance in themselves, yet are the source of further incalculable benefits, inasmuch as they place us in direct commercial communication with the countries of warm climate, and hence that they exercise an incalculable influence on our navigation and on our export of manufactures, and that they benefit our manufactories of machinery more than any other branch of manufacture. ... [W]e cannot see why we should not gradually protect the spinning of yarns from one number to another, in such a way that in the course of five to ten years we may be able to spin for ourselves the greater part of what we require. (Ibid.)

This again illustrates List's awareness of various 'linkage effects'. Hence, one can label it a 'backward linkage' when he predicted that the establishment of spinning of cotton and linen yarns and woollen materials would 'offer us the means for establishing extensive machine manufactories'.

Nor does the spillover effects stop there, for that in turn would spur 'the development of a race of competent technical instructors and practical foremen' (ibid., p. 427).

This progression in tariff legislation, as it relates to 'upstream industries' like machine manufacturing, ties in with the discussion in the last subsection where it was illustrated that List favoured low or no duty initially on the importation of machinery, at least until these nations are 'in a position to produce them as readily as the most advanced nation' (ibid., p. 314).

Prescriptions to Mitigate the Potential Drawbacks of his Programme

List definitely understood the potential drawbacks of tariffs and other aspects of his broader industry promotion programme as well. This is evidenced by what he proposed to mitigate these drawbacks.[48]

Although he did not formulate anything explicitly that resembles the 'Mill test', List did consider how one could perhaps decide whether protection was accomplishing its objective. In this connection he surmised that,

> where any technical industry cannot be established by means of an original protection of forty to sixty per cent. and cannot continue to maintain itself under a continued protection of twenty to thirty per cent. the fundamental conditions of manufacturing power are lacking. (Ibid., p. 313)[49]

How long should protection be continued? At one point he ridiculed Say for proposing 'to allow a nation merely a *few years* for the task of bringing to perfection one great branch of national industry or the whole industry of the nation' (ibid., p. 319, emphasis original). Elsewhere, he suggested that after prolonged wars brought into existence manufacturing power in the 'second and third rank' manufacturing nations, 'possibly it only required another ten or fifteen years of strict protection in order to sustain successfully free competition with English manufactures' (ibid., p. 184).

List was conscious of the possibility that the protected domestic manufacturers could become complacent. One method that he proposed to address that potential problem was for the state to offer awards and prizes to encourage product quality improvements, efficiency in production, consistency in such quality and efficiency performance, and technical knowledge acquisition and sharing. Hence,

> [i]f a government observes that manufacturers are producing goods lower in quality and higher in price than those made abroad and if it is satisfied that this is the fault of the local industrialists it should offer substantial prizes as a reward to those manufacturers who, within a specified period, are able to make goods which approach those made abroad in quality and price. The ability to manufacture such goods regularly should also be considered when awarding prizes. Acceptance of

> such an award should be conditional upon a firm allowing workers employed elsewhere to visit its factory so as to improve their technical knowledge. ([1837] 1983, p. 120)

On the other hand,

> [s]hould a government decide that manufacturers have failed to make products which are as good as those made abroad simply because they have not been able to secure the services of a sufficient number of hardworking skilled men it should offer prizes to workers who reach a high standard of technical skill. It should also offer prizes to firms which, in a particular period, have succeeded in attracting foreign workers of proven skill and reliability into their employment. (Ibid.)[50]

Obviously, allowing a certain amount of competing imports could also check that problem. Indeed, there were times when List recommended duties that were low enough so as to allow some imports to spark competition. In one instance, again referring to the Germans, he opined that,

> they can further their manufacturing power advantageously only by protective duties previously fixed, and on a gradually increasing scale at first, but afterwards gradually diminishing, and that under all circumstances partial but carefully limited foreign competition is really beneficial to their own manufacturing progress. ([1841] 1991, p. 188)

The importation of foreign goods will trigger competition between rival firms at home. Nevertheless, foreigners 'should be allowed no more than a fair share of the annual expansion in the demand for manufactured goods' ([1837] 1983, p. 115).

Obviously, how much competition there could be depends, among other considerations, on the size of the domestic market. In this connection List cautioned that, 'A small State can never bring to complete perfection within its territory the various branches of production. In it all protection becomes mere private monopoly' ([1841] 1991, p. 176; see also [1837] 1983, p. 43). The critic would interject that an 'outward-oriented' trade policy, rather than the 'protectionist' policy that List was allegedly advocating, is the solution to this market-size problem. What did List have to say?[51]

8.6 SECURE HOME MARKET, EXPORT TO FOREIGN MARKETS

It was mentioned in passing in the third subsection in the previous section that List was not advocating the promotion of industries for the sole purpose of serving the domestic market. Export promotion (EP) was also definitely on his mind.[52] In fact, in marrying these two objectives he can be regarded to have anticipated the idea of 'import protection as export promotion' (Krugman, 1984) and other related ideas on strategic trade policies. It is worth quoting one of his discussions of this subject at length. Thus, in his *Outlines* he observes,

> Everybody knows ... that the cost of production in manufacturing business, depends a great deal on the quantity that is manufactured. A man may manufacture 1000 yards of broad cloth a year, and sell a yard for six dollars, and he may lose money; but he may manufacture 20,000 yards of the same quality, and get not more than four dollars a yard, and he may make money. This circumstance has a mighty influence on the rise and fall of manufacturing power. ([1827] 1996, p. 105)

List considered the implication of this observation with reference to a hypothetical English manufactory that was being 'protected' in the home market while being able to sell to another country that had an 'open' market. According to his reasoning,

> If the large supply of the home market is secured to an English manufactory, a steady sale of that quantity which is necessary to sustain his establishment, is secured to him thereby. He is, for instance, sure to sell ten thousand yards of broad cloth a year in his own country for six dollars a yard, to cover thereby the expenses of his establishment, and to clear besides a sufficient sum of money for himself. By this home market he is enabled to manufacture yet other ten thousand yards of broad cloth for the foreign market, and to accommodate his prices to the existing circumstances abroad. The expenses of his establishment being already covered by the sales at home, the costs of producing other 10,000 yards for the market abroad, come by far less high, and he may still profit by selling them for three or four dollars a yard; he may even profit in future if he gains nothing at present. Seeing the manufacturers of a foreign country lying in distress, he may sell for some years without any profit, in the hope to get seven or eight dollars a year ... after the foreign manufactures are dead and buried.

How would this impact upon the manufacturer in the 'open' country?

> [T]he manufacturer of the open country is struggling against a daily loss, ... leading him at last to a certain, inevitable, and radical ruin. This unhappy man ... the little he sells makes his produce dearer and his losses larger. He is forced to enhance his prices for the first years, whilst his competitor is enabled to diminish them.
>
> ... This contest cannot last long without national interference. (Ibid., pp. 105, 107)[53]

This Listian insight briefly resurfaces in the *National System*, where at one point List takes issue with Dr Bowring. The latter allegedly said in a report[54] that German manufacturers at that time could not compete in foreign markets because they could not produce cheaply, given that 'cheap production will not consist with the existence of the protective system [in Germany], inasmuch as the object of that system is to secure higher prices to the manufacturers'. To this List responds, 'Dr. Bowring cannot deny that the manufacturer can offer his products at cheaper prices, the more he is enabled to manufacture – that, therefore, a manufacturing Power which exclusively possesses its home market[55] can work so much the cheaper for foreign trade. ... [I]n the same proportion in which the German manufactories have acquired possession of their own home market, their export of manufactured goods has also increased' ([1841] 1991, pp. 396–7).

Alas, during List's time the temperate zone newly industrialising countries were not in a position to compete with England. Hence, when he considered their external commerce he had in mind trade with countries in the torrid zone, at least before they could catch up with England. The pattern of exchange would be coarse manufactured products from the former group of countries offered for food and raw produce from the latter group. Given what List believed to be ample room for primary production expansion in the latter group, he reasoned that that would imply also ample room for expansion in the production of manufactures and the exports of such from the former group of countries (ibid., pp. 191–3, 265–7).[56]

8.7 CONCLUDING REMARKS

Schumpeter once noted that, 'Even as a scientific economist ... List had one of the elements of greatness, namely, the grand vision of a national situation'. 'Nor was List deficient', he added, 'in the specifically scientific requisites that must come in to implement vision if it is to bear scientific fruits' (1954, p. 504). Unfortunately, the mainstream interpretation of List's works has tended to lead to the belief that he was nothing more than a simple-minded 'protectionist' who based his case on a crudely formulated infant-industry argument, thereby sterilising his broader conception of how development could be promoted.

List could be argued to have mirrored Hamilton in arguing why it would not be advisable for a country to remain largely, not to mention entirely, agricultural. His arguments for why manufactures should be established also show a parallel with those of Hamilton. However, he took the case further by introducing the concept of 'productive powers' and 'reciprocal effects'. He had in mind a much more sophisticated approach to foster and sustain economic, cultural, social, and political development. Indeed, suggestions of similarities with Rosenstein-Rodan (Hoselitz 1960, p. 202, n. 18) and with

Myrdal (Clairmonte 1959, p. 41; Gomes 1987, p. 272; Haberler [1959] 1988, p. 25, n. 10; Ho 2006) have been made.[57]

Except for agricultural products, List was not in favour of free trade for countries like France, the German states, and the United States of his time. Although given the then existing intellectual and political environment he felt compelled to devote most of his effort to making a case for restricted trade in selected sectors, it is clear he treated the tariff as but one of a wide variety of instruments that the state should employ. In some contexts the tariff and these other policy actions were treated as mutually supportive, while in others List did observe that there could be better alternatives to a trade intervention. Besides, the development programme (including the sectors under protection) would have to be adjusted as development advances. Safeguards would have to be instituted to reduce complacency or otherwise negate some of the drawbacks of some state actions. In the meantime, trade between the newly industrialising countries and the torrid zone countries should be encouraged so that exports of coarse manufactures by the former could benefit from scale economies.

It is interesting to note that List at one point made a 'daring suggestion' of convening a world trade congress to 'pave the way for the conclusion of advantageous commercial treaties'. This congress 'should consider the varied interests of regions and societies at different stages of economic development ... It should examine the needs of countries which have reached the second or the third stage of industrial development in relation to the world's leading manufacturing country'. List was of the opinion that 'France and the United States should, in their own interests, take the lead in calling a world trade congress. There are reasons to believe that a suggestion of this kind would be supported by all the countries on the [European] Continent. If these countries collaborated it can hardly be doubted that England, too, would send representatives to the proposed world trade congress' ([1837] 1983, pp. 126–7). The parallel with the desire on the part of today's less-developed countries to secure SDT from MTNs under the auspices of GATT and the WTO is unmistakable.[58]

Referring to Mill's infant-industry case for protection, Irwin (1996, p. 128) remarks that, 'The endorsement by an economic theorist of first rank was not so easily dismissed as similar statements coming from a Hamilton or a List'. The previous chapter on Hamilton and this one on List have hopefully revealed that the statements are not that similar. The arguments presented by both Hamilton and List, as well as the nuances in their conceptualisation of policy action, show a lot of sophistication that is simply not found in Mill's endorsement passage.[59] Yet, the latter, for merely mentioning the word 'subsidy' in several pieces of personal correspondence, has won all the praises.

From the perspective of the economics mainstream, Mill's endorsement has the advantage of allowing the analysis to readily compress the full complexity in the cultivation of an economy-wide indigenous technological capability into the promotion of one single industry (see section 6.5 above). Hamilton's and List's original treatments, especially the latter's consideration of breeding productive powers, do not allow for such compression unless one is prepared to distort. Manoïlesco, the focus of the next chapter, in a sense introduced such a compression with respect to List's ideas. The result was that even though he came up with a case for protection that was much ado about nothing, the economics mainstream has fallen in love with it for it is amenable to being easily portrayed as a case of labour-market failure in hindering industrial development.

NOTES

1. Sections 8.1 and 8.7 of this chapter contain passages from sections 1 and 5 in Ho (2005). The subsections in section 8.5 are largely reproductions of subsections 4.1–4.4 from the same work, while section 8.6 is essentially subsection 4.5 therein. Section 3 in Ho (ibid.) has been expanded into sections 8.2–8.4 in the present chapter.
2. Hereafter his three major works are referred to as *Outlines*, *Natural System*, and *National System* respectively (where for the last title, reference will be made to Lloyd's translation). On the importance of studying List's *Natural System* in appraising his works, see Henderson (1983a, p. 5) and Blaug (1984, p. 368).
3. Hamilton's name is one among a dozen mentioned at one point in List's *Outlines* and collectively these were regarded by the author as 'the most enlightened men of all ages' ([1827] 1996, p. 41). In the same year that the *Outlines* was first published List made a passing reference, but without elaboration, to 'Hamilton's celebrated work' during a speech at a dinner given in his honour by the Pennsylvania Society for the Encouragement of Manufactures and the Mechanic Arts (List [1837] 1983, p. 172, n. 2). Hamilton is again credited in the *Natural System* when List praises that 'he [Hamilton] carried out his task [in preparing a full report on American manufactures] in a very able manner' (ibid., p. 172). For hints of, or speculations on, Hamilton's influence on List, see Hirst ([1909] 1965, pp. 114–6), Notz (1926, p. 262), Schumpeter (1954, p. 505), Dorfman ([1946] 1966, p. 577), and Henderson (1983b, p. 155). On this subject Tribe concluded that 'List had certainly read Hamilton, if only because the Pennsylvania Society reprinted the *Report* in 1824 and 1827, but, in any case, by the 1820s the text had passed into the realm of those texts which are cited more than read' (1988, p. 26). See also Yaffey (1998, pp. 101–3). The works by Hirst, Notz, Dorfman, and Henderson just referenced also contain hints or discussions of the influence of a lesser known American 'protectionist', Daniel Raymond, on List.
4. Others who subscribe to this include, for instance, Viner (1929, p. 365; 1953, p. 41), Little, Scitovsky and Scott (1970, p. 118), Johnson (1972c, p. 308), Blaug (1984, p. 368), Irwin (1996, p. 124), and Corden (1997, p. 139).
5. Recall from the discussion in section 6.4 above that this was also how Austin portrayed List when he reviewed the *National System* in 1842.
6. For a fuller description of this analogy of raising the wind, see the end of section 8.4 below.
7. Three notable exceptions are Chang (2002) and Shafaeddin (2000, 2005b). The former has a title that was inspired by a passage in List ([1841] 1991, p. 368). Through employing an historical approach, its main objective is to critique today's popular discourses on 'good policies' and 'good governance' rather than to illustrate how List's ideas have been distorted by those who are in support of the trade-policies part of the Washington

Consensus. The two papers by Shafaeddin are attempts to clarify List's infant industry argument, and as such, share an objective similar to the present chapter. However, except for occasional references through secondary sources, Shafaeddin (2000) does not incorporate List's *Outlines* and the *Natural System*. Shafaeddin (2005b) makes references to the *Outlines* but not the *Natural System*. It appeared in the same year as Ho (2005), upon which, as described in n. 1 above, the present chapter is largely based. The present author agrees with Shafaeddin's observation that 'the outstanding and innovative aspect of List's infant industry argument ... is that it was formulated in a wider context of development rather than as an instrument of trade policy' (2005b, p. 45). By incorporating the *Natural System* in addition to the *Outlines* and *National System*, it is hoped that the present chapter would shed further light on the complexity and distinctiveness of List's ideas as they relate to the promotion of national development.

8. Gide and Rist observed that 'List borrowed this enumeration of the different economic states, almost word for word, from Adam Smith [Book II, Ch. V, *Wealth of Nations*]' (1948, p. 280, n. 1).
9. Specifically referring to the Corn Laws, List thus remarked that they would 'make it somewhat difficult for the agriculturist of those countries which deal with England to pay with his own produce for the manufactured goods which he consumes' (op. cit., p. 171, see also pp. 244–5).
10. See also List ([1837] 1983, p. 56).
11. List provided figures indicating that while in 1816 American cotton-growers sold 81 million pounds of raw cotton for $24 million, in 1826 they had to sell 204 million pounds for merely $25 million (op. cit., p. 137). These figures were reproduced in List ([1837] 1983, p. 175; [1841] 1991, p. 378).
12. Hamilton noted that 'the labour employed in Agriculture is in a great measure periodical and occasional, depending on seasons, liable to various and long intermissions ... The farmer, from the peculiar fertility of his land, or some other favorable circumstance, may frequently obtain a livelihood, even with a considerable degree of carelessness in the mode of cultivation' ([1791b] 1966, p. 241). Compare with List, who observed that, '[a]ccustomed to reap only after a long lapse of time where he [the agriculturist] has sown, and to leave the success of his exertions to the will of a higher power, contentment with little, patience, resignation, but also negligence and mental laziness, become to him a second nature' ([1841] 1991, p. 197).
13. A fifth circumstance considered by Hamilton concerns how establishing domestic manufactures would give occasion to the exertion of a greater quantity of industry ([1791b] 1966, pp. 252–3). To List, 'a mass of mental and bodily powers, of natural powers and natural resources, and of instrumental powers too (which latter the prevailing school terms 'capital'), is brought to bear, and brought into use, which had not previously been active, and would never have come into activity but for the formation and development of an internal manufacturing power' ([1841] 1991, p. 148, see also pp. 211–12).
14. List reiterates in his *National System* that '*the closer the agriculturist and manufacturer are placed to one another, and the less they are liable to be interrupted in the exchange of their various products by accidents of all kinds*' ([1841] 1991, p. 157, italics original, see also p. 142).
15. At one point in his *National System* List notes, 'Smith affirms that the division of labour is less applicable to agriculture than to manufactures' ([1841] 1991, p. 151).
16. List's shrewd observation in his *Natural System* that the productive powers of industry, when brought together in a locality, could create some synergetic effects resulting in their expansion appears to anticipate some of Marshall's discussions of external economies. See, for instance, Marshall ([1920] 1961, Bk. IV, Ch. X). Interestingly, he adds that '[t]his is why the population of an industrialised society is brought together in a few conurbations in which are concentrated a great variety of technical skills, productive powers, applied science, art and literature. Here are to be found great public and private institutions and associations in which theoretical knowledge is applied to the practical affairs of industry and commerce' (List op. cit., p. 69). However, while Marshall had acquainted himself with some of List's ideas, it is not clear that he had ever read the *Natural System*.

17. This definition by Say is repeated in List (op. cit., pp. 355, 356). In one of his rare mentioning of Ricardo, List did not miss the opportunity to point out how the latter also stated in his *Principles* that, '"The chief object of political economy is to determine the laws by which the produce of the soil ought to be shared between the landowner, the farmer, and the labourer"' (ibid., p. 361).
18. In his *Natural System* List observes that 'it is possible to give up "exchange value" to increase productive power', although the result 'is not immediately apparent' ([1837] 1983, p. 35). Later in the same work and with dramatisation that is characteristic of some of his illustrations, he declares that the developmental benefits would obtain 'not just in a few years but in hundreds – even thousands – of years in the future'. In fact, the developments would take place 'throughout the whole life of the nation'. Members of Smith's school had forgotten that from this perspective 'the theory of value does not come into the picture at all' (ibid., p. 181).
19. Compare with this observation of Kaldor as he pondered how to replace 'equilibrium economics': 'The difficulty with a new start is to pinpoint the critical area where [equilibrium] economic theory went astray. In my own view, it happened when the theory of value took over the centre of the stage – which meant focusing attention on the *allocative* functions of markets to the exclusion of their *creative* functions – as an instrument for transmitting impulses to economic change' (1972, p. 1240, italics original). See also Young (1928).
20. Among other commentators, this passage of List on the crucial importance of acquiring the 'power of producing wealth' caught the attention of Ohlin (1967), who interprets List's argument as one that is desirous of augmenting a 'new manufacturing' country's supply of 'technical' or 'skilled' labour broadly in the long run. As such, he proposes that '[t]he "infant industry argument" should be called instead the "infant country argument"' (pp. 205–6). On the apparently similar notion of 'infant economy argument', see n. 46 below.
21. To be fair to Smith, he does mention in Bk. I, Ch. I of the *Wealth of Nations* not just a separation of workmen by 'trades', but also by 'occupations', consequent upon the process of division of labour and the introduction of machinery. At one point he specifically alludes to the 'assistance and co-operation of many thousands' ([1776] 1979, p. 23).
22. For a discussion of how the division of labour, or the 'division of products', would increase the output of agriculture, see List ([1837] 1983, pp. 62–3; [1841] 1991, p. 151).
23. List indicated that the quotation is from Bk. I, Ch. I of the *Wealth of Nations*. As is often the case with him, it is actually a paraphrase and summary of some passages, in this case apparently of Smith ([1776] 1979, pp. 22–3).
24. For an illustration involving an 'iron-master' that yields an identical message, see List ([1837] 1983, pp. 72–3).
25. Compare with: 'The productive powers of every separate manufactory are also increased in proportion as the whole manufacturing power of the country is developed in all its branches, and the more intimately it is united with all other branches of industry' (List [1841] 1991, pp. 152–3).
26. Compare with: 'the success of one particular branch of industry depends on that of several other branches' (List [1841] 1991, p. 39).
27. On a related note, List deduced that '[n]o factory reaches its maximum efficiency unless all the factories with which it is linked have also reached their maximum efficiency' ([1837] 1983, p. 73). His emphasis of the importance of the interconnectedness of different industries has escaped the attention of many commentators, excepting Hoselitz (1960, p. 202, n. 18), Haddad (1987, pp. 10–11), and Daastöl (1999, p. 389).
28. At a later point in the *National System* List repeats, 'It is evident that canals, railways, and steam navigation are called into existence only by means of *the manufacturing power*, and can only by means of it be extended over the whole surface of the country' ([1841] 1991, pp. 201–2, italics original). 'Manufactures as the basis of a large home and foreign commerce are also the fundamental conditions of the existence of any considerable mercantile marine' (ibid., p. 268).
29. At one point in his *National System*, where List considers well proportioned labour and resource flows between the manufacturing and agricultural sectors of a hypothetical nation,

he projects that 'agricultural and industrial productive power will increase reciprocally, and indeed *ad infinitum*' (op. cit., p. 155). See also List (ibid., pp. 185–6, 233) for yet further discussion of the 'reciprocal action' and 'reciprocal inducement' between these two sectors. For a similar consideration of the relationship between towns and country districts, see List (ibid., p. 204; [1837] 1983, pp. 62–5).

30. For a similar description of a process of cumulative causation, see List ([1837] 1983, p. 93).
31. Among other areas, the effects of these progresses and perfections would be extended to agriculture, in the form of 'more perfect agricultural machines and implements', and the improved 'intelligence' with which agriculture is practised. 'Under the influence of manufactures', List thus concluded, 'agriculture itself is raised to a skilled industry, an art, a science' (op. cit.).
32. In discussing the development experience of some European states, List also mentioned in passing the 'reciprocating influences of industry and freedom' (op. cit., p. 115) and the 'reciprocal influence material wealth and political power exercise on each other' (ibid., p. 140; see also List [1827] 1996, pp. 29, 31).
33. List's consideration of this rich network of reciprocal effects, which blends together economic and non-economic elements, sets him apart from many other supporters of industry promotion. It resembles one of the emphases that Myrdal put in his works. See Ch. 11 below.
34. At another point in the same work he states, 'The Christian religion, monogamy, abolition of slavery and of vassalage, hereditability of the throne, invention of printing, of the press, of the postal system, of money, weights and measures, of the calendar, of watches, of police, the introduction of the principle of freehold property, of means of transport, are rich sources of productive power' (op. cit., p. 139). In his *Natural System* List is careful to maintain that 'there are even significant differences between the productive powers of the adherents of various Christian churches' ([1837] 1983, p. 185).
35. Hence, 'we believe that there should be complete freedom of trade between all nations with regard to raw materials and foodstuffs' (List [1837] 1983, p. 90). In that connection he felt that England should repeal the Corn Laws ([1841] 1991, p. 216).
36. For a detailed description of this process of awakening, see List (op. cit., pp. 54–6). See also List ([1841] 1991, pp. 154, 191).
37. Nor would the manufacturers be the only group who wanted a change in development policies, for 'those who work on the land [also] come to appreciate the fact that the home market is much larger, more stable, more certain, and more profitable than foreign markets' (List [1837] 1983, p. 56). See also List ([1841] 1991, pp. 110–11), where, by referring to the use of 'a system of *restrictions, privileges, and encouragements*, to transplant ... the wealth, the talents, and the spirit of enterprise of the foreigners' (italics added) from the advanced to the less advanced nations, a hint is given for the content of the discussion to come in section 8.5 below.
38. 'He [Smith] falsely maintains that these manufactures have originated in the natural course of things and of their own accord; notwithstanding that in every nation the political power interferes to give to this so-called natural course an artificial direction for the nation's own special advantage' (op. cit., p. 227).
39. The last part of the passage quoted here reads: 'or that those manufactures which have originated in consequence of the commercial interruptions caused by war should be able, "in the natural course of things," to continue to maintain themselves' (op. cit.). This is a reminder that apart from thinking about development somewhat abstractly as a process that goes through stages, List was deeply moved by what he saw in some parts of Europe of 'the admirable effects of what is called the continental system and the destroying effects of the return of what they call trade after the downfall of Napoleon' ([1827] 1996, p. 41).
40. See Backhaus (1992) for a related objection to the use of the theory of domestic divergences to evaluate the soundness of List's argument for development intervention.
41. Contrast this broader appreciation of what constitute the sources of productive powers with the approach adopted by Mill and his followers which narrowly focused on one single industry.

42. This subsection echoes Chang (2002, pp. 65–6), who observes that 'tariff protection ... was ... by no means the only, nor even necessarily the most important, policy tool used by those [now-developed] countries in promoting infant industries'. Shafaeddin (2005b, p. 50) makes a similar observation.
43. Darity regarded Chs. 21–26 of that book as 'a short-hand manual for the conduct of trade policy' (1985, p. 495).
44. Given that most of the non-tariff policy actions enumerated here and in the previous subsection would have to be funded by the state, the reader might wonder what List had to say with regard to the sources of funding. He did not address this question explicitly. It is, however, quite clear List had in mind that some tariffs should serve revenue-generating purposes ([1837] 1983, pp. 116, 118, 120–21, 123; [1841] 1991, p. 308). At one point he was explicit in linking such revenue raised to funding some projects and policy actions ([1841] 1991, p. 435). In any case, on this subject List showed an awareness of alternative methods and did not regard imposing a tariff as the only way of generating revenue for such purposes.
45. Advocating free importation of agricultural produce and raw materials into an industrialising country for its benefit by keeping costs down 'has a deeply Ricardian ring' (Darity 1985, p. 495).
46. Contrast with Corden's portrayal of List's '*infant economy* argument', which, to him, is 'for general protection of the whole manufacturing sector of an economy' (1997, p. 147, italics original). Senghaas (1991, p. 457) and Shafaeddin (2005b, p. 50) both point out that List had in mind a selective rather than universal protection of manufactures.
47. This evolving and dynamic feature of List's programme did not escape Shafaeddin's attention (2005b, p. 50).
48. As Levi-Faur observed, 'As a bureaucrat as well as a Professor of Public Administration, List was well aware of these potential problems [of power abuse by politicians and the inefficiency of public bureaucracies]' (1997a, p. 170). The suggestions described in the present subsection share very much the same spirit as the effort, witnessed in East Asia, to manage 'economic rents' (Akyüz, Chang and Kozul-Wright 1999, pp. 15–16). For List's specific caution on the use of protection, including his understanding that different countries faced different circumstances, see List ([1827] 1996, pp. 33, 35, 77; [1837] 1983, pp. 35, 44, 75–6, 105–7; [1841] 1991, pp. 83, 112–13, 217, 324). Some of these passages resonate with the discussion in the middle subsection of section 8.4, in that List regarded it proper for a country to be 'far advanced in agriculture and civilisation' and possess 'the necessary moral qualities or natural advantages' before it should contemplate promoting development through state intervention. See also Shafaeddin (2005b, pp. 51–2).
49. To this List immediately added that some causes of such incapacity can readily be removed. See the last paragraph in the first subsection ('A Broad Set of Policy Actions to Promote Industries') of the present section.
50. The shrewd reader will detect that these passages indicate yet another instance (in addition to the three examples in the subsection, 'Awareness of the Possible Need to Weigh Some Policy Alternatives') when List appeared to apply something akin to the principle of targetting.
51. One option considered by List was 'the union of the interests of various states by means of free conventions' ([1841] 1991, p. 176). Although this is not further discussed here, the reader will recognise that it relates to his proposal to establish a *Zollverein*. It finds parallels with the post-World War II attempts at South–South trade promotion and, of course, the formation of preferential trade agreements. See also Yaffey (1998, pp. 98–9).
52. Shafaeddin (2005b, p. 53) also notes that for List, 'infant industry protection should eventually lead to massive exports of manufactured products'.
53. This last sentence raises the possibility of retaliation by the erstwhile open country, which List did not explore further. Note, however, his proposal of a world trade congress for the negotiation of commercial treaties that presumably would accommodate the aspirations of second- and third-rank industrial countries to catch up with England. See List ([1837] 1983, pp. 126–7) and section 8.7 below.

54. *Report on the German Zollverein to Lord Viscount Palmerston*, by John Bowring, 1840, cited in List ([1841] 1991, Ch. XXXIV).
55. This deviates from what was discussed in the last subsection in section 8.5 above, namely that List seemed to favour a certain amount of competing imports to create competition with domestic manufacturers.
56. For those temperate zone countries that possessed colonies, List also considered the stimulative effect on their economies when they traded with those colonies. In particular, 'the production of the manufactured goods which are required to pay for the colonial products, occupies a larger number of manufacturers; manufactories and manufacturing business can be conducted on a much larger scale, and consequently more profitably' (op. cit., pp. 264–5).
57. Hoselitz (op. cit.) observed that at some point List 'comes close to the postulate of external economies to an industry'. In that connection it is most interesting to note that Marshall ([1920] 1961, p. 767) calls List a 'brilliant genius'.
58. Levi-Faur also pointed out how the world trade congress proposal anticipated the GATT and noted that List was 'probably the first to aspire to a world congress as a means to regulate all international economic relations' (1997b, pp. 366–7).
59. On this the present author differs from Shafaeddin (2005b, pp. 55, 53), who concludes that 'though brief and lacking in detail, Mill is strikingly reminiscent of List's reasoning' as far as the former's endorsement passage in his *Principles* is concerned. Also, 'his [List's] ideas on the importance of trade for development, by and large, were similar to those of Mill'.

9. Manoïlesco: Supporting the Expansion of Superior Productive Sectors through Tariffs or Subventions

9.1 INTRODUCTION

What has lent coherence to the discussion in the last two chapters is the fact that Hamilton and List are both regarded in the economics mainstream as central figures in formulating and popularising the infant-industry argument for tariff protection. Yet, careful re-examination of their works indicates that their visions for development promotion are much broader than what the standard mainstream version of the infant-industry argument would convey. Besides, they both offered policy proposals that are much more sophisticated and thoughtful than merely tariff protection.

At first sight, the works of Mihaïl Manoïlesco[1] pose some challenges to maintaining this coherence. The chief reason is that in the economics mainstream he is often not associated with the infant-industry, although he is credited with another, argument for tariff protection. Specifically, that argument is variously labelled as 'imperfections in the labour market' (Gomes 1990, p. 88) or 'different wages for identical labor' (Bhagwati, Panagariya and Srinivasan 1998, p. 323).[2]

Having attached that label to his argument, the next step – and here one finds consistency with the mainstream treatment of Hamilton and List – is to portray Manoïlesco as someone who knew no better than advocating tariffs to correct the 'market distortion' that he had laid his finger on. Thus, in Haberler's opinion, 'Manoïlesco tries to base an argument for tariffs upon the existence of permanent differences in wages between different industries and employments, which are due, in his opinion, to differences in the marginal productivity of labour' (1937, p. 196, n. 1). In the words of Viner, 'Manoïlesco contends that ... predominantly agricultural countries will raise their *per capita* incomes if by establishing tariff protection for manufactures they increase the proportion of the labour force engaged in manufactures' (1953, p. 46). Gomes, who gave Manoïlesco's argument one of the labels listed in the previous paragraph, went on to add that upon this rests his 'case for industrial tariff protection' (1990, p. 88). Putting it differently, 'the central issue in Manoilescu's argument ... ultimately turned on the possibility of transforming (through industrial tariff protection) an agrarian and overpopulated country into an industrialised economy – one with a higher level of productivity' (ibid., p. 89, n. 10; see also Irwin 1996, p. 153).

Have these interpretations and labels done justice to Manoïlesco's works, or have the latter been distorted and misrepresented? These will be explored in the following discussions and these are organised as follows.

Section 9.2 lists the reasons why he thought it advantageous for backward countries to become industrialised and examines why he thought state support would be needed for industrialisation. Section 9.3 presents his criticism of the static version of the classical trade model, where his emphasis was on Ricardo, although Smith and Mill did not escape his attention. By reconfiguring the static Ricardian trade model, he thought he succeeded in showing rigorously the circumstances under which an agricultural country should industrialise. However, by following up on a hint provided by Ohlin (1931), his reconfigured illustrations will be shown in this section to be fatally flawed.

Some sort of conception of 'productivity' figures prominently in both sections 9.2 and 9.3, namely that industries in general show superior productivity over agriculture (section 9.2) and that the classical economists had allegedly failed to make that distinction in their static model (section 9.3). Section 9.4 puts Manoïlesco's formulation of this conception to closer scrutiny and argues that it is devoid of considerations of development *as a process*. One recalls, in contrast, how Hamilton's and List's discussions are very much rooted in some such processes. But despite an apparently strong influence on his thoughts by List (but not Hamilton), Manoïlesco tweaked his (List's) conception of productivity and rendered his (Manoïlesco's) argument easily hijacked by the economics mainstream. It is turned into nothing but a static case of market distortion. Interestingly, while in the mainstream portrayal of Manoïlesco's model an alleged labour-market distortion exists in the less-developed agricultural country, in Manoïlesco's reconfigured illustration that is shown in section 9.3, there is arguably no distortion there. If there were any distortion, it actually exists in the industrial country.

Section 9.5 represents the policy measures that Manoïlesco considered to engender industrialisation, which include 'subventions'. Section 9.6 indicates his rather casual portrayal of a world order that is without 'disadvantageous discrimination' against the agricultural countries such that they would be allowed to industralise. Section 9.7 sums up the discussion in this chapter.

9.2 DISADVANTAGES OF BEING AGRICULTURAL: A CASE FOR STATE-AIDED INDUSTRIALISATION

Considerations of Unequal Exchange, Domination, and Exploitation

Unlike the rationales that Hamilton and List provided for diversifying into manufacturing industries, Manoïlesco emphasised the inequity in the *exchange* between predominantly industrial and predominantly agricultural countries, and how the former thus dominated over and exploited the latter.

He thus claims in the Preface to his *Theory of Protection* that '*it is the nature of international exchange which is the determining factor of the wealth of nations*' (1931, p. xiii, italics original). '[F]rom the economic point of view', he elaborates, 'the most significant thing for all countries of the world is *the quality* of their imports and exports' (ibid., p. xiv, italics original). For it is this quality 'that decides the favourable or unfavourable character of exchange operations' and '[t]he country becomes rich if it exports goods of high productivity and imports goods of small productivity' (ibid., p. 168). On the other hand, '[w]hen a people exports the produce of the work of ten of its workmen in order to buy the produce of the work of a single foreign workman, this exchange can be only disadvantageous' (ibid., p. xiv).[3]

To Manoïlesco, this is precisely what takes place when backward agricultural countries trade with industrial countries given that industry possesses what he termed 'superior productivity'. Hence, 'when an industrial product is exchanged for a primary, and especially an agricultural product, then, owing to the superior productivity of industry as compared with agriculture, *the product of the labour of an industrial workman is almost always exchanged for the product of the labour of several agricultural workmen*' (ibid., p. vi, italics original). He concluded that the advantage of this kind of exchange '*exists only for industrial countries, ... and it does not exist for agricultural countries*'. '*[C]ould we call the historical fact of the rapid enrichment of industrial countries compared with agricultural countries anything but a paradox*', he rhetorically asks, '*if the exchange of industrial products for agricultural products cannot assure any particular advantage or superiority to industrial countries?*' (ibid., p. ix, italics original).

According to Manoïlesco, this pattern of inequitable exchange was observed between industrial Europe and other continents in the nineteenth century and was 'extremely favourable' to the former. Within Europe, there were the rich industrial countries like England, France, and Germany on the one side, and the poor agricultural ones like Russia, Romania, Yugoslavia, and Bulgaria on the other. To underscore his claim, he concludes that '[t]hese two Europes show in an approximate manner – before entering into scientific demonstrations – *that it is the structure of a country's exchange, the nature (and not the quantity) of its exports and imports, which determine its state of wealth and capacity for increase of wealth*' (ibid., p. xiv, italics original). Here one finds a rare instance when he refers to the 'capacity' to increase a country's wealth. This is despite what he proclaims at one point in his *Theory of Protection* as he praises List, 'And his famous sentence: "The capacity to produce wealth is much more important than wealth itself," remains a *vade mecum* for economists and statesmen of all time' (ibid., p. 242).[4] And even though it is mentioned, notice that that 'capacity' is regarded as being determined by the structure of a country's exchange.

Manoïlesco laments that this pattern of trade and uneven distribution of wealth as exhibiting 'economic domination' by the industrial over the backward agricultural countries (ibid., pp. vii–viii). He also characterises this as '*invisible exploitation which decides the economic position of peoples*' and as 'exchange slavery' that was 'obtained by the free exchange of products' (ibid., p. viii and p. 148, n. 2, italics original).

It was thus to counter this inequitable outcome in exchange, and to end the domination and exploitation, that Manoïlesco wished to see the backward countries become industrialised.[5]

Why State-Aided Industrialisation?

But why would industrialisation require state support of some sort? This is one area where Manoïlesco appeared to be borrowing a little bit from List, although, as it will become clear, he also obfuscated his (List's) discussion by adding his own touch.

Thus, recall the discussion in section 8.4 in the last chapter that referred to List's juxtaposition of national economy on the one hand, and personal and cosmopolitical economy on the other. Somewhat in parallel with List's consideration of personal versus national economy, Manoïlesco compared an individual's exchange with that of a nation and titled section IV, Part II, Ch. I of his *Theory of Protection* 'Individual and International Exchange'.[6] There he begins with the observation that, 'The most important argument of free-traders is that a nation, like an individual, must buy the goods it requires as cheaply as possible' (ibid., p. 64). To illustrate, he appends to this observation a footnote in which he quotes from Lujo Brentano: '"The tailor does not manufacture the shoes he wears: he buys them from the shoemaker; the shoemaker does not make his clothes: he buys them from the tailor. What is wise in the economy of a household cannot be foolish for a nation"' (ibid., p. 64, n. 1).[7] It is only fair to suggest that Brentano had paraphrased Smith's passage, which is precisely the same one to which List retorted (see section

8.4 above). Among other things, List insisted, 'that may be wisdom in national economy which would be folly in private economy, and *vice versâ*; … that a tailor is no nation and a nation no tailor' ([1841] 1991, p. 165). As for Manoïlesco, he offers: 'But the interests of a nation must not be considered as the interests of a private person, and must not be referred to in a certain moment only. The life of nations is eternal' (1931, p. 244n). He quotes from the Preface to List's *National System* where he (List) asserts as 'the distinguishing characteristic of my system, NATIONALITY' (List [1841] 1991, p. xxix)[8] and concurs that,

> This is what we all must do. And this is the basis of all our theory when we always justify protection from the point of view of the interests of a nation considered as a whole, and discuss only on a secondary plane the influence of the protectionist system on the classes and individuals of each nation. (Manoïlesco 1931, p. 250)

List earned Manoïlesco's praise for transferring, 'in a wonderful manner, the idea of nationality from ideology to economics' (ibid.).

In his elaboration Manoïlesco makes two further distinctions. The first such distinction is made early on in his *Theory of Protection* and is between *individual* profit and *national* profit. By the former he refers to the profit or gain of the individual capitalist, while by the latter he was pointing to national gain, advantages or benefits (ibid., pp. 17–19). At one point he suggests that it would include 'the total of the individual profits of workers [who receive high wages], creditors [who receive interest], the State [which receive taxes] and the capitalist'. As such, '[n]ational profit is a sum: the individual profit of the capitalist is an item of this sum' (p. 19, n. 1). Now, '[i]f on account of the free-trade system, this [individual] profit does not exist, production will cease' (p. 18). Nevertheless, one should '[c]ertainly not' believe that in such a case there is no national profit. On the other hand, it is possible for a produce to 'compete with world prices and the capitalist receive large profits', but yet the national gain is small compared with other production activities (p. 19, n. 1). This echoes something that List argues in his *Natural System*, when he insists that '[o]ne cannot strike a balance of commercial gains and loss from a national point of view by examining the profits and losses of individual merchants'. '[C]ommerce in general can be threatened and can be destroyed root and branch', he further adds, 'although at the same time some of the merchants engaged in foreign trade are making handsome profits' (List [1837] 1983, p. 102).[9] But why might there be a difference in decisions made based on individual as opposed to national profit? Manoïlesco does not give an answer in his *Theory of Protection*. He simply claims that there is an 'antithesis between national and individual profit'. Thus, '[i]t is true that capital always looks for the most profitable investments which may be offered at a certain moment, in its own interest.

But the order of these investments is quite different from the order suggested by national interest and national profit' (1931, p. 133, n. 1). He refers to this 'antithesis' at another point when he considers the trade theories of Ricardo and Mill, cautioning that 'the existence of individual profit of traders is not a proof of real profit to a nation nor of the profitable character of these operations for the nation as a whole' (ibid., p. 126). This is an instance when he seems to connect this distinction between individual and national profits with his other distinction. 'National interest', he thus maintains, 'requires that not only the exchange operation but also the production operation be considered' (ibid.).

On this second distinction Manoïlesco contends that, 'For an individual, the buying problem is a strictly commercial problem; for a nation the buying problem is never a strictly commercial problem – it is always at the same time a production problem' (ibid., pp. 66–7). But why is the individual's buying problem a strictly commercial problem? Manoïlesco regards that '[a]n individual may, usually, have at a given moment only a single profession which brings him in a definite income',[10] while '[a]t the same time, an individual does not generally create, through his own activity (except he be an agriculturist) many of the utilities he consumes'. Hence, 'the question for him is to buy the cheapest in order to get the best return from his fixed income. There is no connection between the productive activity which secures his income and his buying activity' (p. 64). On the other hand, '[a] nation satisfies a great part of its needs by its own labour. By changing the structure of its productive apparatus, it can satisfy a larger number of its needs, and thus diminish the number of the necessaries which have to be imported from outside' (pp. 64–5). Lest this confirms the reader's suspicion that Manoïlesco had only in mind IS and self-sufficiency, it should be pointed out that he also considered, albeit rather superficially, the importance of exports. For a nation would still need to 'buy' imports, only that, unlike individuals, these 'are not paid for out of a settled income'. And contrary to the 'free-traders', 'the cheapness of imported goods is not sufficient to give an idea of the advantage of the operation'. Rather, '[t]he advantage or disadvantage of the buying operation depends very much on the power and facilities to produce goods which serve for exchange' (p. 65).[11] 'So all the buying problem of a country depends not only on what is bought', he proclaims, 'but also on what is produced, in order that it may purchase' (p. 66). The 'production factor' is 'very often neglected in the conclusions of free-traders, or at best it is mixed up with the exchange factor, so that one is unable to distinguish the influence of either' (p. 68). A consideration of the 'synthetic advantage of commerce and of production' is subsequently referred to as the 'synthetic point of view' or the 'integral economic point of view' (p. 103, n. 1 and p. 153).

This last part smacks of the idea that trade could be viewed as an 'indirect method of production' (Maneschi 1998, p. 36). Indeed, as Manoïlesco puts it, '[t]here are only two means of obtaining wanted goods: by producing them directly, or by producing exchange goods in order to acquire them. In both cases the question is production, and the exchange problem cannot fail to be a comparison of the two production processes' (1931, p. 67, n. 1). He also refers to this key consideration as '"how buying capacity may be created"' (ibid., p. 65). Hence, '[a]ccording to the larger or smaller capacity of any industry to supply international buying capacity (with the same disposition of workmen and capitals), this industry is more or less of interest to national economics' (p. 64). But Manoïlesco must have something else in mind, for otherwise he would exactly end up with the classical trade theory which he vehemently seeks to reject in his *Theory of Protection*. His emphasis on the 'power and facilities to produce goods' may appear to some to be reminiscent of List's emphasis on 'productive powers' (see also the discussion leading to n. 4 above). However, his conceptualisation of productivity renders his treatment totally alien to List's approach. That will be one of the subjects of discussion in section 9.4 below. Before then, it is still not clear that he has made a compelling case for state-aided industrialisation.

Having addressed individual versus national exchange in the early part of his *Theory of Protection*, Manoïlesco waits until much later in that same work to turn his attention to dispute the 'natural harmony of the interests of all countries' that is asserted as 'simple and automatic' by the free-traders. He ridicules the 'non-existence and impossibility of this automatism' (ibid., p. 212), adding that,

> the automatic realisation of harmony, has never led to any end, it has had to be recognised as too chimerical.
> For the theory on which this idea was founded was wrong.
> ...
> According to this theory, the problem of international co-operation does not exist. According to us, it does exist, and is really very important. To speak the truth, it is unsolvable. (Ibid., p. 213)

Then he sought to contrast 'national aims' with those of 'humanity'. In a rather clumsy way he stitches together one of his generalisations and one supposition that he makes in this part of his work to claim that national aims are too important to ignore. Specifically, having suggested that industries are more productive than agriculture and having granted, for the sake of discussion, that free trade would indeed be 'followed by a maximum production for the whole world', he concludes that,

> The free-trade system ... is [under the supposition] to represent the highest formula for humanity, but is not to be the best formula for each particular country. Then the average production per inhabitant would be the greatest possible for the whole of humanity, but there will still be countries for which the average production might be greater under protection than under free-trade.
> It therefore means that, giving up protection, those countries will give up a national positive advantage for the sake of humanity, which means a direct and concrete sacrifice.
> Therefore, from this point of view, national aims do not coincide, at least for certain nations, with the aim of humanity at large. (Ibid., p. 220)

'Can we impose upon a nation the renunciation of its own aims to follow those of humanity?', he asks rhetorically. And, 'Is the principle of the economic forces of humanity (the principle of highest output) to be set above the principle of the liberty of nations?' (ibid.). List's influence can again be detected here, this time traceable to his distinction between national versus cosmopolitical economy. Manoïlesco, in tying this with his earlier reference to domination and exploitation, proclaims that '[i]f free-trade is incapable of securing for all nations a larger prosperity than protection, if there are nations which lose under free-trade and gain under protection, free-trade is for such nations nothing but a system of constraint against nature (why should we not risk the words a *system of slavery*?)' (p. 221, italics original).[12]

9.3 CRITIQUE OF THE STATIC RICARDIAN MODEL

Given how influential 'the theory of international trade' (that is, the static classical theory) was during Manoïlesco's time, it was only natural for him to attempt a critique of it so that he could win wider acceptance of his policy proposal for state-aided industrialisation. Indeed, a good part of his *Theory of Protection* is devoted to this end.

Interestingly, he sees with clarity the same lineage in the theory's development that is identified in Chapter 2 above. Thus, after noting that the theory was developed by Smith, Ricardo, and Mill, he points out that while 'Smith laid down the principle of international division of labour', 'Ricardo went further with ... the principle of comparative advantage' (1931, p. 70). He adds that, 'If Ricardo's principle is right, *a fortiori* Smith's will be right too' (ibid., p. 70, n. 1). What about Mill? '[I]n sifting to the bottom Ricardo's theory, [he] was able to establish according to what laws the profit of international trade is divided among the countries that have exchanged goods', and 'Ricardo's deductions, together with ... Mill's idea, form the culminating point of the theoretic basis for the political promotion of free-trade' (p. 70 and p. 71, n. 3).

In Chapter 2 above, Ricardo's England–Portugal model is labelled as the 'anchor' in the mainstream history of thought story as it pertains to trade theories. To Manoïlesco, '[t]he heart of the theory ... is formed by Ricardo's famous declaration upon comparative advantages', for 'it is admitted by everyone to be the strongest point of the free-trade theory'. As a result, '[t]his central stronghold must be taken if we want to conquer the whole town' (ibid., p. 71). That pretty much sums up Manoïlesco's strategy as he attempts a critique of the classical trade models in his *Theory of Protection*.

On Ricardo's England–Portugal Model[13]

He thus zeroes in on the England–Portugal model and complains that Ricardo only 'considers a single production factor, labour, and admits it has a character of uniformity which it is far from having' (ibid., p. 77, n. 1).[14] 'The greatest errors of political economy', he laments, 'are due to the fact that the importance of the *quality* of labour is not recognised'.[15] He is convinced that the introduction of 'the notion of quality or, better, *productivity*' would enable him 'to put the phenomena of production and exchange in a suitable light and to prove clearly by many examples the errors of certain conclusions upon international exchange, conclusions up to now irrefutable' (p. 10, italics original). He proceeds to do so by reconfiguring the static Ricardian model to reflect that industry possesses productivity superior over that in agriculture and then he illustrates the 'buying problem of a country' as spelled out in section 9.2 above.

These reconfigurations are reproduced below. Following some of his original notations, A (Agricultural) and I (Industrial) are country labels; a (agricultural) and i (industrial) are product labels. Let l denote a workman, where the superscript indicates the country in which the workman labours and the subscript denotes the sector in which the workman is employed. Assume for the moment that l_a^A is identical with l_i^A and l_a^I is identical with l_i^I.

Table 9.1 *The static Ricardian model with Manoïlesco's notation*

	Product a	Product i
Country A	$100\ l_a^A \rightarrow Q$ of a	$100\ l_i^A \rightarrow Q_1$ of i
Country I	$(100.q_a)\ l_a^I \rightarrow Q$ of a	$(100.q_i)\ l_i^I \rightarrow Q_1$ of i

Table 9.1 then indicates that 100 workmen in A can produce Q of a, or Q_1 of i, over a certain period. In I, it takes $100q_a$ and $100q_i$ of its workmen to produce Q of a and Q_1 of i respectively over the same period.[16] Manoïlesco set $q_a > q_i > 1$ in order to represent A as superior to I in producing both a and

i, but that A 'has a comparatively larger superiority' in producing a (1931, pp. 100–101).[17]

In order to deliver illustrations that recognise the different qualities or productivities of labour between sectors a and i, he needs to distinguish l_a^A from l_i^A, and l_a^I from l_i^I. He introduces a coefficient K for this purpose, where $l_i = K.l_a$. Obviously, if $K = 1$, then one obtains the standard static Ricardian model. On the other hand, one expects $K > 1$ based on what Manoïlesco has claimed to be the superior productivity of industry.

He applies a separate coefficient K for each country, so that the Ks employed in the illustrations below all have country superscripts. However, what is strange and is crucial to note is that he introduces K^I and K^A into two separate reconfigured illustrations.[18] That is, K^I and K^A are *not* incorporated simultaneously into one single illustration. Recall that in the static Ricardian model one set of numbers illustrates the claim that trade is mutually beneficial if the terms of trade lie strictly between the pre-trade domestic price ratios. But Manoïlesco has to reconfigure that model in two separate attempts, one case is such that $K^I > 1$ and $K^A = 1$, and the other is such that $K^I = 1$ while $K^A > 1$. He thus essentially employs two sets of numbers to make two claims. One relates to how it would 'nearly always' be advantageous for the agricultural country to produce rather than import industrial products. The other pertains to how exporting industrial to obtain agricultural products is always advantageous for the industrial country.

Thus, in Table 9.2 he relaxes the assumption that l_a^I is identical with l_i^I by introducing K^I, where $K^I > 1$, such that $l_i^I = K^I.l_a^I$. It denotes 'the ratio of productivities' between i and a or '*the intrinsic superiority or the qualitative superiority*' of i compared with a (ibid., pp. 101, 103, italics original). Specifically, every industrial workman counts as productively as K^I agricultural workmen, so $100q_i$ industrial workmen are as productive as $100q_iK^I$ agricultural workmen (p. 102). This is, of course, a step to add 'quality of labour' considerations to the simple labour theory of value. However, notice that for this reconfiguration he reserves this distinction only for country I, which is why K is attached with an I superscript. He does not apply it to country A, or, in other words, he has simply set $K^A = 1$. Hence, in that table $l_a^A = l_i^A = l^A$.

Table 9.2 *Reconfiguring the static Ricardian model to determine if the agricultural country should industrialise*

	Product a	Product i
Country A	$100\ l^A \rightarrow Q$ of a	$100\ l^A \rightarrow Q_1$ of i
Country I	$(100.q_a)\ l_a^I \rightarrow Q$ of a	$(100.q_i.K^I)\ l_a^I \rightarrow Q_1$ of i

Manoïlesco thinks he is then ready to determine whether there would be any advantage for *A* to specialise in producing *a* and exporting it in exchange for *i* from *I*, or whether it is more advantageous for it to produce *i* itself. First, *A* is supposed to produce *Q* of *a* and export that to *I* in exchange for *i*. At what terms of trade? He implicitly assumes it to be at *I*'s domestic price ratio (ibid., pp. 101–2). That means *Q* of *a* exported by *A* could be exchanged for $(1/K^I)(q_a/q_i)Q_1$ of *i*. Second, if *A* were to produce *i* with the labour that it requires to produce *Q* amount of *a*, how much *i* could be produced? It is Q_1. Hence, the ratio between 'indirect production' and 'direct production' obtained with the same amount of labour is: $(1/K^I)(q_a/q_i)$ (p. 103). If $(1/K^I)(q_a/q_i) < 1$ or $q_a/q_i < K^I$, then direct production is preferable to the 'trading solution'. In other words, if the comparative superiority of agriculture (q_a/q_i) is less than the intrinsic (qualitative) superiority of industry (K^I), direct industrial production is 'more profitable' and industry would have a 'right to exist' in *A* (p. 113, see also pp. 103, 104, 106 for alternative ways in which this is stated). On the other hand, if $(1/K^I)(q_a/q_i) > 1$ or $q_a/q_i > K^I$, the trading solution is preferable to direct production. To Manoïlesco, those who reason within the context of Ricardo's England–Portugal model conclude that the trading solution is better simply because they do not make a distinction therein between the productivity of industrial and agricultural sectors. In that case, $K^I = 1$, and $q_a > q_i$ will ensure that $(1/K^I)(q_a/q_i) > 1$. However, Manoïlesco claims that 'the intrinsic (qualitative) superiority of industry is twice as great and *even more*'. He thus cautions that 'this condition [$q_a/q_i > K^I$] is very difficult to fulfil, and therefore it is very seldom fulfilled' (p. 105, italics original). In other words, 'the solution of direct production nearly always outweighs the commercial solution' (p. 110).

Having examined the reconfigured static Ricardian model from the viewpoint of country *A*, Manoïlesco then considers the situation from the viewpoint of country *I* and queries 'whether an industrial country has an advantage in producing only industrial articles … in order to buy with these agricultural articles from an agricultural country, or whether it has an advantage in producing the agricultural articles itself' (ibid., p. 107). However, instead of continuing to work with Table 9.2 and to consider *I*'s situation based on it,[19] he introduces a different reconfiguration which is reproduced here as Table 9.3:

Table 9.3 *Reconfiguring the static Ricardian model to illustrate that the industrial country tends to always gain from trade*

	Product *a*	Product *i*
Country *A*	$100\ l_a^A \rightarrow Q$ of *a*	$(100.K^A)\ l_a^A \rightarrow Q_1$ of *i*
Country *I*	$(100.q_a)\ l^I \rightarrow Q$ of *a*	$(100.q_i)\ l^I \rightarrow Q_1$ of *i*

Notice that in this new table he no longer makes any distinction between l_a^I and l_i^I by implicitly setting $K^I = 1$. As a result $l_a^I = l_i^I = l^I$. On the other hand, he starts making a distinction between l_a^A and l_i^A. Specifically, $l_i^A = K^A.l_a^A$, where $K^A > 1$. That is, in *A*, every industrial workman is as productive as K^A agricultural workmen (ibid.).

Manoïlesco follows basically the same steps as in the previous case in determining if there would be any advantage for *I* to specialise in producing *i* and to export it in exchange for *a* from *A*, or whether it is more advantageous for it to produce *a* itself. Thus, *I* is first supposed to produce Q_1 of *i* and export that to *A* in exchange for *a*. This time he implicitly assumes the terms of trade to be at *A*'s domestic price ratio.[20] That means Q_1 of *i* exported by *I* could be exchanged for K^AQ of *a*. Next, if *I* were to produce *a* with the labour that it requires to produce Q_1 amount of *i*, how much *a* could be produced? It is $(q_i/q_a)Q$. Hence, the ratio between 'indirect production' and 'direct production' is $K^A(q_a/q_i)$ (ibid., p. 108). Obviously, if $K^A(q_a/q_i) > 1$, then for *I* the 'commercial solution' is preferable to 'direct production'. Now having assumed that *A* possesses 'comparative superiority' in *a*, $q_a/q_i > 1$. Then having observed that industry is more productive than agriculture, $K^A > 1$. So $K^A(q_a/q_i)$ 'is always greater than unity; so for the industrial country the commercial solution is preferable to direct agricultural production' (ibid.).

Manoïlesco thinks that he has successfully illustrated the disadvantages of being agricultural in accordance with the discussion in section 9.2 above and that he has buttressed his case for supporting industries. But as is obvious to the reader, his illustration can run into difficulties when it is recognised, as it should be, that K^I and K^A should not be considered separately in two configurations (that is, separately in Tables 9.2 and 9.3 above). As Ohlin remarked, 'The question becomes more complicated only in so far as there is an intrinsic superiority ... in manufacturing industries than in agriculture in A also, not only in I' (1931, p. 33).[21] When K^I and K^A are combined into one single table and when both are larger than unity, then the situation is represented in Table 9.4:

Table 9.4 *Representing industrial workers as more productive than agricultural ones in both countries*

	Product *a*	Product *i*
Country *A*	$100\ l_a^A \rightarrow Q$ of *a*	$(100.K^A)\ l_a^A \rightarrow Q_1$ of *i*
Country *I*	$(100.q_a)\ l_a^I \rightarrow Q$ of *a*	$(100.q_i.K^I)\ l_a^I \rightarrow Q_1$ of *i*

Now when one forms the pre-trade price ratios using the labour theory of value, then given that $q_a > q_i$, one definitely returns to a conclusion that is completely consistent with that of Ricardo's England–Portugal model if $K^I =$

K^A. That is, given that A is assumed to be comparatively superior in producing a and I is comparatively superior in producing i, then A would find it 'cheaper' and hence advantageous to import i from I by exporting a. Manoïlesco has basically made this confession at one point:

> It is interesting to notice that if $K^I = K^A = 1$ – that is, if the agricultural article has the same productivity as the industrial article, and *there is no absolute superiority of industry* – in this case … [b]oth countries have profited by confining themselves to their 'natural' productions. This is the only instance in which Ricardo is right. (1931, p. 108, italics original)

Of course, as claimed above, it is sufficient for $K^I = K^A$ and they do not have to be equal to unity for the Ricardian conclusion to be valid.

Interestingly, Manoïlesco indeed observes at one point that K^I and K^A are 'not being too different' (ibid., p. 109). Then noting that the two product terms – $(1/K^I)(q_a/q_i)$ and $K^A(q_a/q_i)$ – '*are* [consequently] *about in inverse ratio*', he draws this conclusion that suggests that K^I and K^A, though incorporated into separate tables, should be considered together:

> *When the intrinsic (qualitative) superiority of industry compared with agriculture … increases, the disadvantage of the commercial solution … gradually increases for agricultural countries, while the advantage of the commercial solution for industrial countries … gradually increases in about the same proportion.*
> *What the agricultural country loses is gained by the industrial country. The contrast and the distance between the disadvantage of the first and the advantage of the second depend on the value of* K^I and K^A *– that is on the intrinsic (qualitative) superiority of industry compared with agriculture.*
> *When this absolute superiority of industry becomes more accentuated, the contrast is greater; when the superiority decreases, the contrast is less; when it does not exist, the contrast disappears and agricultural countries reap the same benefit from exchange as industrial countries.* (Ibid., italics original)

Without considering the terms of trade, the last part of the last paragraph quoted is a *non sequitur*.

Now if $K^I \neq K^A$, then everything hinges on how K^A/K^I compares with q_i/q_a. A conclusion consistent with Ricardo's England–Portugal model will obtain if $K^A/K^I > q_i/q_a$.[22] Given that $q_a > q_i$ (or $q_i/q_a < 1$) in Manoïlesco's illustration, then that type of conclusion will obtain *a fortiori* if $K^A > K^I$ (or $K^A/K^I > 1$). Recall that K^A and K^I are, respectively, the ratio of industrial and agricultural productivity in A and I. Indeed, he observed at one point that 'the contrast between industrial and agricultural productivity is greater in backward and agricultural countries and smaller in advanced and industrial countries' (ibid., p. 43).[23]

It is not clear whether Manoïlesco was oblivious to the problems with his illustration or that he simply chose to ignore them. Having satisfied himself that he has proven Ricardo wrong in the aforementioned parts of his *Theory of Protection*, he presses on to comment on Smith and then Mill.

On Smith's Principle of Absolute Advantage

Manoïlesco thus turns his attention to the case where '*an agricultural country, being superior to the industrial country for agricultural produce, is inferior for industrial produce*' (ibid., p. 110, italics original). In line with his criticism of Ricardo, he laments that Smith considered human labour 'as a uniform element' (p. 233). With the modification of the pattern of superiority in production, but maintaining the criticism relating to uniform labour, he essentially goes back to Table 9.2 and now sets $q_i < 1 < q_a$ (ibid., pp. 110–11). Consequently, whether 'indirect production by commercial means' would be more advantageous for *A* than 'direct production' still depends on whether $(1/K^I)(q_a/q_i)$ is greater than unity or whether q_a/q_i is larger than K^I. But he aptly notes that $q_i < 1 < q_a$ means that,

> the ratio q_a/q_i is much larger [than] in the case of the comparative advantage [of Ricardo] we have just had. It follows that there are more chances than in the preceding case for the commercial solution to be the most profitable, because even with a larger K^I, the congruity $q_a/q_i > K^I$ may easily be realised. (Ibid., p. 111)[24]

Having conceded that, he nonetheless insists that $q_a/q_i < K^I$ 'may also happen, [in which case] the commercial solution is disadvantageous compared with direct production' (ibid.). Then just a page later he combines Ricardo's and Smith's cases, and claims more boldly that 'in both cases ... it may happen, and it often does happen, that the direct production of industrial articles by an agricultural country is more advantageous than their importation' (ibid., p. 112).

Manoïlesco then briefly considers in a footnote the following modified version of Ricardo's England–Portugal model that he dubs 'Adam Smith's case':

Table 9.5a *Manoïlesco's alleged 'Adam Smith's case'*

	Wine	Cloth
Portugal	$80\ l^P$	$125\ l^P$
England	$120\ l_w^E$	$100\ l_c^E$

where *P* (Portugal) and *E* (England) are country labels, *w* (wine, which is treated as an agricultural product) and *c* (cloth, which is treated as an industrial product) are product labels. The direct labour-input coefficients are implicitly indicating what is required for a unit each of *w* and *c* to be produced per period of time in the two countries. He does not distinguish between the Portuguese labour employed in producing w and those producing c, and hence, no subscript is attached to l^P. However, a distinction of this nature with respect to the English labour is made. Specifically, he sets $K^E = 2$ so that $l_c^E = 2l_w^E$ (1931, p. 111, n. 1). Applying the expression $(1/K^I)(q_a/q_i)$ from Table 9.2, he obtains, with modifications in notations, $(1/K^E)(q_w/q_c) = 15/16 < 1$ and he thinks that he has proved his point, that is, it does not pay for the agricultural country (Portugal) to specialise in w and exports it for c. However, notice that Table 9.5a can be rewritten as:

Table 9.5b *Reconfiguring Manoïlesco's alleged 'Adam Smith's case'*

	Wine	Cloth
Portugal	$80\ l^P$	$125\ l^P$
England	$120\ l_w^E$	$200\ l_w^E$

Written this way and after obtaining the pre-trade domestic price ratios, one can see even Ricardo would have concluded that Portugal should be exporting c rather than w. It is again not clear that Manoïlesco, using his approach to emphasise the superior productivity of industries, has succeeded in constructing illustrations that could enable him to draw conclusions distinct from those drawn from the static classical trade models. In spite of that flaw in his illustration he feels so contented that he boasts, 'Not only have we refuted Ricardo's theory of comparative advantage, but at the same time we have refuted Adam Smith's theory of absolute advantage' (ibid., p. 113, n. 1). He feels fully prepared to take on Mill.[25]

On Mill's England–Germany Model

Manoïlesco thinks he sees some indications in Mill's *Principles* that suggests that he (Mill) was aware of the alleged defect in the classical trade models that he (Manoïlesco) is trying to get at. He quotes (ibid., p. 68) as evidence the following passage from Mill's *Principles*:

> There are two senses in which a country obtains commodities cheaper by foreign trade; in the sense of Value, and in the sense of Cost. It gets them cheaper in the first sense, by their falling in value relatively to other things … But in the other sense, that of Cost, … cheapness in a great measure depends upon a cause of a different nature: a country gets its imports cheaper, in proportion to the general productiveness of its domestic industry; to the general efficiency of its labour. (Mill [1871] 1965, p. 615)[26]

Judging from the 'synthetic point of view' (see section 9.2 above), he concludes that 'John Stuart Mill was aware – better than any other writer – of the two quite different factors which determine the advantages of international trade: the exchange factor and the production factor' (1931, p. 68).

Manoïlesco hastens to add, however, that,

> Unfortunately, the meaning John Stuart Mill gives to the idea of efficiency does not seem to be that of the absolute productivity which characterises one merchandise compared with another which forms our essential idea, but the meaning – following Ricardo – of the comparative advantage of one country over another in the production of the same goods. (Ibid., pp. 68–9)

Indeed, he (Mill) constructed '[a]n example of comparative advantage in international exchange' that is 'almost as famous as Ricardo's' (ibid., p. 122). Here Manoïlesco is referring to Mill's England–Germany model first introduced in his *Some Unsettled Questions* and then essentially reproduced in his *Principles* (Bk. III, Ch. XVIII). He (Manoïlesco) attempts to graft it onto his illustration that is represented in Table 9.3 above. That table, where A is replaced by G (Germany), I by E (England), a by n (linen), and i by c (cloth), is reproduced here as Table 9.6, from which he infers that q_n/q_c = 1.33 > 1 (1931, p. 123).

Table 9.6 *Manoïlesco's representation of Mill's England–Germany model*

	Product n	Product c
Germany	$100\ l^G \rightarrow 20n$	$100\ l^G \rightarrow 10c$
England	$100\ l^E \rightarrow 15n$	$100\ l^E \rightarrow 10c$

Then he supposes that 'the productivity of cloth in Germany is twice the productivity of linen' (ibid., pp. 123–4, n. 1). That is, he sets $K^G = 2$ so that $l_c{}^G = 2l_n{}^G$, but he implicitly leaves $K^E = 1$ so that $l_n{}^E = l_c{}^E = l^E$. Now recall the purpose of Table 9.3 above. Manoïlesco wanted to show that if, following from that table, $K^A(q_a/q_i) > 1$, then for the industrial country the 'commercial solution' is preferable to 'direct production'. Here with Table 9.6 he actually wants to argue that Germany (the agricultural country) should produce c (the industrial product) domestically and not import it (ibid.). In accordance with the discussion associated with Table 9.2 above, he should thus have worked with $K^E > 1$ and set $K^G = 1$. Indeed, if $K^E = 2$ (and if $K^G = 1$), then the expression $(1/K^I)(q_a/q_i)$ from manipulating Table 9.2 will become $(1/K^E)(q_n/q_c) = 1.33/2 < 1$. Germany should, under such circumstances and according to Manoïlesco's own reasoning, be directly producing c. But instead of supposing that $K^E = 2$, he has supposed, as indicated at the top of this paragraph, that $K^G = 2$. And then later in the same lengthy footnote, he indicates that $K^G = K^E = 2$ when he asserts that 'Germany must produce only cloth, because in this *article* the productivity in both countries is approximately twice as large as that of linen' (ibid., italics original). Little does he realise in this instance, based on the illustration associated with Table 9.4 above, that, given $q_n/q_c > 1$, if $K^G = K^E$, then the Ricardian solution, not his own, would apply.

Nevertheless, Manoïlesco thought that he has completely and thoroughly proved the classical trade models wrong. Despite what he has perceived to be signs of Mill's awareness of the alleged defect of the classical trade models, he regards him (Mill) to have 'ended his investigations' prematurely (ibid., p. 69). He is aware of Mill's attempt to determine the distribution of the gains from trade between two countries (ibid., pp. 122–5). However, satisfied with his illustration of the problem with Mill's England–Germany model, he reaches the conclusion that 'it seems useless to continue Mill's reasoning' on this distribution issue (p. 125, n. 1).

9.4 SUPERIOR PRODUCTIVITY: ALLOCATION PROBLEM OR RESULT OF DEVELOPMENT PROCESS?

Manoïlesco regretted that the 'economics' that he had criticised was unfortunately, '[just] as other fine products', imported by the agricultural countries the betterment of which he concerned himself. 'It is the science … particularly of those who are in a quite opposite economic situation and who naturally and unconsciously stress the benefits of foreign trade, which are not general, but particular, for each country' (1931, p. 166). To him, the 'cherished and hackneyed ideas' had to be 'relinquished in order to attain to a fresh conception of economics' (ibid., p. 224).

It should be clear from the discussion in sections 9.2 and 9.3 that Manoïlesco thought that he would break new ground by building his analysis upon his idiosyncratic concept of productivity. To recapitulate, industry was regarded as exhibiting productivity superior to that in agriculture. When this is recognised, then he believed that the static trade models of Ricardo, Smith, and Mill could all be shown to be deficient. Having cast doubt on the effectiveness of his illustrations in section 9.3, this section examines his conception of productivity more closely in order to fathom why his thesis is both problematical as well as controversial.

Neglecting the Process of Development that Enables Overall Productivity to Improve

Viewed from a development rather than a static allocation perspective, it is obvious that Manoïlesco's conception of productivity is totally devoid of any content of development as a process. In almost all of his consideration of shifting resources (chiefly labour) from agriculture to industries under conditions that he deemed suitable, it is as if that could be effected and would pay off instantaneously. Regarding instantaneously effecting the shift of resources, this is implicitly assumed in the reconfigured illustrations that are reproduced in section 9.3 above and is, of course, no different from the standard assumption of perfect mobility of resources within each country in the textbook Ricardian and Heckscher–Ohlin–Samuelson models. Regarding the immediate pay-off, he made it clear that '[o]ur theory seeks the immediate, direct, economic advantages of a convenient and well-constructed protection. ... [U]nder certain conditions, it promises sure results in favour of protection' (ibid., pp. 59–60). Armed with this confidence in his theory he asserted that '[n]ational revenue is not a fixed thing. ... In particular, the displacement caused by a rational protection, in the sense of the most productive activity, is followed by an increase of national revenue, therefore by an increased buying capacity' (ibid., p. 207).[27] Similarly, he suggested at one point that 'it is much easier to found a new and more productive branch than to increase the productivity of an existing one' (ibid., p. 152, n. 1).[28] In another instance, referring to the Ireland, Portugal, and Turkey of his time, he had this portrayal:

> Under this system [where agricultural countries export cereals and raw materials and import industrial articles], Ireland loses more labour in one week than it would require *once and for all* to create the necessary modern industrial plant which might increase its production; in the same way, Portugal and Turkey lose in one day more money than they would require for creating all the industrial machinery needed to found a national industry in cloth. (Ibid., p. 164, italics added)

Although he hastened to admit that '[n]o doubt there are some exaggerations' (ibid.), these nevertheless contribute to belittling the difficulties of the process of setting up new industries, bringing them to operating at decently competitive levels, sustaining their growth, and setting the stage for future diversification and differentiation.

Contrast this with Hamilton's and List's approaches to development as a complex process. Those necessitate considerations of mobilising resources and cultivating their productive potential. Industrialisation appealed to them not only because industry itself as a sector was regarded as exhibiting superior productivity over agriculture, but also because industrialisation is a necessary component of the development process that, if successfully carried out, would awaken productive powers and raise the overall level of productivity of the country concerned, and would continue to elevate it into the future.

At one point in section 9.2 above attention is drawn to how Manoïlesco praised List for championing the importance for agricultural countries to cultivate their capacity to produce wealth. Unfortunately, this admiration did not translate into any serious and thoughtful attempt to consider how that cultivation should proceed. Instead, his employment of the static classical trade framework had destined him to trivialise this process. In this connection, it should be noted that while he laments at one point in his *Theory of Protection* that the 'production factor' is 'very often neglected in the conclusions of free-traders, or at best it is mixed up with the exchange factor, so that one is unable to distinguish the influence of either' (ibid., p. 68), he himself has turned out to neglect it also in that work.

One can thus say that Manoïlesco had skirted over a whole host of developmental problems. He did so, inadvertently or otherwise, by telescoping a process of development that might be realised by backward agricultural countries into the present as a certain outcome. It is as if the quality and productivity of industrial labour that was so prized by him could instantaneously be acquired by merely transferring workers from the farms to the factories. If this feature of his analysis is not really questioned, which, not surprisingly, is indeed the case as far as mainstream economists are concerned, then it is as if he had merely laid his finger on a static allocation rather than a development problem.[29]

Productivity Differences as Market Distortions and Static Allocation Problems

Hence, mainstream economists who have conceded that Manoïlesco was onto something, even if it is 'one [very tiny] grain of truth which is embedded' (Viner 1932, p. 125), have turned their attention to the nature of sectoral productivity (wage) differences and how such differences could be rationalised *in a static world* as nothing but market distortions. Thus characterised, the focus then shifts to ranking possible policy instruments that correct such distortions with the aim of rendering the static allocation more efficient.

At the risk of oversimplification, one can classify these distortions into two types. One type is policy-induced distortions, due, for instance, to the activities of trade unions or the impact of social legislation (Ohlin 1931, p. 39; Viner 1932, p. 125; Haberler 1937, pp. 196–7). Not surprisingly, trade protection is deemed inferior, if considered at all, as a means to correcting this distortion. Some propose measures 'to increase the labour mobility and do away with the watertight labour compartment' (Ohlin 1931, p. 44). Others simply insist on a policy of free trade to break the monopoly power of the trade unions, reduce wages, and restore allocative efficiency (Viner 1932, p. 125 and Haberler 1937, p. 198).

The second type relates to market imperfections that manifest themselves as sectoral differences in wages, and hence marginal productivity of labour (Haberler 1937, p. 196, n. 1 and p. 198; Hagen 1958, pp. 504–5; Magee 1973, pp. 11–13; Corden 1984, p. 90; Gomes 1990, p. 88; Maneschi 1998, p. 230).[30] Invariably, the focus is solely on one country, essentially country *A* in Manoïlesco's examples. Besides, the small-country assumption is implicitly made. One can liken this as solely focusing on something akin to Table 9.2 in section 9.3 above but without considering the separate reconfiguration in Table 9.3, not to mention the combination of some features in each of these two tables in Table 9.4. When the focus is thus solely placed on country *A*, the labour-market distortion that is analysed in these works has accordingly to be detected in that same country. To come up with their labour-market distortion, these authors considered there to be no difference between l_i and l_a as far as 'real labor costs' are concerned. But when the wages paid, denoted as w_i and w_a for the *i* and *a* sectors respectively, are such that $w_i > w_a$ in accordance with the (marginal) productivity differences between the sectors, then there allegedly exists a distortion and the employment level in both sectors would be suboptimal. While there is perhaps room for disagreement on whether Manoïlesco's employment of the variable *K* is or is not related to 'real labor cost' considerations, one should recall that in Table 9.2 above, the *K* that is employed is for country *I*. To recapitulate, he assumes that $l_i^I = K^I.l_a^I$, where $K^I > 1$. If one reads, as the mainstream theorists tend to do, his sectoral productivity distinctions as indicative of labour-market distortions, then it is actually a distortion that is located in country *I* rather than country *A*. Given that for that same table he assumes $l_a^A = l_i^A = l^A$, there is *no* market distortion in country *A*![31]

Regardless of which of the two types of distortions one refers to, all mainstream commentators are, with the exception of Ohlin (1931), oblivious to the bizarre feature of his illustrations that is pointed out in section 9.3. To recapitulate, although Manoïlesco has maintained that industry exhibited productivity that is superior over that in agriculture *in all countries*, in the illustrations that are reproduced in Tables 9.2 and 9.3 above that is not the case when he sets the '*K*' in one of the two countries to unity. In some sense it is then un-Manoïlescan for mainstream economists to consider situations that have 'market distortions' in one but not in the other country.[32]

If Manoïlesco did not succeed in making any case for protection and all his reconfigurations of the static classical trade model in an attempt to make that case were much ado about nothing, then what are claimed to be interpretations of his case – especially the second type of distortions identified above – are really not his. Rather, they are the results of misinterpreting him. As the misinterpretation passes on, he has become a poster child for 'protectionists' who supposedly had no clue that in his alleged case a subsidy to encourage employment in the high-wage *i* sector is a better policy than a protective tariff. But was Manoïlesco really prescribing nothing but tariff protection?

9.5 USING TARIFFS OR SUBVENTIONS TO SUPPORT SUPERIOR PRODUCTIVE SECTORS

As it turns out, Manoïlesco does not only prescribe tariffs when he proposes to support sectors that demonstrate superior productivity in his *Theory of Protection*. One instance when he says this loud and clear is worth quoting at full length:

> In all our demonstration and throughout our book we consider customs taxes the only means of protection, but our demonstration is quite valid if, instead of customs taxes, subventions or other direct advantages are granted to national industry, provided that these advantages represent the same value as customs taxes for every unit of produced goods. So our theory is a general theory of protection, not merely a theory of customs taxes. (1931, pp. 134–5, n. 2)

Then a little over 30 pages later, while considering a situation where 'home' goods could use state support, he considers 'the assistance of a subvention equal to the difference of the two prices for each unit produced, or with the assistance of a customs tax (the effect is exactly the same in both cases…) equal to this difference' (ibid., p. 169). In several other places he mentions protective (or customs) taxes and subventions (or subsidies) together (pp. xxii, 35, 136, 169, 173, 175).[33]

Nevertheless, unlike Hamilton and List, Manoïlesco does not make any effort to compare the pros and cons in deploying each of these instruments in specific situations. One can perhaps come to his defence by suggesting that his chief intent in the *Theory of Protection* is to make a case for state action to support sectors of superior productivity. He is clearly aware that the arsenal of instruments contains more than tariffs but to compare these instruments might be beside his main intent in that book.

Nor is he unaware of the possible pitfalls with 'protection' in general. He is thus leery of 'the selfishness of the directly interested minority, *i.e.* the industrial magnates of every country', observing that '[t]he lower the general morality of a country, the more the danger of partiality and corruption menaces the codification of tariffs' (ibid., p. xxiii and p. 8). Somewhat naïvely, he proposes that the real culprit '*lies largely with economic science*, which has not succeeded in giving tariff problems *a standard*, based on exact and measurable economic criteria, quite apart from the subjective ideas of men' (pp. 8–9, italics original). For '[i]n the absence of any objective criterion, it is the intense struggle of private interests which must decide the destiny of different branches of production' (p. 7).

Scale considerations could also become important. Thus, there are industries which, 'owing to their form of productions demand an enormous territorial market, even a world market' and the factories for such 'could never limit their production to the territorial market of a single small country'. An example that he mentioned was factories which manufacture special plant for other factories (ibid., p. 177).

Last but not least, there is the consideration of fallacy of composition. Hence, the critic of his policy proposal may warn that,

> Pursuing the 'fanciful' idea of continual rising on the productivity scale, and encouraging all countries to act in the same way, we can only come to a general fall of industrial productivity. The ladder on which we are all mounting, in emulation of each other, will begin to slip down, and will draw us all down with it! (Ibid., p. 146)

Manoïlesco indeed concedes at one point in his *Theory of Protection* that the price of industrial articles could fall in relation to all other products, predicting that 'there will be a fatal decline in the prices of industrial articles' (ibid., p. xvi),[34] though assuring at another point that 'this evolution will be gradual' (ibid., p. 146). Then he introduces the distinction between the 'absolute productivity of industrial activity (measured in goods units)' and the 'relative productivity of industry' in relation to agricultural productivity (ibid.). The former, he simply asserts, 'will increase according to the technical improvements in industry' (ibid., p. 146, n. 2).[35] This *deus ex machina* enables him to claim that '[o]ur assertion concerning the tendency of the fall of prices of industrial articles, made in the interests of scientific truth, cannot destroy our productivity theory' (ibid., p. 148, n. 2).

9.6 A DIFFERENT WORLD ORDER AND DEMOCRACY OF NATIONS

If Manoïlesco has thus belittled the fallacy of composition problem for the late industrialising countries, he certainly treats another aspect of it much more seriously, namely, changes in the 'world's physiognomy'.

Specifically, he considers the possibility of a dwindling volume of world trade, although he portrays conflicting scenarios. In one instance he suggests that,

> [t]he tendency to manufacture raw materials at the place in the very country of their production would considerably reduce the volume of international trade. It would stop the export of a part of the raw material (namely, the part necessary for manufacture of finished goods in the country until home demands were completely supplied), and would stop the import of fine products for the same consumption. (Ibid., p. 194)

For such considerations he deems raw and manufactured materials the 'compressible part of world international trade' (ibid.). Such a scenario would be a menace to Europe in particular, 'not only by the possibility of a less favourable exchange, but also by the eventual inability of placing its products at all in other continents' (ibid., p. xvi). It is as if he had the foresight of what would unfold in the global economy 60 years or so after the publication of the *Theory of Protection*: he predicts that '[t]he industrial decentralisation of the world, the industrial evolution of India and China, the industrial progress of the new countries will possibly impede Europe, in the future, from placing its products' (ibid.). He adds that,

> There would no more be, as to-day, exclusive industrial supremacies ... Each country would have the opportunity of satisfying, with a large number of fine goods, its home consumption; of course, each nation would have a smaller export possibility for those goods, for the sole reason that it could not be admitted that at the same time all countries should export the same industrial article. (Ibid., p. 174)

Simply put, '[t]he world's physiognomy would then be greatly changed' (ibid.).

But elsewhere Manoïlesco paints a more optimistic scenario and this optimism is based on the 'relatively larger elasticity of the market for industrial articles than of the agricultural market'[36] and a belief in the 'automatic extension of consumption of industrial articles, since industrial countries are always the greatest consumers of industrial articles' (ibid., p. 146, n. 1). He takes the former as a fact and regarding the latter, he has this elaboration:

> there are two leading causes for the large consumption of industrial articles in the modern world: first, the extension of comfort and the refinement of tastes, which demand an abundant production and a great variety of industrial articles, and second, the rapid multiplication of necessities of other production means constantly created by industry.[37]
>
> These two causes apply especially to industrial countries which also have a high social level and an intense need of production means.

> This is the reason why industrial countries are important consumers of industrial articles.[38] (Ibid., p. 198)

These give him comfort and he becomes more firmly convinced in his support of industrialising the backward agricultural countries. He feels more assured that, if successful, this effort would not endanger 'the economic equilibrium of the world'. Referring again to India and China, but adding Russia, he anticipates that,

> in the day when the Russian, Indian and Chinese peasant will become richer by the progressing industrialisation of their countries, the buying capacity of these countries will also increase correspondingly.
>
> They will then be more capable of absorbing the industrial production of Europe than they are at present, inasmuch as the civilisation which we have so well managed to introduce to countries of other continents will develop new tastes, new desires, for whose satisfaction they will make all sacrifices. (Ibid., p. 198)

All in all, 'by stimulating the industrialisation of those countries, raising their buying capacity and improving their standard of living, there will be created for countries at the highest industrial development a sure basis of prosperity and constant progress' (p. 200).

Manoïlesco seems oblivious to the incongruity between this optimistic scenario and his portrayal of self-sufficiency through industrialisation elsewhere in the *Theory of Protection.* While content that the economic equilibrium of the world would not be endangered, he realises that the new development would be 'demanding a new adaptation of this equilibrium' (ibid., p. xvii). There would be a problem of the 'proper co-ordination of production in the various countries of the world'. 'Has this problem a solution', he asks, 'and in which direction may it be found?' (p. 204).

The concern that Manoïlesco has expressed here is with economic dislocation among the industrial countries and what they might do as a result to frustrate the industrialisation effort among the agricultural countries. In this connection, he denounces the ideal of 'universal free trade' advocated by the League of Nations of his time. He rhetorically asks,

> In the name of what principle may we forbid to a nation (free-trade does forbid it) to realise for itself a limitless prosperity, even if this prosperity should divert the whole world from the highest level of production it could attain?
>
> Democracy presupposes, and demands also, respect of the individual in the pursuit of his own aims; could we forbid nations to pursue their own aims, when it might be possible for some of them to attain a larger prosperity by sacrificing the interests of humanity – even if this interest were certain? (Ibid., p. 221)

The implementation of free trade, he claims, would amount to 'a system of disadvantageous discrimination' and would constitute 'the absolute antithesis of the democracy of nations' (p. 222).

9.7 CONCLUDING REMARKS

Manoïlesco cannot be said to have furthered the analysis of Hamilton and List. In fact, by portraying superior productivity as attainable simply through a static reallocation of resources from the agricultural to the industrial sector, his *Theory of Protection* represents regress rather than progress as far as development analysis is concerned. Besides, his reconfiguration of the static Ricardian trade model to illustrate the conditions under which industries would have a 'right to exist' in agricultural countries is fatally flawed. As a result, his whole exercise turns out to be much ado about nothing.

Yet, because it embodies the feature of static reallocation of resources to achieve industrialisation, mainstream theorists have been more than eager to seize the opportunity to make it into a case for state support of structural change due to a labour-market distortion. 'Although his exposition left much to be desired', Irwin thus argued, 'Manoïlescu's methodological approach, though expressed in an extreme way at times, was unreproachably economic' (1996, p. 164). Specifically,

> [t]he argument that countries specializing in agricultural products and importing manufactures were depriving themselves of greater output in high-wage, high-productivity sectors was not only as compelling as the *more narrow* concept of infant industries, but it even proved (initially) to be a *stronger* broadside into the free trade argument. (Ibid., p. 160, italics added)

Thanks to the theory of domestic divergences, that 'broadside' was countered by a 'first-best' policy of an employment subsidy instead of a tariff. In the meantime, List is further relegated through the allegation that he had 'neglected the issue of wage differentials between sectors within a country, *despite its similarities to the infant industry argument*' (ibid., p. 160, n. 12, italics added).

Into the post-war period, it was some of the development economists who attempted to challenge mainstream trade theories yet again. It would be argued that in doing so, the stronger voices all sought to make cases in some frameworks of development rather than static resource allocation. Needless to say, there have also been efforts on the part of the mainstream theorists to distort these. The next three chapters examine the works of Prebisch, Myrdal, and Singer respectively to illustrate where the misrepresentations have been introduced and how their original frameworks of analysis could perhaps be clarified.

NOTES

1. Reference is made almost entirely to *The Theory of Protection and International Trade* (Manoïlesco 1931), hereafter abbreviated as *Theory of Protection*. His last name is spelled slightly differently by various authors. Those differences will be maintained in passages that are quoted from the works of these authors, but otherwise it will be spelled as the name appears in Manoïlesco (1931).
2. But see n. 29 below.
3. Recall the discussion in Ch. 3 above, to which n. 14 is appended, that there are two passages in Smith's *Wealth of Nations* that contain a similar message.
4. The way that List worded it was: '*The power of producing wealth* is ... infinitely more important than *wealth itself*' ([1841] 1991, p. 133).
5. One implication of the discussion thus far is that if, hypothetically, there could be an international scheme to redistribute the gains from trade among countries, then that could be a reason to support free trade. Indeed, according to Manoïlesco, '[t]here is a case – a single one – where the absolute and universal free-trade system might be justified (keeping in mind, of course, the supposition that this would mean the best solution for humanity) – it is the case where the disadvantages of free-trade to certain nations could be corrected by certain conscious measures of distribution' (1931, p. 222). For a discussion of the 'supposition' alluded to in the middle of the quotation, see Manoïlesco (ibid., pp. 219–20, and p. 219, n. 2). However, he recognised that '[i]t is impossible to regulate distribution among different nations' and '[t]his is what all free-traders ought to understand'. 'International *political* organization', he thus concluded, 'is the indispensable condition for equitable free-trade' (ibid., pp. 222–3, italics original).
6. Contrast with the suggestion of Love (1996, p. 253, n. 84), who writes that, 'On this matter, Manoilescu followed in the century-old tradition of the Scot John Rae, who argued, contrary to Adam Smith, that national interests and individual interests were not identical'.
7. According to the footnote, the source is Lujo Brentano (1901), *Das Freihandelsargument*, Berlin: Schöneberg, p. 4.
8. This part from List's *National System* is quoted in Manoïlesco (1931, p. 250) with some variations in translation.
9. Although Manoïlesco had definitely consulted parts, if not the entirety, of List's *National System*, it is not clear that he had looked at List's *Natural System*. The latter is not included in the Bibliography section in the *Theory of Protection*, but List did also express his suspicion toward the individualistic decisions of 'merchants' in his *National System* (for example, pp. 259–60).
10. Manoïlesco does not really entertain in this part of his discussion the possibility for an individual to change his profession, insisting that 'changing his profession is not for him a commercial problem' (op. cit., p. 65). That is ironic when the crux of his policy proposal is to move individuals from low-productivity to high-productivity sectors.
11. Alternatively, 'to be able to judge the advantage of a buying operation between two countries, one must also examine the exchange goods which are exported' (op. cit., p. 154).
12. 'The real independence of a nation is only obtained', Manoïlesco accordingly concludes, 'by creating industrial means which secure national defence and national wealth. In a modern nation, independence spells wealth' (op. cit., p. 227).
13. The representation of Manoïlesco's criticism of Ricardo in this subsection corresponds to what he deems the 'Second Revision' of that trade theory, one that he regards as 'a rigorously scientific presentation' (op. cit., p. 72). Readers interested in the 'First Revision', which he regards as 'less precise', can refer to Manoïlesco (ibid., pp. 72–90). As he intends

it, 'The first ... prepares for the comprehension of the second' (ibid., p. 72), though the reader should judge whether that has turned out to be the case.

14. One should perhaps not treat this as a misrepresentation of Ricardo given what Manoïlesco discusses in another footnote that is inserted several pages before (on which see n. 15 below). But in the last part of the footnote from which the sentence quoted in the main text is taken, he adds this: 'he [Ricardo] thinks that production is proportional to labour without taking into consideration the eventual variation according to the law of less than proportional or more than proportional output' (op. cit.). This distortion is not corrected by him in the *Theory of Protection.*
15. In a lengthy footnote Manoïlesco (op. cit., pp. 72–5, n. 2) demonstrates his awareness of Ricardo's qualifications made in the latter's *Principles*, Ch. I, section II, which has the heading, '*Labour of different qualities differently rewarded. This is no cause of variation in the relative value commodities*'. This prompts him to claim that 'Ricardo himself did not support it [the exchange rule of equal labour for equal labour in interior trade] in the theoretical part of his work, merely slipping it into the framework of this [England–Portugal] example, by making, unfortunately, this assumption the basis of the theory of comparative costs of production' (1931, p. 96).
16. The q and q_1 employed in Manoïlesco (1931) have respectively been replaced by q_a and q_i, where the subscripts *a* and *i* should serve as more informative labels.
17. Among other things in his *Theory of Protection*, Manoïlesco criticises 'the unreal character of the concrete facts contained in Ricardo's hypothesis'. Specifically, he takes issue with the assumption that in the England–Portugal model Portugal has an advantage over England in producing cloth, and that within Portugal and according to his definition of productivity, the wine sector has superior productivity over that of cloth (op. cit., p. 77). Yet in the reconfigurations reproduced here in this subsection, he grants to himself that '[n]o matter what the character of these two exchanging countries, and no matter what the article with a superior productivity might be, the theoretical conclusions we shall come to in the end do not change' (ibid., p. 100, n. 2, see also pp. 113–14).
18. The K and K' employed in Manoïlesco (1931) have respectively been replaced by K^I and K^A, where the superscripts *I* and *A* should serve as more informative labels.
19. Had he stuck with Table 9.2, then the assumption that *A* could trade with *I* at the latter's domestic price ratio implies that *I* would experience no gain from trade.
20. Thus, in Table 9.2 *A* exports to *I* at the latter's terms of trade, while in Table 9.3 *I* exports to *A* at the latter's terms of trade. To the best of the present author's knowledge, Ohlin (1931) is the only commentator who has caught this bizarre feature of Manoïlesco's illustrations, saying that 'he makes assumptions which amount to that both countries at the same time reap the whole benefit although he does not observe this consequence' (ibid., p. 32). Elsewhere in the *Theory of Protection*, Manoïlesco indicates that he is making the small-country assumption (op. cit., pp. 61, 144–5). That still cannot explain away the above bizarre feature.
21. Again, to the best of the knowledge of the present author, Ohlin (1931) is the only commentator who has noticed this feature in Manoïlesco's illustrations.
22. Using reasoning that associates higher factor prices (remunerations) with superior productivity, Ohlin (1931, p. 33) arrives at essentially the same conclusion, namely that if $q_a/(K^I q_i) > 1/K^A$, then 'manufactures [in *A*] will be unable to compete with imports'. Notice that he follows Manoïlesco's notations almost entirely. Once K^A is introduced in addition to K^I, where $K^I > 1$ and $K^A > 1$, the decision on whether to 'directly produce' *i* in *A* should, in accordance with Manoïlesco's reasoning, strictly depend on a comparison of $q_a/(K^I q_i)$ with $1/K^A$. The comparison is between $q_a/(K^I q_i)$ and 1 only when $K^A = 1$. It thus appears to be incorrect for Ohlin (ibid.) to revert back to checking whether $q_a/(K^I q_i)$ is less than 1 and then summarises the 'condition of a loss' from trade for *A* to be $1 > q_a/(K^I q_i) > 1/K^A$.
23. Manoïlesco also observes in the Preface to the English edition of his *Theory of Protection* that 'the contrast of productivities, and particularly the contrast of agricultural and industrial productivities, is much greater in the agricultural countries of Europe than anywhere else' (1931, p. x; see also p. 207, n. 1).

24. Keep in mind that q_a, q_i, and K^l are respectively the replacements for q, q_1, and K in Manoïlesco's original notations.
25. Manoïlesco also employs a notion of 'average productivity' to further explain his points, sometimes supplemented by illustrations involving money (*lei*). See, for instance, the second part of Ch. III in Part II and Ch. I in Part I of his *Theory of Protection*. That notion and the monetary illustrations are both utterly confusing.
26. There are some differences, arising probably from the translations, between the quotation in Manoïlesco (op. cit., p. 68) and the passage as quoted directly from Mill's *Principles*.
27. In this connection Manoïlesco ridiculed List for suggesting that a country would first have to make sacrifices before it could reap the fruits from state-aided development (op. cit., p. 241). However, he also conceded elsewhere that '[i]n reality a protected industry requires a *visible* sacrifice and offers a country much greater *invisible* advantages' (ibid., 1931, p. 144, italics original).
28. Manoïlesco's confidence and certainty seem to wane in the following instance: 'Indeed, one is not always very sure of being able to indicate exactly the degree of productivity in which to take refuge if required to give up the production of exportable goods; therefore the exact national gain resulting from the augmentation of productivity is not always visible and measurable' (op. cit., p. 173). Earlier in the *Theory of Protection* he also admits at one point that 'the question of "difficulties" is very important. Inferior industries are simple (from the point of view of their plant and organisation), superior industries are complex' (ibid., p. 133).
29. Two mainstream economists considered reasons to interpret Manoïlesco's discussions as leading to something akin to the infant-industry argument for protection. Ohlin (1931, p. 45) distinguishes between 'the effects of protection in changing the quality of labour rather than on its ability to cause a transfer of labour'. To introduce protection to achieve the former goal is '[f]or all practical purposes ... the same as the infant industry argument for industrially young nations'. Haberler (1937, p. 284) believes that '[a]n increase in the social product comes about ... if the "nursing" attracts workers from employments where their marginal productivity was smaller', in which case one has 'the "dynamic" argument for tariffs'. But contrast with Irwin (1996, p. 160), who regards 'the argument that countries specializing in agricultural products and importing manufactures were depriving themselves of greater output in high-wage, high-productivity sectors was not only as compelling as the more narrow concept of infant industries, but it even proved (initially) to be a stronger broadside into the free trade argument'. He further accuses that 'Friedrich List neglected the issue of wage differentials between sectors within a country, despite its similarities to the infant industry argument' (ibid., p. 160, n. 12).
30. Many mainstream commentators have also considered the possibility that the wage rate differences across sectors are nothing but 'equalizing differences' of some sort, for example, regional variations in cost of living, different degrees of irksomeness of work, and so on (Ohlin 1931, pp. 38, 40; Viner 1932, p. 123; Haberler 1937, pp. 196–7). The policy prescription in such a situation is neatly represented by Gomes (1990, p. 89), namely, 'there is no justification for protection, since specialisation according to money costs will then be in accordance with comparative real costs (measured in terms of 'disutilities') although not in accordance with labour-time costs, i.e. with wages and value of marginal products lower in agriculture'.
31. Conceivably, if the price of industrial products from country *I* are pushed up by its trade unions, then this creates precisely the kind of unequal-exchange type of situation that Manoïlesco so desired to counter (see section 9.2 above). Indeed, at one point in his *Theory of Protection* he makes a reference to 'monopolies' in the industrial countries (1931, p. 215, n. 1). Almost ten pages later he warns, 'The world must not be dominated by monopolies and the threat of exclusiveness' (ibid., pp. 224–5). Still, none of these relate to the labour-market distortions that the mainstream theorists have alleged to exist in the less-developed countries.
32. That is not to deny that those cases of market distortions considered by the mainstream could be of some interest for other reasons.

33. In one instance he refers to 'grants to new industries, the free sites given for constructing factories, the exemption of taxes' (op. cit., p. 175).
34. 'When, thanks to protection in all countries, the development of industries, and especially of industries with great productivity ..., will supply the world with an enormous quantity of industrial products, prices of industrial products will fall very much in comparison with prices of other produce and services, and especially in comparison with prices of agricultural articles and raw material' (op. cit., p. 146).
35. This, of course, smacks of infant industries maturing over time.
36. Compare with the disparities in the income elasticity of demand between manufactured and primary products that Prebisch would draw attention to. Despite the similarity with Manoïlesco's notion of 'relatively larger elasticity' for industrial articles, Prebisch employed the distinction to partly account for the persistent disequilibrium between imports and exports in the periphery thanks to its specialisation in primary products. See section 10.4 below.
37. This is an instance when Manoïlesco steps out of the static framework that he employs in most of his *Theory of Protection*, and considers something akin to linkage effects and Smith's productivity theory.
38. Indeed, 'agricultural countries which, according to certain theories, should be the "natural market" of all industrial articles, have rather a small buying capacity, quite insignificant in comparison with the same capacity in industrial countries' (op. cit., p. 199). As examples, Manoïlesco contrasts the 'poor market' presented by 'agricultural Russia' for the industrial products of 'occidental Europe' with that presented by England (ibid., pp. xvi–xvii). In 1913, 'of the international trade in Europe 64 to 66% was inter-European trade'. He also notes that Europe's second customer around that time was America (p. 206, n. 2). In making these observations he was far ahead of most economists – of his and later times – in demonstrating an awareness of the significance of intra-industry trade.

10. Prebisch: Infusing Dynamism into Development Processes via Raising Investment and Technological Densities, and IS and EP Industrialisation

10.1 INTRODUCTION

Whereas the last three chapters are chronologically arranged in accordance with when Hamilton, List, and Manoïlesco contributed to the development and trade literature, this and the next two chapters are respectively devoted to three development economists who were essentially contemporaries to each other: Prebisch, Myrdal, and Singer.[1] Their contributions to development studies were made in the more modern period, when the 'protectionist' label has frequently assumed the interchangeable tag of supporters of IS. For their alleged support of IS and for some other considerations to be discussed later, the three have indeed been grouped together on the list of 'usual suspects' (Meier 1958b, pp. 285–6; 1963, p. 55, n. 18; 1980, p. 282; and Balassa 1989, p. xix).[2]

Two years before his death in 1986 Prebisch summed up his thinking on development as having gone through five stages (Prebisch 1984).[3] Commenting on that summary, Bhagwati (1984, p. 198) notes that it is the second stage, from the late 1940s to late 1950s, 'that is best known to economists outside Latin America'. Specifically, '[i]t relates to the period when he developed the thesis that the prospect of declining terms of trade for Latin American primary products implied the desirability of import substituting (IS) industrialization'.

It is fair to say that during that period it was Prebisch's *Economic Development of LA* that caused the biggest uproar in the mainstream economics profession. That is only to be expected considering that that work, which Hirschman (1968) dubs Prebisch's 'manifesto', opens with this provocative sentence: 'In Latin America, reality is undermining the out-dated schema of the international division of labour' (1950a, p. 1). In searching for the reasoning upon which this conclusion is based, attention has mostly zeroed in on the statement that 'the price relation turned steadily against primary production from the 1870's until the Second World War' (ibid., p. 8). That would later be known as the PST.

Not surprisingly, this promptly triggered an onslaught by the economics mainstream (for instance, Viner 1953; Haberler 1957, 1963). Writing in the early 1960s Hyde observed that, 'The focal point for most of the attack is the alleged deterioration in the terms of trade for primary products. This is logical, in view of its importance to the general thesis' (1963, p. 472). One can say that not much has changed in the decades after. Witness how protracted the statistical debate revolving around the PST has been![4]

But before one gets mired in that aspect of the debate, would it not be more fundamental to ask what framework the mainstream critics have employed to consider the implications of the PST? How does that compare with the analytical framework that Prebisch himself employed? What insight into the development process, if any, can one get from each respectively? Finally, has the fixation on the terms-of-trade debate distracted attention from other important messages for development promotion that he attempted to get across?

The framework employed by the mainstream was the one outlined in sections 6.2 and 6.5 above. Essentially, it poses this question: If the prediction of the PST indeed holds and if structural changes in the primary exporting country concerned do not take place spontaneously, what might be the market failure that prevents them from happening? In Haberler's succinct words,

> The mere historical proposition [by Prebisch and others] that the terms of trade have deteriorated in a certain way does not prove anything, unless it can be proved that the economy for one reason or the other has failed to adapt itself fully to the changed conditions. If the latter is claimed, then it has to be shown in which way or for what reasons the adaptation has failed to occur. According to the answer given to that question the argument then becomes a species of one of the familiar *genera*: the infant industry argument for protection; the unemployment (including disguised unemployment) argument; or the lower productivity in agriculture than in industry argument. (1963, p. 287; see also Krueger 1984, p. 526, n. 10)

Pursuing this question-begging exercise further in accordance with the theory of domestic divergences, one can ask if Prebisch might have laid his finger on a 'trade distortion' rather than a 'domestic divergence'. Indeed, some in the economics mainstream have in this manner sought to 'rationalise' Prebisch's alleged case for protection. Bhagwati (1984, p. 202, n. 11), for instance, concludes that 'Prebisch … and others … were elasticity pessimists and therefore were essentially arguing for IS strategy on optimal-tariff grounds'.[5]

However, this 'rationalisation' does not appear to rest on much textual evidence. As Flanders (1964, p. 316) observes, 'The significance of price-inelastic demand for primary products has been given much more attention in the "commentaries" than in Prebisch's own work'. Instead, as section 10.4 below illustrates, his emphasis was rather on the disparities in the income elasticity of demand between primary and manufactured products. In the relatively few moments when he referred to the low price-elasticity of demand, he was careful to distinguish between the options that were open to 'a relatively small and isolated primary producing country' versus the hard realities facing those countries 'as a group' (1950b, pp. 36–7; 1951a, pp. 34–5).

More fundamentally, the 'rationalisation' raises more questions than it answers and they rhyme with the critique launched by Stiglitz and Charlton (2005) on such trivialisation of development by the subscribers to the theory of domestic divergences (see section 1.1 above). Thus, consider the situation where a tariff is deemed the optimal policy of intervention when one considers a country that is large enough to exercise a monopoly power in trade. Through the optimal tariff the diagrammatic illustration shows the country reaching a higher community indifference curve. However, it is far from clear what that framework can offer in furthering one's understanding of development as a process. All the complexities in that process in a supposedly large country have been reduced to a situation that calls for one policy action, namely the imposition of an optimal tariff. The result: this large country is able to attain a higher level of welfare. Keeping in mind that distributional problems are typically assumed away in the neoclassical world, everyone in that country can live happily thereafter. But how in practice does that intervention translate into a lengthy historical sequence of economic and social events that constitute a sustained process of development? In the real world underdeveloped countries, even ones with market power in some primary products, all have far more formidable challenges to confront as they seek to engender and sustain development. Reaching a higher indifference curve in one world and achieving development in the other are two totally different things.[6]

What about the kind of diagnosis, that is, identification of market failures (or more generally, barriers and obstacles to development), that Haberler and others had proposed? Thanks to its fixation of attention on the statistical aspect of the debate concerning the PST, the mainstream has yet to systematically carry out that kind of examination of Prebisch's works, not to mention properly situating any market failures (or barriers and obstacles) in the broader context of his discourse. That is what this chapter purports to do.[7]

The rest of the chapter is organised as follows. Section 10.2 argues that Prebisch sought to better understand and perhaps undo the uneven development, based upon differential technological progress, between the centre and periphery. Hence, the main thrust of his development effort is actually about a sustained improvement in productivity among Latin American and other peripheral countries in both agriculture and industries, and an infusion of 'dynamism' into their development processes so that they would no longer lag behind the centre's development, at least not by as much as previously.

Although Prebisch employed the term 'dynamism' (and other 'dynamic' notions) quite frequently, he did not appear to have ever given a concise definition of what he meant by it. Nevertheless, a meticulous perusal of his works strongly indicates that the main barriers and obstacles that have, in inter-linked manners, prevented the unleashing of sufficient dynamism include the 'chronic savings gap' that is largely governed by a state of underdevelopment and low income, and the consumption behaviour of social groups that enjoy distributional privileges (section 10.3), the peripheral economies' 'inadequate absorptive capacity' of 'surplus manpower' or 'redundant labor force' (also in section 10.3),[8] the 'persistent trend towards external disequilibrium' (section 10.4), the lack of dynamic industrial development (section 10.5), and an inadequate 'technological density' (section 10.6),[9] (Prebisch 1963, p. 79; 1968, pp. 3, 8, 59–60; 1971a, pp. 3–4, 234; 1976, pp. 14–15).[10]

Section 10.3 thus illustrates the emphasis that Prebisch had consistently put on stepping up the rate of investment so that the periphery could participate in the rapid technological progress and keep its labour at a reasonably high employment level. He was deeply concerned that that was not happening to the extent that it should in many of the peripheral countries because of the 'chronic savings gap'. That concern is in turn intimately connected with his distress about the 'persistent trend towards external disequilibrium' in many peripheral countries, for the simple reason that such disequilibria constrain growth and development. In that connection it will be argued in section 10.4 that Prebisch's case for state-aided development rests more primarily on the persistent disequilibrium in the peripheral countries' balance of payments, which constrains their 'capacity to import' for development, than on their declining CTT.[11] In the light of that clarification section 10.5 examines his support for industrialisation. It illustrates that he had never pushed for this process to the neglect of the agricultural sector. It also indicates that while he supported IS since the 1940s (if not before then) till the end of his life, he had never lost sight of the importance of exports and indeed started actively advocating EP in manufactured goods since the late 1950s. Permeating his desire for productivity improvements in the peripheral countries through higher investments, and industrialisation via IS and EP was an understanding that an indigenous 'technological density' would have to be established and be enabled to grow over time. This consideration of his is illustrated in section 10.6.

For each of these factors considered in sections 10.3 to 10.6 that constrains dynamism, section 10.7 illustrates why Prebisch did not believe that the free operation of market forces would spontaneously override them to unleash the dynamism. Where applicable, it also indicates his recommendation for policy actions. Section 10.8 spells out his suggestions for international co-operation, especially as they relate to trade and investment. Section 10.9 sums up the discussion in this chapter.

10.2 ARRESTING UNEVEN DEVELOPMENT: INCREASING PERIPHERAL PRODUCTIVITY AND INFUSING DYNAMISM

Unlike those who have interpreted him to be simply making an optimal-tariff argument for protection, Prebisch was under no illusion that the development problem could be solved simply by improving the CTT *per se*.

From the very beginning when Prebisch's work caught the attention of economists outside of Latin America, his principal focus was on technological progress: on the sharing of the fruits resulting therefrom, but more importantly, on engendering and sustaining such progress within the periphery itself. 'Modern technology', if assimilated quickly, would enhance the possibility of 'extirpating poverty and its inherent evils' in the developing world (1962, p. 26; see also 1963, p. 4; 1964, p. 6). To him, 'technical progress seems to have been greater in industry than in the primary production of peripheral countries' (1950a, p. 8) and the 'increment of productivity' is greater in the former than in the latter (1951a, p. 47). During the years that he devoted himself to development studies, industries were clearly concentrated in the centres, while primary production accounted for a predominant proportion of the periphery's economies.

In *Economic Development of LA* he thus complains about how 'the *advantages* of technical progress have been mainly concentrated in the industrial centres and have not directly extended to the countries making up the periphery of the world's economic system' (1950a, p. 8, italics added). In *Economic Survey of LA* he laments that '[t]he spread of technical progress … has … been relatively slow and irregular' and 'development was very uneven' (1951a, pp. 3, 4). Such 'uneven development of productive technique and the unequal distribution of its benefits' have resulted in 'disparities or differences in income and productivity' especially between the centre and periphery (ibid., pp. 80, 74).

This focus was maintained by Prebisch in his other publications in the 1950s (for instance, 1951b, pp. 117–18, 125–6; 1959a, p. 251).[12] By the 1960s, specifically in *Global Strategy*, he even sounded a little bit Myrdalian. But instead of employing the terms 'spread' and 'backwash' effects (see Chapter 11 below), he proclaims in that work 'the illusion that the economic progress of the centres would permeate into the rest of the world and promote its development has been dispelled'. 'The industrial centres', he explains, 'did not have the radiating power that was sometimes imagined'. 'Capital, which the periphery needs more and more, is being allowed to flow into the centres ... And, what is much more serious, skilled men are also being attracted from the periphery to the centres ..., to the serious detriment of the periphery's development' (1968, p. 70). One continues to detect this emphasis in the 1970s (for instance, 1978, p. 222). It is noteworthy that in his 1984 summary of his five stages of thinking about development he reports that, 'In formulating my point of view I mentioned from the beginning the role of *technological progress*. In particular, my interest was attracted by the question of the international dissemination of technology and the distribution of its fruits' (1984, p. 176, italics added).

Hence, in some fundamental sense Prebisch was deeply concerned with an uneven development process that has manifested itself in the form of the 'technological lag of the periphery' (1985, p. 15). How perhaps can this uneven process be arrested, even if only partially?

There is a little noticed distinction that Prebisch has made in his 'manifesto' that indicates how he would reply to that question.[13] In section VI of that work, he observes that 'the economic growth of Latin America depends on the increase of the average income per inhabitant ... and on an increase in population' (1950a, p. 43). But how could the former increase be brought about? His answer is,

> An increase in the average income per inhabitant could be achieved in only two ways: first, through *an increase in productivity*; and second, assuming a certain level of productivity, through an increase in income per man engaged in primary production, in relation to the income of the industrial countries which import part of that production. (Ibid., italics added)

Four pages later he restates the second way as 'a readjustment of income from primary production so as to lessen the disparity between it and income of the great industrial countries' (ibid., p. 47). For those who are familiar with the earlier sections of that work, that readjustment would have been realised if there could be a better CTT for the Latin American countries.

Of these two ways of increasing average income, which one does Prebisch regard as fundamentally more important? His conviction is that,

> The second result can be achieved only in so far as the first is accomplished. As productivity and the average real income from industry increase in the Latin-American countries, wages in agriculture and primary production in general will have to rise, as they have in other countries.
> The effect will be gradual. (Ibid.)

Put differently, development cannot simply be realised by directly changing the CTT. The primary focus should be on improving productivity in suitable ways and the CTT would improve accordingly. 'The fundamental economic problem of Latin America', he repeats in *Economic Survey of LA*, 'lies in increasing its real *per capita* income by virtue of an increase in productivity, since the raising of the living standards of the masses by means of the redistribution of income is very strictly limited' (1951a, p. 9). Then in one of many instances when Prebisch linked under- or sluggish development with insufficient or inadequate 'dynamism' in the economy and society, he declares in *Global Strategy* that, 'If the rate of growth is to be accelerated and the inadequacy of the economy's dynamism is to be remedied, productivity in the various sectors must be raised' (1968, p. 9).

10.3 RAISING THE RATE OF INVESTMENT

One of the deceptively obvious courses of action to raise productivity and average income in the peripheral countries is to step up their rate of investments. In *Economic Development of LA* Prebisch indeed suggests that,

> The raising of the standard of living of the masses ultimately depends on the existence of a considerable amount of capital per man employed in industry, transport *and* primary production, *and* on the ability to use it well.
> Consequently, the Latin-American countries need to accumulate an enormous amount of capital. (1950a, p. 5, italics added)

He would in his subsequent works frequently repeat this policy objective (for instance, 1951a, pp. 71–2; 1963, pp. 11, 35; 1968, p. 60; 1976, p. 23). That course of action could also infuse dynamism. Hence, as he declares in *Dynamic Development Policy*, 'the problem of lack of dynamism in development brooks no further delay. Accordingly, attention must first be centred on measures aimed at a swift increase in capital formation' (1963, p. 31; see also 1971a, p. 11).

Although this appears to be a most ordinary policy objective for the underdeveloped countries, there are two subtle features in the quotation above from the *Economic Development of LA* that are worth pointing out. Firstly, increased investments should not, as the quotation insinuates, just be confined to industry. The reader will be reminded of this in first part of section 10.5, where it will be pointed out that Prebisch never advocated industrialisation to the neglect of agriculture.[14] Secondly, the country should cultivate an 'ability' to use capital and technology well. As Prebisch would reiterate later in the same work, 'to achieve this increase in productivity, capital, *per capita*, must be considerably increased and the technique for its effective use acquired' (p. 44). This subtle feature will be expanded in section 10.6 below, which is on 'technological densities'.

Noting that 'the margin of savings depends ultimately upon the progressive increase of labour productivity' (1950a, p. 37), Prebisch understood fully well that peripheral countries could be stuck in a 'vicious circle[,] in which incomes are low because investments are inadequate and investments are inadequate because incomes are precarious', if the rate of investments is not increased (1964, p. 124).

But to effect this increase and to better utilize modern technology to raise productivity bring about certain 'contradictions' (Prebisch 1968, pp. 1–3; 1971a, p. 191). One that occupied his attention a lot was the productivity-enhancing but labour-saving effect of investments that utilise modern technology developed in the centre, all set against a background of relatively rapid population growth in most peripheral countries. The growth of the primary sector was regarded as generally hindered by low income elasticity of demand for its products (on which more in section 10.4). Productivity-enhancing investments in this sector, which are not precluded as the discussion above suggests, further drive the population in this sector to look for opportunities in industries or services. Yes, investment in these latter sectors would be stepped up. But would it be rapid enough to absorb those 'redundant labor' driven from the primary sector, those found in the industrial and service sectors employing 'pre-capitalist or semi-capitalist methods of production', and those displaced in these two sectors due to labour-saving investments?[15] This contradiction was one that he wrestled with since at least the 1950s (for instance, Prebisch 1950b, Ch. III; 1954, Ch. III, section II; 1963, part B, Ch. I, section I; 1971a, Ch. 2; 1978, pp. 175–6). Toward the latter part of his life he still insisted that '[t]he insufficient rate of capital accumulation holds the key to the insufficient dynamism of peripheral capitalism, i.e., of its inability to absorb, in conditions of ever-increasing productivity, the continuous increment in the labour force' (1976, pp. 14–15). Hence, this contradiction further underscores the need for stepping up the rate of investments.

But this brings to the fore another contradiction, the 'chronic savings gap' problem, and this manifests itself as the 'latent conflict' between the desire on the part of 'relatively high income groups' in the peripheral countries to imitate the ways of life in the advanced centre and the need for higher savings to enable higher investments (1950a, pp. 6, 37; 1964, p. 114). Early on Prebisch noted the power of advertising (1950a, p. 52). The 'struggle to emulate' was intensified by 'remarkable progress achieved in mass communication techniques' (1968, p. 2). Into the latter 1970s and early 1980s, he further analysed this contradiction in terms of a 'privileged consumer society' versus a 'sub-consumer society' (1976, pp. 9–10; 1978, p. 160). Groups belonging to the former, thanks to their imitative culture of consumption, were not generating adequate savings to unleash sufficient dynamism in the economy through investments. That would leave more workers unemployed than if investments were at a higher level. And even for those who were employed, the weak investment, through the preservation of many 'layers of technology' on the relatively unproductive side, also meant that there would be many whose income remained rather stagnant, thereby condemning them to the 'sub-consumer society'. In short, the 'chronic savings gap' generates an inadequate level of investment, which sustains the uneven income distribution that, given the imitative consumption culture, contributed to the creation of the gap in the first place.

10.4 PERSISTENT DISEQUILIBRIUM BETWEEN IMPORTS AND EXPORTS AS A CONSTRAINT ON DEVELOPMENT

However, there was another problem that Prebisch devoted his attention to that was at least as vexing as the 'chronic savings gap', and that was the 'persistent tendency toward disequilibrium' in the balance of payments of the peripheral countries.[16] Writing in the early 1950s and with Latin America in mind, he lamented that a situation of 'no disequilibrium' simply 'has not been the general experience in the Latin-American countries during the last twenty-five years' (1951a, p. 11).[17] In fact, it is this 'disequilibrium' that destroys the basic premise underlying, and thus renders 'out-dated', the schema of the international division of labour that he daringly declares in the opening part of his 'manifesto' (1950a, p. 1).

This disequilibrium that Prebisch considered was mostly discussed in connection with the trade deficit, although he was fully aware of the difference between that and a current account deficit. As mentioned near the end of section 10.2 above, he concludes in the *Economic Survey of LA* that '[t]he fundamental economic problem of Latin America lies in increasing its real *per capita* income by virtue of an increase in productivity'. However,

> when income increases at a greater rate than population, economic development is accompanied by phenomena of disequilibrium, which occur because exports are not then adequate to meet the demands of the development. In other words, the

> *capacity to import* does not grow in proportion to the necessity to import. (1951a, p. 11, italics added)[18]

When the need to import to meet the demands of development – for example, 'greater imports of capital goods in order to increase productivity' – is not met, there would be 'consequent effects upon the domestic economy' (ibid., pp. 10, 9).[19]

Under slightly different labels over time, this 'disequilibrium between imports and exports' (ibid., p. 10) was also raised as a deep concern in many of Prebisch's other works because it constrains growth and development. Hence, in *Problems of Economic Growth* he states that '[t]he elimination of external disequilibrium is essential to the achieving of a regular and orderly form of economic development', noting that in actual fact development 'has been retarded or halted in order to correct the disequilibrium' (1950b, pp. 28, 20). In *International Co-operation* he alludes to the dilemma that a peripheral country would likely face as it attempts to narrow its development gap with the centre. For,

> if ... [it] is not to develop at a slower rate than the centres, if it wishes to develop economically and to reduce – or at least maintain – the difference in income between them, there will be a persistent tendency towards disequilibrium because its industrial imports will tend to increase more than its primary exports. ...
> In any case, the reduction of imports to the level of the payments' capacity is inevitable. The fundamental distinction lies in whether restrictions are applied spontaneously to the detriment of the rate of growth or whether they are part of a deliberate policy favouring that rate. (1954, p. 63)[20]

Right before he assumed his role, and during his term as the Secretary-General of the United Nations Conference on Trade and Development (UNCTAD), he continued to draw attention to the challenges posed by the 'latent tendency towards disequilibrium', the 'external bottleneck in economic development' (1963, pp. 7, 68), the 'persistent tendency towards external imbalance associated with the development process' (1964, p. 3), and the 'trade gap' (1968, p. 3).

How would the possible decline in the CTT enter into this disequilibrium picture? It is clearly enunciated in *Economic Survey of LA* that it is part of the picture, but Prebisch can arguably be regarded as putting more emphasis on the 'capacity to import', which 'depends fundamentally upon the volume of a country's exports *and* the price relationship between its exports and imports' (1951a, p. 15, italics added, see also pp. 17–18).[21] This emphasis is also evident in several other instances (for example, 1951b, p. 120; 1963, p. 8; 1964, p. 4; 1968, p. 15). Obviously, that capacity to import could decrease even 'on the hypothesis of terms-of-trade stability', only that '[if] there happened to be a deterioration, the disequilibrium would be much greater'

(1968, p. 15). That is, during any period the capacity to import could decrease more than the volume of exports if the trend of the CTT is unfavourable. Indeed, he observed that '[t]he adverse effect of the world economic crisis [Great Depression] upon exports is impressive' and '[u]nfortunately, the terms of trade, so far from offsetting this movement, tended to sharpen its effects' (1951a, pp. 15, 18; see also 1964, p. 19 and 1971a, p. 77).[22]

Notice that this interpretation of Prebisch in no way downplays the significance of the statistical debate concerning the PST. Quite the contrary. It argues that he regarded the persistent disequilibrium problem could be a serious one even if the CTT were to remain stable. When the CTT declines it becomes, *a fortiori*, more serious.[23] Besides, the interpretation is consistent with the clarification advanced in section 10.2, namely that engendering development by way of an overall productivity improvement in the peripheral countries is more fundamental than simply improving their CTT. In that connection, a deterioration of the CTT is seen as 'aggravating the external bottleneck and exerting a marked depressive influence on domestic capacity for capital formation, to the detriment of development itself' (1963, p. 8).

Nor does this interpretation disregard that for Prebisch, the CTT determines how the 'fruits of technical progress' are shared between the centre and periphery, which is after all a major theme in his 'manifesto'. There is, obviously, the possibility of insult being added to injury. For instance, at one point in his *New Trade Policy* he considers a situation in which, 'owing to the transfer abroad of income caused by the deterioration in the terms of trade, the capacity for capital formation [in the developing countries], intrinsically very feeble, will be further diminished' (1964, p. 16). However, at a later point in the same work he allows that there could be 'a case in which the benefits of technological progress would be transferred abroad in the form of lower prices corresponding to lower costs, which would only be acceptable if it was accompanied by a substantial increase in export volume' (ibid., p. 46).

As far as the PST is concerned, Prebisch acknowledged in the latter part of his life that, 'Set forth in somewhat simplified fashion, the thesis aroused criticisms which sometimes made useful contributions to its refinement' (1978, p. 226). However, it should be noted that early on he had anticipated some of these criticisms, and had expressed sensible reservations and qualifications toward certain conclusions. He thus cautioned against 'unwarranted generalizations' of the situations in the peripheral countries (1951a, pp. 5, 53, 83; 1959a, p. 260).[24] He alluded to the problem of varying results depending upon the starting year of observation of the CTT movements (1964, p. 81). At one point in the *Economic Survey of LA* he notes that 'the price indices of industrial exports, used in calculating those relations, do not allow for the improvement in quality of the goods, and yet this has certainly been much greater than in the case of raw materials' (1951a, p. 19).[25] At another point in the same work he refers to what is essentially the single factoral terms of trade (FTT) to illustrate that a declining CTT for peripheral exports 'does not [necessarily] mean that primary producers are worse off than they were before', for '[e]verything depends on the degree of increased productivity reached and the extent to which it is transferred to industrial manufacturers' (ibid., p. 47). That illustration is worth quoting in full:

> If the index [of terms of trade] falls [from 100] to 80, for instance, primary producers will be able to obtain 20 per cent less manufactured goods than they did before, for the same amount of primary goods. However, if to obtain that same amount they need work only half as long as before, one hour's labour would now allow them to purchase 60 per cent more manufactured goods, instead of 100 per cent more, as would have been the case had they received the full benefits of their own technical progress; or an even greater quantity had they been able to share in the benefits of technical progress achieved in the industrial sector, should such progress be greater than that achieved in the field of primary production. (Ibid.)[26]

He laments that 'due to the lack of data concerning the increment of productivity in primary production it is not possible to ascertain the extent of such benefits and what part of them has remained in the primary producer countries'. Nevertheless, he speculates that between the 1870s and the early 1950s '[t]he indices ... seem to indicate that something of this sort has occurred' (ibid., pp. 47–8). All in all he shows keen awareness that the empirical exercise 'is not merely a question of analyzing export and import prices' (p. 18).

It has to be pointed out that the above illustration anticipates one of a similar nature that Haberler (1963, p. 276) outlines as part of his critique of Prebisch and others who subscribed to the PST.[27] The former concedes that,

> even if a given deterioration of the commodity terms of trade is fully or more than fully accounted for by an increase in the productivity of the export industries (that is to say, if the single factoral terms of trade have not worsened), it is still true that the country would be better off if the foreign demand for its exports had been infinitely elastic so that the commodity terms of trade had remained unchanged. (Ibid., p. 277)

While one can say that 'the more elastic the foreign demand and hence the better the terms of trade, the better for the country', it is also the case that 'the less elastic the foreign demand, hence the worse the terms of trade, the worse for the country' (ibid.).

Prebisch certainly regarded many primary commodities to exhibit a low price elasticity of demand, such that 'the concerted effort of the primary producing countries to increase the volume of exports substantially, without regard to the rise in income in the industrial centres, would be attended by so great a price decline that the value of exports would not increase and might even be lower than previously' (1950b, p. 36). This 'concerted effort' might in some sense have materialised in the latter part of the nineteenth century, in manners that smack of what Torrens and Mill proposed England should do as discussed in Chapters 4 and 5 above. In fact, the passage from the *Economic Survey of LA* (Prebisch 1951a) that was quoted in section 5.8 precisely hints at the possible link between the spread of primary production to the 'newer areas' on the one hand, and the declining CTT that they had experienced on the other.

Aside from low price elasticity of demand, Prebisch also drew attention to other features of demand for primary products, or factors pertaining thereto, that while contributing to the tendency of the CTT for such products to decline, also accounted for the persistent disequilibrium in the exporting countries' balance of payments. In particular, he dwelled upon the disparities in the income elasticity of demand between industrial (manufactured) and primary products (1950b, p. 30; 1954, p. 63; 1959a, p. 252; 1962, p. 27; 1963, p. 7; 1971a, p. 194; 1984, pp. 177–8).[28] Harking back to the theme in section 10.3 above that 'any acceleration in the rate of growth requires additional investment', he observed that 'the import content of this investment is normally much higher than that of income as a whole. Consequently, … imports would have to rise at a rate somewhat higher than that of total income' (1964, p. 4).[29]

On some occasions Prebisch spelled out how technological progress had also skewed demand away from certain primary commodities. Thus, such progress enabled 'better utilization of raw materials, sub-products and by-products' (1950b, p. 29), including the substitution of these by synthetic materials (1962, p. 27). On some other occasions he alluded to increasing, or the maintenance of, trade protection of primary commodities in the centres during various periods (1950a, p. 22; 1959a, p. 266; 1968, p. 3). That had frequently and unfortunately accentuated the disparities in income elasticities of demand (1959a, pp. 252, 264; 1964, p. 30).[30]

However, all of these factors that account for the deterioration of the CTT and persistence of external disequilibrium were, to Prebisch, revealing a more fundamental problem, and that was the lack of 'dynamism' in the peripheral economies to respond to changing conditions in world markets. Thus, in *Dynamic Development Policy* he concludes that '[t]he disparity [in income elasticities of demand] need not necessarily bring about any decline in primary prices so long as production adjusts itself continually and easily to the tempo of demand' (1963, p. 78). But in reality, 'deterioration is caused by the lack of dynamism in development, which hinders or precludes absorption of the surplus manpower resulting from the sluggish growth of demand and higher productivity in primary activities' (ibid., p. 79). Thirteen years later, in a *CEPAL Review* article, he reiterates that '[t]his disparity between exports and imports is structural in nature, and is basically due to the lag in industrialization'. And,

> if the industrial development of the periphery had been parallel to that of the centres, it would have been possible to meet, through its own diversification and industrial trade with the centres, the requirements in respect of manufactured goods which the high income-elasticity of demand for them would have entailed. (1976, p. 65)[31]

Hence, industrialisation was looked upon as providing the 'solution for the problem of insufficient dynamism' (1971a, p. 234). This it would accomplish partly by playing 'the dynamic role of absorbing directly the redundant labour force' (1950b, p. 43), and 'obtaining a share of the benefits of technical progress and of progressively raising the standard of living of the masses' (1950a, p. 2). It is 'an inescapable part of the process of change accompanying a gradual improvement in per capita income' (1959a, p. 251). Industrialisation 'is the only way to correct the effects on peripheral growth of disparities in foreign trade elasticity' (ibid., p. 253).[32]

10.5 INDUSTRIALISATION: IS AND EP

Industrialisation without Neglecting Primary Production

Before examining Prebisch's support of both IS and EP, a short subsection that clarifies that it was never his intent to favour industrialisation at the expense of primary production is warranted.

Thus, shortly after he declares in the opening section of his 'manifesto' that the schema of the international division of labour is 'out-dated' and starts advocating peripheral industrialisation, he maintains that,

> The industrialization of Latin America is not incompatible with the efficient development of primary production. ... [T]he availability of the best capital equipment and the prompt adoption of new techniques are essential if the development of industry is to fulfil the social objective of raising the standard of living. The same is true of the mechanization of agriculture. Primary products must be exported to allow for the importation of the considerable quantity of capital goods needed. (1950a, p. 2, see also p. 5)

In the *Economic Survey of LA* he starts to think in terms of interdependence between various sectors, pointing out that

> technical progress forges links of interdependence between the various branches of economic activity ... Just as the development of industry, transport and trade, as well as services, needs the labour which is no longer necessary to primary production, the latter in its turn could not expand further without a corresponding development of these other activities. (1951a, p. 13; see also 1950b, p. 101)

At one point in *Change and Development* he even sounds a little Listian when he refers to a situation where, should industrialisation succeed in unleashing dynamism, 'agriculture and industry will derive a more powerful stimulus from their reciprocal demand and will give each other mutual support, propagating their growth throughout the rest of the economy' (1971a, p. 7; see List [1841] 1991, p. 155).

He singles out Argentina in his 1959 *American Economic Review* (*AER*) article for having followed 'the very mistaken policy of trying to stimulate industrialization to the detriment of agriculture, instead of promoting a balanced growth of both' (p. 252). As will be indicated in the following subsection, he was also critical of some adverse impact of IS on the agricultural sector.[33]

Support of IS Industrialisation with Caution

IS industrialisation was already being implemented in Latin America when Prebisch started to provide theoretical justification for it in the late 1940s and 1950s (1984, p. 177). What was his conceptualisation of that strategy? How might it have changed over time?

In his *Problems of Economic Growth* he clarifies that, given the problem of persistent external disequilibrium as a constraint on development, IS 'does not involve a concept of self-sufficiency, nor of pursuing a systematic reduction of imports; instead, it implies importing as much as exports and foreign investments may allow. ... [Also,] the *possibility of increasing exports adequately must by no means be overlooked*' (1950b, p. 8, italics added). On the import side it also meant that the 'composition of imports' should be adjusted, although at this stage he did not appear to be prepared to differentiate IS into different phases (1950a, p. 45; 1950b, p. 44).[34]

At one point in his 'manifesto' he reasons in 'classical terms' to determine the theoretical 'limits of industrialization'.[35] The situation that he considers is: 'if Latin America, being in a position to maintain exports and imports at a specified level, were deliberately to lower it, sacrificing part of its exports in order to increase industrial production as a substitute for imports', would that trade-off be worthwhile? To decide, one simply finds out 'whether the increase in industrial production brought about by the factors diverted from primary production was or was not greater than the amount of goods formerly obtained in exchange for the exports'. 'This then', he claims, 'is one of the most important limits of industrialization' (1950a, p. 45).[36]

In *International Co-operation* he argues that protection is necessary given the existing productivity differences between the centre and periphery.[37] However, in that particular work he does not consider himself to be making an infant-industry argument. His distinction proceeds from the assumption that, consistent with the discussion in section 10.3, '[t]hese [productivity] differences are explained basically by the great disparity in the capital per occupied person and in the technical skills which they possess' (1954, p. 61). To narrow, let alone close, this productivity gap would require the periphery to correct that particular disparity and this simply 'could not occur in reality in the foreseeable future'. He thus believes that his argument 'demonstrate[s] the inevitability of protection [and] enlarges the scope of classical reasoning', for his 'new approach ... establishes the need for protection so long as productivity continues to be lower than that of more advanced countries and to the extent that the difference in productivity is not offset by differences in wage levels' (p. 62).[38] 'From a strict development point of view', he thus concludes, 'protection is not an exceptional or short-term need; it is a systematic long-term necessity' (p. 66).

The persistence of productivity gaps in individual lines of manufacturing production between the centre and periphery is consistent with an overall improvement in productivity in the latter through IS in Prebisch's framework. Thus, a 'considerable improvement in productivity' was thought to be realised through the 'industrial employment of the unemployed, or ill-employed' (1950a, p. 5).[39] For '[e]ven if *per capita* output is smaller in industry than in exports, it is much higher than in the rest of the activities into which modern production techniques have barely penetrated', including agriculture for internal consumption, cottage industries, and the vast range of personal services. Consequently, 'a shifting of manpower from these relatively unproductive activities into industry and other more highly productive activities, at a rate commensurate with the growth of the active population, represents a net increase in the average *per capita* product for the economy as a whole' (1961a, p. 14).[40, 41]

Many in the economics mainstream are not aware that Prebisch was quite critical of the manner in which IS was carried out and the problems that it had engendered, especially in Latin America. For those – within the mainstream or without – who have paid attention, it would seem that he became so beginning from the late 1950s. Thus, according to his discussions since then, many of these problems have their roots in the haphazard origin of the strategy (1961a, pp. 4–5, 14; 1961b, p. 625; 1962, p. 32; 1963, p. 71;

1964, p. 22). That in turn translated into situations where protection was carried to extremely high levels (1959a, p. 265; 1961a, pp. 2–3; 1963, p. 71, 1971a, p. 214; 1978, p. 184). Competition was choked off, breeding inefficiencies and destroying incentives for productivity improvements (1959a, p. 259; 1961a, p. 16; 1962, pp. 33–4; 1963, pp. 46–7, 71, 92; 1964, p. 22; 1968, pp. 7, 25; 1971a, p. 193). It hurt the agricultural sector (1961a, pp. 3, 15; 1963, pp. 41–2; 1971a, pp. 40, 209).[42] It also discouraged exports, both primary and manufactured,[43] thereby enhancing the periphery's 'external vulnerability' (1961a, pp. 3–5, 14–5; 1962, pp. 31–3; 1963, pp. 42, 72; 1964, pp. 21–2, 74–5, 108; 1971a, p. 210).[44]

However, a careful re-examination of Prebisch's works provides hints that he was alert to many of these problems even in the early to mid-1950s. Thus, regarding haphazardness he writes in *International Co-operation* that 'no country in Latin America developed a policy of protection which, besides being based on logical criteria of economic soundness, took account of the import substitution necessary for economic development, so as to give investments their indispensable order of priority' (1954, p. 10; see also 1950b, pp. 18, 84). In the *Economic Survey of LA* he laments that 'it generally occurs in the process of industrialization that each country within its own frontiers attempts to develop both industrial and agricultural production of a type similar to that carried on across the frontier without regard either for specialization or consumption capacity' (1951a, p. 84). A few years later he reiterates in *International Co-operation* that 'industrialization is developing in "water-tight" compartments of national economies, and trade in industrial products between Latin American countries is very rare'.[45] Understandably, 'high cost production will often result from the inadequacy of the domestic market' (1954, pp. 72, 73). Going back a few years now to his 'manifesto', he warns that such 'higher cost of internal production' could result in a loss in real income. 'It is conceivable', he thus reasons, '[that] the precariousness of natural resources and the inefficiency of workers or management might be such that the loss through increased costs would absorb an excessively large part of the increase in real income gained through greater employment. The seriousness of this difficulty cannot be denied' (1950a, p. 53). Last but not least, in *Problems of Economic Growth* he draws attention to 'cases in which exaggerated emphasis has been placed on certain domestic activities, whilst disregarding the possible margin of profitable development in *exports*' (1950b, p. 21, italics added).[46]

The increasing seriousness of these problems throughout the 1950s had probably enabled Prebisch to better understand their nature, to sharpen his critique, and to come up with recommendations on how industrialisation should proceed in the ensuing phase. Indeed, in his 1959 *AER* article one finds him offering a more nuanced characterisation of IS based on stages or phases of progress. Thus,

> [t]he development process requires a continual change in the composition of imports. These changes usually start with the decline in the proportion of imports of light consumer goods in favor of imports of basic material, capital goods, and durables. At more advanced stages of industrialization, when import substitution of these light consumer goods has been nearly completed, new changes relating to the other categories of goods are necessary, so that by reducing or eliminating imports of some of them it is possible to increase imports responding to the needs of the development process. (p. 264)

Heading into the 1960s and early 1970s he repeatedly issued warnings that the initial stage of easy and simple substitution had reached its limits in those countries where industrialisation had proceeded the most (1963, p. 69; 1964, p. 21; 1968, p. 8; 1971a, p. 46).[47]

However, the move into the next stage was by no means spontaneous. This is the one where imports of intermediate products and capital goods should begin to be substituted. That necessitates heavier investments and the use of technologies that are more complex, but 'neither exports nor foreign capital will suffice to finance all the imports necessary for the accumulation of the vast stock of capital required' (1959b, p. 143). Prebisch fully understood, in the context of Latin America in the late 1950s, that the further IS should proceed, 'the greater will be the attendant difficulties, if the process continues to develop within the twenty watertight compartments represented by the individual country markets' (ibid.). Besides, for those countries that had more or less completed the first phase of IS,

> accentuated by adverse trade conditions, they have compressed their import requirements to a series of goods absolutely essential for the maintenance and growth of their economy and have lost the margin for the further reduction in imports which they had when they imported consumer goods. Thus an unfavorable fluctuation in exports tends to have critical effects on economic development far more so than when, as in former times, vulnerability was more on the demand side. (1959a, p. 268)

Consequently, they had paradoxically become more 'externally vulnerable' (see also 1961a, p. 5; 1963, pp. 69–70; 1964, p. 22; 1978, p. 226).[48]

Prebisch thus realised that a policy was needed 'to encourage these changes in composition in order to accelerate the rate of economic growth, so that imports are adapted to the need for greater technical progress in primary production and for more intense industrial development' (1959a, p. 265). And that prompted him to put more emphasis on EP than before.[49]

Support of EP, but Not Abandoning IS

As the reader has seen in some passages from Prebisch's works that are quoted in the earlier parts of the present chapter, there are strong indications that he was quite aware of the importance of exports to peripheral development. As further evidence, he stresses as early as his 'manifesto' that,

> The more active Latin America's foreign trade, the greater the possibility of increasing productivity by means of intensive capital formation. The solution does not lie in growth at the expense of foreign trade, but in knowing how to extract, from continually growing foreign trade, the elements that will promote economic development. (1950a, p. 2)

One should thus not forget, he reminds the reader, 'that the greater the exports from Latin America the greater may be the rate of its economic development' (ibid., p. 46; see also 1950b, pp. 8, 60, 81).[50]

An early instance when Prebisch considered the benefits of promoting manufactured exports can be found in an interesting passage in the *Economic Survey of LA*. There while discussing what Japan's development experience might offer in terms of lessons to the periphery, he observes that,

> Japan was able to assimilate modern technique rapidly but did not raise wages to the levels of the great industrial countries. ... Japan's incomes thus remained lower than those of other industrial countries; nevertheless, through industrialization Japan was able to increase considerably *per capita* productivity with an evident net increase in income, *which would probably not have been possible without the expansion of exports*. (1951a, p. 77, italics added)

Although he does not make the explicit label, he is probably referring to its manufactured exports, however simple they might be at that time.

Though Prebisch was harbouring that thought even in the early 1950s, it was not until the late 1950s that he started to more explicitly give it support.[51] Thus, referring to the external disequilibrium problem discussed in section 10.4 above, he considers in his 1959 *AER* article a situation where both the centre and periphery in a two region model are growing at the same rate, but where the latter has a higher income elasticity of demand for the former's products than vice versa. He concludes that in the periphery, 'either the rate of increase of demand for imports would have to fall ... by means of *import substitution, or industrial exports* would have to be added to the primary ones, *or a combination of the two*' (1959a, p. 254, italics added). Reiterating this point a couple of years later in his article in the *Economic Bulletin for Latin America*, he proclaims that 'import substitution (and the development of industrial exports to the centres) is a *sine qua non* for rectifying these differences [of elasticity]' (1961a, p. 4). 'It is common knowledge', he adds, 'that the economic development of a peripheral country is very closely linked to the course that its exports follow. ... [For] the rate of growth of its exports sets a limit to spontaneous economic development' (ibid., p. 2; see also 1963, p. 7).[52]

Prebisch continued with this promotion effort in his capacity as the Secretary-General for UNCTAD. Observing the size of the trade gaps typical among peripheral countries at that time, he dismissed as mere 'palliatives' measures that sought to expand primary exports.

> Hence, the absolute necessity of building up trade in industrial exports. Exports of manufactures ought to have been the natural complement of the industrialization of the peripheral economies. (1964, p. 20)
>
> The development of industrial exports, in addition to counteracting the potential trade gap, will make it possible gradually to increase the advantages of industrialization by correcting its defects. (Ibid., p. 22)

And for those peripheral countries that relied on food imports, industrial exports could help pay for them (ibid., p. 55; see also 1968, p. 20).

After leaving UNCTAD and refocusing his attention on Latin America, he harks back to the term 'dynamism' in *Change and Development* and remarks that,

> The process [of IS] bears within itself the seeds of its own loss of dynamism, since industrial development takes place within a closed circuit of costs and prices which, because it has no contact with the world market, discourages exports of manufactures; and these are really essential, for industry needs to stretch outward in order to develop inward in depth. (1971a, pp. 193–4)

'[A] new type of development in Latin America', he declares, 'cannot be based solely on import substitution, but must entail a major effort to promote exports to the rest of the world and, in particular, intraregional exports' (ibid., p. 48, see also pp. 18, 173; 1976, pp. 64–5; 1985, pp. 14, 15).[53]

On this last point of promoting intraregional trade within Latin America, Prebisch started entertaining the idea since the early 1950s, if not before (for instance, 1951a, p. 84). But in the late 1950s, with his deeper appreciation of the problems with IS and the need for the promotion of industrial exports, this began to crystallise into something more concrete. Thus, referring to the 'costliness of the substitution process', he argued that '[t]he only basic solution ... is to break up the out-dated mould [where inter-Latin American trade was very slight] ... by means of the gradual and progressive establishment of the common market and the consequent diversification of imports and exports' (1959b, p. 144). More generally for peripheral countries, '[i]f the trend towards external disequilibrium is to be progressively eliminated, this excessive protection will have to be gradually dismantled, starting with the liberalization of trade' among themselves (1968, p. 25).

Recall that in Chapter 8 List suggested the second-tier industrialising countries of his time like France, the German States, and America to export 'coarse manufactures' to the 'torrid zones' to find markets so that their products could be refined and improved over time to catch up with England's. In advocating a Latin American Common Market, or South–South trade in general, Prebisch understood that such efforts 'can help considerably to achieve more efficient production by expanding markets, encouraging specialization and facilitating competition', and '[t]he resulting reduction in industrial costs will have an important bearing ... in the [world] export market' (1961b, p. 627; see also 1959a, p. 268).

It must be stressed that at no point did Prebisch imply that EP should replace IS. Rather, the two should be implemented in some combined ways. He thus puts it very tersely in *New Trade Policy* that '[t]he stress ... laid on industrial exports does not mean that import substitution policy should be abandoned. On the contrary, it should be maintained' (1964, p. 25). Later in the same work he elaborates that,

> There is no conflict between import substitution and export promotion. Industries that begin by catering to the domestic market may, as they gain experience and efficiency, branch out into export markets. (p. 76)

> The fact is that the development of the domestic market and the promotion of exports are not two alternative or mutually exclusive propositions. The two processes must take place simultaneously and in a co-ordinated manner. (p. 115)[54]

The important feature to remember, he adds, is that IS be implemented 'within groupings of countries', that is, 'be resolutely founded on regional and subregional integration of basic industries' when it comes to capital and intermediate goods (1964, p. 123; 1971a, pp. 106, 236).

Intraregional trade – including trade in certain capital and intermediate goods within a region – aside, what did Prebisch envisage the emerging trade pattern between the centre and periphery to be like? It might at first appear that he was talking here in terms of static comparative advantage. Thus, at one point in the early 1960s he wrote,

> The greater our traditional exports and the exports of industrial goods in which we have comparative advantages, the larger will be our own imports of other industrial goods whose production in Latin American countries would still be relatively costly in relation to the levels prevailing in the more advanced industrial centers. (1962, p. 37)

Trade would then be conducted 'on a basis of reciprocal benefits' (1963, p. 73; see also 1964, p. 25). But there is more, as the next section will illustrate.

10.6 INCREASING INDIGENOUS TECHNOLOGICAL DENSITIES IN THE PERIPHERY

The term 'technological density' is not one that Prebisch employed too often in his works, at least not frequently explicitly. Partly as a consequence, its content can benefit from further clarification and refinement. Nevertheless, when one takes heed of how he conceptualised it on the occasions that he used it, then one realises that the concept actually permeates many important areas of his works and has quite an important role to play.[55] In fact, it even appears to contain traces of Lall's concept of 'technological capabilities' (Lall 1992, 1993).

It is contended in section 10.2 that Prebisch was deeply concerned with the uneven development that, to him, was based on the uneven technological progress between the centre and periphery. In his 1959 *AER* article he alludes again to 'the uneven form in which technical progress has spread into the world economy'. He laments that that has brought 'very great disparities in technological densities. That is to say, the amount of technological knowledge as well as the real aptitude for using it in production' (1959a, p. 261).

In section 10.3 attention is drawn to Prebisch's awareness, shown in his 'manifesto', that the periphery should cultivate an 'ability' to use capital and technology well. In the *Economic Survey of LA* he elaborates that,

> The assimilation of modern productive technique with its increasing complexity was not spontaneous but deliberate, and required considerable effort and persistence. This is all of great importance to the development of Latin America, since the differences in the standard of living between the developed and the developing countries does not only depend on the differences between their respective natural resources but to a great extent on the *effective capacity to assimilate technique*, build up the necessary savings and make the best use of both. *The development of this capacity will therefore be a predominating factor in the economic evolution of the countries which are now in the growing stage.* (1951a, p. 73, italics added; see also 1971a, pp. 206–7)[56]

Recall the discussion in section 10.2 on his emphasis on improving overall productivity in the periphery. With the importance of technological density in mind he cautioned that while it was 'essential' to increase the capital used per man, it was certainly 'not the only condition for increasing productivity'. Rather, '[t]he ability to organize, manage and administer on the one hand,

and the technical skill of labour on the other, are also of great importance' (1951a, p. 71). Put differently, 'productivity involves two closely connected factors: first, the investment of savings in capital goods, and second, the investment of savings in the training of men who can make the best use of these goods at the various stages of production' (ibid., p. 72; see also 1954, p. 42; 1960, p. 107; 1976, p. 23; 1979, p. 171).[57]

This last distinction between two factors also hints at the importance of ensuring that technological density has a certain indigenous base in the periphery. 'Economic development', he thus characterised at one point, 'is basically a process of training and perfecting *national* aptitudes in respect to technique and production' (1962, p. 36, italics added). While he believed that there were 'forms of advanced technology' that were within the reach of the developing countries, there were others that were beyond that reach. Aside from the relative lack of capital, 'the main limiting factor is each country's technological density in the sense of available techniques and skills'. He went on to add that,

> This technology generally requires a high input of capital per person employed.[58] *Capital goods can be imported into the developing countries, but not technological density which has to evolve gradually. Only isolated special skills or techniques can be imported.* A clear distinction must, therefore, be drawn between capital goods and technological density. There are industries which employ advanced and complex capital goods but which do not require great technological density to develop; if there are a few special skills, or if they can be imported, this is enough to ensure their smooth operation. (1964, p. 59, italics added)

But apart from the 'general education and technical training of the masses', what else might facilitate this acquisition of 'national aptitudes'?

Not surprisingly, based on the discussion in the previous section Prebisch believed that IS would play a contributory role. Thus, 'it has helped to build up a measure of managerial skill and to develop industries which would hardly have been likely to spring up on their own' (1971a, p. 46). However, '[p]rotection *carried to excess* affords no encouragement to train efficient workers and make good use of their services. Production equipment is often misguidedly used'. Theoretically speaking, these problems can be solved 'provided [that] private enterprise does not confine its efforts to the initial functions of promotion. It must also be indefatigable in its endeavours to increase yields and reduce costs. And this is where nothing can replace the spur of competition' (1963, p. 47, italics added).[59]

The promotion of industrial exports is one way to spur competition. However, such export promotion was not conceived by Prebisch to be merely in accordance with static comparative advantage, as the quotation at the end of the previous section might have otherwise suggested. In that connection, he made it very clear in his capacity as Secretary-General of UNCTAD that export expansion by the periphery 'is not just a matter of filling the void left by declining industries' in the advanced countries. Nor should the promotion be just a matter of steering existing industries outwards (1964, p. 60). Rather, industrial exports, 'besides their primary aim, must be an effective instrument for promoting technological progress'. That is, they must be a means of changing the forms of production 'where developing countries merely export simple manufactures' (ibid., p. 59). It would be wise, for instance, to 'concentrate on the new industries or the new lines of production in existing industries which, with some support in the local market, or preferably in the wider market constituted by a grouping of developing countries, could be launched in the search for external markets' (ibid., p. 60; see also 1968, p. 57).[60] The periphery should also explore subcontracting opportunities involving 'the possibilities of manufacturing certain types of intermediate goods and components in the developing countries for use in the industries of developed countries' (1964, p. 76).[61, 62]

Another way of spurring competition is to pit transnational corporations (TNCs) against indigenous enterprises through the attraction of FDI. While Latin America and the periphery in general could additionally count on such foreign capital to augment investments, Prebisch was quite conscious of many of the pitfalls of too much of such reliance. He thus repeatedly emphasised the important role to be played by indigenous enterprises and strongly cautioned that '[h]ealthy competition must be based on equality of conditions; otherwise it leads to the destruction or subordination of the weaker part' (1961b, p. 631; see also 1962, p. 37; 1963, p. 55). Perhaps not yet with TNCs in mind, he thus states in *International Co-operation* that, 'It is indispensable to guarantee the Latin American entrepreneur easy access to sources of international capital and techniques, thus offering him opportunities comparable with those enjoyed by the foreign entrepreneur' (1954, p. 8). A few years later he explicitly considered foreign private enterprises' presence in the periphery and argued that,

> private enterprise from abroad, valuable as its contribution might be, could not play so effective a part as is often exaggeratedly supposed. … [U]nless at the same time energetic measures were adopted to promote the training of local technicians and the formation of entrepreneurs, a disturbing situation might arise. Generally speaking, the developing industries of Latin America have not reached a technical level at which they could withstand a very strong current of foreign private enterprise. … [I]f the country's own private enterprise is not to face failure …, it must be given financial assistance to enable it to hold its ground *vis-à-vis* private enterprise from abroad. (1958, pp. 48–9)

Thus, while 'not advocating the exclusion of private foreign enterprise from Latin America' and maintaining that 'it should fulfil a most useful function', he insisted that 'a concentrated and unflagging effort should be made to improve, strengthen and expand Latin American enterprise ... by means of far-reaching technical and financial co-operation programmes on an international basis' (ibid., p. 50; see also 1959a, p. 269; 1961b, pp. 624, 633).[63]

If these programmes work out as desired by the periphery (on which more in the following section), then not only would it better succeed in adapting technology from the centres, it would be in a position to participate in the 'creation of technology' as well so that it could 'make up its technical deficiency in the vast process of transfer of world technology' (1971a, pp. 207, 239). And 'as the technological density of each developing country increases and as its ability to compete abroad improves, new lines of manufactured exports will come to the fore encouraged by the dynamism of demand for a series of products' (1964, p. 60). 'It must not be forgotten', he reminded the reader, 'that *the objective is to lessen the technological disparity between the developing countries and the industrial centres*, even though this cannot be done rapidly given the latter's pace of advance' (ibid., italics added).[64] In declaring so, he also joined Hamilton and List in strongly believing that technological prowess in producing manufactured products is not naturally given, but can be acquired.

10.7 MARKET INTERFERENCE AND POLICY ACTIONS

Thus far in this chapter the discussion has focused on portraying what Prebisch felt should happen in the periphery as it sought to improve productivity and infuse dynamism: higher investments, improved external balance, industrialisation, and enhanced indigenous technological densities. Did he expect that spontaneous market forces would bring these about? If not, what policy actions did he propose to make them happen?

On all counts his conclusion was that a country could not completely rely upon spontaneous market forces. Thus, regarding the need for higher investments, '[t]here is nothing in the spontaneous play of economic forces which makes for adjustment of the rate of capital accumulation to the dynamic requirements of the economy' (1976, p. 29; see also 1962, p. 29; 1971a, p. 200). On external disequilibria, '[n]o instrument exists in the economic system of the periphery which might provoke the spontaneous readjustment of imports, in order to prevent such disequilibria' (1950b, p. 44; see also 1971a, p. 201). 'The industrialization of the periphery has not been a spontaneous phenomenon', he also suggested (1976, p. 61). The 'free interplay' of economic forces 'cannot spontaneously generate the far-reaching changes that will have to take place in the patterns of production and the structure of the ... economy, or create the conditions and incentives that private enterprise requires if it is to enact its primary role in economic development' (1958, p. 48). Finally, as far as technological density is concerned, '[t]he assimilation of modern productive technique with its increasing complexity was not spontaneous but deliberate' (1951a, p. 73). The aspect of it that is related to the training of skilled labour 'is guided only to a slight extent by market forces. In the main, it requires deliberate and far-sighted State action' (1976, p. 34).

While Prebisch was clearly not keen on furnishing abstract theoretical details to buttress claims like the above, he was also not simply making assertions either, at least not in all cases. Thus, in *Dynamic Development Policy* he alludes to some cases – for instance, energy, transport, public utilities – in which 'investments take a relatively long time to bring in a return and price is no guide'. He proposes that, 'This is where the State must supply other pointers to make up for the lack of spontaneous indicators, and provide inducements to private enterprise to follow the pointers in question'. However, he thinks that this would not apply to most other goods and services, in which case 'the State usually has no reason to intervene, except when the operation of competition is distorted' and 'it can enable individuals to make their own forecasts on the basis of better information on market movements and the probable course of future demand' (1963, p. 61; see also 1950b, p. 43). But even for these other goods and services, as he clarifies in *Change and Development* with a 'big push' flavour, 'neither industry nor the other economic activities can provide their own stimulus. What is required is an overall increase in demand which will simultaneously encourage the whole body of economic activities and speed up their expansion' (1971a, p. 133).[65]

Then there are cases for state actions to avoid 'an excessive concentration of economic power ... in private hands', and for the 'taking-over by the State of enterprises that by their nature are monopolistic, or of activities which might otherwise be carried out by international combines that limit competition, and are unfavourable to certain national development aims' (1963, p. 63). The latter includes the 'business methods' of certain TNCs and their practices of exploiting their innovations that are covered by patents, licenses or trademarks (1954, p. 39; 1963, p. 55; 1976, p. 70; 1978, pp. 221, 231).

To Prebisch, each of the areas thus requires state actions to compensate for the inadequacy of market forces. Limited by space, the discussion is here confined to policy actions that pertain to implementing IS and EP, as well as the deployment of investment measures that direct the behaviour of TNCs.[66]

When it comes to implementing IS, he talked in quite general terms of relying on 'import restrictions' or 'customs protection'. For those who wonder if he distinguished between tariffs and subsidies, the answer is that sometimes he did not and sometimes he did. Thus, in the *Economic Survey of LA* he indicates that subsidies could take the form of 'customs duties' or 'compensatory payments' (1951a, p. 76). In another publication in the same year he echoes that '[i]mport restrictions ... are, ultimately, a form of internal subsidy' (1951b, p. 127). In *International Co-operation*, he briefly makes comparisons between tariffs and subsidies on the one hand, and direct import restrictions on the other, concluding that 'if the spontaneous development of industry is impracticable and uneconomic, protection alone, either through customs tariffs *or* subsidies, would remain to offset the differences in productivity, since direct import restrictions are usually less advisable as a measure of industrial policy, unless of a temporary nature' (1954, p. 61, italics added).[67] In his 1959 *AER* article, the comparison is made between tariffs and subsidies on the one hand, and currency depreciation on the other. To quote,

> Protection (or subsidies) seems a more direct and simple solution, as it limits the adjustment to those new branches of industries *that should be developed within a given period of time*. To obtain the same result, depreciation forces the adjustment of the whole price system.[68] ... A selective protection policy is a preferable instrument, notwithstanding the obstacles that have to be overcome in practice; and if it is applied gradually, higher import prices, affecting a relatively small proportion of imports each time, could be absorbed by general increments of productivity without affecting the price level of the entire economy, provided that protection has not been exaggerated to shelter inefficiency. (1959a, p. 257, italics added)[69]

In his 1961 article in the *Economic Bulletin for Latin America*, he finally compares tariffs with subsidies, saying at one point that,

> If the new substitution activities are protected by subsidies instead of customs tariffs, a rise in the cost of activities which in one way or another affect the level of living of the broad masses can be prevented. The impact varies according to the items for which substitution is undertaken. If they are consumer items for the high-income groups, we need only concern ourselves with considerations of economic feasibility in substitution activities. But if these items affect the level of living of the community at large, recourse to subsidies would ensure that the social cost of economic development is defrayed by the groups which can better afford to absorb it. (1961a, p. 14)

Fifteen years later, in his article in *CEPAL Review*, he states that, 'With respect to import substitution, subsidies would undoubtedly have been better than protection, mainly because they would have made industrialization more rational, since they would have provided incentive for both import substitution and industrial exports' (1976, p. 63). Nevertheless, the prospect that the centres might take 'compensatory measures to protect themselves against the competition of the periphery' had served as 'a strong deterrent' to the deployment of subsidies (ibid.).[70]

As his caution on IS suggests, Prebisch fully understood that protection could become excessive and adversely impact exports, in which case some corrective measures are called for in order to facilitate EP. He thus laments in *Change and Development* that, 'Export opportunities have often been missed because of the negative effects of certain measures, or for want of a policy of steady encouragement' (1971a, p. 11). For instance, '[c]hronic overvaluation of currencies and needless impediments have done serious harm to the export trade' (1976, p. 64). Without going into too much detail, he proposes that some taxes that increased industrial costs should be abrogated, technical and financial assistance (including export credits) be offered, market studies be conducted, and export subsidies be instituted (1961a, p. 5; 1971a, p. 110). He observes in the early 1970s that 'few countries have taken positive steps to promote exports', and 'while it is true that exports have grown relatively slowly, it is equally undeniable that some countries have managed to take better advantage of their export possibilities than others' (1971a, pp. 77, 48). In fact, '[t]he encouraging results of the export policies of some countries show what has been lost by not having ventured in this direction long ago' (1976, p. 64).

But as the discussion in the latter part of the previous section indicates, be it IS or EP, Prebisch was interested in supporting indigenous enterprises, entrepreneurs, managers and technicians as strong participants in the industrialisation process. Included in what he referred to as technical co-operation programmes are various forms of technical assistance (1954, Part I, Ch. III), the 'training of local staff at all technical levels' and the 'training and strengthening of domestic enterprise' (1962, pp. 53, 54), 'co-operative activities of a strictly technical nature' or licensing arrangements (ibid., p. 56), and joint-enterprise efforts (1950b, p. 13; 1968, p. 57). He deemed that '[a] selective policy is a necessity' in attracting TNCs, in that no such effort would be necessary in sectors 'where production techniques are already familiar' to peripheral entrepreneurs, but then it would be desirable for those sectors where such techniques 'are not accessible for the time being or where foreign experience might be of great value' (1971a, p. 239).

More generally, out of balance-of-payments considerations Prebisch had mentioned various investment measures. These would direct the behaviour of TNCs with a view to restricting their profit remittances (1954, p. 38), reducing imports (1950a, p. 42), or promoting exports (1964, pp. 77–8; 1978, p. 231). And out of anti-competitive concerns, he proposed that '[i]ntergovernmental agreements could be envisaged aimed at ensuring that the business methods of large [transnational] corporations should be subject to adequate standards of control' (1954, p. 39).

10.8 DIFFERENTIAL TREATMENTS IN INTERNATIONAL CO-OPERATION

Obviously, aside from the capacity and determination of individual peripheral countries in deploying investment measures and instituting development policies, there is also the consideration of whether the affected countries, especially those in the centres, would acquiesce to them. Would 'differential treatment' of some sort be extended by the latter to the former?

Investment measures were not really part of the agenda in the rounds of the MTNs prior to the Uruguay Round and Prebisch's death fell on the same year as the latter commenced. Hence, this section focuses on differential treatments relating to trade, although one could speculate that he would not be receptive to the shape that the Agreements on TRIMs and TRIPs were to take when that round was concluded.[71]

In trade, while Prebisch put some responsibilities on the peripheral countries to get their policy actions in order, he also felt that without differential treatment in consideration of the situations in the periphery in international co-operations, the challenge to spur development would be much more formidable. To that end he lobbied for such co-operations early on from the Latin American perspective and he ardently continued with that effort from a global perspective in his capacity as Secretary-General of UNCTAD (Prebisch 1954; 1964; 1968; 1971a, Part III).

It should come as no surprise that someone who labelled the post-war schema of international division of labour as 'out-dated' would take issue with some of the notions behind the GATT. Given his preoccupation with the problem of external disequilibrium, Prebisch understandably targeted his criticism, for instance in *New Trade Policy*, at the 'abstract notion of economic homogeneity' and the 'classic concept that the free play of international economic forces by itself leads to the optimum expansion of trade and the most efficient utilization of the world's productive resources' (1964, pp. 6, 28). To him, the assumption of homogeneity 'conceals the great structural differences between industrial centres and peripheral countries', which then makes it appear that the 'free play concept is admissible'.[72] With that concealment the 'principle of conventional reciprocity' gained legitimacy, and according to it both the centre and periphery should make equivalent trade concessions regarding their respective imports from each other. He was deeply convinced that such concessions 'would intensify the trend towards trade imbalance inherent in the disparity of international demand, instead of helping to correct it' (ibid., pp. 6, 29, 30).[73] A few years later in *Global Strategy*, he concludes that 'the fundamental mistake was made [in the Havana Charter] of thinking that the peripheral countries could participate as equals in the policy of world-wide trade liberalization without passing through a long transitional phase during which the congenital weakness of their economies would be remedied'. Those countries simply 'cannot offer immediate reciprocal benefits in exchange for the concessions they expect from the industrial centres' (1968, pp. 50, 72).

While he thus subscribed to the principle of 'non-reciprocity' (with reference to what he deemed 'conventional reciprocity') as a differential treatment for the periphery, Prebisch believed that the structural differences between the centre and periphery would guarantee 'implicit' or 'real' reciprocity should the former unilaterally offer trade concessions to the latter. For when the peripheral countries were facing persistent disequilibrium in their balance of payments, and given their need to make substantial necessary imports for development, the more they could export to the centre, the more that they would also import from it.[74] Thus, in *International Co-operation* he concludes that 'reciprocity is found to be implicit in the functional nature of the centre, since, if imports [by peripheral countries] are increased simultaneously with [their] exports, compensation is spontaneous and it is unnecessary to manipulate the tariffs of other countries in order that this may take place without any difficulties' (1954, p. 69; see also 1959a, p. 264; 1962, pp. 37–8; 1964, p. 31; 1985, p. 15).[75]

'There is no suggestion', Prebisch clarified in another context, 'that ... nothing at all should be done about customs tariffs in developing countries' (1963, p. 75). While based on the argument in the last paragraph their protective barriers would not have to be removed in order to apply the concept of reciprocity, 'from the standpoint of development itself revision is necessary, so as gradually to correct the serious shortcomings of [IS] industrialization'. That is, the rationales would be 'in the light of economic expediency' as well as 'to ensure that industry is constantly encouraged by external competition to narrow the gap in productivity *vis-à-vis* the major centres'. Nevertheless, he cautioned that,

> A reform of this kind obviously cannot be carried out where an increasing bottleneck exists. Relief must come rather from the external sector, in the shape of speeding-up in the tempo of the export trade. In other words, *a rational customs tariff must be part of an international plan to expand trade on new bases. Tariff reform cannot be a prelude to such a policy, but must stem from it.* (Ibid., italics added)

In short, '[a] more liberal import policy cannot be applied unless exports also develop more freely' (ibid., p. 72; see also 1964, p. 32; 1968, p. 50; 1985, p. 15).

It is in the expansion of industrial exports by the periphery that Prebisch felt very strongly that the centres should also do their part to facilitate such trade. He laments in his *New Trade Policy* that although the tariff reductions agreed among the industrial countries in the 1960s were extended under the most-favoured-nation clause to the peripheral countries, they 'had no significant effect on them, since the goods to which they applied were usually those of interest to the former countries and not to the latter'. In the meantime there was a lack of determination to reduce 'differential tariffs' which 'seriously hamper the processing of raw materials in the developing countries, because ... they rise in proportion to the degree of processing' (1964, p. 23; see also 1963, p. 73).

More generally, there was another differential treatment that Prebisch thought should be offered by the centre to the periphery, namely the general 'preferential treatment for exports of developing countries'. In *New Trade Policy* he explains that,

> The case is ... a logical extension of the infant industry argument. ...
> In order to be efficient, those industries must have access to wider markets; otherwise they may not be able to break out of the vicious circle of low output and high costs. Such markets must be sought in the developed countries as well as in other developing countries. (1964, pp. 65–6)

He expects this treatment to be only a 'temporary measure' because when the industries of developing countries could enjoy wider market access, that 'would enable them to lower their costs and thus compete on world markets without the need for continuing preferences' (ibid., p. 65; see also 1968, p. 24).[76] Given its 'interim' nature, he reasons that it would be important 'for the peripheral countries to demonstrate in practice their determination to avail themselves of the trade opportunities thus offered to them' (1968, p. 60).[77]

Prebisch did not favour a system of preferences that was based on products, insisting that 'a better and simpler approach would be for preferential treatment to be granted in principle to all imports from the developing countries' (1964, p. 69). He also proposed to distinguish between the peripheral countries, suggesting in *Global Strategy* that,

> [s]ince the more developed peripheral countries are pressing for the markets of the industrial centres to be opened up to their manufactures and semi-manufactures, and rightly so. It follows that they, in their turn, should follow suit, open their own doors to the manufactures and semi-manufactures of the less developed peripheral countries and introduce a preferential system in their favour, to the extent that the

> latter do not benefit from the concessions granted by the industrial centres. (1968, p. 29)[78]

While this would amount to giving 'different degrees or kinds of preference to countries according to their per capita income or stage of development', he was realistic to understand that 'the scope for a gradation of preferences may not be very great'. Besides, 'the greater the administrative complications, the smaller the chances that anyone at all will benefit, since the scheme may prove unworkable' (1964, pp. 72, 73).

10.9 CONCLUDING REMARKS

In commenting on Prebisch's 'manifesto' shortly after its publication, Viner[79] remarked that it 'belongs to the same school of thought' as that of Manoïlesco (1953, p. 46).[80] 'All that I find in Prebisch's study and in the other literature along similar lines emanating from the United Nations and elsewhere', he lamented, 'is the dogmatic identification of agriculture with poverty', where such poverty is predicated on the claim that 'agricultural products tend to exchange on ever-deteriorating terms for manufactures' (ibid., p. 44).

As the discussion in the previous chapter should have made clear, while Manoïlesco was concerned with 'inequitable' exchange between industrial and agricultural countries because workers in the former (or generally in industries) possess 'superior productivity', he did not suggest that the latter's products would be subject to declining CTT. If anything, as the discussion toward the end of section 9.5 indicates, he briefly considered, but did not believe seriously in, the scenario where an *increasing* number of countries becoming industrialised might gradually depress the CTT of their exports to the agricultural countries.[81]

So while both Manoïlesco and Prebisch strongly advocated industrialising the agricultural (Manoïlesco's label)/peripheral (Prebisch's label) countries, one must be careful in distinguishing between their reasoning.[82] It was contended in the previous chapter that Manoïlesco's argument for state-supported expansion of superior productive sectors is about static allocation of labour and is devoid of a substantive dissection of the process of development. In this chapter it is argued that Prebisch's support of industrialisation is part of a larger plan for development that had overall productivity improvements and infusion of dynamism as its objectives, in order that the periphery could narrow the technological gap with the centres. Apart from the lag in industrialisation, he regarded the lack of savings, the persistence of external disequilibrium (of which any declining CTT may aggravate the problem), and the lack of technological density in the periphery as barriers and obstacles that interweave to pose extremely formidable 'structural' challenges to development.

Instead of responding to this structural analysis offered by Prebisch, the economics mainstream has chosen to fixate its attention on the statistical debate that has arisen from the PST. In an entry on Prebisch in *A Biographical Dictionary of Dissenting Economists*, Palma shrewdly notes that,

> It is not clear whether Prebisch saw this [PST] as the most important part of his work, but this hypothesis was a seductive challenge to that part of the North American academic establishment which is ever anxious to extract from the structuralist approach unidimensional hypotheses referring to clearly established variables for its own consumption. (1992, p. 442)

To reduce his analysis to one nothing more than an optimal-tariff argument for protection does him tremendous injustice. To insist that even if the thesis is valid, then it remains for him to make a case for state action in accordance with 'a species of one of the familiar *genera*' is simply an insistence on adhering to the *modus operandi* of the economics mainstream that compartmentalises problems that are otherwise interlocking, and that will grossly distort his analytical approach.

In the later years of his life when he refocused his attention on Latin America, Prebisch broadened the content of his structural analysis as he became disillusioned with certain trends and events. While still maintaining that the market could not be 'the supreme regulator of development', he lamented that,

> [n]or has the State often shown in peripheral capitalism any great aptitude for taking deliberate steps to influence the forces of development. Governed as its action also is by the play of power relations, it has shirked the fundamental changes without which it will be impossible to infuse sufficient dynamism into development. In default of such measures, it has come to interfere in the market, to hamper its movements, and to attack only the outward symptoms of deep-seated ills. (1976, p. 20)[83]

Although his earlier works already showed some awareness, he started to more explicitly declare that 'development could not be confined within the narrow bounds of an economic theory, since in it intervene technical, social, political and cultural factors, in addition to those of a strictly economic character'. '[T]he time has now come', he concluded, 'to deal with them in all their intricate complexity and elucidate their inter-relationships' (1978, p. 172). This is the position that the development economist re-examined in the following chapter, Gunnar Myrdal, took right from the beginning when he devoted himself to studying underdevelopment.

NOTES

1. Singer (1992) calls it a 'triple alliance'. His recollection is that, '[I]t was between presenting my paper to the AEA in December 1949 and its publication ... in the summer of 1950 that I discovered that Raul Prebisch ... had developed very similar opinions and had also put the problem of poor terms of trade for primary products into the centre of thinking of the Economic Commission for Latin America ... We formed a close alliance of ideas and were twinned in the economic literature ... Subsequently I discovered a similar sympathetic bond with Gunnar Myrdal who was Prebisch's counterpart in Geneva as Director of the UN Economic Commission for Europe. It was this triple alliance cemented by personal friendship which gave me the strength to survive the dreadful McCarthy years in the UN' (p. 528).
2. Recall that n. 21 in Ch. 1 above draws attention to the attempt by Linder (1961) to capture through a model for what he calls the 'u-countries' some of the essence of the works of the three. Thus, he regards that 'at the heart of their argument lies an allegation of a terms-of-trade squeeze of underdeveloped countries'. To him, this squeeze implies 'a pronounced lack of reallocative ability', and the inability of the u-countries to respond to the challenge of trade and economic change explains the fact that they 'benefit less from trade than they "should"'. He seems to intend this explanation to constitute an alternative to that contained in the three's works that make references to the 'monopolistic plot or greedy unwillingness to trade on more favorable terms on the part of the industrialized countries'. In doing so, he misleadingly claims that 'they have not come to look upon their investigations as a study of the effects of trade on countries lacking reallocative and growth ability' (ibid., p. 45). Little is he aware of that fact that his notion of a 'lack of reallocative ability' partly mirrors Prebisch's desire to infuse 'dynamism' into the periphery (section 10.2), Myrdal's emphasis on breaking 'rigidities' in the underdeveloped world (Ch. 11), and Singer's desire to build a 'capacity to create wealth' in the poorer countries (section 12.3). Not surprisingly, the broader contexts in which these latter notions are situated in Prebisch's, Myrdal's, and Singer's works are things that Linder has largely failed to capture. Nevertheless, he does caution that their works 'contain many elements' and thus 'it is impossible to do justice to these contributions in a short presentation' (ibid.).
3. His more important works which are cited below will be given abbreviated titles. *Economic Development of Latin America and Its Principal Problems* and *Economic Survey of Latin America 1949* will be called *Economic Development of LA* and *Economic Survey of LA* respectively. The other abbreviations are: *International Co-operation in a Latin American Development Policy* as *International Co-operation*; *Theoretical and Practical Problems of Economic Growth* as *Problems of Economic Growth*; *Towards a Dynamic Development Policy for Latin America* as *Dynamic Development Policy*; *Towards a New Trade Policy for Development* as *New Trade Policy; Towards a Global Strategy for Development* as *Global Strategy*; and *Change and Development – Latin America's Great Task* as *Change and Development*.
4. For some recent discussions see Sapsford and Chen (1998, Part I) and Cuddington et al. (2007), and the extensive references contained therein.
5. See also Bhagwati (1988a, p. 28, including n. 3 and n. 4). This 'rationalisation' does not get very far because '[t]o produce an argument in support of protection for manufactures, you would have to throw in something more to demonstrate that the market signals and incentives would not translate into the appropriate degree of pattern of industrialization' (Bhagwati 1988b, p. 46).
6. See the first part of section 12.6 below for a similar distinction drawn by Singer.

7. With respect to the quotation in n. 5 above, Bhagwati (1988b, p. 46) allows this: 'I have no doubt Prebisch and ECLA [Economic Commission for Latin America] did [throw in something more]; but I frankly have never seen what exactly that extra element was'. Writing in the mid-1960s Flanders (1964, pp. 305–6) shrewdly notes, 'There have, indeed, been many exegeses of his [Prebisch's] text, but in the main these have involved emphasis on one or two aspects of his argument, ignoring the others'. It should be added that that article by Flanders is solely based on a reference to Prebisch (1950a, 1959a). Even on that restricted a basis she draws the conclusion that 'his work, by its very nature, defies any attempt to present a single, simple, summary statement of it' (ibid.) and that 'many of Prebisch's "asides" are extremely perceptive, thought-provoking and ... more useful and relevant to the problem than much of the "formal" analysis' (ibid., p. 316, n. 1). The present chapter, in examining a much wider set of works by Prebisch, attempts to advance a more or less coherent framework for interpreting them.
8. Prebisch's employment of such terms certainly invites a comparison with the analysis by W. Arthur Lewis. Limited by the scope of the present work, that would not be pursued here. It should be added, however, that Prebisch was acting quite freely in employing a number of similar terms interchangeably. Thus, in addition to 'surplus manpower' and 'redundant labor force', he has also mentioned 'real or virtual surplus of the labour force' and 'concealed agricultural unemployment' (1950b, pp. 60, 61), 'disguised unemployment or downright unemployment' (1959a, p. 252), and 'superfluous manpower' (1963, p. 25).
9. An inadequate technological density was not mentioned by Prebisch, at least not explicitly, as contributing to inadequate dynamism. Nevertheless, as will be illustrated in section 10.6 below, he could be regarded as implicitly reasoning in that manner.
10. Prebisch identified 'external economic vulnerability' as yet one more factor in restricting dynamism. This is briefly considered in section 10.5 below.
11. A much earlier attempt to portray Prebisch's thought by di Marco (1972) focuses on the CTT, not the ITT, although he does at one point allude to balance of payments problems.
12. This focus was apparently also detected by Frankenhoff, who, in reviewing Prebisch's works up till the early 1960s, wrote: 'The dynamism for growth is furnished by technical progress. The problem for the periphery country is two-fold: how to achieve greater technical progress per capita; how to retain the benefits of increased productivity for a balanced economic development' (1962, p. 188).
13. The passage is also quoted in Flanders (1964, p. 320), but not for the same purpose that it is quoted here in the present chapter. On the other hand, di Marco (1972, p. 9) points to the importance of increasing productivity in the periphery but without textual support.
14. In the same year Prebisch would write in *Problems of Economic Growth*, 'In agriculture, as in industry, transport and other fields of economic activity, the problem of productivity is in the last analysis a problem of investment. The level of productivity cannot be constantly raised unless the amount of capital is likewise increased' (1950b, p. 20).
15. Prebisch noted that as 'one of the great paradoxes of development', 'an increase in productivity may intensify rather than lessen the inadequacy of the economy's dynamism, if the redundant labour thus generated is not absorbed through capital investment over and above that entailed by the increase in productivity' (1968, p. 61).
16. Prebisch was cognizant of exceptions like the oil-exporting countries.
17. On how the situation was different pre-Great Depression, see Prebisch (1954, p. 67; 1959a, p. 266; 1963, p. 69).
18. In the 'manifesto', he expresses it this way: that in the course of development, a 'high level of employment entails increased imports of consumer goods, ... and very often exports are insufficient to provide for them' (1950a, p. 3).
19. To be sure, imports would not merely be in the form of capital goods to meet the demands of development. They would certainly include items demanded by groups in the privileged consumer society, as '[n]ew tastes are created [by advertising] which must be satisfied by imports'. There are necessities as well, including 'new necessities' that continuously surface as new products are constantly developed (1950a, pp. 17–18).
20. See Thirlwall (1983) for similarly drawing attention to this emphasis in Prebisch's works.

21. Ch. II of this work is titled: 'Weakening of Latin America's capacity to import during the past twenty-five years'. Haberler labelled the product of the index of the CTT and an index of the volume of exports alternatively as the 'income terms of trade' or an 'index of the export gains from trade'. Prebisch's notion of 'capacity to import' in the *Economic Survey of LA* caught Haberler's attention, who remarked that it 'seems to me a much more appropriate description and application than to regard it [the ITT] as a measure of the gain from trade or an indicator of welfare change' (1963, p. 279).
22. Contrast with this consideration by Viner, that a 'favourable' factor, such as 'growth in the volume of trade', may 'more than counterbalance the loss from the adverse movement of the terms of trade' (1953, p. 112).
23. Flanders (1964), who, as indicated in n. 7 above, regards it not easy to boil down Prebisch (1950a, 1959a) to one single summary statement, attempts to ferret out from those works a 'single, "minimum" model which would be sufficient to justify the policies he proposes'. She concludes that for one to obtain a deterioration in the CTT for the primary producing country in a two-country framework, there is 'no need to appeal to differences in market structure, the mechanism of wage determination or any other asymmetrical imperfections in the working of the market mechanism'; 'it stems from the assumption of different income elasticities of demand' and '[t]he problem ... is essentially a balance-of-payments problem' (ibid., p. 322).
24. Contrast with Haberler (1963, pp. 280–81).
25. In his 'manifesto' he expresses that, 'It is regrettable that the price indexes do not reflect the differences in quality of finished products' (1950a, p. 8). That clearly anticipated Viner's and Haberler's criticisms along this line (Viner 1958, p. 53; Haberler 1963, pp. 279–80) by quite a bit. 'Changes in quality' is a point that Singer (1949b, Appendix A) has even earlier considered. Based on the story told by Toye and Toye (2003), it is possible that Prebisch might have become alerted to this issue after coming across Singer (ibid.).
26. Although this illustration shows that a decline in the CTT for a primary exporting country does not necessarily mean that its producers are worse off, it actually also underscores the importance of productivity improvements.
27. It is puzzling that Haberler (op. cit.) does not mention Prebisch's illustration given that he had read at least some parts of the *Economic Survey of LA*. See n. 21 above. Viner (1958, pp. 53–4) points out that 'the single-factoral terms-of-trade index, though inconclusive, is clearly and unquestionably superior to the net barter or commodity terms of trade index as representing the trend of national gain from trade'. However, there is no indication that he was aware of the illustration in the aforementioned work by Prebisch.
28. In an instance in which he drew a distinction between agricultural and mineral products, Prebisch noted that imports of many of the latter 'tend to rise as industrial development progresses'. The contrast between the former products and 'minerals which western Europe does not produce for itself', he added, 'is very striking and indicates the possibilities for increases in imports where protectionism is less significant' (1964, p. 49). An instance, one shortly before his death, where he made a crude distinction between demand growth for different manufactures can be found in Prebisch (1986, p. 4), where he observes that the periphery's exports 'generally correspond to types of manufactures where the growth of demand was relatively slow'. This is more than two decades after he actively started to emphasise the importance of promoting manufactured exports. See the subsection on 'Support of EP' in section 10.5 below.
29. See Dutt (1988) for an attempt to capture the possible connections between relatively low income elasticity of demand, international demonstration effects, and uneven development.
30. In the *Economic Development of LA* there is quite a bit of discussion of how the different extents to which labour markets were unionised in the centre versus the periphery would explain the movement of the CTT to the favour of the former (1950a, pp. 13–14; see also 1963, pp. 82–3). Note, however, that the conclusion from that discussion pertains more to the movement of the CTT rather than to the persistence of balance of payments disequilibrium.
31. Prebisch had in mind, behind his reference to the disparities in income-elasticities of demand between industrial and primary products, ongoing 'diversification' processes. Thus,

through new inventions and designs, industrial goods are constantly being diversified. However, the room for diversification of demand for primary products is comparatively far more limited. See Prebisch (op. cit., pp. 65, 81–2). An earlier consideration of this process can be found in Prebisch (1950b, p. 30).

32. 'If all the productive factors of our countries could be channelled into exports without raising their cost or substantially reducing their prices, there would be no need to industrialize. But the reality of the matter is different' (Prebisch 1961a, p. 14).
33. Hyde (1963, p. 470) thus concludes that Prebisch 'does not advocate a one-sided industrialization program. He sees industry and technical advance in primary production as complementary. But he clearly feels that industry plays the more dynamic role, and that it can give off desirable effects to backward sectors'. This feature has also not escaped the attention of di Marco (1972, p. 10). Contrast with the discussion in Viner (1953, p. 52).
34. In a section in Ch. II in *Problems of Economic Growth* Prebisch employs neoclassical theoretical tools and considers the 'Optimum Distribution of Factors in Different Sectors of Domestic Production'. He regards that the 'principle of marginal productivity' of capital 'offers a basis on which to determine the best means of utilizing the limited capacity to import, that is, which products that were formerly imported should be replaced by domestic production, and which it is more advisable to continue importing'. The choice of industries 'will depend on the comparative increases of production which can be obtained in the different activities'. He concludes that 'if the distribution of savings is carried out so that the productivity of the marginal increment of capital per gainfully employed person is the same in all branches of economic activity, production will be maximized' (ibid., pp. 42, 46). However, he warns that 'the maximization of productivity ... does not always imply that a satisfactory means of maximizing income has been found'. Some activities that are not as productive might nevertheless be desirable because they could 'diminish a country's vulnerability to foreign fluctuations and contingencies' (p. 43). It does not appear that in works subsequent to this one, he actually applied this principle to help him consider how to adjust the composition of imports. For a brief description of his early belief in, but subsequent rejection of, neoclassical theories, see Prebisch (1984, p. 175).
35. This is yet another sign that despite his rejection of the neoclassical logic that supports free trade Prebisch still, occasionally in those years, employed neoclassical theoretical tools.
36. He develops this consideration numerically in *Problems of Economic Growth* and adds the twist that the price of primary products would drop should export expand (1950b, pp. 37–9). One million (mln.) workers are assumed to be employed in primary production and export in a *group of countries*. At that output level, each worker earns $100 per year, of which all is spent on importing manufactured products. Then he brings into the story a marginal bundle of 0.1 mln. workers. Should that be employed in primary or manufactured production? Prebisch assumes that should this bundle be deployed for the latter purpose, it would yield $70 per worker for a total of $7 mln. in manufactured products valued at world prices. When added to the capacity to import generated by the 1 mln. workers engaged in primary production, these countries could consume $107 mln. worth of manufactured goods. On the other hand, if the marginal bundle were to be added to the 1 mln. workers already hired in primary production, he figured that most likely there would be a decrease in the price for the primary product. If that decrease is such that each worker then earns only $97.30 (which is rounded from $107 mln./1.1 mln. workers), then one has computed the 'neutral point' where, were the price to drop below it, then 'it would be advantageous' to utilise the marginal bundle in manufactured production. Given that he was considering a group of primary exporting countries, it is consequently not a situation of one country with market power that could consider imposing an optimal tariff of some sort by itself. See also the next note below.
37. In *Problems of Economic Growth* Prebisch concludes that protection would be necessary based on differences in production cost of manufactures. Thus, he compares two numbers in the illustration summarised in the previous note to claim that 'the cost of [manufactured] production for domestic consumption would be considerably higher than that of the imported article'. Specifically, 'at the neutral point a worker engaged in export activities could obtain 97.3 dollars worth of imported products through trade, in domestic activities

he would obtain only 70 dollars worth of the same products' (ibid., p. 39). This is actually misleading, for it compares an average magnitude in one scenario ($97.30) with a marginal magnitude in the other ($70). These numbers are income figures. If Prebisch had computed the average income for each worker out of the 1.1 mln. total, then that number should be $97.30 in both scenarios. Had he considered the marginal income of each worker in the marginal bundle, then that number should be $70 in both scenarios. Notwithstanding, he concludes that '[d]omestic production could not be fostered unless it were protected against foreign competition' (ibid.). He further deduces that, 'The concept of economic advantage should be based on the total available supply of goods for the population. It has been shown that a greater volume of goods is obtained despite higher costs' (ibid., p. 40). The conclusions that he draws here are repeated in several instances in some later works (1954, pp. 30, 65; 1959a, p. 255; 1961a, p. 5).

38. See n. 69 in section 10.7 below and the main text to which it is appended for a hint of a different case for protection.
39. 'Ill-employed' was defined as including those making hand-made goods and certain types of personal services (op. cit., p. 44).
40. See also Prebisch (1950b, p. 32; 1951b, p. 123; 1971a, p. 46) for other instances when he made a similar point.
41. This is a different way of rationalising IS than the one contained in the illustration that was reproduced in n. 36 above. What is implicit here is the existence of a fair amount of unemployed or 'ill-employed' workers. In the illustration in n. 36 there was full employment and it showed how it might be more socially beneficial to deploy a marginal bundle of inputs to industries than to exports that experience a certain level of declining CTT, where the latter applies to a *group* of countries. Notice that in the general form of the consideration that led up to the illustration under which he determined the 'limits of industrialization', he added that '[t]here is no sign that Latin America is approaching this limit. It is in the initial stage of the industrialization process and in most cases the man-power available as a result of increased productivity is still amply sufficient for industrial growth' (1950a, p. 45).
42. Prebisch occasionally alerted the reader to 'import substitution possibilities' in agriculture, for that could make a 'contribution to the elimination of the external bottleneck' (for instance, 1971a, p. 103).
43. This caution caught the attention of Corbo (1988, p. 176), who thus reminds the reader that 'despite Prebisch's prescription of government intervention to pursue import substitution, he expressed early concern about the anti-export bias of existing import-substitution policies. Indeed, after his period as director of ILPES [Latin American Institute for Social and Economic Planning] Prebisch's move into the United Nations Conference on Trade and Development (UNCTAD) showed his clear interest in improving the trade prospects of developing countries'.
44. On the impact of IS on uneven income distribution, Prebisch noted that, 'Excessive protectionism frequently sheltering industries adds a further privilege to those already existing in the distribution of income' (1964, p. 114; see also 1971a, p. 195).
45. The portrayal of IS industrialisation as taking place in 'water-tight compartments' was repeated by Prebisch numerous times in his subsequent works. Later on, he occasionally described IS as 'progressing within a number of industrial microcosms' (1971a, p. 193) or as contributing to the 'fragmentation of the periphery' (1978, p. 226).
46. These illustrations were probably in the mind of Dell (1986, pp. 9–10), who notes that '[e]ven in his [Prebisch's] earliest writings, when he was pointing to the inevitability of import substitution policies, he repeatedly stressed the dangers of costly mistakes in the application of such policies. He did not need the big studies of such economists as Bhagwati, Krueger and Little to convince him – he had been fully aware of the pitfalls long before these studies appeared'. See also Dell (ibid., pp. 12–13).
47. In *Dynamic Development Policy* Prebisch declares, 'This internally-geared development has already fulfilled its most important role ... But while the result was definitely positive, it could have been better' (1963, p. 69).

48. On top of all that, 'The further substitution proceeds in respect of some imports, the more other imports grow because of the heavier demand for capital goods and, subsequently, because of the effects of higher income' (1964, p. 9).
49. Despite all these cautions Balassa (1980, p. 7) writes that '[i]n Latin America, the choice of this strategy [of second-stage IS in the postwar period] reflected the ideas of Raul Prebisch, in whose view adverse foreign-market conditions for primary exports and the lack of competitiveness in manufactured exports would not permit developing countries to attain high rates of economic growth by relying on export production. Rather, Prebisch suggested that these countries should expand manufacturing industries oriented toward domestic markets. This purpose was to be served by industrial protection'. This prompts Prebisch (1988, p. 36) to retort, 'Obviously, he [Balassa] has had only a fragmentary acquaintance with our studies, culled from quotations at second or third hand, generally mutilated or incomplete'.
50. As Flanders (1964, p. 306) indicates, 'a careful reading of Prebisch shows him to be much less of an "autarkist" than either his detractors or his supporters seem to think'.
51. Writing in the early 1960s Prebisch recalled that, 'Until recently, circumstances did not favour expansion of foreign trade. In the years during which the effects of the great depression and the post-war period – not to speak of the Second World War itself – were still making themselves felt, there was no reason to think that the major industrial countries would open their doors to exports of peripheral manufactures, or that the Latin American countries would be prepared to strive for a foothold in the external market, so long as easy import substitutions offered them a growing and reliable internal market, protected against imports in every possible way. Hence, there was no vital need to export industrial goods' (1963, p. 71; see also 1978, pp. 222–3). About two decades later Singer would also make the same point. See section 12.6 below.
52. Also, 'continuous fluctuations in this rate contribute to serious internal instability' (op. cit.).
53. Prebisch's early effort in advocating EP has escaped the attention of most mainstream economists. An apparent exception is Bhagwati, who took note of 'his early expression of the view that the import-substitution strategy should be tempered by regional trade liberalization: a view that gathered momentum in the 1960s and preceded the major work on trade-and-developmental strategy ... that has resulted in the current thesis that export-promoting strategy has many economic advantages over the import-substitution strategy' (1983, pp. 46–7; see also Finger 1991, p. 205). It should be clear from the discussion in the main text of the present chapter that Prebisch's support of EP was not confined to regional trade liberalisation. It will also be clarified shortly below that he did not regard EP to be superior to IS in the sense that Bhagwati and others do.
54. Bhagwati (1988b, p. 46) chimes in on the spat between Prebisch and Balassa (n. 49 above) by pointing out that one could not claim that one 'was for EP too' by a 'solitary quote'. (The said quotation is presented in Prebisch (1988, p. 36) and it was originally from Prebisch (1961a, p. 5).) Hopefully, the illustrations provided in the present subsection will show that it is much more than a 'solitary quote'. Bhagwati (ibid., p. 47) is careful to suggest that 'the documented excesses of the IS strategy in Latin America cannot be blamed on Prebisch' and that 'it is doubtful whether Prebisch's prescriptions for the *type* of IS strategy that he desired were in consonance with the *actual* outcomes that we have long criticized' (italics original). But Bhagwati (ibid., p. 46) also insists that 'on EP versus IS, you simply cannot have it both ways'. Note, however, that he himself (for instance, 1987a, pp. 258–9) has adopted definitions of IS and EP that is based on average price incentives for producers who are deciding on producing for the home versus the foreign markets. Those definitions have room for sectoral variations, where some sectors are in the category of IS activities while others are of the EP type.
55. Flanders (1964, p. 314) refers to the 'disparities in technological densities' mentioned in an illustration in Prebisch (1959a, p. 262). The nature of that illustration requires Prebisch to simply refer to the *consequences* of those disparities rather than to the *causes*. Flanders (ibid.) appears to be oblivious to that distinction and she does not draw attention to the importance of the concept of 'technological densities' as is being done here.

56. Enhancing the periphery's technological density is one sure way of better positioning it to harness the 'radiating power' (a term mentioned in section 10.2) of the centres.
57. This is one area in Prebisch's conceptualisation of technological density that could benefit from refinement. Critics could conceivably dismiss this as simply a cry for investment in building human capital.
58. Prebisch was quite aware that the advanced technology could be inappropriate for the periphery because of its tendency to 'economize manpower' (1962, p. 28). Singer expressed similar concerns. See, for instance, the last subsection in section 12.3 below.
59. Prebisch was mindful that the content of international trade was not static even during his time. Thanks to the persistent technological evolution in the centres, new products and new designs of existing products were constantly emerging. He also understood that, partly because of that, new import requirements were bound to be arising in the periphery, on top of those that already existed. He struck a sensible balance by stating that, 'In some cases it will be both possible and desirable to replace these imports by domestic production, whereas it will be inadvisable to do so in others, both on the grounds of cost and in order to keep abreast of technical progress by continuing to import products that are representative of it' (1963, p. 77).
60. 'Exports of manufactures ..., together with import substitution, will enable their [periphery countries'] industrialization to be made increasingly efficient and, at the same time, promote their technological development. ... [T]his advance would make it possible to increase the exports of goods which are at present not technologically accessible to the periphery' (Prebisch 1985, p. 20).
61. One advantage of subcontracting arrangements, Prebisch thought, was that no elaborate efforts of marketing or merchandising would be required of the peripheral producers as the export sales concerned would be closely integrated with the production processes in the developed countries. Moreover, he believed that it would tend to build a complementary relationship between industries of developed and developing countries rather than to intensify competition. Nevertheless, he was also alert to the possibilities of 'excessive dependence on external factors or an unduly specialized industrial structure such as might result from industrial development of this type' (op. cit.).
62. It must be noted Prebisch admitted that 'the policy advocated in this report [*New Trade Policy*] is based on the opportunities offered by a wide range of articles for which demand is growing rapidly' (op. cit., p. 63). One thus comes across optimistic notions like the 'dynamism of demand', 'fast growing demand', or 'very rapidly growing demand'. That was 1964.
63. Prebisch's conviction in the possibility of rapidly assimilating advanced production techniques by the periphery was reinforced by the experience of the then Soviet Union. Referring to Lenin he thus noted that 'his resolute efforts to ensure the rapid assimilation of capitalist production techniques in the Soviet Union yielded results so impressive that they have come to constitute, despite the magnitude of the political and social sacrifices involved, a potent source of faith and inspiration for vast areas of the world' (1958, p. 47).
64. Prebisch noted that '[t]he main industrial centres of the world have attained considerable technological density in the course of time; they are not limited to just this or that speciality [sic] but have at their disposal a whole complex of specialities [sic] and techniques which tends to extend over a growing proportion of the economically active population and which is reflected in a vast range of skills, from the manual worker right up to the senior technician and the alert and capable executive' (op. cit., p. 59). A comparable technological density was what he wished the periphery could attain.
65. For his distinction between 'the interest of the entrepreneur and the general interest of the economy' when it comes to investment decisions and the consideration of technological unemployment, see Prebisch (1950b, pp. 54–5; 1963, p. 29; 1971a, p. 205; 1976, pp. 30–31).
66. For the other areas, tax and other fiscal measures were proposed to discourage 'nonessential consumption' on the one hand and stimulate private investment on the other (1971a, p. 139). The correction of external disequilibrium did involve exchange controls, which 'was not the result of a theory but was imposed by circumstances' in the 1930s (1950a, p. 29).

67. Prebisch reiterates in *Change and Development* that 'to restrict certain imports ... it seems desirable for this to be done through general measures rather than by means of direct controls' (1971a, p. 137).
68. To Prebisch, 'a policy of depreciation or devaluation should be used only to correct an externally overvalued currency and not as an instrument for effecting structural changes in the economy' (op. cit.). See also Prebisch (1985, p. 16).
69. There are elements in this passage that suggest that Prebisch was thinking in terms of infant-industry protection.
70. Prebisch did not raise the question of how subsidies might be funded. Nor did he consider how the revenues generated through tariffs might be put to use.
71. For those who are interested in what Prebisch had to suggest regarding financial co-operation, including schemes to aid primary exporting countries, see Prebisch (1964, Part Two, Ch. III; 1968, Ch. III).
72. 'The free play concept is admissible in relations between countries that are structurally similar', Prebisch thought, 'but not between those whose structures are altogether different as are those of the industrially advanced and the developing countries' (op. cit., p. 29).
73. On the other hand, '[t]he request for [conventional] reciprocity in negotiations between countries which have not structural disparity in their demand is logical. Indeed, it is essential for the stability of the world economy that any expansion of exports which a given country achieves on the basis of concessions from the others should be accompanied by concessions granted to the latter, so that its imports from them can increase' (op. cit., pp. 30–31).
74. Writing in the early 1960s Prebisch remarked at one point that, 'To accumulate foreign exchange, rather than to import, when its exports increase is not typical of Latin America. A more characteristic trait is a tendency to import beyond its capacity to do so' (1963, p. 75). See n. 76 in Ch. 11 below on how Myrdal shared a similar belief.
75. Based on this distinction between conventional and real reciprocity Prebisch also illustrated the asymmetrical effects of protection as practised by the centre versus that instituted by the periphery (1954, pp. 67–8; 1963, pp. 73–4).
76. In *New Trade Policy* Prebisch considers preferences to be offered for only a ten-year period, 'unless it could be shown, to the satisfaction of an appropriate international authority, that special circumstances warranted their continuation' (1964, p. 69). In *Global Strategy* he appears to give more thought to 'reason[s] for not sticking to rigid limits' (1968, p. 22).
77. Prebisch's proposal earned this critical reaction from Johnson (1967, p. 31, n. 26): 'The logic is indeed the infant-industry logic of protection – temporary protection of an industry that requires a "learning period" to become competitive – reinforced by recognition of the need for a market on a scale larger than the domestic economy can provide; but the traditional argument called for transitional support of the industry at the expense of the consumers of the developing country, whereas the argument for preferences calls for support at the expense of the consumers of the developed countries (indirectly, by foregoing tariff receipts) thereby introducing an implicit transfer of resources from the developed to the developing countries. In short, the argument for preferences asks the developed country to contribute a part of the cost of the "investment" made in the learning process'. See also Johnson (ibid., pp. 32, 73–4).
78. This resembles, in spirit though not in details, the Doha Round Market Access Proposal discussed in Stiglitz and Charlton (2005, pp. 94–103).
79. Viner's attack is chiefly contained in the third of six lectures that he delivered at the National University of Brazil in 1950, which lectures were published in 1953. Frankenhoff (1962, p. 189) characterises that attack as 'a brief but vigorous pummeling' of Prebisch's position.
80. According to Love (1980, p. 61), a political scientist by the name of Philippe Schmitter has also suggested that Manoïlesco seems to have anticipated some of the points of the ECLA doctrine.
81. Love (1980, p. 62) seems to have interpreted Manoïlesco's consideration of this kind of scenario as indicating that he 'differed sharply with Prebisch and ECLA on one critical point'. According to Love, Manoïlesco asserted that 'as the process of industrialization

spread from one country to another, there was a long-term tendency for the prices of raw materials and agricultural products to rise, relative to prices of industrial goods' (italics added). Prebisch would not rule out this possibility if indeed industrialisation *spreads* and results in an *increasing* number of industrial countries. Also recall n. 36 in Ch. 9.

82. In a correspondence with Prebisch in 1977, Love was able to confirm with him that he had not been influenced by Manoïlesco's works (Love 1986, p. 132, n. 28). Did Prebisch draw any inspiration from the works of Hamilton or List? The former's name appears to have never been mentioned. In fact, there is a conspicuous absence in Prebisch's works of any reference to America's protectionist past when it diversified from agricultural to industrial activities. It is surprising, and to some even disappointing, that he would observe, 'The United States' astounding development in the past seemed to testify to the efficacy of the free and spontaneous interplay of economic forces, guided only by the "invisible hand" of the classical economists' (1971a, p. 225). On the other hand, he was more than cognizant of America's protectionist turn subsequent to the Great Depression. Apparently Prebisch had also not referred to List, although there are definite signs that some in Latin America were familiar with his works leading up to World War II (Love 1986, p. 129, n. 16; 1988, p. 19; 2005a, p. 157). However, Seers revealed, without the provision of details, that Prebisch once told him that 'he had been influenced by List' (Seers 1983, p. 52).
83. For additional discussion on this theme see Prebisch (1983, 1985).

11. Myrdal: Harnessing Spread, while Curtailing Backwash, Effects with a Multitude of Policy Actions

11.1 INTRODUCTION[1]

Unlike Hamilton and List who reacted against largely the works of one economist, namely Smith, by the time Myrdal cultivated a serious interest in development studies he had to do battle with economic ideas that had been refined and polished by an economics profession for more than a century since the classical period. He attacked the 'equilibrium' analyses adopted by the mainstream of that profession, claiming that their limitations were amply exposed in accounting for the sustained and, in some respects, growing international inequalities between the underdeveloped and developed countries.[2] He grouped various forces that bear upon these inequalities into 'backwash' and 'spread' effects on the underdeveloped regions as the developed regions grew and expanded. The forces materialise and interact in ways that are characterised by the principle of circular and cumulative causation, with growing inequalities the result when backwash effects dominate over spread effects.

Mrydal's criticism, especially the aspect directed against 'conventional' trade models, understandably caused ire among mainstream economists. Haberler ([1959] 1988, p. 27) classifies him as one of the 'protectionist writers', adding that his theory 'bears a most striking similarity' to that of List even though the latter's policy recommendations are 'more moderate' than his (ibid., p. 25, n. 10).[3] His concept of the 'backwash effects' is denigrated as one that 'flies in the face of classical trade theory' and '[i]t is very difficult to come to grips and find out precisely what these effects are' (pp. 45, 47). Haberler's verdict is that, 'He makes a molehill out of a mountain and views the problem of how development spreads from the growing points to the surrounding area from an exceedingly narrow and overly static and myopic point of view' (ibid.).[4] Backwash and spread effects are dubbed by Knox (1960, p. 281) as 'rather emotional language' and it 'does not look altogether unlike a process of international specialization'.

Johnson reacted by observing that the logic of Myrdal's analysis 'is not altogether impeccable, *at least on the assumption of a world economy without barriers to capital movements and migration*' (1967, p. 48, italics added). Meier responded by alleging that 'Myrdal attributes more to the factor price equalisation theorem than do its expositors' (1958a, p. 254). Myint complained that his conceptualisation of the principle of cumulative causation is sketchy (1984, p. 168).

'Once the unbalanced structure of the underdeveloped economy is attributed to the working of international forces', mainstream trade theorists like Meier would hasten to conclude, 'it is but a short step to advocating an "infant-economy" type of argument for protection' (1958b, p. 278). Drawing inspiration from one of the pioneers in the development of the theory of domestic divergences, specifically Meade (1955, Ch. XIV), but still writing at a time before that theory had reached fuller development, Meier (1958a, p. 254) then cautions that '[t]he assessment of commercial policy must ... focus on the questions of to what extent there has been a divergence from the optimum, and whether a policy of protection would allow a closer approach to the optimum'. Generally, '[t]he protection argument is a "second-best" argument, and *domestic* policies might be more suitable for removing the divergences between marginal values and costs' (ibid., p. 251, n. 1, italics added). On this basis he concluded that Myrdal's 'protection' argument is 'misdirected' and he submitted that 'Myrdal's enthusiasm for protection must be considerably tempered' (1958b, p. 282; 1958a, p. 247). Echoing Meier, Myint (1984, p. 169) concludes that 'Myrdal favors a protectionist policy' and reminds that '[t]he conventional neoclassical free-trade economist would insist on appropriate *domestic* economic policies' (italics added). At another point he characterises Myrdal as favouring 'an inward-looking policy toward foreign trade and investment' (ibid., p. 170). According to Kindleberger (1987, p. 401), 'he opposed export-led growth'.

Do these representations and conclusions do justice to Myrdal's works?[5] Or are there misrepresentations and distortions, of a similar nature as those applied to the works of Hamilton, List, Manoïlesco, and Prebisch? The discussion in the rest of this chapter is organised as follows. Section 11.2 lays out Myrdal's major reasons for rejecting stable equilibrium analyses while championing the principle of circular and cumulative causation. His application of this principle, including the associated concepts of backwash and spread effects, to interpret uneven development is illustrated in section 11.3. A closer look at how he applied the principle to a domestic setting of underdevelopment is contained in section 11.4. This section also clarifies that his vision of development promotion is far more sophisticated than just advocating industrialisation. His views on commercial policies are similarly sophisticated and nuanced. These are outlined in section 11.5 to point out that he emphasised EP as well as IS. His awareness of the relative merits of different policy instruments under certain contexts is also illustrated. His caution against the use of non-discretionary controls leads the transition into section 11.6, where his discussion of 'soft states' is examined. Myrdal's considerations here on the one hand serves as a reminder that he was fully aware of all kinds of implementation and enforcement problems that could confront his policy proposals, but on the other hand his treatment of these 'obstacles' is also distinct from that of the literature on directly unproductive profit-seeking activities in the economics mainstream. Section 11.7 highlights his thoughts on institutional reforms at the international level. Parallels with the concerns of the 'southern' countries in today's MTNs will be noted. Section 11.8 consists of concluding remarks for this chapter.

11.2 REJECTING STABLE EQUILIBRIUM IN FAVOUR OF CIRCULAR AND CUMULATIVE CAUSATION ANALYSES

To begin, it is perhaps most useful to recognise that Myrdal strongly rejected analyses and policy prescriptions that were based on the 'stable equilibrium concept' that predominated in 'conventional' or 'traditional' economics.[6] In his *Economic Theory* he thus argues that 'the notion of stable equilibrium is normally a false analogy to choose when constructing a theory to explain the changes in a social system' ([1957] 1963, p. 13).[7] Why?

One of the standard assumptions behind conventional equilibrium analysis is that economic decision units are 'atomistic' and competition is 'perfect'. In his rather neglected 1951 article, 'The trend towards economic planning', Myrdal laments that,

> This perfect market has never existed. ... [F]or a long time reality has been moving steadily further and further away from this liberal idealisation. Technological and organisational developments have been increasing the size of the units in relation to the market. At the same time the individual units have found the means to combine. They have thereby come into a position where they can influence the market and manipulate the price. ... The markets have become consciously 'regulated' by the participants, and when the atomism is gone, the assumed static institutional framework is not protected any longer. Instead of obediently adjusting themselves to a given framework of society, which was the liberal dictum, the individuals are starting to adjust society according to their own interests. (Ibid., p. 9)

He concluded that 'equilibrium' might no longer be guaranteed as an automatic result of atomistic adjustments. 'The organisation of the market', he thus summarises, 'leads to the disorganisation of society and calls for State intervention' (ibid., p. 12; see also [1957] 1963, pp. 49, 141).

It should thus be kept in mind that when Myrdal mentioned 'market forces' as governing the interactions between the developed and underdeveloped countries and shaping the results, he was not entertaining the illusion of perfect markets within which those interactions were played out. At one point in *The Challenge of World Poverty* he reminds the reader thus,

> The market forces [in colonial times] did not, as in abstract economic theory, work under free competition. There were many elements of monopoly, almost always working in favor of businesses in the metropolitan country and usually, to an extent, condoned or even promoted by the colonial government. In this chapter I include them in the term 'market forces'.
>
> This process is continually in operation. Decolonization has not by itself changed much of this situation. And I have inserted this section in the book in order to stress the fact that *the underdeveloped countries have been and are still largely at the mercy of the play of the market forces.* (1970a, p. 284, italics original)

These forces, he added, 'are adverse to their [the countries'] strivings for development' also '[b]ecause of their status of underdevelopment' (ibid.). Part of this status of underdevelopment manifests itself in the form of imperfect or non-existing markets in the underdeveloped countries (1968, pp. 19, 745, 916, 952, 1951; 1970a, p. 225; 1970b, p. 233), but where terms like imperfections and non-existence are used 'in a considerably broader sense than is normal in economic analysis' (1968, p. 745).

Indeed, notice that in the passage quoted above from his 1951 article Myrdal's reasoning is not simply couched in terms of the economic effects of perfect versus imperfect competition. He refers to 'organisational developments' and changes in the 'institutional framework' as competition evolves, and that relates to another criticism of equilibrium analysis that he launched, which is the tendency of subscribers to that analysis to focus merely on 'economic' factors. In his *Economic Theory* he declares that 'it is useless to look for one predominant factor, a "basic factor" such as the "economic factor" ... and still less understandable how it can be "basic", as everything is cause to everything else in an interlocking circular manner' ([1957] 1963, p. 19). Clearly, he came out way ahead of Prebisch (end of section 10.9) as far as taking this position is concerned.

Myrdal instead proposed the adoption of what he called the 'principle of circular and cumulative causation'.[8] In this approach, 'everything is [indeed] cause to everything else in an interlocking circular manner'. In his monumental *Asian Drama*,[9] he thus proclaims that,

> there are no exclusively 'economic' problems; there are simply problems, so that distinctions between 'economic' and 'non-economic' factors are, at best, artificial.

> ... The only worthwhile demarcation – and the only one that is fully tenable logically – is between relevant and less relevant factors, and the line of demarcation will vary with the characteristics of the environment under study. (1968, p. 42; see similar statements in 1970a, p. 13 and 1978, p. 772)

'Economic analysis', he concluded, 'will have to deal with all the relevant factors if it wants to be realistic; general economic theory will have to become social theory' ([1957] 1963, p. 100).[10]

Where then do 'cumulative' changes enter into the consideration? When one considers, Myrdal thus suggests in *An International Economy*, the interdependence between all the factors in a social system,

> any change in any one of the factors will cause changes in the other factors; these secondary changes are generally of a nature to support the initial change; through a process of interactions, where change in one factor continuously will be supported by reactions of the other factors, the whole system will have been given a momentum to move in the direction of the primary change, though much further. (1956, p. 16; see also [1957] 1963, p. 13)[11]

In *Asian Drama* he clarifies that,[12]

> circular causation will give rise to a cumulative movement only when, by the interaction of all conditions in the social system, a change in one of the conditions will ultimately be followed by a feed-back of secondary impulses to a further change of that particular condition big enough not only to sustain the primary change, but to push it further. Mere mutual causation is not enough to create this process; otherwise the ubiquity of mutual causation would be inconsistent with the widely observed stability of social systems. The relationship between the size of the coefficients of response and the speed of the response will determine whether mutual causation results in stable, neutral, or unstable equilibrium. (1968, p. 1875)[13]

It is his conviction that this 'contains *in nuce* the approach to a more realistic analysis of social change – indeed a vision of the general theory of under-development and development which we are all yearning for' ([1957] 1963, p. 12, see also p. 23). On the other hand, 'the equilibrium assumption falls to the ground' in the realm of social reality because the 'non-economic factors' are kept out of equilibrium analysis by abstraction. 'Those non-economic factors cannot be taken for given and static; when they react, they normally do so in a disequilibrium way' (ibid., p. 10, see also pp. 30, 153). Myrdal was quite aware that some neoclassical economists had made attempts to research into certain of these 'non-economic factors'. However, those attempts 'generally do not intrude upon the main economic analysis' (1981, p. 506).[14] 'The non-economic factors', he insisted, 'cannot simply be added to a supposedly pure economic theory', just as 'it is not possible to throw the yeast into the oven after the bread has been baked' (1970a, p. 15).[15]

The equilibrium approach can thus be regarded as entailing what Myrdal elsewhere described as 'illegitimate isolation', the practice of isolating variables for a model and concentrating on them 'without regard to their inseparability from variables that are left out of consideration' (1968, p. 1953). In turn, '[i]llegitimate isolation is a specific manifestation of the assumption that all other conditions remain constant and [are] adapted to development' (ibid., p. 1954), which he dubbed 'adapted *ceteris paribus*' and 'automatic *mutatis mutandis*' (pp. 1947–8). There is 'illegitimate abstraction', he cautioned, 'if conditions are assumed to be constant whose change is either necessary to the required results or makes an important difference in their direction, speed, and size' (p. 1954). Alternatively, as happens frequently and implicitly, 'unanalyzed conditions are assumed to vary to the required extent' to accommodate whatever changes that one wishes to take place (p. 1948, n. 3).

The application of the principle of circular and cumulative causation permeates Myrdal's works on development, as is illustrated especially in sections 11.3, 11.4, and 11.6 below.

11.3 UNEVEN DEVELOPMENT: BACKWASH VERSUS SPREAD EFFECTS AT THE INTERNATIONAL AND LOCAL (DOMESTIC) LEVELS

To Myrdal the uneven development between the underdeveloped and developed countries was a phenomenon that clearly illustrated the limitations of the equilibrium approach while it showed the promises of thinking in terms of cumulative causation. It was too clear to him that the equilibrium approach as applied to this situation – typified by certain predictions of the classical trade theory on the one hand and the H–O–S model on the other – simply could not shed light on that process. His attack is strongly present in *Economic Theory* ([1957] 1963, especially Ch. 11), although it can also be detected in his later works like *The Challenge to World Poverty* (1970a, Ch. 9).

In section 6.2 of Chapter 6 above the faith held by the classical economists regarding the spontaneity of structural changes in the primary exporting countries, or the automaticity in the spread of industrialisation to them, was highlighted. Myrdal simply did not share this optimism. Rather than directly addressing the relevant passages from the works of the classical economists,[16] he criticised Viner's expression of this optimism as he stated in his lectures delivered at the National University of Brazil in 1950. To recall,

Viner, whom Myrdal characterised as 'the foremost exponent in our generation of the great theoretical tradition of the classical economists' ([1957] 1963, p. 150), believed that 'free-market conditions' would 'bring spontaneously into action forces tending to industrialize' an agricultural country (Viner 1953, p. 113).[17] But as Myrdal puts it in *Economic Theory*, '[t]his is a very inaccurate description of what has actually taken place, and is taking place, in the under-developed parts of the world' ([1957] 1963, pp. 150–51, n. 2). Among other reasons, there could be very few entrepreneurs in these countries to seize opportunities to make profits or there could be a severe lack of skills (ibid.).[18] These and other 'bottlenecks', 'rigidities', and 'inhibitions', though they were not more fully spelled out until *Asian Drama* was written, are obstacles that would not vanish by simply assuming 'free-market conditions' to apply. '[T]he point is', he thus remarks, 'that such an assumption is totally unrealistic'. In fact, 'it remains an unanswered question what precisely this assumption means in the actual cultural, social, psychological and economic conditions in under-developed countries; if this question is not answered ... this whole way of thinking remains meaningless; and it becomes wrong if any inferences as to reality are drawn' (ibid.).

With respect to the H–O–S model, he felt compelled to respond to the prediction of 'the equilibrating and equalising effects of international trade' on factor prices.[19] '[I]nstead of an equilibrium, as the theory of international trade would demand', he thus countered, 'we are facing *a cumulative process away from equilibrium in factor proportions and factor prices, engendered by international trade*' (1956, p. 225, italics original). For '[u]nder the contrary and more realistic assumption, that more often the economic process is cumulative because of circular causation, the role of international trade becomes ... rather the opposite one of being one of the media through which the market forces tend to result in increased inequalities' ([1957] 1963, p. 152).

The mainstream's reaction to these criticisms was already illustrated in the introductory section of this chapter. If one were to confine oneself to a narrow sample of Myrdal's works, then it is possible for one to come away with the impression that his formulation of certain ideas appears to be sketchy. Thus, in those parts where he juxtaposed his analysis with the prediction based on conventional trade models, it is understandable that he only explicitly referred to international trade as an activity through which uneven development could result. However, it is very obvious from perusing his works more thoroughly that there are other activities – for instance, capital flows, migration, and, to a lesser extent in his discussion, technological and product innovations – through which uneven development could be engendered. For instance, he linked many of the problems associated with enclave development in resource-rich underdeveloped countries, both during and subsequent to the colonial period, to the inflows of foreign capital ([1957] 1963, pp. 4–5, 53, 58; 1968, pp. 148, 448–9, 452–3, 477, 582, 683). This is comparable with the concerns that Singer (1950) has expressed towards such inflows (on which see section 12.4 below).

These activities all indeed have international dimensions, but it shows clearly that Myrdal was considering more than just trade. What impact various activities could trigger also depends on the institutional set-up in the underdeveloped countries in which those activities take place. Put differently, domestic institutional factors also enter into an account of uneven development at the international level.

What matters to him are thus partly the direction and content of these activities. For activities like trade, capital flows, and innovations, it is also pertinent to consider the relative market power of those who are involved, as manifested in what Myrdal referred to as 'market forces' (see section 11.2 above). The impact of various activities on the countries, especially the underdeveloped ones, also depends on the level of social and economic development of the countries concerned, which is in turn the outcome of the complex interaction of 'economic' and 'non-economic' factors within the peculiar institutional set-up in each social system ([1957] 1963, p. 34).

Conceptualised in this manner, Myrdal then defined all relevant adverse impact or changes, caused outside a locality (nation), as the 'backwash effects' of economic expansion in that locality (nation). These could comprise, but are by no means restricted to, the brain drain and capital flight from, and deindustrialisation in, those localities (nations) outside of the centre of expansion ([1957] 1963, pp. 27–30, 51–3, 58). They are engendered '*via* migration, capital movements and trade as well as all the effects *via* the whole gamut of other social relations ...; and the term refers to the total cumulated effects resulting from the process of circular causation between all the factors, "non-economic" as well as "economic"' (ibid., pp. 30–31). At the international level, '*scientific and technological advance in the developed countries has had, and is now having, an impact on the underdeveloped countries which, on balance, is detrimental to their development prospects*'. Such advances could render it even more difficult for the underdeveloped countries to compete in their agricultural and manufactured exports, and could mean more formidable competition for natural versus synthetic raw materials (1970a, pp. 40–41, italics original; see also 1968, pp. 698–700).

By implication, the 'spread effects' of momentum from a centre of economic expansion – again operating through the activities of trade, capital movements, migration, technology diffusion, and so on – refer to all favourable impacts or changes experienced outside that centre, and these could likewise 'weave themselves into the cumulating social process by circular causation' ([1957] 1963, p. 31). They could arise from increased demand by the centre for agricultural products and raw materials; stimulation of technical advance; something akin to the various linkage effects spelled out by Hirschman (1977); the emergence of new secondary centres of expansion; or how industrialisation may inculcate 'a new spirit of rationalism, enterprise, discipline, punctuality, mobility, and efficiency' ([1957] 1963, p. 31; 1968, pp. 1186–7, 1196).

Depending on which set of effects predominate in a setting, the cumulative process could evolve upwards, as in the 'lucky' localities (nations), or downwards, as in the 'unlucky' ones ([1957] 1963, p. 27). Nevertheless, at one point in *Economic Theory* Myrdal asserts that, 'Internationally, ... the backwash effects of trade and capital movements[20] would dominate the outcome much more, as the countervailing spread effects of expansionary momentum are so very much weaker [on the underdeveloped countries]' (ibid., p. 54). Thirteen years later, in *The Challenge of World Poverty* he reiterates, 'The fact is that, contrary to that [H–O–S] theory, *international trade – and capital movements – will generally tend to breed inequality, and will do so the more strongly when substantial inequalities are already established*' (1970a, p. 279, italics original).

What is especially important to note based on the discussion thus far in this section are three things. Firstly, although technological considerations surfaced here and there, Myrdal tended to attribute uneven development more explicitly to other factors. This is in contrast with Prebisch and Singer, who, as the previous chapter has illustrated and the following chapter will show respectively, were more concerned with uneven development driven by uneven technological progress.[21]

Secondly, it is the relative magnitudes of the backwash and spread effects that determine the developmental outcome in any country. With respect to the attack on Viner and the attribution of uneven development to trade and capital movements, Myrdal was in particular emphasising weak *spread* effects.[22] For obvious reasons, national boundaries constitute 'barriers to the spread of expansionary momentum' (1956, pp. 54–5). However,

> more important as impediments ... are the very facts of great poverty and weak spread effects *within* the under-developed countries themselves. ... Basically, the weak spread effects as between countries are thus for the larger part only a reflection of the weak spread effects *within* the under-developed countries themselves caused by their low level of development attained. (Ibid., p. 55, italics added)

At another point he also mentioned that backwash effects and 'unfavorable trends are usually stronger, the lower the levels of income – and of education and a number of other "non-economic" factors' (1970a, p. 280). In these circumstances, he concluded, 'market forces' would tend cumulatively to accentuate international inequalities (1956, p. 55; 1970a, p. 279). On the other hand, 'the higher the level of economic development that a country has already attained, the stronger the spread effects will usually be'. For typically the 'high level of development is accompanied by improved transportation and communications, higher levels of education, and a more dynamic communion of ideas and values – all of which tends to strength the forces for the centrifugal spread of economic expansion or to remove the obstacles for its operation' (1956, p. 34, see also p. 41). Put differently, internal inequalities – associated with a low level of development – and international inequalities are 'inextricably woven together by mutual causation in a circular fashion' (ibid., p. 60, see also p. 50). As will be further illustrated in sections 11.4 and 11.6 below, this should serve to remind the reader that Myrdal was emphasising *domestic* reforms at least as much as *international* institutional changes when it comes to arresting uneven development.[23]

Thirdly, and partly related to the last point, to better harness the spread, and curtail the backwash, effects from the perspective of an underdeveloped country, it does not mean for Myrdal that the most sensible policy action is to apply trade protection. Selective restrictions on specific merchandise may indeed be warranted in certain situations. But it is at least equally important to alter the directions and contents of some activities, like moving away from 'enforced bilateralism' ([1957] 1963, pp. 57–8; 1968, p. 594), diversifying exports in addition to pursuing IS, and reforming the social system in the country concerned to better position it to exploit the spread, and neutralise the backwash, effects. The implications of this for his discussion on commercial policies will be illustrated in section 11.5 below.

11.4 DEVELOPMENT: IMPROVING AGRICULTURAL PRODUCTIVITY, PROMOTING INDUSTRIES, AND IMPLEMENTING SOCIAL REFORMS

So exactly how did Myrdal apply the principle of circular and cumulative causation in a domestic setting of underdevelopment? A useful example is contained in the following passage from *Asian Drama*, where he seeks to enumerate the factors that 'together are responsible' for the low average incomes and low standards of life with respect to the South Asian countries in the 1950s and 1960s:

> [P]oor nutrition and housing, poor schooling and training, poor sanitary and other health facilities. Very low living levels decrease the amount of labor input and

> also the intensity and efficiency of the work actually performed on the land by the labor force. Low incomes are only the other side of low labor productivity; a vicious circle makes poverty and low level of living, or low labor productivity, self-generating. Behind this unfortunate causal mechanism there is, besides the parameter of climate, a social system of institutions and power relations, particularly in regard to the ownership and utilization of land resources, that is severely inimical to productivity, at the same time as low productivity establishes itself as the norm. And within this social system, both shaped by it and upholding it, are the ingrained attitudes of people in all classes. Among the non-physical factors that keep down labor productivity are also the primitive techniques employed in agriculture, likewise both a function of the existing social system, which deprives the tillers of both capital and incentives to greater effort, and a prop to that system. (1968, pp. 433–4)

This passage has, indeed, the 'political, social, psychological, and technological causal interrelations' all in one place.[24]

Could Myrdal then single-mindedly count on industrialisation to lift the underdeveloped countries from the situation that they were trapped in? With reference to South Asia in particular, he did grant that 'no substantial development ... is possible *over the long run* unless these countries can employ a much larger part of their labor force in modern industry or other productive non-agricultural occupations' (1968, p. 1185, italics original). Elsewhere, he also provided some rather commonly cited reasons for industrialisation: that increasing returns prevail in industry and that is where more rapid increases in productivity are possible (ibid., pp. 1156–7); and manufacturing industry represents 'a higher stage of production' (1956, p. 226). At one point he even sounded Listian, observing that 'modern civilization in almost all its more sophisticated forms is rooted in, and depends upon, city life; urbanization is not possible without some measure of industrialization. Indeed, a broad association seems to exist between industrialization on the one hand, and social and economic change on the other' (ibid., pp. 226–7). Finally, '[i]ndustrialization creates a technology which can then be applied to agriculture but not vice versa' (p. 227).

But one should recall that for Myrdal, the social system includes both economic and non-economic factors, where the latter set comprises the levels of consumption – private and collective – by various groups; levels of education and health, and the facilities to promote both; the distribution of power in society, including economic, social, and political stratification; institutions and attitudes, and so on (ibid.; see also 1973, p. 190). It is then only logically consistent for Myrdal to proclaim that, 'By *development* I mean the *movement upward of the entire social system*' (1974, p. 729, italics original) and '[e]conomic development is much more than industrialization' (1968, p. 1842).

Between industries and agriculture, he did not favour the former over the latter in development programmes in general.[25] The industrial revolution in the advanced countries, he thus shrewdly noted, was preceded by, or concomitant with, radical advances in agriculture and transport, and it was never narrowly concentrated on manufacturing industries (1956, p. 228; see also 1968, p. 1249). '[H]igher agricultural output per unit of land is an essential condition for ... supporting industrialization' (1968, p. 417). 'A one-sided industrialization policy that neglects to provide for a simultaneous – or, if possible, earlier – development of agriculture', he thus concluded, 'is almost doomed to frustration' (1956, p. 271).[26]

From the perspective of the agricultural sector, there are additional reasons why it should not be neglected. The first of these has to do with the broad developmental objective of increasing productivity, incomes and living standards among the great masses in the underdeveloped countries. This is in recognition of the fact that, '[h]owever rapidly industrialization proceeds, the great masses of their working population will for decades and, perhaps, generations be employed in agriculture, and the levels of living of the rural masses will mainly be determined by their productivity there' (ibid., p. 227). This also serves as a reminder that with the generally rapid rate of population growth among these countries, industrialisation, especially given that the initial base was relatively small, could never be speedy enough to absorb the rise in agricultural working population. 'For this reason alone', Myrdal thus concluded, 'a major problem of economic development that immediately faces underdeveloped countries is, therefore, how to raise the productivity of the land and of the peasants' (ibid., p. 206; see also 1968, pp. 1173–4, 1183; 1970a, p. 93).[27]

Secondly, there is a reason that shares the same objective as in the first one but has traces of influence by Prebisch, Singer, and (W. Arthur) Lewis. Thus, with reference to the primary exports by these countries, Myrdal concurred at one point that those exports 'often meet inelastic demands in the export market, often also a demand trend which is not rising very rapidly, and excessive price fluctuations' ([1957] 1963, p. 52).[28] Coupled with an abundant supply of unskilled labour, 'any technological improvement in their export production tends to transfer the advantages from the cheapening of production to the importing countries'. In these circumstances, 'what would be rational [in a broader perspective and from a long-term point of view] is above all to increase productivity, incomes and living standards in the large agricultural subsistence sectors, so as to raise the supply price of labour' (ibid.; see also 1956, pp. 231–3, including n. 17, where Lewis (1954) is cited).[29]

Thirdly, by improving productivity in agriculture, underdeveloped countries can 'increase the international space [relax the foreign exchange constraint] for their industrial development' (1956, p. 274).

And fourthly, 'effective measures to raise productivity in agriculture are bound up with land reform, literacy drives, and other fundamental political and social changes that turn against the entrenched vested interests of the privileged classes in society' (ibid., p. 228).

These 'social reforms', of course, are consistent with what Myrdal strongly believed to be necessary to spur development, that is, the broad need to break rigidities. Indeed, it is most important to note that interspersed in his considerations of industrialisation and raising agricultural productivity are threads of recommendation for social reforms. One very clear instance when such reforms were summarised is found in *Asian Drama*:

> [T]he prospects of breaking down the barriers to development in the South Asian countries would be quite different if in a country like India, for example, the government were really determined to change the prevailing attitudes and institutions and had the courage to take the necessary steps and accept their consequences. These would include the effective abolition of caste, prescribed by the constitution, and measures, accepted in principle, that would increase mobility and equality, such as effective land reform and tenancy legislation; a rational policy for husbandry, even if it required the killing of many half-starved cows; eradication of corruption at all levels; enforcement of tax laws; effective taxation on income from land; a forceful attack on the problem of the 'educated unemployed' and their refusal to do manual work – in general, enactment and enforcement, not only of fiscal, but also of all other obligations on people that are required for development. It would mean mobilizing the underutilized agricultural labor for permanent improvements in agricultural production and creation of social capital; a large-scale and effectively carried out campaign to spread birth control; and so on. (1968, pp. 1909–10)

Thus, '[t]he industrialization the underdeveloped countries need is … a much broader social reform than one concentrated on the growth of manufacturing industry' (1956, p. 228). And the call for 'social reform' would later become a call for 'radical institutional reforms', under the banner of which he grouped land reform; reforms relating to population policy, education, and health services; and administrative reforms to strengthen the 'soft states' (1981, pp. 508–20).[30]

What can be done to increase productivity, incomes, and living standards in both agriculture and manufacturing industries? Myrdal was very explicit that 'trade by itself does not lead to such a development' ([1957] 1963, p. 52). '*By itself*, in fact, '"freer trade" would even tend to perpetuate stagnation in the underdeveloped regions' (1956, p. 2, italics original).

11.5 COMMERCIAL POLICIES: EP AND IS

However, to claim that Myrdal was mainly advocating IS at the expense of EP (for instance, Myint 1984, p. 170) cannot be more misleading. He was rather emphasising both sound import restrictions and EP.

Foreign Exchange Shortages and the Importance of EP

Thus, to Myrdal, a 'master bottleneck' faced by most underdeveloped countries was foreign exchange shortages (1968, pp. 919, 2078; 1970a, p. 225). Consequently, in a fundamental sense import restrictions were considered by him as essential ingredients of a development policy because of balance of payments reasons. 'The development plan of an underdeveloped country', he observes in *Economic Theory*, 'will as a rule require large purchases of capital equipment from abroad' ([1957] 1963, p. 92).[31] He further observes in *An International Economy* that the policy to spur development is 'creating at the same time new incomes and causing old incomes to rise, with the consequence that consumption demands [for imports] will also rise' (1956, p. 270). As the pressure on exchange resources mounts, an underdeveloped country 'will be compelled to apply import restrictions in order to protect its exchange balance, *quite apart from any other* [protective] *reasons*' ([1957] 1963, p. 93, italics added). 'Import restrictions are forced upon them as a consequence of the development policy ... In a sense, the[se] ... countries, when they have once gone in for economic development, are forced to be protectionists' (1956, p. 288, see also p. 275).

That is not to say that Myrdal did not list other reasons for import restrictions. Indeed, in his words in *An International Economy*, '*the underdeveloped countries have quite a number of other sound reasons, based on their peculiar situation, for using these restrictions for protective purposes*' (ibid., p. 276, italics original). Nevertheless, Myrdal dubbed the argument for import restrictions which is balance-of-payments-related the '*immediate reason*' for applying such restrictions, adding that the 'additional motives ... are ... mainly operative only in the directing, weighing, and implementing of the restrictions which they [the underdeveloped countries] must anyhow apply because of the scarcity of foreign exchange' (pp. 276, 288, italics original).[32]

But if the main determinant of a country's capacity to import capital goods is its ability to export, would it then be too one-sided for Myrdal to dwell upon import restrictions? In this connection, it should be noted that in criticising IS trade regimes that purport to stimulate industrialisation and ease balance of payments pressure by reducing imports, mainstream theorists always draw attention to how such a regime has the effect of hurting exports and thus aggravates balance of payments problems.[33]

Myrdal did not suffer from this blindness. 'A useful starting point for the discussion of the national commercial policy of underdeveloped countries', he thus argued, 'may be to recall that these countries have a vital interest in high exports in order to enable them to raise their necessary imports of capital goods for economic development' (ibid., p. 254).[34] Consequently, an underdeveloped country has 'powerful reasons for maximizing the total value of its exports' (ibid., p. 229).[35]

Also, harking back to his caution about the limited employment effects of the industrialisation process, where 'the *direct* employment effects ... are small' in the initial stages while 'the *backwash* effects may be considerable' (1968, p. 1177, italics original), at least the backwash effects could be curtailed if the process is 'restricted to production of *exports* or import substitutes' (ibid., italics added).

Pitfalls of Relying on Primary Exports: Echoing the PST?

But what could they export? Myrdal realised that, given the typical initial situation that these countries found themselves in as they embarked upon more rapid development after gaining independence, it was inevitable that they would have to continue to rely on quite a bit of foodstuff and/or raw material exports. But he had reservations about the promise of continuing on this path of development. Because of them, or more exactly, because of the common perceptions of those who hold such reservations, his name became associated with the PST.

'Myrdal has', Meier thus accused, 'overdrawn the significance of the argument that poor countries have suffered a long-term deterioration in their commodity terms of trade and that this has inhibited their development' and 'in giving content to the assertion that for underdeveloped countries the general level of their export prices has been "too low" Myrdal does lend support to the Singer–Prebisch thesis' (1958b, pp. 285–6).[36] Together, these three development economists interpreted 'international market forces ... as a mechanism of international inequality, setting up disequalizing forces and backwash effects to the detriment of poor countries' (Meier 1980, p. 282, including n. 7). Similarly, Lal lamented that '[t]he most extreme form in which these ideas [export pessimism,[37] declining terms of trade] coalesced was the assertion by Mrydal ... that ... a liberal international trade and payments régime ... was really a "zero-sum game" enabling the rich advanced countries to prosper at the *expense* of the poor backward ones' (2000, pp. 22–3, italics original).

However, a more careful reading of Myrdal's works suggests that he was at times circumspect about the PST. For instance, he noted that in the mid-1950s the industrially advanced countries produced more than two thirds of the industrial raw materials (including those originating from agriculture) and deduced that '[a] general comparison between the long-term development of prices of primary goods and manufactured goods cannot be very relevant to our problem' (1956, p. 230). Besides, the 'trade positions' of different underdeveloped countries could vary substantially given that '[t]he trend of relative prices of primary products has not been the same for all products'.[38] And over time, 'the quality of different commodities has changed in different ways and to different degrees', thereby rendering the statistical measurement of the terms of trade 'exceedingly difficult and uncertain' (ibid., pp. 230, 231).[39]

Yet, there are other instances when he seemed to concur with Prebisch and Singer. Thus, both claimed that the rise in productivity has generally been more rapid in the advanced countries (centres) than in the underdeveloped ones (periphery). According to 'economic equilibrium theory', which was the term that Myrdal preferred to employ, 'gains from higher productivity in one sector would be passed on to the whole trading community in the form of lower prices for the produce of that sector' (ibid., 232). But this did not materialise between the two groups of countries. 'While it should have improved the underdeveloped countries' terms of trade substantially', he bemoaned, 'quite the contrary seems actually to have occurred' (ibid.).[40]

Still at other moments Myrdal showed more concern toward the fact that many of the underdeveloped countries, at least up till the late 1960s, had exports concentrated on one or two main commodities. 'Putting all the eggs in one basket', he warned, 'is a dangerous way to live and an improbable basis for steady development' (1968, pp. 509–10; see also 1956, pp. 255–6).[41] The danger is, of course, a reference to the 'very large short-term fluctuations of their export prices'.[42] That combined with large changes in export volume resulted in great fluctuations in export proceeds (1956, pp. 229, 239). And unfortunately for a lot of these products, 'the world demand is not very elastic and the demand trend is not rising'. Income elasticity is low and innovations have economised their use or have allowed them to be replaced by synthetic materials.[43] He was keenly aware that in such circumstances, by raising its output and exports of such commodities, 'one underdeveloped country may gain some advantage at the expense of its competitors – who are also to a large extent underdeveloped'. If this country happens to occupy so important a place in the world market in respect to one commodity, then 'an increase of its supply would bring down the price substantially and, consequently, increase its export proceeds less than proportionally – perhaps even reduce them'.[44] By the same reasoning, 'if all underdeveloped countries did their utmost to increase their present staple exports, they might end up poorer than they were' (ibid., pp. 254–5; 1968, pp. 683–4, 1160; 1970a, p. 286).

Hence, by recommending 'high exports' by the underdeveloped countries Myrdal '[did] not imply simply that it is in their interest to press on with their traditional exports'. Rather, '[t]hey should ... take a good look at the composition of these exports and at their prospects in the world market and then make up their minds about which exports they should try to increase and which they should rather leave alone or reduce. They should seek out for themselves the dynamic commodities with rising demand trends and with high income and price elasticities and try to get away from those with a doubtful future' (ibid., p. 254, see also p. 268). Export diversification was what most underdeveloped countries urgently needed. Not only was this point stressed in *An International Economy*, he continued to emphasise it in *Asian Drama* (1968, p. 1160).

Diversifying into Manufactured Exports

But what could they diversify into? It could be other primary products, which Myrdal did not regard to be a promising option. Thus, '[i]f the diversification of exports were to be limited entirely to primary products, the opportunities may perhaps not everywhere amount to very much'. How about diversifying into manufactures? Here he noticed a 'taboo' against such exports in the underdeveloped countries. Specifically, while '[i]t is gradually becoming recognized that it is a rational element in their economic development policy that they should build up industries and increase their production of manufactured goods; ... it is taken more or less for granted that these should be for domestic consumption only and not to compete in the world market' (1956, p. 257).

While Myrdal sympathised with the difficulty of competing with the developed countries, he did not think that the industries built in the underdeveloped countries should be relegated altogether to the latter's home market. 'From the point of view of international division of labor', he reasons in *An International Economy*, 'this would be entirely unsound, and many opportunities of coming into such export lines where price and income elasticities are great and demand trends rising would be lost'. Harking back to his emphasis on breaking rigidities, he adds that '[t]he development of industrial exports is generally apt to instill more of a dynamic spirit of enterprise and competition into a stagnant economy'.[45] Indeed, 'if economic development is to amount to anything – if stagnation is going to be broken – one underdeveloped country after another will have to enter the world market for manufactured goods in a big way' (1956, pp. 257–8). He reiterates in *Asian Drama* that 'manufactured commodities offer the main prospect for diversification'. He urges that 'the effort to gain a place in the world market with manufactured goods cannot be given up' and that 'exports must be pushed by systematic government action' (1968, pp. 650, 717, 1160). '[T]he achievement of viable and dynamic economics in the underdeveloped countries', he predicts in *The Challenge of World Poverty*, 'rests largely on the chance of these countries to increase exports of manufactured goods' (1970a, p. 293).

While envisaging that the promotion of manufactured exports could aid in breaking rigidities, Myrdal was under no illusion that the diversification from an initial reliance on primary production and exports would be automatic and spontaneous. In yet another instance of invoking the principle of the 'vicious circle of economic stagnation', he thus lamented that,

> it is their underdeveloped status, with all that that implies of rigidity and lack of enterprise, that explains why they have been sticking so tenaciously to the bad risks in [primary] production and export and not been reorienting their economy and shifting their resources more rapidly to adjust to the changing opportunities. (1956, p. 231)

Their ability to adjust to changes in the relative prices in the international market was simply hampered by 'rigidity' and they could not effectively 'exploit advantages and escape disadvantages' (ibid., p. 233; see also 1968, pp. 582–3, 684, 2200).[46]

Import Restrictions and Substitution

That Myrdal did list reasons other than balance of payments concerns for import restrictions is mentioned in the first subsection in the present section. Although to him they did not constitute the 'immediate' reason, he nevertheless refers to them at one point in *An International Economy* as 'sound' reasons for restrictions for protective purposes.[47] At another point some of these are deemed 'special reasons for industrial protection', namely 'the difficulties of finding demands to match new supply, the existence of surplus labor,[48] the large rewards of individual investments in creating external economies, and the lopsided internal price structure disfavoring industry' (1956, p. 279).[49] In other contexts, he also talked about the desirability of greater 'self-sufficiency' (ibid., pp. 257, 268–9, 279–80; [1957] 1963, p. 94; 1968, p. 717).

Nevertheless, it is worth repeating that Myrdal had put at least equal emphasis on EP. Thus, with respect to the first of the four 'special reasons for industrial protection' enumerated above, he notes in *An International*

Economy that while 'import restrictions afford a means of ... creating at once the necessary demand for a particular domestic industry', the 'export market affords a similarly available outlet for increased production' (1956, p. 276). At another point in the same work he mentions briefly the possibility of turning previously import-substituting industries into new export lines, urging that '[t]he development of domestic industry should be pushed in order to substitute domestic for import goods and eventually to furnish new exports' (ibid., pp. 268–9). Both effects, he notes, would provide increased resources for imports of capital goods. Given his recognition of how underdeveloped countries bent upon development would need to preserve their foreign exchange balance, he concludes that they would 'be compelled to take measures to restrict imports *and* push exports' (p. 279, italics added). Finally, when he turned his attention to planning he maintains that, 'In any well-balanced development plan the expansion of export production along lines where new supply is likely to meet high income and demand elasticities and rising demand trends must be given its place alongside the building up of import-competing industries by protection' (p. 274).

By the time he wrote *Asian Drama* Myrdal appeared to have become more convinced of the great 'difficulties' and 'obstacles' faced by the South Asian countries as they promoted their exports of manufactures, some of which are spelled out in section 11.7 below. As a result he suggests at one point in that work that, 'import substitution ... offers a more promising prospect' (1968, p. 1203, see also pp. 279–80, 669–70, 1160, 1175). Nevertheless, he cautions elsewhere in the same work that '[i]mport substitution ... is no shortcut to engendering development' (ibid. p. 672). Reminding his reader once more of the importance of exports, he observes that although '[p]rotectionism played its role in many of the now developed Western countries, ... all of them, unlike the South Asian countries today, had access to growing export markets. There is no historical example in the Western world of economic development based on a policy of self-sufficiency and import substitution' (p. 684).

The discussion in this last paragraph should serve as a reminder that, in addition to the supply-side obstacles mentioned at the end of the previous subsection, Myrdal was no less aware of the demand-side obstacles to a policy of EP. His reference to the Western countries' experiences at the end of this last paragraph is also an occasion to note a significant change in the circumstances between List's and his time. Recall the discussion in section 8.6 in Chapter 8 that List proposed the temperate zone newly industrialising countries of his time to export 'coarse manufactures' to the 'torrid zone countries' in order to advance their manufacturing industries to catch up with England. When Myrdal brought himself back to List's time, he concurred that the then industrialising countries 'were in the fortunate situation of being surrounded by an underdeveloped world which they could use as a market for cheap manufactured goods and as a source of supply for food and industrial raw materials'.[50] He deemed that as 'one of the inestimable advantages in being ahead of the rest' at that time. But in his own time, '[t]he latecomers are obviously not able to follow the same simple pattern' (1956, p. 257). That is because they could no longer 'advance as industrial islands in a surrounding world of backward nations which they could exploit as markets for manufactured goods and as sources of raw materials' ([1957] 1963, p, 98; see also 1968, p. 684). To him, the more important markets for them to gain access to would be those in the developed countries.[51] How this translates into a 'double-standard morality' in commercial policies for Myrdal is discussed in section 11.7 below.

Policy Measures

There was hardly any systematic discussion up to this point in the present section of what policy measures to employ to promote industries. At one point in the chapter on 'Commercial Policy of the Underdeveloped Countries' in *An International Economy*, Myrdal rather casually refers to 'import restrictions' as including 'customs duties as well as exchange and other quantitative restrictions' (1956, p. 276).[52] That would, by itself, add to the suspicion on the part of the mainstream theorists that Myrdal was just another simple-minded protectionist, as indicated in section 11.1 above.

Indeed, if one solely focuses on the 'special reasons' for trade restrictions enumerated in the previous subsection and disregards Myrdal's concern with balance of payments as well as his emphasis on EP, then one might think that one has found the 'smoking gun' in possession by the usual 'protectionist' suspect. For instance, Meier concluded that the aforementioned 'special' reasons 'are inter-related and may be interpreted as an extension of the infant industry argument to the "growing up" of the economy as a whole.[53] In combination, they constitute an "infant economy" case for protection' (1958a, p. 247). He proceeded to consider each of the reasons in turn, and as reported in the opening page of this chapter, he concluded that Myrdal's protection argument is 'misdirected' and that 'domestic policies might be more suitable for removing the divergences between marginal values and costs'.

But that would do great injustice to him. Recall that by development he meant 'the *movement upward of the entire social system*' (1974, p. 729, italics original). To him, this movement 'can be effected by measures applied to one or the other of several points in the system'. This is a hint that similar to List, Myrdal was ready to deploy a variety of policy measures to spur development. Nevertheless, he cautioned, 'this certainly does not imply that from a practical and political point of view it is a matter of indifference where and how a development problem is tackled' ([1957] 1963, pp. 19–20).[54] Hence, it should not be inferred that Myrdal was oblivious to the relative merits and demerits of various measures. In fact, when he discussed such merits and demerits, he appeared to be invoking something akin to the 'principle of targetting' and he also showed a good amount of awareness of the possible adverse effects of some of these measures.

There are, for instance, indications that Myrdal was quite inclined to employ subsidies and other non-trade measures to promote industries and exports. Thus, with respect to three of the 'special reasons for industrial protection' cited in the previous subsection, he mentioned using subsidies to effect such promotion. '[I]t may be entirely sound economics for a poor country with a large surplus working population', he thus proposed, 'to subsidize an industry to encourage its growth and to make it competitive. The workers who thereby become employed would have to be sustained in any case and the real cost of labor is thus lower to the nation than the wages paid' (1956, p. 258). Then while referring to potential external economies to be gained from an individual investment, which is relatively large in underdeveloped countries, he labelled it 'a rational motive for subsidizing industries, including the export *as well as* the import-competing industries' (ibid., p. 277, italics added).[55] The state could also be 'providing facilities for training workers, foremen, and technicians on all levels, as well as business executives, giving managerial advice, making capital available, often subsidizing or protecting new industrial enterprises, and sometimes actually establishing and operating them' (ibid., p. 209).[56] In still another instance he observed that 'an under-developed country will often even have good reasons for subsidising its exports in certain directions' ([1957] 1963, p. 94). Finally, with regard to the structure of internal costs and prices in an underdeveloped country tending to be lopsided as between industry and agriculture, he contended that industrialisation will be hampered 'if industry is not protected and encouraged by fully compensating import restrictions *and* export subsidies or by a system of multiple exchange rates having that effect' (1956, p. 277, italics added).[57]

Myrdal seemed to be aware of the possible advantages in certain contexts of a subsidy as opposed to other instruments. He thus states in *An International Economy* that, 'In theory, … incentives applied in order to start and sustain the development process can be given many forms'. 'From many points of view', he ventures in the same work, 'direct subsidies represent the cleanest solution' (1956, p. 279). Elsewhere, however, he recognised that 'the markets for labour, capital and products are usually highly imperfect or non-existent' in the underdeveloped countries. Hence, 'the subsidies, in particular, can seldom be given by means of general, non-discretionary interventions through the price mechanism' (1970b, p. 233).

At the same time his defense of the use of tariffs in certain contexts anticipated a number of reasons commonly cited in the theory of domestic divergences. Thus, '[a]n underdeveloped country would have more initial inhibitions against doing it [relying mostly on direct subsidies] because of its greater difficulties in raising taxes to pay for the subsidies' (1956, p. 279).[58] In contrast, tariffs can possibly generate revenue.[59] In fact, '[t]he consequent increase in the internal price of the products [due to import restrictions] provides the necessary subsidy in an uncomplicated way which involves neither direct taxation nor the actual disbursement of funds'.[60] These restrictions 'require a minimum of direct interference with the price mechanism', and to Myrdal, that explained their 'great popularity'. It should be an especially important advantage in an underdeveloped country, 'as one of its many weaknesses is in the field of administration' (ibid., p. 281).[61]

Among the different styles of tariff imposition Myrdal thought that the underdeveloped countries 'have reasons to consider carefully … a simple, flat-rate discrimination in favor of manufactured products as a basis for their commercial policies'. The rationales that he provided reflects the broad spectrum of policy objectives that he always kept in sight, as opposed to the relatively narrow focus that is typical of the mainstream literature on commercial policy, and is worth quoting at length:

> Such a policy would quite particularly fit the … special reason for protection … [that has to do with] the lopsided cost and price structure in underdeveloped countries as between industry and agriculture – but would in a general way accommodate the others too. It would also ease the exchange situation by applying an indirect tax on a large number of import goods; it would not worsen its terms of trade as a devaluation often would.[62] Its purpose would be to offset to some extent the general handicap of underdevelopment and provide a general momentum to industrialization, while removing the responsibility for discriminating between different industries from the government.
>
> It could … be supplemented by special levies on luxury imports – and corresponding internal taxes on home produce – not only in order to carry out a desired redistribution of real incomes and discriminate against certain consumption, but also in order to make the system sufficiently effective in bringing down imports. (Ibid., pp. 281–2)

Having said that, Myrdal was also shrewd to point out that given the problem associated with the widely fluctuating export proceeds that the underdeveloped countries constantly had to wrestle with, a variety of short-term interferences (for example, quantitative restrictions (QRs) or controls) would still be necessary. Even over the long term, it is doubtful if any underdeveloped country 'would leave so much of its development policy to the free play of market forces [implied by a flat-rate ad valorem duty]' (ibid., p. 282, see also p. 283).

An alternative tariff regime would be 'regular tariffs, fixed at different levels but embodied in semipermanent legislation'. He argued that this would seem superior to quantitative controls of various types.[63]

It is in making this comparison that Myrdal demonstrated a keen awareness of the limitations of the latter type of instrument, and thus at least partially anticipated one more charge by the mainstream theorists, namely that QRs create adverse incentives. Thus, because they can be changed by administrative ruling and they are 'subject to constant pressures from interested parties at home and abroad', they add uncertainty. If such controls take the form of import licenses, then unless they are auctioned, 'they create unearned windfall profits … for those who … acquire import licenses' (ibid., pp. 282–3).[64] Besides, they have 'destroyed business morale'. Specifically,

> [t]he system tends easily to create cancerous tumors of partiality and corruption in the very center of the administration, where the sickness is continuously nurtured by the favors distributed and the grafts realized and from which it tends to spread out to every limb of society. Industrialists and businessmen are tempted to go in for shady deals instead of steady, regular business. Individuals who might have performed useful tasks in the economic development of their country become idle hangers-on, watching for loopholes in the decrees and dishonesty in their implementation. This is all the more dangerous as a general weakness in underdeveloped countries, inherited from a long history of stagnation, is that their business classes are too much inclined to look for easy profits in place of sustained enterprise. (Ibid.)[65]

Thus recognising the serious difficulties that such controls create for economic development, Myrdal recommended that 'even at the sacrifice of a degree of much-needed flexibility, import restrictions should be carried out to the greatest possible extent by the regular means of tariffs or multiple exchange rates, which are easier than *ad hoc* administrative rules to protect from the worst type of mismanagement'. 'For the rest, serious study and relentless efforts should be devoted to simplifying and rationalizing the direct controls and to getting them administered with scrupulous honesty' (ibid., p. 284).

While Myrdal thus attempted in some ways to compare the appropriateness of different commercial policy instruments for the underdeveloped countries, he did not compartmentalise his analytical treatment of various cases for intervention. His constant focus on the interrelatedness of various rigidities, and hence his broad policy objectives, enabled him to avoid the trap of making cut and dry ranking of instruments in very narrow contexts that the literature on commercial policy always leads one to fall into. To recall, he argued that 'an upward movement of the entire system can be effected by measures applied to one or the other of several points in the system'. 'Nevertheless', he hastens to caution in *Economic Theory*, 'it is unlikely that a rational policy will work by changing only one factor' ([1957] 1963, pp. 19–20).[66] 'Interferences in international trade', he accordingly reminds the reader, 'are only part of the general efforts, defined in the national plan, to recondition the price system in such a way that a sustained cumulative process towards economic development is engendered' (ibid., p. 95).[67]

His desire to take on the obstacles to development *en masse* actually necessitates a certain amount of pragmatism as far as evaluating policy instruments are concerned. Specifically, various instruments have to be considered within much broader contexts, where the merits of some might be enhanced, while the demerits of others might appear to be less unacceptable. Such pragmatism also implies that one will find Myrdal to be more inclined to recommend the deployment of some sort of combinations of the policy instruments, the specific mixture of which depends on the particular circumstances facing any underdeveloped country. This is in sharp contrast to the often knee-jerk reaction on the part of the mainstream theorists to denounce any trace of trade intervention.

11.6 THE SOFT STATE AND THE NEED FOR ADMINISTRATIVE REFORM

Nevertheless, Myrdal would admit '[i]t should not be concealed that balancing the interventions in trade is a difficult problem' (1956, p. 280). 'The fact that protectionism can be proved to be rational in an under-developed country', he further added, 'should not, of course, be used to conceal the other fact that the interferences with international trade, as today actually applied are grossly irrational in perhaps most under-developed countries' ([1957] 1963, p. 96). His extreme caution toward the deployment of QRs, expressed at least as early as in *An International Economy*, has already been pointed out in the previous section. In a more general form, he states in *Asian Drama* that 'we assume as a derived value premise that discretionary controls should be kept to a minimum' (1968, p. 2077).

More fundamentally, Myrdal was duly concerned with the problems of implementing development plans under the guidance of what he dubbed 'soft' or 'weak' states.[68] For the discussion being conducted here the most important feature of a soft state to note is 'a widespread disobedience by public officials on various levels to rules and directives handed down to them, and often their collusion with powerful persons and groups of persons whose conduct they should regulate' (1970a, p. 208; 1981, p. 518). This is a manifestation of what he characterised as a 'fragmentation of loyalties', where little loyalty is devoted by different groups to the community as a whole while stronger loyalty is exhibited to 'less inclusive groups' like caste, ethnic, religious or linguistic community. This has invited 'nepotism', encouraged 'moral laxity', and resulted in a 'prevalence of corruption' (1968, pp. 949–50, see also pp. 895–6).[69]

Myrdal traced the historical origins of these soft states chiefly to colonialism.[70] From that historical experience various groups of power elites were bred and had descended. Whatever 'authoritarian tradition' there was in the pre-colonial times was 'strengthened by colonial rules and transformed into paternalism' (1970b, p. 232). This could account for the 'general preference for individualized, administrative, discretionary controls of private business' among the governments that came to power after gaining independence (1970a, pp. 225–6). In turn, the widespread use of such controls 'increases the temptations to bribe and to take bribes' (1973, p. 121).

These three elements – an upper-class power elite, widespread use of discretionary controls, and a pervasiveness of corruption – then feed on each other in circular causation with cumulative effects to maintain the state as soft (1970a, p. 208). Thus, '*fundamentally the main explanation of the soft state is that all the power is in the hands of the upper class who can afford egalitarian laws and policy measures but are in an unchallenged position to prevent their implementation*' (ibid., pp. 221–2, italics original). Put differently, 'those in power, responsible for reforms, often share these [established] attitudes and have a stake in preserving the institutions through which they are molded; in other words, they suffer from what we have called inhibitions' (1968, p. 1910; see also 1970a, p. 414). These administrators and politicians would 'have an interest in preserving and building up discretionary controls that give them the opportunity to enrich themselves' (1968, p. 933). But then '[i]n a system of operational controls ... the application of one set of controls has a tendency to make necessary the application of others. ... There is thus a self-perpetuating and expansionary tendency in every system of negative discretionary controls' (ibid., p. 923).[71] More controls breed yet more corruption and the spread of corruption 'gives corrupt politicians and dishonest officials a vested interest in retaining and increasing controls of this type' (1970b, p. 241). In all, '[i]t is the general setting of the soft state that makes corruption possible, while, in circular causation with cumulative effects, the prevalence of corruption is a mighty influence to keep these countries soft as states' (1970a, p. 233, see also p. 236; 1970b, p. 240).

What did Myrdal propose to strengthen some soft states? One suggestion that was made was 'retrenchment' regarding legislations. This entails 'making their *legislation more functional*, ... less full of loopholes, and backed by effective sanctions. ... It is of doubtful value to legislate reforms that have no chance of being realized for the time being' (1970a, p. 242, italics original).

There should also be retrenchment from the excessive use of discretionary controls. This follows from his earlier observation that controls tend to self-propagate. Thus, on a few occasions in separate works, Myrdal lamented that the deployment of 'positive controls' to encourage private enterprise – import restrictions, direct subsidies, cheap foreign exchange rates, low interest rates on capital, low prices for goods and services from the public sector, tax exemptions, and so on – had increased the need for 'compensatory negative controls', because 'private enterprise ... has actually been encouraged to the extent that it has had to be curbed by discretionary controls'. He likened this to 'driving a car with the accelerator pushed to the floor but the brakes on'. Obviously, '[w]ith somewhat less encouragement, there would be less need for curtailment. The important point to stress is that encouraging private enterprise beyond practical limits makes necessary a gargantuan bureaucratic system of administrative discretionary controls to harness it' (1968, pp. 923–5; see also 1970a, pp. 223–5; 1970b, pp. 235–6; 1973, pp. 121–2). Lest the mainstream economist mistakes this as an instance where Myrdal contradicted his otherwise ardent support for state interventions to promote development, it should be emphasised that he was simply insisting that in many situations the discretionary controls 'are not needed to the extent actually practiced' and that it is 'not a plea for less control over private business but for its being carried out by different means and thereby more effectively' (1970a, p. 243).[72]

Such retrenchment from an excessive reliance on controls, if achieved, can weaken the links through which corruption thrives. Indeed, on different occasions Myrdal accorded the fight against corruption a 'high priority' and regarded it to be of '*crucial and strategic importance*' in improving administration (1970a, p. 246, italics original). '*[T]he efforts should first be directed*', he proposed, '*toward punishing corruption of these higher up*: ministers and higher officials. Also, the big bribers in the business class should be brought to court. If the disease is not attacked on that level, corruption all the way down will be protected' (ibid., p. 247, italics original).

Making legislation more effective, cutting back on discretionary controls, and suppressing corruption are all part of a larger effort of administrative reform. Myrdal proclaims in *Asian Drama* that 'one of the first conditions for development in the South Asian countries is improvement of government and administration' (1968, p. 2005). He realised that this could be immensely difficult. However, unlike many in the mainstream who crumbled under the fear of government failures, he maintained the faith, as is evident in *An International Economy*, that '"it takes good administration to improve bad administration"', and that an inefficient and dishonest political and administrative machinery 'is another vicious circle that creates deadlocks and obstructions, if it is not broken by vigorous and successful action' (1956, p. 204).[73]

Such administrative reforms are in turn part of the social reforms that were alluded to in section 11.3 above. To Myrdal, the onus for carrying out these reforms rests squarely with the country where the reforms are called for. He thus declared that, '*The strengthening of social discipline in an underdeveloped country and the overcoming of the inhibitions and obstacles for development inherent in its being a soft state must be accomplished by that country itself*' (1970a, pp. 248–9).[74]

11.7 DOUBLE STANDARD MORALITY IN INTERNATIONAL INSTITUTIONAL REFORM

While underdeveloped countries should urgently consider domestic social and administrative reforms, there are nevertheless international institutional reforms that Myrdal recommended that would require the support and even some sacrifice by the developed countries.

Based on his conceptualisation of 'market forces' (section 11.2 above), he understandably regarded that 'on all levels of the economic processes, efforts toward the monopolistic organization of markets are bound to be much more effective in industrially advanced countries than in underdeveloped ones; and ... the bargaining power of underdeveloped countries has been, and remains, relatively very weak' (1956, p. 233).[75] Besides, '*the commercial policies of the developed countries are almost systematically rigged against the efforts of underdeveloped countries to rise out of underdevelopment*' and, as in colonial times, '*have further discriminated against*' them (1970a, pp. 294, 292, italics original). 'These policies become the more damaging', he noted, 'as they add their influences to the adverse effects of the play of the forces in the market' (ibid., p. 294).

In what ways have the commercial policies of the developed countries been rigged? Myrdal lamented that these countries 'have protected and subsidized their own primary production – particularly agriculture' (1956, p. 233; see also 1970a, p. 293). In the meantime they exhibited a 'cold-hearted disinclination ... to do anything at all in order to stabilize the prices of raw materials and staple agricultural commodities of the underdeveloped and very poor countries' (1956, p. 46, see also pp. 250–53; 1970a, pp. 305–6). It is partly because of these challenges that Myrdal strongly recommended, as illustrated in section 11.5 above, diversification into the export of manufactures. However, in doing so 'the opposing forces' in the form of 'restrictive import policies of the industrial countries' have turned out to be very strong (1968, pp. 583, 652). Among various standard measures, that of 'rising protective walls' (that is, tariff escalation) did not escape his attention (ibid., p. 684; see also 1970a, pp. 37–8, 293). While Myrdal advocated the employment of subsidies to encourage production and export of manufactures (section 11.5 above), he was not oblivious to the fact that the advanced countries would 'try to close their markets to "dumping" from the underdeveloped countries' and he cited the history of Japan's long struggle to get into the world markets with its industrial products to buttress his point (1956, p. 258). Elsewhere, he alluded to how 'export subsidies [deployed by the underdeveloped countries] are apt to meet more dislike abroad than [their use of] import restrictions' (ibid., p. 280).

Interestingly, in as early as *An International Economy* Myrdal sees the need for a system of trade arrangements that would confer differential treatments between the underdeveloped and developed countries. He writes,

> Looking back, we in the advanced countries have good reason to ask ourselves whether one policy line – basic, in a sense, to both the Bretton Woods agreements and the abortive attempt to create the International Trade Organization – was not downright wrong ... I mean the idea that all nations are equal, and that the international community should be based on principles and rules that are applied to all. It is an ideal that they *should* be equal but if, in fact, they are not, equal treatment becomes inequality. (1956, p. 291, italics original)

That leads him to suggest that a 'double-standard morality' in commercial policy could be rationally motivated. This is because the underdeveloped countries 'not only have good reasons but are virtually forced to control their imports *and* subsidize their exports – indeed, to practice systematic protection – if they are not to give up their drive for economic development' (ibid., p. 292, italics added). Consequently, as he continues on this in *Economic Theory*,

> [t]he under-developed countries have rational grounds for asking the developed countries to liberalise their trade unilaterally. They need to be staunch free-traders, and even preserve for themselves the right to give export subsidies, so far as the advanced countries' imports from them are concerned, but restrictionists in respect of their imports. And they have valid arguments against anyone who would call this attitude logically inconsistent. ([1957] 1963, pp. 96–7)

'[I]t cannot be stated', he boldly asserts, 'that it is in the interest of the world that they relinquish import restrictions *and* abstain from export subsidies' (1956, p. 291, italics added).[76]

This double standard was not merely a passing thought that Myrdal entertained only in the 1950s. He refers back to it again in *The Challenge of*

World Poverty, arguing that 'for once [here is a demand for reform involving] a double standard to the advantage of the weak and not the strong as usually has been the case in a world which is ruled by power and not by moral considerations' (1970a, pp. 294–5). Two years before, in *Asian Drama*, he also cautions that measures of 'tax advantages or subsidies' offered by the governments (in South Asia) to encourage the exports of manufactures 'will require of the wealthier nations a greater degree of understanding in their approach to the underdeveloped countries and a greater willingness to resist powerful domestic pressures for short-run protective measures than they have hitherto shown', or else '[n]othing effective can be accomplished along these lines' (1968, p. 652).[77] Then in *Against the Stream* he once more urges the underdeveloped countries to 'press for changed policies on the part of the developed countries and obtain not only their abstention from discriminatory commercial policies but their finding means of positively promoting the export interests of underdeveloped countries' (1973, p. 125).[78]

While in supporting this 'double-standard morality' in commercial policy Myrdal wished for policy space for the underdeveloped countries in managing international trade to better harness spread, but curtail backwash, effects arising from that economic activity with the developed countries, section 11.3 above illustrates his understanding that there were other activities that also precipitated international inequalities. Among those, that section alludes, albeit briefly, to problems of enclave development associated with certain capital inflows. It is thus not surprising that, here and there, he had expressed some need for deploying investment measures on the part of the underdeveloped countries. These include preferences for investments that would 'not raise any demand for foreign exchange, especially if it promises to save exchange through import substitution or the building up of export potential' (1968, pp. 823–4). There could also be advantages in having 'a say in deciding in what branch of industry the foreign enterprise is to be undertaken', including 'joint enterprise' arrangements so that those countries could obtain not only capital inflows 'but also the technical know-how, management, and particularly familiarity, etc., with markets' (1970a, pp. 326–7, see also p. 332; 1956, p. 108). In this connection he attempted to popularise Rosenstein-Rodan's idea of 'management contracts', which are means for transferring technology and management in addition to some capital, but he did not find much success in doing so (1970a, p. 330–31; see also 1956, p. 117). Elsewhere he also showed an awareness of how royalties (from conferring privileges in exploiting resources) and taxes could be 'actually used for the further development of the economy' provided that they are not 'being squandered on luxuries or whittled away in the form of private hoardings of gold or foreign exchange' (1956, p. 107). One can safely speculate on his stance if he had lived long enough to have the opportunity to advise the underdeveloped countries when they were pressured to negotiate on the issues that led to the Agreement on TRIMs during the Uruguay Round of MTNs.[79]

11.8 CONCLUDING REMARKS

In his review of the book edited by Dostaler, Ethier and Lepage (1992) that honours Myrdal's works, Reisman (1995, p. 246) laments that, 'For an author of such stature, the secondary literature is deplorably thin'. Worse still, as the discussion in the present chapter amply illustrates, mainstream interpretations of Myrdal's works are grossly distorting and misleading. Thus, while he has been portrayed as a protectionist and staunch supporter of IS, the discussions here clearly show his support of EP. He did endorse IS too, but in far more nuanced and intelligent ways than the representation by the mainstream would suggest. He also put at least equal emphasis on domestic reforms to better position the underdeveloped countries to harness the spread, but curtail the backwash, effects. In believing that soft states, at least most of them, can be strengthened, he did not throw in the towel regarding development promotion by the state like those in the mainstream who are haunted by government failures. Regarding institutional reform at the international level, one can safely label him a supporter of SDT of the underdeveloped countries. And as the latter part of section 11.7 hints, he would probably have voiced very strong opposition against the Agreement on TRIMs reached in the Uruguay Round of MTNs.

In the meantime Myrdal's works have quietly exerted an influence on a few others who are also critical of the mainstream approach to development analysis. It is the works of one such researcher, Hans Singer, that the following chapter seeks to re-examine.

NOTES

1. Some of the passages contained in sections 11.1, 11.3, and 11.5 of this chapter are reproduced from Ho (2009) with permission.
2. One criticism that will not be openly explored here pertains to the claim by, or otherwise belief on the part of, the neoclassical economists that their analyses are 'objective' and value free. The interested reader can consult, for instance, Myrdal ([1957] 1963, Chs. 9, 10; 1968, Prologue, section 9). For a critique of Myrdal on this point, see Little (1982, pp. 5–6).
3. Haberler (op. cit.) finds it puzzling 'that Myrdal, who quotes copiously from earlier and contemporary writers … fails to mention List'. See, however, n. 13 below.
4. Elsewhere in the same work Haberler complains that '[there are] changes … induced by trade and changes in trade including changes in trade brought about by trade policy. Favorable as well as unfavorable trade-induced changes are possible and have to be

considered. Alleged unfavorable trade-induced changes have received so much attention from protectionist writers from List to Myrdal (which has induced trade economists, too, to discuss them at great length), that there is danger that the tremendously important favorable influences be unduly neglected' (op. cit., pp. 26–7).

5. Constrained by space, this chapter only focuses on those of Myrdal's works that pertain to the theme of the present book, which practically began to be published in the 1950s. For an assessment of his earlier works in economics, see Dostaler (1990) and Angresano (1997, Chs. 2, 3). For a briefer consideration, see the first half of Dopfer (1988). His *Economic Theory and Under-Developed Regions* will hereafter be abbreviated as *Economic Theory.*
6. Importantly, Myrdal noted that '[t]he earliest classical authors themselves had, besides their short-term equilibrium theory, an analysis of long-term economic development – in fact they had more of it than the neo-classical authors – and part of it went far outside the framework of equilibrium analysis' ([1957] 1963, p. 144). It is perhaps not unreasonable to expect that he would have regarded the re-interpretation of classical trade theories advanced in Part I of the present work as falling into that realm.
7. Myrdal allows that 'the stable equilibrium concept ... might occasionally play a useful role in the study of some problems, in particular when only a short period is under consideration' (op. cit., p. 157).
8. As Myrdal himself was to recall, his application of this principle to development studies was based upon Wicksell's hints of 'circular and cumulative causation' (1984, p. 152). Incorporating unpublished materials from the Karl William Kapp Archive, including the Myrdal–Kapp correspondence and Kapp's lecture notes on circular cumulative causation, Berger (2008) sheds light on the cooperation between the two in refining the principle. Others have suggested that Myrdal borrowed the principle from Veblen (Dopfer 1988, p. 230). For his own account of how he came into contact with some American institutionalists in the 1930s, see Myrdal (1978, pp. 771–2).
9. This was published in three volumes, totalling almost 2,300 pages. The most thorough coverage is given to India, although it also touches upon Pakistan, Ceylon (Sri Lanka), Burma (Myanmar), Indonesia, Malaysia, the Philippines, Thailand, Cambodia, Laos, and South Vietnam.
10. Myrdal identified such a 'holistic' approach to development studies as an 'institutional' approach (1974, p. 730). See also Myrdal (1978).
11. Myrdal did allow that the 'secondary changes' would 'not always' work in the same directions. See, for instance, Myrdal (1974, p. 730; 1978, p. 774). For some examples of the negating forces see Myrdal ([1957] 1963, pp. 35–6). Even when forces are generally working in the same direction, they could be working at different speeds (ibid., p. 18).
12. This clarification was prompted by Swan (1962). See Myrdal (op. cit., p. 1875, n. 1).
13. The processes of 'circular and cumulative' or 'mutual' causation in some significant ways resemble List's 'reciprocal effects' discussed in Ch. 8 above. For this and other similarities between List's and Myrdal's ideas, see Ho (2006). In this connection, it is worth noting that Myrdal (1978, p. 773) regards List as an institutional economist.
14. A specific example that Myrdal had brought up on a few occasions relates to the treatment of education in neoclassical analysis, what he referred to as 'investment in man'. See, for instance, Myrdal (1968, Ch. 29). One can only imagine how he would evaluate the currently fashionable 'endogenous growth theory'.
15. '*The true institutional approach*', Myrdal thus declared, '*must work with concepts that are adequate to reality from the beginning, i.e. in the very approach to a problem*' (op. cit., italics original).
16. Myrdal's evaluation of classical trade theories could benefit from a more systematic approach. At one point in *Economic Theory* he contends that '[t]he classical economists cannot be accused of having overlooked the importance of non-economic factors' ([1957] 1963, p. 152). Based on the discussions in Chs. 2 to 5 in the present work, that might be truer when it comes to their studies of England but not as true when England's trading partners are concerned.
17. With reference to the distinctions made near the end of section 11.2, this position of Viner qualifies as an instance of 'automatic *mutatis mutandis*'.

18. For one of the reasons for this shortage, see n. 42 below.
19. While this is commonly associated with a theorem derived from the H–O–S model, at one point Myrdal indicated, without elaboration, that the trade-initiated 'tendency towards a gradual and partial equalisation of factor prices in different countries ... was implicit already in the exposition of the classical economists' ([1957] 1963, p. 148).
20. 'Migration' is left out of this quotation because Myrdal notes the general changes in legislations and sentiments since the First World War that has rendered this activity as relatively immaterial ([1957] 1963, p. 54).
21. In the first of two interviews that Angresano conducted with him, Myrdal made the following confession: 'Technology has never played a fundamental role in my thinking. Of course, behind it all, improvement of productivity, investment and all of that but it's not the fundamental concept as it is for [Clarence] Ayres. Technology has never been a large part of my theory' (Angresano 1997, p. 160). Note that he was only referring to the 'old institutionalists' in answering the question concerned.
22. Compare with Prebisch's brief reference to the lack of 'radiating power' from the industrial centres in section 10.2 above.
23. But writing a few years before his death in 1987, Myrdal seemed to have forgotten about this important distinction that he had made. 'In this [*Economic Theory*] and in other early writings of mine', he thus confusingly recalled, 'there was *no* thought that the existing great inequality of resources and power within the underdeveloped countries themselves could be part of the explanation of their underdevelopment' (1984, pp. 152–3, italics added).
24. See also Myrdal (op. cit., Appendix 2, Part II).
25. '[H]e does recognize the indispensable role of agriculture ... But his emphasis is certainly on industrialisation' (Meier 1958a, pp. 251–2; see also 1958b, pp. 280–81).
26. For clear indications of his inclusion of the agricultural sector in his outline of the capital allocation aspect of national plans, see Myrdal ([1957] 1963, pp. 81, 88).
27. The employment creation ability of industries is even more limited if one takes into consideration the backwash effects that the more modern industries might exert on crafts and traditional industries (Myrdal 1968, p. 1174; 1970a, p. 396).
28. Myrdal's position on the PST thesis will be considered in section 11.5 below.
29. For comparison with Prebisch, see Prebisch (1950a, pp. 8–10). See also n. 40 below. For comparison with Singer, see Singer (1950, pp. 478–9).
30. This grouping system first takes shape in *Asian Drama* (1968, vols. II and III). It is refined in *The Challenge of World Poverty* and is clearly laid out in Myrdal (1981). Administrative reforms to strengthen 'soft states' will be considered in section 11.6 below.
31. See Myrdal (1968, pp. 510–11, 677) for his consideration of raw material imports as an added burden on the balance of payments situation.
32. 'My argument for protection', Myrdal qualifies in *An International Economy*, 'does not ... apply to the score or more of underdeveloped countries whose governments for the time being seem to be satisfied with the existing relative stagnation or, anyhow, have not yet got down seriously to the task of starting on their economic development. They usually have plenty of import restrictions which, however, cannot be justified by the reasons accounted for' (1956, p. 269, see also p. 293).
33. Myrdal was also keenly aware that in the short run an IS policy might actually aggravate a country's balance of payments problems. This is in view of the fact that 'the initiation of new industries requires large imports of capital goods, and often continuing imports of spare parts, raw materials, and semi-manufactured goods; the building up of ancillary industries to make the countries independent of these other and continuing import needs will again create a need to import capital goods' (1968, p. 685, see also pp. 669–70, 1161; 1970a, p. 39).
34. While reiterating the same point later in the text Myrdal added the observation that, 'Neither is this point missed by Nurkse and Prebisch' (op. cit., p. 268). Nurkse is also, of course, one of the 'usual suspects' for allegedly advocating IS to the neglect of EP.
35. Myrdal's emphasis on EP must not have registered with Myint when the latter wrote a review of *Asian Drama*. Thus, although the former stressed that 'it is vitally important for these countries to expand their export trade' (Myrdal 1968, p. 1159), the latter remarked

that 'the book treats the role of export expansion in the economic development of the smaller Asian countries in a rather cavalier manner' (Myint 1968, p. 243). It was only ten years earlier that in another publication Myint drew attention to Myrdal (1956, p. 274), where the latter pleaded for vigorous export drive policies among the underdeveloped countries (Myint 1958, p. 336, n. 1).

36. On the point made by some that export prices were 'too low', Myrdal's actual reaction was that '[t]he exact meaning of such an assertion is difficult to clarify as there is no objective norm of comparison available' (1956, p. 232). Also recall n. 2 in Ch. 10 above indicates that Linder (1961) is another who links Myrdal to the PST.
37. Myint also asserted that Myrdal 'has always been prone to export pessimism' (1984, p. 170).
38. This is one of many instances when Myrdal made distinctions among the underdeveloped countries, which is contrary to the claims made by Bauer (1959, p. 109) and Knox (1960 p. 281) that he assumed, even if implicitly, homogeneity within that group of countries.
39. These last two points are considerations that Prebisch was also aware of. It should also be remembered that by primary commodities Prebisch was most of the time referring only to agricultural products. That is definitely not the case for Myrdal.
40. Compare with Prebisch (1950a, pp. 8–10; 1951a, p. 47) and Singer (1950, pp. 478–9). Myrdal went on to observe that, 'The plight of the underdeveloped countries stems *mainly* from a low level of productivity and a slow rise – if any – of this level. The point here is, however, that this fundamental disadvantage has not been counterbalanced by favorable changes in the terms of trade' (op. cit., 232, italics added). This appears to echo Prebisch's position that of the two ways of raising average income, through increases in productivity or improvements in the terms of trade, that it was the former that was more fundamentally important. See section 10.2 in the previous chapter.
41. The recommendation to diversify exports was thus intended to 'spread' or 'even out' risks. But it would also, according to Myrdal, strengthen an underdeveloped country's bargaining power (1956, pp. 256, 268).
42. Myrdal suggested that there was a connection between price fluctuations and the 'relative lack of entrepreneurial spirit' in the primary exporting countries. Specifically, 'the wide price fluctuations have deterrent effects on recruiting brains and initiative for industry and enterprise. Speculation and the gamble of trading under conditions of high risks and high profits will attract venturesome youth, while the prospects of laboring for mass production with low profits, which must be the goal for successful industrial development, will become unattractive. This is the more damaging, since in most underdeveloped countries there is the recognized difficulty of changing the traditions of whatever small business class there is from seeking easy profits through trade and speculation to embarking upon sustained enterprise' (1956, pp. 243–4, see also pp. 202–3, 282–3).
43. Myrdal did not, at least not explicitly, put the kind of stress on 'disparities in income elasticity of demand' that Prebisch did. Nevertheless, his concern with foreign exchange shortages, dubbed the 'master bottleneck', runs parallel with the latter's emphasis on the problem of persistent external imbalance. See section 10.4 in Ch. 10 above.
44. This is, of course, what later came to be labelled as 'immiserizing growth'. See Bhagwati (1958).
45. Elsewhere, Myrdal predicted that spreading exports over a wider range of commodities 'is the only practical means of overcoming the basic weakness of underdeveloped countries in international trade, which is rigidity, and of acquiring the flexibility in their economy which is a precondition for greater success in exploiting the new opportunities and releasing themselves from the less remunerative lines of export. The only way of doing so is continually to seek out new products for sale and so build up gradually a greater number of export outlets. In this field – as, indeed, generally – they must overcome tradition and acquire the pragmatic and experimental habits of modern business' (1956, p. 256, see also p. 268).
46. These points are echoed by Bruton (1965, p. 346).

47. As late as the *Asian Drama* Myrdal would still write, 'Import restrictions are designed primarily to close the exchange gap: the fact that they protect production for the home market is in a sense incidental' (1968, p. 1158).
48. At one point in the *Asian Drama* Myrdal argues that 'chronic underutilization of labor provides grounds for protection' (1968, p. 2085).
49. Save for 'find[ing] demand to match supply', the other reasons are also mentioned in Myrdal ([1957] 1963, p. 95). In *Asian Drama*, though not in a context of discussion of commercial policies, he notes that 'the need for research and for training of workers and specialists on all levels cannot be expected to be filled by industrial entrepreneurs' and 'the magnitude of the individual investment' would provide added reasons for state support (1968, pp. 717, 810).
50. Myrdal did not subscribe to the 'pessimistic geographical determinism' implied in List's position. He nevertheless regarded climatic constraints to be important considerations for development and lamented the effort to ignore them in the post-World War II period (1968, pp. 677–81; 1981, pp. 505–6).
51. Myrdal also considered the potential advantages of IS if practised on a regional basis. See, for instance, Myrdal (1968, pp. 656–7, 1161). Both Prebisch and Singer also gave that approach some attention.
52. At one point in *Asian Drama*, he lists customs tariffs, multiple exchange rates, exchange taxes, import surcharges, and import licenses as examples of 'non-discretionary import controls' (1968, p. 2083).
53. In spelling out the 'special reasons' Myrdal did not mention infant industry considerations. He does mention 'infant industries' protection in passing in *Asian Drama* (1968, p. 2085). At one point in *Economic Theory* he suggests that '[t]he development of the "infant industry" argument, and many other special considerations already taken account of by classical economists, ... contained *in nuce* hints of a much more realistic approach to the problems of the under-developed countries' ([1957] 1963, p. 157).
54. In *Economic Theory* there are references to a 'co-ordinated system of state interferences', a 'system of purposefully applied controls and impulses', and a 'system of interferences with the price system' ([1957] 1963, pp. 80, 95). In *Asian Drama* he talks in terms of 'a rationally coordinated system of policy measures' (1968, p. 58).
55. For traces of influence of the 'balanced growth' idea on him, see Myrdal (1956, p. 202; 1968, p. 694). See Myrdal (1968, pp. 1935–7) for his brief evaluation of balanced versus unbalanced growth.
56. Referring to small-scale enterprises Myrdal suggested that their productivity and competitive strength could be improved 'by securing them access to capital, raw materials and other productive necessities, tools and machines, and plants or workshops. Included, too, are measures that provide the technical assistance and training that are needed'. He added that these 'usually imply some subsidy' (1968, p. 1225).
57. Further caution towards two of the special reasons for industrial protection was voiced when Myrdal indicated that, 'The element of surplus labor, which is a valid reason for subsidy, has to be looked into carefully; there may be alternative uses where the relative productivity is different. Likewise, the effects on external economies must be carefully estimated and compared' (op. cit., pp. 280–81).
58. One can compare this with the discussion in Corden (1997, p. 50).
59. Regarding revenue considerations from various trade taxes, Myrdal notes at one point in the *Asian Drama* that, 'As for foreign trade, convenience alone requires that the state use its control to acquire a "tax handle"'. He specifically mentioned how the Ceylon and Malaya of the 1960s, thanks to their relatively sizeable imports and exports at that time, were able to do so conveniently (1968, p. 814, 2096).
60. Contrast with the discussion in Corden (1997, p. 38).
61. On the other hand, given the imperfection and non-existence of the markets for labour, capital, and products that Myrdal alluded to, subsidies would often be '[m]ixed with ... other types of inducements ... [and] have ... to be distributed by ... discretionary controls'. In the case of India, these arrangements 'overtax the weak administration and open up a vast new field for corruption' (1970b, p. 234).

62. On his caution toward devaluations, see Myrdal (1968, pp. 2081–2).
63. But Myrdal deemed this 'alternative tariff regime' as less desirable than the 'flat-rate ad valorem duty' (op. cit.). This is different from List and Prebisch, who both favoured more selective interventions, but with adjustments over time. See sections 8.5 (third subsection) and 10.5 (second subsection) above.
64. Myrdal attributed the 'unearned windfall profits' to 'unplanned protection', which is in turn due to the fact that 'import controls were adopted for foreign exchange reasons' and thus 'ordinarily give a greater – often a much greater – degree of protection than the planners and the government would find justified, if protection were the primary motive for introducing this type of regulation' (1968, pp. 2085–6). In the meantime, governments are 'unwilling or unable to expropriate by internal excise duties or other devices the profits over and above those needed to make production for the home market a profitable venture'. '[T]he result[ing] ... high prices and high costs in the home market ... are deterrents to the growth of export industries' (ibid., 1158, see also pp. 670, 1161; 1970a, p. 287; 1984, p. 158, n. 7).
65. Contrast with the essence of the literature on directly unproductive profit-seeking (DUP) activities (for example, Bhagwati 1982). These were observations and comments that Myrdal made in the 1950s. They were elaborated upon in the 1960s and 1970s when he devoted more attention to the problem of 'soft states' in most underdeveloped countries. See Myrdal (1970b, 1981).
66. 'Even if those impulses [that a plan has imparted to a few conditions] were sufficiently strong to spread widely', Myrdal also notes in *Asian Drama*, 'development would be slower than if change had been induced directly in many other conditions *at the same time* and efforts had been *coordinated*' (1968, p. 1901, italics original).
67. Nevertheless, he asserts in *An International Economy* that '[t]he underdeveloped countries' way of handling their commercial policy will be one of the most significant factors in determining whether they will fail or succeed in their drive for economic development' (1956, pp. 253–4).
68. Myrdal intended to include under the term 'state' 'all organised interferences with the market forces'. He argued that the state 'has in fact become the main manifestation of this organised society, and has established itself as the controlling framework for practically all the interferences by other institutions and power groupings within a country' ([1957] 1963, p. 42).
69. Myrdal took pride that he 'became the first economist to write about the "soft state" and to have a chapter on corruption', in which he 'showed how its prevalence was hampering economic growth' (1984, p. 154).
70. For some comparisons with the West's experience with the emergence of 'strong' states, see Myrdal (1956, pp. 203–4; 1970a, pp. 245–6).
71. This insight of Myrdal into the drawbacks of discretionary controls seems to have escaped the attention of the economics mainstream, with the exceptions of Myint (1971, p. 296) and Little (1982, pp. 72–3).
72. Talking about economic planning in *Economic Theory*, Myrdal remarks that '[t]here is reason to expect numerous mistakes and in many cases total failure; but the alternative to making the attempt is continued acquiescence in economic and cultural stagnation, or regression, which is politically impossible in the world of today' ([1957] 1963, p. 84).
73. Contrast with the analysis of the political economy of economic development by Krueger (1993) that uses notions of virtuous and vicious circles under outer-oriented and IS regimes respectively. It is of interest to note that while in formal trade and commercial policy models the mainstream economists stick to equilibrium analysis and shun the notion of such circles, the latter are invoked by them in political-economy models as these appear to buttress their attack on IS.
74. About ten years later there was a hint that Myrdal started to believe there was a role to be played by the developed countries in shaping domestic institutional reforms in the underdeveloped countries. He thus lamented that 'in the developed countries very little attention is being paid to the prevailing inegalitarian power structure in most underdeveloped countries and, in particular, to the need for radical institutional reform to

make possible not only greater equality but economic development'. 'Ordinary people' in the former group of countries 'should be prepared to explore the grossly inegalitarian social and economic situation in most underdeveloped countries and give rational reasons for institutional reforms, thereby strengthening those who are fighting for reforms against heavy odds' (1981, pp. 523, 524).

75. For Myrdal's brief references to some of the problems caused by industrial cartels and the dim prospect in the 1950s of controlling them, see Myrdal (1956, pp. 47, 254, 264–5; [1957] 1963, pp. 65, 71).
76. Similar to Prebisch's notion of 'implicit reciprocity' (section 10.8 above), Myrdal believed that the underdeveloped countries would generally be 'compelled to use the whole of their export proceeds, foreign credits, and aid so as to keep imports up to the highest level. From this point of view import restrictions in underdeveloped countries are simply a shift of import demands from some commodities to others, and generally to goods needed for economic development. They do not imply a diminution of total imports. *Their import restrictions and export subsidies do not, therefore, decrease total world trade*' (1956, p. 288; see also 1970a, p. 295).
77. He also appealed to 'preferential treatment', 'freer entry to Western markets', and how the advanced countries should 'subsidize imports from these [underdeveloped] countries' (Myrdal 1968, p. 687).
78. Writing just a few years before his death, Myrdal recalled that in *The Challenge of World Poverty* he 'dealt with the responsibility of the developed countries' and he 'criticized their trade policies, and particularly their aid policies'. He then continued, 'Fresh thinking that could change my views I have done only in regard to the aid problem; otherwise – and I feel with good reason – I have retained my views from earlier periods' (1984, p. 159). The discussion in the present section thus far should suffice to illustrate to the reader that his criticisms of developed countries' trade policies date back much earlier than *The Challenge of World Poverty*. But even his reservations on aid policies might not be entirely new. Thus, in as early as *An International Economy* he suggests that '[m]igration, capital movements, *international aid*, and trade are not the primary means of achieving this closer [international] integration. ... They can help, but they cannot be relied upon to do the job. The major task is first to force economic development in the underdeveloped countries [through their national integration] to the point where a more unified world system can be solidly built' (1956, pp. 2–3, italics added).
79. Nevertheless, he continued to emphasise the indispensable role of domestic reforms in the underdeveloped countries. He thus contended that 'no realistic and truthful discussion of their international relations can be carried out, when abstracting from conditions and developments at home. A study of the effects of transnational corporations becomes defective without consideration of the power relations and the propensity to corruption among the rulers in the underdeveloped countries where they operate' (1981, p. 524).

12. Singer: Correcting Maldistribution of Gains from Progress by Tackling International Technological Dualism

12.1 INTRODUCTION

It is described in Chapter 10 that Prebisch begins his 1950 'manifesto' with the provocative line, 'In Latin America, reality is undermining the out-dated schema of the international division of labour' (1950a, p. 1). In that same year, in his article in the *AER* that is titled 'The distribution of gains between investing and borrowing countries', Singer declares that,

> in the interest of the underdeveloped countries, of world national income, and perhaps ultimately of the industrialized countries themselves, the purposes of foreign investment and foreign trade ought perhaps to be redefined as producing gradual changes in the structure of comparative advantages and of the comparative endowment of the different countries rather than to develop a world trading system based on existing comparative advantages and existing distribution of endowments. (1950, p. 484)

Both Prebisch and Singer, in these respective works, advanced the declining CTT thesis, giving rise to what is today commonly referred to as the PST. As indicated in Chapter 10, Prebisch's 'manifesto' triggered an onslaught by the economics mainstream. For being one of the two prime figures who advanced the PST, Singer was treated no differently.[1]

Would it not be more fundamental to ask, as in Chapter 10, what analytical framework Singer himself employed, not merely in Singer (1950) but also in subsequent works? And has the fixation on the statistical aspect of the CTT debate distracted attention from other important messages for development promotion that he attempted to get across?[2]

The organisation of the rest of this chapter is as follows. Section 12.2 argues that it was not Singer's intention to solely focus on the CTT in his analysis. The emphasis was rather on the ITT. Indeed, soon after the publication of Singer (1950) he proceeded to extend his framework of analysis to one that is much broader and richer than the one that is narrowly focused on the CTT.

The key direction in this extension, as section 12.3 points out, relates to technological factors. There appears to be traces of influence by List when he emphasised the utmost importance of a country's capacity to create wealth rather than the creation of wealth itself. There are definite signs of Myrdal's influence when he drew attention to international dualism, although he particularly attributed that to the dualism in science and technology.

It is far from trivial that the above quotation alludes to foreign investment as well as foreign trade. Section 12.4 thus builds on the discussions in section 12.3 to illustrate the role of FDI in Singer's analysis of 'international dualism' or North–South uneven development. It also shows why he did not pin much hope on FDI as an effective way of transferring technology and closing the technological gap.

Section 12.5 elaborates on Singer's critique of mainstream trade theories that is implied in the above quotation. However, following from the discussions in sections 12.3 and 12.4, one should come to appreciate that the critique is not a narrow one in the form of the PST that is concerned with the static distribution of gains from trade as the CTT allegedly declines for the underdeveloped countries.

Based on the discussions in sections 12.3 to 12.5, it should become obvious to the reader that the promotion of IS could in no way be the main, let alone the only, policy recommendation that Singer made. Section 12.6 describes how he reached a position of supporting IS that would be interweaved with EP. Section 12.7 explains his thoughts on regulating FDI and promoting the cultivation of indigenous technological capabilities in the underdeveloped countries. Although there appear to be not many indications in print that Singer actively engaged himself with the mainstream theory of commercial policy, he was fully aware of many of the drawbacks of trade protection. In some situations he was also ready to compare different policy instruments. The policy actions suggested in sections 12.6 and 12.7 necessitate certain policy space for the underdeveloped countries to act. Section 12.8 illustrates Singer's appeal for such space under the labels of 'compensatory action' and 'positive discrimination'. Section 12.9 is for concluding remarks for this chapter.

12.2 'TERMS' VERSUS 'FRAMEWORK' OF TRADE

Given the attention that the PST has generated and the controversies that it has stirred up over the decades, it is not surprising that Singer himself had carefully reflected on it on many different occasions. To help himself delineate some of these phases, he designated Singer (1950) as *Singer I* in a paper that he presented in 1971. That paper itself, which is titled 'The distribution of gains revisited', is labelled as *Singer II* (Singer [1971a] 1975). In 1984 he again commented on the terms of trade controversy when he contributed a chapter to the *Pioneers in Development* volume that was edited by Meier and Seers (Singer 1984a). He reviewed it yet again in 'Terms of trade: new wine *and* new bottles?' in 1991. Then he published 'Beyond terms of trade: convergence/divergence and creative/uncreative destruction' in 1998. These are in addition to many other instances of such reflection that would be hinted at in the rest of this chapter.[3]

What resulted from these reflections? For the sake of discussion the rest of this section will focus on his emphasis on different measurements of terms of trade, and more importantly, his efforts to situate considerations of the causes and consequences of their movements in contexts of development that are broader than the mainstream critics have recognised.

Which Terms of Trade?

When Singer wrote in *Singer I*, 'It is a matter of historical fact that ever since the [eighteen] seventies the trend of prices has been heavily against sellers of food and raw materials and in favor of the sellers of manufactured articles' (1950, p. 477),[4] the consensus among commentators is that he was talking about the CTT. Forty-eight years later, he opened the discussion in his 'Beyond terms of trade' article with the observation that the attention on the subject 'has perhaps unduly concentrated' on the simple proposition regarding the movement of the CTT (1998a, p. 13). '[I]t deserves to be emphasised', he added, 'that the PST – although statistically mainly discussed in terms of barter terms of trade – was intended as a contribution to the analysis of income terms of trade' (ibid., p. 15).

Where are the signs that early on he did not solely focus on the CTT? Singer recalled 'the emphasis on lower price elasticities and income elasticities for primaries in the early formulations of the PST' (ibid.). Indeed, one finds in *Singer I* his observation that,

> the rise in real incomes generates a more than proportionate increase in the demand for manufactures ... In the case of food, demand is not very sensitive to rises in real income, and in the case of raw materials, technical progress in manufacturing actually largely consists of a reduction in the amount of raw materials used per unit of output, which may compensate or even overcompensate the increase in the volume of manufacturing output. This lack of an automatic multiplication in demand, coupled with the low price elasticity of demand for both raw materials and food, results in large price falls, not only cyclical but also structural. (1950, p. 479)

'Nor can it be said', he added, 'that the fall in their relative prices has been compensated by its *total revenue effects*' given this 'notorious inelasticity of demand' (ibid., italics added). Lamenting how the reduced export revenues had limited the importation of capital goods, he contended '[t]here is little doubt that a sufficient stream of additional capital goods flowing into the under-developed countries to maintain, shall we say, the 1913 quantum relations, over the last two generations could have transformed the economic picture in many of these countries' (1949a, p. 4).[5]

This is very much in line with Prebisch's concern with the 'persistent disequilibrium between imports and exports' rather than the CTT (see section 10.4 above), except that Prebisch's emphasis on 'external disequilibria' was much more explicit from early on. It was not until decades after *Singer I* that he put it explicitly and loudly that, 'For purposes of providing resources for developmental imports (but, alas!, also for debt service) it is the income terms of trade rather than the barter terms of trade which matter' (2000, p. 37).[6] Perhaps it is partly because, as he recalled, commodity prices were buoyant at the beginning of the 'Golden Years', peaking in 1951 at the time of the Korean War. Besides, developing countries like India, Argentina, and Brazil 'had accumulated important foreign exchange reserves during the war which could be gradually drawn upon' and that 'there was no major debt problem' *circa* 1950 (1989a, p. 13; 1991a, p. 345). However, '[t]his happy situation did not last' (1989a, p. 13). Indeed, even in the years shortly thereafter and leading up to the first oil crisis in 1973, the so-called 'period of great buoyancy' of the global economy, 'the balance of the evidence is in line with the earlier predictions, certainly if real export earnings (capacity to import) as well as only relative prices are taken into account' (1984c, p. 82).

On the subject of debt service, between the late 1980s and throughout the 1990s Singer connected the turmoil in the international financial markets and the most catastrophic worsening of the debt position among many of the underdeveloped countries on the one hand,[7] with his terms of trade analysis on the other. While doing so he placed further emphasis on the ITT.

'The debt situation and the terms of trade problem', he thus suggested, 'are deeply entangled with each other in a process of mutual causation' (1989b, p. 3).[8] Specifically, 'the debt-service pressure leads to deterioration of terms of trade' (1991a, p. 348) as these countries were 'compelled to export and earn foreign exchange at any price' (1998a, p. 18).[9] On repeated occasions he extended this to a critique of the practice of the International Monetary Fund (IMF) and World Bank that 'urge[d] countries to be outward-oriented and improve their debt servicing capacity and balance of payments by increased exports, and to do this on a country-by-country basis and without much co-ordination between the different structural adjustment programmes', which thereby further strengthened the 'fallacy of composition' (ibid., p. 19).[10] But to complete the 'mutual causation', he noted that '[t]he deterioration of terms of trade, in turn, intensifies debt pressure: by reducing export earnings it increases the debt-service ratio'. With especially some parts of Latin America in mind, he described this as 'a clear case of "immiserizing growth" – a deterioration of income terms of trade as well as of barter (although not necessarily of factoral) terms of trade'.[11] Viewed from another angle, it could also be regarded as a 'variation of Fisher's paradox: "The more you export, the greater your foreign-exchange squeeze"' (1991a, p. 348; see also 1996, p. 157).

But the vicious circles do not end there when one considers the import 'strangulation' or 'compression' that is implied by the 'debt pressure'. Thus, import compression 'reduces the availability of intermediate and capital goods which are critical inputs in export production' ([1989c] 1998, p. 87). There emerges a new vicious circle: 'import reduction – export reduction – less foreign exchange – more import reduction' (ibid., p. 88; see also 1991a, pp. 348–9).

Did Singer consider the FTT? He claimed that he did as early as *Singer I*, albeit rather implicitly.[12] Thus, at one point therein he observes that '[a]ll the evidence is that productivity has increased if anything less fast in the production of food and raw materials, even in the industrialized countries but most certainly in the underdeveloped countries, than has productivity in the manufacturing industries of the industrialized countries' (1950, pp. 477–8). Looking back at the terms of trade controversy in 1984 as a 'Pioneer in Development', he recalled that observation and argued that

> if productivity in manufacturing increases faster than productivity in primary production – surely a justifiable assumption then and now – it must be assumed that the distribution of welfare gains based on double factoral terms of trade (allowing for change in productivity in the production of exports and imports) would a fortiori become even more unequal (unfair, undesirable). (1984a, p. 284)

Several years later, with collaborators, he summarised it in a way that also included a defense of Prebisch.

> It was explicit in Prebisch (1950) and implicit in Singer (1950, 1975)[13] that this downward movement in the CTT of primary products exporting LDCs does not reflect a faster rate of productivity improvements in the manufacturing sectors of the DCs and so implies an even greater loss in the LDCs' double factoral terms of trade. (Sapsford, Sarkar and Singer 1992, pp. 316–17)[14]

Singer regretted that 'many critics overlooked this point' and continued to criticise Prebisch and himself 'for using the CTT as a measure of gains from trade' (ibid., p. 317).

All said, Singer did not solely refer to the CTT in his analysis. The fact that the PST has mainly been discussed in terms of barter terms of trade in the statistical debates is largely because of the limited availability of data on labour or total factor productivity (Singer 1991a, p. 340). When his observations on productivity trends are taken into consideration, his analysis has direct implications for the double FTT. Last but not least, he did emphasise the ITT in his works, especially more clearly so beginning from the 1980s. In line with the re-interpretation of Prebisch advanced in Chapter 10, he understood that '[t]he tendency for lower income elasticity [of demand for primary commodities] than for manufactures (e.g. Engel's Law) is well established and largely uncontroversial' (1998a, p. 15).

Broadening the Analysis: From 'Terms' to 'Framework' of Trade, and Switching Emphasis from 'Commodities' to 'Countries' in the PST

There is a broader purpose that the considerations in the previous subsection serve. It is obvious from the quotation from *Singer I* in the Introduction section of this chapter that he rejects mainstream trade theories. (On this more will be said in section 12.5 below.) It is only natural that in the process of constructing his critique, he also sought to formulate some alternative framework of analysis. In this connection it is most important to note that in his contribution to the *Pioneers in Development* volume in 1984, he said that he 'should have avoided [in *Singer I*] the use of "terms of trade," with its narrower professional meaning of net barter terms of trade relating to prices only, and used instead "framework of trade" (or perhaps "Terms of trade" with a capital *T*) or some similar concept' (1984a, p. 286).[15]

One can indeed tease out certain ingredients of this alternative framework based on the materials presented in the previous subsection. Within the framework of mainstream trade models, the CTT has direct bearing upon the distribution of gains from trade. In rejecting that framework, Singer sought to consider more than just that static distribution. He felt the current of an unfolding process of uneven development, thus his reference to 'productivity trends'. Instead of being a static phenomenon, there are 'vicious circles' interlinked in processes of cumulative causation, and these have sustained the uneven distribution of not just gains from trade, but more broadly, from progress. The ability of the underdeveloped countries to reap more from the gains from progress depends, *inter alia*, on their ability to import capital and intermediate goods. Alas, the weakening ITT, and thus the capacity to import, essentially means that this channel is not functioning as effectively as it has been hoped for.

Separately, in commenting on Kindleberger (1958), Singer (1958a) realises that the emphasis in *Singer I* 'was too much on primary commodities and their characteristics, and not enough on underdeveloped countries and their characteristics'. 'The real problem', he continues, 'is not in the relation of primary commodities and manufactured goods: it is in the relation of underdeveloped countries to developed countries' (pp. 88, 87).[16] Indeed, *Singer II* put 'more emphasis on relations between types of *countries* rather than types of *commodities* (following Charles P. Kindleberger) and on the nature and distribution of technological power' (1984a, pp. 283–4, italics original).

This list of ingredients is only suggestive and is by no means complete. The next section seeks to make it more so by illustrating the central role played by the technological factor in Singer's 'framework of trade'.

12.3 CAPACITY TO CREATE WEALTH AND INTERNATIONAL TECHNOLOGICAL DUALISM

Capacity to Create Wealth: List's Influence?

In the years that elapsed between *Singer I* and *II*, he researched into what might at first appear to be an area that is not directly related to the PST. There was a pre-World War II view that generally showed pessimism toward further growth in the developed countries ('D pessimism') but reflected optimism toward growth and development among the underdeveloped countries ('U optimism').[17] In the early 1960s Singer argued that the mood should perhaps be switched to D optimism and U pessimism. Why? His answer sounded surprisingly Listian, for he proclaimed that, 'The fundamental problem [of growth and development] is no longer considered to be the creation of wealth, but rather the creation of the *capacity* to create wealth. Once a society has acquired this capacity to create wealth, the creation of wealth itself becomes almost incidental; it follows quasi-automatically' (1961a, p. 107, italics original; see also 1964a, p. 19). What did he mean by the capacity to create wealth? In his words, 'Essentially it resides in the *people* of a country. It consists of *brain power*, it is based upon the application of systematic research to the problems of production and of the best organization of the economic institutions of a country, research systematically pursued and systematically applied' (1961a, p. 108, italics original).

Singer also summarised the 'new factor' that converted D pessimism to optimism in the words '"technical progress" and "human capital"'. Anticipating part of the new or endogenous growth literature that emerged in the 1990s, he believed that 'a systematic expenditure on brain power and the application of its results to production is not subject to the law of diminishing returns. Quite the contrary, it is governed by increasing returns' (ibid., pp. 108, 109). To add more to the Listian flavour of these considerations, he noted that 'there is a further factor which would serve to produce increasing rather than diminishing returns in research and development. This is the mutual cumulative propagation of science and industry' (1964a, p. 20).[18]

Ten years before he called attention to the 'capacity to create wealth' he emphasised something similar in the process of development, namely investment in 'intangible capital'. This consists of 'intangible things of knowledge, of scientific tradition, of skill, of a scientific organization that is conducive to economic progress or economic development' (1951a, p. 2). Associating physical capital with the visible part of an iceberg and intangible capital with the submerged portion of it, he then explained that,

> Economic development consists in increasing the iceberg – both above water and below water – not only the tangible capital but also the intangible capital. The health of people, the strength of people, the skill of people, the education of people, scientific tradition, social co-operation, efficiency of government, good legal institutions, good economic institutions – these things are not capital assets, they would not go into your capital budget, yet they benefit the future just as surely as expenditure on dams and irrigation channels, machinery and all those things you can touch and feel. (Ibid., p. 77)

This serves to caution that 'development planning which concentrates entirely on physical projects to the neglect of intangible capital, of high standards of education, of good health, of a scientific tradition, of research, etc., is not likely to be a good development programme'.[19] In fact, 'It does not follow that expenditure which does not create tangible capital assets, is not true development expenditure in the same sense as expenditure on your capital project – it may be better development expenditure' (ibid., pp. 2, 78).[20]

It is the capacity to create wealth as he has conceptualised it that Singer thought was severely lacking in the underdeveloped countries and 'where this underlying capacity ... is missing, neither economic challenges nor economic windfalls create the kind of response which will lead to a closing of the [economic] gap [between nations]' (1964a, p. 23).

International Dualism: Myrdal's Influence

Singer's analysis of this gap between nations – 'international dualism' or 'dualism in the world economy' – is the counterpart to Prebisch's investigations into centre–periphery uneven development and Myrdal's studies of 'international inequalities'.[21]

Myrdal, in particular, appears to have a more visible influence on Singer in this regard. Thus, in another work that appeared in the same year as Singer (1961a) where he drew attention to the importance of the 'capacity to create wealth', he pointed out that '[o]ne of the clearest connections between the postward [sic] trend toward D optimism and that toward U pessimism is evident in the so-called "backwash" theories, associated with the name of Gunnar Myrdal'.[22] According to them 'the growth of D, apart from any beneficial or "spreading" effects on U, also exerts there certain harmful or "backwash" effects ... Up to World War II the spreading effects were more emphasized ... Now in the postwar decade the 'backwash' effects received more attention' (1961b, pp. 394–5).[23] However, he did not simply repeat what Myrdal had identified as the agents or causes of backwash effects. Rather, he added to the list, claiming that those 'backwash elements' had been witnessed variously in the following:

> colonialism,[24] capitalism, export of unsuitable science and technology, brain drain, private foreign investment, one-sided or harmful international division of labour, harmful trade policies, harmful aid policies (or even harm done by the concept of aid itself), creation of élites in poorer countries, unsuitable methods of training for unrealistic professional standards, demonstration effect in luxury consumption,[25] etc. ([1969b] 1975, p. 69)

As a result, '[t]he interrelations between the richer and the poorer countries ... contain elements which make the rapid growth of the former only doubtfully helpful and possibly positively harmful to the development of the latter' (ibid.).

As Singer continued to grapple with these issues, he started to characterise the factors as 'divergent forces' versus 'convergent forces' at work. 'There is the divergence principle of "cumulative causation," as Myrdal has called it – broadly speaking, "to him who hath shall be given." ... But equally, there is also such a thing as a process of "catching up," of "spread effects" or "trickle-down effects"' (1980, p. 71; see also 1984a, p. 287). Having sketched out a broader framework within which to situate the PST, he thus clarified that its 'real objective' is 'to argue for a tendency for international trade and investment to be a factor contributing to international divergence rather than convergence' (1998a, p. 16).[26] To underscore that he had since *Singer I* broadened his framework, he hastened to add that, 'It [the PST] is of course only one factor out of many'.[27] Besides, '[t]he PST leaves open the possibility that other forces making for convergence are stronger and overrule the tendency towards divergence'. Nevertheless, it 'introduced a discordant element in the optimism of convergence ... [and] argued that there are also elements of divergence operating in the world economy' (ibid., pp. 16, 18).

Hence, while Singer was able to talk about increasing divergence between the North and many countries in the South, he was also able to refer to the growing divergence within the latter group when he considered the rapid transformation of the NICs in relation to the rest in that group. In one instance he even, somewhat carelessly, viewed the rise of the NICs 'as an element of convergence, of catching up' with the North (1980, p. 72). He attributed this to 'the existence of stronger technological capacity, especially in human capital, in the tiger economies enabling them to retain the fruits of technical progress and move rapidly into the more knowledge-intensive types of manufactured exports, thus avoiding deteriorating terms of trade' (1998a, p. 17). As the ensuing discussion will suggest, if this is convergence, then it has not been achieved through freely operating market forces.

International Dualism Mirrored in Science and Technology

Among the various forces that contribute to divergence, the one set that received the most attention by Singer is the one related to technological considerations: the historical emergence of a North–South gap in their respective technological capacities to create wealth, and how that gap has been sustained and widened through a process of cumulative causation.

The seeds for such considerations were sown in *Singer I*, where he laments at one point that foreign investment by the industrialised countries 'has ... diverted the underdeveloped countries into types of activity offering less scope for technical progress, internal and external economies taken by themselves, and withheld from the course of their economic history a central factor of dynamic radiation which has revolutionized society in the industrialized countries' (1950, p. 477).[28] Consequently, they might possibly have passed up opportunities to engage in 'producing manufactured goods ... with superior efficiency' (ibid., p. 476).[29]

With the technological gap thus created, factors that are both internal and external to the underdeveloped countries would come into play that, if not suitably neutralised by policy actions, would handicap their abilities to learn and apply science and technology, and thus aggravates the divergence. Many of these factors are interconnected in processes of cumulative and mutual causation.

A couple of years before *Singer II* was presented, he thus declared in an article that is titled, 'Dualism revisited', that '[t]he international dualism in the world economy ... is mirrored in the crucial field of science and technology' ([1969b] 1975, p. 70). Therein he proceeds to systematically consider four interconnected dimensions of 'international dualism in science and technology' that have contributed to 'chronic widening inequalities'. While this is his first systematic effort to group these dimensions together, he had in his earlier works – even in the early 1950s – hinted at the first, and perhaps the more fundamental, among them. This is yet another reminder of how, soon after *Singer I*, he commenced on broadening his framework of analysis.

This first dimension has to do with the 'unequal distribution' of 'the process of scientific and technological advance in all its stages – basic research, applied research and blueprinting', where the heavy concentration was (and still is) in the richer countries ([1969b] 1975, pp. 70–71). By this he was not just referring to volume distribution; he was also concerned with whether the content or composition of what was mostly advanced by one would be appropriate for use by the other.

As early as the 1950s he was already pointing out how imported capital goods and the 'standard of technology' would be 'more advanced than what would naturally correspond to the circumstances of the under-developed group' because '[m]odern technology – which is equivalent to technology evolved by and for industrialized countries – is both deliberately and innately determined by the requirements and factor endowment of industrialized countries' (1952, p. 7; 1953, p. 24; see also 1961a, p. 111; 1961b, p. 395).[30]

In 'Dualism revisited' he laments that 'although the total *volume* of available knowledge has rapidly increased, at the same time its *composition* has changed so as to become increasingly less relevant for the underdeveloped countries' ([1969b] 1975, p. 73, italics original). Writing in the late 1960s he estimated that about 98 per cent of R&D expenditures were made by the richer countries. These were spent on solving problems,

> which concern the richer countries, according to their own priorities, and on solving these problems by the methods and approaches appropriate to the factor endowment of the richer countries. In both respects – selection of problems and methods of solving them – the interests of the poorer countries would be bound to point in completely different directions. (Ibid., p. 71)

Indeed,

> there is little or no technological progress in areas where the problem does not exist in the richer countries (typically, problems of tropical agriculture, problems of small-scale production, problems of utilization of natural raw materials specific to the underdeveloped countries, problems of subsistence farming and of subsistence crops). (Ibid., p. 74)[31]

Unless special efforts are undertaken at the international level to deliberately address these issues, 'agriculture, rural, small-scale production as well as production utilizing indigenous material and local labour, will be technologically neglected and backward' (ibid.).[32]

None of this is restricted by the distinction made in *Singer I* between primary producing and industrial countries. As indicated near the end of section 12.2, the kind of discussion above led *Singer II* 'to a realization that, for purposes of analysis, simple manufactured products (of the type capable of import-substitution in developing countries) share many of the characteristics which Singer I attributed to primary commodities ("unwrought commodities") as against manufactured goods ("wrought commodities")' ([1971a] 1975, p. 65). 'The manufactures exported by developing countries', he thus observed, 'tended to be technologically simpler than the manufactures imported from developed countries' (1998a, p. 14). It is simply a reflection that the technological gap, and the cumulative process that sustains or widens it, remain in place even after the underdeveloped countries industrialised.

To state this point differently,

> Singer I assumed the central/peripheral relationship to reside in the characteristics of different types of *commodities*, i.e. modern manufactures versus primary commodities, Singer II now feels that the essence of the relationship lies in the different types of *countries*. The investing countries are the seats of the multinational corporations, the homes of a modern autonomous appropriate technology ... Being all this, the investing country will tend to be the chief gainer from *any* kind of relationship, whether the trade or investment or transfer of technology involves primary commodities or manufactured goods. Vice versa, the 'borrowing' country will not gain, for lack of a modern autonomous appropriate technology, except perhaps for groups which are geographically part of the borrowing country, but are being drawn into the nexus of the investing or dominant country. ([1971a] 1975, p. 59, italics original)

Once the 'richer' countries have reached this position of superior technology and of monopoly in determining the direction of technological progress, they have also gained superiority in accessing the necessary information for bargaining and policy-making. One finds here a cumulative process at work, for, in the words of *Singer II*,

> Information, like technology, feeds upon itself. If you do not have enough information to begin with to know where to look for the information that you need, or to know what new information could be assembled, your initial inferiority is bound to be sharpened and perpetuated. And if innovation becomes increasingly complex and difficult to comprehend, the information gap is bound to increase further. This unequal bargaining situation will affect *all* relations between the investing and borrowing countries, whether labelled aid, trade, investment, transfer of technology, technical assistance, or any other. ([1971a] 1975, p. 63, italics original; reworded and reproduced in Singer and Ansari 1988, p. 30)[33]

In this manner he regarded the concentration of technical progress within the richer countries as '*the* basic determinant of the uneven distribution of gains from trade and investment' ([1971a] 1975, p. 65, italics original).[34]

Yet there are additional vicious circles at work. There is the problem of 'brain drain'. To the extent that the institutional environment and economic situation in the underdeveloped countries do not provide sufficient appeal to absorb and utilise certain kinds of workers and they emigrate to the advanced countries, Singer called it an *external* brain drain. Within many underdeveloped countries, a large portion of the already tiny amount spent on research and development could also be 'devoted to the problems and methods determined by the richer countries', thereby resulting in what Singer dubbed an *internal* brain drain. These respectively constitute the second and third dimensions of the international dualism in science and technology (ibid., pp. 71–2; see also [1970b] 1975, p. 193).[35]

The three dimensions considered thus far beg the question of why the stock of scientific and technological knowledge has not diffused rapidly from the advanced to the underdeveloped countries. The difficulties associated with this process constitute the fourth dimension of the dualism in science and technology. Thus, from a viewpoint internal to the underdeveloped countries, 'the transfer of technology may not be useful or even possible unless there is a domestic infrastructure available in the importing underdeveloped country capable of providing the capacity to select, adapt and introduce the appropriate technologies'. Sadly speaking, '[t]his domestic capacity ... is largely lacking' ([1969b] 1975, p. 72). There were 'obstacles to the application of new technologies arising from underdevelopment itself'. This engenders a vicious circle given that 'the resolution of many of the problems of the developing economies requires the application of science and technology to production, yet the conditions of underdevelopment itself tend to limit the possibilities for their application' ([1970b] 1975, pp. 195, 203). Then there are 'problems in organization of science', 'weakness of scientific institutions', and 'weakness of the extension and service types of institutions' (ibid., pp. 195, 197). 'The little that is done in the developing countries [also] fail to reach the minimum scale at which it is effective' (p. 192).

This serious lack of an indigenous technological capability in many underdeveloped countries in turn tends to sustain the circular and cumulative process of uneven development. For instance, 'the lack of endogenous appropriate technology prevents the domestic production of capital goods, while the lack of domestic production of capital goods and the need to import them from more advanced countries in its turn prevents the development of appropriate technology' (1984b, p. 428).

Externally to the underdeveloped countries, the transfer of technology is rendered difficult given that a substantial part of that knowledge is protected or kept in secrecy by all kinds of restrictive arrangements. When it is offered for sale, it typically comes at a hefty price to the less-developed countries. Finally, TNCs could be agents of such transfer, except that that 'raises problems of its own' ([1969b] 1975, p. 72). These and related considerations are the subject of section 12.4 below.

From International Dualism to Internal Dualism: Employment Crisis

The preceding discussion of tendencies in the field of science and technology – its increasing capital intensity, and the increasing dominance by the needs of the richer countries and lack of direct relevance for the needs of the developing countries – are 'closely associated with growing unemployment and under-employment in various forms within the developing countries' ([1969b] 1975, p. 67). Those tendencies, coupled with the generally rapid increase in the population and labour force, 'means that the total number of new jobs which can be created in the sectors reached by modern technology is insufficient to cater for the increase in population which cannot be productively absorbed in agriculture through the cultivation of more land' (ibid., p. 77).

Increasingly to Singer, 'the relevant forms of dualistic fission run along the line of employed versus unemployed rather than the more traditional distinctions between rural and urban sectors, traditional versus modern sectors, etc.' (ibid., p. 67). The result of widely adopting modern technology 'is bound to be uneven growth, economic dualism, inequalities, and lack of development in the sense of failure to reduce poverty [in poor countries with a low capital/labor ratio]' (1977, p. 3). The 'one-sided concentration' of the power to develop new technology in the advanced countries 'creates a condition both of continued and sharpening technological dependency and of continued and sharpening unemployment and internal inequalities within the developing countries' ([1971a] 1975, p. 61).

12.4 FOREIGN DIRECT INVESTMENT AND DUALISM

From early on when he turned his research attention to the underdeveloped countries, Singer was very alert to the possible impact of FDI on development promotion. Over time, the links between international dualism, FDI, and internal dualism were established with even more clarity.[36]

Singer I thus observes that 'the specialization of underdeveloped countries on export of food and raw materials to industrialized countries … [is] largely … a result of investment by the latter' (1950, p. 477). What one sees as the 'import of capital into underdeveloped countries' served, and still serves in many cases, the purpose of 'making them into providers of food and raw materials for the industrialized countries'. In passing, he mentions as examples '[t]he tea plantations of Ceylon, the oil wells of Iran, the copper mines of Chile, and the cocoa industry of the Gold Coast' (ibid., p. 476).

This investment process is, of course, in full harmony with the alternative interpretation of classical trade (and investment) models that was advanced in Part I of this book.[37] One can thus recall that it was Torrens's and Mill's recommendation that England invest more overseas and create more colonies to improve its CTT so that its accumulation could be maintained at high rates.[38] *Singer I* adds that '[t]he capital-exporting countries have received their repayment many times over', thanks to,

> (*a*) [the] possibility of building up exports of manufactures and thus transferring their population from low-productivity occupations to high-productivity occupations; (*b*) enjoyment of the internal economies of expanded manufacturing industries; (*c*) enjoyment of the general dynamic impulse radiating from industries in a progressive society; (*d*) enjoyment of the fruits of technical progress in primary production as main consumers of primary commodities; (*e*) enjoyment of a contribution from foreign consumers of manufactured articles, representing as it were their contribution to the rising incomes of the producers of manufactured articles. (Ibid., p. 480)

These considerations are also in line with the alternative interpretation advanced in Part I of the present work.[39]

But while '[t]he industrialized countries have had the best of both worlds, both as consumers of primary commodities and as producers of manufactured articles', *Singer I* laments that 'the underdeveloped countries had the worst of both worlds, as consumers of manufactures and as producers of raw materials' (1950, p. 479).

Among other considerations, '[t]he main secondary multiplier effects [from foreign investment] ... took place not where the investment was physically or geographically located but (to the extent that the results of these investments returned directly home) they took place where the investment came from'. This is where he cautions that economists should not become 'slaves to the geographers' (ibid., p. 475). Secondly, 'past foreign investment, and the type of foreign trade which went with it, failed to spread industrialization to the countries in which the investment took place' (p. 483). One result is that the 'differential in productivity between the export sectors and the domestic sectors of the underdeveloped countries' has persisted and 'the more productive export sectors – often foreign owned – have not become a real part of the economies of underdeveloped countries'. In that regard, 'they were really an outpost of the economies of the more developed investing countries' (p. 475).[40] All considered, he concludes that there is perhaps some 'legitimate germ of truth in the charge that foreign investment of the traditional type formed part of a system of "economic imperialism" and of "exploitation"' (pp. 479–80).

If the message in *Singer I* was not forceful enough, then *Singer II* was to put this 'rather more strongly and more systematically' ([1971a] 1975, p. 59). To fully appreciate this one has to recall the discussion in the previous section, which shows that leading up to *Singer II*, he had already broadened his framework of analysis by incorporating concepts like capacity to create wealth, international dualism (fundamentally rooted in science and technology), and internal dualism. Also, in accordance with his and others' advice, many underdeveloped countries had in the meantime commenced on industrialisation especially via IS.

In retrospect, 'Singer I took it for granted that new manufacturing industries would prove to be the "growing points" of a developing economy, in line with the prevailing "infant" theory' (ibid., p. 66).[41] He lamented, with the benefit of hindsight, that 'the new industries turned out to be infants all right, but sired by another man – the developing countries find themselves cuckolded in their infants. And the *recherche de la paternité* leads us to the MNC [multinational corporation] and the RMT (Rich Man's Technology) as the parents' (ibid.). *Singer I* describes 'the "infant" argument for protection ... [as] a sickly and often illegitimate offspring' (1950, p. 477), meaning so 'in the purely intellectual sense of the genesis of ideas' ([1971a] 1975, p. 66). By *Singer II* he was 'more inclined to view the infants themselves with a critical eye as to signs of illegitimacy' and was concerned about how many potential domestic entrepreneurs were 'displaced or aborted by MNC/RMT' (ibid.).

Thus, *Singer I* might have left the reader with an impression that any interaction between the enclaves or outposts created by FDI and the rest of the economy was essentially absent due to the 'lack of interacting multiplier effects or spread effects to the rest of the economy'. It suggests that 'the mechanism of international trade *cum* investment was not an efficient engine of growth, because in fact it might be disconnected from the borrowing country and more connected with the industrial or investing country' ([1971a] 1975, pp. 59–60). *Singer II* goes further by implying that,

> the engine of growth might in fact be effective, but pull the car in an undesirable direction, perhaps towards a precipice and catastrophe; or – an alternative metaphor – the engine of growth might work all right in the sense of taking the car at reasonable or even high speed, but at the same time the exhaust may fill the car with poisonous fumes, killing off the passengers (except perhaps the lucky one who sits at the steering wheel!). (Ibid., p. 60)

That is, *Singer II* points out that there is interaction between the enclaves and the rest of the economy, except that it is 'of such a kind as to lead to polarization (or sharpened dualism) within the economies of the borrowing country. Hence it clashes with objectives ... [that] are conceived in terms of reduction of poverty and more equal income distribution' (ibid., pp. 59–60).[42]

Implicit behind *Singer I* and *II* is the consideration also of the immense market power that many of these TNCs wield. Thus, writing for the *Pioneers of Development* volume in 1984, he first recalled that *Singer I* 'mixed together, without clear distinction, elements in the supply/demand analysis (such as Engel's law and low-income elasticity) pointing to deteriorating terms of trade, and elements relating to market structure and technological-financial power'. This 1984 article is the same piece where he indicates that he should not have used 'terms', but rather 'framework', of trade. With the benefit of hindsight, he regards *Singer I* as 'based on a view of commodity markets in which less emphasis is placed on the traditional neoclassical competitive market paradigm and more on bargaining power, financial powers and control of marketing, processing, and distribution'.[43] '[I]nternational trade between primary exporting developing countries and industrial countries', he thus concludes, 'is as much a question of power relationships as of classical markets and comparative advantages' (1984a, pp. 286, 285, 287).[44] Collaborating with Ansari in the late 1980s, they reiterated that 'the structure of international markets is an important determinant of the impact that trade can have on development'. 'The terms on which the developing countries can obtain foreign exchange, capital and technology', they warned, 'reflect the relationship between the rich and poor countries in the world economy. ... They [the poor countries] are also "takers" in trade negotiations and trade policy formulation' (Singer and Ansari 1988, pp. 62, 19–20).

Indeed, the discussion in section 12.3 above directly raises the question of how much TNCs could be counted upon to address the international dualism in technology. Singer's contributions to this subject were more noticeable in the period between 1964 and 1970, during which he focused first on patents and on the related subject of licensing the use of technologies (Singer 1964b). He was fully aware of the 'handicaps and possible abuses from which under-developed countries may suffer in connexion with patent licensing' (ibid., p. 43). For instance,

> undue financial sacrifices may appear not only in the form of excessive royalties, but also in excessive prices paid for materials or components or for the services of technicians obtained from the patentee, or an undue share of profits or an undue amount of equity transferred to the patentee in return for the use of his patent or for his technical services, unduly high management fees, etc. (Ibid.)[45]

He was aware of the TNC practices of shifting profits and resources between various subsidiaries to take advantage of tax differentials, foreign exchange restrictions, and the differential treatment of foreign exchange transfers under the labels of 'profits', 'export proceeds', 'import requirements', or 'royalties' ([1970c] 1975, p. 213). 'All these categories can be largely arbitrary substitutes in the internal accounting and transfer pricing' of the TNC (ibid.). In *Singer II* he linked these TNC practices with the perpetuation of external disequilibria in many underdeveloped countries, which linkage is worth quoting at full length:

> The condition of foreign exchange shortage, caused by the tendency for lagging export proceeds, would make the typical developing country highly dependent on foreign investment or aid, even for its import-substituting industrialization programme. ... This position of dependency will tend to create a situation where the real net export proceeds or real net import savings, even from successful industrialization, will be low and insufficient, *after* allowing for repatriation of profits, dividends, management fees, salaries of expatriate staff, impact of internal transfer pricing by foreign investors, etc. All these factors (transfer pricing particularly clearly) will result in unfavourable terms of trade and other transactions for developing countries generally, in so far as even their exports of manufactured products and their imports of equipment, spares, materials, etc., will be at prices expressing the conveniences of transfer within multinational corporations rather than genuine market forces. ... In this way, the export difficulties arising, perhaps initially, from the characteristics of primary commodities or simple manufactures, and their markets, lead to an on-going process in which the foreign exchange difficulties tend to be perpetuated, and the poor terms of trade generalized to *all* dealings between richer and poorer countries. ([1971a] 1975, p. 64, italics original)

In hindsight he felt that *Singer I* only 'saw the first link in this chain of events, but not the whole chain itself' (ibid., p. 64).

Singer expanded on the subject of licensing by 1970 (Singer [1970c] 1975; Schiavo-Campo and Singer 1970). He also started to pay closer attention to joint ventures (Schiavo-Campo and Singer 1970, Ch. 7).[46] He continued to hold reservations toward these arrangements. For 'essentially the foreign company will tend to treat the host country as a source of production and profit, while keeping the processes of research and development, of management policy and of output decisions centralized elsewhere, usually at its headquarters. It is also relevant that the foreign company will largely be concerned with larger-scale units of production where R & D work is normally concentrated' ([1970c] 1975, p. 210; see also [1969b] 1975, pp. 75–6). Not surprisingly, one finds him considering the deployment of 'investment measures' of different kinds to possibly better enable the underdeveloped countries to absorb more from the technology transfer. These will be illustrated in section 12.7 below.

12.5 CRITIQUE OF MAINSTREAM TRADE THEORIES

Even before one reaches the passage in Singer (1950) that is quoted in the Introduction section of the present chapter, one actually finds him boldly claiming that, 'The principle of specialization along the lines of static comparative advantages has never been generally accepted in the underdeveloped countries, and not even generally intellectually accepted in the industrialized countries themselves' (p. 476). In the light of the discussions in the last two sections, on what grounds then did he reject mainstream trade theories upon which the static principle of comparative advantage is derived?

Classical (Ricardian) Trade Model

Although he does not identify it by name in *Singer I*, he would later critique what he labels as the 'classical (Ricardian)' model in *Singer II*. There he observes that the implication for income distribution arising from the 'classical (Ricardian) theory ... leads to [two] optimistic conclusions for the developing countries'. Firstly, it implies 'a tendency towards improvement of terms of trade for primary products as against manufactured products'.[47] (Even though *Singer I* does not explicitly refer to the classical model, therein he does challenge this first conclusion.) Secondly, the classical theory 'suggests a higher marginal productivity of capital in the developing countries compared with the richer countries in which much capital has already been accumulated' and this would render it profitable for rapid capital accumulation in the former countries ([1971a] 1975, pp. 64–5), which is part of the reason behind the pre-war 'U optimism' that was mentioned in section 12.3 above.

In *Singer II* he explicitly points out that '[t]he more realistic introduction of technical progress destroys both these favourable conclusions at the same time' ([1971a] 1975, p. 65). How so? Recall that in the beginning of the third subsection in section 12.3, the reader is reminded that the underdeveloped countries have been diverted by FDI into activities that promise 'less scope for technical progress' (1950, p. 477). Implicitly, there is an element in the PST which 'emphasised the greater scope for technical progress in industry compared with primary production' (1989b, pp. 1–2).[48] This is traced to Smith, for 'he was quite definite that technical progress in manufacturing and industry is faster than in agriculture and primary production, due to greater possibilities of division of labour, introduction of machinery and increase in the "dexterity" of workers' (Sapsford, Sarkar and Singer 1992, p. 316).[49] This technical progress, 'by being specifically oriented towards raw material saving and substitution and thus counteracting the law of diminishing returns, ... destroys the basic Ricardian assumption of better terms of trade for primary producers' ([1971a] 1975, p. 65).[50]

Besides, technical progress 'keeps the marginal productivity of capital in rich countries higher than in poor countries, because it is concentrated in the richer countries and capable of effective application only in them or by them' (ibid.). This should be clear in the light of the discussion in section 12.3 above.

H–O–S Model

Given his recognition of the North–South technological gap and yet the tendency by many in the South – through hosting Northern TNCs, licensing, etc. – to utilize Northern technologies, *Singer II* went on to discredit the H–O–S model by drawing a distinction between factor endowment versus factor use.[51]

If one follows the reasoning behind the H–O–S model, then the labour-abundant and capital-scarce developing country would employ labour-intensive techniques in specialising in the production and export of labour-intensive products. This yields 'the happy result for developing countries of tending towards full employment (or at least fuller employment), more equal income distribution, saving of scarce capital and gradual factor price equalization [with the developed countries]' (Singer [1971a] 1975, pp. 61–2).

However, as Singer would contend based on the considerations indicated in the last subsection in section 12.3 above, 'the unemployment situation and absence of labour-intensive technologies in developing countries indicate … [that] factor *endowment* as such does not seem to be very effective as a determinant of factor *use*'. Rather, considering that the technologies employed by the developing countries in their modern sectors are 'capital-intensive, raw material-saving and raw material-substituting', he reasoned that 'it is the *technology* which imposes constraints and which determines the production mix and the factor endowment, at least in the sense of factor *use*' (ibid., p. 62, italics original). This led him to propose to substitute the logical chain 'factor endowment – product mix – technology – factor use' with the sequence 'technology – factor use – unemployment – unequal income distribution' (ibid.).

The upshot, albeit an unfortunate one, is that 'growing unemployment and inequality act as equilibrating factors which reconcile the prevailing technology (that of the richer countries) with the factor proportions of the poorer countries'. To *Singer II*, this is 'a deeper explanation of the maldistribution of benefits from trade and investment than the previous emphasis by *Singer I* on deteriorating terms of trade and foreign trade restrictions' (ibid.).[52]

As the second subsection in section 12.3 above indicates, this rejection of the model's prediction of a tendency towards 'global convergence' reveals the influence of Myrdal on his thoughts.

It is important to note that it is not only 'technical progress' and the associated North–South technological gap that Singer regarded as missing in mainstream trade theories. In that connection it should be recalled that *Singer I* is not just about foreign trade and income distribution. FDI plays a crucial role in the story told therein, as illustrated in section 12.4 above. Structural differences are shaped and reinforced by the historical emergence of international dualism in science and technology, with unregulated FDI as an agent that has in some ways reinforced that dualism.

12.6 NOT JUST IS, BUT IS INTERWEAVED WITH EP

While there is no doubt that Singer advocated industrialisation in the underdeveloped countries, there are some aspects of his case that remain to be clarified, including the kind of industrialisation that he would like to see.

Industrialisation: Which Cases?

Singer definitely did not make a simple-minded case for infant-industry protection in the compartmentalised manner found in the mainstream literature on commercial policy. His mentioning of this case by name can only be detected in several rather casual instances. Thus, in *Singer I* he reminds the reader that foreign trade 'may have had very different effects if we think of it not from the point of view of static comparative advantages but of the flow of history of a country. Of this latter school of thought the "infant" argument for protection is but a sickly and often illegitimate offspring' (1950, p. 477).[53] When he elaborates further in the same work on why industrialisation should be pursued, he actually sounds Listian. Thus,

> [i]n the economic life of a country and in its economic history, a most important element is the mechanism by which 'one thing leads to another,' and the most important contribution of an industry is not its immediate product (as is perforce assumed by economists and statisticians) and not even its effects on other industries and immediate social benefits (thus far economists have been led by Marshall and Pigou to go) but perhaps even further its effect on the general level of education, skill, way of life, inventiveness, habits, store of technology, creation of new demand, etc. And this is perhaps precisely the reason why manufacturing industries are so universally desired by underdeveloped countries; namely, that they provide the growing points for increased technical knowledge, urban education, the dynamism and resilience that goes with urban civilization, as well as the direct Marshallian external economies. (Ibid., pp. 476–7)

One could even detect here hints of his desire to cultivate a 'capacity to create wealth' that was discussed in section 12.3 above.

Based on the simple representation of the PST, the critics might regard Singer's case for industrialisation as directly derived from the pessimism toward commodity prices implied therein. A few decades after *Singer I*, he insisted that '[t]he advocacy … of industrialization in preference to primary commodity production … was never entirely or even mainly based on price pessimism alone'. Harking back to *Singer I*, he maintains that it was advocated because it was 'associated with greater linkages, more dynamic effects, economies of scale, learning-by-doing and skill development' (1984c, p. 82).[54]

Nor should the simple version of the PST be regarded as suggesting that Singer was implicitly making a case for the deployment of an optimal tariff by an underdeveloped country which happened to enjoy monopoly power in the market for a certain commodity. In the mainstream version of this case, the optimal tariff improves the imposing country's CTT, thereby enabling it to reach a higher social indifference curve and everyone in that country lives happily thereafter. It is not that simple for Singer. Collaborating with Ansari and making reference to the experience of the OPEC countries, they contended that the rise in the income of those countries during 1973–83 'clearly cannot be compared with the rise that resulted from the early industrialization of Germany or Japan' because this increase 'has not been occasioned by the emergence of a private or state entrepreneurial class that has enhanced productivity levels' (Singer and Ansari 1988, p. 24). Just a year later, authoring on his own, he concluded that '[t]he lesson of events of the 1970s for the developing countries was that assertion of commodity power without control of financial institutions, and not backed up by technological power, is empty and temporary' (1989a, p. 33). A few years later, working with Roy, they reasoned that, 'While it is essential for an open developing economy to have a strong trading position, this by itself is unlikely to be sufficient to ensure development'. Then making reference to Nigeria specifically, they pointed out that, 'In spite of the "golden opportunity" in the 1970s Nigeria failed to transform her economy. The sharp fall in the price of oil exports exposed the persistence of deeper problems, with Nigeria falling into the "debt trap" of the 1980s' (Singer and Roy 1993, p. 164).

Limitations of IS

In the first decade or so since the late 1940s when Singer turned his attention to the underdeveloped countries, IS was the widely adopted strategy as those countries pursued industrialisation. Singer had never appeared to have given any formal and detailed definition of what exactly that strategy would entail. It is as if everyone who was involved understood what it was about.

Not surprisingly, one could pick up from his works in that period and a little beyond references to trade instruments like 'protective tariffs', 'import quotas', and 'overvalued exchange rates' (1953, p. 27; 1959, p. 277; [1970c] 1975, p. 220). However, Singer was not oblivious to the potential pitfalls in employing some of the trade instruments. Thus, protective tariffs 'may saddle underdeveloped countries with permanently high-cost projects which constitute a continuing drain on national resources and thus prevent the very development they are supposed to promote' (1953, p. 27). He lamented the 'difficulty of terminating protection given to infant industries' and that 'there is the ever-present danger that "nothing is so lasting as the provisional"' (1958c, p. 95). In the case of an overvalued exchange rate, it is 'an obstacle to the development of local sources of supply in that it makes it profitable to the foreign company to import' ([1970c] 1975, p. 220). So although '[t]he strategy advocated ... accepts the need for pursuing protectionist policies in the Third World[,] ... such policies must be selected with care and executed with flexibility and skill' (Singer and Ansari 1988, p. 149).

Besides, he also referred to employing 'subsidies', promoting the 'growth of a capital market', establishing 'trading estates' (or industrial estates) that would be supported by basic services and 'general technical assistance', obtaining state 'provision of buildings and equipment' (1951a, pp. 72, 90; 1964a, p. 207), and setting up of 'pilot' or 'demonstration' factory (Schiavo-Campo and Singer 1970, pp. 130, 132). There was the recognition that 'important differences [exist] between infant industry protection through national tariffs and infant industry protection through preferences' (Schiavo-Campo and Singer ibid., p. 202).

Nor did he ignore the importance of having a strong agricultural sector while pursuing industrialisation. He proclaimed early on that, between those two sectors, 'it is a [mutually] cumulative relation and not a competitive relation' (1951a, p. 5).[55]

He also did not belittle the importance of promoting exports. Consistent with his attention to the ITT he thus indicated in the late 1950s that,

> The earning of foreign exchange by underdeveloped countries is crucial for attempts to step up rates of investment, for development, and for short-run considerations. This means the utmost promotion of primary commodity exports (without impairing the development program) and of import substitution, with maximum allocation of the foreign exchange earned to essential investment. (1958a, p. 86)

While he recognised that '[w]ithin limits, the effects of export promotion can also be achieved by import substitution', he understood that it could be so 'only within limits'. That is because 'import substitution will itself require investment with an import content; hence it may add to the immediate problems even where it holds prospects of a long-run solution'. Besides, 'import substitution may adversely affect exports' and 'it may result in uneconomic industries'.[56] As early as then he was claiming that '[e]xport promotion, *and* import substitution, will often offer the only immediately possible solutions to some of the problems posed by resource immobility' (1958c, p. 94, italics added).

By the late 1960s and early 1970s, when his reflections on the PST over the years became systematically crystallised into *Singer II*, he also came to be more critical of the IS as practised in many underdeveloped countries. Thus, employing the term 'genuine import saving' to indicate 'the need for combining import substitution with measures and policies to maintain productive efficiency, and the development of local supplies for the import-substituting industries', he concluded that '[m]uch of present import substitution is not genuinely import-saving' (1970a, p. 353; see also 1989a, p. 15).[57]

To say that there was an inadequate development of local supplies for the import-substituting industries is the same as saying that the attempt to hasten the cultivation of an indigenous capacity to create wealth via IS did not succeed, at least not to the extent that it should be hoped for.[58] There was continuing, perhaps even increasing, 'technological dependence' by the underdeveloped on the advanced industrial countries. This arose from the 'one-sided distribution of technical progress' ([1971a] 1975, p. 65). As explained in section 12.3, there are circular and cumulative forces that tend to render this dependency a 'continuing self-reinforcing relationship'. This would, as *Singer II* puts it, 'ensure that the real terms of trade continue to go against the developing countries and in favour of the advanced countries from which the intermediate inputs flow'.[59] Sadly speaking then, 'import-substituting industrialization becomes a part of the deteriorating terms of trade syndrome, rather than an escape route from it' (ibid., pp. 65, 66; see also Singer and Ansari 1988, p. 27).[60]

IS Interweaved with EP to Achieve Integrated Industrialisation

As indicated in the last subsection, Singer did not downplay the importance of exports. In fact, just the consideration of how important it would be to augment foreign exchange resources so as to alleviate the difficulties typically caused by resource immobility and inelasticities of supply 'would give export promotion a high priority in many actual situations in underdeveloped countries'. Besides, 'export promotion also offers an escape from the limitations set by the narrowness of domestic markets'. Thus, EP, '*where possible*, appears to be the natural answer to some of the fundamental dilemmas of economic development' (1958c, p. 94, italics added).[61]

With the benefit of hindsight, Singer reminded his critics that 'the development of manufactured exports (export substitution) by developing countries was difficult to visualize in 1949–50 to the extent in which it actually later happened' in the NICs (1984a, p. 287). 'ISI should have been proposed as a temporary and transitional strategy only; more attention should have been paid to the time sequences and linkages binding the growth of the domestic market with the development of exports' (1984c, p. 82).[62] 'The question is not whether EOI [export-oriented industrialisation] is *desirable* but whether it is *possible*' (Singer and Alizadeh 1986, p. 196, italics original; repeated in Singer and Ansari (1988, p. 113)).

A consideration that pertains to feasibility is that of 'fallacy of composition', that is, even if EP might work out for some countries at a certain moment, it does not imply that it would be workable if more than a certain number of countries were to adopt it. '[T]here must be scepticism', Singer thus wrote in 1980, 'as to whether such a performance [of strong export by countries like Brazil and Korea] could be generalized without coming up against immovable bottlenecks and resistances. As it is, the export success of the NICs, taken together with the world recession of the 1970s, has already brought formidable protectionist and restrictionist reactions from the industrial countries' (1980, p. 75; see also Singer and Alizadeh 1986, pp. 185, 196; Singer and Ansari 1988, p. 113; Singer [1989c] 1998, p. 91).[63] One should also recall from the discussion in section 12.2 above that he expressed the same concern against the push by the IMF and World Bank toward heavily indebted underdeveloped countries to export more so as to better service their debts.

But more fundamentally, he warned that some kind of EP, just like IS, could become a part of the deteriorating CTT syndrome rather than an escape route from it ([1971a] 1975, p. 66).[64] 'Just as import substitution *à tout prix* very quickly passes through its "easy phase" and then comes up against increasing difficulties and results in increasing distortions', Singer thus observed, 'so also does a policy of increasing the gross value of exports *à tout prix*' (1980, p. 77).[65] In other words, a country could remain trapped in 'technological dependence' regardless of whether it pursues IS or EP.

What strategy did Singer propose then? It should be one, he argued, where IS could be selectively and flexibly interweaved with EP.

Unlike many of the IS critics, Singer thus emphasised the importance of 'a previous phase of IS as a necessary base for subsequent or even simultaneous export-led growth' (Singer and Alizadeh 1986, p. 186). At one point he declared that 'perhaps it takes a dash of Japanese [to export]!' That is because that country 'could serve as a reminder that the development of a prosperous home market base has never yet hurt a country in developing its exports as well' (Singer 1971b, p. 196).[66]

In 1980 he labelled the desired strategy as 'export-oriented import substitution', under which industrialisation would be 'based as much as possible on processing and manufacturing of domestic resources, maximum cultivation of national linkages, and maximum promotion of domestic capital-goods production and national technology' (1980, p. 77). 'The watchword of the new synthesis', to put it differently, 'must be "Integrated Industrialisation"' (Singer and Alizadeh 1986, pp. 190–91).

By the mid-1980s, he even characterised the whole debate of EP versus IS as 'an absurd and silly discussion'. It is 'a combination' of the two that is desirable (1986b, p. 4).[67] Specifically,

> [w]e want export promotion but the exports must be based on indigenous inputs. Otherwise, ... the balance of payments contribution of these exports will be very small and so will be their contribution to the learning process and to indigenous technological capacity. In the same way, the development of import-substituting industries with a secure home market can, with proper policies, be the best basis for subsequent exports ... But, like export promotion, it can also be self-defeating if it itself develops a voracious appetite for imported capital goods and intermediate goods, and fails to lead on to a 'higher stage import substitutions' after the exhaustion of its easy first stage. (Ibid., pp. 4–5)

What is needed is 'an interplay between inward-oriented or import substitution efforts (where regional co-operation also has a great role to play) and export promotion'. He added that 'Prebisch saw this clearly' (ibid., p. 5).

Summarising his thoughts on this debate once more in the late 1980s, he stated that '[t]he truth broadly is that ... inward orientation is right for certain countries, certain sectors and in certain conditions and outward orientation for other countries, sectors and conditions, while usually a selective and phased mixture of inward-oriented and outward-oriented measures is best' (1989a, p. 2). However, as he clarified in collaborative works published at about this time, this is not the same as supporting an industrialisation strategy 'which is "neutral" as between IS and EO' that was favoured then, among others, by the World Bank. Instead, 'what is suggested is a systematic combination of IS and EO, with a different emphasis on IS and EO at different periods and for different sectors'.[68] Given the developmental situation in many underdeveloped countries,

> the sequence from IS to EO will be more frequent than the reverse, both in time and for given sectors. But EO itself will also lead to new opportunities for IS, to reduce the import content of exports and increase linkages from the export sector to the rest of the economy. (Singer and Alizadeh 1986, p. 192; reproduced verbatim in Singer and Ansari 1988, p. 149)

That should contribute to 'preventing dualism and a disarticulated industrial structure'.[69]

12.7 PRE-INVESTMENT, ENHANCEMENT OF TECHNOLOGICAL CAPACITY, INVESTMENT MEASURES

While the implementation of IS that is considered in the previous section would certainly involve, *inter alia*, the deployment of some protective tariffs, Singer was quite aware early on that that would only partially address the problem of technological dualism. Thus, just a couple of years after he indicated the importance of building up 'intangible capital' (section 12.3 above), he noted that underdeveloped countries imposed protective tariffs when they mistook 'the absence of a technology which is ... modern (in the sense of incorporating the latest contributions of scientific knowledge) and in harmony with the[ir] factor endowment' as 'merely an ailment of infancy'. 'Often, however', he understood, 'there is no real alternative. The only remedy would be the development of a different kind of technology, and this is beyond the resources of underdeveloped countries. This is indeed a formidable dilemma' (1953, p. 27).

While he thus advocated that IS should be interweaved with EP, he also emphasised the utmost importance of developing indigenous scientific and technological capacities within the underdeveloped countries. During the 1960s he expressed it as a need to establish some sort of 'human, technological, and data infrastructure', in short a 'pre-investment infrastructure' (1964a, p. 21). This is intended to address the 'inadequacies in trained and skilled people, in technical experimentation, in knowledge suitable to a capital-poor resource endowment, [and] in the power to identify and formulate concrete opportunities for a productive combination of factors of production' (1961b, p. 402) so that those countries could become 'capable of providing the capacity to select, adapt and introduce the appropriate technologies' ([1969b] 1975, p. 72). By the 1970s he described it as the need to support 'basic and applied research', 'pilot and prototype developments', and the 'necessary infrastructure of scientific and technological services – laboratories with their equipment, research institutes, patent offices, scientific and technological laboratories, training institutions, etc.' ([1970b] 1975, p. 191). That was the time when he wrote *Singer II* and he declared that he 'now would see salvation not in industrialization, but rather in the building up of indigenous scientific and technological capacities within the developing countries, or other ways of reforming the present system of concentrating R & D on problems and methods irrelevant or harmful to the developing countries' ([1971a] 1975, p. 61). If that could be accomplished, 'the uneven distribution of gains from trade and investment will begin to look after itself' (ibid.) and the 'technological dependence' on the part of the poor countries could be corrected and they could 'emerge from the depths of poverty' (Singer and Ansari 1988, p. 28).

To those who suggest that the underdeveloped countries should not waste their resources in developing 'national capacities' given that they could conceivably import from abroad all the technology which they need, Singer reminded them that the technology which those countries specifically need might often 'simply not exist'. He further retorted that,

> more importantly, the statement is inconsistent: a country which has no national capacity cannot know what technology is available to be imported, what the most suitable technology for itself is, where the best sources for such technology are, and what the best forms are in which such technology should be embodied – let alone bargain effectively about the terms on which such imports take place. ([1970b] 1975, p. 204)

What those countries should do is to 'find and select those parts of modern technology which are of value, and combine them with developments oriented in a labour-intensive, yet modern direction. This should be the real meaning of the search for an "intermediate" technology' ([1969a] 1975, p. 138).

Based on the discussion in section 12.4 above, it is to be expected that while part of the underdeveloped countries' efforts to build indigenous scientific and technological capacities will involve the TNCs that invest in them, Singer would consider deploying some investment measures to better accomplish this objective. As early as *Singer I* he advocates the 'absorption of profits by fiscal measures and their utilization for the finance of economic development' in the underdeveloped countries, and the use of 'royalties and other income from foreign investment ... for the transformation of their internal economic structure', except that such chances were 'more often missed than caught by the forelock!' (1950, pp. 484, 475, n. 3). FDI could be directed toward the 'more essential' projects or schemes (1951a, p. 88).[70] With the African countries in mind, he proposed 'a system of subcontracting and ordering' so that the TNCs investing there would source more components locally (1964a, p. 206).[71] With respect to the middle-income countries, he advised them to fend off 'restrictive conditions concerning the use of local suppliers, local products, or the local spreading of technological know-how' that various TNCs might impose (1980, p. 78). Most fundamentally, '[i]t is of extreme importance that the state should not be allowed to "wither away" in the LDCs but should actively seek to influence the decision of the multinationals investing in its country' (Singer and Ansari 1988, p. 260).[72]

On a related note, Singer feared that patent protection 'limits competition in the supplying countries and retards the immediate spread of the new lower cost processes, [and] it may fortify the dominant position of the suppliers vis-à-vis the under-developed countries' (1964b, p. 47). The governments of the latter countries should appropriately insist on 'royalty limitations' against the foreign patentees, 'requirements of local training, local management and capital participation, prohibition of unduly restrictive features as to supplies, markets', and 'compulsory licensing'. These are reflections of his firm belief that 'the patent system should not be used to retard and block local production and invention rather than promote it' (ibid., pp. 42, 49). In fact, anticipating some of the subsequent debates surrounding the Agreement on TRIPs reached in the Uruguay Round of MTNs as it relates to products like pharmaceutical items, he suggested that '[i]n spheres of production vital to the national interest and the development of special resources, or to public health, limitations on patentability or provision for limiting the scope of the patent grant by special working or compulsory licensing in the public interest are natural' (ibid., slightly abbreviated and reworded in Schiavo-Campo and Singer 1970, p. 119). More generally, 'it would be equally clearly wrong to devote some of the … scarce scientific resources to the building of the patent offices examining claims for patents to the detriment of other uses for those resources. In this later context, non-examination systems of patent issue might recommend themselves specifically to under-developed countries since they obviate much of the staffing requirements for patent offices' (1964b, p. 49). Even if one accepts the claim that patent protection in the underdeveloped countries could have a discernible effect in promoting R&D in the supplying countries, 'it would have to be questioned whether it is to the interest of the world economy that the poorer countries should be expected, by way of higher prices for their imports, to contribute to the recoupment of research expenditures in the richer countries' (ibid., p. 46).

12.8 COMPENSATORY ACTION AND POSITIVE DISCRIMINATION

The discussions in sections 12.6 and 12.7 are strongly indicative of Singer's belief that there could be policy actions that the underdeveloped countries could pursue to produce 'gradual changes in the structure of comparative advantages and of the comparative endowment of the different countries'. Such changes are expressed in the indented quotation on the first page of the present chapter and that passage is taken from *Singer I*. In response to the critical comments made by McLeod (1951) on the latter, Singer contended he did not believe that 'the present [early 1950s] distribution [of those advantages and endowment] is providentially sanctified, or that it is necessarily the best for the world as a whole'. While he understood that '[d]evelopment certainly is not a matter of willing it alone', he was also under the conviction that 'there are particular international arrangements under which an under-developed country *can* will economic development, and others under which it cannot' (1951b, p. 420, italics original).

The evolution of 'international arrangements' up till the 1980s led Singer to lament that '[t]he assumption of equal exchange in impartial "fair" markets seemed in conflict with the facts of unequal market *and* technological power. The dice were loaded against one of the trade partners' (1984a, pp. 280–81, italics added). There are 'elements' in such arrangements 'which work to the advantage of the rich and the disadvantage of the poor'. Specifically, '[t]o have a near-monopoly of technological capacity, research and development … capacity, know-how, financial power…, investment resources, entrepreneurial capacity, information, and briefing and negotiating techniques, will give the richer industrial countries an edge in trade, investment, growth capacity and indeed in all the bargaining and negotiations relating to economic contacts' (1983d, p. 195). These 'built-in disequilibrium in advantages', he added, '*does* constitute a *prima facie* moral (and perhaps also economic) case for compensatory action, i.e. aid in one form or another' (ibid., italics original).

What might be the content for such aid? It may take the form of 'tariff preferences, better prices for their [the LDCs'] export commodities, liberalised migration, etc., rather than aid in the narrower direct sense', and also 'with some degree of emphasis on technical assistance' (ibid., pp. 195, 196).[73] Elsewhere he also referred to some of these as 'acts of positive discrimination' (1984a, p. 281).

However, it should not be a surprise to the reader that based on the thrust of Singer's analysis as clarified in this chapter, the most fundamental problem to tackle is the North–South technological gap. This is stated most clearly in a co-authored passage that is quoted here at full length:

> The Third World countries cannot overcome the problem of underdevelopment as long as efforts are not made to bridge the technological gap that separates them from the richer countries. The poor countries must somehow obtain and apply a technology that takes into account their factor endowment and fits their needs and requirements. The key to the whole issue is to reorient the system of trade, aid and other forms of resource flows and transfer that characterizes the relationship of the rich and poor countries. If a method can be devised and built into the various transfer mechanisms that ensures that the poor countries successfully adapt technological developments to their own requirements and also create their own indigenous technology based on their own resource potential, every form of

> association and contact between the rich and poor countries will be of much enhanced use to the latter. If the technological gap is not overcome, no form of assistance, trade concessions, aid, grants, technical assistance or fortuitous price rises will prove to be outlasting value. (Singer and Ansari 1988, p. 31)

Hence, '[i]nternational cooperation policies must be devised that serve to remove this fundamental obstacle in the path of development' (ibid.).

All said, it is safe to speculate that Singer would have supported affording SDT to the underdeveloped countries in various agreements reached during MTNs. The discussions in section 12.7 would also lead one to expect that he would not approve of the Agreements on TRIMs and TRIPs in the form that were reached in the Uruguay Round, not to mention subsequent attempts to further extend them to the advantage of the developed countries.[74]

12.9 CONCLUDING REMARKS

Tagged as one of the two originators of the PST, Singer's contributions to development analysis received the same distortionary and misleading treatments as those of Prebisch. This chapter has sought to re-examine his works to clarify those contributions.

It is contended that while *Singer I* contains claims that have prompted critics to fixate their attentions on the movement of the CTT, he actually intended to put more emphasis on the ITT. In fact, his other works clearly indicate that shortly after *Singer I* was published, he sought to broaden the discussions from 'terms' to 'frameworks' of trade. The key consideration here is the 'capacity to create wealth', which hinges on the indigenous scientific and technological capacities possessed by a country. Influenced by Myrdal, he lamented how international trade and investment have over time, through processes of cumulative causation, precipitated 'international dualism', especially as it relates to the comparative scientific and technological capacities between the developed and underdeveloped countries. As he put it succinctly, '[t]he basic problem to tackle for the international community is the one-sided relationship under which the possession of know-how and capital resources are so unequally distributed' (1964b, p. 44).

To then claim that he was solely preoccupied with advocating IS to promote development cannot be more misleading. He was well aware of the limitations of that approach to spur development. Hence, among other suggestions, he proposed to interweave it with EP. But even then development could be limited if there were an inordinate amount of technological dependence by the underdeveloped on the developed countries. Hence, he emphasised the importance of cultivating indigenous scientific and technological capacities among the former group of countries. To this end he proposed establishing 'pre-investment infrastructures', suitably deploying investment measures to extract more benefits from FDI, and various means of technological transfer. These do not add up to a negotiation stance that is solely focused on trade, not to mention that the part that relates to trade is also not just preoccupied with tariff protection. Unfortunately, the distorting and misleading representations of his works have served to bury his substantive contributions that could otherwise have usefully informed the underdeveloped countries when they participated in the Uruguay Round of MTNs.

NOTES

1. Toye and Toye (2003) meticulously provide an account of the events surrounding the ECLA conference in Havana in May 1949, at which Prebisch made a presentation that was subsequently published in English as Prebisch (1950a). That account reveals 'Prebisch did not discover independently that the terms of trade of primary products were secularly declining, but relied wholly on the previous work of Singer' (p. 439). That 'previous work' is the advance version of Singer (1949b) and is titled, *Post-war Price Relations between Under-developed and Industrialized Countries*. It appeared on 23 February, 1949. Toye and Toye (ibid.) further explain the circumstances that resulted in an asymmetric application of the UN rule, that authors of its publications remain anonymous, to Singer and Prebisch. That is, Singer's name is not attached to *Post-war Price Relations* nor to Singer (1949b), but Prebisch's name is shown in Prebisch (1950a). According to Toye and Toye (ibid., p. 459), 'The main result of identifying the author was that the polished and polemical Prebisch rapidly gained greater recognition in Europe and North America as a "UN economist" than did the more understated Singer, who had published under his own name only in academic journals'. This could possibly explain, at least partly, why the mainstream onslaught on the PST has tended to give more attention to Prebisch.
2. Raffer (2005) is a recent 'eclectic summary' of Singer's works that, among other areas, touches on the PST. It also considers his writings on soft financing and food aid. The latter two subjects are omitted from the present chapter. In putting the PST in a broader framework, this chapter seeks to focus attention on Singer's emphasis on international technological dualism, which is partly created and sustained by colonial and/or FDI activities. This broader framework can better enable the reader to appreciate the thrust and nuances of his policy recommendations as much more than just the support of IS.
3. Shaw (2002) provides the first biography of Singer and contains an Appendix that lists his publications in a detailed fashion.
4. With reference to the story told by Toye and Toye (2003) that is alluded to in n. 1 above, one should thus also note that Singer had written earlier that 'from the latter part of the nineteenth century to the eve of the Second World War, a period of well over half a century, there was a secular downward trend in the prices of primary goods relative to the prices of manufactured goods' (1949b, p. 7, see also p. 22, Table 5).
5. Singer (1949b) also refers to the ITT, although in hypothetical situations of improved CTT. He thus notes at one point that 'changes in terms of trade should be analysed and evaluated jointly with changes in the quantum of foreign trade. It is only when improved export prices relative to import prices are not attributable to a reduced volume of exports that results are uniformly favourable' (p. 122). If, for instance, '[a] rise in export prices ... due to a restriction in supplies [is] of such degree that total export receipts (which are the joint product of price and quantity) are diminished rather than increased', then '[i]n such case, the total imports which can be obtained after the "improvement" in terms of trade are

reduced, rather than increased' (p. 121). By the late 1990s he would recall 'it was assumed that the income elasticity as well as the short-run price elasticity of primary commodities was lower than for manufactures, hence the income terms of trade would contribute even more to international divergence than the barter terms of trade' (1998a, p. 15).

6. Singer (1949b, p. 123) observes that '[u]nder-developed countries often have import surpluses representing borrowing abroad and foreign investment'. He also wrote in the late 1950s that 'the development of under-developed countries ... depends on investment, and that investment in turn depends on imports of capital goods, and that imports in turn depend on foreign exchange earnings' (1959, p. 276).
7. Even an oil-exporting country like Nigeria did not escape unscathed. See Singer and Roy (1993, p. 164).
8. This is just one of many instances where Singer's thought process, involving portrayals of forces of circular and cumulative causation, showed signs of Myrdal's influence. See, in particular, the second subsection in section 12.3 below.
9. 'During the period of the big debt build-up in Latin America between 1973 and 1982, no less than 30% of this deterioration can be statistically ascribed to the deterioration of terms of trade' (Singer 1991a, p. 348).
10. Singer drew attention to the parallel with Keynes's (1929) analysis of the German reparations problem. See, for instance, Singer (1989b, pp. 4–5).
11. There is certainly some immiserising-growth flavour *à la* Bhagwati (1958). However, Singer should not shortchange himself but should indicate that there is no cumulative causation in Bhagwati's portrayal of immiserising growth.
12. But note this sentence in Singer (1949b, p. 126), where he claims that '[i]f the deteriorating terms of trade for under-developed countries reflect a more rapid increase of productivity in primary commodities than in manufactured goods, the effect of worsened terms of trade would ... be less serious'.
13. Singer (1975) in this quotation corresponds to Singer ([1971a] 1975) in the present work.
14. 'The core of the P–S thesis ... related to a widening gap, or deteriorating trend in the double factoral terms of trade ... With productivity tending to increase faster in the industrial countries, the deterioration in the double factoral terms of trade is even larger than shown by our study of barter terms of trade' (op. cit., p. 328).
15. Despite Singer's effort in Singer (1984a) and other works to broaden his framework of analysis beyond one that narrowly focuses on the movements of the CTT, Balassa (1984), who comments on Singer (1984a), states that '[t]he terms of trade issue was central to Singer's 1950 article as it is to his present paper' (Balassa 1984, p. 304).
16. 'All the under-developed countries are agricultural (or mining) countries, but not all agricultural (or mining) countries are under-developed' (Singer 1951b, p. 419).
17. On the application of Keynes's notion of marginal efficiency of capital in making this distinction and how that application could be usefully informed by the notion of capacity to create wealth, see Singer (1961b, p. 401; 1964a, pp. 19–20).
18. Three years earlier he wrote something similar, saying that '[a]nother aspect of ... cumulation of discoveries is the mutual propulsion of science and industry, with each advancing the other'. In that connection he noted that there were 'mutually fructifying, supporting and stimulating elements' in the 'infrastructure' in the developed countries (1961b, p. 401).
19. A year after he introduced the concept of 'intangible capital', Singer made a related distinction by way of a critique of the mainstream notion of marginal productivity of capital. In underdeveloped countries, he argued, 'it is rarely possible simply to add a piece of directly productive equipment, and at the same time observe the ceteris paribus of marginal productivity. ... [A]lthough marginal productivity in under-developed countries may be assumed to be high, in view of the universal shortage of capital, in fact it is an irrelevant concept. The relevant concept is the productivity of the complete "package" of directly productive capital equipment plus that required to produce components or complementary goods, plus the provision of basic services required for the new investment' (1952, p. 8).

20. These passages serve to remind the reader that Singer's use of the term 'human capital' should be sharply distinguished from that employed by the economics mainstream. His distinction between tangible versus intangible capital led him to warn in the 1960s that there were weaknesses with the 'human investment model'. Specifically, 'above all it treats human welfare as an instrument, while it treats the increase of GNP or the accumulation of physical capital as a final value' (1965, p. 4). He went on to point out that, 'There is something, not only degrading, but also misleading and leading to wrong policy approaches, in the notion of "human investment" or "human capital." ... [A]ny improvement in human welfare which leads to an increase in income or capital will be called "productive investment," while any increase in human welfare which does not do this will be called "consumption." But this is obviously unreal'. Instead, a 'rational development policy' must look at 'social' and 'economic' development 'as a single entity' (ibid., pp. 4, 5). These were written at the dawn of the creation of the UN Research Institute for Social Development. Decades later he returned to the distinction of how the concept of 'human capital' had been used in various ways, but this time his attention was focused on how it is differently employed by 'the Chicago school' on the one hand and by the UNDP on the other. Thus, while many associated 'human capital' with 'Lucas and Romer', 'some of us also associate with the United Nations Development Programme's Human Development Reports, [and the concept] is clearly multifaceted: low human capital can be the result of low income, poor education, poor health, poor training, lack of employment opportunities, and so on' (2001b, p. 147).
21. See Ho (2008) for a short illustration of this commonality among the three, including the implications for arguments for 'policy space' for the underdeveloped countries.
22. Might Singer have applied the principle of circular and cumulative causation to development analysis even before Myrdal did, although he gave that principle a different label? He thus wrote in 1951, 'The principle of accumulation indicates that in economic life, in economic planning, we are dealing with a world which is rather different from the mechanical world. In the mechanical world, you have relation of cause and effect between different factors. A causes B. ... In economics, you have no cause and effect. What you have in economics is a movement of cumulation. If you do something, the position does not come to rest, but the movement goes on and something else happens. A causes B and B causes C and C causes D and in the end D causes a change in A again. Economic development is a cumulative process of this kind. The secret of development planning is to set in motion such forces of cumulation' (1951a, pp. 1–2). And then: 'I want to emphasize very strongly that there is hardly any development problem which can be treated as a purely technical problem. ... [W]hen you go into it, you have to take into account matters which relate to the economy as a whole' (ibid., p. 16). By 2001 he claimed that 'we have come to realize that "poverty" is multifaceted and requires action in many different fields and by many different actors... In the process, the subject is becoming more and more interdisciplinary' (2001c, pp. 517–8).
23. These and other passages from Singer (1961b, pp. 394–5) that are quoted in the rest of this subsection are reproduced in rewritten form in Singer (1964a, pp. 12–13). For additional instances when Singer credited Myrdal, see Singer ([1969c] 1975, p. 35; 1984a, pp. 279–80).
24. At one point Singer briefly considered the so-called 'restitution argument' and concluded that '[t]here is an economic linkage between generations which may take several forms' and '[t]here is no radical disjuncture between past and present' (1983d, p. 197).
25. Elsewhere Singer also included forces 'leading to imitation and thus promoting a premature desire for high-level consumption or premature ideas about such goals as the welfare state, social insurance, minimum-wage legislation' as elements of backwash effects (1961b, p. 395).
26. An earlier hint of this 'real objective' was indicated 37 years before this quoted sentence was penned. He alluded back then to the backwash effect where 'technical progress, with its attendant economy of raw materials, development of new synthetic materials, and changes in industrial structure, might recoil to the disadvantage of the underdeveloped countries by

leading to a chronic weakness in their terms of trade'. He further mentioned that, 'This line of inquiry was particularly closely explored by Raúl Prebisch' (Singer 1961b, p. 395).

27. It is worth noting that in Singer (1949b, p. 121) he states that '[t]he terms of trade ... are only one factor – and not generally the most important single factor – in determining national income and funds available for economic development. Nor does an increase in export prices, relative to import prices, automatically further economic development'.
28. As he put it more tersely decades later, 'Primary production ... tends to keep the exporting country much more in a technological trap' (2000, p. 37).
29. Regarding the gap in productivity improvements, Singer noted at one point that 'there has been an increasing gap in labour productivity in manufacturing in the industrial centre and the Third World periphery, from 1.8% p.a. (4.1% in the centre and 2.3% in the periphery) over 1960–70 to 2.4% p.a. (2.8% in the centre and only 0.4% in the periphery) over 1970–80' (1991a, p. 341).
30. In a moment of despair Singer complained that '[t]he adaptation of the mechanized technology in the direction of the smaller scale and demechanization is as difficult as it is to unscramble scrambled eggs' (1964a, p. 200).
31. Writing almost 20 years later with a collaborator, Singer pointed out that '[t]he ... poorer countries ... need research to design simple products, to develop production for smaller markets, to improve the quality of and to develop new uses for tropical products, and above all to develop production processes that utilize their abundant labour. Instead, emphasis [in the richer countries] is placed on sophisticated weaponry, space research, atomic research, sophisticated products, production for large high-income markets, and specifically a constant search for processes that save labour by substituting capital or high-order skills' (Singer and Ansari 1988, p. 44). He concluded that 'the spectrum of technologies available to developing countries is not widened; on the contrary, the range of suitable technologies – suitable that is for the LDCs [less developed countries] – is constantly diminished' (ibid., pp. 44–5). See also Singer ([1970b] 1975, p. 200).
32. Just a year later he represented the situation as a 'very lop-sided nature of the ... international division of labour in science and technology', 'problems of access by the developing countries to world science and technology', and the '"weight" and orientation of advanced country science and technology and its impact on the developing countries' ([1970b] 1975, p. 195).
33. 'The exception', Singer noted, 'would be aid or technical assistance directed towards equalizing access to information by supplying relevant information to the developing countries, or strengthening their information-gathering capacity' (op. cit.).
34. Almost 20 years later, working with a collaborator, he concluded that 'the poverty of the Third World countries reflects essentially the technological gap between them and the rich countries' and '[t]he real source of the maldistribution of the gains from trade and investment lies in the nature of modern technology and the process of its development' (Singer and Ansari 1988, pp. 25, 28).
35. Singer was to identify a third type of brain drain, which he called 'fundamental brain drain'. By this he means 'the failure of human brains to develop to their full potential as a result of malnutrition of young children in the crucial period of nine months after birth until three years after birth (when most of the human brain should be developed)' ([1970b] 1975, p. 193). This is just one of the many signs of his deep concern towards the well-being of children.
36. Bhagwati (2004, p. 163) labels Singer as one of the early development economists who 'complained that multinationals created enclaves within countries, with no spillover effects, good or bad, for the host counties'. While this applies to *Singer I*, *Singer II* does suggest that the spillover effects are bad. See the ensuing discussions in the present section.
37. Given that Singer rejected the H–O–S model, it is probably safe to suggest that he was not considering the impact of FDI within that framework. Had he not rejected it and subscribed to, among other assumptions, identical technology between countries, then with factor-price equalisation the *raison d'être* for FDI becomes non-existent.
38. It is obviously conceivable that such investments by various colonial powers in an earlier age and by the TNCs of the modern era could be at a scale that they contributed to

suppressing the CTT for the former colonies and present day underdeveloped countries. 'It is possible', Singer (1949b, p. 127) indeed suggests, 'that the stimulation of production of primary products through foreign investment was a contributing factor the relative decline of the prices of primary products'. It is also 'theoretically possible' that 'when the terms of trade show an improvement, such improvement will mainly benefit foreign companies operating within the under-developed country' (ibid., p. 123). He would later point out that one implication of *Singer I* is that 'the LDCs, even during the 1950s and 1960s, by providing the industrial countries with steady supplies of primary commodities (and also, I would now add, of simple manufactures and labor), on terms increasingly favorable to the industrial countries, were an engine of growth for the industrial countries throughout the twenty-five "golden years" after the end of the war' (1984a, p. 284). Appended to this is the footnote: 'Not least by enabling them to concentrate on high-technology lines of activity and to consolidate their technological leadership' (ibid., n. 24).

39. Although it was not brought up in *Singer I*, Singer (1951b, pp. 419–20) warns about the danger of 'foreign indebtedness'. In Singer (1984a), where he reflects on the terms of trade controversy and reminds the reader that *Singer I* incorporates FDI activities into its discussions, he suggests that it thus 'implies a concept of the terms of trade based upon the national retained value from exports rather than conventionally measured prices for export products' (p. 285). While this adds a pertinent and significant dimension to the conceptual basis behind the PST, it involves elements that are complex in nature and difficult to measure. Indeed, Singer did not attempt to estimate this in his engagement in the statistical debates revolving around the PST. Rather, his suggestion here is a reminder that he made quite an effort in his many works to consider the general impact of FDI on the development of the underdeveloped countries.
40. This second point resurfaces in Singer and Ansari (1988, pp. 241–2) but the discussion there is specifically geared toward the colonial period. There the authors also credit the 'seminal work' of Myrdal ([1957] 1963), noting that economic theory since then 'has held that private investment within the colonial framework and the pattern of international trade that goes with it have been the prime factors that have led to the growth of this structural deformity in most LDCs'.
41. See the illustration of Singer's thoughts on infant industries in the first subsection in section 12.6 below.
42. One could detect these arguments even a couple of years before *Singer II* was presented. 'The tendency for technological developments to produce internal dualism in the underdeveloped countries', he thus argued in 1969, 'is further strengthened by a number of factors, including the association of modern technology with foreign investment' ([1969b] 1975, p. 67). 'Since modern technology is imported from abroad by way of transfer, and for lack of an indigenous scientific and technological capacity inside the underdeveloped countries, the imported technology does not take root and is not adapted or sufficiently developed in line with the requirements of the country. This means that where modern technology is used its use remains limited to the specific area where it has been introduced, but it thus becomes an enclave of modernity' (ibid., pp. 74–5). Nevertheless, it is far from the case that Singer never considered the possible benefits for development that are derived from FDI. See, for instance, Singer (1951a, pp. 102–7) for a rather casual discussion.
43. Singer (op. cit.) indicates that this position of *Singer I* is shared by Helleiner (1981). Just a few years later he suggested in another article that, 'With international trade, and specifically also trade in primary commodities, dominated by monopolistic and oligopolistic production and trading structures, it is to the theory of imperfect competition [with contribution by Joan Robinson] rather than to the analysis of Marshallian elasticities that we must look for understanding and policy guidance' (1987a, p. 67). However, it should also be noted that in response to Kindleberger (1958), he remarked that he 'cannot see how "monopolistic practices on the part of the industrial countries" come into the picture [of accounting for the adverse CTT movements]' (1958a, p. 87).
44. It should be noted that by 'power relationships' he meant the ones between industrial and developing countries as well as those within industrial and developing countries.

45. Singer did not lay the blame solely on the then existing patent arrangement. Whatever abuses there existed were 'basically due to the monopoly of technical knowledge, management knowledge, capital resources and marketing access enjoyed by the firms and economies of the more advanced countries, rather than to the existence of patents as such. ... If only the existence of patent protection and nothing else prevented the transfer of new technology to under-developed countries, excessive royalties and other excessive restrictions under licensing agreements would hardly be possible to the extent to which they exist now' (1964b, pp. 43–4). He did not, however, make it clear whether the kinds of 'monopoly' that he alluded to can be attributed to the patent system in the first place.
46. According to the Preface in Schiavo-Campo and Singer (1970), Singer was 'mainly responsible' for Parts Two and Three therein and also Appendices A, C, and H (ibid., p. ix). Part Three consists of Chs. 6 and 7, which are on technological issues. Some parts of Ch. 7 and Appendix C are based on Singer (1964b). Parts of Ch. 7 are also based on Singer ([1970c] 1975).
47. Years later, Singer (collaborating with Sapsford and Sakar) brought Smith into this 'classical' theory too by recognising Smith's insight into how manufactures enjoy increasing returns. Specifically, '[t]he classical belief in a secular improvement in the terms of trade ... of primary products follows from two classical laws – the operation of the law of diminishing returns in the primary producing sectors and the law of increasing returns in manufactures' (Sapsford, Sarkar, and Singer 1992, p. 316).
48. Singer appeared to contradict himself on this when he wrote at one point in the late 1980s that '[t]his belief has proved largely unjustified, as shown by the tremendous increases in agricultural productivity in North America, Europe and the Far East, where technical progress in agriculture proved to be at least as fast as in industry' (1989a, p. 18; see also 1991a, p. 342). However, it is important to note that those increases did not occur independently within the agricultural sector itself. They happened *after* substantial progress and advances have been made in industry and science.
49. Recall that n. 15 in Chapter 3 above draws attention to how in the early 1990s Singer suggested that the policy conclusion following from the PST, namely that developing countries should seek their future in industrialisation rather than through exports of primary commodities, 'would be fully approved by Adam Smith, Ricardo, Malthus, John Stuart Mill et al.' (1991a, pp. 339–40).
50. It is not clear that just this aspect of technical progress would be sufficient. Elsewhere, Singer also referred to income elasticity of demand considerations and Engel's law. He thus gave credit to Kindleberger, noting that '[i]n 1943 ... Kindleberger published an article in the American Economic Review pointing out that the operation of Engel's law would create a presumption of deterioration for the terms of trade of primary commodity exporters' (1991a, p. 339). A year later, writing with collaborators, he reiterated that 'the credit for first turning the classical proposition "upside-down" should go to Kindleberger' (Sapsford, Sarkar and Singer 1992, p. 316). These technical progress and income elasticity of demand considerations are in *Singer I.* See the first indented quotation in the subsection 'Which Terms of Trade?' in section 12.2 above.
51. Two years before presenting *Singer II,* Singer, without naming the Heckscher–Ohlin Theorem explicitly, lamented that 'trade has not in fact played this major role conceptually attributed to it' in accordance with that theorem. Nevertheless, at that time he thought 'it still remains true that potentially this could be the case' ([1969a] 1975, p. 141).
52. The passages quoted in the present subsection have been reproduced with some rewordings in Singer and Ansari (1988, pp. 28–9).
53. Contributing to the *Pioneers in Development* volume in 1984, Singer recalled that in *Singer I* 'it did seem to be legitimate to ask further questions as to who gains [from trade]', which then led him 'to consider the possibility that in a certain institutional and power set-up the longer-term and dynamic impact on one of the trading partners could be negative, and that at least temporary delinking might be preferable until a better basis for trade with more evenly distributed gains could be developed. That, after all, was no more than an extension of the old infant industry argument into an infant economy argument' (1984a, p. 287).

54. For Singer's changing stance on pursuing 'balanced growth', see Singer (1951a, p. 103; 1960, pp. 79–80; 1961b, p. 404).
55. Singer's early conceptualisation of forces of 'mutually cumulative relation' was mentioned in n. 22 above. For details of how he applied this to industry–agriculture relations, see Singer (op. cit., pp. 4–5).
56. Singer's criticism of inefficient IS would continue in his later works. He thus lamented the tendency that resulted in 'rent seeking rather than efficiency as a basis of profits in protected import-substituting industries'. He was critical of the 'tendency to adopt imported capital-intensive technologies; concentration on items of luxury consumption of the type previously imported; absence of sufficient vertical deepening of the import-substituting industries, in particular a failure to develop local capital goods industries' (1989a, p. 14). Such criticism can also be found in his works with collaborators. See, for instance, Ballance, Ansari and Singer (1982, pp. 41–3, 46), and Singer and Ansari (1988, p. 110).
57. Writing in the late 1980s he observed that, 'Efficient import substitution with delinking from the foreign exchange bottleneck proved to be beyond the unaided capacity of most developing countries. The compensating adjustments have happened only for the limited group of Asian Tigers and, to some extent, in India and China' ([1989c] 1998, p. 89).
58. '[T]he sequence of import substitution pictured by economists implied the existence of a systematic body of measures to encourage the development of different types of industries in different phases of the development process. ... The relative protection accorded each category should have changed accordingly, favouring first one set of industries and then another. With few exceptions, this pattern of tariff setting failed to materialize' (Ballance, Ansari and Singer 1982, p. 41).
59. One can clearly sense Singer's effort to relate the problems of pursuing IS with his analysis of international technological dualism that is represented in section 12.3. Recall that at the end of that section, there is a subsection on 'internal dualism'. An earlier attempt of his to connect 'internal dualism' with the problems with IS can be found in Singer (1975, pp. 19–20), where these pages are part of a postscript that was written in 1975, not in 1960.
60. As he put it while collaborating with Alizadeh in the mid-1980s, 'The terms of trade of the "old" industrial consumer products versus the "new" and capital goods, may be no more favourable than those of primary commodities; hence old-style ISI often proved a dead-end way out of "unequal exchange"' (Singer and Alizadeh 1986, p. 191).
61. This does not come from *Singer I* but appeared eight years later. While commenting on Singer (1984a), Balassa (1984) nonetheless complains that '[o]ne finds no prescription for export expansion in the 1949–50 article or in any of the contributions to the Prebisch–Singer thesis ... Rather, the prescription – widely cited in the literature – called for introducing an anti-export bias in the system of incentives, with a view to improving the terms of trade of the developing countries and accelerating their economic growth' (p. 308).
62. These are points that Singer, sometimes with collaborators, had repeated quite a few times. See Singer (1989a, p. 14; 1999, p. 911); Singer and Alizadeh (1986, pp. 185–6, 193); and Singer and Ansari (1988, pp. 105, 114–15).
63. Singer also made brief references to the problem of tariff escalation in the developed countries ([1971a] 1975, p. 62; [1973] 1975, pp. 102, 106–7).
64. Singer mentioned that this warning was also echoed by others. See, for instance, Helleiner (1973).
65. In this connection he cautioned against the use of most international trade statistics because they were recorded in terms of gross value of exports, thereby concealing the fact that value added by exports within the exporting country would be much lower if the import content of the exports remained high (op. cit., p. 76).
66. Singer promptly cautioned that 'there is also a counter-lesson from Latin America: the building up of a pseudo-prosperous home market under the banner of import substitution may be more of a hindrance than help in export development' (op. cit.). However, 15 years later he cited Teitel and Thoumi (1986) to support the point that in Argentina and Brazil, 'the process of import substitution and development of domestic markets has served to develop technological capacity, experience, skills, economies of scale, linkages and

infrastructure which subsequently provided a useful basis for vigorous exports of manufactures' (Singer 1986b, p. 5).

67. See also Singer (1984c, pp. 86–7) for a similar position. There, and in Singer (1986b, pp. 6–7) as well, he singled out Park (1977) for having provided the 'best description of the purposeful interweaving of ISI and EOI'.
68. Contrast with Bhagwati (1988b, p. 46), who insists that 'on EP versus IS, you simply cannot have it both ways'. See Ch. 10, n. 54.
69. Not surprisingly, Singer also considered the appeal of South–South trade, noting that, 'The very divergence within the Third World creates new opportunities for intensified trade and other international flows, including specifically also interchange of technology within the Third World countries. ... [There are] tremendous opportunities for expanded trade to which the increasing divergences among Third World countries in factor endowment, structure of production, technological capacity, etc. should further powerfully contribute' (1980, p. 73).
70. Singer (op. cit.) realised it could be that 'in certain situations, the price of having foreign capital to help you with your more essential projects is to admit foreign capital in certain projects which you think less essential'.
71. Close to 20 years later, with collaborators, he proposed that, 'Domestic linkages can be fostered by promoting local subcontracting. ... An export orientation may be stimulated by emphasizing the establishment of joint ventures between TNCs and leading domestic exporters' (Ballance, Ansari and Singer 1982, p. 239).
72. Collaborating with Ansari, Singer proposed 'a revival of the discussion for the formulation of an international code of conduct for the transnational corporation, which has been stalled within the UN since 1979' (Singer and Ansari op. cit., p. 264). Into the new millennium, he continued to argue that, 'The problems of "governance," including the "governance" of transnational corporations, are increasingly important in development studies' (Singer 2001c, p. 518). While the initial cultivation of an indigenous technological capability would partly rely on attracting FDI, the long-term objective is not to become overly dependent. In his words, 'the extension of the PST from commodities to countries ... involved a shift from emphasis on industrialisation and diversification to an emphasis on building up technological capacity, entrepreneurial skills, and of "human capital" in general. Without such a technological capacity, a shift into manufactures required foreign investment or aid' (1998a, pp. 14–15).
73. It is interesting to note that in *Singer I* he said, 'The emphasis on technical assistance [to underdeveloped countries not necessarily linked with actual trade or investment] may be interpreted as a recognition that the present structure of comparative advantages and endowments is not such that it should be considered as a permanent basis for a future international division of labor' (1950, p. 484).
74. In an unpublished paper that is titled 'The Uruguay Round of GATT negotiations and Third World trade and development problems' but which was written prior to the conclusion of that Round, Singer asserts that 'regional or global preferential agreements among developing countries could certainly be beneficial to them' (1991b, p. 15). He shrewdly notes that 'the subject of the global multinational corporations is on the agenda only to the extent that it relates to questions of transfer of technology and treatment of foreign investment. (TRIM) Yet this has an impact on the prices of exports of developing countries, and even more of their import prices, and hence on their benefits from trade' (p. 4). Similarly, while services were on the agenda, they were 'not in the form most favourable to developing countries'. Thus, 'labour services – a major interest of the developing countries – is not on the Uruguay agenda' (p. 2).

13. Some Concluding Thoughts

13.1 SUMMING UP THE DISCUSSIONS

It was pointed out in Chapter 2 that the static classical trade model has earned and retained its place in mainstream trade theories because it is a special case of the two-party exchange the benefit of which is a fundamental premise of mainstream economics. However, there is in that two-party exchange story only static allocation but no process of development. What if production is added to render it a production-and-exchange model? As long as production technologies are assumed to be given and 'well-behaved', and resources are assumed to be fully employed, adding production does not really change anything fundamentally. There are simply additional marginal conditions to be specified in characterising the attainment of Pareto efficiency, but it is still through exchange – of goods within and between countries, and of factor-inputs between their owners and competitive firms within each country – that efficiency is attained.

That also means there is no room in the model for a process of uneven growth and technological development. Although in the static classical model the relatively backward country is, by construction, employing less productive technologies, emphasis is placed on the gains from trade that would nevertheless materialise if that country possesses comparative advantage in producing something. There will indeed be a gap in the *per capita* consumption levels between the advanced and the backward countries because the relative wage remunerations in the two countries must appropriately reflect the given technological differences. Barring exogenous changes in the given data (namely preference, technology, and/or endowments), that gap will stay put *ad infinitum* but will otherwise not change. Similarly, although the H–O–S model is not subject to detailed scrutiny in the present work, one can quickly recall the assumption made therein that countries – developed and underdeveloped alike – have access to identical technologies. It can thus be said that in order to focus attention on the crucial role of free trade in achieving efficient resource allocation, mainstream trade theories essentially presuppose that development has already been engendered in all countries, including the underdeveloped ones. This is especially the case when it comes to technological development. In other words, it is through trivialising the development process that mainstream theories succeed in putting a sharp focus on the benefits of free trade.[1]

Chapters 3, 4, and 5 advance an alternative interpretation that links together certain elements in the classical growth, trade, and investment analyses of Smith, Ricardo, Torrens, and Mill. It proposes that Smith's 'productivity theory' and Ricardo's argument against the Corn Laws can be regarded as constituting a powerful two-pronged case for the England of their times to push for free trade with her trading partners. If the suggested trade pattern – with her specialising in and exporting manufactures, while importing food and raw produce – materialised, then she could reap the division-of-labour benefits that were more richly associated with manufactures than agriculture, while she could bypass to an immense extent the barriers to growth posed by the natural impediments in primary production. Torrens and Mill both subscribed to the recommendation based upon this two-pronged case. However, both anticipated that when England would consequently advance more rapidly than her trading partners – through speedier accumulation and technological progress – the uneven growth and development would at some point necessitate renewed efforts on her part to colonise, or undertake foreign investment in, other parts of the world. Unlike the static version of the classical trade model that has long been popularised by the mainstream, this alternative version starkly reminds the reader of the historical process of uneven economic and technological development that has unfolded concomitantly with the expansion of the global trade and investment network. Thanks to this re-interpretation of the classical growth, trade, and foreign investment analyses, there may after all be valid reasons to be sceptical about the benefits of free trade (and investment) from the perspective of certain countries, namely those that are falling behind in the process of uneven development!

While Chapters 3, 4, and 5 illustrate that the classical economists hardly devoted any serious attention to the development situation in those parts of the world that were lagging behind England, Chapter 6 points out that this could be partly accounted for by their rather simple-minded belief in how structural changes could spontaneously be triggered in those economies under free trade conditions. Mill later broke ranks and offered a most cogent, albeit qualified, endorsement of infant-industry protection. With refinement of it over time in the form of the theory of commercial policy and thanks to the compartmentalisation of different sources of market failures, cases for trade protection (among which the infant-industry case is arguably the most important) have evolved to yield the impression that technological advancement and development is simply one market-failure correction away from happening. In most cases of such failures, the first-best policy calls for a domestic intervention (for example, through some sort of a non-trade subsidy) rather than a trade intervention. Should the country concerned happen to possess monopoly power in the international market for the tradable item under consideration, then an optimal tariff can be considered first-best. The message is that the 'protectionists' or supporters of IS were/are not even smart enough to know this possibility of policy-ranking. They are regarded as generally not too alert to the inefficiencies and limitations of an over-emphasis on IS; by implication, they have also underestimated the possible promises of EP.

Where the classical economists did not seriously direct their analyses – the trading partners of, and recipients of investment from, England (and later the industrial centre, when the late industrialisers in the West caught up with or surpassed England) – the developmentalists devoted their attention. Most of those re-examined in Part II explicitly concurred with Smith that there would be more scope for division of labour in manufactures than in agriculture. Hamilton and List (Chapters 7 and 8) thus pointed out the disadvantages for countries that remain largely, even if not purely, agricultural and the advantages of introducing manufactures. List also portrayed it more broadly as the social benefits of unleashing the powers of producing wealth when reciprocal effects could be harnessed between different parts of a society, including between agricultural and manufacturing activities. For Prebisch and Singer (Chapters 10 and 12), when Smith's observation on the different scope for division of labour between primary production and manufactures (including the implication of how an industry could, and did actually, emerge at some point that produces synthetic substitutes that would replace their natural counterparts) is combined with the generally higher income elasticity of demand for manufactures and the historical process of investment flows from the advanced to the less-developed countries to expand the production of primary products, the latter group would very likely experience persistent difficulties in their balance of payments.[2] That poses a serious handicap as they pursue development. Although he did not characterise the problem in exactly the same manner, Myrdal's 'master bottleneck' to development (Chapter 11) is a reference to essentially the same situation. For all five, to engender development, resources have to be mobilised[3] and be put to employment, not in occupations found in relatively stagnant but rather in dynamic economic structures. Among other things, that entails technology acquisitions, upgrading, and indigenous development of capabilities. These are necessary in order to narrow, even if not completely close, the gap with the advanced countries.

What emerges then when the mainstream version of history of thought is juxtaposed against the alternative developmentalist version here advanced is a fundamental difference in how the process of development is conceptualised. Through the lens of equilibrium analysis, the mainstream views development as achievable through efficient static allocation of resources. Underdevelopment exists and persists when market failures block efficient resource allocation. By implication, development is achievable as long as those market failures can be corrected. Compartmentalising different types of market failures, as the mainstream theory of commercial policy does, then becomes a necessary first step for the systematic treatment and diagnosis of policy alternatives within the mainstream theoretical framework. Based as it is on the Theory of Second Best, many mainstream trade theorists recognise that when there are constraints on deploying first-best instruments or when there exist more than one market failure, then probably some bets are off when it comes to policy-ranking. This is certainly an important caution. Nevertheless, one can judge for oneself how frequently it is hidden under the rug in the literature on the theory of commercial policy, thereby giving the impression that the development process is merely one market-failure correction away from being unleashed.[4] Effectively it is as if this important caution has hardly been offered. Rather, it is a sort of face-saving device that is retrieved in certain moments to cover up problems with the theory of commercial policy by arguing that, 'of course, the theory does allow for certain anomalies'.

With the exception of Manoïlesco, none of the six developmentalists re-examined in Part II employed a static allocative framework of analysis that is akin to mainstream trade theories. By seeking to challenge the textbook Ricardian model within the confine of the static allocative focus of that model, Manoïlesco's case for trade protection (Chapter 9) can readily be hijacked by the mainstream and labelled as one that is indicative of how *a* market failure is preventing the achievement of static efficient allocation of resources through trade. Refinements of that model then focus on how to rank different policy instruments that can correct that one single market failure.

On the other hand, Hamilton, List, Prebisch, Myrdal, and Singer followed a totally different approach. While these five also challenged the classical trade model, they sought to break away from that static allocative framework of equilibrium analysis. Explicitly or implicitly, they thus studied obstacles and barriers to the process of development that are inter-linked by the principle of circular and cumulative causation. Under the free operation of market forces, they regarded the development process as one that would tend to engender disequilibrium and uneven outcomes. As they articulated their respective perspectives of how the process of development could be unleashed, they understandably focused on these barriers and obstacles. There are three inter-related features to note in their analyses, however.

First, given that the developmentalists did not employ the static equilibrium framework, the notion of 'market failure' that is defined in that framework should, where appropriate, be carefully distinguished from what they referred to as barriers and obstacles to development. While in both cases conclusions could be drawn that some market interventions would be warranted, there could be substantive differences regarding the nature, extent, and possible sequencing of such interventions.[5]

Second, contrary to the portrayal by the mainstream, the developmentalists were quite aware of the domestic roots of some of these barriers and obstacles. To imply that they were oblivious to the domestic source of some of them, and that they consequently ignored the possible crucial role of some domestic policies, is to do them tremendous injustice. Indeed, as the chapters on Hamilton, List, and Myrdal clearly illustrate, these developmentalists were quite aware of the possible desirability of using some sort of domestic subsidies, or other non-trade interventions, over the reliance on trade protection in certain situations. This awareness was also demonstrated, albeit to a lesser extent, by Prebisch and Singer. And let it not be forgotten, even Manoïlesco mentioned that 'subventions' could serve as substitutes for tariffs.

Thirdly, they did not compartmentalise those barriers and obstacles into individually standing market failures, and trivialised the full complexity of the development process. Their holistic approach thus tends to yield policy suggestions that are multifaceted, unlike the advice of piecemeal market-failure corrections that are typical of the mainstream trade and development literature. The cut-and-dry policy ranking was simply not what they thought was generally possible in the underdeveloped world that they studied. Not surprisingly, one finds them supporting a variety of policy actions and instruments, with the hope of suitably impinging on different strategic phases of the process of circular and cumulative causation, and setting off virtuous circles that spur the catching-up process on the part of the less-developed countries.[6]

Keeping these three features in mind, one can better understand why the instruments that they proposed included not just tariffs but subsidies. There were not only trade but also non-trade interventions. All of them, especially Prebisch, Myrdal, and Singer, expressed reservations about trade protection and policies that were overly inward-oriented. List, Prebisch, Myrdal, and Singer explicitly emphasised the importance of interweaving EP with IS. Prebisch, Myrdal, and Singer, especially the latter two, all advocated the implementation of some social policies to tackle issues related to health, education, and/or housing. And all, excepting Manoïlesco, indicated their awareness of the significance of not neglecting the promotion of agricultural growth. List, Prebisch, Myrdal, and Singer, in one way or another, considered some sort of policy-sequencing. All six understood very well the importance of cultivating technological capabilities on the part of the less-developed countries.[7] While Manoïlesco's reformulation of Ricardo's England–Portugal model suffered from the defect that higher productivity could instantaneously be realised merely by reallocating workers from agriculture to industry, the other five realised the formidable challenge or even immense difficulty for the underdeveloped to cultivate their indigenous technological capabilities. In that connection it is worth remembering that none of these developmentalists, not even Manoïlesco, were solely considering trade policies for advancing development. In fact, it is perhaps more accurate to state that they, excepting Manoïlesco, were fundamentally more preoccupied with (or at least were quite aware of the importance of) policies that cultivate indigenous technological capabilities. Trade policy is only one part of this. Of greater fundamental importance are policies relating to technology acquisition and its domestic development (which included technology piracy or attracting skilled immigrants during the times of Hamilton and List, and attracting but regulating FDI during the times of Prebisch and Singer).

It remains for future research to further clarify and extend the developmentalist framework that is portrayed here. Recalling the note on omission of some authors at the end of section 1.1 in Chapter 1 above, one component of this future research should incorporate the insights of other thoughtful developmentalists – for example, Rosenstein-Rodan, Nurkse, and Hirschman – who have made significant contributions to improving the understanding of the process of industrial development. In that connection it should be pointed out that some of these three's (and Myrdal's) insights did catch the attention of certain mainstream economists. Thus, among others, Murphy, Shleifer and Vishny (1989) and Krugman (1992b, 1994) have made attempts to formalise certain aspects of their works on industrial development.[8]

13.2 IMPLICATIONS FOR MTNs AND THE SDT ISSUE

But even when one is just equipped with the re-interpretations advanced in the earlier chapters, it is quite clear that the significance of the differences between the mainstream economists and the developmentalists in how they have conceptualised development cannot be exaggerated. This is especially the case when it comes to evaluating the outcomes of past MTNs and pondering the future direction in which they should aim. From the perspective of the underdeveloped countries, the key but most controversial issue in such negotiations has to be SDT.[9]

When List made the 'daring suggestion' of convening a world trade congress to 'pave the way for the conclusion of advantageous commercial treaties' that would take into consideration 'the varied interests of regions and societies at different stages of economic development' (section 8.7), when Manoïlesco called for an end to the 'system of disadvantageous discrimination' that the implementation of free trade would entail (section 9.6), when Prebisch criticised the 'abstract notion of economic homogeneity' behind GATT because it 'conceals the great structural differences between industrial centres and peripheral countries' (section 10.8), when Myrdal proposed a 'double-standard morality' in commercial policy 'to the advantage of the weak and not the strong' (section 11.7), and when Singer called for 'compensatory action' and 'positive discrimination' in favour of the poorer countries to better counter the otherwise 'unequal market and technological power' of the richer ones (section 12.8), they were essentially all pleading for some form of SDT for the less-developed countries so that a sensible amount of policy space for state-supported development could be preserved.

But what would the SDT cover and what kind of policy space might the two approaches to conceptualising development respectively focus one's attention on? It would be useful for the ensuing discussion to strike a distinction between GATT-defined SDT on the one hand, and SDT that was for a while implicit and not explicitly defined by the GATT in the course of its history up till the Uruguay Round (hereafter implicit SDT) on the other.[10] It will be contended that, guided as it has been by its own version of history of thought on trade and development, the mainstream has mostly, if not entirely, focused on the allegedly harmful role on development played by GATT-defined SDT. On the other hand, the alternative conceptualisation of development suggests that sensibly utilising the policy space under GATT-defined *and* implicit SDT might be pivotal to engendering development.

The most obvious form of GATT-defined SDT is, of course, contained in Article XVIII, which is entitled 'Government Assistance to Economic Development'. In the words of Dam, 'The theory of the article is quite simply that less developed countries should be freer than developed countries to impose quantitative and other restrictions in order to protect infant industries and to combat payments imbalances' (1970, p. 227). 'The upshot', as Hindley put it, 'is that developing countries are able to adjust their tariffs and impose QRs almost at will' (1987, p. 68).[11] This focus on protection through trade instruments is fully consistent with the concern of mainstream theorists.

Two other forms of GATT-defined SDT that have received attention by the mainstream are 'non-reciprocity' in MTNs and the Generalized System of Preferences (GSP) beginning from 1970.[12] GSP has made possible conditional access for selected exports by selected underdeveloped countries to the markets in the developed countries. Thanks to 'non-reciprocity', the underdeveloped countries were not expected to reciprocate when such market access was conferred. That is, they did not have to lower their trade protection to reciprocate. Mainstream economists claim that as a result, the market access attained through GSP has been limited; the less-developed countries would gain more by abandoning non-reciprocity.

The discussions in Chapters 7 to 12 have hopefully convinced the reader that the developmentalists were much more sophisticated and nuanced in their policy thinking when it came to development promotion. Make no mistake that any of the six ever advocated complete autarky. All wanted the underdeveloped countries to trade, only not in free and unimpeded ways, but rather in manners that are suitably managed and directed by those countries. Most were aware of how industrialisation that merely aimed at serving the domestic market behind excessive trade protection would hurt development. They did not advocate that approach and it does them tremendous injustice to portray them as such. But even if one accepts for a moment that GATT-defined SDT is the only kind of SDT that is at stake, one can still find major differences in the positions taken by the mainstream theorists and the developmentalists. As explained above, the former would certainly advocate reductions in protection and a return to reciprocity on the part of the underdeveloped countries. On the other hand, the latter would caution that if such reduction is prematurely undertaken, it could mean that the policy space for deploying trade instruments as provided by the GATT-defined SDT is dangerously eroded.[13]

And as the discussions in Chapters 10 to 12 have made clear, when it comes to trade policies, Prebisch, Myrdal, and Singer recommended preserving policy space so that state actions could be taken to both protect against imports and promote exports. The latter effort does not just depend upon GSP. It could be facilitated by export subsidies and the ability on the part of the underdeveloped countries to utilise these had for a while constituted an implicit SDT. That was rendered explicit in the Tokyo Round of MTNs when one of the codes addressing non-tariff barriers explicitly excused those countries from the prohibition on such subsidies on non-primary products to which the developed countries were subject.[14]

Together with the GATT-defined SDT, the aforementioned area of implicit SDT had enabled a managed trade policy that was part of a larger picture of an effort to engender development. The chapters in Part II thus clarify that the developmentalists were also aware of the possible advantages of deploying non-trade interventions in certain situations, including different kinds of domestic subsidies. Prior to the Uruguay Round, the ability to deploy most of these subsidies again constituted an area of implicit SDT. In principle, countervailing duties (CVD) could possibly be applied to retaliate against both developed and underdeveloped countries that allegedly subsidise their producers in some ways. Nevertheless, when it came to the 'nonviolation nullification or impairment' claim, the latter group of countries could be regarded as 'off the hook' to the extent that the principle of non-reciprocity still applied.[15]

The developmentalists, excepting Manoïlesco, also emphasised the importance of policies that would encourage and induce the cultivation of indigenous technological capabilities. To the extent that such cultivation could be assisted through hosting FDI, then there is the additional consideration of sensibly regulating and directing FDI activities to that end (which was not an issue that had emerged in its modern form during the times of Hamilton and List). In yet another way prior to the Uruguay Round, the underdeveloped countries enjoyed implicit SDT when it came to intellectual-property rights (IPR) protection and the use of TRIMs. Thus, the fact that these were not on the agenda while there existed non-GATT agreements among the developed countries on some of these subjects meant *de facto* that the underdeveloped countries enjoyed some implicit SDT in those areas.[16]

All said, prior to the Uruguay Round of MTNs the policy space for deploying export and domestic subsidies, using TRIMs, and implementing less restrictive IPR protection were all possible thanks to what can retrospectively be labelled as the implicit SDT that was in place. Thus, the SDT that the developmentalists could count on, explicitly and implicitly, was not just confined to the policy space for restricting imports. It extends to the space for employing subsidies (and other domestic policies), policies that pertain to the cultivation of indigenous technological capabilities, and the regulation and direction of FDI activities. The mainstream portrayal that the less-developed countries, in pursuing development promotion policies, mainly, if not entirely, wanted SDT to afford trade protection against imports is thus badly missing the point.[17] Combining the GATT-defined and implicit forms of SDT, one obtains a relatively holistic definition of the policy space for development promotion. Instead of a narrow focus on static resource allocation through trade with given technological capabilities as in the mainstream approach, it draws attention to how by deploying a multitude of policy instruments and establishing supporting institutions, sustained development could be engendered through interweaving IS with EP, sensibly regulating FDI, and the cultivation of indigenous technological capabilities.

13.3 IMPLICATIONS FOR EMPIRICAL STUDIES

The existence of policy space – from both GATT-defined and implicit SDT – is one thing, the capacity for, and the capability to put to, actual and effective use of that space has obviously varied significantly across the less-developed countries. What policies had various less-developed countries actually deployed that were allowed in the policy space as defined under *both* kinds of SDT? Could there be some significant differences between the successful developing countries (for example, the Asian Tigers) and the less successful ones in how the policies allowed under the two forms of SDTs were combined and used? Is there any possibility of generalising how certain combinations of instruments or actions might tend to more likely yield desirable/undesirable effects in some sense?

As is to be expected, the mainstream version of history of thought in trade and development has informed and shaped, in a dominant fashion, the conduct of empirical research in ascertaining the impact of trade policies on economic performance. Considering how voluminous that body of research work is, this section can only offer brief and rather suggestive comments.

Given the misrepresentation and distortion in that version that resulted in the creation of the 'protectionist' straw-man, one will understandably expect attempts to measure the level of 'protection' or the 'degree of openness' of different countries over some sample period or of a certain group of countries over different periods. The goal is to determine if such measurements might turn out to correlate with different levels of economic performance (for instance, different rates of growth).

Beginning from the 1970s the economics mainstream appeared to be able to gather an increasing volume of empirical evidence from some less-developed countries in the post-war period to buttress its theoretical position. Indeed, it has generally focused on some relatively narrow characterisation of IS and then sought to empirically show that that would not be as effective in engendering growth as EP (or regimes of more liberalised trade). One significant representation of this type of exercise is the World Bank (1987),[18] although in some fundamental ways Little, Scitovsky and Scott (1970), Balassa and associates (1971), Bhagwati (1978), and Krueger (1978) have laid the conceptual foundation for it.[19] Into the 1990s, the push for trade liberalisation gathered further momentum thanks to the results of additional empirical work by, for instance, Dollar (1992), Sachs and Warner (1995), Edwards (1998), and so on.

Interpreting such findings within the framework that is founded upon its version of history of thought, it should be of no surprise that within the economics mainstream many have argued, at times vehemently, that GATT-defined SDT has proven to be undesirable or even a hindrance in promoting development (Srinivasan 1982; Hindley 1987; M. Wolf 1987; Balassa 1988; Finger 1991). Finger concluded in the early 1990s, when the Uruguay Round of MTNs was still proceeding, that 'the GATT has come to institutionalize a set of economic presumptions shown to be inappropriate' (1991, p. 203). Attributing the views that supported the 'right to asymmetric trade policies' to the ECLA, Sachs and Warner (1995, p. 17) lament that 'this "right" was the proverbial rope on which to hang one's own economy!' In a similarly dismissive tone Bhagwati (2008, p. 28) retorts to the claim of a 'need for policy space' by caricaturing that, 'Once a man shot himself in the foot and, when asked why he had done so, explained that he was exercising his "policy space"'.

The first significant empirical attempt to 'question the dogma that protectionism has necessarily a negative impact on an economy' has to be the works of Bairoch in the late 1980s and early 1990s (Bairoch 1989, 1993). Focusing on nineteenth century world economic history he concluded from the cases he studied that 'protectionism [had] led to, or at least was concomitant with, industrialization and economic development'. On the other hand the 'compulsory economic liberalism' imposed on the 'future Third World' of that time 'is a major element in explaining the delay in its industrialization' (Bairoch 1993, pp. 54, 53).[20] Directly or indirectly, his works have stimulated further mainstream research – for instance, O'Rourke (2000), Clemens and Williamson (2001), Irwin (2001, 2002b) – that attempt to resolve the so-called 'tariff-growth paradox'.

Having meticulously established the alternative developmentalist interpretation in the earlier chapters of the present work, it is not totally clear whose theory these aforementioned empirical exercises are intended to discredit or support.[21] None of the developmentalists, not even Manoïlesco strictly speaking, drew the simple conclusion that tariffs *per se*, or trade protection generally, would necessarily promote growth. In that regard, the mainstream version of history of thought has misguided, in quite an unfortunate manner, the conduct of research in hunting for the key to unleashing development. There are some, probably still strongly conditioned by that version of history of thought, who regarded '[t]he construction of a superior index of *protection*, on a uniform basis, for as many countries as possible during the late 19th century should be a major research priority' (O'Rourke 2000, p. 476, italics added). Others appear to resign to the fact that 'the effects of trade policy on growth are probably swamped by *other* policies and unrelated factors so that one cannot isolate the true impact of *trade* policy' (Irwin 2001, p. 20, italics added)[22] or have become 'skeptical that there is a general, unambiguous relationship between *trade* openness and growth waiting to be discovered' (Rodríguez and Rodrik 2000, p. 266, italics added).

Over the last two decades or so some other researchers, most of which can be regarded as seeking to study development with approaches that are alternative to the mainstream, have posed serious challenges to, or offered forceful critiques of, the aforementioned mainstream empirical exercises and interpretations. These include, but are by no means restricted to, Pack and Westphal (1986), Amsden (1989), Wade (1990), Lall (1996, 1999), Nelson and Pack (1999, 2003), Chang (2002), and Shafaeddin (2005a).[23] One should not confuse them as merely making efforts to support Bairoch's hypotheses. At the risk of over-generalising, their works can collectively be regarded as illustrating the importance of cultivating indigenous technological capabilities in achieving development (thereby rendering trade considerations as secondary to technological ones in some sense), demonstrating how IS has been interweaved with EP, and showing that both trade and non-trade instruments have typically been deployed simultaneously in the successful development programmes in East and Southeast Asia. If the countries in these latter regions that have shown signs of successful development can be argued to have achieved this thanks to not just GATT-defined, but also to the implicit forms of, SDT, should the mainstream conclusion on the ineffectiveness of the protectionist aspect of GATT-defined SDT then be qualified?[24] Writing more than ten years after the publication of his *Governing the Market*, Wade (2003, p. 636) thus concludes that,

> the central challenge of national development strategy is to combine the principle of comparative advantage with the principle of import replacement in a way that generates pressure for upgrading and diversifying national production. This does not always imply protection. Strategic economics prescribes free trade, protection, subsidies, or some combination, depending on a country's circumstances and level of industrialization. In some sectors and at some times, a country should give little weight to import replacement and a lot to comparative advantage; and vice versa.

These appear to rhyme with what the developmentalists had advocated: utilising a multitude of policy instruments to unleash productive powers and reciprocal effects (List); to infuse dynamism (Prebisch); to harness spread, while curtailing backwash, effects (Myrdal); and to correct the maldistribution of gains from progress due to international technological dualism (Singer). That suggests that in addition to the component of future research that is indicated at the end of section 13.1 above, one should also seek to explore possible connections between certain aspects of the works of the developmentalists and those by the researchers enumerated above. For instance, can one regard List's emphasis on unleashing the 'power of producing wealth', Prebisch's consideration of 'technological densities', and Singer's stress on cultivating the 'capacity to create wealth' as receiving more concrete treatment in, for instance, Lall's research into the cultivation of indigenous technological capability, Nelson's study of national innovation systems, the assimilation theories of Nelson and Pack, and Wade's prescriptions for 'governed market policies'? Given the overarching goal of knowledge acquisitions, capabilities cultivation, and technology upgrading, can one harmonise the better practice of regulating and directing FDI with the principles spelled out by the developmentalist on this subject? Within the policy context of achieving these, in what desirable manners and with what policy instruments might IS and EP be fruitfully interweaved?

13.4 CAPACITY BUILDING: FOR WHICH PATH OF DEVELOPMENT?

If these latter empirical (or case) studies have indeed uncovered some evidence that supports the policy implications of the developmentalist version of history of economic thought, then should the outcomes of the Uruguay Round of MTNs be regarded as significantly anti-development, given that in some important ways they curtail, or even terminate, the implicit forms of SDT? For the Agreement on Subsidies and Countervailing Measures (SCM) that was reached in that round divides subsidies into 'prohibited' and 'actionable' categories. Other than slight differentiations in implementation grace periods that agreement has brought, or threatens to bring, the kind of implicit SDT that involves the policy space to deploy export and many domestic subsidies to termination.[25] At the conclusion of that same round, the deployment of some TRIMs and the maintenance of less restrictive IPR protection came to be explicitly curtailed with the implementation of the Agreements on TRIMs and TRIPs, again other than slight differentiations in implementation grace periods.[26]

But none of that might matter. Almost two decades ago when the East and Southeast Asian development experiences were attracting more and more attention, and the mainstream attempted to respond to some of the case studies and empirical works mentioned in the latter part of the previous section, it expressed doubts on the administrative capacity of other countries that attempted to imitate the successful cases. For instance, the World Bank (1993, pp. 25–6) claims '[w]e have shown that the HPAEs [High-performing Asian economies] used an immense variety of policies to achieve three critical functions of growth: accumulation, allocation, and productivity growth'. However,

> [t]he sheer diversity of these policies precludes drawing any simple lessons or making any simple recommendations, except perhaps that pragmatic adherence to

> the fundamentals is central to success. These market-oriented aspects of East Asia's experience can be recommended with few reservations. More institutionally demanding strategies have often failed in other settings and they clearly are not compatible with economic environments where the fundamentals are not securely in place. ... In parts of Sub-Saharan Africa and Latin America, and elsewhere in Asia where such institutional conditions are lacking, activist government involvement in the economy has usually gone awry.

In short, 'the fact that interventions were an element of some East Asian economies' success does not mean that they should be attempted everywhere, nor should it be taken as an excuse to postpone needed market-oriented reform' (ibid.).

Curiously, in the aftermath of the conclusion of the Uruguay Round of MTNs, there have been talks of 'capacity building'. As Whalley (1999, p. 1065) observes, while the pre-Uruguay Round consideration of SDT emphasised 'special rights to protect and special rights of access to export markets', the Uruguay Round and after saw situations 'where in the name of SDT and special adjustment problems a whole array of delays on implementation, exemptions, and best efforts endeavours were introduced'. Notice that he does not draw the distinction between GATT-defined versus implicit SDT that is made in section 13.2 above. Nevertheless, his distinction between the two periods is significant. As Singh (2005, p. 237) echoes, the post-Uruguay Round SDT measures have been different. The emphasis has become 'assist[ing] developing countries in implementing the WTO disciplines'. Those countries have been 'offered extra time, and technical assistance to enhance capacity, in order to facilitate their adjustment into the new World Trading System'.

That appears to be the bandwagon that some in the mainstream have joined. From attacking the harm for development that GATT-defined SDT has caused, these mainstream economists have now turned to support the need for trade-related capacity building (TRCB). In the conception of Prowse (2002, p. 1236), this involves a two-pronged effort. Firstly, an underdeveloped country should be offered help to 'formulate appropriate trade positions as well as to place trade reform in the context of the country's overall development strategy that will promote a supply response and facilitate pro-poor growth'. Secondly, at the global level the rule-making process should 'ensure that implementation of WTO rules and efforts to negotiate and implement future disciplines makes sense from a development perspective and that assistance is considered in the context of other competing development needs'. Similarly, Hoekman, Michalopoulos and Winters (2004, p. 502) indicate that '[w]hatever specific new framework for SDT is adopted in the WTO to recognise capacity and related differences across countries, the primary objective of such a new framework should be to ensure that rules are only implemented if this is appropriate from a national perspective'. They even hint at the 'numerous actions that could be taken by developed countries to assist developing countries acquire and absorb knowledge and technology', including 'capacity building in intellectual property rights and technical regulations and standards, establishing public and public-private research facilities, facilitating technology-related services trade, and training programmes in the functioning of modern technology markets' (ibid., p. 501).

The gist of SDT has evolved, from the pre-Uruguay one that was centred upon the right of the state in the less-developed countries to take certain actions to promote development, to the post-Uruguay one that is about assisting these countries to build the capacity to integrate them into the global economy. Whether one finds this worrisome crucially depends on how development as a process is conceptualised. For those that approve of the evolution, the implicit assumption is that integration essentially means development. The rules and agreements that have been reached thus far, especially with reference to the latest changes reached in the Uruguay Round, are all development facilitating and should not be considered for re-negotiations. Instead, the focus should be on how to assist these countries to institute the capacities to implement them over time, with some sort of vague allowance for respecting their own development goals. What if the national sentiment and expression of priority is such that there is a desire to imitate the successful Asian countries in utilising GATT-defined as well as the implicit SDT to promote development? How then might the TRCB effort accommodate it? And does the proposal of technical assistance sound anything but hypocritical? If the developed countries could ram the Agreement on TRIPs down the throat of the underdeveloped countries, how can the latter now be convinced that such assistance will amount to anything that is substantive (from the perspective of national development)?

This is a reminder that the term 'capacity building' should be considered with extreme care. What conceptualisation of development is the selection of specific kinds of capacity based upon? Is it with a view to integrate into the global economy through further liberalisation, or is it with a view to develop one's economy by managing that integration? Seen from a different angle, how might the selection and emphasis of different kinds of capacity building destine a country to different paths of development? If different paths of development entail somewhat different kinds of capacity building, who decides on the specific content of the capacity to be built?

Amidst the talks of TRCB today there is the belief that, if the right kind of assistance be provided, the less-developed countries have a capacity to implement and enforce all kinds of trade or trade-related agreements, to adopt technologies so that they are in better positions to provide supply responses, and more generally to set and pursue their own development goals. The contradiction reflected between the pessimism expressed on the one hand by the World Bank (op. cit.) on the availability of a certain kind of capacity, and the faith expressed on the other hand by those who push for TRCB in their ability to build another kind of capacity, is puzzling. There was no consideration that if the diagnosis of the kind performed by the World Bank suggests the prime source of the problem to be a lack of administrative capacity to imitate the HPAEs, then should the 'first-best' policy in accordance with the principle of targetting be channelling some resources to building administrative capacities in those less-developed countries that attempt such imitation? As Lall (1999, pp. 16–17) puts it when he concludes his own study of the HPAEs minus Japan, '[I]f government capabilities to intervene properly are insufficient, the first remedy must be to improve upon those capabilities'.

13.5 OTHER POST-URUGUAY AND DOHA ROUND DEVELOPMENT

It is an understatement to say that switching the SDT debate from one that is primarily focused on capacity building for global integration back to one that emphasises the right of states to promote development is an uphill battle. Huge global imbalances in trade that have been built up between the successful developing countries and some developed countries especially since the turn of the millennium pose as formidable roadblocks.[27] The Great Recession that has besieged many parts of the global economy in the last couple of years would make that switch even harder.

Although the bulk of Chapter 9 above may come across as not very kind to Manoïlesco's contributions in his *Theory of Protection* in general, one should perhaps take heed of his brief but insightful discussion of the broader implications of the changes in the 'world's physiognomy' (section 9.6). He even appeared to have anticipated the rise of China and India. He foresaw a problem of the 'proper co-ordination of production in the various countries of the world' (1931, p. 204). He also considered the possible fallacy of composition problem for the late industrialising countries (end of section 9.5). In that connection, some may cite as a piece of supporting evidence how the rapid rise of China and India, among others, have allegedly contributed to 'favourable' CTT movements for exporters of many primary commodities in recent years (which, however, were curtailed or reversed by the onset of the Great Recession).

It is a reminder that while the discussion in this book has almost entirely been couched in terms of developed versus less-developed countries, some in the latter group have surged ahead to close their development gaps with the former group and are actually caught in the controversy surrounding the huge trade imbalances that the former group has been experiencing. If their success can indeed be attributed to their ability to sensibly utilise the GATT-defined and implicit SDTs as suggested above, then the erosion and curtailment of both forms of SDT would bring back uneven development, albeit in a different world that has a new constellation of forces of circular and cumulative causation. For if one thinks in terms of Myrdal's backwash effects, then while the successful developing countries might continue to experience certain backwash effects originating from the developed countries, they in turn generate some backwash effects that are felt by the lesser or least-developed. There are spread effects to consider, too, as in the 'favourable' CTT movements alluded to in the previous paragraph, although the caution that should be voiced about that is that one should probe into ownership and distribution situations in different lines of commodity production, including the part played by speculators in certain commodity markets. Besides, the limited employment opportunities in primary production in general would continue to warrant urging the less-developed countries to diversify, to some extent, into industrial production and/or service provision.

Prebisch, Myrdal, and Singer were not oblivious to the increasing differentiation among the less-developed countries. For instance, one can recall that near the end of section 10.8 above it is mentioned that in *Global Strategy* Prebisch (1968, p. 29) makes a proposal to offer market access among countries that is differentiated in ways that resemble, in spirit, the Doha Round Market Access Proposal (MAP) spelled out by Stiglitz and Charlton (2005, pp. 94–103). Indeed, one thing that is certain is that, if there were any new agreement reached down the road that in some ways restores SDTs in the form of the right of the state in less-developed countries to promote development, it will be tiered in some manners in accordance with the level of development in those countries. Yet a quick look at the MAP will convince the reader how complex it is to design any tiered system that would be widely acceptable across countries.

While the MAP is centred on merchandise trade access, there are notable examples from the post-Uruguay and Doha Round years that key debates and/or battles on the issues of subsidies, TRIPs, and TRIMs have continued to be waged that reminds the reader that the fight to restore and protect SDT in the form of the right of states to promote development is far from over.

Thus, lately there is a suggestion on the part of some that the Agreement on SCM should be relaxed, if not totally rescinded, for the less-developed countries. This would be offered in exchange for some agreement on their part not to resort to undervaluing their currencies as a form of industrial policy (Rodrik 2009a, 2009b). The hope is that the less-developed countries could continue to engender substantial growth and development through increasing the production of 'tradables' as encouraged by forms of industrial policies other than currency undervaluation. If gigantic trade imbalances could be avoided and the domestic consumption of these tradables augmented, it smacks of a new era of IS.[28] With the onset of the Great Recession and a noticeable number of predictions on how long it would take the developed countries to climb out of it, there could be a prolonged period when it would be extremely hard to make much inroad with development promotion through a heavy reliance on EP. In that regard a new era of IS that is suitably balanced with EP (including that practised within some regional blocs) has an understandable appeal.

Separately, after heated debates over the course of a few years, the World Intellectual Property Organization (WIPO) General Assembly adopted the Development Agenda in September 2007. Since its establishment in 1967 WIPO has followed a 'maximalist approach' that pushed for an upward harmonisation of intellectual property (IP) laws throughout the world. That remained the case even after it became a specialised agency of the United Nations (UN) in 1974. In contrast, the Development Agenda 'places the benefits of a rich and accessible public domain, national flexibilities in implementing IP treaty norms, access to knowledge, UN development goals, curbing of IP-related anti-competitive practices, and the need to balance the costs and benefits of intellectual property protection firmly within WIPO's central mission' (Netanel 2009, p. 2). Although it is still too soon to gauge the exact impact of this agenda, it nevertheless 'reflects the developing countries' growing resistance to the upward harmonization of IP protection required by the TRIPS and subsequent "TRIPS-plus" bilateral free trade agreements as well' (ibid., pp. 2–3).

Last but not least, the less-developed countries played a significant role in getting the Multilateral Agreement on Investment, which, beginning in 1995, was pushed by the OECD, rejected by 1998. FDI re-surfaced as one of the Singapore Issues that was considered in the early years of the Doha Round, again with the support of the developed countries. But thanks again to the opposition of most of the less-developed countries, this attempt to effectively extend the Agreement on TRIMs was foiled during the Cancún Ministerial Conference in 2003.

In hindsight one can question if the mainstream's traditional emphasis on trade-barrier reduction might have been improperly placed if one is primarily concerned with development promotion. Might the 'T' in MTNs have diverted attention from other equally (if not more) important issues? Might the obsession with trade liberalisation have caught economists off-guard when issues of IPR protection and TRIMs were added to the Uruguay Round agenda? Had the works of some of the six developmentalists – especially those of Hamilton, List, Prebisch, Myrdal, and Singer – not been distorted and misrepresented by the mainstream, might the underdeveloped countries have become better informed and prepared to resist the Agreements on SCM, TRIPs, and TRIMs in the ways and forms that they were reached during that round?

At the time when the manuscript for this book was finalised, the Doha Round of MTNs has not yet been completed. In fact, at the conclusion of the seventh WTO Ministerial Conference in Geneva in early December 2009, some even wonder if the Doha Round is dead. To recall, paragraph 44 of the Ministerial Declaration at the Doha Meeting in 2001 that kicked off this round declares that,

> We reaffirm that provisions for special and differential treatment are an integral part of the WTO Agreements. We note the concerns expressed regarding their operation in addressing specific constraints faced by developing countries, particularly least-developed countries. In that connection, we also note that some Members have proposed a Framework Agreement on Special and Differential Treatment (WT/GC/W/442). We therefore agree that all special and differential treatment provisions shall be reviewed with a view to strengthening them and making them more precise, effective and operational. In this connection, we endorse the work programme on special and differential treatment set out in the Decision on Implementation-Related Issues and Concerns.

As Singh (2005, p. 234, n. 4) notes, SDT is further reinforced by paragraph 12 of the Ministerial Decision on Implementation Issues. The Doha Round is supposedly a 'Development Round'. But as Stiglitz and Charlton (2005, p. vii) conclude after a few years into the round, it 'did not deserve its epithet'.

If a genuine 'Development Round' is to be informed by development perspectives, then hopefully the present book has made a compelling argument that there is a framework based upon a developmentalist version of history of economic thought that one can adopt to think about the process of development, and that it serves as a useful alternative to the mainstream framework that is based upon its own version of history of thought but which focuses on static resource allocation. The alternative framework does not point to easily reached multilateral agreements that respect the right of less-developed countries to development promotion. But if it succeeds in arguing why mainstream trade and commercial policy theories might be of limited use in helping solve the problems of uneven development, and if it encourages more to step and think outside the mainstream theoretical box as they conduct further research on the subject, then perhaps a step in a useful direction in thinking about possible solutions is being taken.

NOTES

1. Certain societal and market institutions would also have to be established *pari passu* the course of development. One can argue that mainstream theories also take that establishment for granted. Recall Mydral's criticism of 'automatic *mutatis mutandis*' in section 11.2.
2. Those producing and exporting petroleum certainly constitute a notable exception. But, of course, petroleum enjoys a much higher income elasticity of demand than most other primary products and one can only dream of discovering viable synthetic substitutes for it!
3. Some would have to be imported and this is one reason why balance of payments disequilibria would handicap development.
4. Consider, for instance, how often it is assumed when a tariff is analysed that the tariff revenue is simply distributed in a lump-sum fashion to economic agents. Implicitly, there is no other market failure the correction of, or social programme the implementation of, which would require the revenue to be so deployed.
5. Recall the reference to Lall and Latsch (1999) in n. 22 in Ch. 1 above. These authors draw a distinction between 'strategic' and 'tactical' interventions, where the former deals with 'broad issues that the market failure approach does not address', and the latter with 'narrower issues that can be considered as remedying market deficiencies' (p. 46, n. 33). All six developmentalists re-examined in Part II supported 'tactical' interventions. With the exception of Manoïlesco, they also advocated 'strategic' interventions in one way or another. It is also safe to imagine that some of them, especially Myrdal and Singer, would introduce certain 'social policies' into the mix. Recall also from the same endnote in Ch. 1 the reference to R. Nelson (2009), who suggests that building 'effective innovation systems' is simply not the same as correcting 'market failures' in static frameworks.
6. That is not to say that among these developmentalists 'anything goes' when it comes to development promotion. There is not even the slightest hint of this in their works. What is clear is that there is no knee-jerk conclusion against trade intervention while they express at the same time a healthy amount of caution against the possible drawbacks of the trade instruments. See, for a similar line of thinking, the consideration of a 'comprehensive' approach to development in Stiglitz (2006, p. 48).
7. Bhaduri (2005) can also be regarded as advocating that IS and EP be interweaved. However, he cautions that productivity growth should 'not [be viewed] primarily as a tool for international competitiveness, but as a source of greater availability of goods and services at home' (ibid., p. 77). He thus draws attention to the importance of balancing the emphasis that national governments place on the internal versus the external markets. He concurs that these governments should not be deterred from spending more on the social sector (pp. 76–7). He also underscores the importance of a 'faster diffusion of learning of processes and products' in the conduct of international economic activities (p. 70).
8. The reader should take note of what briefly drove Krugman to revive what he dubbed 'high development theory'. 'This set of ideas', he thus proclaimed, 'was and is highly persuasive as at least a partial explanation of what development is about … Yet in the late 1950s high development theory rapidly unraveled, to the point where by the time I studied economics in the 1970s it seemed not so much wrong as incomprehensible' (1994, 39). The theorists were 'having a hard time expressing their ideas in the kind of tightly specified models that were becoming the unique language of discourse of economic analysis. They were faced with the choice of either adopting that increasingly dominant intellectual style or finding themselves pushed into the intellectual periphery. They did not make the transition, and as a result high development theory was by and large purged from economics, even development economics'. 'The irony is', he concluded, 'we can now see that high development theory made perfectly good sense after all. But in order to see that, we need to adopt exactly the intellectual attitude Hirschman [and others] rejected: a willingness to do violence to the richness and complexity of the real world in order to produce controlled, *silly* models that illustrate key concepts' (ibid., p. 40, italics original). What Krugman and others who think like him did not consider is: what if the 'richness and complexity of the real world' is *the* key message that the developmentalists wanted the readers of their works

to take? Employing 'silly' models to represent their ideas could then probably result in deforming and distorting that message, especially when the identification and portrayal of 'key' concepts are significantly restricted by the formal techniques that are known to the theorist who employs them. Indeed, readers who are familiar with the original works of these 'high development theorists' can readily tell the substantive differences between the original works and the 'silly' models that seek to represent them.

9. Hudec (1987, p. 4) observes that '[t]he history of the GATT's legal relationship with developing countries is primarily the history of these [countries'] demands for special status'. Recall that SDT is the abbreviation for 'special and differential treatment', a term that was first introduced in Ch. 1 above. Chang (2006, p. 631) contends that calling it 'special treatment' may connote that the countries which are conferred that treatment are 'getting an unfair advantage', whereas in fact 'they are just differential treatment for countries with differential capabilities and goals'.
10. An apparently similar distinction is made by Jackson (1989, p. 277) when he observes that 'many developing countries are able to take advantage of either explicit or implicit exceptions in GATT so as to pursue almost at will any form of trade policy they wish'. However, in giving examples to illustrate, he merely refers to 'the balance-of-payments rules of Article XII and XVIII of GATT' (ibid.).
11. This was not the case for the first eight years or so after the GATT was first signed. As Hudec (1992, p. 69) notes, 'The 1946 negotiations resulted in minimal recognition of S & D treatment in the original GATT. Developing countries were granted a few rights to employ prohibited trade barriers, but the qualified nature of these privileges made them of little practical value'. In 1955, '[t]he text of a few provisions was changed to legitimize the concept of S & D treatment, and developing countries' legal rights to use quotas for balance of payment reasons were expanded' (ibid., p. 70).
12. A non-binding statement of special, but not legally binding, commitments to create opportunities for developing countries to trade was added to GATT in 1964 when it adopted Part IV on *Trade and Development.* In 1968 some developed countries started to grant tariff preferences under the GSP, although GATT did not adopt a waiver allowing for these programmes until two years later (Hudec 1992, p. 72).
13. Some of the sticky points regarding the 'Market Access for Non-Agricultural Products' (NAMA) negotiations in the Doha Round can certainly be seen in this light. Prebisch was alone among the six developmentalists in suggesting that perhaps the more that the centres could accommodate and facilitate the manufactured exports by the periphery, the more feasible tariff reduction in the latter would become (section 10.8 above). Writing around the mid-1980s, Díaz-Alejandro and Helleiner (1987, p. 511) similarly echo that '[t]he most effective means of expanding northern exports to the South is now, as it has always been, for the North to import more goods from the South'. Recall also the discussion in section 11.6 above that indicates that Myrdal was supportive of policy 'retrenchment' in some situations for certain countries, although by that he was actually pleading for the search of more effective control over certain private economic activities.
14. Hudec (1992, p. 73) remarks that '[t]he 1979 Tokyo Round Agreements represent the high-water mark of S&D treatment'.
15. Thus, a change in a domestic subsidy programme subsequent to a tariff concession could, in principle, by putting imported goods in disadvantageous competitive positions relative to domestic producers in the sector concerned, deny the benefits associated with that concession. See Sykes (2005, p. 94). However, should non-reciprocity still apply, the underdeveloped countries would not be making tariff concessions in the first place. Nevertheless, that is not to say that the developed countries may not find other reasons to apply measures like CVD against the underdeveloped countries.
16. For instance, it should be recalled that some less-developed countries did not join the Paris Convention. Those that did often used procedural mechanisms (for instance, reservations to specific clauses of the Convention) to avoid implementing terms that were deemed unsuitable or unfavourable to their needs and interests (Gana 1996, p. 745).
17. Within the mainstream this focus on GATT-defined SDT dies hard. A few years after the Doha Round commenced, Hoekman, Michalopoulos and Winters (2004, p. 484) still report

that '[t]he discussions to date have not focused on the economics of SDT rules, that is, on the costs and benefits of alternative options. Instead, developing country proposals have largely emphasised the need for more flexibility and "policy space", and implicitly if not explicitly the need to be able to *restrict trade to promote development*' (italics added).

18. It is of interest to note the following confession therein: 'The evidence ... strongly suggests that outward-oriented trade policies have been more successful than inward-oriented trade policies. It is a harder task to explain precisely why ... The best that can be achieved in practice [in attempting to provide a full answer] is to consider the broad economic themes that seem to be at work' (op. cit., p. 88).
19. In what could be a rather telling instance, it was actually admitted by Bhagwati during the mid-1970s when the results of the NBER Bhagwati–Krueger project were coming in, that 'we will not find in our standard Bhagwati–Ramaswami–Johnson models the sources of superior performance [of a country like Korea]' and thus '[w]e have to look elsewhere' (Bhagwati 1975, p. 514).
20. Bairoch (op. cit.) also adds that in a few examples of periods of liberalism in Europe there were 'negative or very negative consequences'. Elsewhere, focusing specifically on 1892–1914 and expressing himself in 'simplistic but dramatic terms', he provocatively suggested that 'protectionism = economic growth and expansion of trade; liberalism = stagnation in both' (1989, p. 69).
21. In a misleading manner Bairoch (1993, p. 33) notes, 'The major contribution of Hamilton is the emphasis he put on the idea that industrialization is not possible without *tariff* protection' and his *Report* 'is considered to be the first formulation of modern protectionist theory' (italics added). He also labels List an 'apostle of protectionism' (ibid., p. 21).
22. Irwin (op. cit.) then suggests that '[j]ust as the positive correlation between tariffs and growth in the late nineteenth century does not necessarily imply that tariffs caused that growth, the late twentieth century correlation between low tariffs and growth does not necessarily imply that free trade was responsible for that growth'.
23. Singer (1988) is a short but forceful response to the World Bank (1987).
24. Put differently, if the chapters in Part I have established in a compelling way how the process of uneven growth and development will obtain when 'market forces' operate freely in the conduct of trade and FDI, and if the chapters in Part II have clarified how it might be possible to arrest, even if partially, this uneven process through some technological-capability cultivation policies (of which infant-industry support through trade protection is merely one element), then the wisdom of designing empirical works that determine the relationship between liberalising trade on the one hand, and engendering growth and development on the other, should be carefully reconsidered.
25. 'Prohibited' ones include export subsidies and those that are contingent on the use of domestically produced over imported goods. An 'actionable' subsidy is one that is specific and is regarded as causing injury to a domestic industry in, or impairment of the benefits of a tariff concession extended to, another WTO member. Or it results in serious prejudice to the interests of another member (Sykes 2005, p. 96). The Agreement on SCM originally contained a third category of subsidies that were 'non-actionable'. This category existed for five years and was not extended after it expired on 31 December, 1999.
26. As n. 74 in Ch. 12 indicates, Singer did critically comment, in an unpublished paper in the early 1990s, on some aspects of the then ongoing Uruguay Round.
27. These trade imbalances, though currently chiefly blamed on China, can more generally be regarded as a reflection of the success of the HPAEs in engendering industrial development. The surpluses registered by the oil-exporting countries are not considered here. Rodrik (2009b, p. 5) notes that China did not start to run huge trade surpluses until 2001, coincidentally the year when it became a member of the WTO.
28. In that connection, recall n. 7 above that indicates that Bhaduri (2005) also discusses the importance of balancing the emphasis that national governments place on the internal versus the external markets as they pursue policies to improve industrial productivity.

Bibliography

Akyüz, Yilmaz, Ha-Joon Chang and R. Kozul-Wright (1999), 'New perspectives on East Asian development', in Yilmaz Akyüz (ed.), *East Asian Development: New Perspectives*, London: Frank Cass.

Amsden, Alice H. (1989), *Asia's Next Giant: South Korea and Late Industrialization*, New York: Oxford University Press.

Anand, Sudhir and Vijay Joshi (1979), 'Domestic distortions, income distribution and the theory of optimum subsidy', *Economic Journal*, **89** (354), 336–52.

Angresano, James (1997), *The Political Economy of Gunnar Myrdal: An Institutional Basis for the Transformation Problem*, Cheltenham, UK and Lyme, USA: Edward Elgar.

Arestis, Philip and Malcolm Sawyer (eds) (1992), *A Biographical Dictionary of Dissenting Economists*, Aldershot, UK and Brookfield, USA: Edward Elgar.

Ashley, Sir William [1909] (1987), 'Bibliographical appendix', in John Stuart Mill, *Principles of Political Economy with Some of Their Applications to Social Philosophy*, edited by Sir William Ashley, Fairfield, NJ: Augustus M. Kelley, Publishers, pp. 981–1004.

Austin, John (1842), 'Review of List's "Das Nationale System der Politische Oekonomie"', *The Edinburgh Review*, **LXXV** (CLII), 515–56.

Backhaus, Jürgen G. (1992), 'Friedrich List and the political economy of protective tariffs', in S. Todd Lowry (ed.), *Perspectives on the History of Economic Thought Volume VII – Perspectives on the Administrative Tradition: From Antiquity to the Twentieth Century*, Aldershot, UK and Brookfield, USA: Edward Elgar, pp. 142–56.

Baer, Werner (1962), 'The economics of Prebisch and ECLA', *Economic Development and Cultural Change*, **X** (2), 169–82.

Bagchi, Amiya K. (1982), *The Political Economy of Underdevelopment*, Cambridge: Cambridge University Press.

Bagwell, Kyle and Robert W. Staiger (2006), 'Will international rules on subsidies disrupt the world trading system?', *American Economic Review*, **96** (3), 877–95.

Bailey, Samuel (1825), *A Critical Dissertation on the Nature, Measures, and Causes of Value: Chiefly in Reference to the Writings of Mr. Ricardo and His Followers. By the author of Essays on the Formation and Publication of Opinions*, London: Printed for R. Hunter.

Bairoch, Paul (1989), 'European trade policy, 1815–1914', translated by Susan Burke, in Peter Mathias and Sidney Pollard (eds), *The Cambridge Economic History of Europe, Vol. VIII, The Industrial Economies: The Development of Economic and Social Policies*, Cambridge: Cambridge University Press, pp. 1–160.

Bairoch, Paul (1993), *Economics and World History: Myths and Paradoxes*, Chicago: The University of Chicago Press.

Balassa, Bela (1980), *The Process of Industrial Development and Alternative Development Strategies*, Essays in International Finance, no. 141, Princeton: Princeton University, Department of Economics, International Finance Section.

Balassa, Bela (1984), 'Comment [on Singer (1984a)]', in Gerald M. Meier and Dudley Seers (eds) (1984), *Pioneers in Development*, New York: Oxford University Press, pp. 304–11.

Balassa, Bela (1988), 'Interest of developing countries in the Uruguay Round', *The World Economy*, **11** (1), 39–54.

Balassa, Bela (1989), *New Directions in the World Economy*, New York: New York University Press.

Balassa, Bela and associates (1971), *The Structure of Protection in Developing Countries*, Baltimore: The Johns Hopkins Press.

Baldwin, Robert E. (1956), 'Patterns of development in newly settled regions', *Manchester School of Economic and Social Studies*, **XXIV** (2), 161–79.

Baldwin, Robert E. (1969), 'The case against infant-industry tariff protection', *Journal of Political Economy*, **LXXVII** (3), 295–305.

Ballance, Robert H., Javed A. Ansari and Hans W. Singer (1982), *The International Economy and Industrial Development: The Impact of Trade and Investment on the Third World*, Totowa, NJ: Allanheld, Osmun Publishers.

Bardhan, Pranab K. (1964a), 'External economies, economic development and the theory of protection', *Oxford Economic Papers*, **16** (1), 40–54.

Bardhan, Pranab K. (1964b), 'Factor market disequilibrium and the theory of protection', *Oxford Economic Papers*, **16** (3), 375–88.

Bastable, C. Francis (1887), *The Theory of International Trade with Some of Its Applications to Economic Policy*, Dublin: Hodges, Figgis, & Co.

Bastable, C. Francis (1912), *The Commerce of Nations*, 6th edition, London: Methuen & Co., Ltd.

Bauer, Péter T. (1959), 'International economic development', *Economic Journal*, **69** (273), 105–23.

Bauer, Péter T. (1972), *Dissent on Development: Studies and Debates in Development Economics*, Cambridge, MA: Harvard University Press.

Belshaw, James P. (1959), 'Gunnar Myrdal and Friedrich List on economic development', *Indian Economic Journal*, **VI** (4), 415–37.

Ben-Atar, Doron (1995), 'Alexander Hamilton's alternative: technology piracy and the Report on Manufactures', *The William and Mary Quarterly*, 3rd series, **LII** (3), 389–414.

Berger, Sebastian (2008), 'Circular cumulative causation (CCC) à la Myrdal and Kapp – *political* institutionalism for minimizing social costs', *Journal of Economic Issues*, **XLII** (2), 357–65.

Bhaduri, Amit (2005), 'Toward the optimum degree in openness', in Kevin P. Gallagher (ed.) (2005), pp. 69–79.

Bhagwati, Jagdish N. (1958), 'Immiserizing growth: a geometrical note', *Review of Economic Studies*, **25** (3), 201–5.

Bhagwati, Jagdish N. (1968), *The Theory and Practice of Commercial Policy: Departures from Unified Exchange Rates*, Special Papers in International Economics, no. 8, Princeton: Princeton University, Department of Economics, International Finance Section.

Bhagwati, Jagdish N. (1975), 'What we need to know: panel discussion', in Peter B. Kenen (ed.), *International Trade and Finance: Frontiers for Research*, Cambridge: Cambridge University Press, pp. 506–16.

Bhagwati, Jagdish N. (1978), *Foreign Trade Regimes and Economic Development: Anatomy and Consequences of Exchange Control Regimes*, Cambridge, MA: Ballinger Publishing Company.

Bhagwati, Jagdish N. (1982), 'Directly-unproductive profit-seeking (DUP) activities', *Journal of Political Economy*, **XC** (5), 988–1002.

Bhagwati, Jagdish N. (1983), 'Comment [on Prebisch (1983)]', in Shigeto Tsuru (ed.) (1983), pp. 46–51.

Bhagwati, Jagdish N. (1984), 'Comment [on Prebisch (1984)]', in Gerald M. Meier and Dudley Seers (eds) (1984), *Pioneers in Development*, New York: Oxford University Press, pp. 197–204.

Bhagwati, Jagdish N. (1987a), 'Outward orientation: trade issues', in Vittorrio Corbo, Morris Goldstein and Mohsin Khan (eds), *Growth-Oriented Adjustment Programs*, Washington, DC: International Monetary Fund and the World Bank, pp. 257–90.

Bhagwati, Jagdish N. (1987b), 'Trade in services and the multilateral trade negotiations', the Symposium Issue on the Multilateral Trade Negotiations and Developing Countries' Interests, *The World Bank Economic Review*, **1** (4), 549–69.

Bhagwati, Jagdish N. (1988a), 'Export-promoting trade strategy: issues and evidence', *World Bank Research Observer*, **3** (1), 27–57.

Bhagwati, Jagdish N. (1988b), 'Comments on "Dependence, development, and interdependence"', in Gustav Ranis and T. Paul Schultz (eds) (1988), *The State of Development Economics: Progress and Perspectives*, Cambridge, MA: Basil Blackwell, pp. 42–8.

Bhagwati, Jagdish N. (1989), 'Is free trade passé after all?', *Weltwirtschaftliches Archiv*, **CXXV** (1), 17–44.

Bhagwati, Jagdish N. (1994), 'Fair trade, reciprocity and harmonization: the new challenge to the theory and policy of free trade', in Alan V. Deardorff and Robert M. Stern (eds), *Analytical and Negotiating Issues in the Global Trading System*, Ann Arbor: University of Michigan Press, pp. 547–98.

Bhagwati, Jagdish N. (2002a), *Free Trade Today*, Princeton: Princeton University Press.

Bhagwati, Jagdish N. (2002b), 'Patents and the poor', *Financial Times*, September 16.

Bhagwati, Jagdish N. (2004), *In Defense of Globalization*, New York: Oxford University Press.

Bhagwati, Jagdish N. (2008), *Termites in the Trading System: How Preferential Agreements Undermine Free Trade*, New York: Oxford University Press.

Bhagwati, Jagdish N., Arvind Panagariya, and T. N. Srinivasan (1998), *Lectures on International Trade*, 2nd edition, Cambridge, MA: The MIT Press.

Bhagwati, Jagdish N. and V. K. Ramaswami (1963), 'Domestic distortions, tariffs and the theory of optimum subsidy', *Journal of Political Economy*, **LXXI** (1), 44–50.

Bharadwaj, Krishna (1978), 'The subversion of classical analysis: Alfred Marshall's early writing on value', *Cambridge Journal of Economics*, **2** (3), 253–71.

Bharadwaj, Krishna (1983), 'Ricardian theory and Ricardianism', *Contributions to Political Economy*, **2**, 49–77.

Blaug, Mark (1984), 'Review of List's *The Natural System of Political Economy* as trans. and ed. by W. O. Henderson', *Economica*, **51** (203), 368–9.

Blecker, Robert A. (1997), 'The "unnatural and retrograde order": Adam Smith's theories of trade and development reconsidered', *Economica*, **64** (255), 527–37.

Bliss, Christopher (1989), 'Trade and development', in Hollis Chenery and T. N. Srinivasan (eds) (1989), *Handbook of Development Economics*, vol. 2, Amsterdam: North Holland, pp. 1187–240.
Bloomfield, Arthur I. (1975), 'Adam Smith and the theory of international trade', in Andrew S. Skinner and Thomas Wilson (eds) (1975), *Essays on Adam Smith*, Oxford: Clarendon Press, pp. 455–81.
Bloomfield, Arthur I. (1978), 'The impact of growth and technology on trade in nineteenth century British thought', *History of Political Economy*, **10** (4), 608–35.
Bloomfield, Arthur I. (1981), 'British thought on the influence of foreign trade and investment on growth, 1800–1880', *History of Political Economy*, **13** (1), 95–120.
Bloomfield, Arthur I. (1984), 'Effect of growth on the terms of trade: some earlier views', *Economica*, **51** (202), 187–93.
Bobulescu, Roxana (2003), '*Protectionism* in retrospect: Mihail Manoilescu (1891–1950?)', *Brazilian Journal of Political Economy*, **23** (4), 114–23.
Boldrin, Michele and David K. Levine (2008), *Against Intellectual Monopoly*, New York: Cambridge University Press.
Bourne, Edward G. (1894), 'Alexander Hamilton and Adam Smith', *Quarterly Journal of Economics*, **VIII** (3), 328–44.
Brewer, Anthony (1990), *Marxist Theories of Imperialism: A Critical Survey*, 2nd edition, New York: Routledge.
Bruton, Henry (1965), *Principles of Development Economics*, Englewood Cliffs: Prentice-Hall, Inc.
Burgstaller, André (1986), 'Unifying Ricardo's theories of growth and comparative advantage', *Economica*, **53** (212), 467–81.
Burgstaller, André (1987), 'Europe's industrialization and colonial underdevelopment in the light of Ricardo's Corn Model', *Journal of International Economics*, **22** (1/2), 157–69.
Cairncross, Alec K. (1961), 'International trade and economic development', *Economica*, **28** (111), 235–51.
Cairncross, Alec K. (1962), *Factors in Economic Development*, London: George Allen and Unwin, Ltd.
Canning, David (1988), 'Increasing returns in industry and the role of agriculture in growth', *Oxford Economic Papers*, **40** (3), 463–76.
Carey, Henry C. (1837–40), *Principles of Political Economy*, vols. I–III, Philadelphia: Carey, Lea & Blanchard.
Carey, Henry C. [1858–59] (1873), *Principles of Social Science*, vols. I–III, Philadelphia: J. B. Lippincott & Co.
Caves, Richard E. (1964), 'Trade and development – traditional view', *Economic Development and Cultural Change*, **XIII** (1), 103–6.
Caves, Richard E. (1965), '"Vent for surplus" models of trade and growth', in Robert E. Baldwin et al. (eds), *Trade, Growth and the Balance of Payments*, Chicago: Rand McNally & Co., pp. 95–115.
Chang, Ha-Joon (2002), *Kicking Away the Ladder: Development Strategy in Historical Perspective*, London: Anthem Press.
Chang, Ha-Joon (2006), 'Policy space in historical perspective with special reference to trade and industrial policies', *Economic and Political Weekly*, **XLI** (7), 627–33.
Chenery, Hollis B. (1961), 'Comparative advantage and development policy', *American Economic Review*, **51** (1), 18–51.
Chenery, Hollis B. and T. N. Srinivasan (eds) (1989), *Handbook of Development Economics*, vol. 2, Amsterdam: North Holland.

Chipman, John S. (1965), 'A survey of the theory of international trade: part 1, the classical theory', *Econometrica*, **33** (3), 477–519.
Clairmonte, Frederick (1959), 'Friedrich List and the historical concept of balanced growth', *Indian Economic Review*, **IV** (3), 24–44.
Clemens, Michael A. and Jeffrey G. Williamson (2001), 'A tariff–growth paradox? Protection's impact the world around 1875–1997', National Bureau of Economic Research (Cambridge, MA) Working Paper No. 8459.
Coats, A. W. (1975), 'Adam Smith and the mercantile system', in Andrew S. Skinner and Thomas Wilson (eds) (1975), pp. 218–36.
Cole, Arthur H. [1928] (1968), 'The background of Hamilton's Report on Manufactures', in Arthur H. Cole (ed.), *Industrial and Commercial Correspondence of Alexander Hamilton Anticipating His Report on Manufactures*, New York: Augustus M. Kelley, Publishers, pp. 231–43.
Cooke, Jacob E. (1975), 'Tench Coxe, Alexander Hamilton, and the encouragement of American manufactures', *The William and Mary Quarterly*, **XXXII** (3), 369–92.
Condliffe, J. B. (1933), 'Review of Manoilesco's "Theory of Protection and International Trade"', *Economic Journal*, **43** (169), 143–5.
Corbo, Vittorio (1988), 'Problems, development theory, and strategies of Latin America', in Gustav Ranis and T. Paul Schultz (eds) (1988), *The State of Development Economics: Progress and Perspectives*, Cambridge, MA: Basil Blackwell, pp. 145–82.
Corden, W. Max (1965), *Recent Developments in the Theory of International Trade*, Special Papers in International Economics, no. 7, Princeton: Princeton University, Department of Economics, International Finance Section.
Corden, W. Max (1984), 'The normative theory of international trade', in Ronald W. Jones and Peter B. Kenen (eds) (1984), *Handbook of International Economics, vol. 1: International Trade*, Amsterdam: North-Holland, pp. 63–130.
Corden W. Max (1997), *Trade Policy and Economic Welfare*, 2nd edition, Oxford: Clarendon Press.
Coxe, Tench [1790] (1979), 'Second draft' of Alexander Hamilton's *Report on the Subject of Manufactures*, in Harold C. Syrett (ed.), *The Papers of Alexander Hamilton*, **XXVI**, New York: Columbia University Press, pp. 632–47.
Creedy, John (1992), *Demand and Exchange in Economic Analysis: A History from Cournot to Marshall*, Aldershot, UK and Brookfield, USA: Edward Elgar.
Cuddington, John T., Rodney Ludema and Shamila A. Jayasuriya (2007), 'Prebisch–Singer Redux', in Daniel Lederman and William F. Maloney (eds), *Natural Resources: Neither Curse Nor Destiny*, Washington, DC: World Bank Publications, pp. 103–40.
Daastöl, Arno M. (1999), 'Friedrich List (1789–1846)', in Jürgen G. Backhaus (ed.), *The Elgar Companion to Law and Economics*, Cheltenham, UK and Northampton, MA, USA: Edward Elgar, pp. 375–91.
Dam, Kenneth (1970), *The GATT: Law and International Economic Organization*, Chicago: University of Chicago Press.
Darity, William, Jr. (1985), 'Review of List's *The Natural System of Political Economy* as trans. and ed. by W. O. Henderson', *History of Political Economy*, **17** (3), 493–6.
Deane, Phyllis (1990), 'Marshall on free trade', in Rita M. Tullberg (ed.), *Alfred Marshall in Retrospect*, Aldershot, UK and Brookfield, USA: Edward Elgar, pp. 113–32.

Deardorff, Alan V. (2003), 'What might globalisation's critics believe?', *The World Economy*, **26** (5), 629–58.
de Cecco, Marcello (1974), *Money and Empire: The International Gold Standard, 1890–1914*, Oxford: Basil Blackwell.
de Marchi, Neil (1988), 'John Stuart Mill: interpretation since Schumpeter', in William O. Thweatt (ed.), *Classical Political Economy: A Survey of Recent Literature*, Boston: Kluwer Academic Publishers, pp. 137–77.
de Vivo, Giancarlo (1981), 'John Stuart Mill on value', *Cambridge Journal of Economics*, **5** (1), 67–9.
de Vivo, Giancarlo (1985a), 'Robert Torrens and Ricardo's "corn-ratio" theory of profits', *Cambridge Journal of Economics*, **9** (1), 89–92.
de Vivo, Giancarlo (1985b), 'The author of the article on Owen in the October 1819 *Edinburgh Review*: some neglected evidence, with a reply by William O. Thweatt', *History of Political Economy*, **17** (2), 199–202.
de Vivo, Giancarlo (1986), 'Torrens on value and distribution', *Contributions to Political Economy*, **5**, 23–36.
Dell, Sidney (1986), 'Raúl Prebisch: his contemporary relevance', *Development & South–South Cooperation*, **II** (3), 8–15.
di Marco, Luis Eugenio (1972), 'The evolution of Prebisch's economic thought', in Luis Eugenio di Marco (ed.), *International Economics and Development: Essays in Honor of Raúl Prebisch*, New York: Academic Press, pp. 1–12.
Díaz-Alejandro, Carlos F. (1975), 'Trade policies and economic development', in Peter B. Kenen (ed.), *International Trade and Finance: Frontiers for Research*, Cambridge: Cambridge University Press, pp. 93–150.
Díaz-Alejandro, Carlos F. and Gerald K. Helleiner (1987), 'Developing countries and reform of the world trading system', in Dominick Salvatore (ed.), *The New Protectionist Threat to World Welfare*, New York: North-Holland, pp. 505–25.
DiCaprio, Alisa and Kevin P. Gallagher (2006), 'The WTO and the shrinking of development space: how big is the bite?', *Journal of World Investment and Trade*, **7** (5), 781–803.
Dimand, Robert W. (1998), 'Rae and international trade', in Omar F. Hamouda, Clive Lee and Douglas Mair (eds) (1998), *The Economics of John Rae*, New York: Routledge, pp. 177–84.
Dixit, Avinash K. and Joseph E. Stiglitz (1977), 'Monopolistic competition and optimum product diversity', *American Economic Review*, **67** (3), 297–308.
Dobb, Maurice (1973), *Theories of Value and Distribution since Adam Smith: Ideology and Economic Theory*, Cambridge: Cambridge University Press.
Dollar, David (1992), 'Outward-oriented development economies really do grow more rapidly: evidence from 95 LDCs, 1976–1985', *Economic Development and Cultural Change*, **XL** (2), 523–44.
Dopfer, Kurt (1988), 'In memoriam: Gunnar Myrdal's contribution to Institutional Economics', *Journal of Economic Issues*, **XXII** (1), 227–31.
Dorfman, Joseph [1946] (1966), *The Economic Mind in American Civilization 1606–1865*, vol. 2, New York: Augustus M. Kelley, Publishers.
Dosi, Giovanni, Keith Pavitt and Luc Soete (1990), *The Economics of Technical Change and International Trade*, New York: New York University Press.
Dostaler, Gilles (1990), 'An assessment of Gunnar Myrdal's early work in Economics', *Journal of the History of Economic Thought*, **12** (2), 196–221.
Dostaler, Gilles, Diane Ethier and Laurent Lepage (eds) (1992), *Gunnar Myrdal and His Works*, Montreal: Harvest House Limited.

Dutt, Amitava K. (1988), 'Inelastic demand for Southern goods, international demonstration effects, and uneven development', *Journal of Development Economics*, **29** (1), 111–22.
Edgeworth, Francis Y. (1894a), 'The theory of international values – I', *Economic Journal*, **4** (13), 35–50.
Edgeworth, Francis Y. (1894b), 'The theory of international values – III', *Economic Journal*, **4** (16), 606–38.
Edwards, Sebastian (1998), 'Openness, productivity and growth: what do we really know?', *Economic Journal*, **108** (447), 383–98.
Ellis, Howard S. (ed.) (1963), *Economic Development for Latin America*, New York: St. Martin's Press.
Ellsworth, Paul T. (1956), 'The terms of trade between primary producing and industrial countries', *Inter-American Economic Affairs*, **X** (1), 47–65.
Elmslie, Bruce (1994), 'Positive feedback mechanisms in Adam Smith's theories of international trade', *The European Journal of the History of Economic Thought*, **1** (2), 253–71.
Elmslie, Bruce and Antoinette M. James (1993), 'The renaissance of Adam Smith in modern theories of international trade', in Robert F. Hébert (ed.), *Themes on Economic Discourse, Method, Money and Trade: Selected Papers from the History of Economics Conference, 1991*, Aldershot, UK and Brookfield, USA: Edward Elgar, pp. 63–76.
Eltis, Walter A. (1975), 'Adam Smith's theory of economic growth', in Andrew S. Skinner and Thomas Wilson (eds) (1975), *Essays on Adam Smith*, Oxford: Clarendon Press, pp. 426–54.
Eltis, Walter A. (1988), 'The contrasting theories of industrialization of François Quesnay and Adam Smith', *Oxford Economic Papers*, **40** (2), 269–88.
Esslinger, Hans Ulrich (1996), '"… More of Keynes and less of Milton Friedman!": Sir Hans Singer's contributions to economics', *Review of Political Economy*, **8** (4), 367–78.
Evans, H. David (1989), *Comparative Advantage and Growth: Trade and Development in Theory and Practice*, New York: St. Martin's Press.
Fetter, Frank W. (1962), 'Robert Torrens: colonel of marines and political economist', *Economica*, **29** (114), 152–65.
Fetter, Frank W. (1990), 'New light on the military career of Robert Torrens', *History of Political Economy*, **22** (3), 545–9.
Fieldhouse, David K. (1966), *The Colonial Empires: A Comparative Survey from the Eighteenth Century*, New York: Delacorte Press.
Findlay, Ronald (1974), 'Relative prices, growth and trade in a simple Ricardian system', *Economica*, **41** (161), 1–13.
Findlay, Ronald (1984), 'Growth and development in trade models', in Ronald W. Jones and Peter B. Kenen (eds) (1984), *Handbook of International Economics, vol. 1: International Trade*, Amsterdam: North-Holland, pp. 185–236.
Findlay, Ronald (1988), 'Trade, development, and the state', in Gustav Ranis and T. Paul Schultz (eds) (1988), *The State of Development Economics: Progress and Perspectives*, Cambridge, MA: Basil Blackwell, pp. 78–95.
Findlay, Ronald and Kevin H. O'Rourke (2007), *Power and Plenty: Trade, War, and the World Economy in the Second Millennium*, Princeton: Princeton University Press.
Finger, J. Michael (1991), 'Development economics and the General Agreement on Tariffs and Trade', in Jaime de Melo and André Sapir (eds), *Trade Theory and*

Economic Reform: North, South, and East, Essays in Honor of Béla Balassa, Cambridge, MA: Basil Blackwell, pp. 203–23.
Finger, J. Michael (2001), 'Implementing the Uruguay Round Agreements: problems for developing countries', *The World Economy*, **24** (9), 1097–108.
Finger, J. Michael and J. J. Nogués (2002), 'The unbalanced Uruguay Round outcome: the new areas in future WTO negotiations', *The World Economy*, **25** (3), 321–40.
Flanders, M. June (1964), 'Prebisch on protectionism: an evaluation', *Economic Journal*, **74** (294), 305–26.
Frank, Andre Gunder (1979), *Dependent Accumulation and Underdevelopment*, New York: Monthly Review Press.
Frankel, H. (1943), 'Industrialisation of agricultural countries and the possibilities of a new international division of labour', *Economic Journal*, **53** (210), 188–201.
Frankenhoff, Charles A. (1962), 'The Prebisch Thesis: a theory of industrialism for Latin America', *Journal of Inter-American Studies*, **IV** (2), 185–206.
Freeman, Chris (1995), 'The "National System of Innovation" in historical perspective', *Cambridge Journal of Economics*, **19** (1), 5–24.
Gafni, A., N. Halevi and G. Hanoch (1963), 'Classification of tariffs by functions', *Kyklos*, **XVI** (2), 303–18.
Gallagher, John and Ronald Robinson (1953), 'The imperialism of free trade', *Economic History Review*, **VI** (1), 1–15.
Gallagher, Kevin P. (ed.) (2005), *Putting Development First: The Importance of Policy Space in the WTO and International Financial Institutions*, London: Zed Books.
Gana, Ruth L. (1996), 'Prospects for developing countries under the TRIPs Agreement', *Vanderbilt Journal of Transnational Law*, **29** (4), 735–75.
Garegnani, Pierangelo (1984), 'Value and distribution in the classical economists and Marx', *Oxford Economic Papers*, **36** (2), 291–325.
Ghosh, Rabindra N. (1967), *Classical Macroeconomics and the Case for Colonies*, Calcutta: New Age Publishers Private Ltd.
Gide, Charles and Charles Rist (1948), *A History of Economic Doctrines: From the Time of the Physiocrats to the Present Day*, translated by R. Richards, Boston: D. C. Heath and Company.
Gomes, Leonard (1987), *Foreign Trade and the National Economy: Mercantilist and Classical Perspectives*, New York: St. Martin's Press.
Gomes, Leonard (1990), *Neoclassical International Economics: An Historical Survey*, New York: St. Martin's Press.
Gomes, Leonard (1993), *The International Adjustment Mechanism: From the Gold Standard to the EMS*, New York: St. Martin's Press.
Gomes, Leonard (2003), *The Economics and Ideology of Free Trade: An Historical Review*, Cheltenham, UK and Northampton, MA, USA: Edward Elgar.
Graham, Frank D. (1923), 'Some aspects of protection further considered', *Quarterly Journal of Economics*, **XXXVII** (2), 199–227.
Graham, Frank D. (1925), 'Some fallacies in the interpretation of social costs: a reply', *Quarterly Journal of Economics*, **XXXIX** (2), 324–30.
Groenewegen, Peter D. (1993), 'Introduction' to Robert Torrens [1808] (1993), *The Economists Refuted and other Early Economic Writings*, Fairfield, NJ: Augustus M. Kelley, Publishers, pp. v–xx.
Groenewegen, Peter D. (1999), 'Adam Smith and Alfred Marshall: some reflections', in Sami Daniel, Philip Arestis and John Grahl (eds), *The History and Practice of*

Economics: Essays in Honour of Bernard Corry and Maurice Peston, vol. 2, Cheltenham, UK and Northampton, MA, USA: Edward Elgar, pp. 81–95.
Grubel, Herbert G. (1966), 'The anatomy of classical and modern infant industry arguments', *Weltwirtschaftliches Archiv*, **XCVII** (2), 325–42.
Gruchy, Allan G. (1972), 'Gunnar Myrdal's economics of integration', in Allan G. Gruchy, *Contemporary Economic Thought: The Contribution of Neo-Institutional Economics*, Clifton, NJ: Augustus M. Kelley, Publishers, pp. 177–236.
Haberler, Gottfried (1937), *The Theory of International Trade with its Applications to Commercial Policy*, New York: The Macmillan Co.
Haberler, Gottfried (1950), 'Some problems in the pure theory of international trade', *Economic Journal*, **60** (238), 223–40.
Haberler, Gottfried (1954), 'The relevance of the classical theory under modern conditions', *American Economic Review, Papers and Proceedings*, **44** (2), 543–51.
Haberler, Gottfried (1957), 'Critical observations on some current notions in the theory of economic development', *L'Industria*, **1957** (2), 373–83.
Haberler, Gottfried [1959] (1988), *International Trade and Economic Development*, reprint of the 1959 Cairo Lectures with a new Introduction, San Francisco: International Center for Economic Growth, pp. 17–53.
Haberler, Gottfried (1961), 'A survey of international trade theory', revised and enlarged edition, Special Papers in International Economics, no. 1, Princeton: Princeton University, Department of Economics, International Finance Section.
Haberler, Gottfried (1963), 'Terms of trade and economic development', in Howard S. Ellis (ed.) (1963), *Economic Development for Latin America*, New York: St. Martin's Press, pp. 275–97.
Haberler, Gottfried (1964), 'An assessment of the current relevance of the theory of comparative advantage to agricultural production and trade', *International Journal of Agrarian Affairs*, **IV** (3), 130–49.
Haberler, Gottfried (1967), 'Import taxes and export subsidies: a substitute for the realignment of exchange rates', *Kyklos*, **XX** (1), 17–23.
Haberler, Gottfried (1987), 'Liberal and illiberal development policy', in Gerald M. Meier (ed.) (1987), *Pioneers in Development*, 2nd series, New York: Oxford University Press, pp. 49–83.
Haddad, L. (1987), 'List revisited: dynamic consideration of trade and protection', *Working Papers in Economics*, no. 100, Department of Economics, University of Sydney.
Hagen, Everett E. (1958), 'An economic justification of protectionism', *Quarterly Journal of Economics*, **LXXII** (4), 496–514.
Hamilton, Alexander [1781] (1961), *The Continentalist No. IV*, in Harold C. Syrett and Jacob E. Cooke (eds), *The Papers of Alexander Hamilton*, vol. II, New York: Columbia University Press, pp. 669–74.
Hamilton, Alexander [1782] (1962), *The Continentalist No. V* and *The Continentalist No. VI*, in Harold C. Syrett and Jacob E. Cooke (eds), *The Papers of Alexander Hamilton*, vol. III, New York: Columbia University Press, pp. 75–82, 99–106.
Hamilton, Alexander [1791a] (1965), 'Prospectus of the Society for Establishing Useful Manufactures', in Harold C. Syrett and Jacob E. Cooke (eds), *The Papers of Alexander Hamilton*, vol. IX, New York: Columbia University Press, pp. 144–53.

Hamilton, Alexander [1791b] (1966), *Report on the Subject of Manufactures*, in Harold C. Syrett and Jacob E. Cooke (eds), *The Papers of Alexander Hamilton*, vol. X, New York: Columbia University Press, pp. 230–340.

Hamilton, Alexander [1928] (1968), *Industrial and Commercial Correspondence of Alexander Hamilton Anticipating His Report on Manufactures*, edited by Arthur H. Cole, New York: Augustus M. Kelley.

Hamouda, Omar F., Clive Lee and Douglas Mair (eds) (1998), *The Economics of John Rae*, New York: Routledge.

Haring, Joseph E. (1963), 'Dynamic trade theory and growth in poor countries', *Kyklos*, **XVI** (3), 371–92.

Harris, Donald J. (1978), *Capital Accumulation and Income Distribution*, Stanford: Stanford University Press.

Heckscher, Eli [1919] (1949), 'The effect of foreign trade on the distribution of income', in American Economic Association, *Readings in the Theory of International Trade*, Philadelphia: The Blakiston Co., pp. 272–300.

Helleiner, Gerald K. (1973), 'Manufactured exports from less-developed countries and multinational firms', *Economic Journal*, **83** (329), 21–47.

Helleiner, Gerald K. (1981), 'The Refsnes Seminar: economic theory and North–South negotiations', *World Development*, **9** (6), 539–55.

Helleiner, Gerald K. (1989), 'Transnational corporations and direct foreign investment', in Hollis Chenery and T. N. Srinivasan (eds) (1989), pp. 1441–80.

Henderson, William O. (1981), 'Friedrich List and the social question', *Journal of European Economic History*, **10** (3), 697–708.

Henderson, William O. (1983a), 'Editor's introduction', in Friedrich List, *The Natural System of Political Economy*, translated and edited by William O. Henderson, London: Frank Cass, pp. 1–14.

Henderson, William O. (1983b), *Friedrich List: Economist and Visionary, 1789–1846*, London: Frank Cass.

Hicks, John R. (1959), 'National economic development in the international setting', in John R. Hicks, *Essays in World Economics*, London: Oxford University Press, pp. 161–95.

Hindley, Brian (1987), 'Different and more favorable treatment – and graduation', in J. Michael Finger and Andrzej Olechowski (eds), *The Uruguay Round: A Handbook on the Multilateral Trade Negotiations*, Washington, DC: World Bank, pp. 67–74.

Hirschman, Albert O. (1958), *The Strategy of Economic Development*, New Haven: Yale University Press.

Hirschman, Albert O. (1968), 'The political economy of import-substituting industrialization in Latin America', *Quarterly Journal of Economics*, **LXXXII** (1), 1–32.

Hirschman, Albert O. (1977), 'A generalized linkage approach to development, with special reference to staples', *Economic Development and Cultural Change*, **XXV** (supplement), 67–98.

Hirst, Margaret [1909] (1965), *Life of Friedrich List and Selections from his Writings*, with an Introduction by Joseph Dorfman, New York: Augustus M. Kelley, Bookseller.

Ho, P. Sai-wing (1989), *Essays on Ricardo's Trade–Growth Analysis, with an Application to the Postwar Growth Experience of Hong Kong*, Ph.D. Dissertation, Stanford University.

Ho, P. Sai-wing (1996a), 'Rethinking classical trade analysis within a framework of capitalist development', *Cambridge Journal of Economics*, **20** (4), 413–32.
Ho, P. Sai-wing (1996b), 'Reappraising Torrens's contributions to the analysis of trade, growth, and colonisation', *Contributions to Political Economy*, **15**, 1–31.
Ho, P. Sai-wing (1997), 'Technological gap and uneven accumulation in a classical production model', *Metroeconomica*, **48** (1), 81–106.
Ho, P. Sai-wing (1998a), 'Foreign trade', entry to Heinz D. Kurz and Neri Salvadori (eds), *The Elgar Companion to Classical Economics*, Cheltenham, UK and Lyme, USA: Edward Elgar, pp. 308–12.
Ho, P. Sai-wing (1998b), 'Multilateral trade negotiations and the changing prospects for Third World development: assessing from a Southern perspective', *Journal of Economic Issues*, **XXXII** (2), 375–83.
Ho, P. Sai-wing (2005), 'Distortions in the trade policy for development debate: a re-examination of Friedrich List', *Cambridge Journal of Economics*, **29** (5), 729–45.
Ho, P. Sai-wing (2006), 'Analyzing and arresting uneven development: Friedrich List and Gunnar Myrdal compared', *Journal of Economic Issues*, **XL** (2), 359–67.
Ho, P. Sai-wing (2008), 'Arguing for policy space to promote development: Prebisch, Myrdal, and Singer', *Journal of Economic Issues*, **XLII** (2), 509–16.
Ho, P. Sai-wing (2009), 'An institutionalist's policy advice to address international inequalities: the contributions of Gunnar Myrdal', *Journal of Economic Issues*, **XLIII** (2), 337–44.
Hobsbawm, Eric J. (1968), *Industry and Empire: The Making of Modern English Society, 1750 to the Present Day*, New York: Pantheon Books.
Hoekman, Bernard (2005), 'Operationalizing the concept of policy space in the WTO: beyond special and differential treatment', *Journal of International Economic Law*, **8** (2), 405–24.
Hoekman, Bernard, Keith E. Maskus and Kamal Saggi (2005), 'Transfer of technology to developing countries: unilateral and multilateral policy options', *World Development*, **33** (10), 1587–602.
Hoekman, Bernard, Constantine Michalopoulos and L. Alan Winters (2004), 'Special and differential treatment of developing countries in the WTO: moving forward after Cancún', *The World Economy*, **27** (4), 481–506.
Hollander, Jacob H. (1911), 'Ricardo and Torrens', *Economic Journal*, **21** (83), 455–68.
Hollander, Samuel (1973), *The Economics of Adam Smith*, Toronto: University of Toronto Press.
Hollander, Samuel (1982), 'On the substantive identity of the Ricardian and neo-classical conceptions of economic organization: the French connection in British classicism', *Canadian Journal of Economics*, **15** (4), 586–612.
Hollander, Samuel (1985), *The Economics of John Stuart Mill*, 2 vols, Toronto: University of Toronto Press.
Hollander, Samuel (1998), 'John Rae and Adam Smith', in Omar F. Hamouda, Clive Lee and Douglas Mair (eds) (1998), *The Economics of John Rae*, New York: Routledge, pp. 199–221.
Hollander, Samuel (2000), *John Stuart Mill on Economic Theory and Method*, New York: Routledge.
Hoselitz, Bert F. (1960), 'Theories of stages of economic growth', in Bert F. Hoselitz (ed.), *Theories of Economic Growth*, Glencoe, IL: The Free Press, pp. 193–238.
Hudec, Robert E. (1987), *Developing Countries in the GATT Legal System*, Thames Essay No. 50, Aldershot: Gower (for the Trade Policy Research Centre, London).

Hudec, Robert E. (1992), 'GATT and the developing countries', *Columbia Business Law Review*, **1992** (1), 67–77.

Hufbauer, Gary C. (1966), *Synthetic Materials and the Theory of International Trade*, Cambridge: Harvard University Press.

Hughes, J. R. T. (1959), 'Foreign trade and balanced growth, the historical framework', *American Economic Review, Papers and Proceedings*, **49** (2), 330–37.

Hyde, G. L. (1963), 'A critique of the Prebisch thesis', *Economia Internazionale*, **XVI** (3), 463–87.

Irwin, Douglas A. (1996), *Against the Tide: An Intellectual History of Free Trade*, Princeton: Princeton University Press.

Irwin, Douglas A. (2001), 'Tariffs and growth in late nineteenth century America', *The World Economy*, **24** (1), 15–30.

Irwin, Douglas A. (2002a), *Free Trade under Fire*, Princeton: Princeton University Press.

Irwin, Douglas A. (2002b), 'Interpreting the tariff–growth correlation of the late 19th century', *American Economic Review, Papers and Proceedings*, **95** (2), 165–9.

Irwin, Douglas A. (2004), 'The aftermath of Hamilton's "Report on Manufactures"', *Journal of Economic History*, **64** (3), 800–821.

Jackson, John H. (1989), *The World Trading System: Law and Policy of International Economic Relations*, Cambridge, MA: The MIT Press.

James, R. Warren (1965), *John Rae, Political Economist: An Account of His Life and A Compilation of his Main Writings*, vol. I, Toronto: University of Toronto Press.

Jensen, Hans E. (2001), 'John Stuart Mill's theories of wealth and income distribution', *Review of Social Economy*, **LIX** (4), 491–507.

Johnson, Harry G. (1959), 'Economic development and international trade', *Pakistan Economic Journal*, **IX** (4), 47–71.

Johnson, Harry G. (1960), 'The cost of protection and the scientific tariff', *Journal of Political Economy*, **LXVIII** (4), 327–45.

Johnson, Harry G. (1965), 'Optimal trade intervention in the presence of domestic distortions', in Richard E. Caves, Harry G. Johnson and Peter B. Kenen (eds), *Trade, Growth and the Balance of Payments*, Chicago: Rand McNally, pp. 3–34.

Johnson, Harry G. (1967), *Economic Policies toward Less Developed Countries*, Washington, DC: The Brookings Institution.

Johnson, Harry G. (1972a), 'The ideology of economic policy in the new states', in David Wall (ed.) (1972), *Chicago Essays in Economic Development*, Chicago: The University of Chicago Press, pp. 23–40.

Johnson, Harry G. (1972b), 'Tariffs and economic development', in David Wall (ed.) (1972), *Chicago Essays in Economic Development*, Chicago: The University of Chicago Press, pp. 271–99.

Johnson, Harry G. (1972c), 'Trade preference and developing countries', in David Wall (ed.) (1972), *Chicago Essays in Economic Development*, Chicago: The University of Chicago Press, pp. 300–321.

Jones, Ronald W. and Peter B. Kenen (eds) (1984), *Handbook of International Economics, vol. 1: International Trade*, Amsterdam: North-Holland.

Kafka, Alexandre (1962), 'A new argument for protectionism?', *Quarterly Journal of Economics*, **LXXVI** (1), 163–6.

Kaiser, Carl W., Jr. [1934] (1939), *History of the Academic Protectionist–Free Trade Controversy in America before 1860*, Philadelphia (University of Pennsylvania Ph.D. dissertation).

Kaldor, Nicholas (1963), 'Stabilizing the terms of trade of under-developed countries', *Economic Bulletin for Latin America*, **VIII** (1), 1–7.
Kaldor, Nicholas (1972), 'The irrelevance of equilibrium economics', *Economic Journal*, **82** (328), 1237–55.
Kaldor, Nicholas (1980), 'The foundations of free trade theory and their implications for the current world recession', in Edmond Malinvaud and Jean-Paul Fitoussi (eds), *Unemployment in Western Countries*, New York: St. Martin's Press, pp. 85–100.
Kalecki, Michał (1938), 'Review of Manoilesco's "Die Nationalen Produktivkraefte und der Aussenhandel"', *Economic Journal*, **48** (192), 708–11.
Kaplan, A. D. H. (1931), 'Henry Charles Carey: a study in American economic thought', *Johns Hopkins University Studies in Historical and Political Science*, **XLIX** (4), 9–93.
Keesing, Donald B. (1974), 'Public finance considerations in tariff theory for developing countries', *Public Finance/Finances Publiques*, **29** (2), 209–13.
Kemp, Murray C. (1960), 'The Mill–Bastable infant-industry dogma', *Journal of Political Economy*, **LXVIII** (1), 65–7.
Kenen, Peter B. (1963), 'Development, mobility and the case for tariffs', *Kyklos*, **XVI** (2), 321–4.
Kerr, Prue (1993), 'Adam Smith's theory of growth and technological change revisited', *Contributions to Political Economy*, **12**, 1–27.
Keynes, John M. (1929), 'The German transfer problem', *Economic Journal*, **39** (153), 1–7.
Kindleberger, Charles P. (1958), 'The terms of trade and economic development', *Review of Economics and Statistics*, **XL** (1, part 2), 72–90.
Kindleberger, Charles P. (1987), 'Gunnar Myrdal, 1898–1987', *Scandinavian Journal of Economics*, **89** (4), 393–403.
Knight, Frank H. (1924), 'Some fallacies in the interpretation of social cost', *Quarterly Journal of Economics*, **XXXVIII** (4), 582–606.
Knight, Frank H. (1925), 'On decreasing cost and comparative cost: a rejoinder', *Quarterly Journal of Economics*, **XXXIX** (2), 331–3.
Knox, A. D. (1960), 'Review of Myrdal's *Economic Theory and Under-developed Regions*', *Economica*, **27** (107), 280–83.
Koo, A. Y. C. (1961), 'An economic justification of protectionism: comment', *Quarterly Journal of Economics*, **LXXV** (1), 133–44.
Kregel, Jan A. (1977), 'Ricardo, trade and factor mobility', *Economia Internazionale*, **XXX** (2–3), 215–25.
Krueger, Anne O. (1978), *Foreign Trade Regimes and Economic Development: Liberalization Attempts and Consequences*, Cambridge, MA: Ballinger Publishing Company.
Krueger, Anne O. (1984), 'Trade policies in developing countries', in Ronald W. Jones and Peter B. Kenen (eds) (1984), *Handbook of International Economics, vol. 1: International Trade*, Amsterdam: North-Holland, pp. 519–69.
Krueger, Anne O. (1993), 'Virtuous and vicious circles in economic development', *American Economic Review, Papers and Proceedings*, **83** (2), 351–5.
Krueger, Anne O. (1997), 'Trade policy and economic development: how we learn', *American Economic Review*, **87** (1), 1–22.
Krugman, Paul R. (1984), 'Import protection as export promotion: international competition in the presence of oligopoly and economies of scale', in Henryk

Kierzkowski (ed.), *Monopolistic Competition in International Trade*, Oxford: Clarendon Press, pp. 180–93.

Krugman, Paul R. (1987), 'Is free trade passé?', *Journal of Economic Perspectives*, **1** (2), 131–44.

Krugman, Paul R. (1992a), 'Does the new trade theory require a new trade policy?', *The World Economy*, **15** (4), 423–41.

Krugman, Paul R. (1992b), 'Toward a counter-counterrevolution in development theory', *Proceedings of the World Bank Annual Conference on Development Economics*, pp. 15–38.

Krugman, Paul R. (1994), 'The fall and rise of development economics', in Lloyd Rodwin and Donald A. Schön (eds), *Rethinking the Development Experience: Essays Provoked by the Work of Albert O. Hirschman*, Washington, DC: The Brookings Institution, pp. 39–58.

Krugman, Paul R. and Maurice Obstfeld (1991), *International Economics: Theory and Policy*, 2nd edition, New York: HarperCollins.

Lal, Deepak (2000), *The Poverty of 'Development Economics'*, 2nd revised and expanded US edition, Cambridge, MA: The MIT Press.

Lall, Sanjaya (1992), 'Technological capabilities and industrialization', *World Development*, **20** (2), 165–86.

Lall, Sanjaya (1993), 'Understanding technology development', *Development and Change*, **24** (4), 719–53.

Lall, Sanjaya (1996), *Learning from the Asian Tigers: Studies in Technology and Industrial Policy*, New York: St. Martin's Press.

Lall, Sanjaya (1999), *Promoting Industrial Competitiveness in Developing Countries: Lessons from Asia*, Common Economic Papers no. 39, London: Commonwealth Secretariat.

Lall, Sanjaya (2005), 'Rethinking industrial strategy: the role of the state in the face of globalization', in Kevin P. Gallagher (ed.) (2005), *Putting Development First: The Importance of Policy Space in the WTO and International Financial Institutions*, London: Zed Books, pp. 33–68.

Lall, Sanjaya and Wolfram W. Latsch (1999), 'Import liberalization and industrial performance: theory and evidence', in Sanjaya Lall (ed.), *The Technological Response to Import Liberalization in Subsaharan Africa*, New York: St. Martin's Press, pp. 26–56.

Landes, David S. (1969), *The Unbound Prometheus: Technological Change and Industrial Development in Western Europe from 1750 to the Present*, New York: Cambridge University Press.

Langer, Gary F. (1982), 'Further evidence for Sraffa's interpretation of Ricardo', *Cambridge Journal of Economics*, **6** (4), 397–400.

Levi-Faur, David (1997a), 'Friedrich List and the political economy of the nation-state', *Review of International Political Economy*, **4** (1), 154–78.

Levi-Faur, David (1997b), 'Economic nationalism: from Friedrich List to Robert Reich', *Review of International Studies*, **23** (3), 359–70.

Levin, Jonathan V. (1960), *The Export Economies*, Cambridge, MA: Harvard University Press.

Levine, David P. (1975), 'The theory of the growth of the capitalist economy', *Economic Development and Cultural Change*, **XXIV** (1), 47–74.

Levitt, Kari P. (2005), 'Raúl Prebisch and Arthur Lewis: the two basic dualities of development economics', in Jomo K. Sundaram (ed.) (2005), *The Pioneers of*

Development Economics: Great Economists on Development, London: Zed Books, pp. 193–208.

Lewis, W. Arthur (1954), 'Economic development with unlimited supplies of labour', *The Manchester School of Economic and Social Studies*, **XXII** (2), 139–91.

Lewis, W. Arthur (1965), 'Economic development and world trade', in E. A. G. Robinson (ed.), *Problems in Economic Development*, London: Macmillan and Co. Ltd., pp. 483–95.

Linder, Staffan B. (1961), *An Essay on Trade and Transformation*, New York: John Wiley & Sons.

Lipsey, Richard. G. and Kelvin Lancaster (1956–57), 'The general theory of second best', *Review of Economic Studies*, **24** (1), 11–32.

List, Friedrich [1827] (1996), *Outlines of American Political Economy*, Wiesbaden: Böttiger.

List, Friedrich [1837] (1983), *The Natural System of Political Economy*, translated and edited by William O. Henderson, London: Frank Cass.

List, Friedrich [1841] (1991), *The National System of Political Economy*, translated by Sampson S. Lloyd, with an Introduction by J. Shield Nicholson, Fairfield, NJ: Augustus M. Kelley, Publishers.

Little, Ian M. D. (1982), *Economic Development: Theory, Policy, and International Relations*, New York: Basic Books, Inc., Publishers.

Little, Ian M. D., Tibor Scitovsky and Maurice Scott (1970), *Industry and Trade in Some Developing Countries: A Comparative Study*, London: Oxford University Press.

Love, Joseph L. (1980), 'Raúl Prebisch and the origins of the doctrine of unequal exchange', *Latin American Research Review*, **15** (3), 45–72.

Love, Joseph L. (1986), 'Manoilescu, Prebisch, and the thesis of unequal exchange', *Rumanian Studies*, **V**, 125–33.

Love, Joseph L. (1988), 'Structural change and conceptual response in Latin America and Romania, 1860–1950', in Joseph L. Love and Nils Jacobsen (eds), *Guiding the Invisible Hand: Economic Liberalism and the State in Latin American History*, New York: Praeger, pp. 1–33.

Love, Joseph L. (1990), 'The origins of dependency analysis', *Journal of Latin American Studies*, **22** (1), 143–68.

Love, Joseph L. (1994), 'Economic ideas and ideologies in Latin America since 1930', in Leslie Bethell (ed.), *The Cambridge History of Latin America*, vol. VI, New York: Cambridge University Press, pp. 393–460.

Love, Joseph L. (1996), *Crafting the Third World: Theorizing Underdevelopment in Rumania and Brazil*, Stanford: Stanford University Press.

Love, Joseph L. (2002), 'Resisting liberalism: theorizing backwardness and development in Rumania before 1914', in Michalis Psalidopoulos and Maria E. Mata (eds), *Economic Thought and Policy in Less Developed Europe: The Nineteenth Century*, New York: Routledge, pp. 105–28.

Love, Joseph L. (2004), 'Structuralism and dependency in peripheral Europe: Latin American ideas in Spain and Portugal', *Latin American Research Review*, **39** (2), 114–40.

Love, Joseph L. (2005a), 'The rise and fall of structuralism', in Valpy FitzGerald and Rosemary Thorp (eds), *Economic Doctrines in Latin America: Origins, Embedding and Evolution*, New York: Palgrave Macmillan, pp. 157–81.

Love, Joseph L. (2005b), 'The rise and decline of economic structuralism in Latin America: new dimensions', *Latin American Research Review*, **40** (3), 100–125.

Lowe, Adolph (1975), 'Adam Smith's system of equilibrium growth', in Andrew S. Skinner and Thomas Wilson (eds) (1975), *Essays on Adam Smith*, Oxford: Clarendon Press, pp. 415–25.
Lunt, Edward C. (1895), 'Hamilton as a political economist', *Journal of Political Economy*, **III** (3), 289–310.
Magee, Stephen P. (1973), 'Factor market distortions, production, and trade: a survey', *Oxford Economic Papers*, **25** (1), 1–43.
Maneschi, Andrea (1983), 'Dynamic aspects of Ricardo's international trade theory', *Oxford Economic Papers*, **35** (1), 67–80.
Maneschi, Andrea (1992), 'Ricardo's international trade theory: beyond the comparative cost example', *Cambridge Journal of Economics*, **16** (4), 421–37.
Maneschi, Andrea (1998), *Comparative Advantage in International Trade: A Historical Perspective*, Cheltenham, UK and Lyme, USA: Edward Elgar.
Maneschi, Andrea (2001), 'John Stuart Mill's equilibrium terms of trade: a special case of William Whewell's 1850 formula', *History of Political Economy*, **33** (3), 609–25.
Manoïlesco, Mihaïl (1931), *The Theory of Protection and International Trade*, London: P. S. King & Son, Ltd.
Marshall, Alfred [1890] (1966), 'Some aspects of competition', reprinted in A. C. Pigou (ed.) (1966), *Memorials of Alfred Marshall*, New York: Augustus M. Kelley, Publishers, pp. 256–91.
Marshall, Alfred [1901] (1966), 'An export duty on coal', reprinted in Arthur C. Pigou (ed.) (1966), *Memorials of Alfred Marshall*, New York: Augustus M. Kelley, Publishers, pp. 320–22.
Marshall, Alfred [1903] (1926), *Memorandum on Fiscal Policy of International Trade*, reprinted in John M. Keynes (ed.) (1926), *Official Papers by Alfred Marshall*, London: Macmillan & Co., Ltd., pp. 367–420.
Marshall, Alfred [1920] (1961), *Principles of Economics*, 9th (variorum) edition with annotations by C. W. Guillebaud, London: Macmillan & Co., Ltd.
Marshall, Alfred (1923), *Industry and Trade: A Study of Industrial Technique and Business Organization; and of Their Influences on the Conditions of Various Classes and Nations*, London: Macmillan & Co., Ltd.
Marshall, Alfred [1923] (1991), *Money, Credit and Commerce*, Fairfield, NJ: Augustus M. Kelley, Publishers.
Marshall, Alfred (1975), *The Early Economic Writings of Alfred Marshall, 1867–1890*, vol. 2, edited by John K. Whitaker, New York: The Free Press.
McCloskey, Donald N. (1980), 'Magnanimous Albion: free trade and British national income, 1841–1881', *Explorations in Economic History*, **17** (3), 303–20.
McCombie, J. S. L. and Anthony P. Thirlwall (1994), *Economic Growth and the Balance-of-Payments Constraint*, New York: St. Martin's Press.
McLeod, Alex N. (1951), 'Trade and investment in underdeveloped areas: a comment', *American Economic Review*, **41** (3), 411–19.
Meade, James E. (1955), *The Theory of International Economic Policy, vol. II: Trade and Welfare*, London: Oxford University Press.
Meenai, Saeed A. (1956), 'Robert Torrens – 1780–1864', *Economica*, **23** (89), 49–61.
Meier, Gerald M. (1958a), 'International trade and international inequality', *Oxford Economic Papers*, **10** (3), 277–89.
Meier, Gerald M. (1958b), 'Myrdal on commercial policy of underdeveloped countries', *Economia Internazionale*, **XI** (2), 247–56.

Meier, Gerald M. (1959), 'Review of Myrdal's *Rich Lands and Poor: The Road to World Prosperity*', *Journal of Political Economy*, **LXVII** (6), 636–7.

Meier, Gerald M. (1963), *International Trade and Development*, New York: Harper & Row.

Meier, Gerald M. (1980), *International Economics: The Theory of Policy*, New York: Oxford University Press.

Meier, Gerald M. (ed.) (1987), *Pioneers in Development*, 2nd series, New York: Oxford University Press.

Meier, Gerald M. (2005), *Biography of a Subject: An Evolution of Development Economics*, New York: Oxford University Press.

Meier, Gerald M. and Dudley Seers (eds) (1984), *Pioneers in Development*, New York: Oxford University Press.

Meier, Gerald M. and Joseph E. Stiglitz (eds) (2001), *Frontiers of Development Economics: The Future in Perspective*, Washington, DC: The World Bank/Oxford University Press.

Michalopoulos, Constantine (1999), 'The developing countries in the WTO', *The World Economy*, **22** (1), 117–43.

Mill, John Stuart [1825] (1967), 'The Corn Laws', *Westminster Review*, April 1825, pp. 394–420, reprinted in *Collected Works of John Stuart Mill*, vol. IV, Toronto: University of Toronto Press, pp. 47–70.

Mill, John Stuart [1843] (1986), 'Torrens's letter to Sir Robert Peel', *Spectator*, 28 January, 1843, pp. 85–6, reprinted in *Collected Works of John Stuart Mill*, vol. XXIV, Toronto: University of Toronto Press, pp. 836–41.

Mill, John Stuart (1848), *Principles of Political Economy with Some of Their Applications to Social Philosophy*, London: John W. Parker.

Mill, John Stuart [1871] (1965), *Principles of Political Economy with Some of Their Applications to Social Philosophy*, J. M. Robson ed., in *Collected Works of John Stuart Mill*, vols. II and III, Toronto: University of Toronto Press.

Mill, John Stuart [1873] (1969), *Autobiography*, London: Oxford University Press.

Mill, John Stuart [1874] (1974), *Essays on Some Unsettled Questions of Political Economy*, 2nd edition, Clifton, NJ: Augustus M. Kelley, Publishers.

Mill, John Stuart (various volumes), *Collected Works of John Stuart Mill*, Toronto: University of Toronto Press.

Murphy, Kevin M., Andrei Shleifer and Robert Vishny (1989), 'Industrialization and the big push', *Journal of Political Economy*, **XCVII** (5), 1003–26.

Myint, Hla (1958), 'The "classical theory" of international trade and the underdeveloped countries', *Economic Journal*, **68** (270), 317–37.

Myint, Hla (1963), 'Infant industry arguments for assistance to industries in the setting of dynamic trade theory', in Roy Harrod and Douglas Hague (eds), *International Trade Theory in a Developing World*, New York: St. Martin's Press, pp. 173–93.

Myint, Hla (1968), 'Review [of Myrdal's *Asian Drama*]', *Swedish Journal of Economics*, **70** (4), 242–5.

Myint, Hla (1969), 'International trade and the developing countries', in Paul A. Samuelson (ed.), *International Economic Relations*, Proceedings of the Third Congress of the International Economic Association, New York: St. Martin's Press, pp. 15–35.

Myint, Hla (1971), 'Market mechanism and planning – the functional approach', in Hla Myint, *Economic Theory and the Underdeveloped Countries*, New York: Oxford University Press, pp. 291–314.

Myint, Hla (1977), 'Adam Smith's theory of international trade in the perspective of economic development', *Economica*, **44** (175), 231–48.
Myint, Hla (1984), 'Comment [on Myrdal (1984)]', in Gerald M. Meier and Dudley Seers (eds) (1984), *Pioneers in Development*, New York: Oxford University Press, pp. 166–72.
Myint, Hla (1987), 'The neoclassical resurgence in development economics: its strength and limitations', in Gerald M. Meier (ed.) (1987), *Pioneers in Development*, 2nd series, New York: Oxford University Press, pp. 107–36.
Myrdal, Gunnar [1939] (1965), *Monetary Equilibrium*, New York: Augustus M. Kelley, Bookseller.
Myrdal, Gunnar (1951), 'The trend towards economic planning', *The Manchester School of Economic and Social Studies*, **XIX** (1), 1–42.
Myrdal, Gunnar (1956), *An International Economy: Problems and Prospects*, New York: Harper & Brothers Publishers.
Myrdal, Gunnar [1957] (1963), *Economic Theory and Under-Developed Regions*, London: Methuen & Co. Ltd.
Myrdal, Gunnar (1961), 'Toward a more closely integrated free-world economy', in Robert Lekachman (ed.), *National Policy for Economic Welfare at Home and Abroad*, New York: Russell & Russell, pp. 235–92.
Myrdal, Gunnar (1968), *Asian Drama: An Inquiry into the Poverty of Nations*, vols. I–III, New York: Pantheon.
Myrdal, Gunnar (1970a), *The Challenge of World Poverty: A World Anti-Poverty Program in Outline*, New York: Pantheon Books.
Myrdal, Gunnar (1970b), 'The "soft state" in underdeveloped countries', in Paul Streeten (ed.), *Unfashionable Economics: Essays in Honour of Lord Balogh*, London: Weidenfeld and Nicholson, pp. 227–43.
Myrdal, Gunnar (1973), *Against the Stream: Critical Essays on Economics*, New York: Pantheon Books.
Myrdal, Gunnar (1974), 'What is development?', *Journal of Economic Issues*, **VIII** (4), 729–36.
Myrdal, Gunnar (1978), 'Institutional economics', *Journal of Economic Issues*, **XII** (4), 771–83.
Myrdal, Gunnar (1981), 'Need for reforms in underdeveloped countries', in Sven Grassman and Erik Lundberg (eds), *The World Economic Order: Past and Prospects*, New York: St. Martin's Press, pp. 501–25.
Myrdal, Gunnar (1984), 'International inequality and foreign aid in retrospect', in Gerald M. Meier and Dudley Seers (eds) (1984), *Pioneers in Development*, New York: Oxford University Press, pp. 151–65.
Nelson, Eastin (ed.) (1960), *Economic Growth: Rationale, Problems, Cases*, Austin: University of Texas Press.
Nelson, John R., Jr. (1979), 'Alexander Hamilton and American manufacturing: a reexamination', *Journal of American History*, **65** (4), 971–95.
Nelson, Richard R. (2009), 'Building effective "innovation systems" versus dealing with "market failures" as ways of thinking about technology policy', in Dominique Foray (ed.), *The New Economics of Technology Policy*, Cheltenham, UK and Northampton, MA, USA, pp. 7–16.
Nelson, Richard R. and Howard Pack (1999), 'The Asian Miracle and modern growth theory', *Economic Journal*, **109** (457), 416–36.
Nelson, Richard R. and Howard Pack (2003), 'Factors behind the Asian Miracle: entrepreneurship, education and finance', in Luigi Paganetto and Edmund S.

Phelps (eds), *Finance, Research, Education and Growth*, New York: Palgrave Macmillan, pp. 105–32.

Netanel, Neil W. (ed.) (2009), *The Development Agenda: Global Intellectual Property and Developing Countries*, New York: Oxford University Press.

Nicholson, J. Shield [1904] (1991), 'Introductory essay', reprinted in Friedrich List [1841] (1991), *The National System of Political Economy*, Fairfield, NJ: Augustus M. Kelley, Publishers.

Notz, William (1926), 'Frederick List in America', *American Economic Review*, **16** (2), 249–65.

Nurkse, Ragnar (1962), *Equilibrium and Growth in the World Economy*, Cambridge: Harvard University Press.

Nurkse, Ragnar (1963), 'International trade theory and development policy', in Howard S. Ellis (ed.) (1963), *Economic Development for Latin America*, New York: St. Martin's Press, pp. 234–63.

Ocampo, Jose A. and Lance Taylor (1998), 'Trade liberalisation in developing economies: modest benefits but problems with productivity growth, macro prices, and income distribution', *Economic Journal*, **108** (450), 1523–46.

Ohlin, Bertil (1931), 'Protection and non-competing groups', *Weltwirtschaftliches Archiv*, **XXXIII** (1), 30–45.

Ohlin, Bertil (1967), *Interregional and International Trade*, revised edition, Cambridge, MA: Harvard University Press.

O'Rourke, Kevin H. (2000), 'Tariffs and growth in the late 19th century', *Economic Journal*, **110** (463), 456–83.

Pack, Howard and Larry E. Westphal (1986), 'Industrial strategy and technological change: theory versus reality', *Journal of Development Economics*, **22** (1), 87–128.

Palma, J. Gabriel (1992), 'Raül Prebisch', in Philip Arestis and Malcolm Sawyer (eds) (1992), *A Biographical Dictionary of Dissenting Economists*, Aldershot, UK and Brookfield, USA: Edward Elgar, pp. 438–48.

Park, Sung Sang (1977), *Growth and Development: A Physical Output and Employment Strategy*, with a Foreword by Colin Clark, New York: St. Martin's Press.

Parks, Robert J. [1963] (1977), *European Origins of the Economic Ideas of Alexander Hamilton*, New York: Arno Press.

Parrinello, Sergio (1988), '"On foreign trade" and the Ricardian model of trade', *Journal of Post-Keynesian Economics*, **X** (4), 585–601.

Pasinetti, Luigi L. (1977), *Lectures on the Theory of Production*, New York: Columbia University Press.

Pasvolsky, Leo (1932), 'Review of Manoilesco's *Theory of Protection and International Trade*', *American Economic Review*, **22** (3), 477–8.

Pollard, Sidney (1981), *Peaceful Conquest: The Industrialization of Europe 1760–1970*, New York: Oxford University Press.

Prebisch, Raúl (1950a), *The Economic Development of Latin America and Its Principal Problems*, New York: United Nations.

Prebisch, Raúl (1950b), *Theoretical and Practical Problems of Economic Growth*, New York: United Nations Economic and Social Council.

Prebisch, Raúl (1951a), *Economic Survey of Latin America 1949*, New York: United Nations Department of Economic Affairs.

Prebisch, Raúl (1951b), 'Interpretation of the process of economic development', the English summary of 'Interpretação do Processo de Desenvolvimento Econômico', *Revista Brasileira de Economia*, **5** (1), 117–27.
Prebisch, Raúl (1954), *International Co-operation in a Latin American Development Policy*, New York: United Nations.
Prebisch, Raúl (1958), 'Soviet challenge to American leadership: America's role in helping underdeveloped countries', in Committee for Economic Development (CED), *Problems of United States Economic Development*, New York, pp. 47–55.
Prebisch, Raúl (1959a), 'Commercial policy in the underdeveloped countries', *American Economic Review, Papers and Proceedings*, **49** (2), 251–73.
Prebisch, Raúl (1959b), 'Statement at the second session of the Special Committee to study the Formulation of New Measures for Economic Co-operation of the Organization of American States', in Economic Commission for Latin America, *The Latin American Common Market*, New York: United Nations, pp. 141–6.
Prebisch, Raúl (1960), 'The structural crisis in Argentina and its prospects of solution', in Eastin Nelson (ed.) (1960), *Economic Growth: Rationale, Problems, Cases*, Austin: University of Texas Press, pp. 104–24.
Prebisch, Raúl (1961a), 'Economic development or monetary stability: the false dilemma', *Economic Bulletin for Latin America*, **VI** (1), 1–25.
Prebisch, Raúl (1961b), 'Joint responsibilities for Latin American progress', *Foreign Affairs*, **39** (4), 622–34.
Prebisch, Raúl (1962), 'Economic aspects of the Alliance', in John Dreier (ed.), *The Alliance for Progress: Problems and Perspectives*, Baltimore: The John Hopkins Press, pp. 24–65.
Prebisch, Raúl (1963), *Towards a Dynamic Development Policy for Latin America*, New York: United Nations.
Prebisch, Raúl (1964), *Towards a New Trade Policy for Development*, Report by the Secretary-General of the UNCTAD, New York: United Nations.
Prebisch, Raúl (1968), *Towards a Global Strategy for Development*, Report by the Secretary-General of UNCTAD, New York: United Nations.
Prebisch, Raúl (1971a), *Change and Development – Latin America's Great Task: Report Submitted to the Inter-American Development Bank*, New York: Praeger Publishers.
Prebisch, Raúl (1971b), *Latin America: A Problem in Development*, 1970/71 Hackett Memorial Lecture, Austin: University of Texas at Austin, Institute of Latin American Studies.
Prebisch, Raúl (1976), 'A critique of peripheral capitalism', *CEPAL Review*, 9–76.
Prebisch, Raúl (1978), 'Socio-economic structure and crisis of peripheral capitalism', *CEPAL Review*, second half of 1978, 159–252.
Prebisch, Raúl (1979), 'Address', delivered at the 18th session of CEPAL in La Paz, April 1979, *CEPAL Review*, 171–3.
Prebisch, Raúl (1983), 'The Latin-American periphery in the global system of capitalism', in Shigeto Tsuru (ed.) (1983), *Human Resources, Employment and Development, vol. 1: The Issues*, New York: St. Martin's Press, pp. 30–45.
Prebisch, Raúl (1984), 'Five stages in my thinking on development', in Gerald M. Meier and Dudley Seers (eds) (1984), *Pioneers in Development*, New York: Oxford University Press, pp. 175–91.
Prebisch, Raúl (1985), 'Power relations and market laws', in Kwan S. Kim and David F. Ruccio (eds), *Debt and Development in Latin America*, Notre Dame: University of Notre Dame Press, pp. 9–31.

Prebisch, Raúl (1986), 'The dynamic role of the periphery', in Krishna Ahooja-Patel, Anne G. Drabek and Marc Nerfin (eds), *World Economy in Transition: Essays Presented to Surendra Patel on His Sixtieth Birthday*, Oxford: Pergamon Press, pp. 3–9.

Prebisch, Raúl (1988), 'Dependence, development, and interdependence', in Gustav Ranis and T. Paul Schultz (eds) (1988), *The State of Development Economics: Progress and Perspectives*, Cambridge, MA: Basil Blackwell, pp. 31–41.

Prebisch, Raúl et al. (1965), *Proposals for the Creation of the Latin American Common Market*, Inter-American Development Bank.

Prendergast, Renee and Hans W. Singer (1991), 'Introduction: development perspectives for the 1990s', in Renee Prendergast and Hans W. Singer (eds), *Development Perspectives for the 1990s*, New York: St. Martin's Press, pp. xvii–xxiv.

Prowse, Susan (2002), 'The role of international and national agencies in trade-related capacity building', *The World Economy*, **25** (9), 1235–61.

Pryme, George (1870), *Autobiographic Recollections of George Pryme, Esq. M.A.*, edited by his daughter, Cambridge: Deighton, Bell, and Co.

Rae, John [1825] (1965), 'Sketches of the origin and progress of manufactures and of the policy which has regulated their legislative encouragement in Great Britain and in other countries', *Canadian Review and Literary and Historical Journal*, no. 3, reprinted in R. Warren James (1965), *John Rae, Political Economist: An Account of His Life and a Compilation of his Main Writings*, vol. I, Toronto: University of Toronto Press, pp. 195–206.

Rae, John [1834] (1964), *Statement of Some New Principles on the Subject of Political Economy, Exposing the Fallacies of the System of Free Trade, and of Some Other Doctrines Maintained in the* Wealth of Nations, New York: Augustus M. Kelley, Bookseller.

Raffer, Kunibert (2005), 'Sir Hans Singer: advocating a fair distribution of fruits of progress', in Jomo K. Sundaram (ed.) (2005), *The Pioneers of Development Economics: Great Economists on Development*, London: Zed Books, pp. 209–25.

Raffer, Kunibert and Hans W. Singer (2001), *The Economic North–South Divide: Six Decades of Unequal Development*, Cheltenham, UK and Northampton, MA, USA: Edward Elgar.

Ranis, Gustav and T. Paul Schultz (eds) (1988), *The State of Development Economics: Progress and Perspectives*, Cambridge, MA: Basil Blackwell.

Reddaway, William B. (1987), 'Some reflections by a Keynesian economist on the problems of developing countries', in Anthony P. Thirlwall (ed.) (1987b), *Keynes and Economic Development*, New York: St. Martin's Press, pp. 36–65.

Reisman, David A. (1995), 'Review of G. Dostaler et al. (eds), *Gunnar Myrdal and His Works*', *Economic Journal*, **105** (428), 246.

Ricardo, David [1815] (1951a), *An Essay on the Influence of a Low Price of Corn on the Profits of Stock*, 2nd edition, in Piero Sraffa and Maurice H. Dobb (eds), *The Works and Correspondence of David Ricardo*, vol. IV, Cambridge: Cambridge University Press, pp. 9–41.

Ricardo, David [1821] (2004), *On the Principles of Political Economy and Taxation*, in Piero Sraffa and Maurice H. Dobb (eds), *The Works and Correspondence of David Ricardo*, vol. I, Indianapolis: Liberty Fund.

Ricardo, David [1823] (1951a), *Absolute Value and Exchangeable Value*, in Piero Sraffa and Maurice H. Dobb (eds), *The Works and Correspondence of David Ricardo*, vol. IV, Cambridge: Cambridge University Press, pp. 358–412.

Ricardo, David [1928] (1951b), *Notes on Malthus's Principles of Political Economy*, in Piero Sraffa and Maurice H. Dobb (eds), *The Works and Correspondence of David Ricardo*, vol. II, Cambridge: Cambridge University Press.

Ricardo, David (1951c), Letters 1810–1815, in Piero Sraffa and Maurice H. Dobb (eds), *The Works and Correspondence of David Ricardo*, vol. VI, Cambridge: Cambridge University Press.

Richardson, G. B. (1975), 'Adam Smith on competition and increasing returns', in Andrew S. Skinner and Thomas Wilson (eds) (1975), *Essays on Adam Smith*, Oxford: Clarendon Press, pp. 350–60.

Robbins, Lionel (1958), *Robert Torrens and the Evolution of Classical Economics*, New York: St. Martin's Press.

Robbins, Lionel (1968), *The Theory of Economic Development in the History of Economic Thought*, New York: St. Martin's Press.

Robbins, Lionel (1970), *The Evolution of Modern Economic Theory and Other Papers on the History of the Economic Thought*, Chicago: Aldine Publishing Company.

Robbins, L. (1998), *A History of Economic Thought: The LSE Lectures*, edited by Steven G. Medema and Warren J. Samuels, Princeton: Princeton University Press.

Rodríguez, Francisco and Dani Rodrik (2000), 'Trade policy and economic growth: a skeptic's guide to the cross-national evidence', *NBER Macroeconomics Annual*, **15**, 261–325.

Rodrik, Dani (1992), 'Conceptual issues in the design of trade policy for industrialization', *World Development*, **20** (3), 309–20.

Rodrik, Dani (2001), 'Trading in illusions', *Foreign Policy*, **123** (2), 54–62.

Rodrik, Dani (2009a), 'Growth after the crisis', unpublished paper, Harvard Kennedy School, http://www.hks.harvard.edu/fs/drodrik/Growth after the crisis.pdf (accessed on January 6, 2010).

Rodrik, Dani (2009b), 'Making room for China in the world economy', unpublished paper, Harvard Kennedy School, http://www.hks.harvard.edu/fs/drodrik/Research papers/Making room for China.pdf (accessed on January 6, 2010).

Rogge, B. A. (1956), 'Economic development in Latin America: the Prebisch thesis', *Inter-American Economic Affairs*, **IX** (4), 24–49.

Rollins, Charles E. (1956), 'Mineral development and economic growth', *Social Research*, **23** (3), 253–80.

Rosenberg, Nathan (1960), 'Some institutional aspects of the *Wealth of Nations*', *Journal of Political Economy*, **LXVIII** (6), 557–70.

Rosenstein-Rodan, Paul N. (1943), 'Problems of industrialization of Eastern and South-Eastern Europe', *Economic Journal*, **53** (210), 202–11.

Sachs, Jeffrey D. and Andrew Warner (1995), 'Economic reform and the process of global integration', *Brookings Papers on Economic Activity*, **1995** (1), 1–95.

Samuelson, Paul A. (1982), 'Bertil Ohlin 1899–1979', *Journal of International Economics*, **12** (supplement), 31–49.

Samuelson, Paul A. (2004), 'Where Ricardo and Mill rebut and confirm arguments of mainstream economists supporting globalization', *Journal of Economic Perspectives*, **18** (3), 135–46.

Sapsford, David and John-ren Chen (eds) (1998), *Development Economics and Policy: The Conference Volume to Celebrate the 85th Birthday of Professor Sir Hans Singer*, New York: St. Martin's Press.

Sapsford, David, Prabirjit Sarkar and Hans W. Singer (1992), 'The Prebisch–Singer terms of trade controversy revisited', *Journal of International Development*, **4** (3), 315–32.

Schiavo-Campo, Salvatore and Hans W. Singer (1970), *Perspectives of Economic Development*, Boston: Houghton Mifflin Company.

Scholte, Jan Aart (2008), 'Defining globalisation', *The World Economy*, **31** (11), 1471–502.

Schumpeter, Joseph A. (1954), *History of Economic Analysis*, New York: Oxford University Press.

Scitovsky, Tibor (1954), 'Two concepts of external economies', *Journal of Political Economy*, **LXII** (2), 143–51.

Seers, Dudley (1963), 'Big companies and small countries: a practical proposal', *Kyklos*, **XVI** (4), 599–607.

Seers, Dudley (1964), 'The mechanism of an open petroleum economy', *Social and Economic Studies*, **13** (2), 233–42.

Seers, Dudley (1983), *The Political Economy of Nationalism*, Oxford: Oxford University Press.

Seligman, Edwin R. A. (1903), 'On some neglected British economists, parts I & II', *Economic Journal*, **13** (51, 52), 335–63, 511–35.

Seligman, Edwin R. A. (1911), 'Ricardo and Torrens', *Economic Journal*, **21** (83), 448–55.

Semmel, Bernard (1970), *The Rise of Free Trade Imperialism: Classical Political Economy, the Empire of Free Trade and Imperialism, 1750–1850*, Cambridge: Cambridge University Press.

Senghaas, Dieter (1991), 'Friedrich List and the basic problems of modern development', *Review*, **XIV** (3), 451–67.

Shafaeddin, Mehdi (2000), 'What did Frederick List actually say? Some clarifications on the infant industry argument', *UNCTAD Discussion Paper*, no. 149, Geneva.

Shafaeddin, Mehdi (2005a), *Trade Policy at the Crossroads: The Recent Experience of Developing Countries*, New York: Palgrave Macmillan.

Shafaeddin, Mehdi (2005b), 'Friedrich List and the infant industry argument', in Jomo K. Sundaram (ed.) (2005), *The Pioneers of Development Economics: Great Economists on Development*, London: Zed Books, pp. 42–61.

Shankman, Andrew (2003), '"A new thing on earth": Alexander Hamilton, pro-manufacturing Republicans, and the democratization of American political economy', *Journal of the Early Republic*, **23** (3), 323–52.

Shaw, D. John (2002), *Sir Hans Singer: The Life and Work of a Development Economist*, with Foreword by Richard Jolly, New York: Palgrave Macmillan.

Singer, Hans W. (1949a), 'Economic progress in under-developed countries', *Social Research*, **16** (1), 1–11.

Singer, Hans W. (1949b), *Relative Prices of Exports and Imports of Under-developed Countries: A Study of Post-war Terms of Trade between Under-developed and Industrialized Countries*, New York: United Nations Department of Economic Affairs.

Singer, Hans W. (1950), 'The distribution of gains between investing and borrowing countries', *American Economic Review, Papers and Proceedings*, **40** (2), 473–85.

Singer, Hans W. (1951a), 'Development projects as part of national development programmes', lectures delivered from October to December, 1950, at the Asian Centre on Agricultural and Allied Projects in Lahore, Pakistan, printed in United

Nations, *Formulation and Economic Appraisal of Development Projects*, Book I, pp. 1–109.

Singer, Hans W. (1951b), 'Reply' to Alex N. McLeod, 'Trade and investment in underdeveloped areas: a comment', *American Economic Review*, **41** (3), 419–21.

Singer, Hans W. (1952), 'The mechanics of economic development: a quantitative-model approach', *Indian Economic Review*, **I** (2), 1–18.

Singer, Hans W. (1953), 'Obstacles to economic development', *Social Research*, **20** (1), 19–31.

Singer, Hans W. (1958a), 'Comment [on C. Kindleberger (1958)]', *Review of Economics and Statistics*, **XL** (1), 85–8.

Singer, Hans W. (1958b), 'Trade fluctuations and buffer policies of low-income countries', *Kyklos*, **XI** (2), 141–54.

Singer, Hans W. (1958c), 'Deficit financing of public capital formation', *Social and Economic Studies*, **7** (3), 85–96.

Singer, Hans W. (1959), 'Introductory statement', *Kyklos*, **XII** (3), 271–82.

Singer, Hans W. (1960), 'The concept of balanced growth in economic development: theory and practice', in Eastin Nelson (ed.) (1960), *Economic Growth: Rationale, Problems, Cases*, Austin: University of Texas Press, pp. 71–86.

Singer, Hans W. (1961a), 'Education and economic development', in United Nations Economic Commission for Africa and United Nations Educational, Scientific and Cultural Organization, *Final Report on the Conference of African States on the Development of Education in Africa, Addis Ababa, 12–15 May 1961*, pp. 107–11.

Singer, Hans W. (1961b), 'Trends in economic thought on underdevelopment', *Social Research*, **28** (4), 387–414.

Singer, Hans W. (1964a), *International Development: Growth and Change*, New York: McGraw-Hill Book Company.

Singer, Hans W. (1964b), 'Effects of patents on the economies of under-developed countries', in UN Secretary-General, *The Role of Patents in the Transfer of Technology to Developing Countries*, New York: United Nations, pp. 39–50.

Singer, Hans W. (1965), 'Social development: key growth sector', *International Development Review*, **VII** (1), 3–8.

Singer, Hans W. (1967), 'Pre-conditions for regional economic integration', *International Development Review*, **IX** (3), 19–20.

Singer, Hans W. [1969a] (1975), 'Employment problems in developing countries', condensed from a paper with the same title prepared for the Human Resource Conference of the ILO, Philadelphia, May 1969, reprinted in Hans W. Singer (1975), *The Strategy of International Development: Essays in the Economics of Backwardness*, London: Macmillan, pp. 133–44.

Singer, Hans W. [1969b] (1975), 'Dualism revisited: a new approach to the problems of the dual society in developing countries', originally prepared for the Conference on the Dual Economy held at Glasgow in September 1969, reprinted in Hans W. Singer (1975), *The Strategy of International Development: Essays in the Economics of Backwardness*, London: Macmillan, pp. 67–90.

Singer, Hans W. [1969c] (1975), 'Keynesian models of economic development and their limitations: an analysis in the light of Gunnar Myrdal's "Asian Drama"', UN Asian Institute for Economic Development and Planning Occasional Papers, December 1969, reprinted in Hans W. Singer (1975), *The Strategy of International Development: Essays in the Economics of Backwardness*, London: Macmillan, pp. 22–42.

Singer, Hans W. (1970a), 'Some problems of international aid', *Journal of World Trade Law*, **4** (2), 347–61.
Singer, Hans W. [1970b] (1975), 'Science and technology for the development of poorer countries', paper mainly derived from the Sussex Manifesto 1970 that was prepared by a group of consultants to the UN Advisory Committee on Science and Technology, reprinted in Hans W. Singer (1975), *The Strategy of International Development: Essays in the Economics of Backwardness*, London: Macmillan, pp. 189–207.
Singer, Hans W. [1970c] (1975), 'Multinational corporations and technology transfer: some problems and suggestions', paper presented to OECD Conference on 'The Transfer of Technology', Istanbul, October 1970, reprinted in Hans W. Singer (1975), *The Strategy of International Development: Essays in the Economics of Backwardness*, London: Macmillan, pp. 208–33.
Singer, Hans W. [1971a] (1975), 'The distribution of gains revisited', paper presented to first Inter PAS Conference at the Institute of Development Studies, May 1971, reprinted in Hans W. Singer (1975), *The Strategy of International Development: Essays in the Economics of Backwardness*, London: Macmillan, pp. 58–66.
Singer, Hans W. (1971b), 'International policy and its effect on employment', in Ronald Robinson and Peter Johnston (eds), *Prospects for Employment Opportunities in the Nineteen Seventies*, London: Her Majesty's Stationery Office, pp. 194–202.
Singer, Hans W. [1973] (1975), 'Trade liberalization and economic development', from 'Trade liberalization, employment and income distribution – A first approach', by Hans W. Singer et al., *Institute of Development Studies Discussion Paper*, no. 31, October 1973, reprinted in Hans W. Singer (1975), *The Strategy of International Development: Essays in the Economics of Backwardness*, London: Macmillan, pp. 91–113.
Singer, Hans W. (1975), *The Strategy of International Development: Essays in the Economics of Backwardness*, edited by Sir Alec Cairncross and Mohinder Puri, London: Macmillan.
Singer, Hans W. (1977), 'Reflections of sociological aspects of economic growth based on the work of Bert Hoselitz', *Economic Development and Cultural Change*, **XXV** (supplement), 1–15.
Singer, Hans W. (1979), 'Poverty, income distribution, and levels of living: thirty years of changing thought on development problems', in C. H. Hanumantha Rao and P. C. Joshi (eds), *Reflections on Economic Development and Social Change: Essays in Honour of Professor V. K. R. V. Rao*, Bombay: Allied Publishers Private Ltd., pp. 29–40.
Singer, Hans W. (1980), 'The role of newly industrializing (middle-income) countries in the world economy', in Economic Growth Department (ed.), *New Directions of Asia's Development Strategies: Proceedings and Papers of a Symposium held at the Institute of Developing Economies on March 13–16, 1979*, Tokyo: Institute of Developing Economies, pp. 71–81.
Singer, Hans W. (1983a), 'Brandt: mutual and conflicting interests in relations with the Third World', *IDS Discussion Essay*, reprinted in Hans W. Singer (1998c), *Growth, Development* and *Trade: Selected Essays of Hans W. Singer*, Cheltenham, UK and Lyme, USA: Edward Elgar, pp. 193–205.
Singer, Hans W. (1983b), 'North–South multipliers', *World Development*, **11** (5), 451–4.

Singer, Hans W. (1983c), 'North–South and South–South: the North and ECDC', in Breda Pavlič et al. (eds), *The Challenges of South–South Cooperation*, Boulder, CO: Westview Press, pp. 317–28.

Singer, Hans W. (1983d), 'The ethics of aid', *Asian Journal of Economics*, **2** (3), 193–207.

Singer, Hans W. (1984a), 'The terms of trade controversy and the evolution of soft financing: early years in the U.N.', in Gerald M. Meier and Dudley Seers (eds) (1984), *Pioneers in Development*, New York: Oxford University Press, pp. 275–303.

Singer, Hans W. (1984b), 'Relevance of Keynes for developing countries', *Estudos de Economia*, **IV** (4), 419–37, reprinted with slight rewording in Harold L. Wattel (ed.) (1985), *The Policy Consequences of John Maynard Keynes*, Armonk, NY: M. E. Sharpe, Inc., pp. 128–44.

Singer, Hans W. (1984c), 'Industrialization: where do we stand? Where are we going?', *Industry and Development*, **12**, 79–87.

Singer, Hans W. (1986a), 'South–South trade revisited, in a darkening external environment', *Development & South–South Cooperation*, **II** (2), 26–30.

Singer, Hans W. (1986b), 'Raúl Prebisch and his advocacy of import substitution', *Development & South–South Cooperation*, **II** (3), 1–7.

Singer, Hans W. (1987a), 'Discussion' of Anthony P. Thirlwall (1987b) and William B. Reddaway (1987), in Anthony P. Thirlwall (ed.) (1987b), *Keynes and Economic Development*, New York: St. Martin's Press, pp. 66–9.

Singer, Hans W. (1987b), 'What Keynes and Keynesianism can teach us about less developed countries', in Anthony P. Thirlwall (ed.) (1987b), *Keynes and Economic Development*, New York: St. Martin's Press, pp. 70–89.

Singer, Hans W. (1988), 'The World Development Report 1987 on the blessings of "outward orientation": a necessary correction', *Journal of Development Studies*, **24** (2), 232–6.

Singer, Hans W. (1989a), 'Lessons of post-war development experience: 1945–1988', *Institute of Development Studies Discussion Paper*, no. 260.

Singer, Hans W. (1989b), 'The relationship between debt pressures, adjustment policies and deterioration of terms of trade for developing countries (with special reference to Latin America)', *Institute of Social Studies Working Paper Series*, no. 59.

Singer, Hans W. [1989c] (1998), 'Industrialization and world trade: ten years after the Brandt Report', *Institute of Development Studies Discussion Essay*, reprinted in Hans W. Singer (1998c), *Growth, Development* and *Trade: Selected Essays of Hans W. Singer*, Cheltenham, UK and Lyme, USA: Edward Elgar, pp. 85–95.

Singer, Hans W. (1991a), 'Terms of trade: new wine *and* new bottles?', *Development Policy Review*, **9** (4), 339–51.

Singer, Hans W. (1991b), 'The Uruguay Round of GATT negotiations and Third World trade and development problems', paper delivered in Vienna at a conference on the GATT negotiations, 28 June.

Singer, Hans W. (1992), 'Hans Wolfgang SINGER', in Philip Arestis and Malcolm Sawyer (eds) (1992), *A Biographical Dictionary of Dissenting Economists*, Aldershot, UK and Brookfield, USA: Edward Elgar, pp. 526–32.

Singer, Hans W. (1993), 'Adam Smith: forebear of development studies', in Anthony Carty and Hans W. Singer (eds), *Conflict and Change in the 1990s: Ethics, Laws and Institutions*, London: Macmillan, pp. 26–34.

Singer, Hans W. (1995), 'Are the structural adjustment programmes successful?', *Pakistan Journal of Applied Economics*, **XI** (1&2), 1–15.
Singer, Hans W. (1996), 'Is a genuine partnership possible in a Western Hemisphere Free Trade Area?', in Marjan Svetličič and Hans W. Singer (eds), *The World Economy: Challenges of Globalization and Regionalization*, New York: St. Martin's Press, pp. 153–64.
Singer, Hans W. (1997), 'Is development economics still relevant?', in Louis Emmerij (ed.), *Economic and Social Development into the XXI Century*, Washington, DC: Inter-American Development Bank, pp. 507–11.
Singer, Hans W. (1998a), 'Beyond terms of trade: convergence/divergence and creative/uncreative destruction', *Zagreb International Review of Economics & Business*, **1** (1), 13–25.
Singer, Hans W. (1998b), 'How relevant is Keynesianism today for understanding problems of development?', in Soumitra Sharma (ed.), *John Maynard Keynes: Keynesianism into the Twenty-first Century*, Cheltenham, UK and Lyme, USA: Edward Elgar, pp. 104–15.
Singer, Hans W. (1998c), *Growth, Development* and *Trade: Selected Essays of Hans W. Singer*, Cheltenham, UK and Lyme, USA: Edward Elgar.
Singer, Hans W. (1998d), 'Modern relevance of Keynesianism in the study of development', in David Sapsford and John-ren Chen (eds) (1998), *Development Economics and Policy: The Conference Volume to Celebrate the 85th Birthday of Professor Sir Hans Singer*, New York: St. Martin's Press, pp. 524–33.
Singer, Hans W. (1999), 'Beyond terms of trade – convergence and divergence', *Journal of International Development*, **11** (6), 911–16.
Singer, Hans W. (2000), 'Some reflections on trade expansion as a measure of globalization', in Martina Metzger and Birgit Reichenstein (eds), *Challenges for International Organizations in the 21st Century: Essays in Honour of Klaus Hüfner*, New York: St. Martin's Press, pp. 31–45.
Singer, Hans W. (2001a), *International Development Co-operation: Selected Essays by H. W. Singer on Aid and the United Nations System*, edited, with contributions, by D. John Shaw, New York: Palgrave.
Singer, Hans W. (2001b), 'Comment' on Irma Adelman's 'Fallacies in development theory and their implications for policy', in Gerald M. Meier and Joseph E. Stiglitz (eds) (2001), *Frontiers of Development Economics: The Future in Perspective*, Washington, DC: The World Bank/Oxford University Press, pp. 147–8.
Singer, Hans W. (2001c), '"Pioneers revisited"', in Gerald M. Meier and Joseph E. Stiglitz (eds) (2001), *Frontiers of Development Economics: The Future in Perspective*, Washington, DC: The World Bank/Oxford University Press, pp. 517–19.
Singer, Hans W. and Parvin Alizadeh (1986), 'Import substitution revisited in a darkening external environment', *Asian Journal of Economics and Social Studies*, **5** (3), 183–203.
Singer, Hans W. and Javed Ansari (1980), 'Trade access and employment in developing countries: a survey', *Canadian Journal of Development Studies*, **II** (2), 288–302.
Singer, Hans W. and Javed A. Ansari (1988), *Rich and Poor Countries: Consequences of International Disorder*, 4th edition, London: Unwin Hyman.

Singer, Hans W. and Sumit Roy (1993), *Economic Progress and Prospects in the Third World: Lessons of Development Experience since 1945*, Aldershot, UK and Brookfield, USA: Edward Elgar.

Singer, Hans W. and Prabirjit Sarkar [1989] (1998), 'Manufactured exports and terms of trade movements of less developed countries in recent years (1980–87)', *Institute of Development Studies Discussion Paper* no. 270, reprinted in Singer (1998c), *Growth, Development* and *Trade: Selected Essays of Hans W. Singer*, Cheltenham, UK and Lyme, USA: Edward Elgar, pp. 159–83.

Singh, Ajit (2005), 'Special and differential treatment: the multilateral trading system and economic development in the twenty-first century', in Kevin P. Gallagher (ed.) (2005), *Putting Development First: The Importance of Policy Space in the WTO and International Financial Institutions*, London: Zed Books, pp. 233–63.

Skinner, Andrew S. and Thomas Wilson (eds) (1975), *Essays on Adam Smith*, Oxford: Clarendon Press.

Smith, Adam [1776] (1979) *An Inquiry into the Nature and Causes of the Wealth of Nations*, Liberty*Classics* reprint of the Oxford University Press edition. Indianapolis: Liberty*Classics*.

Spengler, Joseph J. (1959), 'John Rae on economic development: a note', *Quarterly Journal of Economics*, **LXXIII** (3), 393–406.

Spengler, Joseph J. (1960), 'John Stuart Mill on economic development', in Bert F. Hoselitz (ed.) (1960), *Theories of Economic Growth*, Glencoe, IL: The Free Press, pp. 113–54.

Sraffa, Piero (1951a), 'Introduction to the Principles', in Piero Sraffa and Maurice Dobb (eds), *The Works and Correspondence of David Ricardo*, vol. I, Cambridge: Cambridge University Press, pp. xiii–lxii.

Sraffa, Piero (1951b), 'Note on "Essay on Profits"', in Piero Sraffa and Maurice Dobb (eds), *The Works and Correspondence of David Ricardo*, vol. IV, Cambridge: Cambridge University Press, pp. 3–6.

Srinivasan, T. N. (1982), 'Why developing countries should participate in the GATT system', *The World Economy*, **5** (1), 85–104.

Srinivasan, T. N. (1985), 'Neoclassical political economy, the state and economic development', *Asian Development Review*, **3** (2), 38–58.

Srinivasan, T. N. (1994), 'Development economics, then and now', in Jan Willem Gunning, Henk Kox, Wouter Tims and Ynto de Wit (eds), *Trade, Aid and Development: Essays in Honour of Hans Linnemann*, New York: St. Martin's Press, pp. 15–29.

Srinivasan, T. N. (1999), 'Developing countries in the world trading system: from GATT, 1947, to the Third Ministerial Meeting of WTO, 1999', *The World Economy*, **22** (8), 1047–64.

Steedman, Ian (1979), *Trade amongst Growing Economies*, Cambridge: Cambridge University Press.

Steedman, Ian and J. S. Metcalfe (1973), 'On foreign trade', *Economia Internazionale*, **XXVI** (3–4), 516–28.

Stern, Nicholas (1989), 'The economics of development: a survey', *Economic Journal*, **99** (397), 597–685.

Stigler, George J. (1955), 'The nature and role of originality in scientific progress', *Economica*, **22** (88), 293–302.

Stiglitz, Joseph E. (2006), *Making Globalization Work*, New York: W.W. Norton & Co.

Stiglitz, Joseph E. and Andrew Charlton (2005), *Fair Trade for All: How Trade Can Promote Development*, New York: Oxford University Press.
Streeten, Paul P. (1997), *Thinking about Development*, New York: Cambridge University Press.
Sundaram, Jomo K. (ed.) (2005), *The Pioneers of Development Economics: Great Economists on Development*, London: Zed Books.
Sundaram, Jomo K. and Ben Fine (eds) (2006), *The New Development Economics: After the Washington Consensus*, London: Zed Books.
Sundaram, Jomo K. and Erik Reinert (eds) (2005), *The Origins of Development Economics: How Schools of Economic Thought Have Addressed Development*, London: Zed Books.
Swan, T. W. (1962), 'Circular causation', *Economic Record*, **38** (84), 421–6.
Sykes, Alan O. (2005), 'Subsidies and countervailing measures', in Patrick F. J. Macrory, Arthur E. Appleton and Michael G. Plummer (eds), *The World Trade Organization: Legal, Economic and Political Analysis*, vol. II, New York: Springer, pp. 83–107.
Syrett, Harold C. and Jacob E. Cooke (1966), 'Introductory note' to Alexander Hamilton's *Report on the Subject of Manufactures*, in Harold C. Syrett and Jacob E. Cooke (eds), *The Papers of Alexander Hamilton*, vol. X, New York: Columbia University Press, pp. 1–15.
Tajima, Keiji (1985), 'Alexander Hamilton and the encouragement of manufactures: an interpretation of the Hamiltonian System', *Japanese Journal of American Studies*, **2**, 127–55.
Teitel, Simón and Francisco E. Thoumi (1986), 'From import substitution to exports: the manufacturing exports experience of Argentina and Brazil', *Economic Development and Cultural Change*, **XXXIV** (3), 455–90.
Thirlwall, Anthony P. (1983), 'Foreign trade elasticities in centre–periphery models of growth and development', *Banca Nazionale del Lavoro Quarterly Review*, (146), 249–61.
Thirlwall, Anthony P. (1987a), *Nicholas Kaldor*, New York: New York University Press.
Thirlwall, Anthony P. (ed.) (1987b), *Keynes and Economic Development*, New York: St. Martin's Press.
Thweatt, William O. (1976), 'James Mill and the early development of comparative advantage', *History of Political Economy*, **8** (2), 207–34.
Tinbergen, Jan (1945), 'Appendix I: Professor Graham's case for protection', in Jan Tinbergen, *International Economic Co-operation*, Amsterdam: Elsevier, pp. 182–99.
Torrens, Robert [1808] (1993), *The Economists Refuted and other Early Economic Writings*, edited with an introduction by Peter D. Groenewegen, Fairfield, NJ: Augustus M. Kelley, Publishers.
Torrens, Robert (1815), *An Essay on the External Corn Trade*, London: printed for J. Hatchard.
Torrens, Robert [1819] (1993), 'Mr. Owen's plans for relieving the national distress', *Edinburgh Review*, **XXXII**, 453–77, reprinted in Robert Torrens [1808] (1993), *The Economists Refuted and other Early Economic Writings*, Fairfield, NJ: Augustus M. Kelley, Publishers, pp. 83–103.
Torrens, Robert (1820), *An Essay on the Influence of the External Corn Trade upon the Production and Distribution of National Wealth; Containing an Inquiry into the General Principles of that Important Branch of Traffic; an Examination of the*

Exceptions to Which these Principles Are Liable; and a Comparative Statement of the Effects which Restrictions on Importation and Free Intercourse, Are Respectively Calculated to Produce upon Subsistence, Agriculture, Commerce, and Revenue, 2nd edition, London: Hatchard.

Torrens, Robert [1821] (1965), *An Essay on the Production of Wealth*, New York: Augustus M. Kelley, Publisher.

Torrens, Robert (1827), *An Essay on the External Corn Trade*, London: printed for Longman, Rees, Orme, Brown, & Green, Paternoster Row.

Torrens, Robert [1829] (1972), *An Essay on the External Corn Trade*, New Jersey: Augustus M. Kelley, Publishers.

Torrens, Robert [1833] (1958), *Letters on Commercial Policy*, with an Introduction by Lionel Robbins, London: The London School of Economics and Political Science.

Torrens, Robert [1834] (1969), *On Wages and Combination*, New York: Augustus M. Kelley, Publishers.

Torrens, Robert [1835] (1962), *Colonization of South Australia*, Adelaide: Public Library of South Australia.

Torrens, Robert [1844] (1970), *The Budget – on Commercial and Colonial Policy*, New York: Augustus M. Kelley, Publishers.

Torrens, Robert (1852), *Tracts on Finance and Trade*, Nos. I and II, London: Chapman & Hall.

Toye, John and Richard Toye (2003), 'The origins and interpretation of the Prebisch–Singer Thesis', *History of Political Economy*, **35** (3), 437–67.

Tribe, Keith (1984), 'Review of List's *The Natural System of Political Economy* as trans. and ed. by W. O. Henderson', *Economic Journal*, **94** (373), 198–200.

Tribe, Keith (1988), 'Friedrich List and the critique of "cosmopolitical economy"', *The Manchester School*, **LVI** (1), 17–36.

Tsuru, Shigeto (ed.) (1983), *Human Resources, Employment and Development, vol. 1: The Issues*, New York: St. Martin's Press.

Tucker, G. S. L. (1960), *Progress and Profits in British Economic Thought 1650–1850*, Cambridge: Cambridge University Press.

Vernon, Raymond (1966), 'Foreign-owned enterprise in the developing countries', *Public Policy*, **XV**, 361–80.

Viner, Jacob (1929), 'Review of Friedrich List's *Schriften, Reden, Briefe*, Band IV, *Das naturliche System der politischen ökonomie*, edited by E. Salin and A. Sommer', *Journal of Political Economy*, **XXXVII** (3), 364–6.

Viner, Jacob (1932), 'Review of Manoilesco's "Theory of Protection and International Trade"', *Journal of Political Economy*, **LX** (1), 121–5.

Viner, Jacob [1937] (1975), *Studies in the Theory of International Trade*, Clifton, NJ: Augustus M. Kelley, Publishers.

Viner, Jacob (1953), *International Trade and Economic Development*, London: Oxford University Press.

Viner, Jacob (1958), 'Stability and progress: the poorer countries' problem', in Douglas Hague (ed.), *Stability and Progress in the World Economy*, New York: St. Martin's Press, pp. 41–65.

Von Laue, Theodore H. (1963), *Sergei Witte and the Industrialization of Russia*, New York: Columbia University Press.

Wade, Robert H. (1990), *Governing the Market: Economic Theory and the Role of Government in East Asian Industrialization*, Princeton: Princeton University Press.

Wade, Robert H. (2003), 'What strategies are viable for developing countries today? The World Trade Organization and the shrinking of "development space"', *Review of International Political Economy*, **10** (4), 621–44.

Wakefield, Edward Gibbon [1834] (1967), *England and America: A Comparison of the Social and Political State of Both Nations*, New York: Augustus M. Kelley, Publishers.

Wall, David (ed.) (1972), *Chicago Essays in Economic Development*, Chicago: The University of Chicago Press.

Walsh, Vivian Charles (1979), 'Ricardian foreign trade theory in the light of the classical revival', *Eastern Economic Journal*, **5** (4), 421–7.

Waterbury, John (1999), 'The long gestation and brief triumph of import-substituting industrialization', *World Development*, **27** (2), 323–41.

Watkins, Melville H. (1963), 'A staple theory of economic growth', *Canadian Journal of Economics and Political Science*, **29** (2), 141–58.

Whalley, John (1999), 'Special and differential treatment in the Millennium Round', *The World Economy*, **22** (8), 1065–93.

Williams, John H. (1929), 'The theory of international trade reconsidered', *Economic Journal*, **39** (2), 195–209.

Williams, John H. (1951), 'International trade theory and policy – some current issues', *American Economic Review, Papers and Proceedings*, **41** (2), 418–30.

Winch, Christopher (1998), 'Listian political economy: social capitalism conceptualised?', *New Political Economy*, **3** (2), 301–16.

Winch, Donald (1965), *Classical Political Economy and Colonies*, Cambridge, MA: Harvard University Press.

Winch, Donald (1970), 'Introduction', in John Stuart Mill, *Principles of Political Economy with Some of Their Applications to Social Philosophy*, Books IV and V, edited with an Introduction by Donald Winch, New York: Penguin Books, pp. 11–48.

Wolf, Jr., Charles (1979), 'A theory of nonmarket failure: framework for implementation analysis', *The Journal of Law and Economics*, **22** (1), 107–39.

Wolf, Martin (1987), 'Differential and more favorable treatment of developing countries and the international trading system', *World Bank Economic Review*, **1** (4), 647–68.

Wood, Adrian (1994), *North–South Trade, Employment and Inequality: Changing Fortunes in a Skill-Driven World*, Oxford: Clarendon Press.

World Bank (1987), *World Development Report 1987*, New York: Oxford University Press.

World Bank (1993), *The East Asian Miracle: Economic Growth and Public Policy*, New York: Oxford University Press.

Yaffey, Michael (1998), 'Friedrich List and the causes of Irish hunger', in Helen O'Neill and John Toye (eds), *A World without Famine? New Approaches to Aid and Development*, New York: St. Martin's Press, pp. 84–106.

Young, Allyn (1928), 'Increasing returns and economic progress', *Economic Journal*, **38** (152), 527–42.

Index